ARISTOCRATS OF COLOR

Aristocrats of

THE BLACK ELITE, 1880–1920

INDIANA UNIVERSITY PRESS

Color ◆

WILLARD B. GATEWOOD

BLOOMINGTON & INDIANAPOLIS

First Midland Book Edition 1993

The paper used in this publication meets the minimum requirements of American National Standard for Information Sciences—Permanence of Paper for Printed Library Materials, ANSI Z39.48-1984.

Manufactured in the United States of America

Library of Congress Cataloging-in-Publication Data
Gatewood, Willard B.
    Aristocrats of color: the Black elite, 1880–1920 / Willard B. Gatewood.
      p. cm.
    Includes bibliographical references.
    ISBN 0-253-32552-8 (alk. paper)
    1. Afro-Americans—Social life and customs. 2. Afro-Americans—History—19th century. 3. Afro-Americans—History—20th century. 4. Upper classes—United States—History—19th century. 5. Upper classes—United States—History—20th century. 6. Bruce, Josephine. 7. Bruce, Blanche Kelso. 1841–1898. I. Title.
E185.86.G38   1990
973' .0496073—dc20   89-46000
ISBN 0-253-20850-5 (pbk.)   CIP

3 4 5 6 7 99 98 97 96 95 94 93

For Lu, Bill, and Ellis

Contents ◆

CONTENTS

Illustrations follow pp. 84 and 148.

Preface

To undertake a discussion of class in America is to venture into an area fraught with perils. It may well be, as one authority has suggested, that "class is the toughest, slipperiest opponent in the lexicon," all the more so when applied to Afro-Americans. But failure to consider class division in the black community is likely to contribute to what Bayard Rustin once termed the "sentimental notion of black solidarity" and to the perpetuation of the myth that black society is a homogeneous mass without significant and illuminating distinctions in background, prestige, attitudes, behavior, power, and culture.

Throughout the late nineteenth and early twentieth centuries Afro-Americans challenged what they perceived as the Jim Crow way of viewing black society, which held that among blacks there existed no class distinctions. In the generation following Reconstruction blacks engaged in lively and frequent discussions regarding the significance and implications of the evolving social gradations in the black community. They spoke in terms of a larger lower class, a small but expanding middle class, and a minuscule upper class. The attention devoted to the last group indicated that its significance was vastly disproportionate to its numbers.

Students of the black class structure generally agree that the upper class was exceedingly small, yet they often divide it into two strata: the "old families" as the top tier, newcomers as the second. This study focuses on the "old families," who viewed themselves as the products of a process of natural selection and superior to other blacks in culture, sophistication, and achievement. A sufficiently large segment of the black community shared this self-image to legitimize the notion of an elite or what was described at the time as an aristocracy. The black elite was identified, by itself and by others, in various ways: the "colored aristocracy," "black 400," "upper tens," and "best society." Such terms will be used in this work to evoke and describe the self-perceptions of the elite, but without the imputation that the elite was necessarily superior to other blacks in their values and way of life, or that the "old families" were in fact always as ancient as they suggested.

Recent studies in Afro-American history lend credence to contemporary assessments by blacks regarding the contours of the class structure among Afro-Americans in the period between 1880 and 1920. Such works, which have been used extensively in this study, reveal much about the diversity, tensions, and dynamics of black society in the era and leave little doubt, as one student put it, that "there has always been a Negro elite of some kind." The purpose of this work is to identify the black elite that was predominant in the forty years following the end of Reconstruction, to explore its self-image, behavior, values, strategies, and relationship to the larger society, both white and black, and to indicate changes that occurred in its composition.

The black elite considered in this volume constituted, on its own terms, an "aristocracy," that is, an aristocracy relative to other blacks, and was so described by black contemporaries, but it scarcely conforms to customary usage of the term. In view of the deteriorating status of blacks in general in the era from 1880 to 1920, one does not usually think in terms of black aristocrats or aristocrats of color. What is especially noteworthy about this "aristocracy" was its cross-cutting definition of itself in regard to the black and white worlds, and the tenuous place that it occupied between them. These aristocrats laid claim to elite status within a subgroup, the black Americans, by defining themselves in terms of prestige, tradition, culture, and other considerations reflective of values drawn from the white majority of American society. The aristocrats of color also dramatized the fact that there have been numerous variations of *the* black experience. Because they were upper-class *black* Americans, not simply upper-class Americans, their "we" feeling was defined by both class and race. Their behavior mingled these variables in ways that often perplexed whites and sometimes enraged other blacks.

Each of the four parts of this volume is introduced by an exploration of some aspect or aspects of the life of the family of Blanche K. Bruce, the black United States senator from Mississippi. In many respects members of the Bruce family constituted the ideal or quintessential aristocrats of color. Others rarely achieved such eminence. The Bruces and a few other families obviously bore a closer resemblance to upper-class whites in terms of prestige, education, wealth, political importance, and influential connections than did most other aristocrats of color who nonetheless enjoyed high status in relation to the black population.

Numerous individuals provided valuable assistance in the preparation of this volume. I owe a large debt of gratitude to librarians and archivists at Atlanta University, University of Georgia, Duke University, University of North Carolina at Chapel Hill, the Library of Congress, and the Schomburg Center for Research in Black Culture, New York Public Library. Among the staff members of Mullins Library at the University of Arkansas who always responded to my numerous inquiries and requests, I am especially indebted to Regina French,

Debra Cochran, and Stephen Dew. Gary M. Shepard of the University of Arkansas Media Services displayed great skill and patience in reproducing most of the photographs in this volume. During extensive research at Howard University in Washington many individuals, but especially Esme E. Bhan of the Moorland-Spingarn Research Center, provided extraordinary assistance and called my attention to materials that I undoubtedly would otherwise have overlooked. No less valuable was the help given by Clifton H. Johnson and the staff of the Amistad Research Center, Tulane University, New Orleans, who were as gracious as they were generous with their time. Roberta Church graciously allowed me to use the papers of the Robert R. Church family, located at Memphis State University. Michele Fagan, Curator of the Mississippi Valley Collection at Memphis State, not only made the Church papers available but called my attention to other relevant materials in the collection. Sara D. Jackson of the National Archives was extraordinarily helpful in directing me to individuals knowledgeable about the black community in the District of Columbia. Jane Knowles of the Radcliffe College Archives and Kathleen A. Markees of the Harvard University Archives furnished valuable data on various members of the Bruce family. Gail Lumet Buckley of New York City shared with me useful information gathered during research on her *The Hornes: An American Family.* David Edwin Harrell, Jr., Robert Finlay, Randall B. Woods, Mary Gussman, and Suzanne Maberry read the entire manuscript and gave me the benefit of their wise counsel and perceptive criticisms. While I have drawn upon and profited by the works of numerous scholars, I would be remiss if I did not acknowledge the influence of August Meier and his pioneer investigations of the class structure in black America. Theresa Garrity and Jeanie Wyant, who typed and retyped the manuscript, displayed extraordinary patience and an uncanny ability to decipher my copy. As always, my wife, Lu Brown Gatewood, was a constant source of support and encouragement throughout the research and writing of this project; she was in large measure responsible for its completion.

The illustrations in this book have been reproduced from the following books, magazines, newspapers, and library collections:

Alexander's Magazine: Nos. 4, 5, 22, 48.
Amistad Research Center, Tulane University: Nos. 25, 30.
Colored American Magazine: Nos. 8, 15, 16, 20, 21, 24, 26, 27, 28, 31–37, 40, 43, 44, 45, 46, 49, 51, 57, 63.
D. W. Culp, *Twentieth Century Negro Literature:* Nos. 9, 10, 13, 17, 18, 19, 24, 41, 58–62.
Caroline Bond Day, *A Study of Negro-White Families in the United States,* courtesy Peabody Museum, Harvard University: No. 23.
Indianapolis *Freeman:* Nos. 47, 53.
Daniel Smith Lamb, *Howard University Medical Department:* Nos. 11, 38.

John Mercer Langston, *From the Virginia Plantation to the National Capitol:* Nos. 6, 50.
Library of Congress: No. 12.
Mississippi Valley Collection, Memphis State University: No. 7.
Moorland-Spingarn Research Center, Howard University: Nos. 1–3 (from the Bruce
    Collection) and No. 39.
Voice of the Negro: Nos. 14, 29, 42, 54, 56, 64.
Washington Bee: No. 55.

PART I

◆

Origins

PROLOGUE

Two weddings that took place in Cleveland, Ohio in 1878, a little more than a month apart attracted considerable attention in the nation's press. The first was the highly publicized marriage of Don Cameron, a former secretary of war who had succeeded his father as senator from Pennsylvania in 1877, to Elizabeth Bancroft Sherman, the niece of General William T. Sherman and Secretary of the Treasury John Sherman. The political and social prominence of the two families, combined with the fact that the nineteen-year-old Lizzie Sherman was two years younger than Cameron's daughter by a previous marriage, aroused extraordinary public interest in the union. According to press reports, their lavish wedding on May 9, 1878, in Saint Paul's Episcopal Church, was "one of the most elaborate and costly affairs which the people have ever witnessed." The excitement created by the Cameron-Sherman marriage had scarcely subsided when rumors began to circulate about "another senatorial wedding" in Cleveland.[1]

Close observers of the city's social life had been aware that for over a year Blanche K. Bruce, the black senator from Mississippi, was a frequent guest at Forest City House, a well-known hotel, and that he regularly called at the handsome two-story house at 228 Perry Street, the home of Dr. Joseph Willson, a highly respected black dentist. Several years earlier Bruce had been engaged to marry Miss Namée Yosburgh, whose family had long occupied a place of prominence in Cleveland's black community. In fact, their wedding date had been set when Miss Yosburgh became ill and died within a few weeks. The senator "took her death greatly to heart" and observed a period of mourning for some months. Sometime in 1876 he met Dr. Willson's daughter Josephine Beall Willson, a graduate of Cleveland High School and a teacher in the city's public schools. She was, by all accounts, a striking beauty, with "fine black eyes and an animated countenance" who possessed no visible "trace of her African ancestry." An accomplished linguist, Josephine Willson shared with her mother, Harriet, and her three younger sisters a love of literature and classical music.[2]

Although the Willsons prided themselves on being Philadelphians, Joseph Willson was actually born in Augusta, Georgia in 1817. Educated in Boston, he settled in Philadelphia and for a time was engaged in the printing trade before

[3]

studying dentistry. A modest and reticent man with impeccable manners, he was well informed on books and current events. When his daughter was scarcely a year old, Willson moved his family to Cleveland. Like others in Cleveland who had been free for a generation or so before the Civil War, the Willsons occupied a place at the top of the black social structure. They were among the select black families who belonged to the Social Circle, a club organized in 1869 "to promote social intercourse and cultural activities among the better educated people of color" in Cleveland. In terms of life style, education, income, and even color the Willsons more closely resembled whites of the upper and upper-middle class in Cleveland than they did most blacks. In fact, they often associated and identified with such whites. They were members of an elite white church, Saint Paul's Episcopal; the children attended racially mixed schools; and many of Dr. Willson's patients were white. Josephine's older brother, Leonidus, was an attorney affiliated with one of the best-known white law firms in the city. He married the sister of his law partner, was accepted into a white Masonic Lodge, and ultimately "lost his identity with blacks."[3]

Unlike his fiancée, Senator Bruce was born a slave. His was not the background of an ordinary slave, but rather that of a privileged bondsman who enjoyed an extraordinary position in the Virginia family that owned him. He was born in 1841 to a slave woman and therefore by law he inherited the "condition of the mother." His white master, who may have been his father, took a special interest in his welfare. Bruce shared a tutor with his master's son and experienced few of the hardships associated with slavery. His life as a slave, first in Virginia, then in Mississippi and Missouri, was, as he later recalled, little different from that of the sons of whites. From Missouri he escaped into Kansas and proclaimed his freedom. In 1864 he returned to Missouri and for a time taught school in Hannibal. Following a brief course of study at Oberlin College, he settled in Mississippi in 1868. He acquired considerable property and prospered as a cotton planter in Bolivar County, where he became active in politics. He rose rapidly in Republican Party ranks during Reconstruction and was elected to the United States Senate from Mississippi in 1874.[4]

When Bruce arrived in Washington, he immediately became a favorite of the single ladies among the capital city's black aristocrats. Smitten by his good looks and polished manners, they vied with each other in attracting his attention and interest. But the new senator, while always courteous and solicitous, was not interested in romantic entanglements because he was still grief-stricken over the death of his fiancée in 1874. In order to shield himself from flirtations, he adopted the practice of appearing at social occasions in the company of his friends Congressman John R. Lynch from Mississippi and Miss Emma V. Brown, a well-known Washington school teacher. Compared to the socially prominent belles eager to attract Bruce's attention, Emma Brown possessed little style or beauty. She enjoyed having such a charming and handsome escort, and described Bruce as a "great big good natured lump of fat" always impeccably attired in the finest broadcloth, diamond studs, and kid gloves; he was "gentlemanly and very jolly"—"just the kind of fellow to go around with."[5]

In Washington Bruce quickly acquired a wide circle of influential political friends and commanded the respect of even those who objected to the presence of a black man in the Senate. Most of those who came to know him were impressed by his innate dignity, elegant manners, conservative tastes, and shrewd political judgment. A black acquaintance spoke of him as "an exceptionally cultured and refined man" who had read more widely than most of his Senate colleagues.[6] Not the least among whites who respected and admired Bruce was L. Q. C. Lamar, a Democrat, who joined him as the junior senator from Mississippi. After a private conference with Bruce at the Lamar residence in Washington, he confided to a white friend that his black colleague was a truthful, sensible, and "self-poised man" of principle. "The fact is," Lamar wrote in regard to Bruce, "I believed him to be a noble negro."[7] David S. Barry, a white journalist in Washington for forty years, described Bruce as a man of "high moral, mental and physical standards" whose language was that of a highly educated person and who resembled "a Creole Beau Brummel." According to Barry, the senator was "a handsome man, well-built, with a finely shaped head covered with curly black hair"; his clothes were always of "the best texture and most fashionable cut."[8] Reflecting the perspectives of those whites friendly toward Bruce, the *Boston Herald* succinctly characterized him as "really a whitened African."[9] Though legally born a slave and largely self-educated, by the mid-1870s Bruce had become a man of considerable means with the manners and tastes of a polished Victorian gentleman. His personal attributes, affluence, and prestigious political office combined to make him a worthy suitor of Josephine Willson.

Because the senator and the Willsons disapproved of ostentation, they agreed that the wedding should "make as little display as possible." The ceremony, therefore, was to take place at the Willson residence in the presence of a few intimate friends rather than in a church with hundreds of guests. At the appointed hour on the evening of June 24, 1878, approximately sixty guests in "full dress," a majority of whom were white, arrived at the Perry Street residence. According to one observer, they encountered abundant "evidence of the good taste and enlightened ideas of the occupants," from the Brussels carpets, fine furniture, and oil paintings to the heavy velvet draperies closely drawn at all windows "to keep out the gaze of the inquisitive crowd" that lined the sidewalk in front of the house.[10]

N. S. Rulison, rector of Saint Paul's Episcopal Church, who had officiated at the Cameron-Sherman marriage, performed the ceremony. The bride's sisters—Victoria, Mary, and Emily—served as her attendants. The bride wore a gown of white silk trimmed in satin that had been created for her by a New York designer. Following the wedding ceremony, Joseph and Harriet Willson hosted a catered supper for the guests at which a local orchestra provided music. Their gift to the Bruces was a set of sterling flatware. At 10:30 P.M. Senator and Mrs. Bruce boarded a special railroad car for New York City, where they occupied the bridal suite at the Hoffman House. On June 27, 1878 they sailed for Europe aboard the *Algeria* for a four-month honeymoon.[11] "If half is true that is told of her beauty and accomplishments," the *Washington Post* noted in regard to the senator's new bride, "her entry here as a Senator's wife is likely to create a sensation."[12]

The Bruces' European tour assumed a semi-official status because Secretary of State William Evarts instructed American diplomatic and consular personnel to extend them every courtesy. In England, Senator and Mrs. Bruce toured various historic sites, visited art galleries, and attended the theatre. Their presence attracted considerable attention from the British press. The London *Times* described Bruce as a man of great ability, as "accomplished as any man in the Senate." On the Continent the Bruces toured Belgium, Holland, Germany, Switzerland, and France, where they were honored by receptions and introduced to government officials. During two weeks in Paris, Josephine Bruce spent much of her time acquiring an extensive wardrobe, including a number of gowns that prompted much comment upon her return to Washington. While she was shopping, Senator Bruce met regularly with former President Ulysses S. Grant, who had stopped in Paris during his tour around the world.[13]

The Bruces returned to Washington in time for the reconvening of Congress late in 1878. The senator had leased a large house at 909 M Street, but because it was undergoing extensive renovation they temporarily took up residence near Howard University in the home of Virginia-born John Mercer Langston, who was in Haiti serving as United States minister. The Langston home, a fourteen-room house known as "Hillside Cottage," had for some years been the center of social life for Washington's black elite. Here Caroline Wall Langston had presided over receptions, teas, musicales, and literary gatherings as the grand lady of black society. The new mistress of Hillside Cottage, who was no less skilled in the art of entertaining, continued that tradition.[14]

1

◆

Background and Antecedents

THE IDEA OF A BLACK ARISTOCRACY, a black Four Hundred, or an "old upper class" was so alien to most whites that it regularly encountered ridicule and scorn. In 1873, in a satire on "Negro society," *Harper's Weekly* printed a cartoon grotesquely caricaturing an upper-class black wedding. The caption read: "Mr. Leon de Sooty, the distinguished Society Man, will to-day lead to the altar Miss Dinah Black, the beautiful heiress. . . ."[1] Since most whites in the late nineteenth and early twentieth centuries viewed blacks as a homogeneous mass of degraded people, they were rarely inclined to think in terms of a stratified black society. Rather, the tendency was to classify blacks as "good Negroes" and "bad Negroes" or to designate, for one reason or another, certain black individuals and families as exceptional. But even exceptional blacks were considered inferior to whites. Those who attempted to go beyond vague generalities in dealing with social gradations among blacks invariably were surprised to discover the existence of a well-defined social hierarchy. That the mass of blacks belonged at the bottom of a social pyramid was scarcely unexpected; more surprising was the discovery of a small, but growing, upwardly mobile, middle class which in the phrase of the day had struggled "out of the depths" of bondage. This group appeared to whites to be an example of the rewards of hard work, thrift, and "righteous conduct" that awaited even those among a proscribed race. It was the small group of blacks at the top of the pyramid, the "colored aristocracy," that aroused the greatest curiosity and posed the greatest difficulties for white investigators. What they concluded as a result of first-hand observation, rather than by any close objective analysis, was the existence of a black elite, small in number and light in complexion, whose culture and style of living more closely resembled that of the "better class of whites" than that of the masses of their darker brethren. Even though the distance between the colored aristocracy and the white upper class was as great or greater than the gulf that separated the former from most blacks, the discovery of such an elite group prompted some white observers in the late nineteenth century to question the validity of the common notion that all blacks were "upon an equal plane."

One such individual was a correspondent for the Hartford *Courant* who in 1883 wrote an article entitled "Gradations in the Social Scale Among Colored People," focusing almost exclusively on what was termed "the upper reaches" of black society. Even in slavery, he discovered, "there were distinctions among the Negroes," especially between field hands and house servants. The "culture of the mind and manners" among the latter, not to mention that possessed by blacks who had enjoyed the status of free people of color prior to Emancipation, placed them socially far above the "dusky multitude" and cast them in a leadership role in the post–Civil War era. Impressed by the polish, refinement, and family pride evident among this small elite, the *Courant* correspondent noted that the younger members of the black upper class possessed a "degree of culture unknown to the average white youth." Even more surprising to him was the discovery that the black aristocrats resided in comfortable, tasteful homes and often employed one or more servants. "A few days ago when sitting in the handsomely furnished parlor of an accomplished colored lady who had had many advantages of seeing the world denied her 'plain' compatriots," he noted, "my hostess, instead of telling me of her travels and distinguished acquaintances as I hoped she would do, turned the conversation upon the difficulty of obtaining competent domestics." The existence of a cultured, educated black elite, in the view of the writer, was not without serious implications. In fact, he believed that a major problem confronting Americans was how to make accessible to such blacks "avocations hitherto reserved for the favored race."[2]

In 1887, a white resident of Baltimore, amazed to discover the existence of social gradations among blacks, wrote: "Colored society has rules as strict as the laws of the Medes and Persians. It is full of circles and each succeeding circle holds itself proudly above the one just below it. A colored aristocrat is one of the most perfect pictures of conscious exclusiveness that the world has ever known."[3] One such aristocrat who remained prominent in the social and political life of the national black community for four decades after Reconstruction was James Lewis of New Orleans. A native of Mississippi who grew up in Louisiana, Lewis was the son of a white planter and his mulatto slave. During the Civil War he raised the first regiment of black troops to serve in the United States Army. From the end of the war until his death, he was prominent in the Republican Party and held a succession of state and federal offices. In 1864 he married Josephine Joubert, a member of a slaveholding free family of color. For many years the Lewises lived in a large house on Canal Street across from Straight University.[4] When he died in 1914, the *New York Times* observed: "Lewis was an aristocrat of his race and was not disposed to associate on terms of equality with the mass of his people. He held himself, in a measure, aloof from them, even while working zealously for their betterment."[5]

Twenty years earlier, in 1894, Henry McFarland of the *Philadelphia Record* had reached similar conclusions in regard to black leaders such as Frederick Douglass, Congressmen John R. Lynch and John Mercer Langston, and Senator Blanche K. Bruce. "They have very little to do with the mass of colored citizens . . .," McFarland declared, "except in a business way or by making speeches or addresses to them. With their families and friends these leaders of their race form a society as exclusive as the most fashionable white society, and socially have almost as little to do with their brethren as if they were white, instead of almost so, as most of them are. The colored people do not feel identified with them, and although they are in a way proud of their prominence, they are not fond of them personally. They do not feel that they are being helped very much by these leaders."[6] In 1898, at the death of Senator Bruce, a black acquaintance noted that he "was a man of education and fine tastes" who, though "alive" to the interests of Negroes, did "not have any close fellowship with members of his race" and especially alienated some because while living in Indianapolis he chose to attend a white church.[7] At one time or another in the late nineteenth and early twentieth centuries similar assessments were likely to be made of those who constituted the exclusive black social circles in Detroit, St. Louis, Memphis, Philadelphia, Cleveland, and Boston, not to mention the enclaves of mulatto aristocrats in Washington and Charleston, South Carolina.

Whites who showed interest in the black social structure in general and the colored aristocracy in particular usually tried to explain both through the use of class indices such as wealth, income, education, and occupation traditionally applied to whites. Such criteria or indices, employed within the context of the black experience, were useful but scarcely proved adequate to explain the peculiar place occupied by what became known as the "old black upper class"— described by Constance McLaughlin Green as the few Negroes who from the perspective of those lower may not have appeared as angels "but were scarcely more accessible than the heavenly creatures."[8] More subjective factors related to historical experience and traditions and to a color-conscious society figured significantly in determining the contours of the black class structure. Much of what accounted for prestige and status in the black community had no counterpart in white society. For example, the emphasis that colored aristocrats placed on ancestry and family heritage, or what Charles S. Johnson later termed "a significant family history," was in large measure bound up with blacks' experience with slavery—their place in the slave system, their role in opposing it, and the extent to which their families had been free from it.[9]

Often related to their pride in ancestry and lineage was the question of color or complexion. The existence around the turn of the century of a color complex among some blacks that linked a light skin with high status reflected the extent to which "the Negro community's internal prestige hierarchy was the product of the external pressures exerted by the color caste system" imposed by whites.[10] What made the mulattoes "so aristocratic," explained a character in one of

Sutton Griggs's novels, was: "we blacks like them, the white folks like them, and they like themselves; leaving nobody to like us blacks."[11]

Modern sociologists, whose studies of the black social structure have been less impressionistic but often little more enlightening than those of earlier nonprofessional analysts, seem to have reached at least a measure of agreement about the "inapplicability of 'white' social class indices for the Negro community" and about the substantial differences in the class identification process among blacks and whites. While sociologists still disagree about many aspects of this process among blacks, especially about the relationship between color and status, at least they no longer treat the black social structure as a mere facsimile of that in the white community or attempt to analyze it exclusively in terms of objective criteria applied to white society. "It would appear," one student of social class measurement admitted in 1968, "that the Negro stratification structure is a bigger mystery than has been heretofore imagined." Even though some sociologists take exception to the suggestion that blacks are "more class conscious than whites," few disagree with the notion that race constituted such a cleavage in American society that there existed two "essentially different subjective class hierarchies" for whites and blacks.[12]

Although the hardening of anti-black sentiment in the late nineteenth century encouraged white Americans to view blacks as an undifferentiated mass of inferior beings, the notion of a stratified black society capped by a "colored aristocracy," however vaguely or loosely defined, had existed for well over a half century before the appearance of the article in the *Courant* in 1883. Through their association with blacks in the struggle against slavery, some white abolitionists came to appreciate the significance of class among blacks and to despair of the elitism evidenced by some of their black compatriots. "I mourn over the aristocracy that prevails among our colored brethren," Sarah Grimké wrote Theodore Weld in 1837. "I cherished hopes that suffering had humbled them and prepared them to perform a glorious part in the reformation of our country, but the more I mingle with them, the fainter are my hopes. They have as much caste among them as we have, and despise the poor as much, I fear, as their pale brethren. . . ."[13]

Four years after Grimké's observation, in 1841, Joseph Willson, writing under the pseudonym "A Southerner," explored in considerable detail the question of a black aristocracy in a little volume entitled *Sketches of the Higher Classes of Colored Society in Philadelphia*. Aware that such a title was likely to prompt derision, Willson nonetheless hoped to disabuse whites of their inclination "to regard people of color as one consolidated mass, all huddled together, without any particular or general distinctions, social or otherwise" and to hold the "errors and crimes of one . . . as the criterion of the character of the whole body." Such a view, he argued, imposed upon black society a degree of unity quite contrary to reality. Focusing on the "men of fortune and gentlemen of leisure found among black Philadelphians," Willson maintained that the principal grounds of social distinction were "founded upon wealth, education, station, and occupation." While birth and family connection were important, they alone did not insure a place at the top of the black social structure. Education, in particular, received a high priority, and among no people, according to Willson, was "the pursuit of knowledge more honored" than among Philadelphia's black upper class. While those in this class fully enjoyed the good things of life, they avoided extravagance and vulgar display. They practiced abstinence and sobriety, evidenced a concern for moral conduct that made them "as chaste and temperate as any other body of the population," and adhered so strictly to "the nicer etiquettes, proprieties and observances . . . of the well-bred" as "to render their society agreeable and interesting to the most fastidious in such matters." Always careful to remain "aloof from the vicious and worthless" of their race, upper-class black Philadelphians led such "virtuous and exemplary" lives that they provided the black masses with a model worthy of emulation.[14]

Wishing to present a balanced view of the upper class, Willson was careful to note what he interpreted as its basic weakness. For him the most unbecoming attribute of this group resulted from its division into "numerous distinct social circles," or cliques, each made up of individuals "equally respectable and of equal merit and pretensions," which were locked in competition. Marked by displays of envy, hypocrisy, and deceit, these rivalries had on occasion lasted through several generations. The implication was that upper-class blacks expended so much energy on social feuding that they had little left to devote to more worthwhile causes, such as uplift activities in behalf of the "submerged" masses.[15]

In many respects the black upper class that evolved in communities, large and small, throughout the North resembled that in Philadelphia described by Willson. Differences in environments, settlement patterns, and other factors accounted for variations in the size and character of this class. In New York City, the Dutch influence was evident in the names and traditions of some prominent aristocrats of color as late as the opening of the twentieth century. Fannie Barrier Williams, a native of Brockport, New York, who became a conspicuous figure in Chicago's black society, described herself as a "mulatto in complexion" whose parents and grandparents were free people. In Brockport her only association was with whites. "We suffered from no discrimination on account of color or 'previous condition,' " she later recalled, "and lived in blissful ignorance of the fact that we were practicing the unpardonable sin of 'social equality.' " Her sister, Ella Barrier, was for many years a teacher in Washington's public schools, and her brother George Barrier settled in Detroit and married into the prestigious Pelham family there.[16] In Boston the black brahmins displayed, in their values and life styles, what was termed the influences of "New England ideals of home and society." In a reference to the exclusive social set of black Boston, James Weldon Johnson spoke of those "staid, more or less dark New Englanders" who were sometimes awed and puzzled by the expansiveness and penchant for opulent display exhibited by black Southerners in their midst.[17] Regardless of the differences that existed among the black upper class in various Northern communities, its members displayed pride in a free ancestry and the role that their forebears had played in the struggle against slavery, lived "virtuous and exemplary" lives, and placed a premium on education.

Because of Cincinnati's proximity to slave states, emigrés from the South made up a sizable element in the city's black community. In the relatively free atmosphere of Cincinnati, a host of caterers, barbers, and other entrepreneurs achieved a degree of prosperity that allowed them "ample opportunity for imitation of the aristocratic white people with whom they came in contact." By the 1850s there had emerged an upper class known as "the big families," who enjoyed and dispensed "the amenities of high social life" and spearheaded campaigns that secured educational opportunities for black children. According to one authority, those of the black upper class, including the Harlans, Fossetts, and Schooleys, pursued a life style resembling that of "the aristocratic white people with whom they came in contact." Despite economic reverses suffered by some of the "big families" and the emergence of other blacks claiming elite status, the "small group" descended from the old upper class was "still true to ancient conditions" and manifested pride in being "to the manor born."[18]

The black social structure that emerged in post–Civil War America had its roots not only in the experience of the higher classes of free blacks in the North, described by Willson and others, but also in the experience of those blacks, both slave and free, in the antebellum South. That group known as the "old upper class" or "old families," as distinct from those that later made up an economic elite, was drawn largely from the ranks of free blacks (some of whom owned slaves), house slaves and other privileged bondsmen, and certain immigrants from the West Indies. Class distinctions developed among antebellum free blacks in the South, ranging from those whose poverty, illiteracy, and color placed them closer to the slave masses than to those free people of color whose wealth, education, values, and complexion more closely resembled upper-class whites, with whom they were sometimes related by blood. A free black elite flourished especially in the Southern port cities of Charleston, Mobile, Savannah, Pensacola, and New Orleans.[19]

Daniel Murray, an early twentieth century Afro-American bibliographer and a member of a prominent black family from Maryland, extolled the traditions and contributions of free blacks, especially those in his native state and in North Carolina. He cited in particular the Chavises, Evanses, Greens, and Chesnutts, all antebellum free families of color located in the area around Fayetteville and New Bern, North Carolina. Descendants of these families who lived in Ohio and other states outside the South in the twentieth century continued their families' traditions of achievement and occupied places of prominence in diverse fields. "It is this power of blood inheritance, fully illustrated in the career of colored men from Maryland and North Carolina," Murray declared, "that we find the fullest justification that 'blood will tell.' "[20]

The stratification of free blacks, as Ira Berlin has indicated, was infinitely complex. Substantial differences existed between the class structures of those in the North, upper South, and lower South. Each region "had its own distinctive demographic, economic, social and even somatic charcteristics," which resulted in "different relations with whites and slaves, as well as distinctive systems of values and modes of social action." In the lower South, for example, free blacks tended to think of themselves as a caste apart from slaves and attached greater significance to gradations of color.[21]

The concept of the three-caste society was perhaps more fully developed in Louisiana and Gulf port cities such as New Orleans than anywhere else in antebellum America. Extramarital unions between European males and black females, in addition to liberal manumission policies under the French and Spanish, resulted in a large population of *gens de couleur libre*. It was not unusual for the offspring of such unions to be recognized officially as the children of white fathers, who on occasion provided them with educational advantages and bequeathed to them substantial wealth. In New Orleans the so-called Creoles of color, who were usually fair complexioned and often identified with French culture, thought of themselves as a caste apart from other blacks. They assumed positions of leadership during Reconstruction, and despite pleas from some of their spokesmen for the Creoles of color to abandon their tradition of separatism and make common cause with the masses of freed slaves, old distinctions proved to be extraordinarily difficult to eradicate. Few colored Creoles were willing to accept the notion that their future was "indissolubly bound up with that of the negro." Some attempted to acquire separate and distinct legal rights for themselves, prompting other blacks to fear that the Creoles would "institutionalize themselves into a kind of oligarchy."[22]

The light-skinned black elite whose forebears had been free for one or more generations not only responded differently to Emancipation than did slaves but were also quick to draw distinctions between themselves as free men and the former slaves as freedmen. As one slave recalled, the "freeborns" used "contraband" as a pejorative term to designate newly freed slaves. In 1868 a young, fair-complexioned woman of free ancestry who was a school teacher in Frederick, Maryland exhibited a condescending view toward black freedmen and poor whites that was probably typical of her class. Frederick, she wrote, was populated largely by "poor, mean, sneaking looking whites" and by blacks who were "ignorant and unfit for the society of any who have been blessed with any advantages of cultivation and refinement." As one so blessed, she avoided all contact with both groups and confined her social relationships to a small circle of black friends of comparable refinement that she met at the local Episcopal church.[23]

An institution frequently cited as a symbol of the exclusiveness of free-born mulatto elite was the Brown Fellowship Society of Charleston. Organized in 1790 and limited to fifty free men of color of good character, the Society continued well into the twentieth century. The founders of the Society were members of the white St. Philip's Episcopal Church, "where they worshipped, were baptized and married but could not be interred in its burial ground." Therefore one of the organization's most important functions was the mainte-nance of a cemetery. The membership included men of substantial wealth who owned slaves. In 1859 Richard and Joseph Dereef, whose family was long a part of the slave-owning free black elite of Charleston, together owned real estate valued at more than $40,000 and a total of eighteen slaves.[24]

Also representative of the society's membership was the Holloway family. In 1904, on the 117th anniversary of the founding of the Society, J. H. Holloway, whose father, grandfather, and great-grandfather had all been free men, delivered a moving address in which he discussed its ideals and traditions, noting in particular its commitment to charity, benevolence, and "social pur-ity." Because "our fathers" allied themselves with upper-class whites, Holloway explained, "they had their influence and protection," and "our fathers" had "to be in accord with them and stand for what they stood for." Even if the members of the Brown Fellowship Society had publicly supported the system of slavery, they had "sympathized with the oppressed" for they themselves, though free, had to endure oppression. What Holloway did not emphasize was that members of his society, like the white aristocrats with whom they identified, also exploited the labor of slaves and discriminated against all Negroes of darker complexion, free as well as slave. Through all the tumultuous changes of war and Reconstruc-tion, Holloway declared with obvious pride, he and others in the Fellowship "still kept the compact close" and revered "the heritage of the fathers." A saddle and harness maker by trade, Holloway clearly viewed himself, as did others, as "an aristocrat," unobtrusive, of gentle nature, and "very virtuous." He man-ifested great pride in the accomplishments of his family both before and after the Civil War.[25]

The tradition of civic responsibility demonstrated by Holloway's antebellum ancestors continued after the war with his father, who served as city alderman in Charleston, and a brother who was a presidential elector in 1896. Holloway himself was active in Republican politics and received an appointment as postmaster of Marion, South Carolina. Upon retirement from that position, in 1902, he wrote a friend that he had returned to Charleston to reside in the ancestral home built by his grandfather almost a century earlier on land pur-chased by his great-grandfather in the eighteenth century. Throughout his life he was "true to his convictions" and steadfast in his loyalty to the ideals and "close compact" of the Brown Fellowship Society. It may well be, as a writer suggested in 1925, that Holloway resembled "a priest of a dying cult" but the legacies of that cult continued to exert influence among the "old families."[26]

The "close compact" among upper-class free blacks described by Holloway was also evident among a similar group in St. Louis. In 1858 Cyprian Clamorgan, a free black man of French and Afro-American ancestry who resided in the city, published a slender volume entitled *The Colored Aristocracy of St. Louis* "to show the origins and position of a portion of those whom circumstances have placed in the path of comparative respectability and to whom fortune has been kind in the bestowal of the good gifts of life." By the term "colored aristocracy," Clamorgan meant those blacks in antebellum St. Louis who "moved in a certain circle; who, by means of wealth, education or natural ability, form a peculiar class—the *elite* of the colored race." According to Clamorgan, a "high wall" separated this elite, those of the "first class," from those whom he placed in "the second class"; and the distance between the "first class" and the black masses at the bottom was insuperable. While his account includes numerous references to the elite's emphasis on learning, manners, and style of living, its most distinctive traits were its color and wealth. Except in rare instances Clamorgan's colored aristocrats were fair-skinned mulattoes, a group "separated from the white race by a line of division so faint that it can be traced only by the keen eye of prejudice." Many were blood relatives of "the first families" in the white community. In addition to their fair complexions, the colored aristocrats possessed wealth, some being worth more than $100,000, according to Clamorgan's estimates. While a few had inherited substantial property, in some cases from white relatives, most were self-made men whose own business acumen accounted for their worldly goods. Since barbering was considered a high-status occupation by blacks and was one of the few professions open to them, "tonsorial artists" were well represented among the colored aristocracy of St. Louis. What was also obvious from Clamorgan's account was the extent to which family background—"connection"—was important in establishing one's place among the elite. Clearly too, neither wealth nor color alone or together was sufficient to guarantee acceptance among those of "the first class." Rather, admission to the upper reaches of society required a combination of respectability, moral rectitude, social grace, education, and proper ancestry, as well as wealth and color.[27]

Among those whom Clamorgan described in some detail was Samuel Mordecai, "one of the wealthiest of our colored aristrocats." A Kentuckian by birth and of Jewish-Afro-American ancestry, he had served for many years as a steward on a river boat and had amassed a sizable fortune through his skill with cards. By 1860 he had acquired real estate valued at $14,000. A man of elegant manners and unimpeachable integrity, Mordecai was "quite aristocratic in his feelings" and, according to Clamorgan, possessed "the ability and address" to "be received in the first circles" of any society. He sent his fifteen-year-old daughter to England to be educated and considered moving his family to Paris upon completion of her schooling because "in France a colored man is more respected than in any other part of the world." For some reason Mordecai abandoned the idea of leaving St. Louis, and he and his descendants remained among the city's most socially prominent blacks. One of these in the 1890s was Edith V. Mordecai, "the society queen" of St. Louis, who expressed pride in being a "lineal descendant of the proud blood of the 'Blue Grass' country." A teacher in the city's public schools, an accomplished pianist, and a linguist who spoke German "with the fluency of a Berliner," Miss Mordecai obviously was as gracious and "artistocratic in feeling" as her ancestor.[28]

That an aristocracy of color on a smaller scale than that described by Clamorgan existed in Natchez, Mississippi is evident from the extensive diary of William Johnson, a free man of color, and a barber who acquired considerable wealth from his real estate speculation and money-lending activities. The Johnsons, along with several other free fair-complexioned black families such as the Barlands, McCarys, Fitzgeralds, and Winns, constituted an elite circle whose cultural and social pretensions approximated those of upper-class whites. Some of these families had not only inherited valuable property from white ancestors, but, like Johnson, also owned slaves. Johnson undoubtedly reflected the attitude of "the top bracket of the free Negro group" in Natchez with his disdain for any kind of ungentlemanly behavior, especially that evident in what he called "darky parties," where slaves and lower-class free blacks intermingled. He was a man of elegant tastes, great dignity, and lively intelligence who subscribed to several journals and enjoyed music and the theatre. His home was filled with expensive furniture, carpets, cut glass, and paintings. In fact, Johnson and his close friend Robert McCary, also a barber, maintained life styles that distinguished them from most blacks—and poor whites—whom they referred to as "low minded wretches." Their tastes, values, and outlook more closely resembled that of the white planters with whom they were in regular contact. Despite the proscribed world in which they existed, the Johnsons, McCarys, and the few other families that made up Natchez's free colored upper class not only kept aloof from most whites as well as other blacks, both slave and free, but also identified with the white aristocracy.[29]

Another component of the old upper class among blacks in the post–Civil War era came not from those who had been legally free but from slaves who had occupied a privileged, or at least an unusual, position in the slave system. Among these were the house slaves who in time became the subject of numerous legends. Often ridiculed for aping the ways of their white owners, they were accused on occasion of disloyalty to the race because of their practice of using the influence that they had acquired with their masters "against the interest of the field hands." The idea of a well-developed class system among slaves, in which house servants identified with white aristocrats and drew a sharp distinction between themselves and field hands, appears to be largely mythical, but like most myths, it contains an element of truth. Class consciousness was more likely to be found on plantations large enough to possess clearly defined categories of work among slaves. On most plantations no sharp distinction existed between housework and field duties; hence many slaves moved from one to the other as circumstances required. Although the evidence suggests that "group loyalty overrode tendencies toward class division among slaves," the idea persisted, among blacks as well as whites, that the "aristocracy ethos" absorbed by pampered house slaves prompted them to identify with their white masters and to place distance between themselves and field hands.[30]

In his autobiography, published in 1895, H. C. Bruce, the brother of Senator Bruce and a slave for twenty-nine years, attempted an elaborate, if somewhat convoluted, defense of "favored slaves," whom he considered superior to the "free fellows" even though the latter "felt themselves better" than their brethren in bondage. Convinced that "blood will tell," Bruce explained that blacks, no less than whites, fell into two categories, superior and inferior, as a result of the quality of the "blood in their veins." He did not mean that white blood was superior to black, but rather that some blacks, just as some whites, possessed "inferior blood," which accounted for their backwardness and degraded status. Those blacks who made no progress and remained in menial positions generation after generation obviously did so as a result of their "inferior blood." In contrast, slaves "having superior blood in their veins" never gave up in "abject servility" but held their heads high and "proceeded to do the next best thing under the circumstances, which was to so live and act as to win the confidence of the masters, which could only be done by faithful service and upright life." These were "the reliables," faithful and trustworthy, whose loyalty slave owners rewarded by placing confidence in them. Bruce calculated that there were thousands of such "high toned and high spirited slaves who had as much self-respect as their masters, who were industrious, reliable, and truthful, and could be depended upon by their masters in all cases." From the ranks of these "high-toned" slaves, he argued, came the natural leaders of the race after Emancipation. Their self-confidence, sense of duty, and other admirable traits exhibited in their own lives and instilled in their children meant that the freedmen of "superior blood" were "largely instrumental in making the record of which we feel so proud today."

Bruce's argument could be used to support the view of the favored slave as one who, no matter how "high-toned," was always deferential to whites and all too willing to embrace their attitudes toward the mass of slaves. Clearly that was not Bruce's intention. Rather his aim was to explain the slave hierarchy in terms of character traits in a way that justified the claims of "superior" slaves to positions of high status in the postwar black community. Despite his disparagement of free blacks and their hauteur toward slaves, the attitude of his "superior" slaves toward the "inferior" masses resembled that of the "free fellows" toward slaves in general.[31]

Among the observers of life in the antebellum South who noted that the light-skinned house slaves enjoyed a lofty status in the slave hierarchy was Samuel Mordecai. His *Richmond In By Gone Days*, published in 1860, included a chapter on "the Colored Aristocracy," which described the self-conscious elitism of such slaves and their tendency to imitate upper-class whites in their "high life below the stairs." Sy Gilliant, a fiddler for parties and balls held by the white gentry, was "the most prominent member of the black aristocracy" in early nineteenth century Richmond. Like others of the city's slave elite, Mordecai explained, Gilliant "acquired something of the polite and respectful demeanor which prevailed among the gentility." Highly selective in his choice of associates among blacks, he limited his circle of friends to a few of the "leading stewards, coachmen and head cooks of the best families."[32]

Daniel R. Hundley, whose *Social Relations in Our Southern States* also appeared in 1860, lent support to Mordecai's observations. "The slaves of a gentleman of good family . . .," Hundley argued, "are not only more intelligent than the mass of blacks, but are both polite and well-bred, and in a measure refined and aristocratic. They scorn to associate with common darkeys." Even Frederick Douglass believed that "these house people constituted a sort of aristocracy."[33] Although the distance between such slaves and those in the fields was scarcely as great as sometimes implied, house servants in some Southern cities and on certain large plantations, especially if they were light skinned, probably did approximate an elite class "that lived up to the legends." Certainly the notion of sharp distinctions between house servants and field hands persisted within the black community.[34] In 1906 a black editor, in a scathing denunciation of "big Negroes," likened them to the slaves "up in the big house" who spent so much time currying favor with whites and trying to imitate them that they manifested little interest in the welfare of ordinary Negroes.[35]

Not all house slaves, any more than all free persons of color, entered the ranks of the postwar black upper class. Much depended on one's answer to the question: "Who are your people?" An answer likely to gain one admission into the colored aristocracy would almost certainly convey information about respectability, manners and deportment, education, ancestry and color, family achievement, and perhaps wealth. In explaining what made a family distinguished, historian Carter G. Woodson noted that a black family must early produce "a member who accomplished something unusual and others of his descendants lived up to that record by likewise achieving distinction."[36] That "something unusual" might involve purchasing or otherwise securing freedom from slavery, acquiring an education, or participating in activities associated with the crusade against slavery, as in the case of Frederick Douglass and William and Ellen Craft. Certainly, Douglass and his descendants as well as the Crafts were accorded places in the upper strata of black society.

Another route by which favored slaves gained admission to the social elite was by way of a particular form of the miscegenated family tree. It was what John Mercer Langston later called one of "the many curious things . . . connected with the old institutions of American slavery." Conspicuous among the members of the black upper class in the late nineteenth and early twentieth centuries were the fair-compexioned offspring of white masters and mulatto slaves and the descendants of such offspring. Unlike the mulatto children that resulted from casual liaisons between white men and slave women, who were ignored or abandoned by their white fathers and who, in Roi Ottley's words, constituted the sizable population of "mulatto nobodies,"[37] these individuals were the children of more stable liaisons, sometimes of long duration. They benefited directly from their white parentage by gaining access to education, wealth, or opportunities unavailable to other slaves or even to free blacks.

A number of men prominently identified with Blanche K. Bruce's social circle, including P. B. S. Pinchback, Josiah Settle, Robert Harlan, Norris Wright Cuney, Robert Church, and Henry P. Cheatham, were also slave sons of well-to-do white planters who showed a special interest in their welfare. For example, Harlan, a slave and relative of the Harlan family of Kentucky, who allowed him "unusual freedom," traveled widely in the United States and abroad. A politician of influence and a prosperous businessman with a fondness for thoroughbred racehorses, he and his family were fixtures in the highest social circles of black Cincinnati for a half century beginning in the 1850s. Scarcely less remarkable was Norris Wright Cuney, one of eight children born to Colonel Philip N. Cuney and his slave Adeline Stuart, whom he eventually set free. Colonel Cuney was an indulgent father who provided generously for the education of his mulatto offspring. In 1859 Norris Wright Cuney entered the Wylie Street School in Pittsburgh under the famous educator George B. Vashon. When the outbreak of the Civil War interrupted plans for him to continue his education at Oberlin, Cuney secured a job on a steamboat on the Ohio and Mississippi between Cincinnati and New Orleans. Here he first met and formed lifelong friendships with P. B. S. Pinchback and James Lewis, who, like him, became prominent politically during Reconstruction. A man of considerable wealth who served as collector of the Port of Galveston, Cuney remained the most influential black Republican in Texas until his death in 1898.[38]

Robert R. Church, the wealthy Memphis businessman, banker, and father of Mary Church Terrell, was a close friend of Harlan and Cuney as well as Pinchback and Bruce. Like Cuney, he first encountered James Lewis before the Civil War when both were working on river boats. Church's father was Captain Charles B. Church, owner of two palatial Mississippi River steamboats, who reared his son to be a gentleman and taught him to fight anyone who showed disrespect. Robert Church's mother, Emmaline, was described as "a born aristocrat" with "exquisite manners." Though a slave, Emmaline claimed she was the daughter of Lucy, a beautiful Malay princess who had been enslaved following her family's fall from power. Robert Church never considered himself a slave because of his close relationship with his natural father, whom he adored and respected, and because of the freedom he enjoyed. He amassed great wealth in

Memphis, and when a Southern journal referred to him as a "former slave," James Lewis, his boyhood friend, hastened to complain: "I never heard of you being classified as a slave." Whether technically a slave or not, Church was, according to his daughter, a man of "innate culture" who, "reserved in his manner, was rarely familiar with anybody."[39]

As was often the case of slave sons who enjoyed special treatment, they displayed obvious pride in their background as well as considerable affection for their white ancestors. Aristocrats of color were almost always expert genealogists possessing a detailed knowledge of their miscegenated family trees. Knowledge of one's family history, W. E. B. Du Bois remarked of upper-class black families in New England, "was counted as highly important." In 1907, for example, B. F. Wheeler, a descendant of the Varick family of New York, published a history of the family that covered several generations. Among the family's most notable characteristics were its "lightness of complexion," strength of character, continuous record of achievement, and prominence in the civic and social life of communities from New York to Mobile. Most disappointing in Wheeler's view was the lack of religious fervor in a family whose most famous ancestor, James Varick, was the founder of the African Methodist Episcopal Zion Church. In explaining the strengths of the Varick family, Wheeler placed much emphasis on its "mixture of blood," noting that in its veins flowed "the blood of the firm and tenacious Dutchman, the blood of the alert and unconquerable Indian, and the blood of the religious Negro."[40]

Unlike Booker T. Washington, who never knew the identity of his white father, mixed-blood aristocrats of color could furnish detailed genealogical knowledge about the African kings, Indian chiefs, Malaysian princesses, and distinguished white Americans from whom they were descended. That they acknowledged and sometimes exhibited affection for their white forebears did not mean that they either ignored or were unimpressed by their African ancestors. "One of the marvels of our once divine institution of slavery," John Mercer Langston observed in 1887, "is the product of sons and daughters— slaves, too, by law—who, because of the affection and devotion of their white master-fathers, have been recognized, named, cared for and endowed as offspring, in fact and in law, by fathers who were their owners. How many colored children, sons and daughters in this country bear the name of white, slave-holding families . . . ? How many of them, too, have been educated and located in life and business upon efforts and outlays made by men, their fathers, whose names they bear! How many of such class have won fame and standing in general society and distinction in colored society . . . and have wielded commanding influence throughout the community." The "best representatives" of such miscegenated families, according to Langston, not only identified with blacks but also "exercised a loyalty and devotion to the whole Negro race, to whose welfare they have given their wisest and bravest efforts."[41]

Among those who fit Langston's description of such offspring was Adella Hunt, one of seven children born to Georgia judge Nathan Sayre and Maria Hunt, whose ancestry was white, Indian, and African. A petite, strikingly beautiful woman, Adella Hunt graduated from Atlanta University and joined the faculty at Tuskegee Institute, where she married Warren Logan, the school treasurer, in 1888. Asked on one occasion to provide a biographical sketch, she responded: "There is little to tell, as my busy life has been without romantic event. I was not born a slave, nor in a log cabin. To tell the truth I got my education by no greater hardship than hard work, which I regard as exceedingly healthful." The marriage of Warren Logan, Jr., to the daughter of Hutchins Bishop, rector of St. Philip's Episcopal Church in New York, linked the Logans to one of the most respected old upper-class families of Maryland and New York.[42]

Similar in many respects were the background and experience of Josiah T. Settle of Memphis. He was named after his father, a white planter who lived for a time in Tennessee before settling on a plantation in Mississippi. His father "had a deep and sincere affection for his children and their mother," who was his slave. After several years in Mississippi, Settle manumitted her and his children by her, but still fearing that their freedom was not secure, he settled his mulatto family in Hamilton, Ohio and lawfully married his former slave. He spent part of the year in Ohio and part in Mississippi. Josiah T. Settle, the eldest son of this union, recalled that his father "was a father to him in the broadest sense of the word" and enrolled him in Oberlin College in 1868. Following graduation from Howard University Law School in 1875, Settle married the beautiful and cultured Therese T. Vogelsang of Annapolis, a niece of James C. Bishop. The couple moved to Mississippi, where Settle practiced law and played a prominent role in politics. In the early 1880s they established themselves in Memphis and became a part of the city's black elite.[43] Although it is impossible to ascertain how many free blacks in the South had advantages comparable to those of Adella Logan and Josiah Settle, their background and experience were not unique.

Few mulatto aristocrats benefited more directly from the generosity of their white fathers or evidenced more clearly an aristocratic ethos than the urbane John Mercer Langston. At one time or another he was an attorney, educator, diplomat, congressman, and racial spokesman. His father was a wealthy Virginia planter, Ralph Quarles, who had freed his mother and his "favored slave" before Langston was born. Quarles not only provided for the education of his three mulatto sons but also left them a substantial portion of his estate. Langston graduated from Oberlin College and became a lawyer. He married Caroline Wall, also a student at Oberlin and the daughter of "a very wealthy and influential [white] citizen" of North Carolina. "Reared in a white family, educated in a white school," P. B. S. Pinchback later said of Langston, "he had been in close contact with the best element of refined and Christian white people, and naturally acquired their habits of thought and action and imbibed their self respect and innate feeling of perfect equality with all mankind."[44]

No one can read Langston's autobiography without becoming aware of his class consciousness and the pride that he had in his own family background. He described the ancestry of his father as "distinguished" and claimed that his mother was descended from a "tribe of Indians of close relationship in blood to the famous Pocahontas." Keenly aware of family name and prestige, he largely confined his associations to persons of "high social position." While attending a private school in Cincinnati in 1840, he moved in a social circle that included only "the very best and most highly educated and cultured young colored persons," whose families represented the top stratum of black society. Such families possessed "a reasonable amount of means" and lived in relative ease and comfort. "If there has ever existed in any colored community of the United States anything like an aristocratic class of such persons," Langston later wrote, "it was in Cincinnati. . . . " More than a half century later he still spoke in terms that revealed his class consciousness.[45]

Those who made up the "colored aristocracy" in post–Civil War America inherited from their antebellum forebears ideals, traditions, and patterns of behavior which they perpetuated and which set them apart from other blacks. Central to this legacy was an emphasis on education and the acquisition of what was termed culture, an emphasis articulated by a member of Charleston's free mulatto elite who claimed that education not only sharpened the distinction between free people of color and slaves but also promised to eliminate white prejudice against people like him. Similar sentiments were common among aristocrats of color a half century later. Existing alongside the emphasis on education and often associated with it was a persistent concern with manners, "good breeding," and decorum evident in the writings of Clamorgan, Willson, John F. Cook and numerous others of the antebellum "colored aristocracy." Their children and grandchildren in the postwar era, according to one authority, were not satisfied to exhibit just proper conduct; rather theirs were "exemplary conduct, superior manners" and "superrespectability." Aristocrats of color in the forty years after Reconstruction were no more inclined than their antebellum ancestors to associate with blacks outside their own class, especially those whom William Johnson of Natchez had referred to as "low-minded wretches" or those whom Clamorgan described as persons unmindful of "the proprieties of life."[46] Notwithstanding their aloofness from those blacks whom they considered not of "good society," the antebellum aristocracy of color displayed a deep commitment to "the elevation of the race." In all sections of the country they displayed a deep commitment to education; those outside the South also figured prominently in abolitionist and antislavery movements and in moral reform crusades. Their descendants, who made up a sizable portion of the post–Civil War black aristocracy, inherited a sense of "service to the race" and to the realization of equal rights for black citizens.[47]

In the late nineteenth and early twentieth centuries, black Americans evidenced a keen interest in the question of social "gradations" or classes within the black community. Those who publicly addressed the issue generally agreed that a class hierarchy among blacks did in fact exist, shaped in large part by the slave system with its house servants and field hands, artisans and unskilled laborers, and bondsmen and free people of color.[48] The issue was not whether a class structure existed but what form its development and refinement should take in order to promote "the progress of the race." Of especial concern were the appropriate criteria for delineating between the upper, middle, and lower classes.

In the years immediately following Reconstruction much of the public discussion focused on the need for a simple division between those who were "respectable" and those who were not. There were few references to factors such as ancestry, education, wealth, or decorous behavior. The primary argument was that the "respectables" of the race, those who possessed moral character and virtue, should draw a dividing line between themselves and those blacks lacking such attributes. It was high time, a black editor declared in 1878, to ostracize prostitutes, thieves, loafers, and other "vicious" elements of the race. The failure of respectable blacks to draw such a line themselves would allow whites to continue their practice of considering all blacks as an undifferentiated mass and of judging the entire race by its worst elements. A quarter of a century later, W. E. B. Du Bois counselled blacks on the necessity of observing social distinctions: "A rising race must be aristocratic; the good cannot consort with the bad—nor even the best with the less good."[49]

By the 1890s, when the public discussion of social classes in the black community became more widespread and more heated, the class structure within the black community had undergone substantial evolution. In cities with large black populations, such as New York, Chicago, Philadelphia, and especially Washington, social divisions were clearly defined. Old upper-class families that made up what was known as "the colored aristocracy" had already begun to confront the challenges posed by an upwardly mobile middle class. While a number of factors undoubtedly contributed to the heightened interest in the class issue in the 1890s, including the increasing urbanization of blacks, one of the most significant related to the hardening of racial lines and the proliferation of Jim Crow contrivances. For aristocrats of color who still clung to the idea of "amalgamation" or integration into the larger society, these developments posed special difficulties. Convinced that blacks *en masse* were unlikely to be incorporated into the larger society within the foreseeable future, they tended to place greater social distance between themselves and the masses in the hope of achieving amalgamation on an individual basis. They appeared to believe that to the extent that they succeeded in convincing whites that they were in fact different from other blacks in education, refinement, manners, morals, wealth, and even complexion, they would be accorded the rights and privileges of first-class citizens.[50] Although their efforts to establish class lines prompted black critics to accuse them of being cheap imitations of the white "codfish aristocracy" or, even worse, of racial treason, few upper-class blacks abandoned concern for the "submerged masses." Theirs was an attitude of *noblesse oblige*, an obligation to lift the entire race as its privileged few won acceptance by the "larger society."

Much of the discussion of social classes by blacks took place within the context of the struggle over Jim Crow measures and public debates over the issue of social equality. The "social equality scare" among Southern whites, according to an aristocrat of color in Savannah in 1889, was ridiculous, because "the Negro as a people do not have it among themselves."[51] Two years later J. C. Price, a highly respected black educator and churchman, elaborated upon this theme in an article in *The Forum*. "There is no social equality among Negroes," he wrote, "notwithstanding the disposition of some whites to put all Negroes in one class. Culture, moral refinement and material possessions make a difference among colored people as they do among whites."[52]

W. E. B. Du Bois, while a student at Harvard in 1891, exhibited an attitude toward the Federal Elections Bill that probably was not unusual among others of the black upper class. Critical of the idea that "law can accomplish everything," he maintained that many blacks in the South were "not fit for the responsibility of republican government," and when the region had "the right sort of black voter" there would be no need for election laws. The same class attitude found expression in the arguments made by some black legislators in the South against measures to segregate the races on public conveyances. According to one Louisiana legislator, such laws would constitute an "unmerited rebuke" to colored men and women of culture, refinement, and wealth by forcing them to associate with lower-class blacks.[53]

The black upper class justified its claims to a privileged status on various grounds, including its record of achievement, status as antebellum free people of color, culture and education, and, to a lesser degree, wealth. They viewed themselves as the products of a natural selection from which they had emerged as the strongest and fittest of the race. They stood in sharp contrast to those who belonged to the "submerged masses." The emergence of such a class, though small in size, prompted both pride and resentment in the black community.[54]

One of the most extensive discussions of the black class structure occurred in 1896, when the editor of the Indianapolis *Freeman*, W. M. Lewis, invited Richard W. Thompson, a well-known black journalist, to respond to the question: "Do you think the interest of [black] society would be promoted by drawing lines, not based upon color, but in the same manner as instinct draws them in the race around us?"[55] Basing his observation primarily on his knowledge of Indianapolis and Washington, which he considered prime examples of the "eddying currents of Afro-American society," Thompson began by asserting that class lines already existed among blacks and that these lines had been established as a result of the working out of the "natural order." He emphatically denied that social stratification of blacks should be based on criteria different from those prevailing in the white community because "the Negro lives under the same civilization as his Caucasian brother." Thompson also distinguished between authentic class criteria, such as "character, worth, morals [and] conduct," and transient, superficial considerations, ranging from "the accidental possession of money or position" to the "color of skin and texture of hair." "Mere money, mere complexion, mere pretense, unaccompanied by sterling virtues," he argued, "will not maintain an individual's standing forever, nor garner him enduring fame. Individuals will find their destiny determined not so much by one particular quality or acquirement as by a delicate system of sifting and averaging." Thompson urged upper-class blacks whose aim it was "to assist nature in enforcing the law of natural selection" to "grant labor its dignity," and to avoid the temptation "to leave the race behind" and "withhold the sympathetic aid of a hand grown strong from race support." To commit such an error or to embrace a "false system of education which breeds a contempt for the race" and its masses would ensure the establishment of "a false aristocracy." Although Thompson avoided rendering any judgment on the degree to which the black upper class in 1896 succeeded or failed in measuring up to his standards, he clearly believed that an aristocracy of color did in fact exist.[56]

Dr. J. M. Henderson, well-known black physician and clergyman in New York, who joined in the discussion launched by Lewis and Thompson, agreed that a black aristocracy, "though rudimentary and indistinct," was a reality. Henderson, however, was not reticent about standing in judgment of the aristocracy: he believed that it was more harmful than helpful in promoting racial progress because of its pretentiousness, conspicuous consumption, and disdain of manual labor, not to mention its "whims, vanities and tomfoolery." "The highest expression of the social tastes of the aristocracy," he observed, "is the exclusive dance and the exclusive party." The fate of the Afro-American, according to Henderson, rested with the emerging middle class, which was vigorous, enterprising, aggressive, and intimately identified with the race and its collective welfare. Nor did this antipathy for the aristocrats of color abate with the passage of time.[57] As late as 1907, he was still referring to them as "a tiny class of effulgents" and as "a few puny accidental colored exquisites" who were parasites subsisting on "hand-outs in the way of preferments" from whites. Such people, always preoccupied with promoting themselves as "an exclusive social set," would in the judgment of history go largely unnoticed while the robust middle class would force its way to the front.[58] Others echoed Henderson's criticisms of the aristocracy and praise of the middle class throughout the period from the 1890s to the First World War.[59]

Most black Americans appeared to agree that a "graded social scale" existed in black communities throughout the United States. It was more pronounced in the cities with large black populations but also existed among blacks in small towns and even rural areas. Like sociologists later, black observers in the late nineteenth and early twentieth centuries indicated that the black class structure resembled a pyramid with the overwhelming majority belonging to the lower class at the bottom and a tiny minority constituting the "aristocracy" at the top. Between the two was an emerging middle class, relatively small in size, but steadily growing.[60]

While black writers marshalled evidence to demonstrate the existence of a well-defined class structure among Negro Americans in order to combat the notion that "all Negroes are alike" and hence to strike a blow against segregation efforts, they disagreed over the appropriate criteria to determine the class identification of an individual or a family. Class distinctions, a black Clevelander noted in 1893, "should be made on a positive basis" but "what this basis should be is not universally agreed upon."[61] In identifying the upper class, blacks often placed "intelligence and character" or "character and attainments" as the prime requisites. Only a little less often did they specifically include attributes such as refinement, culture, manners, and education. Ancestry and family background, while obviously considerations of importance, rarely appeared in general discussions of the black class structure, but they invariably received extensive treatment in biographies of and references to those who belonged to the aristocracy. Wealth and color or fairness of complexion as stratifiers, whatever their actual role, were almost universally condemned as "artificial" and "malignant" considerations. Upper-class blacks, J. Simon Flipper, a well-known clergyman in Atlanta, observed in 1902, were those who had "outstripped their fellows in the race of life and attained a standard of civilization commensurate with the opportunities and had proved to the civilized world that under favorable circumstances the Negro is as capable of a high development in civilization as any other race."[62] Like others who analyzed the black upper class, Flipper spoke in Darwinian terms of the "race of life" while simultaneously implying that those who stood at the apex of the black class structure had enjoyed "favorable circumstances," a phrase that could be related to everything from culture and color to education and wealth.

In 1891 an article on "Colored Aristocracy" by Ralph Tyler, a member of a well-known black family of Columbus, Ohio, appeared in many black newspapers throughout the country. The existence of an aristocracy, he argued, was not only indisputable but also evidence of the "rapid progress of Afro-Americans." "The line between the '400' and the masses of the colored population," he declared, "is as clearly drawn as if an ebony Ward McAllister had spent a life time preaching his theories of social distinction." Tyler did not attempt to explain the origins of the black upper class, but focused on its most visible attributes, noting in particular the significance of personal appearance, character, refinement, and education. A black aristocrat always lived in a fashionable neighborhood, and it was virtually impossible for those who lived elsewhere to rise socially. If one were not born into the aristocracy or had not managed somehow to get into it, the prospects for gaining admission "to its clubs and societies" were practically nonexistent. The black upper class spoke flawless English, while those blacks who sprinkled their conversation with "dialect" expressions clearly belonged to "the lower class of colored people." According to Tyler, money had very little weight in determining whether one gained admission to the "upper tendom." The chief requisite for being included among "the chosen few" was education.[63]

Although the wealth of aristocrats of color was small compared to the great fortunes acquired by some whites in the late nineteenth and early twentieth centuries, they did enjoy a degree of financial security unknown to most blacks. Virtually all were working aristocrats whose standard of living and leisure, as well as the educational opportunities provided their children, dramatized the economic gulf between them and other blacks. In addition to those in the professions and in government positions, the black upper class included families identified with such service trades as catering, barbering, and tailoring, which brought them into regular contact with upper-class whites. Some aristocrats of color inherited wealth; others accumulated substantial property, especially in real estate; a few were wealthy by any standard. But Tyler was essentially correct when he later observed that wealth alone did not ensure one a place in the top rung of the black social structure.[64]

The class and color divisions and caste distinctions that developed within the black population before the Civil War did not suddenly disappear with Emancipation: rather they gave rise to a complex class structure topped by those who prided themselves on being "colored aristocrats." Those from the ranks of the elite free black society and privileged bondsmen viewed themselves as natural leaders, superior in culture, sophistication, and wealth to the "parvenu free." According to Langston, the presence in the South of "colored people who had been free for a long time, born so or emancipated," was of "incalculable advantage to those just leaving slavery." The free people of color, born and reared among the very class which had once held them slaves, contributed "much toward influencing and directing those just made free." No other influence, in Langston's view, was "so potent as that of the free colored class" in elevating and directing the thoughts and purposes of the mass of slaves freed by the Civil War.[65]

Although those whom Clamorgan would have designated as belonging to "the first class"—the well-entrenched mulatto elite—often moved in disproportionate numbers into positions of leadership during Reconstruction and afterward, they continually encountered challenges from ambitious, upwardly mobile, darker-complexioned individuals emerging from and closely identified with the black masses. Despite all the rhetoric about unity and racial solidarity, "the advent of freedom exacerbated old differences and introduced new ones" in the black community.[66]

In the decades after the Civil War, the mulatto elite composed of the "old families" and tied by blood as well as culture to the white world, in Joel Williamson's phrase, functioned as the "carriers of whiteness into the Negro community."[67] In 1892 Andrew F. Hilyer, a native of Georgia and a graduate of the University of Minnesota, who was long a fixture in Washington's most exclusive black social circles, spoke directly to this point when he explained the role of the mulatto aristocrats: "The people of mixed blood is the natural bridge between the two races." Although the mixed blood might prefer, as Hilyer indicated, to be identified with "the dominant race" and thereby escape all the disadvantages of being classified as black, whites had "decreed that one drop of African blood" was sufficient to preclude entry into the white world. "No matter how intelligent, learned, cultured, or wealthy any Afro-American may become, or how white he may be, or how straight his hair," he concluded, "he is always classified as colored and as such liable to all the disadvantages under which the mass [of blacks] labors."[68]

Despite repeated charges that mulatto aristocrats embraced the attitudes and ways of whites, they generally took seriously what they considered their mission of service to blacks, utilizing their "superior advantage and opportunities" in behalf of the masses. Although the light-complexioned aristocrats engaged in a wide variety of racial uplift causes and allied themselves, especially in pursuit of political and economic objectives, with the darker "parvenu free," their day-to-day lives continued to be marked by social distance and exclusiveness. In brief, it appears that economic and political distances between the aristocrats and ordinary black folk narrowed at a substantially faster rate than did social distance. In a sense, the aristocracy embraced a modified version of Booker T. Washington's famous hand and fingers analogy: in all things purely social the aristocrats tended to be as separate from other blacks as the fingers, yet one as the hand in all things for racial uplift. Naturally, the social distance maintained by the "old families" was the source of tensions that sometimes disrupted the unity of uplift activities and invited scorn from other blacks. As early as 1872 the *Christian Recorder*, a publication of the African Methodist Episcopal Church, warned the "upper class of Society" about the dangers of ignoring and attempting to separate itself from the "unfortunate creatures of the lower class." The *Recorder* reminded the aristocrats that their fate was bound inextricably with that of other blacks and that the upper class could not succeed "without taking the lower class with it." A quarter of a century later, Francis J. Grimké, a black Presbyterian clergyman, pursued a similar theme in an essay in which he argued that blacks, regardless of social status or complexion, simply could not "get away from each other."[69]

By the late nineteenth century there existed a nationwide network of aristocrats of color who were personally acquainted and often related either by blood or by marriage. The existence of the network owed much to the migrations of blacks, especially free people of color, both before and after the Civil War. Antebellum free blacks left the South in sizable numbers and achieved prominence in various cities beyond Mason and Dixon's line. By the outbreak of the Civil War, free families of color had members in both the North and the South. For example, various members of free families of color in Fayetteville, North Carolina, including those by the name of Leary, Revels, and Chesnutt, lived in Ohio and Indiana; while free black families in Virginia, South Carolina, and elsewhere in the South had relatives in cities all along the Atlantic seaboard. Then, with the beginning of Reconstruction, a host of talented blacks in the North, often native Southerners or relatives of families still in the ex-Confederate States, migrated into the lower South along with some of the mulatto elite of the upper South. Contact and marriage between the elites of different sections provided the underpinning for what became a nationwide network of aristocrats of color, drawn from social circles in all regions that were as "discriminating as actual conditions allow." "These social circles," James Weldon Johnson explained, "are connected throughout the country, and a person in good standing in one city is readily accepted in another." Entry into the charmed circle for those not in good standing, even if they possessed wealth, was difficult if not impossible.[70]

In the late nineteenth century the light-skinned colored aristocrats exhibited a self-conscious elitism: on some occasions it led to condescension and even arrogance toward other blacks, especially the poor, uneducated masses at the bottom of the class structure, who were sometimes referred to as "vicious" and "degraded"; on others this same elitism produced a sense of awesome responsibility that translated itself into a commitment to improve the lot of the race in general.

PART II

◆

People and Places

PROLOGUE

BLANCHE AND JOSEPHINE BRUCE HAD SCARCELY returned from their wedding trip when the press began to speculate on how official white society in Washington would react to the senator's wife. It was by no means certain that Josephine Bruce would receive the treatment accorded the wives of other senators. Her presence posed what was referred to as "the capital social problem." But like several other white newspapers, the *Baltimore American* maintained that her attractive personal traits were sufficient to preclude "any embarrassments." Few journalists failed to comment on her intelligence, refinement, and courtesy. She possessed, one commentator noted, "a quiet dignity . . . that bespeaks the perfect lady" and more education "than most of the women who intend to snub her." Mrs. Bruce's complexion received more detailed treatment in the press than any other of her notable attributes. The *Boston Journal* referred to her as "a great beauty of the Andalusian type," while another white daily asserted that she resembled "what we all imagine a beautiful Spanish lady to be."[1] The *People's Advocate,* a well-known black weekly published in Washington, described Josephine Bruce's complexion as being so fair that even the use of "a microscope" would not detect any evidences of her African ancestry. A white journalist argued that the fair appearance of the wife of the Mississippi senator was proof that all theories about the telltale "signs of African blood" were absolutely false.[2]

That the press devoted so much attention to her color and character suggested that Josephine Bruce was not considered merely as another senatorial spouse. No matter how fair her complexion or how completely she conformed to the image of an ideal Victorian lady, she was still a Negro, the wife of a black senator whose skin color was only a shade darker than hers. But fears that she would be treated as a social outcast in official circles proved to be largely unfounded, at least for a time, in part because of the timing of her arrival in Washington. The "tolerant friendliness" that characterized relations between whites and blacks in Washington early in the decade of the 1870s, while diminished by 1878, still had not disappeared altogether.[3]

[33]

As was the custom, Josephine Bruce designated Thursdays as her "reception days"; her visitors from official Republican circles were numerous, including the wives of cabinet members and congressmen. No Democratic wives paid their respects, and when rumors circulated that the wife of Senator Allen G. Thurman of Ohio had called at the Bruce residence, the senator issued an emphatic denial. Although the Bruces encountered obvious slights from white Democrats, they received invitations to all official Republican social functions, including White House gatherings.[4] A young, upper-class black woman who as a student at Oberlin was a guest in the Bruce home during Bruce's tenure in the Senate later recalled: "With Mrs. Bruce I attended dances and receptions galore, large and small."[5]

The Bruces' own social affairs both at Hillside Cottage and later in their renovated brownstone on M Street invariably prompted flattering comments from both white and black guests about Josephine Bruce's skill and graciousness as a hostess. Those who attended her receptions and teas agreed that "few ladies in Washington can entertain more gracefully." Even fewer were as beautiful or as fashionably dressed. Ten years later, Mrs. Bruce was still "one of the handsomest and best dressed ladies on the avenue." Despite the apparent ease with which she and the senator moved in white social circles for a time, they were scarcely oblivious to the fact that they were included only in social affairs of a more or less official nature.[6]

Nor were the Bruces unaware of the criticism directed at them by certain blacks who claimed that they appeared more interested in associating with whites than with members of their own race. In August 1879 an unsigned letter to the editor of a black newspaper in Washington suggested that Josephine Bruce was the cause of the family's snobbery. When the senator was a bachelor, according to the letter, he had moved easily and often among diverse social circles, but since his return from his European honeymoon and his acquisition of an elegant mansion in "the aristocratic part of the city," no colored person had received an invitation to any of the Bruces' teas or soirées. The anonymous correspondent claimed quite falsely that even the most prestigious black families, including the Douglasses and Cooks, had been excluded from their social life.[7]

By no means were all of Josephine Bruce's efforts focused on social activities. She was knowledgeable about financial matters and managed the household with efficiency and economy. She was in charge of the servants and appears to have encountered the same difficulties as other women of her social status in finding and keeping satisfactory maids and cooks. "Poor old Mrs. Jackson," she complained at one point, "got so good for nothing that I turned her off and now at least have a good, strong, willing girl." A "constant source of worry" for her was Meekins, the coachman long in the employ of the Bruces, who attended to their elegant carriage. Although she objected to what she perceived as Meekins's inefficiency and casualness, she apparently could not bring herself to fire such an old and faithful servant.[8]

The Bruces' only child, a son, was born on April 21, 1879. When the baby was a month old, his parents held a party of their most intimate friends in order to select a name for him. The senator's wishes prevailed, and the child was named Roscoe Conkling Bruce after the Republican senator from New York who had accompanied Bruce to the desk of Vice President Henry Wilson in 1875 to be sworn in, when James Lusk Alcorn, the senior senator from Mississippi, refused to do so. The christening was delayed until Josephine Bruce could take the baby to Cleveland, where the ceremony was performed, according to her wish, by the same Episcopal rector who had officiated at the Bruces' wedding.[9]

The end of Reconstruction and the return to power of white Democrats in Mississippi meant that Senator Blanche K. Bruce's career as an elected official was over. Following his defeat for reelection to the Senate in 1880, he secured a succession of appointments from Republican presidents, first as Register of the Treasury in 1881, as Recorder of Deeds for the District of Columbia eight years later, and finally as Register of the Treasury again in 1897. By the 1890s he had become the senior black official in Washington and enjoyed a degree of political prestige unmatched by any other man of color, except perhaps his close friend Frederick Douglass. During the Democratic interludes under Grover Cleveland, Bruce served the Republican National Committee in a variety of capacities, especially as a campaign speaker among black voters in Northern and Border states. On at least two occasions he was seriously considered for a cabinet post. Always a harmonizer who eschewed violent rhetoric and who was generally seen as an honorable and reasonable man, Bruce believed that whites would continue to dominate American society and that the best hope of black Americans lay in patience, compromise, and education.[10]

For almost two decades following his departure from the Senate, Bruce remained a highly visible figure in the black community. Although the Republican organization in Mississippi remained his political base, he functioned as a national leader of his race who usually found cause for optimism in regard to the "progress of the Negro." A fixture on the lecture circuit, he traveled extensively throughout the United States, often accompanied by his wife, whose presence was considered an ornament at any social occasion. Everywhere, whether in Boston, Memphis, Indianapolis, or Philadelphia, his association with the black masses was largely limited to making addresses at public gatherings or "mass meetings."[11] Whites viewed him as a spokesman for blacks but in fact his contact with blacks was confined to a select few who shared his tastes, interests, and life style, such as John R. Lynch, a friend and political ally in Mississippi, Robert R. Church of Memphis, and James Lewis of New Orleans.

His salary as a federal official, combined with his lecture fees and the rents from his Mississippi plantations, provided Bruce sufficient income to maintain a large house in Washington with several servants and to enjoy travel and other luxuries similar to those of upper middle- and upper-class white families in late nineteenth century America. For a time Bruce operated a successful insurance, loan, and real estate agency and made substantial investments in stocks, bonds, and rental property in the District. He also acquired a large plantation adjoining the one he already owned in Bolivar County, Mississippi. His landholdings in the Delta ultimately amounted to several thousand acres. He always had a keen interest in the development of his plantations and often sought the advice of his Memphis friend, Robert Church, who sometimes acted as his agent. Bruce apparently viewed his plantations as performing a dual function: contributing to the welfare of poor blacks in Mississippi and providing him with a source of income. But he saw the plight of the black masses from afar, and his attitude toward those trapped in the sharecropping system resembled that of paternalistic white planters. Although it is not clear if blacks derived any special benefits from being Bruce's tenants, the evidence suggests that the plantations, which included numerous tenant dwellings, a cotton gin, and a church, were profitable enterprises. Through Bruce's influence a post office was established in Bolivar County, largely to serve his plantations, and was named Josephine, Mississippi, in honor of his wife. [12]

Although the Bruces continued to receive invitations to official receptions and parties, their presence at predominantly white social functions declined sharply after Blanche's departure from the Senate. That Bruce thereafter occupied a relatively minor federal office was probably not the only reason he and his wife appeared less frequently at official social gatherings. The deterioration in race relations in the nation's capital during the 1880s, which differed only in degree from what was happening elsewhere, marked the beginning of what Constance M. Green referred to as "the withering hope" for blacks. The 1883 Supreme Court decision declaring unconstitutional the Civil Rights Act of 1875 served as tangible evidence of the movement to thwart their ambition and aspirations. Those of the upper class, such as the Bruces, were acutely sensitive to the change in the racial atmosphere. [13] Josephine Bruce found polite, social intercourse with the wives of white officials increasingly difficult, and rebuffs became more frequent. At a White House reception in 1884, white women studiously avoided her until Mrs. John A. Logan, the wife of the Republican senator from Illinois, made a point of introducing her to those who had shown little inclination to be hospitable. Mrs. Logan later recalled that when President Chester A. Arthur invited the wife of Senator Bruce to assist at one of his New Year's receptions, no one in the "receiving line acquitted herself more graciously, was more elegantly gowned or more accomplished in her manners than Mrs. Bruce." She was "a handsome, modest, capable and womanly woman" who was in every respect worthy of receiving "all the civilities due the wife of a United States Senator." All the while, according to a white Washington newspaper in

1883, Blanche K. Bruce continued to be "received in courtesy and as a political equal" in official circles, "but there the line is drawn." Anything smacking of social equality was no longer tolerated.[14]

Too proud either to go where they were not wanted or to risk moving backward, black aristocrats withdrew into a world of their own, often as separate from that of other blacks as from that of whites. The Bruces and others like them in Washington created what Jean Toomer later recalled as "an aristocracy such as never existed before and perhaps will never exist again in America—midway between the white and Negro worlds."[15] That peculiar "aristocracy" consisted of members of the old, well-established District families such as the Wormleys, Syphaxes, and Cooks, as well as distinguished newcomers, who constituted what Mary Church Terrell described as "society, spelled with a capital S."[16]

Following the death of her husband in 1898, Josephine Bruce moved to Indianapolis and lived for a time with her sisters Victoria and Mary Wilson, both of whom were principals of public schools in the city. The Wilson sisters, who attended a white Episcopal church and rarely moved outside a small circle of black friends, had "very little association with members of the race." Their exclusiveness prompted resentment among certain blacks who in 1892 tried in vain to have them removed from their principalships.[17] After a little more than a year in Indianapolis, Josephine Bruce accepted an offer from Booker T. Washington, an old friend of her husband, who was emerging as the best-known spokesman for black Americans, to become Lady Principal of Tuskegee Institute in Alabama. The position at Tuskegee allowed Mrs. Bruce an opportunity to return to educational work in a way that satisfied her growing interest in rendering service to the less-fortunate members of her race. Washington could scarcely have found anyone who would function more superbly as a role model for the women students at Tuskegee: Josephine Bruce epitomized the moral rectitude, polished manners, and social grace associated with the genteel lady at the turn of the century.[18]

The news of her appointment to the Tuskegee staff prompted much speculation in the black press. For some it came as a shock to learn that the Northern-born wife of a former United States senator, accustomed to moving in the best black circles and even in the white ones, would abandon the life of a society matron to labor among the "uncouth girls of the rural South." The implication of much of the speculation was that the Bruce family was in dire financial straits and had thrown in its lot with Booker T. Washington as a means of survival. On the other hand, a black weekly in Seattle, edited by the daughter of Hiram Revels, the black senator from Mississippi who preceded Bruce, interpreted Josephine Bruce's move to Tuskegee as evidence of her bravery, magnanimity, and desire "to be useful to the race with which she is identified," especially since she "had no financial reason to do so." Not all blacks, especially those in the

South, took such a generous view of Mrs. Bruce's appointment. One black Southerner viewed it as an example of a well-to-do society woman "cutting some poor deserving young woman out of a job." "What does Mrs. Bruce know of us in the South?" he asked. Despite such occasional criticisms, Josephine Bruce went to Tuskegee in the fall of 1899 as Lady Principal and remained there until 1902. She devoted most of her time and energy to "direct teaching in morals and manners."[19] She returned to Washington by 1906 and resumed her place in the social life of the city's aristocracy of color.

2

◆

Washington: Capital of the
Colored Aristocracy

FROM THE END OF RECONSTRUCTION UNTIL at least World War I Washington was the center of the black aristocracy in the United States. "Among the masses of Negroes," Haynes Johnson later reported, the city was known as the "center of Negro 'bluebloods' and aristocrats."[1] No other city possessed such a concentration of "old families," not merely from the District and nearby Maryland and Virginia but from throughout the United States, whose emphasis on family background, good breeding, occupation, respectability, and color bound them into an exclusive, self-consciously elitist group. Blacks from Philadelphia, Charleston, New Orleans, Boston, and even rural districts and country towns who, for one reason or another, considered themselves to be among the "upper tens" and who in many instances were several generations removed from slavery, gravitated to Washington in sizable numbers because of its educational and cultural opportunities, the availability of white-collar jobs commensurate with their education and aspirations, and the presence of a black social group that shared their values, tastes, and self-perceptions. Intermarriage within the group gave it the appearance of a single family with numerous branches. From Washington radiated a nationwide network of social relationships among individuals and families similar in origins, culture, color, aspirations, and life styles, who generally demonstrated a sense of *noblesse oblige* toward the black masses. Local elites in towns and cities throughout the nation, if not related by blood or marriage to the exclusive circle in Washington, were likely to be acquainted with its members socially.

The so-called black 400 of Washington in reality consisted of fewer than a hundred families out of a black population of 75,000 in 1900. Among the old families of the District with whom the Bruces had intimate social relations, few bore a more prestigious name than the Cooks. The family's most-distinguished ancestor was John Francis Cook, a free man of color, who founded the Fifteenth Street Presbyterian Church in 1841 and conducted a school for blacks for more than twenty years before his death, in 1855. In 1849 a white acquaintance described him as "a thorough gentleman in all his deportment" whose complexion placed him "about half way between the pure Anglo-Saxon and the doomed race."[2] Cook was first married to Jane Mann, whose grandmother was a "full-blooded Algonquin Indian"; and following her death, to Jane Le Count, a member of an old well-known black family in Philadelphia. Two of his sons, George F. T. Cook and John F. Cook, Jr., graduated from Oberlin and achieved great prominence in Washington's black community. George was for a quarter of a century the superintendent of the separate colored school system in the District; and John, who married into the famous Appo family of New York, was for a time District tax collector and generally regarded as the wealthiest black resident of Washington. A third son, Samuel Le Count Cook, was a graduate of the University of Michigan Medical School and a prominent physician in Washington. Their children, in turn, became educators, physicians, and other professionals who perpetuated the high status bequeathed by their ancestors.[3]

In 1869 a white reporter referred to the younger John F. Cook as a "leader of the aristocracy among the darkies," which looked "down on poor blacks and particularly the Virginia contrabands" flooding into Washington. Cook and his friends thought such people "unfit for decent colored society." According to the white reporter, Cook and others of the colored aristocracy clamored "for admission to the theatres on the white level" for themselves but refused to practice the same equality in their dealings with blacks outside their own social circle.[4] Thirty years later, a black critic asserted that John F. Cook was "not identified with the Negro in this city [Washington] although he accumulated a fortune by virtue of being a Negro."[5] Another black critic described his brother George F. T. Cook and his coterie of aristocratic friends in Washington as constituting something of a mutual-aid society which manifested no concern for ordinary blacks and was solely interested in promoting the welfare of their own exclusive group. Although membership in the Cook family carried with it considerable prestige and influence, it also meant, as one observer noted in 1884, that there was always "a little prejudice" against the family within the black community.[6]

Among other old families represented in the circle to which the Cooks and Bruces belonged were the Wormleys, Syphaxes, Shadds, Francises, and Grays. Each possessed "a background of accomplishment" and positions of considerable influence with the District power structure. James Wormley, whose ancestors had been free since the eighteenth century, was the owner of the famous Wormley Hotel. His sons substantially augmented the family fortune by their successes in a variety of business enterprises. In 1871 James Wormley's niece created a sensation by marrying a Frenchman, Paul Gerard, a brother-in-law of the Minister of Portugal.[7] The Syphaxes, who claimed descent from George

Washington Parke Custis, Martha Washington's grandson, through a maternal ancestor, figured prominently in the social, political, and educational life of the black community of the District and nearby Virginia from the antebellum era well into the twentieth century.[8] The Francises, Shadds, and Grays owned restaurants and catering establishments. Measured by the standards prevailing in the larger black community, these families were economically well-to-do and well educated; most were fair complexioned and had been free for a generation or more before the Civil War.[9] After the war, they occupied the most important positions in the District government and educational system. Their children, often educated in private academies and universities in New England, tended to enter the professions of law, medicine, and education. "Where the family was prominent in the business and social life of the colored population before the war," Andrew Hilyer declared in 1892, "their descendants to this day are equally so." Family continuity was, in his view, an essential prerequisite for admission into the colored aristocracy of Washington at the turn of the century.[10]

As was evident from the place occupied by the Bruces in the city's black society, not all of those who belonged to the "Four Hundred" were natives of the District. Rather it included a sizable contingent of individuals from elsewhere in the United States whose ancestry, record of achievement, education, refinement, and other attributes readily admitted them to high black circles. When Rosa Wilder, from a prominent black family in South Carolina, married into an upper-class family in Washington, an observer of colored society in the capital city noted: "[S]he will naturally, by virtue of her social position in Carolina, take a leading place in the same co-equal circle here."[11]

In addition to the Bruces, the colored aristocracy of the nation's capital included the Terrells, Grimkés, Pinchbacks, Purvises, Cardozos, Menards, McKinlays, Douglasses, Murrays and especially families associated with Howard University. The McKinlays, Purvises, and Cardozos were descendants of the free-born mulatto elite of Charleston, South Carolina. The Grimké brothers, Francis and Archibald, were also Charlestonians, the sons of Henry Grimké, a prominent white planter and his slave Nancy Weston. They apparently enjoyed a privileged childhood until the death of their natural father. Both completed their studies at Lincoln University in Pennsylvania; later, Francis graduated from Princeton Theological Seminary and Archibald from Harvard Law School.[12] The descendants of J. Willis Menard, the first Negro congressman from Louisiana, who was reputed to be the grandson of a lieutenant governor of Illinois, continued to live in Washington, where they held lucrative government appointments and occupied a prominent place in the life of the "upper tens" of Negro society.[13] Daniel Murray, of an old and highly respected Baltimore family, was for many years connected with the Library of Congress and ultimately became assistant librarian. His wife was Anna Evans of Oberlin, Ohio, a descendant of Lewis Sheridan Leary, of Harper's Ferry fame. She was largely responsible for the establishment of a kindergarten program in the District's colored schools.[14]

Few of the non-native members of the colored aristocracy were more visible or more socially active than Pinckney Benton Stewart Pinchback of New Orleans, who moved to Washington in 1893. Even fewer were as urbane, worldly, or regal in bearing. Born in 1837, Pinckney was the son of Major William Pinchback, wealthy white planter, and Eliza Stewart, his mulatto slave mistress whom he had freed before the child's birth. The boy was always a favorite of his father. Upon the death of his father, his mother fled to Cincinnati to escape reenslavement by Major Pinchback's white relatives. For a brief period young Pinchback attended the famous Gilmore School in Cincinnati, where other mulatto sons of white fathers, including John Mercer Langston, were enrolled at one time or another. Dropping out of school, Pinchback took a job on the river boats, first as a servant, later as an employee of some well-known gamblers. Ultimately he became a gambler himself; and as he never lost his taste for the racetrack, Saratoga remained his favorite vacation place. In 1860, he married a sixteen-year-old beauty of French and English descent, Nina Emily Hethorn. Two years later, Pinchback joined a regiment of free men of color in New Orleans with the rank of captain. In the postwar era he rose rapidly in Republican politics in Louisiana. Elected lieutenant governor in 1871, he served for more than a month as acting governor during a tumultuous era in Louisiana history, and for the remainder of his life he was known as "Governor" Pinchback. In 1873 the Louisiana legislature elected him United States senator, but after a prolonged and bitter struggle the Senate refused to seat him. Returning to New Orleans, he received several important federal appointments, published a newspaper, practiced law, and operated a profitable commission house. From the late 1870s until a few years before his death, in 1921, he functioned as a political broker. In a manner similar to that of his friend Blanche K. Bruce, he lined up black delegates for Republican conventions and used his influence to secure appointments for friends and acquaintances.[15]

Pinchback, a man of substantial wealth, and his beautiful wife, Nina, entertained lavishly and occupied a prominent place "at the very peak of light society in the Crescent City."[16] In February, 1885, the reception that "Governor" and Mrs. Pinchback gave in honor of their friends visiting the New Orleans Exposition was described as "the most notable event that New Orleans has witnessed since Reconstruction." Those in attendance included colored aristocracy not only of the city and the surrounding area in Louisiana but also from Vicksburg, Little Rock, Cincinnati, and Nashville. "Everybody in New Orleans who received an invitation was there," declared one guest, "and those who were not honored with the handsomely engraved *cards d'invitation* presumably would like to have been." The city's best French orchestra furnished music, and caterers kept the tables constantly replenished with every delicacy and the "silver punch bowls filled with wines of rare old vintages." The elegant and bejewelled ladies, including Nina Pinchback and the wives of James C. Napier of Nashville, Wesley Crayton of Vicksburg, and State Senator Theophile T. Allain of Louisiana, presented what was termed an array of "bewildering beauty."[17]

When the Pinchbacks moved to Washington in 1893, they blended easily and quickly into the colored aristocracy there. The "Governor" built a red brick thirteen-room house on Bacon Street near the Chinese Embassy. Heated throughout by hot water radiators and lavishly furnished, the house contained two large parlors and a fine library. A succession of cooks and maids, in addition to a gardener known as Old Willis, a former slave, attended the house and spacious grounds.[18] Present at their house-warming reception on December 28, 1893 was the "crème de la crème of Washington's colored society": the Langstons, Shadds, Terrells, Bruces, Francises, Hilyers, Hollands, McKinlays, and Cardozos.[19]

A commanding figure always impeccably attired in a cutaway coat, Pinchback so closely resembled Andrew Carnegie that he was often mistaken for the steel magnate. He "loved to be the host and entertain, to be the central figure of an admiring crowd." Alternately indulgent and stingy, he functioned as a domineering patriarch and attempted to maintain a tight rein over his household. In the house on Bacon Street, the Pinchback children—three sons, Pinckney, Walter, and Bismarck, and a beautiful and twice-married daughter, Nina—grew up and moved in a world that Eugene (Jean) Toomer, Nina's son, characterized as existing halfway between the black and white worlds. Pinchback's aspirations for his children were similar to those of most ruling-class Americans of his time. He sent his daughter to a finishing school in Massachusetts and his sons to Yale, Pennsylvania, and Howard to pursue courses in pharmacy, medicine, and law. Although the Pinchback children scarcely measured up to their father's standards of success and the Bacon Street house was the scene of numerous family crises and disappointments, Jean Toomer described his youth there as "a gay, bright, sweet life."[20]

Of the non-native members of Washington's Negro Four Hundred, the Terrells probably best demonstrated the importance of connections with influential, upper-class whites in providing access to opportunities that bestowed high status. Harrison Terrell was a member of a mulatto family in Orange County, Virginia that had been freed before the Civil War. He moved his family to Washington and secured employment with George W. Riggs, the Washington banker, through whom he became acquainted with all the leading families of the District. Later, Terrell served as a nurse companion to General Ulysses S. Grant. Through the influence of his white friends, he secured a minor post in the Department of the Interior which he occupied for more than twenty years, beginning in 1886. Of his three children, the best known was Robert Heberton Terrell, who was educated at Lawrence Academy and graduated from Harvard *cum laude* in 1884. For a time Robert Terrell taught Latin in the District's colored high school. After acquiring a law degree from Howard, he practiced law, held a number of positions in the federal government, and was associated with several business enterprises, including the Capital Savings Bank, in which he was an officer. In 1891 he married Mary Church, a graduate of Oberlin and the daughter of Bruce's wealthy friend in Memphis, Robert R. Church. By the time Theodore Roosevelt appointed Robert Terrell to a municipal judgeship in the District, the Terrells' circle of friends and acquaintances included most of the influential blacks throughout the United States and many well-known whites.[21]

The possession of great wealth, that is, as measured by white standards, was scarcely a prerequisite for membership in Washington's colored aristocracy, but those included in the Four Hundred usually enjoyed a degree of economic security unknown to most blacks and many whites. The economic resources of physicians, public-school teachers and administrators, attorneys, government employees, popular caterers and certain businessmen, Howard University faculty members, and others within the upper reaches of the city's colored society constituted, from the perspective of most other blacks, enormous wealth. For the day laborer or even the skilled worker, the aristocrats represented a degree of wealth almost beyond comprehension, and a few were indeed wealthy by any standard. John F. Cook was probably worth over $200,000. According to a knowledgeable observer in 1895 the other wealthiest black men in the District were: Blanche K. Bruce, $150,000; W. A. A. Wormley, $115,000; P. B. S. Pinchback, $90,000; John R. Lynch, $80,000; Charles B. Purvis, $75,000; Daniel Murray, $60,000; J. H. Meriwether, $60,000; George F. T. Cook, $50,000; Furman J. Shadd, $40,000; and John R. Francis, $35,000.[22] But as one observer noted later, it was a mistake to assume "that high salaries and big incomes are the passports into the best sets of Washington society." Some of those "identified with the most exclusive sets" were "poor in worldly goods" but always possessed "some special qualities that recommend them."[23]

One measure of the economic condition of the colored aristocrats was their life style. Those of substantial means possessed comfortable, tastefully decorated homes in what were considered the respectable and fashionable districts of the city. Disdainful of the gaudy and the ostentatious, they preferred homes and furnishings that exhibited "quiet dignity" and were quick to detect among the nouveau riche any lack of "good taste."[24] After being a guest in the expensive home of a well-to-do black resident of Nashville, Tennessee, Mary Church Terrell noted in her diary: "The decoration of the house was the crudest I have ever seen."[25] The District's colored aristocrats surrounded themselves with books, paintings, fine furniture, and musical instruments. Among their most-prized possessions were family heirlooms, such as the "free papers" or silver pieces of their antebellum ancestors, and mementoes of special occasions. The Bruces proudly displayed the silver cup given to their son by Senator Roscoe Conkling, after whom he was named; and for the Terrells a "solid silver pitcher" had special meaning because it was a wedding gift from Thomas Jefferson Coolidge, the great-grandson of Thomas Jefferson, who was a friend and class-mate of Robert Terrell at Harvard.[26]

A few of the District's "upper tens" not only owned comfortable residences in the city but also possessed what were known as "country places." The Wormleys, Murrays, and several other families had summer homes in nearby Maryland and Virginia. Those who did not own such places escaped the summer heat of the District by taking cottages either in the vicinity of Harper's Ferry, Virginia or at well-known resorts such as those at Cape May and Saratoga which had sizable "colored colonies." The Shadds and the Pinchbacks,[27] among oth-ers, were regular guests at Saratoga Springs in the summer. Late in the 1880s Charles Douglass, the son of Frederick Douglass, purchased a tract of land on Chesapeake Bay, about five miles from the Naval Academy at Arundel-on-the-Bay, to develop a vacation site for Washington's black elite. In attempting to persuade the Terrells to purchase a lot and build a summer house at what he called Highland Beach, Douglass assured them that he intended to develop the property into a resort strictly for what Mary Church Terrell invariably referred to as "our group." By the turn of the century the Terrells, Francises, Wormleys, Curtises, and other aristocrats of color had purchased lots and constructed summer cottages there. At Highland Beach the social intercourse was "easy and pleasant," with "no straining, no pomposity, [and] no posing for the gallery" because it was "so close a corporation."[28]

Despite the hardening of racial practices and the erosion of civil rights for blacks in post-Reconstruction Washington, the colored aristocrats held stead-fastly to the hope that Negroes would ultimately achieve equality. As the exceptional group in the race, they expected to be in the vanguard of those realizing these objectives. Although they by no means escaped the impact of the proliferating discriminatory regulations and practices, they still enjoyed suf-ficient privileges denied ordinary blacks to nourish their hope of being assimi-lated in the larger society. Purvis, Wormley, Terrell, and other "representative men"—a euphemism for exceptional or upper-class blacks—sat on the Washing-ton Board of Trade well into the 1890s. Several black families—the Cooks, Langstons, Lynches, Purvises, Somervilles, and Wormleys—were included in the first issue of the *Elite List* in 1888, the forerunner of the *Social Register*. A few attended white churches; and at least three among the colored aristocrats— Archibald Grimké, Frederick Douglass, and Charles B. Purvis—married across the color line. Even after certain public places, such as hotels and restaurants, closed their doors to blacks, they sometimes made exceptions in the case of "refined and genteel Negroes." While such exceptions became increasingly rare, the practice had not altogether disappeared by the First World War.[29]

For the colored aristocrats of Washington, nothing was more absurd than the idea that all blacks were social equals. They viewed such a notion as utter fiction, based largely on the white man's ignorance of the black community and positively detrimental to racial progress. Whites, they argued, began by insisting that all blacks were alike, then proceeded to judge the entire race by its worst rather than its best elements. Because colored aristocrats viewed themselves as proof that all blacks were not alike, either in culture, sophistication, wealth, or even color, they chafed under a system that placed all Negroes on an equal plane. They were culturally, socially, and spatially remote from the black masses, especially from the thousands crowded into Washington's alley dwellings. The aristocrats lived in comfortable houses in respectable and often fashionable neighborhoods, where their life style and values more nearly resembled those of "the best people" of the "dominant race." Although the colored aristocrats were often embarrassed by the behavior of blacks who made up what they termed the "submerged masses," they were nonetheless sympathetic with their plight, which they viewed from a distance. Their attitude toward the less fortunate of their race was in fact marked by a *noblesse oblige* not unlike that of certain whites concerned about the welfare of the black masses. Like those elsewhere, the colored aristocrats in Washington saw themselves as holding the key to the solution of the race problem. If upper-class blacks "were given rights as rapidly as they merited them," so the argument ran, they would be inspired and in turn would inspire "the fellows of the lower grade."[30]

Long before W. E. B. Du Bois articulated the idea of the Talented Tenth, which claimed that blacks, like other races, would be saved by their exceptional members, the colored aristocrats had been subscribing to and practicing a similar notion. "Among our friends . . .," Mary Church Terrell later recalled, "were doctors, whose practice was lucrative and large, lawyers, dentists, plus real estate men, not to mention Government clerks, who had secured their positions through competitive examination . . . and . . . the officers and teachers in the public schools, some of whom wore Phi Beta Kappa keys given them by the best colleges and universities in the United States."[31]

By 1910 Washington had a black population of 94,000, of whom 1,500 were classified as belonging to the professional class.[32] These numbers, in view of the fact that not all professionals belonged to the Terrells' social circle, suggest how small and restricted that circle was. Those whom Mary Church Terrell counted among her friends were likely to attend the Fifteenth Street Presbyterian Church, St. Luke Protestant Episcopal Church, and one or two others and to hold membership in the same social, cultural, and racial uplift organizations. During the summer exodus from Washington these same people vacationed together at Silcott Springs and Harper's Ferry in Virginia, at Highland Beach in Maryland, on the Jersey Coast, or at Saratoga. With few exceptions they resided in the northwest section of Washington. They dominated the colored school system and occupied the choice positions open to blacks in the federal and District governments and at Howard University.

The proliferation of clubs and societies with identical objectives indicated the existence of numerous factions of cliques within the ranks of Washington's colored aristocracy. Among the best-known and most widely discussed divisions was that between the "old citizens" and the "newcomers." According to the latter, the "old citizens" and their descendants drew a sharp line of distinction between themselves and those from the outside who also possessed "culture and affluence" but who lacked the longevity of residence in the District that presumably bestowed considerable status. Although the newcomers undoubtedly exaggerated the exclusiveness and snobbery exhibited by those known as "old cits," the latter did indeed exercise caution in admitting into their social circle anyone from the outside. They not only thoroughly investigated a newcomer in regard to his or her character, background, education, and respectability, but also required a "proper introduction," meaning that someone inside their circle had to vouch for the newcomer, that is, verify that he or she would not be "uncordial or unfit." Without such an introduction a stranger, no matter how worthy, "would remain unnoticed [for] many months." But newcomers from a "co-equal" social circle elsewhere usually encountered no difficulty in securing the proper introduction.[33]

Although the line of demarcation between "old cits" and newcomers was scarcely as rigid as sometimes implied, certain organizations did tend to remain preserves of old District families. The "old citizens" dominated the Harmony Cemetery Association, a venerable organization founded early in the nineteenth century by John Francis Cook and others; as well as the Banneker Relief Association, organized in 1885 to aid the Sojourner Truth Home and a day nursery; and the Native Washingtonians, a strictly social group, launched in 1902. The Native Washingtonians appears to have become defunct shortly after staging an elaborate ball in connection with the inauguration of Theodore Roosevelt in 1905, but it was succeeded in 1912 by the Association of Oldest Inhabitants. Organized largely in response to the increased influx of Southern blacks into the city and patterned after a white organization with the same name, the association limited its membership to males of good character who had resided in the District at least thirty years and to the sons of such residents twenty-five years of age or older. While its primary purpose was to provide "old citizens" with opportunities for socializing and for preserving "valuable personal and racial history," the organization claimed to be "aggressively alive to every racial interest" and "a liberal contributor to organized uplift effort." By the time the Association of Oldest Inhabitants was launched, many of those who a generation earlier had complained bitterly about the "high wall" that surrounded the "old citizens" had themselves become "old cits" no less inclined to snobbery and exclusiveness. But even in those organizations whose rules allowed only "old citizens" to join, newcomers of sufficient merit, stature, and prestige could be included as "honorary members."[34]

The organization which perhaps best demonstrated a combination of old citizens and newcomers was the Monocan Club, which evolved out of the Cosmos Club. In addition to six regularly scheduled assemblies each year, the

Monocans also "gave a grand ball during inauguration week, during a G.A.R. encampment or any such notable occasion." Its grand ball during the week of Theodore Roosevelt's inauguration in March 1905 was a lavish affair held in the armory of the National Light Infantry. The morning after the ball one participant recorded in her diary: "The great ball . . . was a glorious success. The most distinguished men and women of the race were there. The costumes of the ladies were unusually brilliant." She also observed that the affair "partook more of the nature of a private reception than it did a public ball, although four hundred and fifty were present." By 1912 the leadership of the Monocan Club had passed to the younger generation of colored aristocrats. Its president was Walter Pinchback, the son of "Governor" Pinchback. Its membership was still restricted to twenty-five men, virtually all of whom bore the same family names as its founders. The pre-teen sons of Monocans of Walter Pinchback's generation belonged to an affiliate known as the Junior Monocan Club.[35]

In addition to social functions sponsored by the Monocan Club and similar elite organizations during presidential inaugurations and other special occasions, Washington's colored aristocrats amply entertained their out-of-town guests privately with card parties, luncheons, dinners, and receptions that lent support to their reputation for unstinted hospitality. In 1904 Mary Church Terrell described the customary ritual of entertaining guests from afar: "If a matron or a maid from a sister city visits Washington, her hostess will probably give a reception in her honor so that the stranger may meet her Washington friends. Then there will be a succession of luncheons, dinners, card and theatre parties, and small dances given for the stranger by the friends of the hostess. She will enjoy one or more drives [about the city] and the chances are that she will be taken in a conveyance owned by the friend who invites her."[36]

During the G.A.R. encampment in 1902, which attracted large numbers of upper-class blacks from other parts of the nation to Washington, the elaborately decorated home of the Pinchbacks on Bacon Street was the scene of a reception for forty couples that represented the pinnacle of the national colored aristocracy. During the same week Imogene and Josephine Wormley entertained a friend from Brooklyn, who had accompanied her husband to the encampment, with an elaborate luncheon that included a selection of their own social set. The newspaper account read: "The luncheon consisted of eleven courses. All of the knives, forks and spoons used were of solid gold, and the parlors and dining room were profusely decorated with fragrant flowers and palms."[37]

Although weddings, anniversaries, and notable occasions were important, the routine social life of Washington's colored aristocracy revolved around less-expensive and less-lavish activities, such as intimate dinners; card parties; visits to art galleries, museums, and public concerts; and tennis and croquet. Such activities involved only members of what Mary Church Terrell referred to as "our group." For example, she and her husband regularly played cards, usually

Whist, with their closest friends, Dr. and Mrs. John R. Francis, and occasionally with two other physicians and their wives. One was Dr. James R. Wilder, a descendant of "an ancient line of the South Carolina aristocracy," whose father served for a decade and a half as postmaster of Columbia, South Carolina. The other was Dr. Austin M. Curtis, who in 1900 became administrative head of the Freedman's Hospital. The son of an old and highly respected black family in Raleigh, North Carolina, he married Namahoko Sockoume of San Francisco, a socially and politically active woman of striking beauty. All three of their sons became physicians.[38]

Writing in 1909, a close observer of the Washington social scene described Mary Church Terrell, Bettie Cox Francis, and Anna Evans Murray as the most prominent leaders in the "social world" and in "charity work" in the city. "In fact," he declared, "Madame de Stael never presided over her salon with more grace than these three matrons preside over the social affairs in their homes." While each would undoubtedly have denied being a "society leader," they were nonetheless "very much of and in society."[39]

The black press throughout the nation, not merely the Washington news-papers, faithfully chronicled the social activities of the city's colored aristocrats. The best-known black papers in the country, such as the New York Age, Indianapolis Freeman, and Detroit Plaindealer, regularly published a "Washing-ton Letter," which provided detailed accounts of the "doings of colored society" in the capital city. In some instances the sources of these letters were upper-class blacks from Michigan, Indiana, and elsewhere who held government jobs in Washington. Robert Pelham of Detroit, who was employed in the Government Printing Office, served as correspondent for the Plaindealer, which was owned and published by his family. Willis Menard, the son of the former Louisiana congressman, held a succession of government positions and furnished copy to several black newspapers on life in Washington's black community. Richard W. Thompson, a highly respected black journalist, wrote a weekly column for the Indianapolis Freeman and several other newspapers in which he recounted "society happenings" in Washington. Although Thompson was not an insider in the same sense as Pelham and Menard, he circulated socially on the periphery of the "black 400."[40] That the social life of the colored aristocrats so faithfully chronicled by these writers appeared in columns alongside those devoted to accounts of lynchings, burnings, mutilations, and other atrocities suffered by blacks, especially in the South, served to dramatize the gulf between the black masses at the bottom of the social structure and the few at the top. The high wall that the latter appeared to erect between themselves and other blacks at a time when racial oppression was increasing only invited criticism and scorn.

The criticism directed by blacks at the colored aristocrats assumed diverse forms and often revealed a complex of contradictory sentiments. In some instances the criticism was either frivolous and without basis in fact or merely expressions of anger and bitterness by those who felt that the "upper circle" had discriminated against them personally. In others, the criticism possessed more substance, especially when it focused on the failure of the colored aristocrats to patronize racial enterprises and to provide the type of leadership needed in a time of crisis. Much of the criticism appeared to suggest that the "upper tens" were more interested in monopolizing the choice positions in the government and the public schools than in combatting the spread of Jim Crowism and in elevating the masses. Complaints about the color consciousness of light-complexioned aristocrats surfaced regularly. The charge was that any drawing of the color line within the black community undermined racial unity and therefore weakened movements to combat the proliferation of restrictions and proscriptions. A prominent black resident of Washington declared in 1906 that the colored aristocrats, while "too proud to mix with their own prople" and wholly indifferent to the plight of the black masses, were always receptive to the formation of another "color line" club or another invitation to a select social function.[41]

The record of the colored aristocrats in regard to charity and uplift causes may well have been "distinctly thin," as one authority has suggested,[42] but it was scarcely as barren as some contemporary critics implied. The Banneker Association, the congregations of several so-called aristocratic churches, and the Colored Women's League, all of which included a substantial representation of Washington's "colored 400," contributed to a wide range of charitable institutions and causes. Dr. John R. Francis headed a fund-raising campaign in 1911 for the benefit of the Colored Social Settlement.[43] Whatever the shortcomings of the colored aristocrats in regard to their contributions to charity, their critics often demanded of them far more than they were capable of delivering. Few possessed either the wealth or the time to contribute on the scale that their critics seemed to suggest. The problems of the ever-increasing population of unskilled, low-income blacks in Washington were so numerous and so complex that they were likely to leave even the most civic-minded among the upper class with a sense of helplessness—a condition that tended to heighten the ambiguities evident in the attitude of the colored aristocrats toward the surrounding black community.

If those of the top social stratum manifested an interest in the moral and intellectual uplift of the masses and a commitment to civil rights, they also condemned the behavior of lower-class blacks—those designated as the "unimproved" class—and lectured them on "respectability" and the need to learn what Blanche K. Bruce described as "the laws governing society."[44] For all their references to *noblesse oblige*, the colored aristocrats often found their uplift efforts thwarted by condescension of whites on the one hand and criticism from blacks on the other. Convinced that they suffered from racial stereotypes stemming from the behavior of blacks who possessed little knowledge of or appreciation for "the laws governing society," they attempted to increase the distance between themselves and the black masses, invariably prompting outcries about their exclusiveness and color consciousness.

The effort of colored aristocrats to detach themselves from the black masses was perhaps most evident in the attitude they adopted toward the annual Emancipation Day celebration in April. For most black residents of Washington, it was an occasion for a mammoth parade, numerous rallies, and "general merry making." In 1883 the parade was a mile and a half long and included representatives from such organizations as the Gay Heart Social Club, Galilean Fishermen, Knights of Jerusalem, Paper Hanger's Union, and Solid Yantics. Embarrassed by what they perceived as gaudy and undignified displays by the "worst elements of the race," upper-class blacks disassociated themselves from the Emancipation Day festivities. In 1886 Frederick Douglass publicly condemned the parades and rallies as "tinsel shows" with "straggling processions, which empty the alleys and dark places of the city into the broad day-light . . ., thus thrusting upon public view a vastly undue proportion of the most unfortunate, unimproved and unprogressive class of the colored people." Such displays, he warned, not only repelled "the more thrifty and self-respecting among us" but also invited the contempt and ridicule of whites.[45]

The withdrawal of upper-class blacks from Emancipation Day celebrations, which dramatized their efforts to distance themselves generally from the "unprogressive" masses, prompted considerable discussion in the black community. In 1890 a black newspaper in Washington expressed regret that there were "a few Negroes in the District" who refused to have anything to do with the celebration to commemorate the freeing of black men and women from bondage. Three years later it reported that "the higher class colored element was conspicuous by its absence" from the Emancipation Day activities. In all of his discourse on slavery, freedom, and the failure of "higher class" blacks to take part in the "sacred occasion," the editor failed to mention that many of those whom he so bitterly denounced had less reason to celebrate Emancipation Day than did other blacks, because they or their ancestors had been free people of color and, legally at least, had not been freed by Lincoln's proclamation.[46]

A variety of reasons were given to explain why the Emancipation Day celebration in Washington was "not what it used to be." One was that the slave generation, by the 1890s, had grown old and feeble and hence the ranks of those most faithful in celebrating the "sacred day" had been substantially reduced. Blacks born after the Civil War had never known slavery, so the argument ran, therefore the Emancipation Proclamation had little meaning for them. But for Richard W. Thompson, the Washington correspondent of the Indianapolis *Freeman*, who covered the celebrations for several years, the changes that had occurred in the Emancipation Day festivities were inextricably linked to the evolution of the black social structure. "Gradually," he remarked in 1893, "the most important men . . . like Frederick Douglass and Blanche K. Bruce dropped out, followed by the richer and more respectable . . . until the celebration is left

largely to the lower classes." The black population, he noted, was now composed of many classes differentiated by education, wealth, sophistication, and
other factors. Thompson suggested that Douglass, Bruce, Lynch, and their like
were "as far away from the colored people at the other end of the social scale as
the most exclusive white society man thinks himself to be from the most humble
white laborer." He was certain that if "any of the leading colored citizens of
Washington . . . looked at the Emancipation procession last Monday [1893] at
all, it was just as the leading white citizens looked at it."[47]

The notion that Washington was "the colored man's paradise," in which a
"Negro aristocracy in all its glory" flourished, gained wide acceptance among
blacks and some whites.[48] Despite the exaggerations and condescension that
characterized accounts written by whites of "colored society" in the city, the
consensus was that the District was exceptional in both the quantity and quality
of its black elite. Mrs. John A. Logan, the wife of the Illinois senator who had
befriended Josephine Bruce, was convinced that nowhere but in Washington
was the "educated, well-to-do, light-colored class" of Negroes numerous enough
to "form a society in distinction from the shiftless negroes." In the District, Mrs.
Logan observed, the "genteel colored society" did not "hold itself exclusive of
the less fortunate" blacks "except in purely social relations."[49]

In 1886 the Chicago Inter-Ocean printed a report describing the aristocrats
of color in the capital city, who in its view were quite as exclusive as their white
counterparts. "The focus or pole around which the high toned colored society
revolves," the Inter-Ocean explained, "is the Fifteenth Street Presbyterian
Church which stands in an aristocratic section of the city." The story devoted
special attention to the family of Congressman James E. O'Hara, the son of an
Irish merchant and a West Indian black woman, who represented North Carolina's Second District and was part of the upper stratum of Washington's Negro
society in the mid-1880s. But the O'Haras attended St. Augustine's Roman
Catholic Church rather than the Fifteenth Street Presbyterian. Mrs. O'Hara,
like Josephine Bruce, was a highly educated woman of great beauty; she spoke
French, "played Beethoven, and employed a white governess for her children."
Ironically, O'Hara's identification with Washington's colored aristocracy proved
to be a political liability because it lent credence to charges by his political
opponents in North Carolina that he refused to send his children to colored
schools and kept himself aloof from the black people responsible for his election
to office.[50]

Some whites who devoted attention to the colored aristocracy in Washington attempted to explain why that city more than any other fostered such a
group. Some argued that the most-important factor was the existence of "well
paying government jobs" open to talented blacks, which made possible a life of
relative comfort and ease. Others attached considerable significance to the
presence of the colored school system and Howard University. Many of those
from elsewhere who vied for teaching positions in the colored schools, such as

Ella Somerville of Mobile and the Barrier sisters, Fannie and Ella, of Brockport, New York,[51] possessed the education and intellectual attainments as well as the "proper lineage" and refinement for admission to the upper stratum of Washington's black society. In educational circles the "old families" of the District came together with those from New York, South Carolina, and elsewhere to form the "educational set" within the aristocracy.

Few white observers of Washington's black social structure took exception to Katherine Bishop's observation that "the sense of caste is as strong among Washington's Negroes as among Brahmin." Writing in *Colliers* in 1902, I. K. Friedman insisted that "in Washington the rigid laws and iron rules of caste are applied among . . . the colored people with a severity that marks the white man's exclusion of the black." He claimed that certain restaurants and saloons admitted "only the chosen of the race" and that there existed numerous homes where the ordinary black was "barred from entrance by his limitations of education, conduct and general carriage."[52]

Most white observers also noted that the colored aristocracy in the District was not of a single piece, but was made up of numerous cliques and sets which were often locked in fierce social competition. Those who attempted to sort out and identify the various factions usually had little success, especially in capturing nuances and subtleties. One investigator designated three groupings: the "swell set," made up of the *nouveau riche*; the "old fashioned set," which consisted of members of the old families; and the "smart set," which was composed of the younger members of the old fashioned set. But regardless of how they defined the different cliques or sets, most white observers seemed to agree that the colored aristocracy in Washington adhered to "high standards of excellence" and was very exclusive. Admission to its ranks was "almost as difficult to obtain as into New York's Four Hundred." In addition to being intent upon holding themselves aloof from other blacks, colored aristocrats were "sticklers for the provisions of the civil rights bill" and vigorously opposed any form of segregation that restricted them to "any place marked distinctly 'Negro.' "[53]

In an analysis of "the Washington Negro" in 1892, Henry Loomis Nelson not only paid special attention to the commodious residences and comfortable incomes of the colored aristocrats but also noted that "their women folk have regular reception days and dress themselves in silk and satins, often employing dress makers of their race who cut and sew for their white neighbors." More important, in Nelson's view, was that upper-class Negroes in Washington displayed an independence and self-confidence lacking in other blacks. They never attempted any social "intrusion into the white circle," yet when communication with whites was necessary, they conducted themselves on "the level plane of equality" and were never obsequious or ill at ease. In "dealings between the races," Nelson observed, the colored aristocrat served as "a mediator in behalf of his lowlier brethren," toward whom he assumed an attitude of "patronizing superiority that may be rightly felt by the intellectual equal of whites." The role of mediator or buffer ascribed to the aristocrats by Nelson was remarkably close to their own self-image.[54]

Blacks responded in various ways to commentaries by whites about Washington's "upper ten" Negroes. They universally resented the condescension and prejudice evident in some of these accounts, but whether they approved or disapproved of a colored aristocracy, few were inclined to deny its existence. As early as 1880 the *People's Advocate*, a black weekly in the District, roundly criticized the Washington *Evening Star* for suggesting that "no well defined classes of society" existed in the black community. The *Advocate*'s response was that such a suggestion merely revealed the ignorance of the average white American, whose racial prejudice had so distorted his view of blacks as to allow him to "see nothing but repulsive features—shallow intellect, sordid tastes, blunted instincts [and] groveling appetites." No less than whites, the editor of the weekly contended, blacks had their own stratified society, including an aristocracy at the top, which "commended itself to every lover of progress." Convinced that social classes were continually undergoing change and evolution rather than remaining static, he argued that the criteria for admission to the highest stratum of black society were by no means immutable: "Today it may be military distinction or pride of ancestry that admits you to the charmed circle; tomorrow it may be learning and scientific achievement."[55]

Other blacks responded to discourses by whites on Washington's colored aristocracy by pointing out both factual and conceptual errors. The *New York Globe*, a well-known black newspaper, responded in 1884 to a story in a white daily in regard to colored society in the capital city by taking exception to the idea that the standards and criteria of upper-class status within the black community were different, and by implication, inferior, to those in white society. On the contrary, according to the *Globe*, the same principles that underlay social distinctions in the white world prevailed among blacks, and in both cases, "foolish discriminations" often existed. The differences in blacks and whites of high social status were quantitative rather than qualitative; there were fewer well-educated and refined blacks, and upper-class blacks did not possess great wealth by white standards.[56]

The response to the same analysis of Washington's colored aristocracy by the *Washington Bee*, a black weekly, was less dispassionate but in some respects more revealing. Convinced that the colored aristocracy was "the theme of a thousand tongues that have never seen or felt it" and hence spoke in ignorance, the *Bee* dealt with each of the traits credited to this group by the white daily. It emphatically denied that Washington's light-skinned aristocrats drew the color line against Negroes of darker complexion, a position that it was to contradict regularly in its own editorial columns over the next quarter of a century. According to the *Bee* in 1883, however, there was only one line drawn in black society, that "between the respectable and the disrespectable." "The colored people," it declared, "are too sensible and too generous to create caste distinctions; the rich and the poor, quadroon, mulatto, brown skin and black all associate together [and] are respectable or disrespectable as the case may be." To catalogue the wealth of individual colored aristocrats in Washington, as the white daily had done, was in the opinion of the *Bee* altogether irrelevant, because money "did not regulate social matters" among blacks but rather "merit and respectability." The *Bee* also suggested that the designation of certain well-known colored men as "society" figures was patently ridiculous because most of them, such as the Wormleys, Cooks, and Syphaxes, were too busy devoting their time and energy to full-time jobs and worthwhile enterprises. In referring to Dr. Charles B. Purvis and his white wife, the newspaper quite incorrectly stated that they never went "in society of any kind," because "the white people won't take them and the colored don't like her."[57] Despite the fervor and bluster with which the *Bee* defended Washington's colored aristocracy, its own columns during the years after 1883 echoed many of the same sentiments expressed in the white daily's article. Indeed, the *Bee* specialized in exposing what it perceived as the drawing of the color line by the "white Negroes" of Washington's "upper crust."[58]

If whites on occasion caricatured the colored aristocrats or treated them with condescension, their severest critics were in the black community. Denouncing the pretensions and foibles of the "bon tons" became a favorite exercise of some black journalists and editors. The "colored aristocracy" even became the title of several black minstrel shows. As early as 1877 a lengthy essay entitled "Washington's Colored Society," written by John E. Bruce, who later achieved journalistic prominence as "Bruce Grit," satirized "that abortion miscalled colored society . . . which flourishes under peculiar circumstances at the national capital." The "fust families" that made up the upper stratum of this society, Bruce insisted, were free blacks and their descendants in the District who possessed "more family pride to the square inch . . . than there are fleas on a dog's back." Unalterably opposed to the influx of freedmen into the city, the "fust families" withdrew into a society of their own which emphasized pedigree, "*decayed* respectability," and such evidences of white ancestry as "aristocratic in-steps," "blue veins," and "good hair." They "wouldn't be caught dead with an ordinary Negro" and foolishly expected to "become absorbed by the white or Caucasian race." Most of the "fust families" were pensioners, "provided they or their ancestors lived with the 'bloods' of their day and generation." Characteristically, according to Bruce, whose parents had been slaves and whose mother was a domestic in Washington in the 1860s, such families kept "a servant, two dogs, a tom cat and a rifle that saw service in 1776." If they did not employ a servant, it was a clear indication that they did not have a pension or an inheritance from ancestors across the color line. In Bruce's view Washington's colored aristocracy was "all tinsel, shadow and show," and its very existence retarded the unity and progress of black Americans.[59] For more than a quarter of a century after he wrote this biting satire, Bruce Grit periodically returned to the subject of "colored society," and his criticism, if possible, was more devastating than it had been in 1877.

Throughout the late nineteenth and early twentieth centuries other black critics of Washington's "upper ten" Negroes pursued themes similar to those expressed by Bruce. They too condemned the aristocrats' color consciousness and tendency to identify with whites rather than blacks, ridiculed their emphasis on family pride and efforts to withdraw into exclusive clubs, and even questioned their respectability. The phrase most often used by critics to describe Washington's aristocrats of color was "sham and tinsel." Reverend J. M. Townsend, an important political figure in Indiana who lived in Washington while employed in the federal land office, denounced the "Negro aristocracy in this country and especially in this city as a farce and a disgrace." Following a visit to the capital city, a black resident of New York wrote a letter signed "Aunt Maria" to the *People's Advocate* that described the District's colored aristocracy as "the meanest apology for respectability and morality that I have ever seen." John W. Cromwell, editor of the *Advocate*, whose treatment of the colored aristocracy was more thoughtful and less biased than that of most of his contemporaries, characterized "Aunt Maria's" communication as altogether "gross and malicious." In his view the aristocrats of color might well deserve criticism on various grounds but not in regard to their respectability and morality.[60]

Throughout the eight-year existence of the *People's Advocate* (1876–1884), Cromwell regularly commented on the colored aristocracy and emphasized in particular its responsibility to the black masses. While he condemned whites for their failure to distinguish between the "intelligent and cultured colored people" and those that occupied "the lowest grade of colored society," he argued that at least a part of the responsibility for this condition lay with the aristocrats of color because they often manifested too little interest in the uplift and enlightenment of the black masses whose behavior served as the basis on which whites judged all blacks. Colored aristocrats, he observed, were too "disposed to content themselves in the mere fact of *their* personal improvement, caring little as to what might be the condition of those around them." Although Cromwell believed that "intelligent and well-to-do colored people" should engage in intellectual and cultural pursuits for their own self-improvement, he thought it no less important that they fulfil their duty "to elevate the moral and intellectual tone of the *whole* community." A persistent theme of the *Advocate's* editorials focused on the obligations of colored aristocrats to use their superior talents and means in behalf of lower-class blacks. His idea of a black aristocracy was far more concerned with a civic-minded, educated elite than with what was called the "social society" of Washington's "upper tens." Rather than separating themselves from the race, colored aristocrats were urged to become more actively involved in causes to uplift the masses culturally and materially.[61]

For almost a decade after the demise of the *Advocate* in 1884, no black newspaper in the District provided such a sympathetic and intelligent commentary on the colored aristocracy as Cromwell had. In 1893, when Edward E. Cooper established the *Colored American* in Washington, he assiduously cultivated the city's colored aristocrats and succeeded to a degree in winning their approval and support. He courted the favor of the influential Terrell family in particular. Mary Church Terrell for a time contributed a column to Cooper's paper, "The Woman's World," under the pen name Euphemia Kirk; her brother-in-law William Terrell was on the paper's staff, and her husband allegedly contributed to its financial support. From at least the late 1890s until its demise in 1904, the *Colored American* was subsidized by Booker T. Washington and served as the principal journalistic mouthpiece for his philosophy in the nation's capital.[62]

A self-styled "national negro newspaper," the *Colored American* devoted less attention to District affairs than did its competitor, the *Bee*. Although few copies of Cooper's weekly from its early years are extant, it appears that from its beginning the *Colored American* viewed social stratification within Washington's black community as evidence of racial progress. As a newcomer himself, Cooper maintained that the influx into Washington of cultured, well-to-do blacks from elsewhere contributed significantly to making the city the center of the black aristocracy in America. The city was, in his view, a magnet that attracted those who constituted "the flower of society, politics and religious denominations" from throughout the nation. Those "representatives of culture and civilization" who had won the "plaudits and encomiums of their home people," according to Cooper, gained easy and quick acceptance into Washington's colored aristocracy and moved "along harmoniously as a part of the local machine."[63]

That all was not harmonious between newcomers and "the local machine" was evident in the columns of the *Washington Bee*, which from its beginning in 1882 manifested a keen interest in the affairs of those it called the city's "colored 400." The editor and publisher of the *Bee* for almost forty years was William Calvin Chase, a free-born, educated, and socially prominent native of Washington. Although the Chases had been active in the Fifteenth Street Presbyterian Church since 1844 and were related through Calvin's mother, Lucinda Seaton, to "one of the best and purest families in the Commonwealth of Virginia," they were never quite in the top stratum of Washington's black society, but rather in the rung just below it. The *Bee*'s motto, "Honey for Friends, Stings for Enemies," aptly described both Chase and his newspaper. Other than his attacks on all forms of racial discrimination, Chase displayed little ideological consistency in his editorials.[64] In regard to Washington's colored aristocracy, he alternated between unstinting praise and withering denunciation. In general, the aristocrats felt the *Bee*'s sting far more often than they tasted its honey.

The *Bee* regularly chronicled the "doings of society people" on its editorial page and in a column alternately entitled "Louise to Clara" and "Clara to Louise," which was a hodgepodge of gossip, accounts of social events, and pronouncements regarding the morality and respectability of Washington's "black 400." Only rarely did the *Bee* indicate, as it did in 1883, that colored society in the city was "on a higher and certainly a more incorruptible plane than in the days of yore."[65] Far more frequent were expressions of regret that those who belonged to the contemporary exclusive set fell below the standards adhered to in the past by the old families of the District. "We have among the colored people in Washington," Chase wrote in 1885, "a class of Mugwumps, not political but social, some of whom are too honest to steal and too lazy to work but who nevertheless effect all the airs of a diplomat or millionaire. To remind any of this class that their fathers were good house servants, restaurant keepers, clubhouse men, hotel waiters or artists in lime [white washers] . . . would be an unpardonable sin." Chase objected to these "Negro Mugwumps" not only because they were "foreigners" who did not conform to his notions of respectability and lacked the decorum exhibited by old District families but also because he considered them more "sham than substance."[66]

The *Bee* traced the beginning of the decay of Washington's colored society to the Lotus Club, organized in the 1860s. Chase described its members as insufferable snobs who labored during the Civil War and immediately afterward to force the newly freed slaves flooding into Washington to keep to themselves. In brief, he charged the Lotus Club with promoting a species of segregation. He also claimed that the individuals who belonged to the club were also members of the so-called Bank Ring, those blacks associated with the Freedman's Savings and Trust Company, which failed in the Panic of 1873. Made up largely of "foreigners" with little to offer other than their fair complexions and disdain for ordinary blacks, according to Chase, this group wormed its way into the "best circles." The result was that the old standards of excellence in matters of character, deportment, and civic concern traditionally found among the "first families" were replaced with "sham respectability," "good-for-nothing snob-bery," and the single-minded pursuit of selfish interests. As a descendant of an old District family, Chase regularly railed against foreigners and interlopers, those "social pirates" who had usurped places in Washington's "upper crust" that he believed rightly belonged to him and others descended from the old families of Washington. In 1884 he noted with regret that "the strangers have control of everything, socially, musically, dramatically and otherwise." A quarter of a century later he was still denouncing the Lotus Club and the Bank Ring for establishing among the city's upper class a pattern of discrimination against their own people on the basis of "color and social standing."[67]

The *Bee* never denied the existence of a colored aristocracy, but it regularly bemoaned its inferior quality as compared to that existing before the emergence of the Lotus Club and the Bank Ring. Chase's musings bore a striking resem-blance in this respect to certain whites in the late nineteenth century who were certain that they were witnessing the passing of genteel society. For him the authentic colored aristocracy of Washington was "made up of natives" such as the Cooks, Wormleys, and a few other families; but this authentic aristocracy was constantly jeopardized by the intrusion "of broken down society wrecks" from elsewhere who flocked to the city and quickly joined the Fifteenth Street Presbyterian Church as the first step in gaining admission to "the select fives, tens, twelves, etc."[68] "Our society in years gone by," the Bee noted in 1884, "judged persons by the company they kept and the stock from which they had sprung. . . . The fault with our society [today] is the admission of and too much familiarity with strangers."[69]

The admission of recruits from other cities into the society of Washington's best families without screening them in regard to their ancestry, respectability, and life style, Chase argued, had seriously eroded the quality of the colored aristocracy and damaged its ability to assume a leadership role in the black community. In his opinion the upper social stratum had come to be dominated by "a class of would-be's" from the outside who lacked the family pride, record of achievement, and other attributes that characterized native-born Washingtonians of the elite. Because of the infiltration of newcomers, the city's "high toned society" no longer emphasized education, refinement, and civic duty, but rather "money, color and good looks."[70]

Accompanying this shift in emphasis, according to Chase, was a noticeable decline in the disposition of the upper class "to assist in developing the material interests of the community." As the number of "strangers" who gained admission to this class increased, the more preoccupied it became with maintaining its social distance from other Negroes and with "ostracizing all who do not conform in every aspect to certain established social dogma." Even the People's Advocate suggested that "our most cultured people ought to concern themselves less with purely social chow chow" and more with the elevation of the poor.[71] The Bee was less circumspect; it regularly denounced "high toned society people" for refusing to patronize black enterprises, especially "race journals," and for monopolizing control of black institutions exclusively for their own benefit. Chase's paper undoubtedly reflected the sentiments of many ambitious blacks in Washington outside the upper social stratum who resented the power exercised by the "select few," especially over appointments to positions in the federal and District governments, colored school system, Freedman's Hospital, and Howard University. This "select few," in Chase's words, "played the Negro racket for all it was worth" and was always present "to receive favors from the masses" at the same time that they were busy widening the social gap between themselves and those whom they claimed to represent.[72] That some of the aristocrats also appeared to attach great significance to a light skin only served to deepen the resentment of the dark-complexioned elements in Washington's black community.

A "large portion of Washington's select society" consisted of public-school personnel and college professors. A few families, such as the Cooks, Francises, Terrells, Bruces, Syphaxes, and Shadds, dominated the separate colored school system and often secured for their relatives and friends, including those from elsewhere, appointments as teachers and principals.[73] The control of the colored schools by a certain "social clique," regardless of its persistent efforts to advance the cause of black education, was a perennial source of controversy in Washington's black community. This clique, so the *Bee* argued, "endeavored to run our schools to the detriment of the more deserving." Chase regularly used the editorial columns of his paper to provide Bruce, Francis, and other school trustees with advice on the selection of school personnel and to champion the cause of applicants whom he considered deserving, rather than socially acceptable to the clique in control. He waged a bitter and ultimately successful battle for the removal of Francis Cardozo as principal of the city's colored high school. Although Chase ostensibly disagreed with Cardozo over matters of educational philosophy and policy, clearly some of his hostility was related to the fact that Cardozo was a "foreigner" who had achieved a place of prominence in the city's upper class. Somewhat similar in nature was the opposition that developed late in the 1890s against Mary Church Terrell, a school trustee, who was accused of favoring "society" women for teaching positions over more-deserving applicants outside her own social circle.[74]

Paul Laurence Dunbar, a famous black poet at the turn of the century, lived for a time in Washington next door to Robert and Mary Church Terrell, in a house rented from Mary Terrell's father, Robert R. Church. A frail, dark-skinned man, Dunbar on one occasion when walking in the park with Mary Terrell encountered a barrage of verbal abuse from whites who recognized him as a black man but mistook her for a white woman. Despite his dark skin, Dunbar possessed sufficient literary stature to be what was called an "ornament" of Washington's colored society, a subject that he occasionally discussed in articles in national magazines. In essays on Negro life in Washington published in 1900 and 1901 and addressed primarily to white audiences, he described the city as the place where "the breeziness of the West" met "the refinement of the East, the warmth and grace of the South," and "the culture and fine reserve of the North." The "social life of the Negro," he argued, was more highly developed in Washington than in any other city in the country, and could no longer be "laughed at or caricatured under the name of 'colored sassiety.' " Class lines were "strictly drawn," and one from outside the District would be no more likely to gain admission to the "black 400" without "a perfect knowledge of his standing in his own community than would Mrs. Bradley Martin's butler to an Astor ball." Little wonder, Dunbar declared, that some blacks "wince a bit when we are thrown into the lump with the peasant or serving class." "In aims and hopes for our race," he concluded, "we are all as one, but it must be understood that when we come to consider the social life, the girls who cook in your kitchens and the men who serve in your dining rooms do not dance in your parlors."[75]

Despite the criticism directed at Washington's colored aristocracy, it continued throughout the late nineteenth and early twentieth centuries to be the inspiration and envy of "upper ten" Negroes everywhere in the United States. It was the standard by which others measured their own culture, refinement, and wealth. In 1883, a black resident of Richmond, Virginia boasted that "the culture and tone of society" in his city approximated that in Washington, even though the number of aristocrats in the latter city was much larger. "Washington," he noted with pride, "will always find room for a Richmond son or daughter." Voicing a sentiment expressed by many others, a black journalist in the Midwest claimed in 1895 that it was common knowledge that colored society in the District was composed of "the most cultured, most advanced and intelligent as well as the wealthiest members of the colored race." Almost two decades later the Pittsburgh *Courier* observed that the quality of Washington's colored aristocracy approached that of "the best society of other races."[76]

Such an assessment was in essential agreement with a more-detailed analysis in 1904 entitled "Society Among the Colored People in Washington" written by Mary Terrell, who for a half century after her marriage to Robert Terrell in 1891 was a leader among the city's colored aristocrats. Washington's black upper class, in her view, was not an oddity but rather "much like that of any other kind." No less than that of whites, it was made up of various sets and cliques. "Even if all those who are equal mentally, morally and financially chose to join one grand social union it would be inconvenient to do so," she wrote. "Like other human beings all colored people who are of equal culture, intelligence and affluence do not care to mingle with one another socially. For this reason it would be easier to locate the North Pole than to find 'the great and only' among the numerous colored circles of Washington." But as "Mollie" Terrell indicated, the basic division within the city's upper crust was between the "old citizens" and the "new comers." Viewing themselves as "the elect" and "the chosen," the old citizens believed that longevity of residence in the District coupled with culture and affluence counted "for more than any other combination." In the manner of the "old Knickerbocker set in New York," the old citizens of Washington's colored society maintained a "social sanctum sanctorum" into which "the nouveau riches are not permitted to set their unhallowed feet." Socially prominent newcomers, on the other hand, scoffed at the exclusiveness of the old citizens and described themselves as the ones who were "up and doing things." Although the old citizens and the newcomers exchanged social courtesies and came together in the Monocan Club, the line of demarcation was "never wholly eradicated."[77]

At social gatherings of colored aristocrats, whether they represented old citizens, newcomers, or a combination of the two, Mollie Terrell insisted that one would encounter only people who dressed "tastefully," spoke flawless English, and exhibited all the earmarks of education, sophistication, and wealth. Graduates of Yale, Harvard, Cornell, Oberlin, and "other renowned institutions of learning" were likely to be numerous at such gatherings. Those who made up "society" not only read "the best literature" but also cultivated "a taste for good music" and took "a deep interest in the questions of the day," especially those related to race.[78]

Regardless of the "sub-divisions ad infinitum" within Washington's colored society, Mollie Terrell suggested that those who made up the aristocracy were strikingly similar in origins, life style, and values. Their social lives were closely intertwined: they belonged to a few select clubs, attended two or three high-status churches, vacationed together, and were often related by marriage if not by blood. As Langston Hughes later suggested, those in the social circle represented by Mary Church Terrell perceived themselves as "the best people" and as "the best society." But unlike Hughes and others who were critical of this group, Mrs. Terrell did not stress color as a factor in determining membership in the aristocracy. While the great preponderance of those whom she included among Washington's most-fashionable colored society were light skinned, her only reference to complexion was in connection with a young society woman who looked "as though she might be a beauty from Madrid." Mary Church Terrell, as well as those with whom she regularly associated, would undoubtedly have denied that skin color figured in criteria for admission to the aristocracy. She might well have called attention to dark-skinned individuals within her circle, such as the poet Dunbar and the scholar Kelly Miller. She did insist that the "race problem" was a subject of persistent concern among upper-class blacks and "was constantly discussed of course when two or three are gathered together."[79]

Periodically blacks intimately acquainted with Washington's colored society attempted dispassionate analyses of the city's colored aristocracy and its role in regard to the black masses. One of these was Richard W. Thompson, who in 1895 furnished the Indianapolis Freeman with a series of articles entitled "Phases of Washington Life." Thompson agreed with Mary Church Terrell that there was nothing more futile than attempting to identify the "first circle" among the numerous cliques and factions existing among the upper stratum of Washington's colored society. While Thompson refused to identify the "first circle" within "the class commonly denominated as the aristocracy," he was certain that entry into any circle or clique therein by an outsider required "proper" introduction by an insider. Colored aristocrats, he observed, rarely patronized public balls but tended to confine their social activities to gatherings that included no more than a "double parlor full." They maintained contact with other blacks by attendance at "the great concerts and musicales given frequently at the churches and other places," but even here there was "no social intercourse beyond one's immediate party." Colored aristocrats sometimes opened their homes for church socials, which could be attended by "any person of respectable appearance," but the presence of such persons on these occasions did not constitute anything remotely resembling admission into the "upper reaches" of society. Those who assumed otherwise were immediately and forthrightly made aware of their error.

One point that Thompson stressed was the "uncomplaining acceptance of social distinctions" and of the existence of a colored aristocracy by "the restricted classes." The latter expressed no resentment against the aristocrats because "servants and those employed in menial capacities" did not expect social recognition from "the office-holding, professional and monied classes." Between the aristocrats of color in Washington and those blacks whom Thompson described as "the denizens of the courts, alleys and cheap tenements" there existed a social chasm as vast as that separating the white aristocrat from the common laborer of the same color.

As for wealth, Thompson contended that relatively few aristocrats could be described as rich. Like Calvin Chase earlier, he suggested that wealth was considerably less important than other considerations in determining status in the black community. Nevertheless, many colored aristocrats were constantly in the throes of an economic struggle "to keep up appearances and make both ends meet." The expenses involved in maintaining a residence at a fashionable address and in entertaining properly sometimes resulted in living beyond their means. Nor did Thompson deny that "a vast array of tinsel and cheap imitation" was on occasion evident among those who claimed to be among the exclusive set, but in his view such persons did not really belong to the aristocracy. Rather they were imitators wholly lacking in the intangible qualities that set aristocrats apart. In their style of living the authentic aristocrats of color exhibited "a quiet air of elegance and refinement" found among no other group of blacks anywhere else in the United States.[80]

Eleven years after Thompson's articles appeared in the *Freeman*, Archibald Grimké (the brother of Francis Grimké, pastor of the Fifteenth Street Presbyterian Church), who had moved from Boston to Washington, provided the *New York Age* with a description of "The Four Hundred of Washington." In his opinion the city contained the "best specimens of the race," who had been attracted there from all over the nation by the possibility of white-collar employment in government service and the exceptionally strong colored school system. Those from the outside who held positions in the government and in the schools, "together with those or descendants of those who lived here before the war," constituted "the upper class of colored society in the District of Columbia." The combination of natives and newcomers had built "a strong professional class composed of preachers, teachers, lawyers, doctors, dentists, real estate and note brokers, and professors" who were "well fed, well dressed, well mannered and well educated." "They measure up in all respects to the average American middle class," Grimké declared, "and there are individuals among them who compare favorably with the best of the highest American class in culture, morals, and aspirations." Like Thompson, he denied that the colored aristocrats represented "great wealth . . . such as possessed by whites of the corresponding group at the capital," but he believed that they were acquiring valuable real estate and "growing rich on the quiet."

But Grimké balanced such praise with some serious criticisms. In his view one of the main features of Washington's aristocrats of color was the preoccupation with "pomp and trappings" and the tendency to devote too much energy and money to matters of little significance. The fierce competition of numerous "social factions and cliques" precluded the cohesiveness necessary to advance the race in general. Although the colored aristocrats set a good example for the masses by their cultural sophistication and their acquisition of property, they provided "the worst possible object lesson of improvidence and thriftlessness" by their lavish entertaining and ostentatious display. Grimké reminded his fellow aristocrats that it was their responsibility "always to lift the lower classes upward." "Noblesse oblige," he continued, "is an infinitely nobler motto . . . than that of Eat, Drink and be Merry."[81]

Whatever success the colored aristocrats in the city may have had in disassociating themselves socially from the surrounding black community, they were unable to escape the disabilities and proscriptions imposed upon all blacks by a racist society that adhered to the notion that "one drop" of African blood was sufficient to place a person in the "inferior caste." Beginning in the 1890s, as the economic depression drew a new wave of black migrants into Washington, the legal and extralegal manifestation of an increasingly virulent racism resulted in the "steady paring down of incentive" for blacks, especially that of the upper class. The decline in federal employment of blacks seriously eroded the fragile economic basis on which much of the colored aristocracy rested. The number of black federal employees in Washington shrank from 1,532 in 1892 to 1,450 in 1908. Of the latter only about 300 were clerks; the rest were messengers and common laborers. Promotions became increasingly rare. White-collar jobs in the District government were only a little more accessible to blacks than those in the federal departments. Negro congressmen had usually occupied prominent places in Washington's colored society and provided blacks with access to the federal establishments, but the departure of George H. White of North Carolina in 1901 left Congress without a black member for almost a generation. Opportunities for federal employment declined with the return to power of the Democrats under Woodrow Wilson in 1913. Wilson not only sanctioned a segregation policy within the government departments but also refused to appoint blacks to offices that had come to be viewed as sinecures for blacks. Thus, an American Indian became Register of the Treasury and a white Recorder of Deeds. All the while, white-collar employment opportunities for blacks outside the government steadily declined, and despite the efforts of Booker T. Washington's National Negro Business League, little progress occurred in the development of black business enterprises in the District. The city's only black bank, the Capital Savings Bank, in which John R. Lynch and Robert Terrell were officers, failed in 1903.[82]

The proliferation of Jim Crow contrivances appeared to destroy any hopes that aristocrats of color may have had about being assimilated into American society. By 1892 the names of all blacks, except those of Mr. and Mrs. John F. Cook, had been dropped from *The Elite List*. Despite the persistent efforts of Furman J. Shadd, John R. Francis, Charles B. Purvis, Le Count Cook, and other black physicians to join the Medical Society of the District of Columbia, their applications for membership always met rejections on the ground that their presence was undesirable at meetings in which "papers were read and medical matters discussed in a semi-social manner." After more than a decade and a half of trying to breach the color line, the black physicians organized their own medical society in 1884. The organization became moribund within a few years, but when the District Medical Society refused admission to Dr. John R. Francis in 1894 it became apparent "that the bars were not going to be taken down." The following year the old organization was revived and incorporated under its original name, the Medico-Chirurigal Society of the District of Columbia. Ironically, three of the eight incorporators were white physicians, and whites continued to hold membership in the society throughout most of the first two decades of the twentieth century. But as "the original white members were lost by death, their places were never filled," so that the society at least after 1920 was "composed of, though not limited to, Negroes alone." Writing in 1939, the historian of the society linked it with the colored public school system and Howard University. "The personnel of all three of these groups," he observed, "has been composed of Negroes of a comparable cultural level." In his opinion the society represented "the degree to which values emanating from the School System and University had carried over into the free life of the community."[83]

Increasingly, restaurants, hotels, theatres, and other public places became inaccessible to upper-class blacks. "Every hour in the day," a colored aristocrat observed in 1907 in regard to the electric cars crossing from the District into Virginia, "Jim Crow cars filled with colored people, many of whom are intelligent and well-to-do, enter and leave the national capital." At the same time opportunities for white-collar employment shrank so dramatically that blacks, no matter how well educated or refined, were left with only a few menial occupations open to them. "We can't all be preachers, teachers, doctors and lawyers," one upper-class black resident of Washington despaired. Even the public school system, whose teaching and administrative posts had traditionally been the preserves of the colored aristocrats, was no longer a reliable source of employment. Changes in the system in 1901 resulted in the reduction of the office of Superintendent of the Colored Schools to an assistant superintendency. More important in some respects was the replacing of blacks with whites as directors of departments in the Negro school system.[84]

In no areas, perhaps, did aristocrats of color in Washington confront the color line so persistently as in their efforts to secure adequate housing. As early as 1881 the *People's Advocate* complained about the shortage of "houses for our people," noting that the crisis was especially acute for those of "the official class" because respectable homes were simply out of reach for anyone classified as a

Negro. Cottages and medium-size dwellings in desirable localities were as "scarce as hen's teeth," a member of the black upper class observed in 1895. When Mary Church Terrell began house hunting in Washington, she found that the white residential areas she considered desirable were closed to her because of her color. She and her husband finally succeeded in purchasing a house in Le Droit Park, a fashionable area in the northwest section of the city, which at the time had only one black resident. Mary Terrell maintained that blacks, especially those in what she called "our group," were not obsessed with living in white neighborhoods but that such neighborhoods were the only areas that contained the quality of housing that she and her friends would consider purchasing. She also noted that upper-class blacks were forced to "pay much more for the property they buy than do others." That colored aristocrats managed to purchase decent homes at inflated prices suggested a degree of affluence unknown to the black masses. In the Terrells' case, the money for the residence that they finally purchased at 326 T Street, Northwest, was a gift from Mary's father.[85]

Despite the difficulties of purchasing property in a desirable section, many colored aristocrats did manage to secure commodious residences in "fashionable quarters." The Douglass home at "Cedar Hill" in Anacostia, the Langstons' "Hillside Cottage," and the Pinchbacks' thirteen-room house on Bacon Street were among the largest and most elegantly furnished homes of the colored aristocrats, but others were only a little less so. Henry P. Cheatham, the congressman from North Carolina who later became recorder of deeds, purchased a home on T Street, Northwest, in 1897, that was described as "one of the best pieces of property owned by a colored man in the District." On the same street lived the Terrells and Alice Strange Davis, whose "at homes" were among the most exclusive social gatherings in Washington. The Daniel Murrays, who resided nearby, were for many years the only black residents in the 900 block of S Street, but by 1912 the block had become all black, including two physicians and several Howard University professors. Perhaps "the most commodious house owned by an Afro-American in Washington" was the one built in 1899 by Mr. and Mrs. John F. Cook on 16th Street between L and M Streets. A three-story structure of buff brick and stone, it was decorated inside with "finely finished oak" and contained "all modern conveniences." Some of the old families such as the Cooks, Wormleys, and Francises had acquired extensive real estate in the city before the Civil War and kept it in the family. By the turn of the century such property had appreciated enormously in value. Dr. John Francis, who had inherited property from his father, invested extensively in real estate that included an elegant home on Pennsylvania Avenue adjoining his private hospital. But for most blacks, regardless of their education, wealth, refinement, or fairness of complexion, the securing of housing, other than that already "discarded by discriminating people," involved considerable trouble.[86]

Although Washington's colored aristocrats belonged to the "proscribed race" and were acutely sensitive to the proscriptions imposed upon them, the impact of Jim Crowism on their lives was less pervasive and less brutalizing than it was on the "submerged masses." The aristocrats lived in an isolated social world, removed from whites as well as from lower-class blacks, that enabled them to avoid many of the daily humiliations experienced by ordinary black people. Jean Toomer, who grew up in the Washington home of his grandfather P. B. S. Pinchback, admitted that it was not until his senior year in high school that he "came face to face with the race question in a personal way."[87] In spite of the isolation from whites, they sometimes had access to powerful whites, especially those who held positions in the federal and District governments and who protected them from the more-blatant forms of prejudice and discrimination. Their economic resources enabled them to purchase decent housing, even at inflated prices, and to provide their children with superior educational advantages. Those who found themselves in court were likely to get fairer trials than a black from one of the alley dwellings, because they could afford legal counsel or on some occasions secure the assistance of powerful white friends.[88]

Within the context of their own racist attitudes, some whites, either consciously or unconsciously, recognized the existence of social gradations among blacks and behaved toward those of the colored aristocracy in a manner different from that displayed toward ordinary black folk. The difference in behavior was sometimes subtle, but subtle or not, it was significant, especially for those blacks singled out for respect. Mary Church Terrell, who regularly moved among whites while on the lecture circuit, was always sensitive to the nuances involved in the etiquette of interracial gatherings. That the mayor of Roanoke, Virginia introduced her as Mrs. Mary Church Terrell to a white audience in 1909 impressed her as "an unusual exhibition of breadth" for the South. In 1916, when a new employee of People's Drug Store in Washington refused to serve Mary Church Terrell at the soda fountain, she and her husband formally protested to the store manager, who immediately apologized for "the crass ignorance of the clerk." "We do not care to serve people of any race at our fountain who are not genteel," he wrote Robert Terrell, "but such objection certainly could not obtain against your wife, yourself and any high class colored person." Clearly for some whites the aristocrat of color warranted different and better treatment than did ordinary blacks.[89]

By the outbreak of the war in Europe in 1914 the colored aristocracy in Washington was scarcely the same as in the days when Josephine Bruce as the wife of a United States senator held court and "chose with rare discernment those who would receive one of those coveted missives inviting one to tea at her home." The black population of the city had almost doubled, and from the ranks of slave descendants had emerged a darker, upwardly mobile middle class whose size, wealth, and influence were steadily increasing. Middle-class businessmen, politicians, ministers, teachers, and journalists who embraced Booker T. Washington's philosophy and sought to build self-sufficient, independent black institutions, came to constitute a new economic elite which in time pressed its claim for a share of the social status of the old upper-class families. The District's colored aristocracy, while never a closed group, expanded slowly and admitted only those of the stratum below it who had been carefully screened to ensure that they conformed to the values and expectations of "our group."

Ralph Tyler, a veteran observer of the black upper class, admitted that the "brainy men" associated with Howard University and their families had by 1914 come to dominate the social scene in Washington's black community. But the city's authentic aristocracy, he insisted, was found among the older residents, "among the 'Old Cits' and those whose residence in Washington has covered . . . a quarter of a century or more." Although access to the socially prominent "Old Cits" was much more difficult than to the "Howard Hill set," Tyler observed, those "so fortunate as to meet them" would be profoundly impressed by their refinement and aristocratic manners. "Reserved and sedate, cultured and clever," he declared, "they form a delightful assemblage . . . who impress you with their accomplishments, entertain you with their cleverness and make you feel at home with their unstinted hospitality, the latter being traditional."[90] Caroline Langston and Josephine Bruce, referred to as elderly matrons or dowagers by 1914, represented the older generation of society leaders, whose places had been naturally assumed by Bettie Cox Francis, Mary Church Terrell, and others of the younger generation. Despite the changes that had engulfed their city and its black community, they still constituted the "upper crust," so perceived by themselves and by others. Some others undoubtedly had more money and received more attention in the press, but the upper-class old families possessed the culture, refinement, and sense of tradition that sustained their places at the pinnacle of the city's black social structure. Fully conscious that they constituted the upper class of a minority group classified as inferior by the larger white society, they nonetheless perceived theirs as the role of an aristocracy whose right it was to govern socially and whose responsibility it was to serve by example and take action in the cause of racial uplift.

3

◆

Aristocrats of Color in the South

IN BLACK COMMUNITIES THROUGHOUT THE UNITED STATES, old established families occupied a position comparable to that of the aristocrats of color in the nation's capital. As a black observer noted in 1876, almost all communities possessed "a few thoroughbred families who glory in lineal ancestors and carry wherever they go the tone and flavor of unconscious refinement, [and] social fellowship, or cemented by dear remembrances."[1] Whatever other attributes may have characterized these few thoroughbred families, the pride that they manifested in their culture, achievement, behavior, and ancestry was virtually universal.

In the introduction to his *As We See It*, published in 1910, Robert Lewis Waring, a Michigan-born black attorney whose family had "produced sixty-one school teachers in three generations," spoke for many aristocrats of color when he explained the meaning of his book's title: "By 'We' I mean the educated Negroes, those of cultured families of the third and fourth generations . . . who see things as other men of their mental caliber see them [and] who feel the sting of race prejudice most keenly."[2] Those included in Waring's "We," whether residents of Albany, Detroit, Little Rock, or San Francisco, were acutely conscious of their family background and viewed themselves as heirs of a legacy that commanded authority, bestowed prestige, and imposed responsibility. "In every town," a black journalist observed in 1902, there were inquisitive people who dealt "heavily in family trees."[3] The genealogical charts of such people often included an assortment of European noblemen, white American statesmen, African kings, and Indian chieftains. But no less significant was that their families had enjoyed the status of antebellum free persons of color or favored slaves and had compiled records of achievement. In 1908 Ray Stannard Baker observed: "In Philadelphia I heard of the Old Philadelphia Negroes, in Indianapolis of the old families, in Boston a sharp distinction was drawn between the 'Boston Negroes' and the recent southern importation. Even in Chicago where there is nothing old, I found the same spirit."[4] In their perspective, an emphasis on family, continuity, heritage, and achievement set them apart from other blacks.

If Washington was the "capital of the colored aristocracy," it was also preeminently a Southern city. The best-known old families of the district had originally migrated from Virginia, Maryland, and other Southern states, and an overwhelming majority of those of "co-equal" status from elswhere who later became incorporated into the city's black aristocracy were members of upper-class families in such Southern cities as Baltimore, Charleston, New Orleans, Little Rock, Nashville, and Atlanta. The Southern origins of many of the District's aristocrats of color were significant in shaping their perceptions of class functions and responsibility. Although Washington's "black 400" represented an amalgam of old families from throughout the nation, the Southern influence was obvious in its attitudes, values, and traditions.

Despite the tendency of white Southerners to treat all blacks as an un-differentiated mass of inferior beings, they too recognized and on occasion admitted that such a view scarcely conformed to reality. In 1877, for example, a "South Carolinian," writing in the *Atlantic* about society in his native state, noted that blacks there had "among themselves social rank and aristocracy outrageously severe and strictly discriminated."[5] Eight years later, a well-known Memphis daily with pronounced racist views admitted, "There is as much distinction in the society of colored people of the South as there is among the whites. In every community, town and city the blacks are divided into classes governed by education, intelligence, morality, wealth and respectability. The distinction is scrupulously observed here in Memphis by the colored people. The educated and intelligent who, by honest industry, have acquired a competency and who live exemplary lives create a fashionable social circle of their own."[6]

Whether designated as an "aristocracy" or a "fashionable social circle," a "strictly discriminated upper class" of blacks existed throughout the South in both small towns and large cities. A white observer reported in 1891 that "social differentiation" among blacks was apparent everywhere in the South. "Two aristocracies are appearing in the colored race, the aristocracy of culture and the aristocracy of wealth." As "South Carolinian" noted earlier, many "local variations" underlay class distinctions, but in his opinion, the prime gradations rested on "official station, position in the church, possession of money or real estate, former ownership and city birth." The "color factor" was also important in the stratification process.[7]

Lura Beam, a white teacher in black schools sponsored by the American Missionary Association in Memphis and Wilmington, North Carolina between 1908 and 1919, learned from her students much about the "Negro Aristocracy." She concluded that in their "hair splitting" in regard to matters of class and status, blacks surpassed whites because they not only "added more categories" but also invoked different criteria and applied them more rigorously. At the top of their class structure was the "Negro Aristocracy" that existed and could be recognized even "in lonesome hamlets so small that a few families were considered above the rest."[8] The only sure way to be included in this aristocracy was to be born there, since the black aristocracy "lived by birth, money, education and conduct" and "perpetuated itself by marriage." Education and extraordinary achievement might on occasion entitle someone from the middle class to a place in the "upper ten," but "making a splash with money would not." According to Beam, the black aristocracy in the early twentieth-century South "was, at birth, farther along than the others," because "it was lighter in color and had inherited land or education or money from white or free ancestors."

Having acquired the first higher education and produced the earliest black professionals, the aristocrats of color, at maturity, functioned as community leaders, lived in the best houses, and spent their money for Northern travel, books, musical instruments, and the education of their children. Because they "were deathly afraid of getting dragged back to what their grandfathers had left behind," Beam argued, they placed extraordinary emphasis on education, especially education that equipped one for a profession. To become a physician, for example, was to perpetuate upper-class status. Although the colored aristocrats Beam encountered had relatively little contact with or knowledge of lower-class blacks, they nonetheless felt keenly their responsibility to the less-fortunate masses. They perceived themselves as keepers of high ideals, guardians of culture, and models of proper decorum to be emulated by other blacks. But being "too high on a hill" and too far removed from ordinary black folk made the aristocrats a natural target for "snipers" from below who sometimes regarded them as "stuck up and impossible." The aristocrats of color, as a result, suffered what Beam described as "spells" of adapting the "contemptuous attitudes" of whites toward those at the bottom. Convinced that "the noble would go on raising more noble," they nonetheless despaired at ever seeing the "end of their brotherly responsibility."[9]

Although Beam's analysis of the Negro aristocracy rested on her impressions of a limited number of upper-class blacks in two cities in the South, the evidence suggests that some of her observations were applicable to aristocrats of color throughout the region. Even in the tiny settlement of Anding, Mississippi in 1894, "colored high life" was a term used to describe three or four black families. Studies of black communities in Farmville, Virginia in 1898 and Thomasville, Georgia about 1900 indicated the validity of Beam's claim that a black upper class existed even in "lonesome hamlets." In both, the upper class was made up of prosperous, landowning farmers, teachers, and other professionals who were well-educated, regularly employed servants, and exhibited the highest standards of moral rectitude.[10]

While most probably felt an obligation to reach and reclaim the lowest social strata, they also believed that it was low classes of both races that restricted the opportunities of "better class" blacks, especially those at the top of the Negro social structure.[11] In 1893, a Negro resident of Knoxville, Tennessee, convinced that refined and cultured blacks suffered primarily because of the activities of their lower-class brethren, suggested that the remedy lay in more-rigid social classification among blacks. Such classifications would prevent the "bad element" from intruding into the presence of those with "fine manners" and "social standing." The result, he explained, would remove from the "better element of the colored people" many of the disadvantages under which they labored.[12]

The scrupulous observance of class distinctions was evident even in the small town of Hope, Arkansas, whose "fashionable social circle," known as "the big Nigguhs of Hazel Street," included fewer than a dozen families. What separated these families from other blacks in this town, one resident recalled, was "the fact that they had, and could do, many things the rest of us could only dream about." Such things included the "houses, vacations, educations, transportation, status, clubs, culture, hobbies, luxuries [and] ambitions" of the Hazel Street elite.[13] But in Hope and other small towns it was, of course, more difficult for the upper class to isolate itself from the "submerged masses." As a member of an old upper-class family in Natchez, Mississippi explained in 1903: "You take a small place like Natchez, you are necessarily thrown in frequent contact with persons whom you would not select as your friends. In a large city you can avoid meeting them at all."[14]

The proximity of Washington and Baltimore meant that the aristocrats of color in these cities often "co-mingled" socially. "With her sister city Baltimore just next door," Paul Laurence Dunbar observed in 1901, "the Negro in Washington forms and carries on a social life which no longer can be laughed at. . . ." Upper-class social events in one city almost invariably included representatives of the elite from the other. Many of those who belonged to the "upper tens" in the District of Columbia were either natives of Baltimore or related by blood or marriage to the old families of that city. Daniel Murray, James T. Bradford, and William E. Matthews were members of old, well-known Baltimore families who achieved social prominence in Washington. Ralph V. Cook, the son of John F. Cook, Jr., of Washington and a teacher in Baltimore's Colored High School, married into the socially prominent Mason family of the Monumental City. Frederick Douglass, a native of Maryland who spent eight years in Baltimore as a slave, possessed a wide circle of friends in the city and was a frequent visitor there until his death. According to one scholar, Douglass preferred Baltimore society to that of Washington. Those of "co-equal" status in the two cities regularly vacationed together at Harper's Ferry or Saratoga. The association of the two elites was nowhere more evident than in the shared activities of their prestigious literary societies.[15]

Both before and after the Civil War Baltimore possessed one of the largest black populations of any American city. By the outbreak of the war its black population included 26,000 free people of color.[16] By the late nineteenth century, there had emerged primarily from these free people a favored few families who had been closely identified with the civic, educational, and religious life of the city's black community for several generations. A white historian, writing in 1890 about these "exceptional" black Marylanders, observed that "there are certain families who have long been better off and better educated than the rest of their fellows, . . . who have been better known to, and had more to do with, whites, and there are everywhere differences in social life and mental attainments which mark any people." Like the "larger world about them," black Baltimoreans had their "small fashionable groups" in which "a few privileged daughters are brought out into society by a party or reception." In the black community, he concluded, the behavior and life style of "the prosperous and unpretentious" old families contrasted sharply with those of the "poor and showy."[17]

Among the first families in post-war black Baltimore were those whose forebears had made significant contributions in the antebellum era. The Gilliards, Hacketts, and Cokers, who were related through marriage, provided much of the early black religious leadership in the city, and, in the opinion of one scholar, were "well entrenched in what constituted the best of black life in the nineteenth century." No less prominent in the postbellum era was the Fortie family, which also produced early religious leaders; and the Deavers, whose ancestors had figured prominently in the antislavery cause and antebellum convention movement. One Deaver descendant, James M., was for many years rector of Saint Augustine's Protestant Episcopal Church in Atlantic City and was conspicuous in national Episcopal affairs relating to blacks. Another Deaver, Sarah, married Isaac Myers, who, born free in Maryland, was one of the best-known blacks in Baltimore in the nineteenth century. Active in a variety of civil rights and civic enterprises, he pioneered in the organization of black labor and played an important role in local and national Republican affairs. A man of substantial wealth, he and his family were "social factors" in the city for many years. In 1884, his son, George A. Myers, married Annie Deans, a teacher in Baltimore's Howard Normal School, who, according to the press, was "well connected" and "a society favorite." They settled in Cleveland, where they became fixtures in the city's black social elite.[18]

Other families in Baltimore's black upper class included the Murrays, Lockses, Butlers, Fernandises, Browns, Masons, DeCourseys, Mossells, and Briscoes. Most were educated and relatively well-to-do. No less than their counterparts in other places, Baltimore's first families tended to be bound together through interlocking genealogies. They were often linked through marriage to each other or to upper-class families in Washington, Philadelphia, and other Eastern cities. John W. Locks, the owner of a hack and funeral business and perhaps the wealthiest black man in postwar Baltimore, was the brother-in-law of John W. Fernandis, a prosperous barber who had inherited substantial wealth from his Brazilian father. Dr. H. J. Brown, a prominent physician and the scion of an old antebellum family long identified with civil rights and racial uplift causes, established once and for all his "social imminence [sic]" by marrying the daughter of James H. Fleet, a black physician in antebellum Washington, who was active in the early convention movement.[19]

Few other old upper-class black families in Baltimore were more knowledgeable about their origins and ancestry than the Murrays. George Murray, born free in Maryland in 1773, lived until 1890. Noted for his remarkable memory and his knowledge of the Bible and the writings of the Jewish historian Josephus, he was a Methodist preacher "for fully 80 years" and was closely associated with the greatly revered Daniel Alexander Payne, an educator and bishop of the African Methodist Episcopal Church. Murray's son Daniel (the namesake of Bishop Payne), an assistant librarian of Congress and a bibliographer of Afro-American literature, was primarily responsible for the genealogical findings regarding the family. According to him, the black Murrays of Baltimore traced their origins to Scottish nobility. In the view of a black contemporary, Murray was "a composite subject" whose career was convincing proof "that the mulatto, given an equal chance, will outstrip either of his ancestors."[20]

No black family in the city, or in Maryland for that matter, occupied a higher social status than the Bishops, who as descendants of free people of color had maintained an enviable record of achievement since the eighteenth century. An early ancestor, Hannibal Bishop, had opened a school in Baltimore in 1810. Through the years, the Bishops, both in Baltimore and in Annapolis, had become "well connected" through marriage with other socially prominent families, notably the Prices and Vogelsangs of Annapolis and the Yopps of Albany, New York. William H. Bishop, a colleague of Myers, Locks, and Brown in the cause of racial justice and uplift, was a well-to-do barber and the owner of valuable real estate in Baltimore. For more than a half century he was a vestryman at Saint James Episcopal Church. His sons, William, Jr., and Hutchins C., were also prominent in civic and church affairs. A nephew, also named William and a graduate of Howard Medical School, was a physician in Annapolis.[21]

The prestige attached to the Bishop name was even more evident in the status occupied by the Annapolis branch of the family. James Bishop, brother of the elder William Bishop of Baltimore, was a prosperous sugar manufacturer who resided in an imposing three-story brick house directly across the street from Saint Anne's Episcopal Church. In fact, Bishop owned a pew in this historic church, which he and his family continued to occupy for many years after the Civil War. James and William Bishop were intimately associated with Washington's aristocrats of color, especially the Shadds and Parkes. The Bishop children usually attended preparatory schools and college. James's daughter Charlotte entered Wellesley College in 1896, and William's son Hutchins was the first black graduate of General Theological Seminary in New York.[22]

The Bishops and a few other "favored" families occupied places of leadership in the political, civic, and economic life of Baltimore's black community. They also dominated its cultural organizations, such as Saint Paul's Lyceum, organized in 1876, whose members bore the names of Deaver, Bishop, Myers, and Mason.[23] In 1885 a number of the most prominent members withdrew from the Lyceum to form the Monumental Literary and Scientific Association, which became Baltimore's equivalent to Washington's Bethel Literary and Historical Association. In the view of a black resident of the city the Monumental attracted only "the best classes of our citizens" and was "the pride and glory of educated Baltimoreans." Virtually all of Baltimore's old families were active in its affairs. Any cultural or social event to which the name of a Bishop, Deaver, Fortie, or Brown was attached, according to another observer, was indisputable "evidence of its gentility."[24]

Such gentility was also evident in the more exclusive social affairs of the city's aristocrats of color. As elsewhere, much of the elite's social life was home-centered and included soirées, musicales, and small receptions. A typical press account of such events was one describing a reception hosted by Dr. and Mrs. H. J. Brown in April, 1883: "The elegant residence of Dr. H. J. Brown was brilliantly lighted up on the evening of the 12th inst., the occasion being a reception given for the young ladies and gentlemen who compose the most refined and cultured society of the Monumental City."[25] Those present were the sons and daughters of Baltimore's black aristocracy—the younger generation of Bishops, Deavers, Bradfords, Masons, and Fernandises. Other home-centered events included dinners and receptions to honor upper-class visitors from Philadelphia or Washington, as well as the meetings of small social clubs, which were usually limited to a dozen or so families.[26]

Those who participated in the affairs of a few elite social organizations were likely to worship in one of the four or five high-status churches. Many if not most of the old families had religious roots in Baltimore's Bethel African Methodist Episcopal Church, which was organized in the first decade of the nineteenth century by Daniel Coker. Because of its historic position, Bethel continued to attract representatives of the city's old upper-class families. Several generations of the Bradfords, for example, were closely identified with Bethel.[27] But by the late nineteenth century a disproportionate number of the old upper class was found in such high-status churches as the Protestant Episcopal, Presbyterian, Methodist Episcopal, and Catholic, which though relatively small in comparison to the numerous A.M.E. and Baptist congregations, had existed almost as long as Bethel. Among the most "aristocratic" old churches in black Baltimore were Saint James Protestant Episcopal, Madison Street Presbyterian, and Sharp Street Methodist Episcopal, all dating from the early nineteenth century. In time other high-prestige black congregations were established in these denominations, notably Grace Presbyterian and the Chapel of Saint Mary the Virgin. Spearheading the movement to establish Saint Mary's, a mission chapel of the prestigious white Mount Calvary Protestant Episcopal Church, were William H. Bishop, Jr., Cassius M. Mason, and other younger members of Baltimore's colored aristocracy.[28]

The sanctuaries of Baltimore's high-status black churches were on occasion the scenes of fashionable weddings which united members of local families of social prominence or linked them with upper-class families from elsewhere. In 1879 the marriage of Spencer Murray, Jr., and Maggie Myers, both representatives of old Baltimore families, was performed by Alexander Crummell, the founder and rector of Saint Luke's Protestant Episcopal Church in Washington. In the "fashionable audience" were a number of prominent whites, including Senator and Mrs. William Windom and two former mayors of Baltimore.[29] No less fashionable but without any whites in attendance was the wedding in 1886 of Ione Elvita Brown, the daughter of Dr. and Mrs. H. J. Brown, at Saint Mary's Episcopal Church. The bride's sole attendant was Alida Matthews, whose family had been prominent in Baltimore for several generations. Among the distinguished out-of-town guests were former Senator and Mrs. Blanche K. Bruce and the Bishops from Annapolis.[30]

From Reconstruction to the First World War the high-status black churches in Baltimore engaged in a variety of racial uplift and charitable activities. At one time or another most sponsored day schools, usually for the children of poor black families. The Male Beneficial Society, organized under the auspices of the Saint James Episcopal Church in the 1840s, came in time to represent an interdenominational "brotherhood of a large portion of the reputable and substantial colored men of the city" whose primary concern was "the well-being of the race and the preservation of the highest and best ideals." The Saint James Society, as it was known, aided the sick, buried the dead, and provided "a forum where all things which concerned the advancement of the racial group were discussed."[31] In the mid-1880s the city's black Episcopalians opened "a free kindergarten for colored children . . . gathered from the highways and hedges of southwest Baltimore." In addition to "moral instruction," the kindergarten also provided the children with a noon meal. Later efforts to aid "poor" black children included the activities of the Empty Stocking Circle and the Fresh Air Circle, organizations composed primarily of women from Saint James's, Saint Mary's, Madison Street, and Sharp Street churches. Conspicuous in both societies was the wife of George F. Bragg, Jr., the rector of Saint James for many years and assistant editor of the *Afro-American Ledger*.[32]

Compared to the economic status of the vast majority of Baltimore's large black population, those who constituted the city's aristocracy of color were relatively well-to-do. A black editor calculated in 1890 that about twenty individuals in the city's black community collectively represented a wealth of approximately $500,000. The wealthiest, John Locks, was said to be worth $75,000. Many of those included in Baltimore's black economic elite derived their wealth from catering, barbering, hod-carrying, brickmaking, and caulking. Because of the importance of Baltimore's port and shipyards, according to an early historian, "some of the richest colored men in Baltimore began life, in the old days, as caulkers and stevedores." Many of these individuals invested in real estate, so that by the turn of the century their heirs were often among the wealthiest blacks in the city.[33]

The economic status of Baltimore's black upper class made it possible for them to travel extensively and to vacation with those of comparable social and economic background from other places. The Bishops summered at Harper's Ferry, which for a time was a favorite of Washington's colored aristocrats. The family of James T. Bradford for some years spent a portion of each summer at Cape May, New Jersey, usually at The Banneker, a hotel that catered to black guests.[34] The hotel was inferior to those for whites at the resort, and, according to one black observer, it "never was such a place as the best people coming here [Cape May] wished to patronize." By 1880 it had deteriorated to the point where many of "the best people" sought accommodations elsewhere on the Jersey coast. The Bradfords finally purchased a cottage at Sea Isle City. Others of Baltimore's old upper class joined their acquaintances from Washington in patronizing the exclusive resort at nearby Arundel-on-the-Bay developed by the son of Frederick Douglass. By the First World War Highland Beach, as the Douglass project become known, was the most popular vacation site for upper-class blacks in the Washington-Baltimore area.[35]

As a result of their economic condition, black Baltimoreans in high-status churches and such elite organizations as the Baltimore Assembly lived close together in a particular section of the city. They were, therefore, physically as well as socially and culturally removed from the sprawling slums and unkempt alleys where a majority of the city's blacks resided. Notwithstanding the difficulties that upper-class blacks in Baltimore, like their friends in Washington and elsewhere, encountered in securing decent housing, the Baltimore *Afro-American Ledger* noted in 1906 that they had been remarkably successful in establishing themselves in comfortable and attractive homes on "the better streets." Since 1890, the newspaper noted, "we have seen one of the most beautiful streets in our city, with elegant homes, turned over almost wholly to our people. We speak of Druid Hill Avenue."[36] What occurred in regard to Druid Hill Avenue in Baltimore in the quarter of a century after 1890 paralleled the development of Le Droit Park in Washington as the prime residential area of the city's aristocrats of color. In both, white residents of a "fashionable section" moved out as upper-class blacks moved in.[37]

The struggle for decent housing was only one aspect of a large, pervasive pattern of discrimination encountered by blacks of all social and economic classes in Baltimore. In fact, the movement of blacks into northwest Baltimore and especially the purchase of residences by the "best people" in the "Druid Hill district" ultimately resulted in the passage of residential segregation ordinances. The first such measure, enacted in 1910, was declared invalid, but one passed the following year remained in effect until 1917. The *Afro-American Ledger,* which waged a persistent editorial campaign against the ordinances, interpreted their existence as evidence of an increasingly virulent prejudice displayed by whites bent upon preventing blacks, regardless of their social standing, wealth, or respectability, from residing in "decent, respectable sections of the city."[38]

Throughout the post–Civil War era, Baltimore's aristocrats of color were involved in efforts to thwart the imposition of legal restrictions on the rights of black citizens. Some, like Isaac Myers, employed the tactics of "judicious conservatism"; while others, such as Dr. H. J. Brown and Joseph E. Briscoe, pursued a more aggressive, militant course.[39] These differences in approach contributed to what observers in the early 1890s described as a "serious lack of unity" among blacks that weakened attempts to resist white prejudice at the very time that "prejudice against Afro-Americans in this city is on the increase."[40] Regardless of the validity of such observations, the black upper class was capable of presenting a solid front, as was evident in the opposition to the passage of a separate coach bill in 1902. Six years later members of the old upper class set aside their differences to unite in a successful campaign to prevent the disfranchisement of black Marylanders, thereby preserving for blacks the relatively free use of the ballot, a condition that distinguished Maryland from most states to its south.[41] As in the case of black aristocrats elsewhere, those in Baltimore viewed Jim Crow contrivances as aimed primarily at them—at "the better class of colored people"—rather than at the masses of blacks, as whites often claimed.[42]

Despite increasing racial discrimination, Baltimore's aristocrats of color, even in the second decade of the twentieth century, still possessed contacts with whites and identified with the larger white community. Because they sought integration into the larger society, they eschewed race chauvinism and "found separate Negro business ventures unnecessary and unacceptable."[43] Few manifested any great interest either in Booker T. Washington's philosophy of surrendering political and civil rights for economic progress or in his National Negro Business League, a principal promoter of black capitalism. Although the *Afro-American Ledger* applauded both Washington and Du Bois,[44] few representatives of the city's old upper-class families were found among Washington's vocal supporters. The Baltimore branch of his National Negro Business League was never very active. George F. Bragg, Jr., was among those closely identified with Du Bois's Niagara Movement; and Dr. F. N. Cardozo, a physician and the son of the Washington educator and former Treasurer of the state of South Carolina, was president of the Baltimore branch of the National Association for the Advancement of Colored People.[45]

By the second decade of the twentieth century, the composition of Baltimore black social elite was clearly undergoing changes. Representatives of old upper-class families appeared less frequently in the vanguard of the city's social and civic life. Their declining role and visibility may be explained by a combination of circumstances: Upper-class families tended to have fewer children, many of whom married and moved away from Baltimore to make their mark else-where. At the same time, there was an influx of black migrants from the South that included talented and upwardly mobile individuals, especially professionals such as doctors and lawyers, who assumed the places once occupied by the Bishops, Bradfords, Briscoes, and other old families. Theirs became the names that filled the society section of the *Afro-American Ledger* and appeared most prominently in connection with the activities of the prestigious churches and social and cultural organizations. Among the newer residents of Baltimore who came to dominate the social and civic life of its black community were the families of attorneys William Ashbie Hawkins and H. S. McCard, Dr. F. N. Cardozo and others in the city's substantially expanded corps of physicians, and the educator Mason A. Hawkins. Some of these were obviously families of "co-equal" rank from other places who easily won acceptance into Baltimore's best society; others made up in educational and economic achievement what they may have lacked in family credentials. At any rate, they gained admission to the social circle that still included individuals who bore names such as Bishop, Fernandis, and Mason.

At the mid-winter ball of the Baltimore Assembly during the Christmas season of 1914, even William H. Bishop, Jr., who had been president since its founding, was absent because of illness. Those present included almost as many of the upper class from Washington as from Baltimore, according to one observer. As was usually the case, the mid-winter Assembly was an occasion for homecoming for many of the younger generation of the old families of Baltimore who resided elsewhere. But the largest contingent at the festivities in 1914 consisted of representatives of Baltimore's new social elite—the families of physicians, attorneys, and educators who had established themselves in the city since 1890. So obvious had the change in the clientele of the Assembly become by 1914 that one participant remarked: "There was a noticeable absence of representatives of the old families that have been socially prominent for the past generation or two."[46]

The black elite emerging in Baltimore prior to the First World War was perhaps most visible in the new social and cultural organizations. The older literary societies appear to have gone into eclipse by 1911, when the Baltimore Literary and Historical Association was organized at Bethel A.M.E. Church in the interest of "all the people." The list of organizers contained not a single name associated with the old families. There is no evidence that the association flourished.[47] But an organization that did prosper was the Foster Whist Club, which appeared frequently in accounts of "society happenings" in black Balti-more throughout the second decade of the twentieth century. While the club included two or three couples representing the younger generation of the old families, it was clearly dominated by the new social elite, primarily physicians, attorneys, educators, and their wives. Nowhere was the role of this new elite more in evidence than in the charity balls staged in the interest of Provident

Hospital, a black institution founded in 1894.[48] Whatever differences may have existed between Baltimore's old and new social elites, they had one thing in common—both encountered criticism for being insensitive to the plight of the black masses.[49]

Among black Americans, the aristocrats of color in Charleston, South Carolina, more than those anywhere else in the South, even in New Orleans, had a reputation for snobbery and colorphobia that persisted well into the twentieth century.[50] Both black and white observers traced the origins of Charleston's black elite to the top stratum of the city's sizable community of free people of color in the antebellum era, "who lived in self-satisfied complacency in a little world below the whites and above the slaves."[51] That some of these free families of color were also slave owners made it all the easier for them to assume the outlook and values of whites. In the postwar era, so the argument ran, the descendants of the relatively well-to-do, slave-holding free people of color perpetuated what has been termed the "aristocratic complex" of their forebears. They remained closeted in a world of their own, represented by institutions such as St. Mark's Protestant Episcopal Church, Avery Normal Institute, the Brown Fellowship and the Friendly Moralist societies, the Amateur Literary and Fraternal Association, and other social organizations whose members were usually intricately related by marriage and so fair in complexion that it was "impossible to discern the slightest trace of black blood." At the twenty-fourth commencement of Avery Institute, in 1889, the graduating class consisted of eleven members, ten "young ladies and a gentleman." The latter, according to one observer, "bore the name of De Reef, a family that has stood high for respectability and wealth." For some like J. H. Holloway, the essential prerequisite for admission to Charleston's colored aristocracy was not wealth or complexion but descent from a free family of color, which, of course, was more likely also to be light-skinned and relatively well-to-do.[52]

In 1907 the *Charleston News and Courier*, in a feature story on the city's antebellum free black families of prominence, maintained that "their descendants are still the colored aristocracy of Charleston." Nor was its influence confined to that city: descendants of the Westons, Holloways, McKinlays, and Dereefs who settled elsewhere took with them the class consciousness and "tone and flavor of unconscious refinement" bequeathed by their forebears. They figured prominently in the "upper ten" circles of Washington, Brooklyn, Philadelphia, and other cities. Whitefield McKinlay, well-to-do scion of a slave-holding free family of color, occupied a place of political and social prominence in the District of Columbia from the late nineteenth century until his death in 1941. In Milwaukee, the heir of another elite Charleston family, George H. Dereef, an attorney and businessman, moved among the city's "best people," as did Weston Thorne in Brooklyn, the Grimkés in Washington and Boston, and the Adgers in Philadelphia.[53]

Despite their dispersal throughout the United States, upper-class black Charlestonians maintained a deep affection for their city and spoke with pride of the reputation and traditions of their forebears. T. McCants Stewart, a free-born native of Charleston who lived all over the world, always viewed himself as an exile from his birthplace. Writing in 1908 to Whitefield McKinlay, a friend observed: "Of course you married a Charlestonian. That is almost a proverb when it comes to a gentleman from Charleston getting married. As a rule they go back for a wife."[54]

In addition to the McKinlays, Dereefs, Westons, DeCostas, Bennetts, Holloways, and other old families descended from Charleston's antebellum free people of color, the city's black aristocracy at the turn of the century included an infusion of members of "co-equal" status from both inside and outside South Carolina. Among such families were two physicians: One was William D. Crum, a native of South Carolina, a free person of color of African-German descent, and a graduate of Avery Normal Institute and Howard University Medical School. Crum married Ellen Craft, who was born in England, the daughter of William and Ellen Craft, whose escape from slavery was widely publicized in both America and England. According to a New York *World* reporter, Crum, who resembled a "German burgher," read French literature, spoke some German, attended the theater, dressed as well as any man in Charleston and lived in better style than most of them."[55]

Crum's friend and associate, Dr. Alonzo C. McClennan, also a graduate of Howard Medical School, was a tall imposing figure with blond hair and blue eyes, who "was to all appearances a white man." He was born in Columbia, South Carolina and reared in the home of his uncle, a well-to-do free man of color. McClennan married Ida Ridley, a schoolteacher whose family was among "the best social element" in Augusta, Georgia and closely related to the socially prominent Ridleys in Boston. Like the Crums, Dereefs, Bennetts, and other aristocrats of color in Charleston, the McClennans resided in a commodious residence, always attended by at least three servants. They frequently hosted receptions, literary gatherings, and musicales. With the assistance of friends among the black elite as well as upper-class whites, McClennan, in 1897, established a hospital for blacks that was essentially a charity institution to which he and Crum contributed their services free of charge. A nurses training school existed in connection with the hospital. "The colored people," McClennan's daughter later wrote of her father, "worshipped him and the white people respected him."[56]

In the late nineteenth century, the families of Crum, McClennan, and a few other "newcomers," especially among the professional class, became integrated into Charleston's aristocracy of color. If names such as Kinloch, DeReef, and other families descended from upper-class free people of color of the antebellum era enjoyed a place of honor and respect in Charleston, so did those of McClennan and Crum. In 1890, when T. Thomas Fortune visited Charleston, he was impressed "by the remarkable deference" shown the two physicians by the blacks. "Everybody appeared to know them," Fortune noted, "and it was a novelty to see aged men and women as well as younger members of the race . . . pulling their hats off and bowing and scraping to these gentlemen."[57]

For Charleston-born aristocrats of color and for "co-equals" from elsewhere, the advantages they and their ancestors enjoyed as free people, despite the restrictions under which they lived, endowed them with social status and influence in the post–Civil War era. Belonging to what they termed the "bona fide free," in contrast to the mass of freedmen, the fair-skinned upper class remained "fundamentally integrationist and generally shared the class values of their white counterparts."[58] Despite the involvement of Charleston's aristocrats of color in the establishment of a charity hospital, a free kindergarten, and other civic and racial uplift enterprises, they remained, for many blacks, the symbol of a malevolent force. Critics regularly condemned them as "exclusives" who drew a color line against their darker brethren and refused to recognize that their destiny was inextricably tied to that of the black masses. John E. Bruce, in an outburst against the Charleston "exclusives" in 1903, reminded them that "no matter how great their Caucasian reinforcement," they were "still 'niggers' " in the view of the white man.[59]

Returning to his native Charleston in 1906 for the fortieth anniversary of the founding of Avery Normal Institute, Archibald Grimké took exception to the view of the city's black elite expressed by Bruce. "Nowhere in the United States," he observed, "is a colored society, a group of urban colored people, superior to the colored society of Charleston." A year earlier, William H. Ferris, a graduate of Yale and Harvard, encountered a receptive audience among the aristocrats of color in Charleston when he lectured there on the topic, "The criterion of aristocracy, or who's who in colored society."[60]

Although the aristocracy of color in New Orleans in the late nineteenth and early twentieth centuries resembled, in some respects, that in Charleston, the black community and social structure in the Crescent City, as John Blassingame has noted, "was sui generis."[61] In both Charleston and New Orleans a substantial portion of the postwar colored aristocracy traced its origins to antebellum free people of color, but the free black communities in the two cities developed under different historical circumstances and within different cultural milieux. In New Orleans, as well as in other parts in the Gulf region that were long under Spanish and French control, there existed by the mid-nineteenth century a sizable and significant group known as *gens de couleur libre*, with rights and privileges substantially greater than those enjoyed by free blacks elsewhere in the South. A free man of color from Tennessee, who traveled extensively in antebellum America and was in New Orleans on the eve of the Civil War, claimed that such people "enjoyed more privileges and were more respected by their white neighbors/than in any other city in the United States."[62] Free blacks in New Orleans, according to one authority, could "best be described as quasi citizens."[63]

By the outbreak of the Civil War the population of New Orleans included almost 11,000 free persons of color. Of these many were colored Creoles, a racially mixed group whose number had been augmented by West Indian emigrés fleeing the instability of the Haitian Revolution in the eighteenth and early nineteenth centuries and by French Creoles expelled from Cuba in 1809. Those who made up the community of Creoles of color in New Orleans identified themselves culturally as more French than Afro-American. In 1860 free blacks in New Orleans and the surrounding area possessed stable social institutions, a culture that "was decidedly European in flavor," wealth, education, and a degree of sophistication probably unsurpassed by blacks elsewhere in the nation. Because about three-fourths of the slaves in New Orleans were dark-skinned and about the same proportion of the free people of color were mulattoes, color assumed symbolic significance. The fair-complexioned, educated, wealthier *gens de coleur libres*, some of whom were slave owners and as intent upon protecting the "peculiar institution" as whites, placed great distance between themselves and the poorer, less-skilled, less-educated, dark-skinned free blacks. At the peak of the social structure stood the free people of color whom Alexis de Tocqueville termed the "noirs blancs."[64] Color in New Orleans, as elsewhere, correlated closely with opportunity, hence with the acquisition of education, wealth, refinement, and other attributes of high status. A Creole of color, writing early in the twentieth century about "our people," expressed pride in "being a Frenchman" and in possessing "distinguished ancestry, material wealth, education and respectability." Cited as evidence of their superiority was their enviable record of literary, musical, and artistic achievements.[65]

Individuals from the New Orleans free black community, especially colored Creoles, easily and naturally assumed leadership positions during Reconstruction. In a composite portrait, historian David Rankin described the black politician of Reconstruction New Orleans as a free man at the outbreak of the Civil War, of light complexion, the son of an old New Orleans Catholic family. Literate and educated, he "probably spoke beautiful French" (certainly not the slave dialect), and more than likely worshipped at St. Louis Cathedral. He was usually a successful artisan, professional person, or businessman. Such individuals might well have been members of either the Société des Artisans or the Société d'Economie. The latter "confined its membership to those Creoles with tendencies toward exclusiveness." By 1916 Walter Cohen, an influential and socially prominent Republican politician of Afro-Jewish ancestry, had headed the Société d'Economie for a quarter of a century. Intimately linked to what Rankin described as the most exclusive black community in antebellum America through family connections, friendship, and business, the typical black politician in New Orleans during the turbulent era of Reconstruction possessed "unusual ancestry, uncommon wealth and exceptional ability."[66] In writing about "the aristocratic tendencies" among certain New Orleans blacks in 1879, one commentator claimed that "political distinction" was the one sure step toward acquiring "social favor."[67] Such an observation may well have been valid for dark-skinned politicians with slave backgrounds, but for the majority, high social status predated their entry into politics.

Blacks in New Orleans perceived their city as different from those elsewhere in the South. It possessed, according to one resident, "a peculiar social system," and because of the extensive "mingling of the races" there racial classification was difficult. "Men who elsewhere would be called 'colored' because of their known African origins," he observed, "find their social business level here as Creoles." Writing in 1883, another black resident of New Orleans extolled the city's "cosmopolitan" character, which in his view enabled Negroes to escape the "intense prejudice manifested toward the race in other sections of the South." What opposition there was to blacks attaining all privileges enjoyed by the dominant race came not from the "better class of white citizens" but from a small minority of lower-class whites. Despite this opposition, blacks had made significant strides in gaining civil rights. "The saloons which a year or two ago would refuse a colored man a drink," he noted, "now serve him in the same manner they do a white man." According to him, the same trend was evident in theatres, restaurants, and other public places. Whatever liberalization of racial barriers took place, however, proved to be short-lived.[68]

Even though the Louisiana Supreme Court continued to distinguish between "the terms *negro* and *person of color*" as late as 1910, the so-called mystic letters—F.M.C. (free man of color)[69]—obviously no longer had the same meaning in post-Reconstruction New Orleans as it did in the antebellum era. Creoles of color lost their fight to retain the special privileges associated with their prewar third-caste status; but instead of establishing a closer relationship with the city's larger Negro population, they withdrew further into a world of their own and created a community that accentuated the differences between themselves and Afro-Americans. Those attributes rooted in their exceptional antebellum experiences—such as French language and culture, Catholicism, education, and occupational background—took on a new and special meaning that reinforced their self-perception of distinctiveness. They created for themselves a middle ground between whites and other blacks, a position that was neither recognized nor sanctioned by anyone other than themselves.[70]

Convinced that they were different from and superior to Afro-Americans who were the descendants of slaves and tended to be darker, Creoles of color in New Orleans avoided extensive and intimate contact with other Negroes in the city. They socialized, married, and lived with other colored Creoles. Residential patterns reflected their perception of themselves as distinct from other blacks. Canal Street symbolically separated them from the "uptown" Afro-Americans. Creoles lived "downtown" in the fourth, fifth, sixth, and seventh wards, where

1. Josephine Willson Bruce (1852–1923) at the time of her marriage to United States Senator Blanche K. Bruce.

2. Blanche K. Bruce (1841–1898) was United States Senator from Mississippi from 1875 to 1881, twice Register of the Treasury, and Recorder of Deeds of the District of Columbia.

3. Roscoe Conkling Bruce (1879–1950), educator and realtor in Washington and New York respectively. *Illustrations 1, 2, and 3 courtesy The Bruce Collection, Moorland-Spingarn Research Center, Howard University.*

4. James Lewis, prominent Republican politician and federal office holder in New Orleans.

5. John Mercer Langston—educator, diplomat, and politician—served as congressman from Virginia from 1890 to 1891.

6. Caroline Wall Langston, wife of John Mercer Langston, was the "social arbiter" of Washington's "black 400" for many years.

7. Robert Reed Church, wealthy businessman and banker in Memphis, Tennessee. *Courtesy Mississippi Valley Collection, Memphis State University.*

8. Pinckney Benton Stewart Pinchback (1837–1921) was lieutenant-governor of Louisiana during Reconstruction; he resided in Washington after 1891.

9. Adella Hunt Logan, women's-rights advocate; her husband was Treasurer of Tuskegee Institute in Alabama.

10. Henry Plummer Cheatham (1857–1935), educator and politician, served as congressman from North Carolina in the 1880s.

11. Charles B. Purvis, scion of a famous abolitionist family, professor at Howard University Medical School, and chief surgeon at Freedman's Hospital in Washington.

12. Marian Parke and her cousins, of Washington, D.C., as part of a bridal party in 1882. *Courtesy Library of Congress.*

13. John R. Francis, a prominent physician in Washington, D.C., who owned a private hospital.

14. Bettie Cox Francis, wife of Dr. John R. Francis, was a social leader of the "black 400" in Washington and a member of the D.C. Board of Education.

15. Daniel Murray, scion of an old Maryland family, was assistant librarian of Congress from 1881 to 1923.

16. William Bruce Evans, Daniel Murray's brother-in-law, was an educator in Washington, D.C.

17. Andrew F. Hilyer, author and inventor, was graduated from the University of Minnesota in 1882; he resided in Washington, D.C.

18. James R. Wilder, descendant of a prominent South Carolina family, was a physician in Washington, D.C.

19. Henry E. Baker, a native of Mississippi, was a businessman, banker, and civil servant in Washington, D.C.

20. Archibald Grimké, a graduate of Harvard Law School, practiced law in Boston and Washington and was a founder of the NAACP.

21. Mason Hawkins, a graduate of Harvard, Columbia, and Pennsylvania universities, was an educator in Baltimore and a close friend of W. E. B. Du Bois.

22. James C. Napier, a well-to-do banker, Republican politician, and civil servant from Nashville, Tennessee.

23. The Henry Rucker family. Rucker was a prominent Georgia politician, and his wife was the daughter of Georgia Congressman Jefferson Long. *Courtesy Peabody Museum, Harvard University.*

24. James Weldon Johnson—author, diplomat, lyricist, and civil-rights leader—was a native of Florida.

25. Alonzo Clifton McClennan, a physician in Charleston, South Carolina, where he founded a hospital and a school of nursing. *Courtesy Amistad Research Center, Tulane University.*

26. William Demos Crum, a physician in Charleston, South Carolina, was active in Republican politics.

27. Theophilius G. Minton, an attorney in Philadelphia, belonged to one of the city's famous "catering families."

28. Henry McKee Minton, son of Theophilius G. Minton, was a physician and a founder of Sigma Pi Phi and of Mercy Hospital in Philadelphia.

29. Edith Wormley Minton, the wife of Henry McKee Minton, was a member of the prominent Wormley family of Washington, D.C.

30. Josephine St. Pierre Ruffin, clubwoman and civil-rights advocate in Boston, the wife of Judge George Lewis Ruffin. *Courtesy Amistad Research Center, Tulane University.*

31. Edwin Clarence Howard, prominent physician in Philadelphia.

32. Samuel R. Scottron, inventor and chronicler of "Old New York."

their neighbors might be Jewish, German, or other whites but not dark-skinned Negroes. The Creoles themselves considered the seventh ward as *the* Creole section of the city.[71]

Creoles of color placed a premium on education and evidence of personal refinement. Because they opposed segregated schools in principle and were reluctant to have their children associate with other Negro children, they patronized private schools in the downtown area of New Orleans. One of the most prestigious was St. Mary's Academy for Young Ladies of Color. Incorporated in 1880, St. Mary's was essentially a finishing school for the daughters of well-to-do colored Creoles. A comparable institution for their sons was the St. Louis School. But those who could not afford such private schools and were forced to attend segregated public schools were likely to choose the public school on Bayou Road, which attempted to keep out anyone seen as too dark.[72]

Creoles of color endowed education with a broad meaning, a manifestation of the refinement and decorum of an individual. According to one Creole, it referred to those "people whose background had been such that they had some refinement and culture." Educated Creoles therefore appreciated a well-appointed home filled with "good things," as well as French music and literature. They attended the opera, and their libraries included the works of Molière, Chateaubriand, and other French authors. Although those who possessed wealth were able to acquire more formal education and more of the "good things" associated with the genteel life style, money was not considered a prerequisite for high social standing in the Creole community. "What was important," one scholar has noted, "was the tastefulness and discretion used in spending what [wealth] you had."[73]

To arrest the proliferation of Jim Crow statutes, Creoles of color organized a citizens committee in 1890, supported by L. J. Joubert, Homière Plessy, Aristide Mary, and others of prominence. The committee laid plans to test the constitutionality of the new laws. Joined by James Lewis, P. B. S. Pinchback, and others, they mounted a campaign to defeat the so-called separate coach bill in the Louisiana legislature that year. In opposing the enactment of the measure, Senator Henry Demas, a black who was first elected to the Louisiana Senate in 1874, spoke primarily in class terms and in behalf of upper-class blacks. Convinced that the principal enemies of blacks were whites who lacked any "social or moral standing," he appealed to the sense of justice of "educated and refined" Southern whites. "This state," he declared, "is peopled by a far larger number of cultured and wealthy colored people than is conjectured, and, owing to the intermingling of the races, it is frequently a difficult matter to determine—from the standpoint of color—the white from the Negro. Would it not be unjust, I ask, to relegate this class to a coach occupied by those much inferior to them in life, and by thus doing, humiliate a people accustomed to better surroundings? It would be forcing them to associate with the worst class of the Negro element and be an unmerited rebuke upon the colored man of finer sensibilities."[74] Despite

Demas's appeal and the opposition of various black organizations, the separate coach bill became law, as did other Jim Crow measures in succeeding years.

The Citizens Committee of colored Creoles, making good its promise to test such legislation, championed the cause of Homière Plessy, who was arrested in 1892 when he refused to leave his seat in the white coach on the East Louisiana Railroad bound from New Orleans to Covington. The Plessy case was ultimately argued before the United States Supreme Court, which rendered its famous 1896 decision embodying the separate but equal doctrine. One of the Creoles of color who was a member of the Citizens Committee undoubtedly spoke for all of his colleagues when he declared, "Our defeat sanctioned the odious principle of the *segregation of races.*"[75] In 1902 the implementation of the Jim Crow street car law only deepened the sense of humiliation experienced in New Orleans by the city's aristocrats of color. To exclude them from compartments occupied by white people would, they argued, "be as unjust as it would to force them to sit in compartments with unworthy representatives of their own race, whom they, as much as the white people, despised." Some walked rather than submit to Jim Crow cars; others simply stood on the street car platform rather than behind the wire screens or wooden partitions required by law.[76]

The worsening of the racial atmosphere in New Orleans, combined with the defeat in the Plessy case and the legislation of Jim Crow, had a devastating effect upon the city's black community. A few aristocrats of color either migrated elsewhere or passed for white. While some of those who remained were broken in morale and showed little interest in reviving "their fallen dignity," others continued to participate in the struggle for equality. Assessing the fate of Creoles of color in 1911, Rodolphe Lucien Desdunes took a pessimistic view: "Some Creoles in our own day have fallen to such a point of moral weakness that they have disowned and rejected not only their fellow blacks but even their own kin. These same people, far from seeking deliverance, surrender to their weakness without being able to determine correct principles to follow or to fix upon any resolution, as though they wished to accustom themselves to absolute submission or to forget their individuality. They live in a moral depression that seems to represent the last degree of impotence."[77] Although Desdunes himself died in 1928 in Omaha, Nebraska, at the home of his son, a significant portion of his fellow Creoles remained in New Orleans and retreated "within an increasingly rigid, but secure, system of non-Afro-American values."[78]

The downward mobility of certain aristocrats of color was nowhere more dramatic than in the career of Theophile T. Allain, an Iberville Parish sugar planter who was closely identified with the black elite in postwar New Orleans. Born in 1846, Allain was the natural son of Sosthene Allain, a wealthy white Creole planter near Baton Rouge, and his favorite slave. Allain accompanied his father to Paris, attended a private school in New Jersey, spoke French fluently, and in every respect, except legally, "was raised and educated as a man and a gentleman." He acquired the family's sprawling plantation on the Mississippi, which he called "Soulouque," the affectionate nickname given him by his father, and actively participated in Republican Party affairs. Allain served more than twenty years in the Louisiana legislature and was something of a political boss in Iberville Parish. He and his wife were frequent visitors in New Orleans, where they moved in the "best social circles"; they vacationed at Blount Springs, Alabama, a favorite spa of "the best white Creoles." Their six children were all graduates of Straight University in New Orleans, where they studied under teachers from New England. Accused of corruption in 1887, Allain lost his standing in the Republican Party and his seat in the legislature. During the early 1890s he suffered economic setbacks; he finally abandoned his plantation and moved to Chicago. Through friends on the Republican National Committee he managed to secure several minor patronage positions in Washington. About 1900 he disappeared from public view. A dozen years earlier, when William J. Simmons published his *Men of Mark: Eminent Progressive and Rising,* a kind of black *Who's Who,* the space devoted to Allain was two pages longer than the entry on Frederick Douglass.[79]

Despite the impact of the post-Reconstruction environment on New Orleans's blacks of "finer sensibilities," an exclusive colored aristocracy continued to exist in the city. Though not without contact with aristocrats of color elsewhere, those in the Crescent City tended to be less visible in the upper class's national network. For blacks from elsewhere, New Orleans and the social life of its black community invariably were a source of fascination and no little awe. After a visit there in 1897, Fannie Barrier Williams, who with her lawyer husband occupied a place among Chicago's "upper tens," spoke enthusiastically about the "foreign flavor" of the city's black community and of the "gayety of temperament, polish of manners and sprightliness of personality so characteristic of the French." Although not all blacks in New Orleans were as fluent in the French language as Williams suggested, the colored Creoles with whom she associated probably did speak French as if it were their native tongue. For Williams, who traveled extensively throughout the United States, the "separation between whites and blacks [was] less rigid in New Orleans than in any other part of the South," a condition that she credited to French influence and "the equality spirit of the Roman Catholic church."[80]

Visiting New Orleans five years later, in 1902, following the disfranchisement of blacks through the use of the "grandfather clause," J. D. Howard provided a perceptive appraisal of the complex class structure of its black community. He found that Creoles of color, "so nearly white that the best ethnologist would be put at his wits' end to determine the real from the adulterated article," still occupied the top rung of society. These Creoles lived comfortably; some were wealthy as a "result of liberal bequests from departed kindred," and all were very conservative and mingled "with no one but their own people." They justified their aloofness from other blacks on the grounds that "nothing by way of betterment of their condition could possibly come of a promiscuous association with the various classes of the Negro." The second rung of the social ladder was dominated by those blacks "identified with the trades, professions and politics." The burden "of keeping up the social life of the Negro in New Orleans," Howard observed, rested with this group. In his opinion only Philadelphia's aristocrats of color surpassed them in the quality of their social functions. The third tier in the class structure, embracing the vast majority of the black population, was made up largely of domestics and laboring elements. They took "no part in the social life of the city," or at least not in the social life dominated by the Creoles and the professional and business element. At the bottom of the class structure were the "Demi-mondes and levee class." What disappointed Howard most about New Orleans blacks of the higher classes was their lack of commercial spirit and energy. Of those he listed as the most enterprising blacks in business and professions, only the name of Aristide Dejoie was recognized as belonging to the old upper class.[81]

In 1909 V. P. Thomas, another black writer, reached similar conclusions about the economic backwardness of the Negro community in New Orleans. He claimed that it lagged behind all others of comparable size in the South in the development of business enterprises. Their energies appeared to be devoted primarily to "having good times at picnics, excursions, balls, parades and other such amusements." Thomas admitted that one reason for the lack of business enterprise among the blacks was white racism and the malice that it produced toward any "Negro success in business." But Thomas was also convinced that part of the problem lay in the disunity within the black community caused by the emphasis on class and complexion. The prejudice directed against all Negroes in New Orleans, regardless of their social status or fairness of their complexion, he argued, was "doing for the race what the race has neglected to do for itself," namely, destroying "the passing-for-white habit" by some blacks and bringing about a greater degree of unity, especially in the development of business enterprises.[82]

Although the hardening of white prejudice and the proliferation of anti-black legislation may have had a unifying effect on the New Orleans black community, such unity was far from complete. Creoles of color, those of "the good old genuine stock,"[83] continued to insist on "the right *blood* line" and to remain socially aloof from other blacks in the city. Closely identified with the Catholic church, they exhibited a style that emphasized propriety, good manners, and proper dress, and they often spoke French. Their social lives revolved around old, exclusive organizations such as the Société d'Economie and the Société des Jeunes Amis. Always vigilant to protect what they perceived as their elite status, Creoles of color usually married within their own social circle, and when they married non-Creole blacks, the unions were described as "mixed marriages."[84]

Despite the loss of political rights and the erosion of their economic status, the New Orleans Creoles of color continued to regard themselves as an elite, a perception shared by the city's black population in general. That they considered themselves as occupying "a socially intermediary position between Negroes and whites" was evident in the findings of a team of social scientists who investigated black New Orleans in the 1950s. A portion of their study focused on a colored Creole born there in 1923. A light-skinned, neatly attired man whose speech was that of an educated person, he confined his social contacts to other Creoles of color who lived in his neighborhood. He rarely identified with the aspirations of blacks in general, and even when he did, he displayed hostility and contempt for those of the lower class. Always ambivalent about his racial classification, he lived "in a kind of chronic identity crisis."[85]

Although other Creoles of color were scarcely as neurotic as the subject of this study, they nevertheless thought of themselves as a people apart from either blacks or whites, as a "colored" elite in a biracial society. Even after the civil rights revolution of the 1960s, they refused to describe themselves as either blacks or Negroes. Although they were reluctant to refer to themselves as Creoles, because the term had "bad vibes," they preferred to think of themselves as colored. Rather than being eliminated as a class, some colored Creoles of New Orleans scattered throughout the United States, and those who remained in the city underwent significant change. A black observer in New Orleans in the 1970s noted that the city's society had been plagued by divisions other than "the black-white one." Class divisions, he maintained, had always been important in its black community, and residents of the Seventh Ward, which contained a concentration of Creoles of color, understood the significance of class "better than perhaps anyone else in the whole community."[86]

Cities with sizable black populations throughout the South possessed an "upper ten" group whose background, outlook, and life style, while by no means identical to those of the aristocrats of color in Charleston and New Orleans, were sufficiently similar to create a kind of esprit de corps among the diverse groups. In Memphis, the upper class included the families of Robert R. Church, the son of a white planter and river boat captain; Josiah T. Settle, an attorney who was educated at Oberlin and Howard University and who figured prominently in Republican politics in Mississippi before establishing his practice in Memphis; A. S. J. Burchet, a physician and devout Episcopalian who was "Chesterfieldian in manner"; the Gillis brothers, who were prosperous furniture dealers; and A. E. Clouston, a planter and banker who was a descendant of a well-known antebellum free family of color. Burchett, Settle, and Clouston served on the board of directors of Church's Solvent Savings Bank and Trust Company.[87]

Through their acquaintances with the James C. Napiers of Nashville, the Churches and their Memphis friends, the Settles, often moved in the most select social circle of the Tennessee capital, which boasted a degree of "culture, refinement and intelligence . . . second to none in the United States."[88] Scion of a free family of color who had achieved prominence in Republican politics and business, Napier married the daughter of John Mercer Langston. In mid-September 1907, on her return from Oberlin, where she had enrolled her two sons, Mrs. Settle stopped off in Nashville to visit Nettie Langston Napier and her mother at "Ogedankee," the Napiers' summer home outside Nashville.[89] As in Memphis and elsewhere, the black social elite of Nashville, according to one of its members, tended to be "more or less conservative" and to place a premium on "good breeding, culture and wealth." But what she made clear is that wealth alone would not secure one a place in "our group." While this group included well-to-do businessmen, attorneys, and other professionals, its membership also drew heavily from those associated with the city's institutions of higher education for blacks: Fisk, Meharry, and Roger Williams.[90]

The social elites in other Southern cities were similar in many respects to Nashville's "upper tens." In Louisville, Kentucky, according to one authority, status in the black community by the 1890s was determined not only by skin color and acquaintance with the white elite but also by "having a prestigious occupation, acquiring an education, attending the 'right' church and being involved in fraternal orders and social clubs." If Louisville's aristocrats of color were primarily concerned with obtaining positions for themselves, they also engaged in activities designed "to improve the race morally, physically and financially."[91]

In the mid-1890s, when James Weldon Johnson returned home to Jacksonville, Florida after graduating from Atlanta University, he found that social life among blacks there had assumed "a degree of exclusiveness" that he, at least, had been unaware of previously. Actually, Jacksonville's black society had been plagued periodically throughout the 1870s by fair-complexioned social leaders who were accused of drawing a color line against their dark-skinned brethren, but Johnson and his upper-class friends, the Menards and the Gibbses, had apparently been oblivious to this criticism. Twenty years later the most elite social club for men was The Oceolas, whose membership included doctors, lawyers, teachers, bricklayers, carpenters, barbers, waiters, and Pullman porters. Lest the diversity of occupation represented in the club suggest laxness, Johnson pointed out that what the members had in common was not wealth but proper family background. Men of property and wealth might be refused admission, but not those who possessed "old family" connections.[92]

In the black communities of old cities in Georgia, such as Augusta and Savannah, there existed by the end of the Civil War a "choice group." With roots in the antebellum free black community, it stood at the apex of the social structure. In describing the black society of Augusta during his boyhood, John Hope, the well-known educator and member of an elite, fair-complexioned free family of color, explained that this choice group had two primary components: those who defied circumstances and rose to the top; and those "who independent of particular merit on their part, but because of circumstances, their

relationships to their masters, received additional money and additional education and were to that extent ahead of the people who had no money, no
education, nothing." In the Augusta in which Hope grew up, there existed by
the end of the war "a rather well organized Negro society, with its social metes
and bounds, with its ideals, and a great deal of culture."[93] Among the aristocrats
of color in Augusta were the families by the name of Ladeveze, Harper,
Cumming, White, and Hope, many of whom were related to each other by
marriage and to prominent white Augusta families by blood. As a group they
were well educated and fair of skin. The social life of Augusta's black elite
centered in several exclusive literary and social clubs and in the Trinity Methodist Episcopal Church. An Augusta native and childhood friend of Hope, Chan-
ning Tobias, who became head of the Phelps-Stokes Fund, later referred to the
"indefinable something in the atmosphere" of late nineteenth- and early twentieth-century Augusta that made it possible for "a Negro . . . to aspire to the
heights and to receive encouragement from white people for so doing."[94]

As in Augusta, the mulatto aristocracy in Savannah had its origins in the
antebellum free people of color, whose ranks included a number of West Indian
emigrés. A black resident of Savannah in the 1890s characterized the city as
more cultured than Augusta and as more liberal in its attitude toward blacks in
general. In the postwar generation, the Deveaux, Toomer, Porter, Desverney,
and Scarborough families were among the most prominent blacks in Savannah,
socially as well as politically and economically. Their social lives revolved
largely around a few exclusive clubs and St. Stephen Episcopal Church and its
annual bazaar. They affected "aristocratic graces, traditions, and manners" that
bore a striking resemblance to their upper-class relatives across the color line. In
some cases Savannah's aristocrats of color were the children or descendants of
well-known whites "who had thoughtfully made provisions for them." Fair in
complexion and "naturally clannish," they "thought and felt differently" from
the ignorant, brutalized lower-class blacks of slave origins.[95]

Because Atlanta was a relatively young city, founded a little more than a
dozen years before the outbreak of the Civil War, it lacked an antebellum free
black population comparable to that in Savannah and Augusta. The upper class
in Atlanta, including many who were non-natives, traced its origins primarily to
the "house-servant group" of mixed ancestry. In some cases, they continued to
have close relationships with prominent whites to whom they had belonged and
on occasion were related. David T. Howard, for example, who was the slave and
son of Colonel T. C. Howard of Atlanta, invested his small inheritance from his
white father in an undertaking business that in time became the largest in the
state. Howard's daughter Fannie married Joseph Douglass, the grandson of
Frederick Douglass. Alexander Hamilton, a leading building contractor, also an
ex-slave, had served in the Union Army and in the Alabama legislature before
settling in Atlanta in 1877 and marrying a "genial, cultured lady" from an old
elite family in Charleston, South Carolina.[96] Atlanta's most prominent Repub-

lican politican for almost two decades beginning in the 1890s was Henry A. Rucker, who owned a barbershop frequented by prominent whites. He married the daughter of Jefferson Long, Georgia's black congressman during Reconstruction, and in time acquired valuable real estate in the city. Rucker, John Deveaux (a member of Savannah's black aristocracy), and Judson Lyons of Augusta (an attorney and John Hope's brother-in-law) constituted what was known as the ruling Republican triumvirate in Georgia.[97]

Walter Francis White, who was born in 1893 and later became famous as executive secretary of the NAACP, was a member of one of the city's elite black families. His father attended Atlanta University and was in the Postal Service. His mother, a schoolteacher before her marriage, was described as a striking beauty with "severely aquiline features," blue eyes, and golden hair.[98] The Whites, along with the Ruckers and other families in Atlanta's black upper class, attended the First Congregational Church and Atlanta University, one of five black institutions of higher education created in the city between 1867 and 1885. Like the upper class in Nashville, Atlanta's social elite included a substantial number of those associated with its colleges, such as George Towns, William H. Crogman, and W. E. B. Du Bois. The popular image of Atlanta University and Spelman College, in particular, was that they catered to upper-class blacks. Spelman was known as the black "Mount Holyoke of the South." According to James Weldon Johnson, who attended Atlanta University in the 1890s, the majority of the women students at least were from "the best-to-do colored families of Georgia and the surrounding states." Although the issue of exclusiveness based on fair complexions occasionally cropped up in political struggles, the color factor does not seem to have been as prominent as in Savannah, Augusta, and some other cities. A black resident of Atlanta claimed in 1894 that the prime requisites for admission to the highest stratum of the city's black class structure were "education, wealth and respectability." Because of the concentration of black colleges in the city, Atlanta often vied with Nashville in being the premier center of culture and learning among blacks. "Atlanta," one native boasted in 1897, "has more eminently cultured Negroes than any city in the union."[99]

Although Little Rock, Arkansas was a small city, which even in the late nineteenth century had not entirely shed its frontier character, the upper class in its black community resembled, in some respects, that in Atlanta. In both, this class traced its origins primarily to slave families and to emigrés of high status. In Little Rock the antebellum free black population amounted to fifty-six persons in 1842 and declined steadily thereafter. Those who occupied the top rung of the black class structure for several generations after the war included members of slave families who had enjoyed what one referred to as "peculiar privileges." Such privileges belonged to house servants and skilled artisans who "hired out" and often "lived out." Their status, according to one authority, derived from their contribution to the well-being of the slave community. As a liaison to prominent, paternalistic whites, they assumed a leadership role "in obtaining, protecting and extending customs, privileges or knowledge on which a relatively free social life was based."[100]

Among this group were the Rectors, Richmonds, Andrews, Winfreys, and Sanderses, whose members furnished a disproportionate number of educators, politicians, and entrepreneurs in the postwar era. The most notable were the Rectors and the Andrews, who had been owned by Chester Ashley, a wealthy aristocrat and an indulgent master. The Ashley slaves, who enjoyed privileges unknown to rural "field hands" and to few urban bondsmen, acquired the education and other skills necessary for assuming positions of leadership after Emancipation. One of the Ashley slaves, Charlotte Andrews Stephens, the Oberlin-educated daughter of William Wallace Andrews, was a teacher in Little Rock for over a half century. She later recalled that "class distinction" existed among Little Rock slaves "perhaps to a greater extent than among the white people." Those of the highest class cultivated exquisite manners, proper language, and "good form" in receiving guests.[101]

Little Rock's aristocracy of color in the late nineteenth and early twentieth centuries also included people who moved into the city during and after the Civil War. Among the earliest of these was the red-haired, fair-complexioned John E. Bush, born a slave in Tennessee and brought to Little Rock with his mother early in the war. He ultimately amassed a sizable fortune as the founder of the Mosaic Templars. A man of wealth, he continued to receive lucrative appointments as a reward for his services to the Republican Party long after the end of Reconstruction. Bush solidified his place at the top of the social structure by marrying the daughter of Soloman Winfrey, a building contractor and long-time resident of the city. Isaac Gillam, who was also born a slave in Tennessee, served in a black regiment during the war and later settled in Little Rock. A blacksmith and dealer in horses, Gillam acquired substantial property and during the 1870s served as a member of the city council and as a member of the state legislature. His children, including a son who graduated from Yale, were teachers and administrators in the city's public schools and private black colleges.[102]

During the early 1870s, in the midst of Reconstruction, Little Rock witnessed the arrival of several individuals and families who, though sometimes viewed as black carpetbaggers, became permanent fixtures in the "upper crust" of the black community. Among the best known of the emigrés who acquired prominence in Little Rock was Mifflin Wistar Gibbs, a native of Philadelphia. His brother, Jonathan, a graduate of Dartmouth and Princeton, was a Presbyterian clergyman who achieved political prominence in Florida during Reconstruction. Mifflin Gibbs lived in California and Canada before settling in Little Rock in 1870, where for more than four decades he was prominently identified with virtually every political, social, and economic enterprise of any consequence undertaken by blacks in the city. As a politician, businessman, and banker who had traveled extensively and resided in various places, Gibbs was acquainted with numerous black men of prominence in the nation, including Blanche K. Bruce, whom he accompanied on occasion to Hot Springs, the famous Arkansas spa.[103]

At about the same time that Gibbs moved to Little Rock, John Henry Smith, a free-born black dentist from Delaware, settled in the city. For almost a half century, Smith enjoyed "a large and lucrative practice," chiefly among the wealthy white class. He was a man of considerable education, an inventor, and a painter of merit. In 1906 he wrote a lengthy novel, *Maudelle*, whose principal theme was miscegenation. Smith's daughter, Florence, who married a Little Rock attorney, Thomas Price, became a well-known Afro-American composer.[104]

Of the emigrés who settled in Little Rock in the early 1870s, few figured so long or so conspicuously in the life of the city's black community as the Ish family. In 1873, Jefferson Gatherford Ish and his wife, Marietta Kidd Ish, both college graduates and teachers, arrived in Little Rock and secured jobs in the public school system. They became prominent educators and "social factors" in Little Rock, and also acquired extensive and valuable real estate in the city. In 1880 they built a large two-story home on Scott Street; according to an observer in 1968, it "has ever remained an uncelebrated bridge between the Negro and white communities." Their son Jefferson Ish, Jr., who graduated from Yale, was for many years an educator in Arkansas before becoming associated with the insurance division of John Bush's Mosaic Templars; their other son, George William Stanley Ish, a 1909 graduate of Harvard Medical School, practiced medicine in Little Rock for over a half century and resided in the family home on Scott Street. Two of his sons also became physicians.[105]

Despite the hardening of racial proscriptions following the collapse of Reconstruction and the proliferation of racial violence in Arkansas, the upper class of Little Rock's black community continued to have access to opportunities unavailable to the masses. According to William Grant Still, the famous Afro-American composer, his mother believed that Little Rock was one of the most enlightened communities in the South. Those who composed what Still called "our group" were educated, lived in comfortable residences often in racially mixed neighborhoods, traveled extensively, and entertained regularly. Their cultural life centered around musical and literary activities associated with organizations such as the Lotus Club and Bay View Reading Club; the two black colleges in the city, Philander Smith and Arkansas Baptist; and the black high school, originally called Union High School, where various members of the Ish, Rector, and Gillam families, as well as Still's mother, Carrie Still Sheppardson, taught. Although members of the upper class were found in the congregations of the oldest and most prestigious Baptist and African Methodist Episcopal churches, perhaps the most exclusive black church in Little Rock was the First Congregational, whose membership included the Winfreys, Ishes, and "many of the best people of the city." Dr. Smith's family was Presbyterian; others of the upper class attended the Episcopal church, whose communicants, according to an observer in 1901, were "known here as the blue veins." The children of Little Rock's black upper class often attended prestigious white and black colleges: Yale, Harvard, Oberlin, Wilberforce (where Still enrolled), Howard, and Talladega. Dr. Smith's talented daughter Florence was graduated from the New England Conservatory of Music, where she "passed" as a "Mexican" and listed her hometown as Pueblo, Mexico, presumably in an attempt to avoid any encounters with racism.[106]

In towns and cities throughout the South, a clearly identifiable black elite existed in the generation following the end of Reconstruction. Often the descendants of free people of color or privileged slaves, they occupied positions of leadership in black communities as teachers, physicians, lawyers, and politicians. A few carved out special niches for themselves in the Southern economy that allowed them to become wealthy. These aristocrats of color, or "best people," were often in the vanguard of movements that led to the establishment of schools, homes for the aged, and other institutions that served the needs of the black masses.

4

♦

The "Upper Tens"
in the Northeast

BY THE LATE NINETEENTH CENTURY, a well-defined "colored aristocracy" existed in black communities throughout the Northeast. Proud of being "old Philadelphians" or belonging to the "old Knickerbocker set," they viewed the masses of untutored blacks, especially those in the rural South, with a mixture of pity and condescension. But those from the South whose ancestry, education, and genteel behavior qualified them for "co-equal" status rarely had much difficulty finding a place within the upper stratum of even Boston's exclusive black society. As a result of the antebellum migration of free people of color from the South to northern cities, some of those considered "old families" in Philadelphia and New York by the turn of the century were actually Southern in origin and still had relatives south of Mason and Dixon's line. Old upper-class families of Charleston, for example, were well represented in northern cities in the postbellum era. Nor was it unusual for aristocrats of color from Boston and elsewhere in the Northeast to marry into the "black 400" of Washington or to seek employment in the city, especially in its schools. Despite the fear expressed by some about what they perceived as the deepening alienation between Northern and Southern blacks, aristocrats of color in the two regions maintained relationships that cut across sectional lines to form a nationwide network of families whose values, tastes, and outlook were remarkably similar.

Those who formed the "aristocracy of the Negro population" of Philadelphia at the turn of the century had inherited a long tradition of leadership from forebears active in educational and religious affairs and in abolitionist, civil rights, and moral reform movements. Some possessed substantial wealth, and all maintained impeccable credentials of respectability. At the opening of the twentieth century, when Arthur Shadwell, an Englishman, visited Philadelphia, he believed that he had discovered "the home of the coloured aristocracy" in America. After visiting a worship service in one of the African Methodist Episcopal churches in Philadelphia, Shadwell observed that it was "practically indistinguishable from a high church (not ritualistic) Anglican one in England, except that the surpliced choir was formed of women."[1]

The old families of Philadelphia contained three distinct components. One was made up of native Philadelphians such as the Forten family; a second by a so-called West Indian group, especially those from San Domingo and Haiti, such as the Augustins, Appos, de Baptists, and Le Counts, who settled in the city and established businesses there in the late eighteenth and early nineteenth centuries; and a third element, known as the "southern contingent," mostly fair-complexioned, free-born mulattoes from South Carolina, Virginia, and Maryland, which included the Purvises, Adgers, Mintons, and McKees.[2] The descendants of these families, along with those of Cyrus Bustill of New Jersey and his Indian wife, who settled in Philadelphia in the mid-eighteenth century, constituted what became known as the "upper ten" Negroes in the city. Among later arrivals who won ready acceptance into this circle were Dr. Edwin Clarence Howard, a Harvard-educated physician, and his sister Joan Imogene, a graduate of New York University. The Howards were an old and highly respected Boston family whose members had figured prominently in the Underground Railroad and in the city's cultural and social life in the antebellum era. The black aristocrats of Philadelphia were closely identified with the abolitionist cause, several benevolent societies, various civic and religious enterprises, and especially the prestigious Banneker Institute. They usually worshipped at Saint Thomas Protestant Episcopal Church, which was established in 1794, the Bethel A.M.E. "Mother Bethel," which emerged from it some years later, or one of several Presbyterian churches.[3]

Some of the old families prospered in the catering business and accumulated substantial wealth. "No other city in America," Henry Minton wrote in 1913, "has been so famed for its efficient and successful caterers as this. . . ." Among the early Philadelphia caterers, few rivaled Robert Bogle, a waiter who "conceived the idea that instead of those who desired to entertain being inconvenienced by having to temporarily enlarge the retinue of their kitchens to prepare the viands for a formal dinner, he would contract to furnish the entire meal with his own help." Bogle, a man of polished manners, counted among his patrons the white elite of Philadelphia, including the banker Nicholas Biddle, who in 1829 composed a lengthy "Ode to Bogle." A local historian writing in 1913 claimed that Bogle "set in motion catering as it is known today." In addition to acquiring substantial wealth from catering, Bogle also demonstrated his business acumen as a popular "conductor of funerals." Active in the civic life of Philadelphia's black community and a prominent member of Saint Thomas Episcopal Church, he was the father of three daughters, "all highly educated and school teachers." Although the Bogle name disappeared at his death in 1837, his descendants continued to be prominent members of Philadelphia's black aristocracy. In the early twentieth century perhaps the best known of his direct descendants was Charles Bogle Truclear.[4]

Among others who prospered as caterers were James Le Count, James Prosser, Jeremiah Bowser, and Peter Augustine. Their descendants remained prominent members of Philadephia's black community throughout the nineteenth and early twentieth centuries. Peter Augustine established a catering firm in the city in 1816, and it was still in existence a century later. His catering establishment was later rivaled by those of Cyrus Bustill, Henry Minton, Thomas Dorsey, and others, so that blacks monopolized the catering business in the city for over a century. Their clientele included the most prestigious whites of Philadelphia. Perhaps the wealthiest of this group of caterers was John McKee of Alexandria, Virginia, who arrived in Philadelphia in 1821 and secured a job in the catering house of James Prosser. He married Prosser's daughter and ultimately assumed direction of his business. Like Henry Minton and other caterers, McKee invested heavily in real estate. He also engaged in land development and by the time of his death in 1902 was reputedly a millionaire. Throughout the nineteenth and early twentieth centuries, intermarriage was common among these old Philadelphia families, so that in one way or another, they were often related, as was the case with the Mintons and McKees and the Purvises and Fortens. Henry M. Minton, a well-to-do pharmacist in Philadelphia at the opening of the twentieth century, was the son of Theophilius J. Minton, a prominent attorney; the grandson of Henry Minton and John McKee; and the great-grandson of James Prosser.[5]

By the late nineteenth century, the Warricks had produced a succession of teachers, ministers, and social and civic leaders in Philadelphia. One member of this family, William W. Warrick, resided temporarily in Raleigh, North Carolina, where he operated a school for freedmen during Reconstruction. His kinsman Richard Warrick continued the family tradition of involvement in the social and civic life of Philadelphia's black community. His son, Richard, started as a barber but entered the catering business and belonged to what has been termed "a special class of blacks" in Philadelphia. He married Emma Jones, a descendant of Absalom Jones, and amassed a considerable fortune in catering and real estate investments. Their daughter Blanche married Francis Cardozo, Jr., of Washington; another daughter, Meta Vaux Warrick, gained a national reputation as a sculptor. Their son, Richard, a well-known dentist, was closely associated with Dr. Henry Minton and others of a "privileged" background; he figured prominently in the founding of Mercy Hospital in Philadelphia. Throughout the late nineteenth and early twentieth centuries the Warrick family was a part of the most exclusive social set in the city's black community.[6]

Among others who added luster to Philadelphia's catering tradition and whose families were conspicuous members of the city's black upper class in the late nineteenth century were Andrew F. Stevens and Levi Cromwell, the brother of John W. Cromwell, the Washington editor and teacher. Along with the Mintons, Dorseys, and divers descendants of Prosser and McKee, the Stevenses and Cromwells were invariably present at the most elite social functions in the city and were often guests of upper-class gatherings in Washington, New York, and Baltimore. Representatives of virtually all of Philadelphia's "old families" attended the annual ball of the Crescent Club, the city's most exclusive black social organization, founded in 1877. Referring to black society of Philadelphia a dozen years later, a visitor to the city observed: "If you are a caterer, you are 'in the swim'; if not, then you're 'in the soup.' "[7]

Another old Philadelphia family, the Bustills, according to a descendant in 1925, had maintained a "continuous record" of achievement since 1732. They were well connected through marriage to aristocrats of color in Philadelphia and in other cities. Gertrude Bustill became the wife of Nathan F. Mossell, a physician from Lockport, New York, who established his practice in Philadelphia and founded Douglass Hospital. Through marriage their children and grandchildren linked the Bustills and Mossells with the Tanners and Alexanders, two other prominent families associated with "old Philadelphia." One observer noted in regard to the Bustills in 1914, "the present generation has yet to show its mettle." Even so, because the family belonged to "the innermost inner circle" of black society in Philadephia, its position was "secure for all time."[8]

No less secure was the social position of the Durhams, represented in the late nineteenth century by Elizabeth Stephens Durham, the widow of Samuel Durham, and their son, John Stephens Durham. Although the family had modest means, their proud heritage and record of achievement, dating from the eighteenth century, entitled them, regardless of their economic status, to a place in the top rung of Philadelphia's black social structure. Elizabeth Durham's forebears had migrated from Virginia, where they reputedly figured prominently in Nat Turner's Rebellion. Samuel Durham's ancestors, according to one commentator, had "been noted for their personal beauty, social culture, intellectual attainment and leadership in church affairs." Two of them, Clayton Durham, a caterer, and Jeremiah Durham, a teacher, had joined Richard Allen in the founding of the African Methodist Episcopal Church. The best-known member of the Durham family in the late nineteenth and early twentieth centuries was John Stephens Durham—engineer, teacher, journalist, and diplomat—who had been educated in Philadelphia at the Institute for Colored Youth and at the University of Pennsylvania. He served as United States Consul at Santo Domingo in 1890 and as Minister to Haiti from 1891 to 1895. Upon his return to Philadephia, he practiced law and resumed a conspicuous place in the civic and social life of the city's black community. In 1900 he represented the United States before the Spanish Treaty Claims Commission in Cuba, where he later managed a sugar plantation. After Durham married "across the color line," he and his wife lived for a time in Germany before moving to London, where he practiced law until his death, in 1919. Handsome, sophisticated, and well educated, he exemplified "the personal beauty, social culture and intellectual attainment" which his family had long exhibited. Although Durham became closely identified with Booker T. Washington and the Tuskegee philosophy, his place in Philadelphia's black upper class was never in doubt. Durham's sister Mary married William Maurice Randolph, a native of Virginia and a well-to-do attorney in Pittsburgh, where they were leaders of black society.[9]

Commenting on "our best society" in 1884, a black Philadelphian noted that a true upper class was still in the process of evolving: "The most that has been done so far, and the most that could have been done in so short a time, is the formation of a nucleus for society upon which the future can build." In his view Philadelphia's "social society" had not yet excluded from its midst certain "objectionable elements." By most accounts the elimination of such elements was virtually complete by the 1890s. The exclusiveness in the social life of Philadelphia's aristocrats of color was abundantly evident in the series of receptions, dinners, and dances sponsored by The Assembly during the Christmas season beginning in 1889. In an account of one of The Assembly's events the following year, a newspaper correspondent described the impressive decorations at Natatorium Hall and the tasteful attires of Philadelphia's "prominent society people" and their guests who had gathered for a dance on Christmas night: "Mothers and chaperons looked on approvingly, while the most charming belles and gallant beaux of Philadelphia, Washington, Wilmington and other cities, beautifully attired, worshipped at the shrine of terpsichore until early morn."[10]

In his classic study, *The Philadelphia Negro*, published in 1899, W. E. B. Du Bois described and analyzed the "aristocracy of the Negro population" in the city. In some respects his observations bore considerable resemblance to those of Joseph Willson, whose *Sketches of the Higher Classes Among the Colored Society in Philadelphia* appeared more than a half century earlier. The caterers, clerks, teachers, professional men, and small merchants whom Du Bois termed the "picked class" were generally educated and well-to-do. They lived in homes which exhibited "good breeding and taste"; their social life revolved around small receptions, musical events, and private parties attended only by individuals of their own class. Philadelphia's aristocrats of color, according to Du Bois, had little social contact with the black masses; they were never found at "ordinary assemblages of Negroes nor in their usual promenading places." Largely Philadelphia-born by 1899 and of light complexion, the old families manifested interest in the doings of blacks of comparable status in New York, Washington, and other cities. They readily engaged in discussions of "questions of the day and less willingly on the situation of the Negro."[11]

Aristocrats of color in Philadelphia, as well as those elsewhere, attached great significance to what was usually termed "good breeding." While they admitted that regular association with those of high rank could on occasion "make a man polished and refined in deportment," they were rarely willing to concede that environment alone was sufficient to secure authentic gentility. Generally speaking, polish and refinement were outward evidence of qualities inherent in a person that "no amount of training" would produce. The essentials of "high accomplishment," a member of an old Philadelphia family observed in 1888, were more closely related to birth and inheritance than to training; the qualities essential to achievement were "created in a person when conception took place."[12]

Those at the top of Philadelphia's black class structure constituted what an observer in 1905 termed the "innermost inner circle." Their place in society was "secure for all time," unlike that of upwardly mobile, well-to-do middle-class folks with social ambitions. The "old Philadelphians" had a long and distinguished record of leadership in the cultural, religious, and political life of the city's black community. Their members had been continuously identified with organizations such as the Free African Society, formed in 1787; the Philadelphia Library Company of Colored Persons, established in 1833; and a variety of literary and debating societies that originated before the Civil War. By the 1880s many in the city's "innermost inner circle" were conspicuous in the affairs of the Scientific and Art Association of Philadelphia. The Fortens, Bustills, Mintons, and other old families, secure in their lofty status, engaged in numerous efforts to "uplift" the masses and to advance the cause of civil rights for blacks, but they and their social life remained far removed from "ordinary Negroes." They bore an "air of aristocratic superiority and consequence" and subscribed to the adage: "familiarity breeds contempt." Such attitudes were clearly evident in the Bachelor Benedict Club, which dominated the social life of Philadelphia's black community after 1910.[13]

Other observers corroborated Du Bois's findings about the exclusiveness of Philadelphia's black elite. A black visitor from Indiana in 1889 pronounced Philadelphia's colored society as "rather pretentious and perhaps that is all." "A person may visit the city and be entertained by individuals," a black writer noted in 1902, "but when the knock vibrates on the portal of the social realm, the response is not a rushing one." But whenever an outsider was allowed entry into the social realm, he encountered not only "grace and beauty, but intellect as well." Such a description fit the annual reception given by the Crescent Club, the most prestigious black social organization in Philadelphia in the late nineteenth century. In 1888, its reception included not only the aristocrats of color in the city but also an extensive list of guests from elsewhere, including the Marses and Downings from New York and the Wormleys and Shadds from Washington.[14]

"Old Philadelphians" figured prominently in the works of Philadelphia-born black novelist Jessie Fauset, who described in detail their emphasis on "birth, gentility [and] decency." Malory Forten, a character in one of her novels, was the scion of an old catering family who viewed himself as an authentic aristocrat. He looked with equal disdain on the new rich and on the impoverished masses. Even at the age of twenty, Forten, according to Fauset, held definitely fixed views: "[He] believed in the church, . . . in the family, in the Republican party, in moderate wealth, a small family, a rather definite place for women." He represented those whom lower-class blacks resentfully referred to as "them hincky culled folks" who consciously segregated themselves from others of their race. They fiercely guarded the status their ancestors had won through hard-fought struggles. Malory Forten belonged to the cream of "his own racial group." Others might be wealthier, but he "believed complacently no one could surpass him", and except in rare instances, he cared "surprisingly little for those who could not equal him."[15]

No less than in other cities in the North and Midwest, social and economic changes in Philadelphia during the first two decades of the twentieth century, occasioned in large part by the influx of black migrants from the South, had a significant impact upon its black community. Not all of the recent migrants from the South were unskilled, lower-class people. Their ranks included talented, upwardly mobile individuals who acquired wealth and assumed positions of leadership. Their presence complicated the class structure, especially for those "Old Philadelphia" families who shared the views and attitudes of the fictional Malory Forten and who for a time appeared to belong to a species in the process of extinction. "Look over the list of colored clergymen, physicians, lawyers, dentists, and businessmen right here in Philadelphia," the city's leading black newspaper observed in 1917, "and you will find that the great majority are not natives of the North."[16] Rather, Southerners dominated these fields. Ten years earlier, when the flow of migrants out of the South was noticeable but less dramatic, the scholar Richard R. Wright claimed that criteria for entry into "the best type of Negro Society" in Philadelphia were already changing. Admission into the highest social stratum, he argued, was based chiefly on culture rather than on wealth or ancestry, even though he admitted that the acquisition of culture required sufficient wealth "to permit a comfortable living" and that some black Philadelphians could trace their ancestry "to Revolutionary personages."[17]

Despite the disruption prompted by the "great migration," the old families proved sufficiently adaptable to retain their position at the pinnacle of the class structure. Descendants of the old catering families in particular appear to have fared well; many perpetuated and even strengthened family claims to high social status by entering the professions of medicine, law, and education or by becoming businessmen. Although they admitted to their ranks individuals of comparable standing from elsewhere and cooperated with middle-class people on a variety of specific goals, they were not disposed to obliterate all lines of demarcation in the purely social realm no matter how loudly critics complained of their snobbery, blue-veinism, and racial treachery. Family name and tradition (inextricably linked to an emphasis on and access to education, the white power structure, and a relatively high standard of living, as well as culture, style, and aspirations) continued to function as social stratifiers. The social distance between the small upper class and the rest of the black population that Du Bois detected in Philadelphia in 1897 existed there twenty years later. No organization or institution better exemplified this distance than Sigma Pi Phi, or Boulé, the first black Greek-letter fraternity in Philadelphia, organized in 1904 and limited to "men of like qualities, tastes and attainments."[18]

The old upper class of New York closely resembled that in Philadelphia. In both, the black community was old and included families which had long occupied positions of leadership in civic and racial causes. By the Civil War, one historian has written, the Negro community in New York "had a small social aristocracy which seems to have led a gay life, emphasizing balls, soirées, dancing classes and musicales." In fact, aristocrats of color in the two cities, in part because of their proximity, not only shared a common social life on occasion but also were often related by blood or marriage. A member of Philadelphia's "higher classes" who moved to New York readily gained acceptance into comparable circles in New York. Charles A. Dorsey, the Oberlin-educated son of a well-to-do Philadelphia catering family, served for a generation beginning in 1863 as a teacher and principal in one of Brooklyn's best-known public schools and always occupied a place among the city's "upper tens." He was related by marriage to the Harlans of Cincinnati, the Murrays of Washington, and the Evanses of Ohio. His brother, Thomas G. Dorsey, a graduate of Harvard Medical School, was a conspicuous figure in the black society of Washington.[19]

As in Philadelphia, in the late nineteenth century the old black upper class in New York represented a fusion of several different elements. One consisted of native New Yorkers, including some who traced their lineage to the days of the Dutch settlement and who bore Dutch names, such as Ten Eyck and Van Vranken. Forebears of the Downings, Reasons, Rays, Petersons, Whites, and Eatos had figured significantly in the educational, religious, and civic life of black New Yorkers since the late eighteenth century. Among the enterprises that attracted the continuous support of these families was the New York African Society for Mutual Relief, incorporated in 1810. For more than a century membership in the society, according to one black New Yorker, carried "with it a greater sense of special worth or ability" than identity with any other black organization in the nation. "The taint of slavery," Mary White Ovington wrote in 1911, "was far removed from these people who looked with scorn upon the new arrivals from the South."[20] In fact, upper-class black New Yorkers preferred to "forget that the race was ever held in bondage"; hence they opposed "celebrating any event in their history which refers to their former condition of servitude." "It has not been customary," the New York Age observed in 1889, "to celebrate Emancipation Day in this city" because "there has never been a sympathetic opinion to inspire and sustain it."[21]

A second component of New York's old upper class was made up of emigrants from elsewhere in the United States whose long residence in New

York, coupled with their achievements, family background, respectability, and values, placed them among the city's elite. Among this group were those of Northern birth, such as the Scottrons, Lansings, Marses, Vosburghs, and Dorseys, as well as those with roots in the South. The latter included Hutchins Chew Bishop, a member of a well-known free-born family in Maryland, who served as rector of St. Philip's Protestant Episcopal Church in New York from 1886 until 1933. The third element in New York's black upper class included West Indian emigrés such as the Guignons and Livelys. By the late nineteenth century, these three elements had combined through marriage, as was the case with the Rays, Whites, Guignons, and Scottrons, to form a close-knit, socially exclusive group that constituted the city's "best society." They belonged to the same clubs and social organizations, dominated civic and political enterprises, vacationed together, and usually worshipped at St. Philip's, Siloam Presbyterian, St. Mark's Methodist Episcopal, and other select churches known for their "conservative respectability."[22] As early as 1880, a white New York newspaper observed that there was "a colored aristocracy in this city as distinct and as exclusive as that of Murray Hill." Black New Yorkers who were well-to-do and belonged to the old families fully agreed. Samuel R. Scottron devoted much energy in his later years to extolling "the ancient colored New Yorker," whose virtues and achievements were, in his view, vastly superior to those of blacks in the early twentieth century.[23]

Few black families were more socially prominent in New York in the late nineteenth and early twentieth centuries than those of James W. Mars and Charles Henry Lansing. The son of a famous Connecticut abolitionist, Mars was for many years caterer to the Hanover National Bank. He served as senior warden of St. Philip's church and was conspicuous in the club life of New York for a generation. In fact, an invitation to a musicale, reception, or supper at the "Mars' mansion" in Brooklyn was indisputable proof of one's membership in the "black 400." Scarcely less significant as a sign of one's social standing was an invitation to the home of Charles H. Lansing, Jr., a native New Yorker who held a white-collar position in the Brooklyn Water, Gas and Electricity Department for more than twenty-five years. Like his ancestors, he was a member of the New York African Society for Mutual Relief and senior warden of Brooklyn's St. Augustine's Episcopal Church. His second marriage, to Katharine White, the daughter of Dr. Philip A. White, merely strengthened his claim to a position among the city's aristocrats of color.[24]

White journalists tended to equate the emergence of a "colored aristocracy" in New York with the acquisition of wealth. They periodically referred to the size of the fortunes and real estate holdings acquired by certain blacks, especially small businessmen, caterers, and restaurateurs such as the Downings, Van Dykes, Rays and Ten Eycks. Measured by the poverty and low income that characterized the vast majority of the black population of Manhattan and Brooklyn, the aristocrats of color were relatively well-to-do, but few could be classified as wealthy by white standards. In 1901 W. E. B. Du Bois estimated that "probably less than ten Negroes in New York own over $50,000.00 worth of property each."[25]

What set them apart from other blacks was not merely wealth and the life style that it made possible; of no less importance was their emphasis on education, pride in family heritage and tradition, and adherence to a rigid moral code and Victorian decorum. Among those who consistently fought for better educational facilities for blacks were various members of the Reason, Ray, Scottron, White, and Eato families, whose members included teachers, school administrators, and other professionals. Philip A. White, a wealthy wholesale druggist who married the daughter of Peter Guignon, the chemist and apothecary, was perhaps the most effective champion of black education in the early 1880s, during his tenure as a member of the Brooklyn Board of Education. After his death, in 1891, he was succeeded on the board by T. McCants Stewart, a prominent Brooklyn attorney. A member of a free family of color, Stewart was born and grew up in Charleston, South Carolina, where his childhood friends included Archibald and Francis Grimké and Whitefield McKinlay.[26]

Though conspicuous in educational, civic, and racial uplift movements, New York's "colored families of high class" attempted, according to John Nail, a well-to-do tavern keeper, to "keep their family and social affairs out of sight of the rest of the world, white and black, as much as they can."[27] The world of blacks in New York City, Du Bois reported in 1901, was "a world of itself, closed in from the other world and almost unknown to it . . . with its own social distinctions, amusements and ambitions." Blacks of the better classes, far removed from "the ignorant and lewd" masses, displayed an intelligence and decorous life style that, in Du Bois's view, "would pass muster in a New England village." Nail explained that the wealthy and educated colored man sought to avoid being "reminded of the fact that the great mass of his fellow citizens despise him on account of his color." Fully aware that they were ignored by whites of similar position, upper-class black New Yorkers, many of whom were well educated, cultured, and refined, sought to avoid being "classed with the most degraded and brutal element of their race" by keeping to themselves and trying to "make their standards as high as they can." The "better element of the race," an Indiana visitor to New York noted in 1887, was never seen parading Fifth Avenue on an afternoon or forcing "its way into theaters"; members of the upper class possessed "a distinct world of their own."[28] Unwelcome in the best restaurants like Delmonico's and Sherry's, they spent "more money on their homes, their dinners, and their parties than white men of the same income would, because they have no place to spend it outside."[29]

As a result, the homes of New York's black families of "high class," especially those in Brooklyn, were occasionally the scenes of sometimes lavish and always tasteful entertainments, including catered dinners of many courses, dances with well-known orchestras, debutante balls, select musicales, and literary gatherings.[30] According to the *New York Freeman*, "the most brilliant event for many years" in New York's black society was the debut of Ellie A. White, the eldest daughter of Philip White, in March, 1886.[31] But whether the affair was a debutante ball or a small literary gathering, certain names regularly appeared on the guest lists—the same names that appeared on the memberships of most exclusive upper-class social organizations.[32]

Throughout the late nineteenth and early twentieth centuries—or until Harlem emerged as the dominant black section—considerable rivalry existed between what was known as the Manhattan "set" and the Brooklyn "set" in black society. In New York, blacks, like other racial and ethnic groups, were a part of the city's constantly shifting population. As Seth Scheiner has noted, "each decade between 1860 and 1920 witnessed some change in the Negro's place of residence, whether he was moving from the Greenwich Village area of Manhattan northward or from the Borough Hall neighborhood of Brooklyn southeastward." The black population of Manhattan Island was 20,000 in 1880 and 36,000 twenty years later. The annexation of outlying districts, including Kings County (Brooklyn), in 1898 meant that the black population of Greater New York was more than 60,000 by the turn of the century.[33]

Beginning with the draft riots of 1863, blacks, especially the more-affluent families, deserted Manhattan for Brooklyn. In 1895 the *New York Times* observed that as soon as black New Yorkers "amass a comfortable fortune, they move across the East River" into Brooklyn.[34] Not all such black families abandoned Manhattan. As a result by the 1880s New York's black upper class was divided into two competing factions. An observer of New York's black social scene commented in 1884:

"The factional differences existing between some of the social aspirants of Brooklyn and New York seem to be kept up with as much vigor as ever, and unlike wine, do not improve with age. Why this feeling should exist is incomprehensible. The majority of the adherents of either side, if asked why they swore allegiance to the social elements of their respective cities, would look askance at the interrogator in open wonder. In all probability they would not understand why the appellations Half Breed and Stalwart applied to them. . . . The relative positions of the two cities almost forbid that there should be any marked differences in their social systems. Upon the surface the cause of this feeling is the outcome of a little jealousy on the part of the women, groundless perhaps. . . . For example, if a few ladies and gentlemen of either city happen to come together for a social evening and fail to invite some if not all the society folks in the other city, the cry is instantly raised that an attempt is being made to draw a line and the side that is left out counters by imitating the example set."[35]

In the first decade of the twentieth century, when James Weldon Johnson of Jacksonville, Florida went to live in New York, he readily recognized that the "real society among colored people" in their city existed only in Brooklyn. There was an active social life among Manhattan blacks—concerts, big dances, performances by the Drury Opera Company, and numerous picnics, but these events were public, and "anyone who paid the price of admission could attend." According to Johnson, "cultivated Negroes living in Manhattan had, for many years, been going to Brooklyn for the social intercourse that is confined more or less to the people one knows or knows about." In Brooklyn one encountered the "older families," some bearing historic Dutch and English names and a few whose wealth had come down through two or three generations.

What impressed Johnson was the similarity of the social gatherings in Brooklyn with those he attended in Jacksonville on his return there after graduating from Atlanta University in 1894. During his childhood, social affairs among blacks in Jacksonville had been public or semi-public, but by the mid-1890s they had assumed a degree of exclusiveness, so that "entertainment among those who went in for society had become largely a private matter." Neither wealth nor reputation assured one admission to Jacksonville's black society, but "anyone belonging to an 'old family,' regardless of his pecuniary condition . . . was eligible." That Johnson was a member of such a family, as well as a graduate of Atlanta University, assured him a secure place in the highest rung of Jacksonville's black social structure. There were, as he was well aware, not only "similar social groupings in all American cities with a sizable black population" but also "an interchange of privileges like those accorded to a member of an [fraternal] order in good standing going from one lodge to another." Hence when Johnson went to New York, he moved easily into the best "Brooklyn set"[36] and ultimately married Grace Nail, daughter of the highly respected tavern keeper John Nail.

The "interchange of privileges" that Johnson experienced also operated for other upper-class blacks visiting New York and for New York's aristocrats of color visiting in black communities elsewhere. When Mary Church Terrell of Washington was in New York in August, 1891, she was entertained by Mrs. J. W. Mars of Brooklyn at a dinner-dance to which the most highly regarded of local black society were invited. A dozen years earlier, according to a resident of Washington, the "marriage of Miss Estelle Mars . . . in Brooklyn took away scores of the 'society people' from the capital city." In 1889, when Philip A. White and his wife attended the festivities in Washington in connection with the inauguration of Benjamin Harrison, the John F. Cooks gave an elaborate luncheon in their honor, and Marion Shadd entertained Mrs. White at a breakfast.[37]

The "interchange of privileges" was perhaps most frequent between the aristocrats of color in New York City and those from nearby places, such as Philadelphia, Boston, Syracuse, and especially Albany. The state capital possessed a sizable black colony of wealth and culture, including some families "who had settled there in earliest times, intermarried with the Dutch and other white settlers and later worked against slavery." Among the most socially prominent old families of Albany, some of whom were related to the first families of Brooklyn and most of whom exchanged visits frequently with their equals downstate, were the Van Vrankens, Topps, Van Burens, Douglasses, Matthewses, Lattimores, Yopps, and Blakes. These and a few others who made up the Home Social Club, Albany's most exclusive club, welcomed upper-class visitors from Manhattan, Brooklyn, and elsewhere to its social functions. Such hospitality was, of course, reciprocated, as when the Van Vrankens and Lattimores visited Washington and were entertained by various aristocrats of color there, including the Somervilles. The John Mercer Langstons were friends of the Blakes and often visited them in Albany. A caterer who accumulated substantial wealth, Adam Blake died at an early age, but his widow, Catherine, continued his business and ultimately became sole owner of the Kenmore House, Albany's most fashionable hotel. The Blakes' daughters, educated at the St. Agnes Convent school, were "belles of colored society"; one of them, Kittie May, counted among her suitors Bismarck Pinchback and Dr. Daniel Hale Williams, although she ultimately married a white attorney.[38]

Some black New Yorkers took special pride in their Dutch blood and Dutch names. They constituted what John E. Bruce, long a resident of Albany, derisively termed in 1899, "the present crop of darky 'vans,' " in reference to the Van Vrankens, Van Dykes, and others with Dutch names. "About a year ago," Bruce wrote, "I asked one of these 'vans' to tell me how he got his name. He began by saying that his great-grandparents were Manhattan Indians, that his grandmother was a queen, that she married a Holland Dutchman of great wealth, etc. ad nauseam." Bruce wondered how a man with so much Dutch and Indian blood could possess "so much kink in his hair and so much of the African in his countenance."[39] Despite the scoff of critics like Bruce, the black "vans" remained proud of their heritage and attempted to keep alive what were believed to be historic Dutch customs.[40]

By 1910, when the black population of New York had grown to almost 92,000, it included increasing numbers of individuals from elsewhere whose education, achievements, and family heritage entitled them to places within the city's black aristocracy. Although the African Society for Mutual Relief and the Society of the Sons of New York continued to be enclaves of the old families of New York, they tended to be less visible than other elite organizations whose members included well-to-do physicians, lawyers, and other professionals of relatively recent residence. By the second decade of the twentieth century, the Pre-Lenten Recital and Assembly, an annual social event usually held in mid-February, had come to represent an amalgamation of the new and the old elite, with the latter clearly dominant. At the Assembly in 1909, according to one observer, "quite a delegation was over from Philadelphia and Boston and shared honors with the Old Knickerbocker set of New York and Brooklyn." The families seated in the choicest boxes at the Palm Garden, where the affair took place, bore such historic names as Downing, Lansing, Peterson, and Mars.

Others who occupied boxes were largely the families of physicians and dentists.[41]

The growing prominence of doctors, lawyers, and other professionals in the elite social life of New York's black community was even more evident in the annual charity balls, begun in 1911, on behalf of McDonough Memorial Hospital. Known as the Charity Ball and Artists' Review and usually held at the Manhattan Casino, the affair invariably attracted a large and fashionable crowd from New York and nearby cities. Spearheaded by doctors, surgeons, dentists, and prominent individuals in other professions, the ball also included representatives of old families. The younger people of both the old and the new elite also dominated the membership of the Bachelor-Benedicts and of the Penelope Club, a women's social club in Brooklyn. The latter included Hutchins Bishop's daughter and descendants of the Downing and Van Vranken families as well as the wives of several prominent physicians whose length of residence in the city was relatively brief.[42] Younger members of the medical profession and descendants of the old New York families combined to form a gentleman's club known as "The Frogs" early in the twentieth century. In 1913 the "Frogs" purchased a ten-room mansion on 132nd Street as the permanent headquarters of the organization. Its annual social event, the "Frolic of the Frogs," took place in June and was considered one of the most exclusive affairs in New York's black community.[43]

No less than did their counterparts in New York and Philadelphia, the aristocrats of color in Boston also placed a premium on family, education, tradition, and respectability. The "real Negro upper class" of the city, comprising an estimated two percent of the black population at the turn of the century, included attorneys, physicians, salaried employees, business proprietors, and "literary and musical people" who held themselves "apart and aloof" from other blacks. Most prided themselves on being "old Bostonians," a designation applied to those whose ancestors resided in the city before the Civil War. Among the old families the names of the Duprees, Haydens, Walkers, Baldwins, Allstons, Lattimores, and Ruffins had special significance. Conspicuous among this group were the numerous descendants of Brazilla Lew, a black Bostonian who had participated in the American Revolution. Although the Lews were not affluent, their family background entitled then to a place at the top of Boston's black social structure. By 1952 eight generations of the Lew family had been prominent in the social and civic life of black Boston.[44]

Blending easily with the black Brahmins was a group of postwar migrants, mostly from the South, such as the Grimkés, Trotters, Ridleys, and Chappelles, whose achievements and family background entitled them to a place among the "upper tens." Among the black New Englanders who settled in Boston after the Civil War and became a part of the city's upper crust was the family of James H.

Wolff, a native of New Hampshire.[45] But whether old Bostonians or Southerners or New Englanders of more recent residence, the city's black upper class manifested "a spirit of abolition" and violently objected to any form of "voluntary racial segregation." From their ranks came the most vocal and persistent critics of Booker T. Washington's tactics of accommodationism.[46]

Boston's aristocrats of color tended to be socially exclusive while also cultivating connections with whites. The overwhelming majority were light-skinned and vehemently objected to the term "Negro." A member of Boston's old black upper class told a white investigator in the first decade of the twentieth century: "When you write of the Negroes of Boston tell about us who are neither Negroes nor whites, but an ambiguous something-between;—a people not yet known or named. While our sympathies tend to unite us with the Negroes and their destiny, all our aspirations lead us toward white."[47] More so than those elsewhere, aristocrats of color in Boston seemed to have attended predominantly white churches, especially Episcopal churches, and to have held memberships in white organizations. Several generations of Ruffins, for example, were patrons of the arts, especially the Boston Symphony Orchestra, and were involved in numerous interracial civic enterprises.[48]

The vocations of black aristocrats also brought them into contact with upper-class whites more often than with lower-class blacks. For example, William H. Dupree was for many years in charge of the largest postal substation in the city; George L. Ruffin, a Harvard-educated attorney, served as a legislator and as a city judge; and J. H. Lewis and T. A. Ridley operated large, fashionable tailoring establishments.[49] James Monroe Trotter, Dupree's brother-in-law, lived in Hyde Park, a white neighborhood, and also held a position in the Post Office. Joseph Lee, who claimed to be descended from the Lees of Virginia, owned a catering establishment that served the "first families of Boston." The children of these men enjoyed exceptional educational and cultural advantages. Trotter's son attended Harvard, while one of Ruffin's sons was a graduate of the Massachusetts Institute of Technology and an engineer. The wives of these men dominated the social life of Boston's black elite for several decades around the turn of the century.[50]

Despite their lack of association with the black masses, the aristocrats of color appeared before the public as intimately acquainted with the needs of their race. Lower- and middle-class blacks, while cognizant of the "superior achievements" of the aristocrats, were nonetheless resentful of their aloofness and often opposed their leadership.[51] Analyzing Boston's black community in 1908, a black writer suggested that its old upper class was beset by two conflicting traditions that prompted other blacks to view it with both pride and resentment: its "spirit of abolition," and its "old-family-class ideas." "On the whole," he observed, "it seems only fair to say that in the class, not only the soul of John Brown, the unreasoning lover of liberty, but as well the soul of John Hancock, the designing, pompous patriot, goes marching on."[52]

Boston's aristocrats of color had a reputation for exclusiveness that went even beyond that of those in Washington or Philadelphia. Black society in the city regularly inspired epithets such as "cold" and "chilly."[53] The old upper-class Bostonians thought of themselves as special, as far superior to other blacks, especially those who emigrated to the city from the South in increasing numbers after the beginning of the twentieth century, and to most "dark-skinned Negroes everywhere." A character in Dorothy West's novel *The Living Is Easy*, described as a "social worker's detailed report on a group of turn-of-the-century Boston-born and bred Negroes," discoursed on the importance of family name, tradition, and class: "Our fathers built a social class for us out of tailor shops and barber shops and stables and caterer's coats. We cannot afford its upkeep because they have taught us to think above their profitable occupations." Another character, Miss Eleanor Elliott, a descendant of an old black family and the daughter of a district attorney, reveled in the "moulted elegance" of her Back Bay drawing room and openly expressed a desire "to preserve her father's world." "With so many of the unfortunates of our race migrating to Boston," Miss Elliott explained, "we find ourselves becoming crusaders for our beloved city."[54]

As in most other cities of comparable size, Boston's black aristocracy was divided into several social cliques, each "with its own peculiar avocations, customs and ceremonies." The two most "fashionable social sets" in Boston in the mid-1890s were the "South End Set," dominated by Mrs. John Lewis, the wife of the prosperous tailor, and the "West End Set," led by the Ruffins and Ridleys. Although the rivalry between them was sometimes fierce, members of the two cliques shared similar backgrounds and tastes and were often related either by blood or marriage. Admission to either set was allowed only after careful scrutiny. The question that every aspirant had to answer satisfactorily was "who are you?" not "how much wealth have you?"[55]

Among the old families of black Boston answers to such a question came easily and naturally in view of their pride in ancestry. One Boston native, Walter J. Stevens, recalled that his father, "a plain man with no special capabilities of any kind," constantly impressed upon his children that their family was of noble birth and that its ancestry could be traced back to the era of Christopher Columbus. According to the elder Stevens, the family name had originally been Estravan, from the Spanish, but had been Anglicized when his forebears took up residence in England. He took special pride in the fact that he was entitled to membership in the Sons of the American Revolution by virtue of the fact that an ancestor, Crispus Attucks, was the first to fall in the War for Independence.[56]

By the turn of the century, the "happy few," as one authority described the elite families, constituted an exclusive circle that was difficult for outsiders to penetrate. They often associated with their white neighbors; employed white servants; attended a few select churches, usually Episcopal; and vacationed together at Saratoga, Newport, and Oak Bluff. They regularly attended performances of the Boston Symphony, the opera, and public events at Harvard. They gathered at Mystic Park to watch the races, where in 1886 John H. Lewis's trotter, Capitola, won the silver cup in the "gentleman's road wagon race." Their children took private lessons in music and dancing. The Lewis Dancing School in Cambridge, directed by Mrs. George Lewis, enrolled as students the children of Boston's most socially prominent black families. "For dignified fun," one student recalled, "there was not a more desirable place for a boy or girl." But more important, as he recognized, was that attendance at the special functions of the school, replete with orchestra, represented "the very heights of social achievement" in black Boston.[57]

The significance that Boston's aristocrats of color attached to family background is apparent in the records handed down from one generation to another. For example, a prosperous free family of color from Virginia, the Ruffins, emigrated to Boston early in the 1850s. George W. Ruffin and his wife, Nancy Lewis Ruffin, who were "free, good livers and highly respected," had eight children of whom the best known were George L. and Powatan Ruffin. Both became prominent in the social and political life of Boston and through their marriages linked the Ruffins to old and highly respected black families of New England. George L. Ruffin married Josephine St. Pierre, a woman of extraordinary ability whose ancestors included African princes, Frenchmen, and Indians. A civil rights activist, Josephine Ruffin was a founder of the Woman's Era Club, one of the first civic associations of black women. Her daughter, Florida Ruffin, a teacher in Boston's public schools and a writer, married a Ridley. She was active in promoting Afro-American history and, like her forebears, manifested great pride in the history of her own family. Among the family heirlooms that Florida Ridley treasured were deeds, mortgages, and other official documents from the St. Pierre line, including a record of a land grant made in 1786 by the General Court of Massachusetts in recognition of services rendered by a St. Pierre in the American Revolution. Memorabilia and documents from the Ruffin family included a will apportioning the "houses, money and furniture accumulated by a Virginia Negro at the end of the seventeenth century." Other family records and portraits provided evidence of their involvement in the Abolition movement and the cultural life of Boston. Contemplating the chests that had housed the Ruffin–St. Pierre mementoes and documents for more than a century, Florida Ridley spoke proudly of her mixed ancestry—of "the instinctive repudiation of trammels inherited from Indian ancestry, the courage and pride of a Negro forebear who broke his chains, the stubborn insistence upon 'rights' of the Yankee backwoodsman who broke into the family." A character in one of her autobiographical short stories protested against "being designated a 'Negro' and saddled with all the shortcomings and vices so carelessly and unconcernedly heaped on those possessing color." Florida Ridley may have belonged to what she termed "the other Bostonians," but she was convinced that her family, in terms of its continuity and achievement, entitled her to a status comparable to those across the color line known as Brahmins.[58]

Throughout the Northeast, the old upper class in small black communities exhibited many of the characteristics of the aristocrats of color in Boston, New York, Washington, and other large cities. Writing in 1940, Robert Warner chronicled the rise and decline of the Negro aristocracy in New Haven, Connecticut. Beginning in the eighteenth century, a few families—such as the Creeds, Duplexes, Lathrops, and Bassetts—made up what was known as the "quality people" in New Haven. Affiliated primarily with the Congregational and Episcopal churches and one or two highly selective clubs, these aristocrats of color formed an exclusive group that admitted to its ranks only those with appropriate family background, refinement, wealth, standard of living, education, and tradition of community service. The influx of foreign immigrants and black Southerners in the post–Civil War decades, in time, disrupted the class structure that had emerged in New Haven's antebellum black community and eroded the fragile foundations on which the Negro aristocracy rested. Often outstripped economically by newcomers, the old families also suffered dilution by the departure of descendants who found greater opportunities elsewhere. "Only the shreds and fragments of aristocracy persist today," Warner noted in 1940. Despite the dilution of their ranks and persistent challenges to their claims to primacy, the aristocrats of color still used their old family status to gain social advantage and, in Warner's words, to buttress "personal dignity and a reason for ambition."[59]

Even in the small black community in Syracuse, New York, according to George S. Schuyler, the well-known black journalist who grew up in the city, "there were definite classes." At the bottom were those blacks associated "with the underworld" and usually found in the midtown area; above them were the laborers and domestics "who were poor but respectable." At the top of the class structure were the chefs, butlers, and other blacks employed by and in frequent association with upper-class whites. Schuyler's father, as head chef in Syracuse's leading hotel, was by the very nature of his position considered "an aristocrat in the colored community." At home the elder Schuyler "affected baronial living replete with Haviland china, silver service and gourmet delights." The family resided in a two-story house on a tree-lined street where they were the only black residents. As a child, George Schuyler associated primarily with white children; the black families in closest proximity to his house were recent arrivals from the South, and his mother considered them uncouth and devoid of moral and social standards. Their white neighbors were "Yankees" and as such were what his mother considered "her kind of people."[60]

Like other aristocrats of color, the Schuylers displayed great pride in their family heritage. They "boasted of having been free as far back as any of them could or wanted to remember"; they looked down on blacks "who had been born in servitude" and they "neither cherished nor sang slave songs." In explaining his family's origins, Schuyler wrote: "On my father's side they came from the Albany-Troy area. A great-grandfather fought [in the American Revolution] under General Philip Schuyler. . . . My maternal great-grandmother came from Madagascar, was bound to service around Freehold, New Jersey, and married a sea captain named Liedendraught from Saxe-Coburg." Somewhere in the remote past, American Indians were also part of the Schuyler family.[61]

Schuyler, who achieved fame as a Negro conservative, credited his mother with playing the decisive role in molding his thinking, manners, and outlook on society. She herself was a true conservative who believed strongly in "preserving the values of society." She took him to theatrical performances of Shakespeare's plays, introduced him to the world of great literature, and imbued in him a taste for gracious living. Theirs was a home in which "order and discipline prevailed" and in which cultural standards, manners, and family traditions had meaning. "Here," Schuyler wrote in his autobiography, "was something to be preserved and improved." He was, therefore, conservative for the same reason that other people, regardless of race or color, were conservative: they felt they had something worthy of conserving.[62]

One of the favorite vacation spots for well-to-do aristocrats of color throughout the East in the late nineteenth century was Newport, Rhode Island. "I doubt," a black vacationer wrote in 1886, "if there is a watering place in America where respectable, refined and well-bearing colored ladies and gentlemen have as little reason to feel their color as in Newport." The black population in Newport fluctuated considerably, rising substantially in summers with the arrival of vacationers from New York, Washington, Philadelphia, and elsewhere. Although the permanent black community in the town was small, its upper class exhibited many of the attributes of the Negro aristocracy in New Haven and was, on occasion, viewed as resembling a microcosmic version of that in Washington. Women in Newport's socially prominent families were known as "parlor ladies" because they did "not take in sewing and the like." They looked down on women who worked and ignored "their claim to social recognition." In addition to several social and cultural societies with highly restricted memberships, Newport's black elite was likely to be found at the Union Congregational Church, where worship was devoid of any "gyrations" or "hankering for plantation melodies."[63]

Although the composition and background of the aristocrats of color in the Northeast, as well as the environment in which they existed, differed from those in the South, there were remarkable similarities between the two groups. Both lived in a social world of their own quite apart from that of other blacks, while at the same time they functioned as racial spokesmen. Like aristocrats of color elsewhere, those in the Northeast preached the gospel of education, promoted a variety of charitable causes, and offered themselves as examples of the "possibilities of the race."

5

◆

Elites in the Midwest and West

IN THE LATE NINETEENTH AND EARLY twentieth centuries the class structure of black communities in the Midwest, both small and large, was similar to that found in the East and South. Differences did exist, in part because of the relatively small size of the black population of midwestern towns and cities before the Great Migration. In 1900 the combined black population of Chicago, Cleveland, and Detroit was less than half that of the District of Columbia. But whether in Chicago, whose black population of 6,480 in 1880 increased more than sevenfold by 1910, or in a small town in Kansas, there existed groups whom blacks described as "aristocrats," the "400," the "upper tens," and "high-toned people." Casual acquaintance with midwestern black communities sometimes led observers to conclude erroneously that no social stratification existed. "The ones who constitute society here," a black visitor to Kansas City remarked in 1897, "are the common every day People and cannot be called high-toned or above anyone; everyone appears to be on an equality here."[1]

Suggestions that a midwestern black community possessed "no society" was certain to prompt vigorous protests from its residents. When such a charge was leveled at blacks in Lawrence, Kansas in 1891, an old resident was quick to respond that the town's black "society people" ranked "with the best anywhere in the West." "The upper class," he explained, "looks upon the lower with some pity but more contempt; the lower looks to the upper with little comparison and much hatred. It has been so from the beginning, it will be so to the end."[2]

In the antebellum era the city of Cincinnati, separated from slave territory by the Ohio River, became the destination of increasing numbers of black immigrants, including bands of manumitted slaves and other free people of color. The city's black population increased from 410 in 1819 to 3,237 in 1850, and by the outbreak of the Civil War its black community possessed a clearly defined upper class. "In and immediately after the fifties," an old black resident of Cincinnati later reported, "colored society was in all its glory." Families who dominated the social life possessed adequate means and "found ample opportunity for imitation of the aristocratic white people with whom they came in contact." A small, self-consciously elite group which had acquired education and affluence before the Civil War, these generally fair-complexioned families constituted Cincinnati's postwar black aristocracy. They usually married within their own social circle and admitted to their ranks only those immigrants whose background, tastes, and aspirations resembled their own. They engaged in a variety of cultural and social activities, spearheaded civil rights and racial uplift movements, provided their children with the educational advantages that perpetuated upper-class status, occupied the choicest positions in the school system, advocated greater educational advantages for blacks in general, and monopolized the political patronage dispensed by the Republican party to its black adherents.[3]

Until his death, in 1897, Robert Harlan exemplified the life style, tastes, and self-perceptions of Cincinnati's black upper class. An "affable courtly gentleman of the old school," Harlan "thought of himself as the descendant of Kentucky aristocrats." His relationships with his white relatives, the Harlans of Kentucky, including his white half brother, Supreme Court Justice John Marshall Harlan, who wrote the classic dissent in *Plessy* v. *Ferguson*, was one of intimacy and mutual respect. Educated by his white family and allowed virtually full freedom, Harlan was "only theoretically a slave." He traveled without restriction and visited almost every state in the Union as well as England and several European countries. Throughout his career Harlan, like P. B. S. Pinchback, prided himself on being an expert on "horse-flesh" and was frequently present at Saratoga and other race tracks. He went to California during the gold rush in 1849 and amassed a fortune, which he invested in real estate in Cincinnati. He also secured formal acknowledgment of his freedom by a payment of $500. In 1852 he married Josephine Floyd, reputedly the daughter of Virginia's governor and President James Buchanan's secretary of war. The Harlans then resided for some years in a large stone-front house in a fashionable area of Cincinnati. Josephine died in 1853, shortly after giving birth to a son, and Harlan married the daughter of the well-known Philadelphia caterer Thomas J. Dorsey. For the next five years, Harlan was active in a variety of "race causes" in Cincinnati, serving as a trustee of the city's colored orphanage and of its black schools.[4]

In order to get "beyond the reach of American prejudice," the Harlans moved to England in 1858, where they remained for a decade. When they returned to the United States, the family possessed only a fraction of its former wealth. Harlan, nonetheless, resumed an active role in the social and civic life of Cincinnati's black community. From 1868 until his death almost thirty years later, he was a conspicuous figure in Republican party affairs. He was a member of the Ohio legislature in 1886 and received a succession of patronage appoint-

ments from Republican presidents. He was widely known among black aristocrats throughout the United States, especially in Washington, where he resided
briefly; in Philadelphia, the home of his second wife; and in New Orleans,
where his racehorses had often been the envy of thoroughbred owners.[5] His son,
Robert Harlan, Jr., a law school graduate, held a responsible office in the
municipal government of Cincinnati and also practiced law in partnership with
George H. Jackson. The latter's position in the city's black community owed
much to the fact that his wife was the daughter of Robert Gordon, a man of
wealth and prestige in the antebellum era. When the wife of Robert Harlan, Jr.,
visited friends in St. Louis in 1891, the city's black upper class accorded her a
welcome clearly indicating that she was one of their own. "The elite of St.
Louis," read one account, "was present at the reception given by Mr. and Mrs.
Samuel Mordecai at their residence 3726 Texas Avenue in honor of Mrs. R. J.
Harlan of Cincinnati. The evening was spent dancing. An elegant supper was
served. It was the most respectable affair given in St. Louis in many months." In
Cincinnati, Robert Harlan and his wife moved in the same social circles as his
father—the circle made up of the Fossetts, Roxboroughs, Lewises, and other
"old families."[6]

Although St. Louis was also a river city bordering on slave territory, it
possessed more of a Southern flavor than did Cincinnati. In 1830 blacks made
up almost a quarter of the population of St. Louis; over the next three decades
the number of blacks declined dramatically so that they constituted only about
two percent of the city's population on the eve of the Civil War. In 1858
Cyprian Clamorgan indicated the existence of a "colored aristocracy" in St.
Louis composed of free blacks "who, by means of wealth, education or natural
ability," formed "a peculiar class." In the postwar era these aristocrats and their
children continued to dominate the social and economic life of the city's black
community. Those whom the *New York Tribune* in 1871 cited as examples of
prosperous freedmen in St. Louis were, for the most part, the well-to-do free
people of color and their kin listed in Clamorgan's tract. But postwar anti-Negro
prejudice severely restricted the opportunities of even the colored aristocrats;
despite their accumulation of substantial wealth, they remained largely confined
to service trades. Because of their wealth and ambition, their children were
educated and became teachers, lawyers, and other professionals who reinforced
the high social status of the old families.[7]

By 1890, the black population of St. Louis had grown so dramatically that it
was surpassed only by a few cities in the East. The ranks of the city's colored
aristocracy had expanded to include a number of blacks from elsewhere whose
family background, education, wealth, and other attributes entitled them to
acceptance in what Clamorgan had earlier referred to as "good society." Among
them were George B. and John B. Vashon, sons of the elder George Boyer
Vashon, a famous teacher, lawyer, and poet who was the first black to graduate

from Oberlin, in 1844. George, a newspaper publisher, along with another well-known black resident of St. Louis, J. Milton Turner, was prominent in Democratic party affairs. John was a teacher who served for many years as principal of one of the city's black public schools. The Vashons manifested great pride in their ancestry: on the paternal side both their grandfather, who was a veteran of the War of 1812, and their distinguished father had been active in the abolitionist movement; on the maternal side they were descended from the Pauls of Boston, whose members were among the best-known black clergymen, teachers, and antislavery activists in the city. The Vashons also "counted among their ancestors Jean Pierre Boyer, once president of Haiti, and François Vashon, chevalier in the American company of the Marquis de LaFayette."[8]

Socially allied with the Vashons in St. Louis was another emigré black family, that of Arthur D. Langston, the son of John Mercer Langston, and his wife, Ida Napier Langston, whose family occupied a unique place in the upper class of Nashville's black community. Langston, an Oberlin graduate and principal of Dumas School in St. Louis, figured significantly in the social and cultural life of the city for a generation. Like the Vashons, he easily and naturally took his place among the Mordecais, Hickmans, Clamorgans, Johnsons, Whites, and other old families. Their social lives revolved around one or two organizations, the most prestigious of which were the Home and Forum clubs. On Sundays they were likely to worship in the Episcopal, Catholic, or a few other elite churches.[9]

No less at home among the old upper class of St. Louis were William Parrish Curtis, a physician and graduate of Howard, and Thomas Austin Curtis, a dentist. Their father, Alexander H. Curtis of Perry County, Alabama, was a barber whose slave background was scarcely that of the stereotypical bondsman. Alexander Curtis was prominent in Reconstruction politics in the state and a key figure in the establishment of public educational facilities for blacks. Through their mother, the Curtis brothers traced their lineage to the "legendary 'African' Princess" (1736–1800). The descendants of the Princess, the Curtis and Childs families (Dr. William P. Curtis married Julia Childs), figured significantly in Horace Mann Bond's study of the "ecology of talent" in assessing the origins of black scholars in the United States. Like the Langstons, Vashons, and Peter H. Clark of Cincinnati (who until 1908 taught at Sumner School, the famous black high school in St. Louis), the Curtises were easily incorporated into the city's black upper class and became leaders in the St. Louis chapter of the NAACP.[10]

In 1905 Dr. William P. Curtis sought election to the St. Louis school board. In a statement to the white press regarding his candidacy, he spoke explicitly about the city's black upper class and about the failure of whites to recognize class distinctions among blacks. Curtis declared:

"White men do not understand the Negro, as a rule, and the high-class gentlemen of the school board do not understand, I am sure, the inner lives of the Negroes of St. Louis. White men will say: 'Oh, yes, I know all about the Negro' and then will tell you they have talked about it to their barber or coachman or Mary, the cook, who has been with them for thirty years.

"But there are other Negroes in St. Louis besides the serving class. There are families who are deeply interested in the education of their children; there are homes where there is culture and polish; there are circles where the cultured white man would be pleasantly surprised were he to enter them. . . . This class of Negroes St. Louis seldom hears about. It hears about Negroes who apply for jobs as janitors in political offices. Well, this movement to place a Negro on the school board is designed partly to show the white people of St. Louis that there are Negroes who take an interest in the public welfare, who do not desire political recognition for the money there is in it, but who are willing to do what they can to aid the white brother to contribute to the public good."[11]

Curtis's remarks touched off a storm of controversy in the black community, especially among those in "the serving class." One critic likened the doctor to "an aspiring knight" who would "weigh upon us as a millstone on our necks." Unlike Curtis, he argued, the cooks, barbers, janitors, and other blacks of "the serving class" were at least "of us and among us" rather than aloof from the black majority whom the elite viewed with considerable condescension.[12]

In the late nineteenth century, Chicago was already the home of numerous and diverse ethnic groups, but none, according to Allan Spear, had a longer local history than Afro-Americans. Although tradition claimed that Jean Baptiste Pointe de Sable, a black trader from Santo Domingo, was the first permanent settler on the site that became Chicago, it was not until the 1840s that an identifiable black community, made up largely of fugitive slaves and free Negroes from the South and East, emerged in the city. Despite Chicago's reputation as "a sink hole of abolition," blacks there lived under a heavy burden of legal and extralegal discrimination. In the post–Civil War era, when the antebellum system of segregation collapsed, black Chicagoans continued to confront discrimination in housing, employment, and even in public accommodations. But they were not yet confined to a ghetto and most lived in racially mixed neighborhoods. Before 1900, the small group of old residents, "usually descendants of free Negroes and of Mixed Stock," made up what was termed the "refined people." Their education and good breeding prompted them to look with displeasure on the less-decorous behavior and life styles of blacks in social strata below them. Concentrated in the service trades and professions, individuals in this group often had economic ties with the white community and counted among their acquaintances whites of comparable social status. Usually linked to the abolitionist movement, they were committed to the ultimate integration of blacks into the mainstream of American life. In Chicago these aristocrats of color dominated the black community until about 1900, when both their status and their adherence to the integrationist's creed encountered increasingly serious challenges from the newer ideology of racial solidarity and self-help associated with the emerging black ghetto and with the teachings of Booker T. Washington.[13]

Perhaps the best known among the socially prominent old residents of Chicago's black community was John Jones, a well-to-do tailor and persistent advocate of equal rights. Born in 1826 in Greene County, North Carolina, Jones was the son of a "free mulatto mother" and a German father by the name of Bremfield. Jones emigrated to Chicago in the 1840s, established a tailor shop in the business district, and, by the time of his death in 1879, had amassed a fortune. Active in a variety of Abolitionist, civic, and racial uplift activities, Jones also figured prominently in politics, serving two terms on the Cook County Board of Commissioners. He bequeathed to his widow and daughters considerable wealth as well as "a name outstanding both in colored and white Chicago." For some years after his death, when Mary Jones, his imperious widow, presided over the family residence on Ray Street, invitations to social and cultural gatherings at the Jones house were reserved for aristocrats of color.[14]

Two individuals who became prominent members of Chicago's black society in the late nineteenth century, Lloyd Wheeler and Daniel Hale Williams, had close ties with the Jones family. Wheeler, a native of Ohio, where his family had been active in the Underground Railroad, was trained as an attorney and for a time practiced law in Little Rock in association with Mifflin W. Gibbs. After his marriage to Jones's adopted daughter, he assumed management of her father's tailoring establishment and was labeled by one hostile observer as the "King" of Chicago's black "upper tens." Wheeler's friend Daniel Hale Williams boarded with Jones's widow while attending medical school in Chicago. A native of Hollidaysburg, Pennsylvania, Williams was the scion of a racially mixed family—German, Welsh, Scotch, and Indian as well as African—on his father's side. His mother, Sarah Price, was a member of a well-known and prosperous free family of color in Annapolis, Maryland, a city that had a sizable free black community. The Bishop family were neighbors of the Prices, and it was while visiting his maternal grandparents that Williams met Hutchins Bishop, who became a lifelong friend. Bishop served for more than three decades as rector of St. Philip's Protestant Episcopal Church in New York. Williams's father was active in the antebellum conventions of free people of color; it was in this connection that he became acquainted with John Jones of Chicago. Jones's widow not only provided the aspiring physician with room and board while he was in medical school but also served as his sponsor when he began his practice.[15]

When Williams moved to Washington to head Freedman's Hospital, he met and courted Alice Johnson, a schoolteacher who was reputedly the daughter of the famous sculptor Moses Jacob Ezekial. Bookish and reclusive, she counted among her highly select circle of friends the daughters of black aristocrats in both the District and nearby Maryland. They included Anna Evans Murray, Nettie Langston Napier, Betty Cox Francis, Caroline Parke Shadd, and the sisters of Hutchins Bishop of Annapolis. After four years in Washington, Dr. Williams returned to Chicago in 1898 with his new bride, who quickly and naturally assumed a place of importance in the social life of the city's aristocrats of color. Alice Williams was openly intolerant of those who failed to measure up to her social standards. "I'd rather stay at home and read a good book," she wrote a friend, "than mingle with ill-bred people."[16]

Such people rarely intruded upon the exclusive circle in which the Williamses moved. Aside from the Joneses, Wheelers, and Dr. Dan's numerous relatives, one of whom married Oscar De Priest, a contractor and politician who later served in Congress, their social activities were likely to include the Avendorphs, Maddens, Smileys, S. Laing Williamses, Morrises, and Bentleys. Julius Avendorph, known as the "Ward McAllister" of black society in Chicago, was an assistant to the president of the Pullman Company. Like Avendorph, both James B. Madden and Charles J. Smiley had close ties with the white community. Madden was a bookkeeper in a white business firm; Smiley, one of the wealthiest blacks in Chicago, was the owner of a fashionable catering establishment that served the city's upper-class whites. Charles E. Bentley was a dentist; his friendship with Dr. Daniel Williams antedated their arrival in Chicago. Two other professional men, Edward H. Morris, a native of Kentucky, and S. Laing Williams, achieved prominence as attorneys. Williams was born in Georgia and grew up in Michigan. A graduate of the University of Michigan and the Columbian Law School in Washington, he settled in Chicago in the mid-1880s. His wife, Fannie Barrier, a native of Brockport, New York, whose father had been an associate of Dr. Daniel Williams's father in the antislavery cause, taught school in Washington before her marriage. A woman of extraordinary energy, she enjoyed a wide reputation as a lecturer, writer, and clubwoman. Throughout the late nineteenth and early twentieth centuries, these families and those of a few other black professionals who measured up to what Fannie Barrier Williams called "gentle folks," formed a close-knit, exclusive social group. They belonged to one or two highly select clubs, worshipped either at white churches or in upper-class black congregations, and cooperated in a variety of civic and racial uplift enterprises, notably the establishment of Provident Hospital.[17]

In 1905 Fannie Barrier Williams was certain that the black aristocracy in Chicago was "better dressed, better housed, and better mannered than almost anywhere else in the wide west." It enjoyed, she argued, an abundance of "material things" and exhibited a wealth of "intelligence and culture." "We are trying our best," she said, "to be the real gentle folks in the highest and best sense of the term."[18]

The rapid expansion of Chicago's black population after 1890 posed a number of challenges for and altered the composition of the city's aristocracy of color. The black population numbered 14,171 in 1890; it more than doubled by the end of the decade and increased to 109,458 by 1920. This rapid growth meant that class stratification among Chicago's blacks underwent constant revision. The influx of migrants from the South swelled the ranks of the lower classes and less dramatically increased the size of the middle class. The class-conscious "upper crust," especially those who considered themselves "old residents," often resisted the mass migration into their city. They sometimes manifested their contempt for the poor, unskilled blacks who poured in from the South by withdrawing into organizations that overtly excluded recent arrivals. Few migrants won ready acceptance into the ranks of those known as "society people." Those who did invariably possessed the necessary credentials of education, wealth, family background, and achievement. When the family of William E. Mollison, a politician and banker from Vicksburg, Mississippi, who was an intimate friend of Robert R. Church of Memphis, and J. Gray Lucas, an Arkansas lawyer educated at Boston University and a former member of the state legislature, settled in Chicago, they easily assumed places in the "upper circles" of black society. [19]

One who waged a persistent struggle to win acceptance by Chicago's black aristocracy was George Cleveland Hall, a native of Michigan and a graduate of an eclectic medical school of dubious quality. A large, dark-skinned, heavy-featured man, Hall was an energetic self-promoter closely identified with the black community and popular with the rank and file. The feud that developed between him and Dr. Daniel Williams, who considered Hall something of a quack, lasted for years and revealed the differences between the aristocrats and the new economic elite. The dispute between Williams and Hall was both personal and ideological. It was by no means confined to the issue of Hall's admittance to the staff of Provident Hospital, Chicago's first interracial hospital, which was founded by Williams and supported by the city's black and white elite. It also involved the acceptance of Hall's wife into the exclusive social circles dominated by Alice Williams, Jennie Avendorph, and a few others. For these staid society women, the towering, red-haired, ebullient Theodocia Brewer Hall was clearly not acceptable. Both "her laughter and clothes were apt to be a little loud." But the Halls were not without substantial resources and influential friends, including Booker T. Washington, in retaliating against these professional and social rebuffs. It was symbolic of the changes that occurred in the composition of the black social structure that in time Hall not only gained a place on the staff of Provident Hospital but both he and his wife were accepted in Chicago's "black 400." [20]

Throughout the late nineteenth and early twentieth centuries debates erupted periodically in the black community over the question of whether Chicago possessed "real society," as did cities in the East. In 1887, a resident of Chicago publicly stated that "society" was "something that has never existed in this city since that war," and he ridiculed what he termed the "H.T.C.P." or "high-toned culled people." Members of Chicago's black upper class were quick to respond to charges that they were discriminatory in the choice of those they admitted to their social circle. "If any person is discriminated against by the society people," one noted, "it is for a just and essential cause. . . . Simply because some of the better class of people do not unhesitatingly take up as their associate every stranger, no matter who, that comes to the city, they must be 'stuck up' and 'would-be high-toned culled people.' Must they take people whom they know nothing about and associate with them because they happen to possess a few good clothes and have a little pocket change?" The writer, in explaining why barbers were sometimes included among Chicago's black elite, emphasized that wealth and occupation counted for less in determining one's status than did family background and culture.[21]

The exchange of views in the press concerning the nature and authenticity of Chicago's black aristocracy had scarcely subsided when it flared again in 1888 because of a remark made by Dr. Daniel Hale Williams. According to reports printed in numerous black papers, Dr. Williams had declared, in the course of an interview, that "the great mistake which white people make is to judge the whole colored race by the sleeping car porter . . . , by the newsboys and roustabouts." The storm of controversy prompted by Williams's statement resembled that created in 1905, when another physician, Dr. William P. Curtis of St. Louis, made a similar reference to black bootblacks.[22]

In the opening years of the twentieth century, as the influx of black Southerners into Chicago increased in tempo, the debate over whether the city possessed an authentic black upper class was renewed. In 1907, Edward E. Wilson, a black lawyer and politician, educated at Oberlin and Williams colleges, who espoused an integrationist posture, published a lengthy critique of Chicago's black community. He carefully distinguished between what he termed "society proper" and the pretentious hustle and bustle of those who, in the process of imitating rich and dissolute whites, entertained lavishly, dressed extravagantly, and possessed few of the attributes of true gentility. The latter were conspicuously lacking in culture, education, manners, family background, and morals. He suggested that no more than a score of persons within Chicago's black community were "fitted pecuniarily to be in society in the proper sense of the word," and their social life was likely to revolve around far less-ostentatious affairs. In these "small circles of friends," who spent many pleasant and profitable evenings "discussing music, drama or literature or whiling away an hour or so at cards," was where one found gentility and the attributes of "genuine aristocracy." But Wilson insisted that those who constituted the real "colored society" occupied a difficult place, because blacks were "not willing to admit that any one of them is superior to the other." "An excess of democracy," he declared, "existed among Negroes which, though beneficial in some respects, has a fatal policy of dragging everything down to its level." Thus, those who manifested pride in their genealogy and claimed social precedence as descendants of distinguished forebears were almost certain to be "overwhelmed by the lusty scorn of a host of upstart nobodies."[23]

Fannie Barrier Williams, who, like Wilson, belonged to Chicago's black upper class, also defended the existence of an aristocracy that placed a premium on "character, intelligence and manners." "We must not despise the coming of the Negro aristocrat," she wrote in 1905. "He is very much needed and has good services to perform. The only hope is that he will not imitate the codfish variety so much in evidence on the other side of the color line. . . . This is not the kind we are developing in Chicago." The development of society was, in Williams's view, nothing more or less than "an effort to escape the rabble, the ignorant and the uncouth." But the escape, as she recognized, was never quite complete and satisfactory. Even those who shared her "real aristocratic instincts" and high level of education and refinement, on occasion were compelled, by "a hostile public sentiment, to accept menial occupations in order to live," thereby being forced "to work and associate with ignorant and uncongenial people."[24]

When in 1923 a black newspaper in Chicago editorialized about the social stratification that was occurring within the black community, it actually was discussing the alteration in the existing class structure, especially in the upper class, prompted by the Great Migration and the development of ghettoes in large cities. The editor noted that teachers and educators, physicians and dentists, and a few clergymen had been "the first in establishing distinctions" and in constituting themselves as the black "upper crust." By the end of the First World War, he noted, black businessmen—bankers, real estate dealers, insurance executives, and others—had joined this group. Status and achievement measured in terms of wealth counted for more in the new era, and education, ancestry, color, and manners counted for less. Stratification in black society, the Chicago editor noted, was "proceeding along its natural course exactly analogous, or at least similar to, the formation of social groups of the white race in this country.[25]

In comparison to Chicago, Detroit possessed a small Negro community. Only sixty-seven blacks lived in the city in 1820. By 1880 the number had increased to 2,821 and by 1910 to only 5,741. Because of the prevalence of Negrophobia and the Blackburn riot in 1833, Negro migrants generally avoided Detroit until the late 1830s and early 1840s. Among those who did settle there in the antebellum era was a sizable contingent of free blacks from Virginia, especially those from Fredericksburg. The "old families" of black Detroit in the late nineteenth century were, for the most part, descendants of the prosperous, free people of color from Virginia, including the Richards, Lees, DeBaptistes, Cooks, and Williamses from Fredericksburg and the Pelhams from Petersburg. Other old families of upper-class status were the Lamberts, Fergusons, Johnsons, and Watsons. Later arrivals who assumed prominent places among Detroit's "cultured, colored '40' " included D. Augustus Straker, a native of the West

Indies and an attorney who had been active in politics and education in Reconstruction South Carolina; and Granville S. Purvis, a druggist, the brother of Dr. Charles Purvis of Washington and the son of the abolitionist Robert Purvis. These families provided the leadership for what one student described as "an exceptional Negro community, adept, frugal and culturally gifted."[26]

By the turn of the century the city's aristocrats of color, like those elsewhere, socialized together, belonged to one or two clubs, cooperated in racial and civic activities, and held the best political jobs and appointments open to blacks. A disproportionately large number belonged to St. Matthew's Protestant Episcopal Church, the first black Episcopal church established west of the Alleghenies. Many of Detroit's black aristocrats were related by marriage: the Pelhams were linked through marriage to the Lewises, Fergusons, and Barriers; Delia Pelham married George A. Barrier, a well-known barber and politician who was the brother of Fannie Barrier Williams of Chicago. D. Augustus Straker, a close personal friend of well-known blacks in Charleston and throughout South Carolina, secured his place among Detroit's elite by marrying the niece of John D. Richards.[27]

In 1902 the Detroit News-Tribune described in detail the forty families who made up the city's black aristocracy. It spoke of the refinement and culture that characterized the city's "most exclusive social clique"—a group that the average white man scarcely knew existed. "There is," the News-Tribune explained, "a colored elite more exclusive than any other society in Detroit, which has its old families, its professional classes, its nouveau riches clamoring for recognition, its afternoon teas, its dances, its club studies, and most of the other duties and diversions which make up the life of white society in its most exalted strata." Within this clique were six physicians, seven lawyers, three dentists, several old residents who had grown wealthy from real estate investments, and employees in the United States post office department. The group also included "men of more humble occupation" whose place within the highest social stratum was assured "by reason of their family connections, their personal worth, or their refinement and culture, which many a wealthy colored family is unable to maintain." Unlike most of Detroit's blacks, those of the "40 families" interacted regularly with whites.[28] Benjamin L. Clark was a black physician who had been educated in Berlin. He resided in Detroit from 1858 until his death thirty-three years later and had a large and lucrative practice among the city's German population.[29] As historian David Katzman has noted, many aristocrats of color enjoyed a common educational experience with white leaders either in Detroit schools or at the University of Michigan, and politics provided them "with a wedge into the white world." Katzman characterized the city's upper-class blacks as a "marginal group whose relative position in the social system was at some point between the white caste and the general black caste."[30]

The Pelhams were perhaps the most visible family among the city's black upper class. The brothers Benjamin and Robert were active in Republican politics for several decades and held a number of choice political appointments. They belonged to the Osceola Club, a gentlemen's organization that limited its membership to twelve individuals.[31] Two other Pelham brothers, Joseph and Frederick, were a school principal and a civil engineer respectively. Their sister Meta, a teacher who had been educated at Alma College, was for some years the driving force behind the family's weekly newspaper, The Plaindealer. Another Pelham sister, Emma, was the wife of William W. Ferguson, a prosperous printer. In 1903, their daughter married Leonard Thompson, an abstract clerk of the Union Trust Company whose family belonged to the city's "40" families. The Detroit Journal described their wedding at St. Matthew's as "the most elaborate social function Detroit colored society has ever known." In 1900, when Robert Pelham was appointed to a position in the Census Bureau in Washington, he and his musically talented wife, Gabriella Lewis Pelham, were readily admitted to the black "upper tens" in the nation's capital.[32]

While the Pelhams and others among Detroit's crème de la crème were active in a variety of civil rights causes and, in general, espoused an integrationist position, they remained socially aloof from the black masses. Newcomers to the city viewed them as snobbish, as "cold and distant," and resented their monopoly on the choicest positions, political and otherwise, open to blacks. For their part, the aristocrats of color were careful to avoid actions that might jeopardize the high status which they believed rightfully belonged to them. The Pelham's Plaindealer undoubtedly reflected the prevailing view of Detroit's black upper class in 1890 when it editorialized: "This is peculiarly an American white man's view, that every Afro-American is his brother's keeper, no matter how low. In thousands of cases the ties of consanguinity between black and white are closer than that existing between black and black." So far as the black aristocrats were concerned, there was "nothing in common between the natures of two Afro-Americans, save that which circumstances has forced upon them."[33]

Such a view was perhaps even more prevalent among the aristocracy of color in Cleveland, where the black community was almost as old as the city itself.[34] "The colored people of this city are not numerous," the Cleveland Herald observed in 1839, "but [are] of the better class of free blacks. They are industrious, peaceable, intelligent and ambitious of improvement."[35] Among the 224 black residents of the city in 1850 were several well-known families such as the Watsons, Vosbughs, and Malvins, who were active in civic and abolitionist causes. The steady growth of Cleveland's black population meant that by 1910 it had risen to 8,448, or about 1.5 percent of the city's total population. The most dramatic increase occurred in the decade between 1910 and 1920, when the number of blacks in Cleveland more than quadrupled. As historian Kenneth L. Kusmer has noted, an atmosphere of racial equalitarianism coupled with the fluid social and economic conditions in this rapidly growing frontier city "made nineteenth-century Cleveland much less oppressive for blacks than most other municipalities in the United States."[36]

Long after Cleveland's commitment to racial equality had been replaced by diverse forms of overt discrimination, black residents extolled their city as having less prejudice than any other in the United States. It possessed, according to a black resident in 1899, "mixed schools, mixed churches . . . and in fact everything mixed."[37] The integrationist stance of and quest for equality by Cleveland's original black leadership were perhaps best exemplified in the career of John Malvin, who resided in the city from 1831 until his death in 1880.[38]

Among Cleveland's aristocracy of color in the late nineteenth and early twentieth centuries were three fair-complexioned families who had settled in the city in the 1850s. One was that of the Philadelphia dentist Dr. Joseph Willson, whose daughter Josephine married the United States senator from Mississippi and whose son, Leon, an attorney, was no longer identified with blacks by the time of his death.[39] The second was the family of Charles Waddell and Susan Perry Chesnutt, whose roots, like those of the Learys, Revels, Perrys, and several other black families of note, lay in the sizable community of free people of color in Fayetteville, North Carolina. So fair as to be "indistinguishable," Chesnutt was a lawyer and court stenographer who achieved national prominence as a writer of fiction.[40] Born in Cleveland in 1858, Chesnutt grew up in Fayetteville and did not return to Cleveland until the mid-1880s. In a thinly disguised reference to Fayetteville in one of his best-known works, *The House Behind the Cedars*, he noted that the free antebellum people of color there were numerous enough "to have their own 'society' and human enough to despise those who did not possess advantages equal to their own."[41]

Like the Chesnutts, the family of John P. Green, also an attorney, came from North Carolina. Born in New Bern, he was the son of "free colored people of mixed blood, and highly respected by people of both races in that community." Green, whose status consciousness was evident throughout his autobiography, *Fact Stranger Than Fiction*, showed great pride in his paternal white ancestors, especially the Stanley family of North Carolina. Green's mother, who possessed "not the slightest suspicion of African blood," nevertheless chose to identify with the "colored race" and "commingled with her colored friends" throughout her eighty-one years. During his long career as an attorney, civil rights advocate, friend of John D. Rockefeller, Ohio state legislator, and federal appointee, Green always emphasized "high bred conduct" and viewed himself as one who exhibited "aristocratic instincts." "It is a maxim," he wrote a friend in 1899, "which the ages have handed down to us: 'blood will tell'; but while this is strictly true, one cannot ignore the fact that *good breeding* will manifest itself at all times and places." He fully agreed with his friend Chesnutt that "Cleveland's *upper crust* is fully equal to anything that this country can produce."[42]

In addition to the Greens and Chesnutts, Cleveland's black aristocracy included the families of William Clifford, Henry T. Eubanks, Jere Brown, and George A. Myers, all of whom were active in Republican politics. Most were descendants of families who had enjoyed freedom either legally or extralegally long before Emancipation. They were relatively well educated, economically better off than the vast majority of Cleveland's black population, and engaged in occupations that brought them into frequent contacts with prominent whites. For example, George A. Myers, a member of an old and well-known free black family in Baltimore, was no ordinary barber. He was a substantial entrepreneur, and his Hollenden House Barbershop was an elaborate establishment with a sizable staff. Its clientele included the most influential white men in Cleveland. Aside from being a man of means and considerable culture, Myers was also an important political figure in the Republican organization of Senator Marcus A. Hanna. Like his close friend John P. Green, he possessed "aristocratic instincts" evident in his courtliness, refined speech and taste for "higher culture." When Myers used the term "our people" in correspondence with Green and a few other intimate acquaintances, it referred not to Negroes in general but to the small group of upper-class black associates in Cleveland. Writing to Green in 1902 about a project to raise money for the Home for Aged Colored People, Myers explained that it was an effort "to reach a class of people, whom our people never come in contact with."[43]

Although Cleveland was widely heralded for its atmosphere of equalitarianism, it was also known as a city in which "blue veinism" was a significant factor in delineating the city's black upper class. Although the black aristocrats were indeed lighter in complexion, evidence that color *per se* consciously figured in their considerations regarding status is inconclusive. Even John P. Green, who apparently was color-conscious, always boasted of his family's identity "with the race" and of its involvement in racial causes. Nevertheless, darker-skinned Afro-Americans and whites accused the light-complexioned elite of "drawing the color line."[44]

Throughout Ohio and the Midwest, black aristocrats in cities both large and small shared many of the characteristics found among those in Cleveland, including the charge of being color-conscious. In the small town of Xenia, Ohio the black upper class consisted largely of families who had enjoyed several generations of freedom and had acquired education. Its ranks included "teachers and other professional classes, entrepreneurs and a few porters and artisans" who "divided into smaller circles of more or less exclusiveness." According to Richard R. Wright, Jr., in 1903, it was this group of blacks which possessed "the confidence of the community of whites." In Toledo's black community in the late nineteenth and early twentieth centuries the greatest prestige belonged to those known as the "refined" element, which consisted of a small group of attorneys, municipal employees, and entrepreneurs active in religious and social affairs. One student has suggested that the most important factors in conferring high status among Toledo's blacks were education and occupation.[45]

In the black communities of St. Paul and Minneapolis, where there was a high degree of correlation between a light skin and social prominence, an aristocracy of a dozen persons dominated intellectual, social, and political life. Among them were Frederick L. McGhee, an attorney who achieved prominence as an opponent of Booker T. Washington's philosophy; Thomas and Amanda Lyles, a barber and a beautician who had amassed considerable wealth and assisted in the founding of St. Mark's Episcopal Church; and John Q. Adams, an Oberlin graduate and newspaper publisher who figured prominently in various civil rights causes. Adams was the scion of an old and prominent black family in Louisville, Kentucky. He was active for a time in Reconstruction politics in Arkansas, where his uncle, Joseph C. Corbin, achieved prominence as a politician and educator. Extraordinarily fair-complexioned, Adams was on occasion accused of attempting to "pass" or of being addicted to "blue veinism." Periodically rumors circulated to the effect that "a blue vein society existed among the mulatto element" in the Twin Cities.[46]

At one time or another aristocrats of color in Topeka, Indianapolis, and other cities in the Midwest encountered similar accusations. By the 1880s the old upper class in the black community of Indianapolis consisted of the Bagbys, Elberts, Christys, McCoys, Hills, Furnisses, Thorntons, and a few other families descended from free people of color or from slaves who had escaped north many years before Emancipation. Characterized by a relatively high level of education and a high standard of living, they furnished the black community with teachers, journalists, physicians, attorneys, and entrepreneurs who dominated its social, political, and cultural affairs. Throughout the late nineteenth century the black press in the Hoosier capital devoted considerable attention to "upper ten circles of Indianapolis' social exclusiveness." It alternately fretted over what was perceived as its qualitative inferiority to the black "society" that existed in Cleveland, Chicago, and other cities and boldly defended Indianapolis' upper class as the equal of any in the United States. Repeatedly, local observers noted that the true "bon tons" in Indianapolis placed extraordinary emphasis on modest reserve, dignified demeanor, refined culture, and high moral standards. Associated with one or two literary and cultural organizations and usually members of either the Methodist Episcopal or Presbyterian churches, Indianapolis' "upper tens" consciously drew the line "against the contaminating touch" of those blacks considered "bad" or "vulgar."[47]

Black communities in the West remained small until the First World War. In 1900, the combined black population of San Francisco, Los Angeles, Seattle, and Denver was 7,191, less than one-eighth that of Philadelphia and less than one-fourth that of Chicago. On the Pacific slope the oldest and most-important black community until the turn of the century was that in San Francisco and the Bay area.[48] The city's black population of 464 in 1852 increased to 1,654 in 1900 and remained at approximately that figure until the First World War.

Diverse in origins, the early black inhabitants of San Francisco included relatively large numbers of foreign-born Negroes as well as those from urban centers in the North. Among the best known of the latter were the educator Jeremiah B. Sanderson of Massachusetts, the journalist Philip Bell of New York, and the shoe retailer Mifflin W. Gibbs of Philadelphia, who returned East and spent the last forty-five years of his life in Arkansas. David W. Ruggles, a native of New Bedford, Massachusetts, was identified with numerous civic and racial concerns. He was employed for many years by the Adams Express Company, and in 1878 he was the first black appointed to a grand jury in California. No less conspicuous in the affairs of San Francisco's black community was the large family of John Francis, who for many years was an employee of the San Francisco Stock Exchange. Another socially prominent family (unrelated to John) was that of Robert and Mary Francis, both natives of Pennsylvania. Mary Francis was a member of the well-known Durham family of Philadelphia and related to the Appos of the same city. Of their three sons, the best known was Joseph Francis, who for many years published the black weekly *Western Outlook* and whose wife was active in the San Francisco Women's Club. Despite the ethnic diversity and the cosmopolitan character of the city, the prevailing attitude toward blacks was scarcely ideal. Yet the anti-Negro prejudice in San Francisco "was always ambiguous, and respect and support coexisted with antipathy."[49]

Characterized by a relatively high degree of literacy and prosperity, black San Franciscans established newspapers, schools, and cultural organizations and waged a campaign for full civil rights. These "pioneer urbanites," whom one scholar has described as substantially different from "the ghetto dwellers of the Great Migration," resided throughout the city rather than in an identifiable "Negro quarter." Following the earthquake and fire in 1906, black residents moved to the suburbs, often acquiring larger homes in Oakland. Among the earliest black settlers in Oakland were Isaac and Elizabeth Thorn Scott Flood. Born a slave in South Carolina, Isaac Flood purchased his freedom and learned to read and write. Attracted West during the gold rush of 1849, he resided in various places in California before settling in Oakland; by the time of his death in 1892, he had lived there for forty-four years. In 1854, he married a widow, Elizabeth Thorn Scott, who, like Jeremiah Sanderson, was from New Bedford, Massachusetts and a teacher. She opened the first school for blacks in Sacramento and taught there until she married Flood. Flood pursued a variety of vocations. In the late 1860s he was in charge of an expedition aboard *The Petrel* in search of the reputed treasure of Cocos Island. Throughout his residence in California he was active in movements to advance the cause of civil rights of blacks. Flood amassed a small fortune as a result of his investments in real estate in Oakland. His eldest son, George, was "the first colored child" born in the city and, like his brother and sister, was a prosperous, socially prominent citizen in its growing black community in the early twentieth century. Flood's daughter, Lydia Flood Jackson, a businesswoman of ability and an active member of several women's clubs, was long socially prominent in the Oakland–San Francisco area.[50]

Within San Francisco's black community class lines remained fluid so long as the population remained small. There is little evidence to suggest that "an elite group dominated the community's social life" before 1890, certainly not to the extent that existed in older and larger black communities in the East.[51] Ancestry, color, and family background appeared to be of considerably less importance in the social stratification of black San Franciscans than in the black communities in Washington, Boston, and Philadelphia. Nevertheless, the East did, in some respects, provide models for black westerners. "Look at the cities of the East!" a black San Franciscan noted in 1874, "They have their debating clubs and lyceums and public lectures."[52] While San Francisco may have lacked a clearly defined black social elite, the more cultured and refined Negroes of the city considered class distinction essential and desirable to thwart the tendency of white Americans to lump all blacks together. Far removed from "the rabble" in black San Francisco was the eminently respectable, cultured gentleman who, according to historian Douglas Henry Daniels, was an "example of Black ideals"—one who combined education and erudition with chivalry, displayed impeccable manners, "read the classics, presented a solid front to the business world and belonged to a men's club."[53]

In time the term "pioneer" in San Francisco assumed a meaning and significance comparable to that of "colored aristocracy," "black 400," and other phrases used to describe the old black upper class in the East and Midwest. Members of a "pioneer" family who possessed education, polished manners, and respectable employment were certain to enjoy high social status. Victoria Shorey, the daughter of the West Indian sea captain William T. Shorey, was active during the 1920s in numerous social and cultural organizations and a leader in what was locally called "the smart set." In describing the wedding of David Ruggles's son to Irene Bell in 1915, the local black weekly wrote: "The groom is a member of a pioneer family, is a native of San Francisco, has been an employee of the Customs House for fifteen years and is a very industrious citizen. The bride, although not a native daughter, is one by adoption. . . . The couple will be a valuable acquisition to San Francisco society." Other members of "pioneer" families who regularly appeared in the society columns of the press were the Townses and Francises. In 1915, when Josephine Bruce and Dr. and Mrs. George W. Cook of Washington were in San Francisco to attend the meeting of the World Purity Federation, they were entertained by the Ruggleses and Francises.[54]

On the Pacific coast the black community in Los Angeles increasingly surpassed that in San Francisco in size as well as influence after 1900. Blacks were present at the founding of Los Angeles in 1781 under the Spaniards, but these original settlers and their descendants apparently died out or became "amalgamated" by the time of the emergence of the city's modern Negro population in 1850. The black population of Los Angeles, listed as 102 in the census of 1880, remained small until after 1900, when a little more than 2,000 blacks resided there. Twenty years later the number of blacks had increased to 15,579, or 2.7 percent of the city's total population. One student suggests that the year 1888 marked the beginning of the first well-defined Negro residential area in Los Angeles, although for some years thereafter blacks were widely dispersed throughout the city.[55]

As in other parts of the West, considerable prestige belonged to those black families of long residence whose members had achieved wealth, education, and political recognition and who enjoyed a life style that distinguished them from the black rank and file.[56] Among the "pioneer" families, most of whom settled in the Los Angeles area in the 1850s, were the Masons, Ballards, and Owenses. Biddy Mason, a slave and the mother of three girls, arrived in California in 1851 with her master. Five years later, when he threatened to return to Texas with his slaves, Biddy Mason instituted a famous legal proceeding and secured her freedom. She supported her family as a midwife and nurse and invested all surplus monies in Los Angeles real estate. When she became wealthy as a result of these investments, she launched projects to aid the poor and unfortunate of her race. Her daughter Ellen married a member of the pioneer Owens family; their son, Robert C. Owens, a dealer in real estate, was reputedly the wealthiest black man in California at the turn of the century. He was a personal friend and admirer of Booker T. Washington and regularly made financial contributions to Tuskegee Institute.[57]

Beginning in the 1890s and continuing into the first two decades of the twentieth century, a succession of black professionals—physicians, lawyers, teachers, and clergymen—and their families settled in the growing metropolis of Los Angeles. By 1909 the city's black professionals included five physicians, two dentists, one pharmacist, five attorneys, and three journalists as well as teachers and ministers. Some were members of "pioneer" families but most were natives of the South.[58] This group, along with the well-to-do "pioneer" families, came to make up the city's black elite. In the second decade of the twentieth century the "pioneers" and "old settlers" withdrew into organizations such as the Native Sons and Daughters of California and The Pioneer Club. The latter consisted of those who had lived in Los Angeles for twenty-five years or longer.[59] It was perhaps more than coincidence that the first decade of the twentieth century witnessed the establishment of two traditionally high-status black congregations in Los Angeles, a Presbyterian and an Episcopal church.[60] At the same time "old settlers," as well as well-to-do newcomers, especially professionals, moved to the West Side, onto what was known as the Furlong Tract. Writing in 1936, J. Max Bond noted that "this section was indeed exclusive." Made up primarily of people of "culture and refinement," the West Side black residents represented, in Bond's words, those who "attempted to escape from the masses and obtain a higher level of culture."[61]

Among those who moved to Los Angeles was Titus Nathaniel Alexander, a native of Arkansas. His family was well known, and they were only technically slaves before Emancipation. His father, James Milo Alexander, a highly literate barber, was a member of the Arkansas legislature during Reconstruction. His brother John attended Oberlin College and was the second black to graduate from West Point. All five of James Alexander's children attended Oberlin, and Titus also spent time at the University of Michigan and at Western University in Pennsylvania. Leaving the South in the 1880s, he lived for a time in Cincinnati and Detroit, where he moved in "best circles." He migrated west and ultimately settled in Los Angeles, where he became identified with the Democratic party at a time when most black voters were loyal Republicans. A proud man who consistently adopted an integrationist position, Alexander was for more than forty years employed in the business division of the municipally owned power and light company. Honored repeatedly by both blacks and whites for his efforts in behalf of civil and human rights, he was a keen student of Afro-American history and was regarded as the outstanding authority on black Los Angeles.[62]

In Seattle, which had a black population of 406 in 1900, the same emphasis was placed on "first" or "pioneer" families. One such family was that of William Gross, a native of Washington, D.C. After accompanying Commodore Matthew Perry to the Orient, Gross settled in Seattle in 1859 and opened what became a fashionable hotel. By the time of his death in 1898 he was one of the largest taxpayers in the city. His son, George Gross, who was for years the poundmaster of Seattle, inherited the prestigious place that his father occupied in the city's black community.[63] In 1907 the Grosses and other "old families" of Seattle's black community organized the Pioneer Social Club. The club met monthly, and its purpose was to provide "for a closer affiliation" of older residents in which "geniality and a moral standard may be maintained." The term "pioneer" was interpreted loosely enough for the club to embrace most members of Seattle's black upper class, including four attorneys whose practice was almost exclusively among whites, three barbers who owned or operated shops in the city's leading hotels, three caterers, a building contractor, and several postal employees. These men also belonged to the Twentieth Century Club, a gentlemen's social club that annually sponsored "a full dress formal after Easter." Their spouses dominated the Quid Nune Club and the Musical Club, and both husbands and wives belonged to the Clover Leaf Whist Club.[64]

Among the aristocrats in Seattle's small black community were Horace and Susan Revels Cayton, publishers and editors of the *Seattle Republican,* a weekly. Cayton, born in Mississippi, was the son of a white plantation owner's daughter and a slave who became a prosperous independent farmer. Susan Cayton was the daughter of Hiram Revels, a member of a free family of color in Fayetteville, North Carolina who became a United States senator from Mississippi during Reconstruction. According to their son, the marriage of Horace Cayton and Susan Revels was one of convenience: it enabled Cayton to "make an alliance with a prominent family of the Negro elite" and Susan Revels to escape the South. Educated at Alcorn College in Mississippi, where ex-Senator Revels was president and where he met Susan Revels, Cayton first emigrated to Salt Lake City and later to Seattle. He prospered in the Northwest, acquired substantial wealth from real estate investments, and for some years lived in comfort. The Caytons purchased a large two-story house on Capital Hill, Seattle's most-exclusive residential area, and employed a Japanese houseboy. Theirs was an existence "in between two worlds," one white, the other black. Susan Cayton "held down the cultural front" and engaged in a variety of uplift activities while her husband busied himself with Republican politics, their newspaper, and real estate interests. They impressed upon their children the necessity of education and of the special obligations placed upon educated blacks in regard to their race. Their children attended public schools and the University of Washington.[65]

Booker T. Washington visited Seattle during the 1909 Alaskan, Yukon and Pacific Exposition, and as was the case when the Wizard of Tuskegee traveled to different cities, he was entertained by the "leading colored people." The Caytons were his hosts in Seattle. Horace Cayton drove Washington about the city in his fine carriage, entertained him lavishly, and introduced him to the city's most prominent citizens, both black and white. Although Cayton was a gracious host, he did not subscribe to Booker T. Washington's race relations formula and philosophy of accommodation and told his guest so. When Cayton, who found W. E. B. Du Bois's philosophy more congenial, criticized Washington for acquiescing in the disfranchisement of blacks and for backing away from a "bold strike for freedom," the Tuskegeean suggested that Cayton was "living in a fool's paradise." Cayton conceded that Washington was "a great man," but insisted that he was "wrong and this young fellow Du Bois is right."[66]

During the First World War the Caytons suffered a succession of economic reverses that dramatically altered their life style and place in Seattle society. Forced to sell their spacious house on Capital Hill, they bought a more modest one in a predominantly Italian residential area. Although they held on to some of their income-producing real estate, both Horace and Susan Cayton had to secure employment of a variety that symbolized just how complete "their come down in the world" was: he became a janitor and she a domestic. Some blacks in Seattle obviously relished "the decline of the proud and arrogant Caytons." Despite their reduced circumstances, the Caytons refused to abandon the values and ideals that had previously shaped their lives. Horace Cayton "maintained his pride and continued to speak with the authority born of his wide acquaintance with rich and powerful white people." Susan Cayton never forgot "that she was the daughter of a United States Senator and that her family belonged to the aristocracy of free Negroes." For them—and for their children—upper-class status involved far more than wealth. It focused on education, family, and a cultured life style.[67]

The Caytons' integrationist stance and social remoteness, on occasion, prompted criticism from blacks who interpreted their behavior as evidence of their unwillingness to be identified with blacks. In 1901, Dr. Samuel Burdette, a dark-skinned, retired army veterinary surgeon who settled in Seattle, roundly condemned Horace Cayton for what he viewed as his social pretensions and efforts to merge into the white world: "Mr. Cayton is not a colored man in one sense of the word. He long ago deserted his race. He affects white society. He attends a white peoples' church."[68] As for Cayton, he stoutly maintained that all blacks were not alike and believed, like the Detroit *Plaindealer*, that in many cases the "ties of consanguinity between black and white" were closer than those between black and black. He and his "cultured" black friends had nothing in common with a bootblack, and he resented even being "indirectly classified with this noble bootblack."[69]

In Denver, where the black community grew from 23 in 1866 to almost 4,000 in 1900, the opportunity for a black family to attend "a white peoples' church," as the Caytons did in Seattle, was practically nonexistent. Although Denver may well have been preferable to the postwar South, it was scarcely a racial utopia. Blacks regularly encountered discrimination that differed more in degree than in kind from that experienced by black residents on the Pacific slope. The opportunity to build fortunes and acquire power in frontier Denver remained the preserve of white men. Not surprisingly, in view of the color consciousness of the city, there was a close correlation between a light skin and opportunity. In the late nineteenth century, the overwhelming majority of Denver's best-known and most-prosperous Negroes were mulattoes.[70]

Among them was Henry Oscar Wagoner, a native of Maryland. His mother was a mulatto slave woman, and his father was a German physician, an affectionate, indulgent man who encouraged his son's fondness for reading. Wagoner himself married an "English woman of good education," and their son and daughter were so fair in complexion as to be virtually white. But there is no evidence that any of the Wagoners attempted to pass for white. On the contrary, Henry Wagoner was active in the cause of Abolition and counted among his friends Frederick Douglass and John Jones of Chicago. A resident at various times of Salina, Illinois, Chicago, and Canada, he moved to Colorado during the Pike's Peak gold rush and lived in Denver for more than forty years. Known as "the Douglass of Colorado," he figured prominently in Republican politics for a generation, held a succession of appointive offices, and amassed a small fortune. His son, a man of "delightful manners and finished education," was a graduate of Howard University and an accomplished linguist. Appointed American consul in Lyons by President U. S. Grant, he died in France while serving in this post. Wagoner's daughter, who was also well educated, lived in Denver and was a fixture in the city's "black society" for years after her father's death in 1902.[71]

The Wagoners and other black families who had emigrated to the Denver area during the gold rush and who had achieved success and respectability enjoyed the status of "pioneers," a designation that conferred prestige. Even those who later suffered financial reverses still occupied a place at the top of the black social hierarchy, as was the case of the Edward J. Sanderlin family. Born in New Orleans and heir to a sizable inheritance from his British father, Sanderlin settled in Denver in 1859. He owned a barbershop, invested wisely in real estate, and accumulated a substantial fortune by 1890. The loss of most of his wealth during the Panic of 1893 did not significantly affect the social standing of the Sanderlin family in Denver's black community.[72]

One of the best-known and wealthiest black residents who, according to Denver calculations, belonged among the "old families" was Barney Ford. A man of elegant demeanor and keen intellect, he was born a slave in Virginia. His mother was a house servant, and he was sold after the death of his mother and his master/father. Ford eventually escaped slavery and found his way to Chicago, where he became a friend of Wagoner, John Jones, and others active in the Underground Railroad. He married Julia A. Lyons, a native of Indiana and Wagoner's sister-in-law. After a brief residence in Central America, Barney Ford settled in Denver in 1860 and was soon joined by his wife and newborn son, Louis Napoleon Ford. Two other children, Sarah and Francis, were born to the couple. At one time or another, Ford was a barber, gold miner, restauranteur, banker, and hotel owner in both Denver and Cheyenne. Ford made and lost several fortunes but he died a man of considerable wealth in 1902. Among his most notable properties was the elegant Inter-Ocean Hotel in Denver's central business district.

Ford was active in a variety of political and civic movements and was for years an important figure in Republican politics in Colorado. Ford, Wagoner, and Edward J. Sanderlin constituted a black political triumvirate that led the fight to win full suffrage and other rights for blacks in Colorado. In fact, Ford traveled to Washington and remained there for some weeks as a lobbyist to ensure that the Colorado statehood legislation would not restrict the civil rights of blacks. In Denver he was a leader in efforts to educate newly arrived blacks, who settled in an area of the city known as the "Deep South," and in a number of other uplift causes.

The Fords purchased a large house in "the heart of Denver's choicest Capitol Hill residence district." Julia Ford was a gracious hostess, and their elegant residence was the scene of frequent receptions, teas, and dinners. Their most intimate social friends were the Wagoners, Sanderlins, and a few other well-to-do and highly respected black "pioneers." On occasion the Fords entertained the leading politicians of Colorado at social events that equaled any in Denver's "best society." Some white politicians even brought their wives to these dinners and receptions. In 1898, the year before her death, the name of Mrs. Barney L. Ford appeared in Denver's *Social Year Book,* an annual social register. While the Fords displayed pride in their Negro ancestry and were always identified as "race" people, they were also acutely conscious of their relations across the color line. In fact, Barney Ford maintained throughout his life an affection for his white half brother, Claiborne, whose poverty-stricken condition following the Civil War was a source of grave concern. At Claiborne's death, Ford paid the burial expenses.

The Fords sent their elder son, Louis, to Howard University and upon graduation set him up in the hotel business in Jefferson City, Missouri. The younger son, Francis, married a San Francisco "society belle" and lived in the Bay City. Their daughter, Sarah, received the attention of numerous suitors, including the son of Edward Sanderlin. She was on the verge of marrying a white man of prominence until he requested $40,000 of her father to compensate for his loss of status in marrying "a colored girl." Sarah ultimately married William H. A. Wormley, a member of one of the nation's most distinguished black families and whose father Ford had known during his sojourns in Washington. Julia and Barney Ford were present at their daughter's wedding in the "summer parlor of the famous Wormley Hotel" in 1892. It was "the social event" of the season for Washington's black aristocracy.[73]

By 1907, the upper class of Denver's black community included an assortment of professionals—seven physicians, two attorneys, two pharmacists—as well as several small entrepreneurs and government employees. Among the most socially prominent of these were P. E. Spratlin, a physician who was active in politics; J. W. Jackson, a shoe and boot dealer and a "political leader of Colorado Colored Republicans"; John R. Jackson, owner of a dyeing and cleaning business; Joseph H. Stuart, an attorney; Edwin H. Hackley, an attorney and municipal government employee; and Joseph D. D. Rivers, a real estate dealer, a proprietor of the *Colorado Statesman,* and a former student of Booker T. Washington at Hampton Institute. The wives of these men were likely to be members of the Booklovers, the Berkeley Art, or the Bon Vivant clubs. Both husbands and wives were members of the Eureka Literary Club, one of the oldest cultural organizations in Denver's black community. In boasting of the longevity of the club, one member declared in 1905, "It was once said of Denver as of a great many other cities of the West that no organization of an intellectual character could remain beyond the space of a year." The Eureka disproved such notions.[74]

While the vast majority of black church members in Denver attended one of the African Methodist Episcopal or Baptist churches in the city, most of the upper class were affiliated with small Methodist Episcopal, Presbyterian, or Protestant Episcopal congregations. The black Episcopal church, the Church of the Redeemer, which had 149 communicants by 1920, appears to have attracted a disproportionately large number of upper-class families and was generally considered the city's most exclusive black congregation.[75]

Among the communicants at the Church of the Redeemer were Edwin and Azalia Hackley from Detroit, who settled in Denver shortly after their marriage in 1894. Both were members of old upper-class families—"old Detroiters"—who were active in a variety of civil rights efforts. Hackley's family was one of the band of prosperous free families of color who emigrated to Michigan from Fredericksburg, Virginia before the Civil War. Hackley attended the University of Michigan, read law, was admitted to the bar, and served as a clerk in the county recorder's office in Detroit. In Denver, where he held a similar post and also practiced law, he was the only "colored member of the Michigan Alumni Association of Colorado." His wife, Azalia Smith Hackley, was the granddaughter of Wilson Beard, "a prominent Old Detroiter" whose associates and acquaintances included the Watsons, Pelhams, Fergusons, and others of the city's black upper class. In Detroit Azalia Hackley grew up "in an aristocratic neighborhood," where hers was the only black family. She graduated from the city's Central High School and from the normal school in Washington, after which she returned to Detroit and taught school. A talented vocalist who ultimately became famous as a professional singer under the name Madame E. Azalia Hackley, she was a member of Denver's leading white choral society. Conspicuous figures in the social life of Denver's black upper class, the Hackleys formed a Whist Club and entertained "their group" at parties and dances. The Hackleys separated in 1910. Edwin remained in Denver, while Azalia pursued her musical career in various parts of the United States and Europe. But as residents of Denver they demonstrated the extent to which members of the black upper class who moved west took with them the style, values, and views of social life drawn from older societies in the East.[76]

Those who made up the black upper class in the West tended to be less tradition-bound and less inclined to view themselves as "aristocrats" than did the "upper tens" in the East. While the upper class placed a premium on refinement and culture, high social standing was related more to wealth than to family background and formal education. Although extant black newspapers published in Western towns regularly included news about blacks in Washington, Philadelphia, and elsewhere in the East and took special note of the "social doings" of upper-class blacks in these places, they seldom if ever referred to the "crème de la crème" of local black society and rarely invoked the usual phrases to indicate one's place in the social hierarchy. Even more than the black press in the East and Midwest, these black journals spoke of status primarily in terms of individual effort and initiative, a version of the notion of the self-made man. The manifestation of "aristocratic instincts" and the life styles and values associated with such instincts were most evident among more-recent upper-class migrants, such as the Caytons in Seattle and the Hackleys in Denver. In time, of course, the term "pioneer family" in the West acquired a meaning and conferred a status roughly equivalent to that of "old family" in the East.

PART III

◆

Color, Culture, and Behavior

PROLOGUE

A STRIKINGLY HANDSOME COUPLE, Blanche and Josephine Bruce exemplified the culture, behavior, and life style of the nation's aristocrats of color. Exhibiting the decorum, dignity, and restraint characteristic of the polite society of which they were a part, they abided by the prevailing canons of proper etiquette and avoided ostentatious display. They held membership in a variety of high-status social clubs and racial uplift organizations, affiliated with what some called "high-tone" churches, and were sufficiently affluent to enjoy the amenities of life denied most blacks. Devoted to the cause of education, they insisted on a classical curriculum for their son but considered vocational education appropriate for the black masses. Despite their support of the educational efforts of Booker T. Washington and their cordial personal relationship with him, the Bruces never embraced the Tuskegee formula of race relations but remained committed to the concept of black equality, especially as applied to blacks of their own class. Their approach was that of conservative assimilation.

The Bruces were obviously aware of the acrimonious debate over the so-called color complex in the black community. Critics denounced what they claimed to be the practice of utilizing color as a major stratifier, with fairer-skinned Negroes occupying places at the top of the social scale and darker people those at the bottom. While it does not appear that either the senator or his wife addressed the color issue in public, they knew from first-hand knowledge and experience that color could and indeed did "cut considerable figure in grouping Negroes."[1]

Blanche Bruce was obviously a "mixed blood." Descriptions of him, especially by whites, rarely failed to mention his swarthy complexion and even his hair, which one observer described as "wavy but parted and brushed like a white man's." While the senator, by the nature of his position, appeared frequently before audiences of dark-skinned Negroes and was associated in an official way with blacks exhibiting an infinite variety of color, his social life was largely confined to those whose complexion was rarely darker, and often fairer, than his own. In 1884 he and his wife served as witnesses at the private wedding ceremony of Frederick Douglass and Helen Pitts, a graduate of Mount Holyoke

[141]

and a "plain, fortyish and efficient" white woman—a marriage that created outrage among blacks as well as whites. That the Bruces stood as witnesses meant that they did not share the disapproval voiced by the many blacks who viewed Douglass's act as one of racial treachery.[2]

On perhaps no other occasion did the light complexion of Josephine Bruce create more difficulties than in her work with the National Association of Colored Women. She aspired to be president of the organization, and at the biennial convention in Detroit in 1906 it appeared that she would realize her ambition. Rather suddenly, she, or rather her color, became the center of the only serious dispute at an otherwise harmonious convention, for opposition to her candidacy centered on the fairness of her skin. Not since she arrived in Washington in 1878 as the bride of Senator Bruce had it prompted so much public comment. A large contingent of delegates felt that she was unacceptable because "the predominance of her Caucasian blood caused her to be considered a white woman," and that would be harmful to an organization that prided itself on being "directed and controlled entirely by women of the colored race."[3] "We prefer," said one delegate, "a woman who is altogether a Negro, because, while the lighter women have been the greatest leaders and are among the most brilliant in the Association, their cleverness and ability is [sic] attributed to their white blood. We want to demonstrate that the African is as talented."[4]

The controversy stirred by Mrs. Bruce's complexion became the subject of news stories from Detroit entitled "Colorline in Woman's Convention." White reporters interpreted this incident as "a new phase of color discrimination" since Josephine Bruce encountered opposition "not because she was too black, but because she was too white." Deeply embarrassed by the whole episode, Josephine Bruce withdrew from contention for the presidency.[5]

The Bruces would undoubtedly have insisted that character and genteel conduct were infinitely more important than color. In their private and public lives they exhibited all the attributes of what Karen Halttunen has described as the genteel performance, "a system of polite conduct that demanded flawless self-discipline practiced with an apparently easy, natural sincere manner."[6] Both the senator and his wife according to all accounts, possessed "elegant manners" and all the attributes of "good breeding." Both were skilled in the art of conversation and practitioners of the most decorous behavior in public, marked by quiet dignity and politeness. They attached importance to proper dress that was conservative in taste and high in quality. In their manner of dress, as in their life style generally, the Bruces were not inclined toward conspicuous consumption.[7]

Like other aristocrats of color, Mrs. Bruce was most likely to exhibit emotion in the form of anger or disgust when she encountered breaches in the genteel performance by those who knew better. For example, she was dismayed by the way the family of her future daughter-in-law, Clara Burrill, "paraded the engagement."[8] In her view their behavior was simply a matter of bad taste and may well have accounted for her reluctance to approve the match.

Although Roscoe Bruce, the son of a United States senator and an honor graduate of Harvard, was obviously considered an ideal husband by the Burrill family, Clara subscribed to the same social code as did her future husband and his mother. She never equaled her mother-in-law in the practice of the genteel performance, but she shared many of the same social values and was no less concerned about proprieties and decorum. Like many aristocrats of color, Clara and her husband were disdainful of the materialism that they believed to be rampant among blacks as well as whites early in the twentieth century.[9] Nor did either Roscoe or Clara Bruce approve of people who made an ostentatious display of their wealth. Such behavior automatically placed such persons outside the "charmed circle" and among the vulgar. From clothing and jewelry to household furnishings, the Bruces preferred "pretty things, simple but elegant."[10]

Perhaps nothing was so indicative of one's degree of gentility as one's use of language. Any trace of what was called "dialect" placed one beyond the pale of polite black society. Despite the meagerness of his formal education, Senator Bruce possessed the vocabulary and language skills of an educated man. His wife not only was a gifted conversationalist, public speaker, and writer but also read French.[11] Their son and daughter-in-law, both of whom enjoyed educational opportunities open to few Americans, regardless of race, were always conscious of correct usage of language. Clara Bruce, on first meeting George Washington Carver at Tuskegee, was appalled to hear him say, "he don't."[12]

Throughout their residence in Washington both generations of Bruces were active in a variety of clubs and voluntary organizations. In addition to being identified with Republican party organizations, the senator figured prominently in several highly selective gentleman's clubs. Because of the prestige that Bruce enjoyed as a senator and as Register of the Treasury and Recorder of Deeds, social as well as philanthropic organizations eagerly sought to have his name associated with their cause. The presence of the Bruces at a purely social function or charity benefit was indisputable evidence that it was an upper-class affair.

Both before and after the death of her husband, Josephine Bruce took an active part in the civic and club life of Washington's black community. In 1892 she was among the female aristocrats of color who founded the Colored Women's League, which sponsored a variety of activities to aid the disadvantaged of their race. After the League merged with similar organizations elsewhere to form the National Association of Colored Women, Josephine Bruce became a prominent figure in a nationwide federation of black women's clubs. In the years following the death of her husband in 1898, "Mrs. Senator Bruce" was almost invariably described as "a woman prominent in club affairs."[13]

Like most of those who belonged to their social circle, the Bruces were keenly interested in education. While the senator had relatively little formal schooling, he read widely and avidly throughout his life. According to a journalist who was often critical of upper-class blacks, Blanche Bruce was not only an "exceptionally cultured and refined man" but also "better read than most men of his class."[14] In his lectures to black audiences throughout the United States Bruce emphasized the critical importance of education in promoting the "progress of the race."

Josephine Bruce was reared in a home in which art, music, and literature received much attention. Following her graduation from Cleveland's Central High School in 1871, she took "the short course required of teachers" and secured a position at Mayflower School, one of the city's public elementary schools.[15] Although she abandoned teaching following her marriage, Josephine Bruce continued to have a keen interest in black education. She and several other socially prominent women in Washington organized a campaign to establish a vocational or industrial high school for blacks in the District. Such a school was designed not for their children but for those of the less fortunate classes. Her experience at Tuskegee following her husband's death appears to have reinforced her commitment to industrial education as the most appropriate solution to the problem of educating the black masses.[16]

The Bruces provided their only child, Roscoe, with all the educational and cultural advantages enjoyed by upper-class Americans, regardless of race. He grew up in a home that bore all the attributes of culture and refinement and attended Washington's famous M Street High School, whose high academic standards attracted the children of aristocrats of color not merely from the District but from other parts of the United States as well. Following his graduation from Phillips Exeter Academy, he entered Harvard College and graduated with honors in 1902. The following year he married Clara Burrill, who was also a graduate of the M Street School and who had attended Radcliffe College. She was, according to one observer, "quite as cultured as her distinguished husband."[17]

Booker T. Washington, who no doubt was fully aware of the prestige attached to the Bruce name and the Harvard degree, persuaded Roscoe to head the academic department at Tuskegee, where he remained from 1902 until 1906. Bruce assisted Washington in a thorough revision of the curriculum through a process known as "correlating" or "dovetailing." To obliterate "differences between the literary department and the industrial department," the revised curriculum required the practice of mathematics in carpentry classes and the writing of essays on plowing or other agricultural subjects in English courses. Although Bruce was at first Washington's principal agent in implementing the new curriculum, he became convinced that it was leading to a steady erosion of the academic component of the school. Regardless of differences that developed between them, Bruce remained on friendly terms with Washington.[18] In 1906 he returned to Washington as principal of one of the Negro public schools. The following year he became assistant superintendent in charge of Negro schools in the District of Columbia, a coveted post that he secured with the aid of Booker T. Washington and held for fifteen years.[19]

The religious life of the Bruce family was, in many respects, typical of that of the aristocrats of color with whom they associated socially. They attended church, but it was not the institution around which their lives revolved. The denominations with which they were identified engaged in formal and liturgical worship and were generally perceived as high-status churches. As a major political figure, Blanche Bruce considered it appropriate to appear frequently before numerous black religious organizations and to attend Sunday worship at various black churches. There is little to suggest that he was especially devout or possessed a deep attachment to a particular creed or faith. Although Bruce joined a group of his close friends in organizing a Congregational church in Washington two years before his death, he was also identified with the Episcopal church during his residence in the city, largely because of his wife's influence. His funeral, in 1898, was perhaps indicative of his ecumenical approach to religion. It was held in the huge sanctuary of the Metropolitan A.M.E. Church in Washington to accommodate the large crowd. Sterling Brown, minister of the Congregational church that Bruce assisted in establishing, presided, while ministers of the Episcopal, Presbyterian, Baptist, and A.M.E. churches participated in the funeral service.[20]

Throughout her life Josephine Bruce remained attached to the Episcopal church, in which she had been reared, although she later joined her husband's Congregational church.[21] In the late 1880s, when the Bruces lived in Indianapolis for eighteen months, they joined Saint Paul's Episcopal Church, a white church, where Mrs. Bruce's sisters, Mary and Victoria Wilson, teachers in the city's public schools, were members.

The decision of the Bruces to attend a white church prompted some blacks to question why a former senator from Mississippi who claimed to be a spokesman for Afro-Americans found no black church in the city to his liking. A well-known black citizen of Indianapolis later claimed that Bruce and his wife "alienated many colored people here" because they did "not go to hear a colored preacher in a church attended by colored people."[22] Other prominent blacks, who identified with predominantly white denominations, such as Congregational, Presbyterian, and Methodist Episcopal churches, encountered similar complaints.

Roscoe and Clara Bruce, like the elder Bruces, found the emotional religion practiced in many black churches distasteful. During a visit to Tuskegee in 1902 before he joined the faculty, Roscoe Bruce likened a revival being conducted on campus to "a reversion to barbarism." "The antics of the preacher and the students," he declared, "were disgusting. Such nonsense ought to be stopped at once. I for one shall never attend such a performance again."[23]

Even though Blanche and Josephine Bruce, as well as their son and daughter-in-law, participated in a variety of racial uplift causes, they scarcely belonged among the vanguard of the civil rights activists of their generation. Neither the senator nor his wife had experienced the bitter realities of slavery or the frustrations of the common freedman. Their encounters with social rebuffs and indignities were relatively few. As a result, the Bruces, like others of their class, viewed the plight of the black masses from a distance. White conservatives in Mississippi liked the senator precisely because he was a "man of moderation and integrity without brilliance or force."[24]

Blanche Bruce and his wife early moved into the circle of Booker T. Washington, whose influence spread rapidly following his Atlanta Compromise speech in 1895. Five years earlier, Washington had invited the ex-senator from Mississippi to deliver the commencement address at Tuskegee.[25] Profoundly impressed by what he observed at Washington's school during this visit, Bruce became an enthusiastic advocate of industrial education as suitable for the educational needs of the black masses.

While Bruce's support of Washington's educational endeavor lent prestige to the Tuskegee idea of education, Washington's alliance with the senator had its advantages for the Bruces. Bruce enlisted Washington's support in obtaining a political appointment in the McKinley administration and in securing the admission of his son, Roscoe, to Harvard. All the while, Josephine Bruce and Washington's wife worked closely in launching the National Association of Colored Women.[26]

While Roscoe Bruce remained on cordial terms with Booker T. Washington until the latter's death in 1915, he was also an early member of the National Association for the Advancement of Colored People, which the Tuskegeean viewed as an enemy and sought to undermine. In a sense Bruce, not unlike other upper-class blacks, became a casualty of his attempt to embrace two movements, one symbolized by Washington and the other by W. E. B. Du Bois. Part of his problem as head of the black schools in the District, according to one critic, was his effort "to please everybody" or at least to please two ideologically antagonistic factions in the black community.[27]

Such a stance sprang from a basic ambivalence which Bruce shared with many of his upper-class associates. They embraced Du Bois's concept of the "Talented Tenth" and its implications, but, at the same time, they recognized and even admired the contributions of Booker T. Washington to the uplift of the black masses. An outspoken advocate of industrial education for the black majority, Bruce considered such a curriculum inappropriate for the elite, especially for his own children, who attended prestigious preparatory schools and liberal arts institutions.[28] Though constantly reminded of racial barriers and restricted in career opportunities by their racial identities, Bruce and those of comparable status in the black community were reluctant to abandon the idea that blacks, especially educated and genteel blacks like themselves, would be assimilated into the larger society. They never doubted that they were indeed different from other blacks. "It is," Bruce's mother observed figuratively in 1902, "the several thousand years of development that makes the difference."[29]

As did others of his associates, Roscoe Bruce tended to think of himself in class, rather than racial, terms. That his son, Blanche and Josephine Bruce's grandson, shared such a perception was abundantly evident in a letter he wrote to his mother about sending Roscoe, Jr., to Exeter. "O, about Exeter, you know mama, little Bubsie [Roscoe, Jr.] would have no trouble of a racial character at all with those boys. They would never in the world *think* of him that way; he doesn't think of himself that way."[30] Young Bruce may not have thought of himself within a racial context or may not have encountered any problems of a racial character among those "fine, clear-eyed, clean-souled New Englanders" at Exeter, but his race assumed great importance when he applied for a dormitory room at Harvard, his father's alma mater.

Bruce's attempt to reserve a room for his son in the freshman dormitory at Cambridge was personally denied by President A. Lawrence Lowell. "I am sorry to tell you," Lowell wrote, "that on the Freshman Halls, where residence is compulsory, we have felt the necessity of not including colored men." In a lengthy reply, Bruce expressed disappointment and dismay that his alma mater had inaugurated such a discriminatory policy, which diverged so sharply from that existing during his days as an undergraduate. "Few words in the English language, I submit," Bruce wrote, "are susceptible of more poignant abuse than the two you have seen fit to employ. The first is 'race'; the second 'necessity.' As the one is often nothing more than a term of social convenience, so the other is quite as often a means to buttress prejudice. But, *Veritas* is less elusive." Bruce concluded by informing Lowell that "no son of mine will ever deny his name or his blood or his tradition" in order to enter Harvard. For Bruce, the "basis of sound nationality" was not race but culture.[31]

The publication of the Bruce-Lowell correspondence in the daily press touched off a storm of protest. Although interviews with Harvard students indicated that they were sharply divided on what came to be known as Harvard's "Negro exclusion policy," the alumni bulletin opposed it as did numerous alumni who interpreted Lowell's action as "an ominous departure from Harvard traditions." James Weldon Johnson of the NAACP lodged a strong protest against Harvard's "Negro policy," describing it as nothing more than "putting into effect the program proclaimed by the notorious Ku Klux Klan." Even though Lowell at one point admitted that he felt like "Saint Sebastian, stuck full of arrows which people are firing at me," he refused to alter his position regarding the exclusion of blacks from Harvard's freshman dormitories.[32]

Roscoe Bruce had rarely confronted such overt racial discrimination as that involved in the Harvard incident. It was all the more devastating because it affected his son. An upper-class black man who took great pride in his Harvard education and refinement, Bruce had, like others of his class, viewed himself as a cultural broker who spoke to blacks and for blacks to whites. Intimately acquainted with the culture of both races, Bruce had for most of his career functioned as a carrier of white culture into the black community. The refusal of his alma mater to extend to his son the same privileges that he had enjoyed twenty years earlier undoubtedly prompted him, as similar incidents did others of the upper class, to reassess his traditional place and role in a biracial society. As a result, their roles as cultural brokers underwent subtle changes, prompting a closer identity with and appreciation of black culture. Like Bruce, they tended to find greater significance in their black heritage—in their name, blood, and traditions as Afro-Americans.

33. Officers of the New York Society for Mutual Relief, one of the most prestigious organizations in New York's black community in the late nineteenth and early twentieth centuries.

34. Joan Imogene Howard, well-known educator, the sister of Dr. Edwin Clarence Howard.

35. Joseph Lee, a wealthy Boston caterer, inventor of a bread-making machine.

36. Mrs. George W. Forbes. She and her husband were associated with the militant *Boston Guardian*.

37. J. H. Lewis, merchant tailor in Boston; his family was socially prominent in the city's black community.

38. Daniel Hale Williams, physician and surgeon in Washington and Chicago.

39. Alice Johnson Williams, a schoolteacher in Washington until her marriage to Dr. Daniel Hale Williams in 1898. *Courtesy Moorland-Spingarn Research Center, Howard University.*

40. George A. Myers, prominent barber, businessman, and politician in Cleveland.

41. John P. Green—attorney, politician, and civil servant—whose family was considered a part of the black upper crust in Cleveland.

42. Fannie Barrier Williams, schoolteacher and clubwoman, the wife of attorney S. Laing Williams of Chicago.

43. Charles H. Smiley's Catering Establishment, Chicago, established in 1883.

44. Cyrus Field Adams, civil servant and newspaper publisher in the Midwest.

45. Charles W. Chesnutt, writer and novelist, resided in Cleveland, where his family belonged to the black upper class.

46. Robert C. Owens, a wealthy businessman in Los Angeles and a member of one of the "pioneer" black families.

47. "Why Not Welcome Him"—a front-page cartoon in *The Freeman* of Indianapolis.

48. E. Azalia Hackley, famous Afro-American singer and music teacher who performed on several continents.

49. Home of George A. Myers, Cleveland.

50. "Hillside Cottage," Washington, D.C., home of Mr. and Mrs. John Mercer Langston.

51. Samuel Coleridge-Taylor, a world-famous, Afro-British composer who enjoyed great popularity among aristocrats of color in the United States.

52. The 1914 Bachelor-Benedict Assembly of New York, an elite social function typical of those held by aristocrats of color in large cities. *Courtesy of* The Crisis.

53. "Ideal Afro-American Lady of the Day," which appeared in *The Freeman* of Indianapolis, was a typical newspaper article of the time.

54. Mary Church Terrell—clubwoman, lecturer, and civil-rights advocate—was the daughter of Robert R. Church of Memphis and the wife of Judge Robert H. Terrell of Washington.

MRS. HELEN A. COOK.

55. Helen Appo Cook, clubwoman, was the wife of John Francis Cook, Jr., scion of one of Washington's best-known and most-prestigious black families.

56. John Hope, a native of Augusta, Georgia, was president of Atlanta Baptist College (Morehouse) and later headed Atlanta University.

57. Spelman Seminary, founded in 1881 in Atlanta, Georgia, claimed to be the first college for Afro-American women in the United States.

58. Henry Hugh Proctor, minister of the First Congregational Church in Atlanta from 1894 to 1920.

59. Sterling N. Brown, a Congregational minister in Washington, D.C., for many years.

60. George F. Bragg, Jr., author and editor, was minister of St. James Protestant Episcopal Church in Baltimore from 1891 to 1940.

61. Francis J. Grimké, a graduate of Princeton Theological Seminary, served for almost a half century as pastor of the prestigious Fifteenth Street Presbyterian Church in Washington.

62. Owen Meredith Waller, an Episcopal clergyman, was a founder of the NAACP.

63. John H. Dorsey (1873–1926), Catholic clergyman and a native of Baltimore, served parishes throughout the South.

64. W. E. B. Du Bois, scholar and civil-rights activist with whom many aristocrats of color identified in the struggle for equality and justice.

6

◆

The Color Factor

PERHAPS AS CLEARLY AS ANY OTHER SCHOLAR, E. Franklin Frazier, in his 1939 classic work on the Negro family, appreciated the complexities involved in the role of the color scale as a stratifier in the black community and warned against "the tendency to oversimplify the problem." Frazier granted that a light complexion was a factor in gaining admission to the upper class, but he was also aware that its significance as a stratifier varied from place to place. More important, he viewed color as an indication of other factors, such as opportunity, acculturation, education, and wealth.[1] More-recent scholars who have studied the importance of complexional differences among blacks, tend to corroborate Frazier's interpretation. John G. Mencke, in his study of mulattoes and race mixture in the United States, argued that "the Afro-American community has in fact always been characterized by conspicuous social stratification in which color plays a significant although not determinant role in affixing an individual's status." In a similar vein, Thomas Holt, in his investigation of black political leadership in Reconstruction South Carolina, spoke of color as essentially "an indicator of a whole complex of interrelated variables" that determined one's place in the class structure.[2]

In the early twentieth century, white Americans generally came to embrace what was known as the "one drop rule," by which a person with even a minuscule amount of Negro blood was classified as a Negro and therefore subjected to all the proscriptions, legal and otherwise, imposed upon black people. Theirs was the perspective of a two-caste system, Negro and Caucasian, rather than a three-caste system which recognized mixed bloods and which existed in various parts of the world, including the West Indies and Latin America. In the United States, therefore, the person of white-African ancestry constituted what has been called an "American anomaly." Described by such terms as "marginal," "tragic," and "mongrel," the mulatto was visible evidence of racial mixing and a contradiction of white notions of racial purity.

From the end of Reconstruction to the First World War, the mulatto was an object of considerable fascination for whites, as was evident from the sizable body of scholarly and popular literature devoted to the topic. Whites tended to view mulattoes as more intelligent than blacks but not the equal of Caucasians. Because mulattoes were intellectually superior to blacks, with whom they were racially grouped, they were leaders in every line of activity undertaken by Negroes. On the negative side, whites believed that "mixed bloods" were hybrids, morally weak, and physically degenerate. Furthermore, they were "stirrers-up of strife," constantly demanding greater rights and privileges for themselves and awakening false aspirations among the black masses. For white Americans the mulatto was a black person, regardless of his or her Caucasian appearance, because as Mencke has noted, "popular understanding of the meaning of race left no room for someone in-between."[3]

During the first decade of the twentieth century, as the Mississippi Way in race relations increasingly became the American Way, some whites did ponder the wisdom of a three-caste system that provided a place for the mulatto "in-between" blacks and whites. Alfred Holt Stone, a Mississippi planter who gained a considerable reputation as an authority on the race problem, addressed the issue of the "mulatto factor" and appeared to be inclined to recognize mixed-bloods as a separate caste, neither black nor white, such as existed in the West Indies. Stone subscribed to most of the popular conceptions of mulattoes, including the notion that they were the real leaders of the Negro race. Free of mulatto or white influence, he argued, the mass of blacks were "docile, tractable and unambitious," totally indifferent to possessing the franchise and to achieving "social equality." Stone's interest in a three-tier caste system, therefore, appears to have been prompted at least in part by his desire to isolate the mulattoes and to relieve blacks of their "harmful" influence.[4]

Two other whites acquainted with blacks through their work with religious organizations concluded that mixed-bloods were moving toward the organization of a separate caste. Writing in 1909, H. Paul Douglass, who described the mulatto elite as the "emerged class" of blacks, applauded their success in developing "manifold organs of social control" and in attaining "a magnificent place of leadership over the general negro mass." According to Douglass, "one of the most fateful questions for the American negro" was whether the mulatto would "attempt to regard itself as an intermediate race between white and black" or continue to accept identification with the black race, to which white sentiment assigned it. "This is the deepest issue within the higher negro classes today," he concluded. "Upon this issue race leaders are divided. . . ."[5]

Mary Helm, like Douglass, was sympathetic to the plight of blacks, but revealed more directly than he the degree to which she accepted the popular notions of whites in regard to mulattoes. She was emphatic in her conviction that "mixed bloods" constituted the vast majority of those in the black aristocracy. In fact she believed that "class distinctions based on color" within the black community were "drawing apart the mixed blood from the full-blooded Negro." The "drawing apart," she observed, was becoming increasingly evident in both social and religious life. She argued that a major reason for the separation was directly related to the fact that Negroes who continued their education beyond the common school were "the mulattoes, quadroons and octoroons." In the natural selection process they proved themselves "mentally fit to survive."[6] Helm pronounced "the social drawing away of the higher class from the masses" as detrimental to the race and condemned the color factor involved in making class distinctions.[7] The inclusion of so many mixed bloods in "upper-tendom," she concluded, seemed to place a "premium . . . on amalgamation resulting from immorality."[8]

By the time Helm, Douglass, Stone, and others were writing, the establishment of a separate mulatto caste in American society was probably less likely than ever before. By the early twentieth century the color line had become more rigid and the "one drop rule" was being applied more inflexibly. Historian Joel Williamson delineates the years from 1850 to 1915 as the time of a "grand transition in race relations," an era in which white America moved from a position of overlooking "some blackness in a person" to one of classifying persons known to possess one "iota of color" as black. He maintains that it was also a period when the mulatto elite effected an engagement with the black masses that profoundly influenced the future of both blacks and whites in America.[9] But the establishment of that engagement was a long and often bitter process that had not been completed by 1915.

Few issues were more emotion-laden in the black community than those relating to the color prejudices and preferences of blacks themselves. While whites drew a single color line between themselves and blacks, multiple color lines allegedly existed in the black community. Those accused of placing a premium on a fair complexion became the targets of bitter criticism by those, usually of a darker hue, who denounced such color consciousness as a major impediment to the "progress of the race."

Although Lura Beam, a white teacher in black schools in the South between 1908 and 1919, fully understood that class distinctions in the black community rested on factors other than complexional differences, her experiences with black students led her to observe that "color appeared mysteriously in everything," especially in the selection of friends and spouses. She recounts the story of a well-educated young black man who was an applicant for a principal-ship of an American Missionary Association school but who, regardless of his qualifications, realized that he was "too black" and that the job would go to one of lighter complexion. According to Beam, a "very dark stranger" even if he were well educated by the standards of the day, would not have been accepted "by the aristocracy in the circles I knew," but if he possessed a doctoral degree from a prestigious northern university "adjustments would be made."[10]

The prevasiveness of color gradations in the black community, not only in the South, was evident in political contests, educational and church affairs, and other areas as well as in social relationships. In Washington the Negro public schools became embroiled in the late 1890s in a "controversy between the 'yellow' and 'black' contingents" when the latter challenged the traditional control exercised by the fair-complexioned elite. In Cleveland, as elsewhere, "blue veinism" was a charge made against the mulatto political leaders. The black press made much of the so-called color line within the Colored Methodist Church in 1910 during the election of an additional bishop. "On the bench of bishops," a West Virginia black weekly editorialized, "there is now but one of the dark hue, all the others being mulattoes, quadroons or octoroons." So, the issue confronting the church, according to critics, was whether to choose a black man for bishop or to continue adhering to its self-imposed color line.[11]

In the late nineteenth and early twentieth centuries, blacks who were most vocal in regard to color gradations in the Negro community devoted special attention to the fair-complexioned upper class. They might vehemently deny that mulattoes were intellectually superior to blacks, but they accepted and embellished upon other aspects of white notions about "mixed-bloods": they emphasized that mulattoes were physically weak hybrids, the progeny of "lower-class" white men, and were the mischief makers in the black community. They claimed that these "few puny colored exquisites"[12] were largely responsible for the concern with color. Most of the direct testimony about the color conscious-ness of black aristocrats came largely from sources outside the old upper class, usually from darker-skinned individuals, rather than from those who allegedly drew the color line against dark members of the race. Because these critics usually couched their accusations in general rather than specific terms, it was often difficult to ascertain whether they were referring to "authentic" aristocrats or to socially ambitious individuals of light complexion whom they sometimes confused with those at the top of the social scale.

Regardless of the group to which they had reference, critics blamed the fair-skinned upper class for the existence of a scale of color among Negroes that perverted the whole system of social stratification. It mattered not, so the argument ran, how cultured, educated, or rich dark-complexioned individuals might be, they were not likely to gain entrance into the ranks of the "upper tens."[13] If they did, their chances of remaining members in good standing were, at best, slim. According to a character in a novel by Sutton Griggs in 1901, "if you are black and don't work with your hands and are smarter than the whole lot of them blue-veiners put together, you will be accepted until they get something on you."[14] On the contrary, a light-complexioned Negro with minimum quali-fications, or qualifications substantially less impressive than those of a black person, was readily accepted into the ranks of the social elite. Personal character and worth were factors of little or no importance in gaining admission to the upper class.[15]

Convinced that this class did indeed place a premium on a fair skin and Caucasian features, critics characterized socially prominent mulattoes as "would-be whites" who, despite being scorned by whites, nevertheless were willing to ape all the vices and none of the virtues of the aristocracy of the dominant race. In the process these "codfish aristocrats" of color functioned as divisive forces in the black community at a time when unity was most needed to combat racial oppression. Although critics of the fair-skinned elite were genuinely concerned about racial pride and solidarity, their rhetoric also revealed envy and jealousy.[16]

On occasion, color became a useful weapon in challenging the social elite for positions of leadership in the black community. Some raised the issue merely to besmirch the reputation of a social club to which they, for whatever reason, had failed to gain admission. Notwithstanding the warning from T. Thomas Fortune that protests directed by blacks at mulattoes would hasten the establishment of a separate caste and thereby rob Negroes of a valuable link with the white world, the barrage of criticism continued through the First World War.[17]

Indisputably, the overwhelming majority of aristocrats of color were indeed mixed-bloods ranging in color from light brown or "yellow" to virtually white. Their appearance was obviously an advantage in a society that placed the highest premium on a white skin. Because whites preferred their Caucasian features and considered them more intelligent than blacks, mulattoes had greater opportunities, especially in securing jobs. But if the advertisements for skin bleaches and hair straighteners that filled the pages of black newspapers were any indication, blacks of all shades and classes admired and aspired to white standards. "The whites," as one black writer declared in 1901, "regulate all of our tastes. . . ."[18]

Critics often conveyed the impression that color alone underlay social stratification among Afro-Americans and that the possession of a fair skin was sufficient to assure one a place at the top of the class structure. But even those blacks most inclined to make such charges knew better, because they were well aware that relatively few of the several million mixed-bloods belonged to the "upper tendom." Even the illiterate, fair-complexioned Negro man who wandered into St. Mark's Church in Charleston in 1866 and who was, by Roi Ottley's definition, a "nameless mulatto nobody," was sufficiently perceptive to appreciate that his light skin alone did not qualify him for intimate association with the city's aristocrats of color.[19]

Nevertheless, critics railed about the "blue veinism," a reference to a skin light enough to reveal one's blue veins, that was allegedly rampant among those who claimed to constitute the elite of black society. Their war on this form of colorphobia became increasingly shrill with the triumphal march of Jim Crowism after 1890, because it thwarted the racial unity and solidarity that the crisis demanded. The social distance that the light-complexioned upper class had traditionally placed between itself and other blacks tended, under the deteriorating racial climate, to confirm the suspicion of dark-skinned critics that their preoccupation with a light skin color was the cause of this obnoxious practice. Social distance allegedly based on a light skin easily became translated into charges that the elite possessed an acute case of "white fever" and was intent upon transforming itself into a separate caste that would win immunity to the proscriptions being placed on all Negroes.

While some black observers regularly pronounced the impending demise of blue-veinism, others were no less convinced that the "disease" was spreading. Nannie H. Burroughs, a highly articulate dark-skinned woman, publicly denounced the color consciousness of the same class. "Many Negroes," she wrote in 1904, "have colorphobia as badly as the white folks have Negrophobia." "Some Negro men have it [colorphobia]. Some Negro women have it. Whole families have it, and . . . some Negro churches have it. . . ." Among the evidence Burroughs cited to prove that colorphobia was spreading even among darker-skinned Negroes were their preference for light-skinned individuals as marriage partners and their increasing use of face bleaches and hair strighteners. "The white man who crosses the line and leaves an heir," she acidly concluded, "is doing a favor for some black man who would marry the most debased woman, whose only stock in trade is her color, in preference to the most royal queen in ebony."[20]

Nannie Burroughs was not alone in believing that color consciousness among Negroes was seriously retarding the progress of the race. A black editor in Pine Bluff, Arkansas insisted that there was "no use talking about the color prejudice of white folks" because it could "not equal the color prejudice among colored folks," for no one would call a dark-skinned man "a 'nigger' so quickly as a light-colored dude."[21] Speaking to the annual convention of the Ohio Federation of Afro-American Women's Clubs in 1902, Sarah Mitchell, a public school teacher, denounced the prevalence of blue-veinism for its disruptive impact on the black community. Fair-complexioned Negroes, she argued, claimed "special consideration of the white factor because they have so small a fractional part of Negro blood," while whites were all too ready to credit the achievements of such people to the predominance of their white blood.[22]

Four years later, in making a plea for racial unity, a writer in the *Colored American Magazine* maintained that the most serious obstacle to its achievement was the system of color "caste" that had developed among Negroes. "We," he observed, "have the blacks despising the lights, since they represent neither one thing nor the other, and the lights priding themselves on their white origins and straight hair. Here is where the trouble begins."[23] In 1910, the preoccupation with color, quality of hair, and other Caucasian features prompted W. A. Majors, a dark-skinned physician, to insist that "every Negro should be dark of complexion" and that those who were not should be regarded as suffering a great misfortune.[24]

Although Edward E. Wilson, a black attorney in Chicago, conceded that color was still a troublesome issue in 1909, he remained convinced that it was a problem that, if left alone, would resolve itself. The "light skins," he argued, could never "form a Negro aristocracy" because they were relatively small in number and because they would not be able to win the support of "a sufficient portion of the Negro intelligence and wealth to give them the force of an aristocracy." Their efforts to get themselves considered a third caste somewhere between whites and blacks was even less likely, because of adherence by whites to the "one drop rule." But according to Wilson, the greatest single deterrent to "light skins" forming an aristocracy lay in their lack of unity. Some stood aloof from and poked fun at their darker brethren while others were among "the staunchest Negroes." At any rate, he claimed that color alone was too artificial a factor on which to build class distinctions. Far more important was education, and with the emergence of a sufficiently large educated or professional class would come a sound basis for social stratification.[25]

But whether critics of color gradations in the black community claimed that the phenomenon was increasing or declining, they were usually quick to challenge claims that mulattoes were intellectually superior to blacks and to offer evidence to the contrary. Among the dark-skinned Negroes regularly cited as proof that the "full-blooded Negro" was the intellectual equal of either whites or mulattoes were Kelly Miller, an erudite professor at Howard; the poet Paul Laurence Dunbar; and William Pickens, an educator who became field secretary of the NAACP in 1920. "The superior race," the Colored American said of Miller, "cannot claim that it has imparted to him any of its powers and gifts."[26]

When a New York Times correspondent claimed that the Negro Building at the 1907 Jamestown Exhibit was actually the work of mulattoes, the black press was quick to denounce the story as "simply another effort of the white man to discredit Negro intelligence." It suggested that the writer confer with Giles B. Jackson of Richmond, Virginia, the father of the Negro enterprise at the Exhibit, because he could "never be mistaken for a mulatto." The whole issue of pure-blood Negroes versus mulattoes was, in the view of the Colored American Magazine, a false one, because "the white man has mixed with us so thoroughly that there are but few full-blooded Negroes left."[27]

Aristocrats of color in almost any city with a sizable population were likely, at one time or another, to become the targets of criticism for their color consciousness. The frequency and intensity of such criticism depended on various factors. Thus, the presence of a large population of West Indian blacks, as in New York and other cities on the eastern seaboard, was likely to accentuate the importance of complexional differences.[28] The attitude of the local black newspapers regarding color gradations among Negroes figured significantly in whether the question became the focus of public discussion. Some refused to become a medium for airing complaints against "blue veinism."[29] Others, such as editors in Washington and Atlanta, kept up a steady barrage of criticism against upper-class blacks, who they believed exhibited a colorphobia more severe than that of whites. Because New Orleans probably came as near as any city to a three-tier caste system, it might be expected to figure significantly in the public debate over color and class, but such was not the case. Blacks as well as whites seemed to agree that the city was unique. Its "peculiar social system," while at once fascinating and puzzling, was viewed as largely irrelevant to that existing elsewhere in the country.

The city of Charleston perhaps served the longest as a reference point for those critical of a color gradation among Negroes. Often cited in this connection were two organizations among free people of color: the Brown Fellowship Society, established in 1790 and confined to light-skinned "free brown men" and their descendants; and the Society of Free Dark Men. A white visitor to Charleston observed in 1847 that what impressed him "as very singular, indeed, was the fact that *blacks* and *mulattoes* did not sit together" in church.[30] But more significant was the role of color in determining the legal "distinctions between citizen and denizen" in South Carolina. Light-complexioned mulattoes apparently had a greater chance of acquiring citizenship than did darker people. In post–Civil War Charleston, according to one scholar, the mulatto aristocrats continued to value their "light complexions as symbols of their privileged positions."[31]

Whatever the role of color in determining status among free people of color in antebellum Charleston, the city's mulatto elite and its history continued, for several generations after the Civil War, to be cited as a prime example of the mischief created by color gradations among blacks. Some claimed that its persistence in the postwar era seriously retarded the "progress of the race" in the city. The old mulatto upper class in Charleston, in Lura Beam's words, "looked into its own mirror, and reveled in a past in which their grandparents owned slaves, Sheraton and Hepplewhite furniture, heavy silver tea services, portraits painted by itinerant artists, and plots in the cemetery for the fair skinned caste." In a world rapidly disappearing, the mulatto aristocrats of the "city by the sea" held tenaciously to forms that tolerated "no black teacher, no black friend, no black graveyard."[32] In 1896 a black native of Charleston, who was well acquainted with its old upper class, recalled that "two of the prime requisites for entrance into the so-called best society were a light complexion and 'good hair,' " and that a Negro "who was light was taught to feel, in consequence of that fact, that he was better than the man who was dark."[33]

Seven years later, in 1903, John E. Bruce, a well-known black journalist, castigated Charleston Negroes for persisting in "drawing the color line among themselves." A black woman of Charleston, agreeing that a color line existed among the city's black population, asserted, "Charleston had two segregations." The ubiquitous "color business" not only retarded black economic development in the city, she observed, but also "mixed up some of the children and teachers at Avery," the American Missionary Association school. Even more critical was Kelly Miller, a South Carolina native and professor at Howard University who had never been a part of Charleston's mulatto elite. Miller claimed that Emancipation destroyed the world created by a small band of fair-complexioned free blacks in Charleston who relished their place in society above the slaves and below the whites. Despite the changes wrought by Emancipation and Recon-struction, they still possessed their color "conceit."[34]

The influence that may have been exerted by members and descendants of Charleston's mulatto elite in establishing and perpetuating this "conceit" else-where is difficult if not impossible to ascertain. What is certain is that a substantial number of those who were identified with the city's old upper-class families and grew up in a color-conscious environment achieved social promi-nence in Washington, Philadelphia, and New York. Some, such as Francis J. Grimké, who was minister of the elite Fifteenth Street Presbyterian Church in Washington, forthrightly rejected the idea of color gradations among blacks. Others, such as various members of the Cardozo family, were closely identified with groups and social organizations that were regularly accused of "colorpho-bia."[35]

In his study of blacks in five southern cities—Atlanta, Montgomery, Nash-ville, Raleigh, and Richmond—between 1865 and 1890, Howard Rabinowitz concludes that little evidence existed to indicate that color conferred special status in these black communities. He suggests that wealth and cultural attri-butes were more significant than color in gaining admission to the upper class. When in 1889 news spread that some light-skinned Negroes had formed a Blue Vein Society in Nashville, a well-known minister publicly attacked the organ-ization, which "evidently did not become an important factor in Negro life" there. Later, in the two decades after 1890, "blue veinism" in Nashville seemed to have been more a topic of whispered conversation than public discussion. But for many years the city's elite black church, First Congregational, was known as the "blue vein" church, or as the "B.V. church."[36] Elsewhere in Tennessee, in the small town of McMinnville, a black resident reported in 1893 that while the "blue vein" element was present there it was not sufficiently "a pest to make the thoroughbred African feel uncomfortable on account of his color, although most of the Negroes [here] are of Caucasian extraction."[37]

While the old families of Baltimore's black community tended to be fair-complexioned, color does not appear to have played the significant role that it did in some other cities. The linking of color and class was not a subject that found its way into published accounts of the city's social life, either in the local press or in other journals that occasionally reported on its "society happenings." Unlike Cleveland, Cincinnati, and especially nearby Washington, where the *Bee* regularly held forth on the "blue veinism" evident in "the 400," Baltimore's best-known and most-respected black newspaper, *The Afro-American Ledger*, omitted references to complexion and forthrightly stated that it took "little stock in the nasty business of color." The *Ledger,* in fact, reminded its readers that historically it had been blacks, such as Toussaint L'Ouverture, rather than mulattoes who had been leaders of movements for Negro freedom.[38]

In the old free black communities of Savannah and Augusta, the color consciousness of the mulatto elite more closely resembled that in Charleston. The dark-skinned Robert Abbott, who grew up in the vicinity of Savannah and became the publisher of the *Chicago Defender,* encountered the snobbery and color consciousness of the city's mulatto upper class. One of only a handful of dark students at Beach Institute, an American Missionary Association school, he was always treated as an outsider. Dominated by Savannah's fair-complexioned aristocrats of color, St. Stephen's Episcopal Church for many years was known as a "blue vein" church. The color question erupted in open conflict in 1872, when the "near white vestrymen sought to exclude all black people" and limit the congregation to individuals and families whose complexion approximated that of Caucasians. J. Robert Love, "a robust black man" from the West Indies who became rector of St. Stephen's, unalterably opposed such a move. He ultimately resigned and led the dark-skinned members out of the congregation to form St. Augustine's Church. Not until 1943, when the two congregations merged to form St. Matthews, was the color question resolved.[39]

Color gradations among blacks in Atlanta, a relatively new city, were undoubtedly less significant than in Savannah and Augusta, at least until the arrival of Benjamin Davis and his Atlanta *Independent.* Always a maverick, Davis became "the champion mulatto baiter," often detecting "colorphobia" among the light-skinned elite where it did not exist and occasionally where it probably did. He regularly aimed his editorial artillery at the alleged color consciousness of the politician Henry Rucker, the minister H. H. Proctor, and various educators, including W. E. B. Du Bois. According to him, Atlanta's black upper class consisted of "the artificials, the superficials, the seemers, would-bes, race leaders, posers, wish-I-was-white social sets, [and] educated idlers . . . ," most of whom attended Proctor's First Congregational Church, which had "an unwritten law that mulattoes were preferred." In 1914 he accused the Georgia State Colored Medical Association of staging a color line, "high yaller ball" that excluded those physicians of dark complexion.[40]

While Davis was perhaps more unrestrained and flamboyant than most journalistic "mulatto baiters," he was by no means unique. On occasion, Julius F. Taylor, editor of the Chicago *Broad Ax,* who specialized in "preacher-baiting," could equal Davis in his condemnation of the color-conscious behavior of that city's black upper class.[41] In the mid-1890s the editor of a black weekly in Indianapolis reacted vehemently to a report that "a blue vein society is on foot" and was closely identified with "a particular church," which he did not name. The editor reminded the social elite that "the complexion of morals should be of more importance than that of the face." After about six weeks, he reported that blue veinism in the city's "strictly social circle" appeared to be on the wane.[42]

Some midwestern blacks described "blue veinism" as a phenomenon that had originated in the East and spread westward.[43] Whether or not their observation was valid, it seems to have been the source of less controversy in the Plains states and farther west than in the East. As was often the case, however, even in these areas references to the color consciousness of the elite appeared not so much in attacks on "blue-vein societies" as in connection with individuals or special events. In 1905, when Mary Church Terrell lectured in St. Louis for the benefit of the colored YMCA, the local Negro newspaper observed that "the black boys were not there, but the yellows were out in number."[44] In Wichita, Kansas, in 1909, rumors of the formation of a "blue-vein exclusive society" prompted a passionate statement from the editor of the city's black weekly. He ridiculed the movement as the folly of "would-be whites" who posed a "threat to keeping the race as a unit."[45]

In various Ohio cities rumors and reports of blue veinism surfaced periodically throughout the late nineteenth and early twentieth centuries. For some years beginning in the mid-1880s rumors of a "blue-vein circle" in Cincinnati abounded. In 1885 a black resident of the city claimed that such a circle had been organized by that class of Negroes "who do not want to be identified with the Negro and the white man will not recognize him." The following year a Cincinnati correspondent printed a blistering attack on the city's fair-skinned blacks, claiming that "no other requisite is deemed essential for membership" in their "blue vein society" than color. "The members of this august and dignified concern," he declared, "are highly distinguished for the absence of brains and consequent force. A few male members aspire to political prominence, supremely unconscious of their lack of ability." Because so little had "been said or written of this delectable body," his love for the black race compelled him to expose the mischievous frauds who composed it. The agitation over color in Cincinnati appears to have originated in a struggle for control of the Colored Orphan Asylum. Darker-skinned aspirants for positions on its board of managers invoked the charge of "blue veinism" against Robert Harlan, Peter H. Clark, George H. Jackson, and other prominent, fair-complexioned men who had traditionally dominated Asylum affairs.[46] The squabble over control of the Asylum indicated the divisive impact that color sometimes had on racial civic enterprises.

In possessing a reputation for a "blue-vein element," few cities equaled that of Cleveland. Throughout the late nineteenth and early twentieth centuries references to its existence regularly appeared in print. By implication rather than direct assertion, the "blue-vein element" in Cleveland was usually linked to the Social Circle, an old organization that included the Chesnutts, Wilsons, Greens, and other fair-complexioned families who were, for the most part, descendants of free people of color. By 1890 a group of black Clevelanders began a concerted campaign to expose and route the "blue-veiners"—the "foolish few"—who had for so long injured the city's Afro-American society and besmirched its reputation abroad. These "foolish few" made up a small clique of light-skinned blacks who were accused of attending white churches and seldom showing "any interest in our local race organizations or efforts" but were always ready to "criticize and make fun of them." In brief, the blue-vein element consisted of a very small minority of light-complexioned Negroes "who want to be white and a few blacks ones who are sufficiently ignorant to apologize for them."[47]

Taking the lead in the campaign against the "blue veins" was Harry C. Smith, editor of the *Cleveland Gazette*. A native of West Virginia and a mulatto, Smith did not belong to the Social Circle. His newspaper maintained a consistently integrationist position, and Smith himself has been described as continuing the protest tradition in "its purest and most militant form." A politically ambitious man who served in the state legislature between 1894 and 1902, he had opposed the election of John P. Green, supposedly one of the "blue veins," in 1885 and later broke with Mark Hanna's Republican machine, which included most of Cleveland's old mulatto upper class.[48] Regardless of the extent to which his political aspirations were involved in his struggle against "blue veins," Smith proved to be one of their most persistent critics. As with most other critics of color consciousness among the black elite, he always insisted that it was a phenomenon that was rapidly disappearing. In 1890 he claimed that the blue-vein element was "groveling in the throes of death."[49] Fifteen years later, another critic of Cleveland's fair-complexioned elite made a similar claim but admitted that blue veinism had not entirely "died away." "The question of tints," another black observer noted, "is one of the racial follies that die hard."[50]

Few journalists wrote more forcefully or for so many years in opposition to the colorphobia of the black upper class as did John E. Bruce, whose column appeared in black newspapers throughout the country for several decades under his pen name, Bruce Grit. Beginning in 1877, when he wrote his critique of "colored society in Washington," he persistently denounced those Negroes who, having narrowly escaped "from being born white," attempted to set themselves as leaders of the Afro-American people exclusively on the basis of their color and Caucasian features. He ridiculed the pride they manifested in their blue veins, small hands, finely chiselled features, "good" hair, and "aristocratic insteps." Bruce, dark-skinned and of a slave background, blamed the fair-complexioned, "pin-headed dudes and dudines" for introducing in the Negro community the whole concept of class distinctions based on color. He thought it absurd that those who were actually "the illegitimate progeny of the vicious white men of the South" should attempt to pose "as representatives of the better class of Negroes." Viewing the color-conscious elite of his generation as the descendants of antebellum free blacks who were "only nominally free and enjoyed no more rights as citizens than the slaves," he characterized both ancestors and descendants as exploitative of the masses in their own struggle for supremacy. In this connection he not only castigated the mulatto elite of Charleston for its colorphobia but also ridiculed the blacks in New York who manifested pride in their Dutch ancestry and insisted on retaining the Dutch prefix "van" in their names. Those of the black upper class who were obsessed with their fair complexions, straight hair, and patrician "blood" lived in a "fool's paradise"; they were nothing more than "mongrels" who possessed the vices of both races and the virtues of neither. Cunning, more loyal to their "white half" than to their "mother race," they were as "treacherous" in their relations with black men as "the worst bourbons of the fire-eating type in the South." Until his death, in 1924, Bruce continued to pour out his venom on the color-conscious, self-proclaimed mulatto aristocrats and to call upon "black men to resent their insolence" and rout them from their positions of leadership.[51]

From at least 1877, when Bruce wrote his scathing critique, "Colored Society in Washington,"[52] the color consciousness of the Negro aristocracy in the nation's capital was a perennial topic of hostile comment. The impression conveyed by contemporary accounts was that Washington, rather than Charleston or New Orleans, was the center of blue veinism. Critics, both inside and outside the city, expressed resentment toward "all the 'big' Negroes [there] with all their aristocracy, color lines, and cornered off classes." Each year, according to one observer in 1886, the city's "blue-vein element" produced a crop of "professional Negroes for political and social purposes"—fair-complexioned individuals who not only monopolized the choicest positions in politics, public schools, and municipal and federal governments and claimed to speak for all Negroes, but also composed an exclusive, snobbish social clique that established a rigid color line against all Negroes of darker complexions. Whether charges of "blue veinism" were leveled against the Orpheus Glee Club, the Monocan Club, or those who taught in and administered the separate school system for Negroes, they almost invariably prompted references to the mulatto aristocrats as "ethnological abortions" or to their illegitimate and "doubtful origins." Despite all their social pretensions and pride in ancestry, so the argument ran, Washington's aristocrats of color were "in the same boat with the flat-nosed, wooley haired, kidney-footed Negro whom they . . . so heartily *despise* in their heart of hearts."[53]

Of all the critical commentators on the color consciousness of Washington's black upper class, few were more persistent or more influential than W. Calvin Chase, editor and publisher of the *Washington Bee*. A "mixed-blood" whose appearance clearly revealed his African ancestry, Chase ranked with Davis of Atlanta, Smith of Cleveland, and "Bruce Grit" as an effective mulatto baiter. For forty years after its establishment in 1882, his *Bee* remained a vocal foe of those upper-class Negroes it characterized as "would-be whites," always eager to win the approval of the "favored race" and skilled at garnering the harvest, however slight, allowed the "oppressed race." Chase and his newspaper detected the "pernicious influence" of their colorphobia virtually everywhere—in the schools, churches, political contests, and especially social relations.[54] Others agreed, claiming as one did that "seven tenths" of all appointments given Negroes under William McKinley's administration went to mulattoes. Black women, in 1909, complained that nurses' training schools for Negroes excluded all those of dark complexion.[55]

A favorite editorial theme pursued by the *Bee* concerned the discrimination allegedly practiced by the fair-complexioned social elite against Negroes of darker skin. "There is more color prejudice among the so-called colored society of this city," the *Bee* declared in 1890, "than there is among white people toward the colored."[56] Similar pronouncements were appearing in the *Bee* twenty years later. The newspaper thought it both ironic and ridiculous that the same color-conscious aristocrats who attempted to isolate themselves from their darker brethren were the ones who clamored loudest for an end to "color prejudice" and discrimination on the part of whites. It was not always clear which clique or faction among the aristocrats that Chase was accusing of color consciousness. Despite his penchant for naming names, he avoided this practice in editorializing on the color-line issue. Only when blacks attempted to "pass for white" during the day, usually in some government office, and moved in "colored circles at night" was he inclined to mention specific names.[57]

According to Chase, the introduction of the color line into Washington's black community was another legacy of the Lotus Club, which had been kept alive ever since the 1860s largely through the steady influx into the city of color-conscious blacks. Such a charge was scarcely unexpected because Chase was protective of Washington's old, native-born, free families, with whom he identified, and inclined to blame "interlopers" for many of the ills of Washington's black community. Regardless of the group responsible for introducing the color line among blacks in Washington, it was a durable topic of private discussion and a persistent source of dissension.[58]

The issue periodically surfaced in connection with the staffing of colored schools. The claim was sometimes made that the fair-skinned aristocrats who controlled the school system gave preference to teachers whose complexions resembled their own and turned down "deserving black teachers."[59] In 1884 the *Bee* claimed that John H. Brooks, a member of an old black family, who was a school trustee, showed rank favoritism toward persons of fair complexion in the selection of teachers. In 1897, when "a crowd of negroes of dark complexion" endorsed Kelly Miller of the Howard University faculty as a school trustee because they wanted "a black man on the board . . . [to] look out for black teachers," the *Bee* suggested that Miller was scarcely the appropriate candidate to defend their interests since he married "a lady almost white."[60]

Weary of the *Bee*'s persistent harping on the color-line theme, one resident of the District wrote Chase a letter in 1916 in which she frankly admitted "passing": "I am a colored woman who can and does attend all the white theatres, and any other place intended only for whites and am proud of it, and am really sorry you can't. Only by delivering a message or package, or if you were the janitor, maybe, they would allow you to see a show now and then. People of your complexion are jealous because they can't pass. . . . My father is pure white and was legally married to my mother who was a creole. Yes, I have the white fever, and truly hope this will help you get over the colored fever."[61] Chase merely identified the letter writer as a public school teacher whose father was employed at the Capitol and who "came from one of the leading families in the city."[62]

What the *Bee* and other black newspapers in Washington suggested throughout the late nineteenth and early twentieth centuries was that, unlike the single color line imposed by whites, there was within the black community a complex system of color grading that ranged from virtually white through "ginger cake" and "yellow pine" to black. The shade of one's complexion was directly related to the social clique or class to which one belonged. Even Chase recognized the extent to which color could be used as a bogus issue, as when he charged that Frederick Douglass and his sons raised the color issue against any individual they could not control. In regard to the appointment of teachers, the issue was often invoked, according to the *Bee*, without the slightest proof or justification by dark-skinned Negroes who were unsuccessful in competing for teaching positions that invariably attracted large numbers of highly qualified applicants.[63]

The question of a fair complexion and lack of identity with blacks periodically figured in discussions of Dr. Charles B. Purvis, a light-skinned physician from a prominent abolitionist family who had "no slave blood in him."[64] In 1882 Purvis became the administrative head of the Freedman's Hospital in Washington. The next year when his name was suggested as a trustee of the city's colored schools, even the *People's Advocate* objected, not because he was "lacking in character or intellectual capacity" but because the position required "one more *generally* and *thoroughly* identified with the colored people" to "look out for their special interests." In 1889 a black critic claimed that Purvis was a classic example of the light-complexioned black man who advanced his own interests by claiming to be a Negro but at the same time disdaining any association with black people.[65] That Purvis had married a white woman and insisted upon sending his daughter to the white public schools in Washington was viewed as evidence of such charges.[66]

In 1885 Chase's newspaper denounced Richard Greener and Robert Terrell, both of whom were affiliated at one time or another with the colored high school, for their attempt to gain admission to the Harvard Club. When the applications of these two honor graduates of Harvard were turned down, presumably on racial grounds, Chase vented his hostility, not on the club, but on Greener and Terrell. He described them as typical examples of the fair-complexioned, well-educated blacks who were always in search of means to abandon "their own race" for "white society." He used the Harvard Club incident as an occasion to discourse on the mischief caused by light-skinned schoolteachers who drew the color line against those of darker complexions. In 1914 he was still complaining that "too many Negro teachers . . . in this city are anxious to be regarded as white."[67]

Few other events prompted so much comment by the *Bee* on the distance that the fair-complexioned, upper-class Negroes placed between themselves and other blacks as the wedding of John R. Lynch, a former Mississippi congressman, and Ella V. Somerville on December 18, 1884. Born in Concordia Parish, Louisiana in 1847, Lynch was the son of Patrick Lynch, an Irish plantation manager, and Catherine White, a mulatto slave. Lynch remembered his white father with obvious affection. Patrick Lynch publicly recognized Catherine as his wife and their two children as his sons. As was the case with Pinchback, Francis and Archibald Grimké, and various other slave children of white fathers, Lynch's father died before arrangements for the freedom of Catherine and his children were completed. As a result, they remained in bondage and were taken to Natchez, Mississippi after his death. Following Emancipation, Lynch entered politics and rose rapidly in the ranks of the Republican party in Mississippi during Reconstruction. He became politically allied with Blanche K. Bruce, who remained his lifelong friend. Described as "aristocratic and handsome," Lynch was a polished orator and skilled political strategist. Elected to three terms in Congress, he used the floor of the House as a forum for championing the cause of civil rights for blacks. A man of considerable means, who owned extensive real estate in the city of Natchez and several large tracts of land in the surrounding area, Lynch later practiced law and headed a black bank in Washington, where he was a close friend and associate of Robert Terrell.[68]

His bride was from a prominent antebellum free family of color in Mobile, Alabama. Ella Somerville's mother, a "colored Creole" noted for her grace and refinement, was a dressmaker. Her father, James A. Somerville, was "a member of one of the oldest and most aristocratic families" in a city that possessed a sizable and prosperous free black community. A cotton sampler who had acquired substantial wealth before the Civil War, he was loyal to the South and invested heavily in Confederate bonds. As a result, he emerged from the war virtually bankrupt. Entering politics as a Republican, he played a conspicuous role in Reconstruction in Alabama and was rewarded with an appointment as customs inspector in Mobile. Although Somerville was unable to regain the fortune he had lost, he remained "a man of high standing, socially and otherwise." He and his wife, who contributed to the family income through her dressmaking, used all the resources they could muster to educate their large family of girls. Sometime in the 1870s the Somervilles moved to Washington, where Lynch's bride, Ella, had secured a teaching position in the colored schools and one of her sisters gained employment in the Government Printing Office. Despite the reduced affluence of James Somerville, his family easily won acceptance into the colored aristocracy in the District. His wife's dressmaking business and his daughters' well-paying jobs enabled the family to live comfortably and even to acquire some valuable real estate. By the time of the Lynch-Somerville wedding they resided in a commodious house on Corcoran Street that the *Bee* described as "the exclusive Somerville mansion."[69]

At one o'clock on the afternoon of December 18, 1884, Francis J. Grimké of the Fifteenth Street Presbyterian Church performed the wedding ceremony at the Somerville residence. This "exclusive affair" was witnessed only by the *crème de la crème* of Washington's "best society." Lynch described his bride as "one of those at whose feet the proudest and finest aristocrats of antebellum days would kneel in recognition of her accomplishments, beauty, charm, personal appearance and attractive bearing." A person of "becoming modesty and good taste," Ella Somerville Lynch gave "unmistakable evidence . . . that her childhood surroundings had been the very best." A woman of striking beauty with "just enough African blood to give her a . . . creamy complexion," she possessed large, penetrating hazel eyes and a nose that "was an exact type of the Grecian." According to Lynch, her "beautiful straight hair" was an "indication of the Indian blood that courses through her veins." An acquaintance of Ella Somerville, who was obviously less enamored of her than Lynch was, described her as one who was "too anxious to impress others with her superiority."[70]

From the perspective of some blacks, the exclusiveness and emphasis on color which the Somervilles allegedly evidenced were sources of great mischief in the District's Negro community. The *Bee* claimed that Ella Somerville's sister who was an employee of the Government Printing Office denied that she was a Negro and eschewed "all identity with the colored race." In its opinion Lynch had seriously damaged his reputation as spokesman for black Americans by marrying into a family that was "so prejudiced against color." The newspaper also reported that the wedding had been followed by two receptions: one in the afternoon for the fair-complexioned aristocrats and one in the evening for the darker "plebeians." At the afternoon reception, according to the report, "a *black* face was not visible except as servants with white caps and aprons." The *Bee* also charged that Ella Somerville had informed the white press that her father was an Englishman and that her "mother had very little African blood in her veins."[71]

After the Lynches had returned from a wedding trip to Niagara Falls and established themselves in Washington, the *Bee* continued to comment on what it perceived as evidences of Ella Somerville Lynch's pretentiousness and preference for white society. It noted that the Lynches had been among the few invited to a reception given by Dr. Charles Purvis and his white wife for his brother who was visiting from Detroit. Ella Lynch had "astonished" the guests by the "pure French which she spoke during the entire evening." In March 1885, when the Lynches issued invitations to their first reception, the *Bee* carefully scrutinized the guest list and observed that, aside from Blanche and Josephine Bruce and a few other members of the "black 400," those invited were for the most part "second class white people from the [government] departments." "I claim that Mr. and Mrs. Bruce are the ornaments of any society," declared the writer of the Bee's "Clara to Louise" column, "and if Mrs. Lynch so soon forgets herself, she should not allow others to be imposed upon. She must have an idea that all white persons are the equals of Mr. and Mrs. Bruce. I have little respect for people who attempt to ignore their own society for that of second-class white people."[72]

In 1910 a much-publicized court case tended to confirm the Bee's contention that the color-conscious upper class suffered from an acute case of the "white fever" and seized every opportunity to abandon association with blacks for that with whites. The case involved the nine-year-old daughter of Stephen B. Wall, Isabel, who entered the Brookland School, a white institution, in September 1909, and shortly thereafter was removed by the principal on the grounds that she was a "colored child." Wall, an employee of the Government Printing Office, was the son of Captain O. S. B. Wall, who had rendered distinguished service during the Civil War. Like his sister, Mrs. John Mercer Langston, Captain Wall had attended Oberlin College and after the war became a prominent member of Washington's aristocracy of color. His son, Stephen, who was of "extraordinarily light complexion," married a white woman who was Isabel's mother.[73]

When the Wall incident came before the District of Columbia Board of Education, three of its members were Negroes, including Mary Church Terrell, who moved in the same social circles as the Walls and Langstons and knew the families intimately. Mary Terrell forthrightly insisted that Isabel Wall should be allowed to remain in the white school. In public she argued that in the antebellum South the child traditionally followed the condition of the mother, and since Isabel's mother was white, the child should be considered white and attend a white school. Later, Mrs. Terrell admitted that the real reason she waged such a fight in Isabel's behalf was her desire to see that the child was classified as white to escape "the hardships, humiliations and injustices" suffered by those "classified as colored" in "a prejudice-ridden city" like Washington. The two other black members of the Board of Education disagreed with Mary Terrell's position on the grounds that to allow Isabel Wall to attend a white school would reflect adversely on the quality of the District's Negro schools. Although the Bee commended Mrs. Terrell's position as entirely honorable, it agreed with the other two black members of the Board and noted that there were other fair-complexioned children, "just as bright as Miss Wall," who were "satisfied with being associated with colored children in colored schools." By a vote of eight to five the Board upheld the Brookland School principal's decision and directed Isabel Wall to attend a Negro school. Mrs. Terrell voted with the minority, the other two black members with the majority.

The adverse decision by the Board prompted Stephen Wall to petition the Court of Appeals in the District to allow his daughter to attend a white school.

His petition both attacked the constitutionality of the separate school system in the District and claimed that Isabel was "not a colored child" within the meaning of the law. To support the latter Stephen Wall cited some family genealogy, noting that Isabel's "great-grandparents were a white man and a very light mulatto woman; her grandparents were a son of said great-grandparents and a white woman; and [her] parents . . . the son of said grandparents and a white woman." Therefore, Isabel's father denied "that she has a distinct and sure material admixture of colored blood." He further denied that he himself was "a colored man" or that he was so recognized by neighbors and friends.

The Court disputed the latter assertion, claiming that while Stephen Wall's present "associations were not largely with the colored race," he had formerly operated "a pool room in a colored neighborhood, that was frequented by colored people." Based on the estimates of the Court, Isabel possessed "Negro blood of one-eighth to one-sixteenth," even though she had blue eyes, blond hair, and an "unusually fair" complexion. In the quaint language of the Court: "There was to be observed of the child no physical characteristic which afforded ocular evidence suggestive of aught but Caucasian." But as the presiding judge pointed out, complexion and physical appearance had little to do with determining one's racial status. Clearly subscribing to the "one drop rule," he maintained that Isabel Wall was indeed "colored" and should attend a colored school, because "persons of whatever complexion, who bear Negro blood in whatever degree, and who abide in the racial status of the Negro, are 'colored' in the common estimation of the people." Having lost their legal battle, the Walls quietly moved to another section of Washington, passed as white, and entered Isabel in another white school under an assumed name.[74]

For Calvin Chase's Bee, the Wall case merely corroborated several editorial themes in regard to colorphobia among upper-class blacks that it had pursued for years. Among these was the idea that no matter how fair-complexioned a mulatto might be, he or she was, in the eyes of whites, a member of an inferior race, subject to the same discriminatory laws as the blackest black. Therefore, all efforts of the light-skinned aristocrats to organize themselves into a separate caste were bound to fail. In the opinion of the Bee the Wall case was little more than another example of the fair-complexioned upper class "trying to get away from the [Negro] race," an enterprise that at best could be described as sheer folly.[75]

The criticisms of Washington's colored society first voiced by Chase and his newspaper in the 1880s appeared more frequently and assumed a more strident tone after the turn of the century. The admission of increasing numbers of "interlopers" from elsewhere into the city's upper class remained, in his view, the primary cause of its deterioration because outsiders strengthened "color prejudice and social fever" and had a devastating effect upon any sense of duty toward the less fortunate black masses.[76] Still complaining about the malevolent influence of "social outcasts" from elsewhere who had invaded Washington's society, Chase remarked to a friend in 1914: "It does seem as if the interlopers have taken the bit in their mouths and run away with society. It used to require a name to get into Washington society." In his view the colored aristocracy of the city no longer deserved the name: it had become all "sham and pretense" with an emphasis on color to the exclusion of everything else.[77]

The increasing colorphobia, or "white fever," that Chase detected among certain blacks in Washington attracted more of his scorn than did some other of their unbecoming traits. He maintained that not only did the so-called better class insist upon using the services of white lawyers and even white undertakers, but also that they had perfected color gradations into something of a science. In 1913 he announced in the Bee that he had discovered the existence of a club in Washington among "society women," including "school teachers and other social flunkies," who made a fetish out of light skin. The club was known as The Kingdom, and admission was based on the skin color, hair quality, shape of nose, thinness of lips, and ownership of an automobile; the organization alleged-ly admitted only those whose color and hair resembled that of whites.[78]

In Chase's view the latter-day aristocrats in the District had little in common with those of a half century earlier who paid little attention to skin color but who closely identified with the black community and provided leader-ship in a wide variety of civic movements. But in the second decade of the twentieth century, as proscriptions against all blacks became increasingly op-pressive, the color-conscious, fair-complexioned aristocrats compounded the black man's difficulties by imposing a color line of their own and by removing themselves from any association with those of more obvious African ancestry. "The Bee means by Negro aristocracy," he wrote in 1914, "those Negroes who have attempted to organize a caste society or a society of alleged select Negroes who live on the earnings of the working class and when they have work to be done, they ignore their own professionals and mechanics and seek inferior white workmen." Two years later, when Chase made a bid to win election as a delegate to the Republican national convention, he claimed that these "select Negroes" of fair complexion had rallied to the support of a socially prominent physician in a vain effort to bring about his defeat.[79]

While Chase's commentaries on Washington's colored aristocracy often contained gross exaggerations and more personal resentment than dispassionate analysis, his criticism of it found considerable support in the expressions of other black observers. James M. Townsend of Indiana, a respected minister and Republican politician who resided for a time in Washington, regularly indicted the city's so-called better class for "continually pulling up their coat sleeves and exposing their blue veins" to prove that they were closer kin to whites than to blacks. For such people to place a premium on a light skin, he argued, was merely to publicize their "illegitimate origins." "We are all classed as Negroes from the whitest to the blackest," Townsend declared, "and there is no sense or reason why the so called better class should persist in making itself ridiculous."[80]

The fair-complexioned aristocrats rarely responded to the charges of color consciousness that were often directed specifically at them. Some undoubtedly attempted to ignore the issue altogether; others, if they considered it at all, did so in private and among intimate friends without leaving any written record of their musings; still others considered all the talk of color gradations among Negroes as the "pernicious" work of individuals and groups who were envious of their status and willing to use any method to attack them. In 1907, Edward Beckham of Philadelphia announced the launching of a newspaper, *The American*, as "a national organ" of the 2,000,000 "mulattoes, quadroons and octoroons" in the United States, but the project failed to elicit any response from the nation's fair-skinned upper class and there is no evidence that the newspaper was ever published.[81] Nevertheless, some aristocrats of color probably did consciously invoke color in determining who was included and who was excluded from their social sphere, but even for most of these people more than mere complexion was involved. Ancestry and family background, as well as evidences of education and gentility, were virtually always seen as important.

Many aristocrats of color probably did not make a conscious connection between social status and a light skin, at least not until the issue became the topic of public discussion. Then it became "a delicate subject," and they probably assumed the position of a member of the New Orleans fair-skinned Negro elite who preferred not to "talk about things like that." Or as an admirer of Washington's Fifteenth Street Presbyterian Church explained the presence of so few "dark faces" in its congregation: it "just happens that way."[82] In his view there was no conscious effort to exclude dark-skinned Negroes; rather the erudite minister Francis J. Grimké and the whole ambience of the Fifteenth Street Church attracted only those Negroes of education and refinement who for the most part happened to possess light complexions. But most members of Grimké's church would have argued that what counted was culture, not color, and they could have also pointed out that few condemned colorphobia among Negroes more forcefully than their minister.

Most aristocrats of color usually referred to themselves as "colored" at a time when a debate raged in the black community over the proper terminology to be applied to persons of African descent. The Florida-born editor of the *New York Age*, T. Thomas Fortune, campaigned for the use of the term Afro-American. In the view of John E. Bruce both "Afro-American" and "colored" were merely terms used by those who, ethnologically "neither fish, nor fowl, nor good red herring," set a premium on hair quality and skin color and claimed themselves as "superior to the blacks." Bruce insisted that the only term appropriate for Americans of African descent, regardless of their color, was Negro, and that the use of any other term was merely a subterfuge by those fair-complexioned "hybrids" who wished to separate themselves from their darker brethren.[83]

Most objectionable of all was the word "nigger," a pejorative term applied to all Negro Americans of whatever hue by some whites. The use of the term by

Negroes had multiple meanings, some of which had no offensive connotation. Like upper-class whites who placed a premium on restraint in all matters including language, aristocrats of color rarely used "nigger," but when they did it usually bore more of a class than a racial connotation. When a member of Chicago's black upper class described Julius Taylor's *Broad Ax* as a "nigger sheet,"[84] he was referring to the editor's breaches of propriety and unmannered excesses characteristic of the lower class, both black and white. Writing to his wife in 1902 about the lack of manners displayed by the son of a well-known black family, John P. Green declared: "That's a 'nigger' for you, isn't it?"[85] Ten years later, when P. B. S. Pinchback, who had moved to New York and fallen victim to declining fortunes, used "nigger," its meaning appeared to resemble that conveyed when whites used it. In a letter to an upper-class friend in which he expressed dismay that so many blacks continued to support Theodore Roosevelt and his Progressive party in the face of its "lily white policy," Pinchback wrote: "Lincoln made a great mistake when he freed the mass of niggers. Quite a number of them up this way are still shouting for Roosevelt."[86] Even though obviously uttered in anger and frustration, Pinchback's reference to "niggers" would have been grist for the mill of the black critics of color consciousness if it had become public. Most upper-class blacks, however, probably would have agreed with the Kansas City editor who specifically characterized "nigger" as a word denoting lower class and who insisted that both whites and blacks had a bountiful supply of "niggers" in their ranks.[87]

Evidence from the nation's fair-complexioned aristocrats of color themselves that color pervaded their thinking and determined their behavior, as claimed by critics within the black community, is at best ambiguous. Madame Azalia Hackley, in providing advice to Negro girls, appeared to apply standards associated with both Negro and Caucasian standards of beauty. Such an approach was consistent with her view that "colored" Americans were "a mixed race" endowed by nature with three rare physical gifts: beautiful eyes, strong and attractive teeth, and "the finest voices in the world." She emphatically denied that either a dark skin or "kinky hair" should be considered a liability. A dark skin indicated, among other positive attributes, the possession of "rare psychic powers." The quality of the Negro's hair was the result of the "torrid sun" of Africa, but through constant care its texture could be greatly improved and "will in time be inherited." Madame Hackley paid especial attention to what were considered the least attractive features of "the colored girl beautiful": the mouth, lips, and nose. The mouth was too large because of "grinning and loud laughter"; the lips were too thick because of allowing the mouth to "hang open too much." To correct the physical feature of the Negro most subject to ridicule, the large, flat nose, Madame Hackley advised that too much grinning widened the nose, "so grinning must cease." She suggested that what was needed was a "hump" in the Negro's nose and counseled girls to "pinch up, think up, will up a hump."[88]

In the voluminous papers of Robert and Mary Church Terrell, as well as in the latter's autobiography and other writings, which provide a detailed chronicle of their social life and thought, there is little direct evidence to suggest that they consciously chose their associates on the basis of complexion. It is possible, however, to conclude from an analysis of Mrs. Terrell's writings, especially her choice of words in describing the physical appearance of individuals, that Caucasian features constituted standards by which she judged personal attractiveness. But even if this was true, it did not distinguish her from a vast number of dark-skinned Negroes outside the upper class. Indisputably, her most intimate friends, those who made up the Booklovers and Matron's Whist Club, were fair-complexioned women who were also well educated and genteel. While she viewed as a model Josephine Bruce, who possessed all the attributes of an aristocrat of color, including a virtually white skin, Mary Terrell also counted among her special friends the dark, tubercular black poet Dunbar, whose claims to her affection were his talent and personality.[89]

Others of Mary Church Terrell's class were no less inclined to ignore color in applauding talent and achievement. In a eulogy of the fair-skinned John Mercer Langston, Pinchback elaborated upon the positive influence that his long and close association with "refined and Christian white people" had on his life, claiming that it was a significant factor in equipping him to become an effective champion of the oppressed black masses. But Pinchback was no less generous in his assessment of the contributions of Oscar J. Dunn, a prominent Negro political figure in Reconstruction Louisiana. He was, according to Pinchback, "as black as the ace of spades, but a grander man from principle never trod God's earth." What Pinchback implied was that not all Negroes who exhibited intelligence and "executive ability" in Reconstruction politics were mulattoes, such as himself, with a privileged background.[90]

Questions about Pinchback's own racial identity were later raised by his famous grandson, Jean Toomer. Toomer on occasion suggested that political ambition rather than racial lineage prompted his grandfather to cast his lot with blacks. He indicated that Pinchback actually possessed no Negro ancestry whatever. On other occasions he claimed that his grandfather merely emphasized the small "fraction of Negro blood in veins" as a means of achieving political power in the Reconstruction era. On still others, he admitted that while Pinchback could scarcely be classified as a Negro, he identified with the freedmen out of genuine sympathy for them. Toomer also claimed that his grandmother, Nina Hethorn Pinchback, was "a white Creole" of English and French descent and that he "never heard any implication she had Negro blood." The family, he said, "had lived between two worlds, now dipping into the Negro, now into the white." Toomer's father, Nathan, appears to have "lived in both the black world and the white." His grandfather's sister, Adeline, who lived in Sidney, Ohio and who encouraged her brother to take his "position in the world as a white man as you are," lived as a white woman.[91]

For aristocrats of color, like other Americans who claimed high status, a knowledge of family history was important. Most did indeed "deal heavily in family trees," and in view of their complexion and other Caucasian features it would have been absurd to attempt to eliminate the white roots of such trees. In some instances the infusion of white blood appeared as early as the eighteenth century; in others, it was of more recent date, but almost always in the antebellum era. Rather than attempt to obscure the existence of white ancestors, most aristocrats of color referred to them rather openly and often with affection and pride. John P. Green spoke of "our white people"; the black Harlans of Cincinnati were fully aware of their relationship to the white Harlans of Kentucky; the Syphax family in Washington inherited property through a white ancestor, George Washington Parke Custis, Martha Washington's grandson. Pauli Murray recalled the counsel of her grandmother in North Carolina: "Hold your head high and don't take a back seat to nobody. You got blood in you—folks that counted for something. . . . Aristocrats, that's what they were, going back seven generations right in this state."[92]

Critics of the mulatto elite, who attempted to denigrate their ancestry by references to illegitimacy, bastardy, and "uncertain origins," may have been technically correct in suggesting that their fair complexion had often been acquired sometime in the past through race mixing outside of marriage. But the genealogical musings of most aristocrats of color show that this white blood came not through casual liaisons between blacks and whites but from long-standing relationships such as existed in the case of ancestors of the Langston, Syphax, and Lynch families. Furthermore, some of these families had acquired education and property through white ancestors.

While aristocrats of color readily acknowledged their white ancestry, they were no less inclined to acknowledge their African and in some cases Indian forebears. As in the case of their white ancestors, they tended to endow the African branches of the family tree with a prominence they did not always possess. Their genealogical charts contained a disproportionate number of African "kings" and Madagascan "princesses." An upper-class Negro woman, in recounting her family history, noted: "My great-grandmother was the daughter of an Indian chief and married my great-grandfather, the son of an African chief." Aristocrats of color were not unlike those across the color line whose genealogies often contained members of European royalty and nobility. No less important in the African branches of the family trees were those who had been active in the antislavery and convention movements and who served in the nation's wars, beginning with the American Revolution. The well-known Downing family of New York manifested pride both in its descent from Sir George Downing and in the role its members had played in the Underground Railroad and the abolitionist cause.[93] But that such people frankly acknowledged their miscegenated family trees, regardless of the affection and pride they displayed in their African ancestors, was sufficient to fuel charges of possessing the "white fever."

Upper-class Negroes of fair complexions, however, could scarcely have been devoid of color consciousness; they were aware of the degree to which, in both appearance and culture, they often resembled Caucasians more than most other Negroes. Charles Chesnutt, for example, wrote in his journal: "I am neither fish, flesh nor fowl, neither 'nigger,' white nor 'buckrah.' Too 'stuck up' for the colored folks, and of course, not recognized by the whites."[94] Mary Church Terrell was once asked if she was a relative of Governor Joseph Terrell of Georgia by someone who mistook her for a white person; she was sufficiently impressed by the incident to record it in her diary.[95] Mrs. Terrell also knew that Fanny Garrison Villard, the daughter of the abolitionist leader and wife of the railroad magnate, considered her "almost white with . . . most pleasing and prepossessing manners." "That one so attractive should, because of this slight indication of color, be judged as belonging to the colored race," Fanny Villard declared, "is truly affecting, and seems in the highest degree unjust."[96] There is no indication that Mary Church Terrell ever entertained any notions that she was anything but a "colored" person. "But never once in my life," she wrote, "have I ever been tempted to 'cross the color line' and deny my racial identity." The fair-complexioned aristocrats of color appeared not so much to approach the color issue from the perspective of belonging to no race but from one that emphasized their kinship to both races. Tied by blood and culture to both black and white society, they viewed themselves as people uniquely capable of building a bridge between the two.[97]

Some members of the Negro aristocracy who were sufficiently light-skinned to "pass" for white disappeared into white society, but others chose to use their fair skin as a means of ascertaining the white man's thoughts on "the race question."[98] What they learned was sometimes so revolting that it removed whatever doubts they may have had about joining the white race.[99] John Hope, who was fair enough to "pass," suffered "through being taken for white" on so many occasions that he admitted that he would "not mind being darker." In a letter to his wife in 1899, in which he discussed his "suffering" caused by being taken for a white person, he wrote: "But honestly from the bottom of my heart, as long as the Negro is the sufferer, as long as the white man makes him suffer, I prefer to be with the oppressed rather than be as puny and mean and un-Christlike as the white man. . . . Of course, when discrimination passes away and all men are equal in the light of the law and public sentiment, then it will not matter what we are. Then, you can set it down that under the most favorable conditions I should be satisfied to be a colored man; and that under unfavorable conditions I *prefer* to be colored."[100] But as some of the light-complexioned members of the upper class learned, it was not always easy to convince others of one's racial identity. Cyrus Fields Adams, who was regularly accused by some blacks of trying to "pass" as a white man, stoutly denied the charge: "My trouble is, all my life I have been trying to pass for colored."[101]

In view of the mixed ancestry of most aristocrats of color—a mixture that

[173]

was barely visible in some of the lighter-skinned people—it was difficult to accept without question the doctrine of racial integrity espoused by many blacks and whites alike. Speaking before the Boston Literary and Historical Association in 1905, Charles Chesnutt denounced the doctrine as the work of whites to "perpetuate the color line" and to preserve their own racial purity because they had "never been unduly careful of the purity of the black race." "I can hardly restrain a smile," he declared, "when I hear a mulatto talking of race integrity or a quadroon dwelling upon race pride." Most people came to America, he argued, "to lose their separate identity," and it should be the same for Negroes. In his view the accomplishment of this goal was to be found in "the admixture of the races" through intermarriage, which he advocated; but he readily admitted that the actual practice bore such serious social penalties that "none but the brave or the reckless would dare it."[102] For some blacks such statements, as well as Chesnutt's stories and novels about light-skinned Negroes, merely reflected the sentiments of Cleveland's "blue vein" elite, of which he was a member.[103]

Among the fair-complexioned aristocrats of color who addressed the question of mulattoes and their status, few were more forthright or more inclined to a positive assessment than Daniel H. Murray, the descendant of a prominent old mulatto family in Maryland, who was for many years a conspicuous figure in Washington's "black 400."[104] He traced the white side of his family to James Stuart, the Earl of Murray, and manifested great pride in his black as well as his white ancestors. As a result of his genealogical and other studies of Afro-Americans, Murray came to believe strongly in what he called "the power of blood inheritance." He cited the careers of a number of descendants of the antebellum free mulattoes as evidence "that blood will tell." Disputing the negative conclusions regarding mulattoes drawn by whites and many blacks, he argued that "the result of amalgamation of the Anglo-Saxon and the African has produced a composite man possessing in full measure the very best qualities of each." This "composite man" was not only "unexcelled in his mental endowment" but also possessed "exceptional virility" and a life expectancy that surpassed that of either Africans or Anglo-Saxons. Mulattoes, he argued, were the "only true Americans outside the Indians." In Murray's view, the intense feeling on the color question was primarily a Southern problem, which would dissipate sooner than some expected, at which time "the relations of the races will be as is now the case in the West Indies and the Island of Mauritius."[105]

Throughout his career as a bibliographer of Afro-Americana and historian of "colored" people in the United States, especially in his research for a proposed encyclopedia, Murray devoted much attention to "mixed bloods" and the "color question." His papers include biographical sketches of hundreds of Afro-Americans, the overwhelming majority of whom were described as of "mixed ancestry."[106] In 1904, in response to an article in a British publication on "Color Problem in America," Murray produced a lengthy list of famous individuals who conformed to his concept of the "composite man," that is, individuals of

Caucasian appearance who possessed African blood. The essay included, among others, the names of Alexander Hamilton, who was identified as an octoroon; Lafcadio Hearn, who was classified as a quadroon; Alexander Pushkin, referred to as an Afro-Russian; and the mulatto family of Vice President Richard M. Johnson. Murray also discoursed at length on Thomas Jefferson as the father of several mulatto children. According to Murray, miscegenation in the United States was "much greater than people suppose, and thousands have sunk their identity and it will never be known." Nor was he unsympathetic to those who had blended into white society. To retain the "preferment and distinction" that they possessed as whites they "had simply to keep their lips sealed."[107]

The "passing" phenomenon—fair-complexioned Negroes passing as whites—which attracted considerable popular interest, was of two basic varieties: permanent, and occasional or temporary. Permanent "passing" referred to those who cut their ties with the Negro world and lived as whites. This form of passing was fraught with high social costs, such as separation from family, loneliness, and, most important of all, the constant threat of exposure. But once individuals made the decision to "pass" permanently, most observers agreed that "it took more than ordinary provocation for colored people to betray them," because Negroes, of all colors, understood both why they did it and "the bitter thralldom and humiliations" that came with exposure. Some claimed that "thousands pass every year," while others, uncertain about the number, almost always claimed to know of someone who "passed" or at least to know someone whose relative had "passed." On the issue of permanent "passing," rumor and hearsay often appeared to count for more than fact.[108]

Among the fanciful tales that circulated among whites about the phenomenon of "passing" was one that involved the Bruces. The story, almost entirely fictional, finally appeared in print in 1931 in a national magazine. The Bruces, according to this account, were "quadroons" and natives of New Orleans, where they had both been house slaves. Blanche Bruce became a congressman from Mississippi during Reconstruction. Their first two children were so fair that they gave them to a "fine white family in Massachusetts" so that they could grow up white and be spared the indignation they were certain to encounter as Negroes. Identified as Negroes themselves, the Bruces longed for a child dark enough for them to keep and rear as their own. They sent their third child, a dark-skinned boy, to Paris for a medical education. Except for Bruce's name, the story, which apparently circulated for many years before appearing in print, was erroneous in almost every detail.[109]

Permanent "passing" was a subject that few aristocrats of color addressed publicly. One who did was Fannie Barrier Williams, a mulatto who was a prominent member of Chicago's upper class. She, like Daniel Murray, was sympathetic to those fair-skinned Negroes who "crossed over" into the white world. Since "passing" was the only means of gaining an equal opportunity, Williams concluded, those who were willing to take the risk could "scarcely be blamed, since they are certainly not responsible for the anomalous position in which they find themselves." As in the case of Murray and Williams, other fair-complexioned aristocrats of color, including Mary Church Terrell, appeared not only to be sympathetic toward those who chose to move into the white world but also to admire their courage in doing so. Almost all of them apparently knew of fair-skinned members of upper-class Negro families, such as members of the Cardozo, Wall, and McCary families, as well as relatives of Bettie Cox and Milton Holland, who had "passed" permanently, but they would not reveal information that might expose or "betray" them.[110]

It is impossible to ascertain why certain fair-complexioned aristocrats of color chose to "pass" permanently and others did not. Regardless of other considerations that may have prompted those who crossed over into the dominant society, the prospect of escaping the restrictions imposed on Negroes and of enjoying the opportunities possessed by whites was of primary significance. Those whose Caucasian features might have allowed them to "pass" but who chose to remain identified with the "oppressed" race—the so-called voluntary Negroes—did so for a variety of reasons other than the fear of ultimate exposure. Among these were the high social costs of cutting ties with family and friends in the black community and a genuine pride in one's African ancestry. Undoubtedly, too, some were unwilling to risk abandoning their status as upper-class Negro Americans and the social and economic benefits, however limited, derived from it for the uncertain status they would occupy in white society.[111]

Some aristocrats of color engaged in the practice of temporary or occasional "passing" as a matter of convenience. In this way they could secure seats at theatres and concerts, get decent accommodations at hotels, and avoid riding in unkempt, smoke-filled Jim Crow railroad cars. This form of "passing" was far more likely to prompt public comment than permanent "crossing over." In Chicago, Dr. Charles E. Bentley and John R. Marshall, among others of the light-skinned upper class, were accused of "getting by" at times. More serious was the case of Dr. J. Frank McKinley, who in 1898 married Maud Cuney, the daughter of Norris Wright Cuney of Texas. At McKinley's insistence the couple passed as Spanish-Americans. When their daughter was born, in 1902, her birth certificate indicated that she was of "Spanish American origin." Their divorce two years later led to a prolonged custody battle during which McKinley's "passing" tactics and alleged anti-Negro sentiments received full airing in the press.[112]

Even Fannie Barrier Williams engaged in temporary "passing" on occasion. During a tour of the Southwest in behalf of the National Associaton of Colored Women, she routinely refused to ride in the Jim Crow railway cars and, having purchased a "first-class ticket," she rode in first-class accommodations with whites. When a conductor asked her, "Madame, are you colored?" her response, which proved to be entirely satisfactory to the conductor, was "Je suis Français." In justifying to herself her game of deception, Mrs. Williams recalled that "there was quite a strain of French blood" in her ancestry, and furthermore the "barbarous laws" of the South "did not allow a lady to be both comfortable and honest."[113]

Scarcely less vexing was the question of racial intermarriage. Such breaches in the color line prompted controversies that revealed how sharply divided the black community was on the issue. In 1884 Frederick Douglass's second marriage, to a white woman, set off an acrimonious debate and outraged a majority of black commentators. Despite such outbursts, interracial marriages continued to be performed in states where they were legal. In his study of Philadelphia, W. E. B. Du Bois found "thirty-three cases of mixed marriages" in a single ward of the city. "It was known," he observed, "that there were others in that ward, and probably a similar proportion in many other wards." In his analysis of the thirty-three interracial couples, he concluded that four were upper class, fifteen middle class, and the remainder lower class.[114]

Early in the 1890s, interracial couples in the Midwest formed an organization known as the Manasseh Society. It is unclear whether it originated in Milwaukee or Chicago, but it existed in the latter city by 1892, and shortly thereafter a similar organization was established in Des Moines. Reverdy Ransom, a well-known A.M.E. clergyman in Chicago who "married 104 Negroes to white women and three white men to colored women," claimed that the Manasseh Society at one time had 700 members and that, contrary to the often expressed opinion, by no means all whites involved in such marriages belonged to the lowest stratum of white society. In fact, the Manasseh Society was highly selective in regard to the interracial couples admitted to membership and turned down all except those of "high moral and intellectual standing." By the turn of the century the Chicago society's annual ball at the Eighth Regiment Armory had become an elaborate and exclusive social affair.[115]

Most blacks, whether they approved or disapproved of interracial marriages, seemed to agree with Ransom that organizations such as the Manasseh Society were necessary because of the anomalous position of interracial couples. The *Cleveland Gazette* contended that they were "ostracized by both races,"[116] while Ransom, whose church included several such couples, agreed that "they were shut out from social intercourse with white people and in most cases received a cold welcome even among the colored people." But in his opinion their rejection was not without positive benefits, because "thus thrown back among themselves, they saved their money and made substantial provision for their personal security and comforts." Their children, whose education was a parental priority, often became attorneys, physicians, teachers, and other professionals. "Quite a few of them with no particular gain for themselves . . .," Ransom maintained, "passed over to the other side, that is to say they 'passed for white.' "[117]

Blacks who opposed the Manasseh Society and what it symbolized embraced a form of ethnocentrism which became increasingly evident in the late nineteenth century. Opposed to "amalgamation" in almost any form, they emphasized group loyalty and race pride and solidarity. Davis's *Atlanta Independent* represented an extreme position on the question of interracial marriage in particular and amalgamation in general. "The *Independent* is unalterably opposed," it editorialized in 1908, "to both social equality and the amalgamation of the races."[118] The latter was "a crime against both God and man." Davis, therefore, was not only opposed to intermarriage but also objected to what was perceived as the practice of dark-skinned Negroes "marrying light." Others who shared such views, even if they expressed them in less strident language, delighted in pointing out that the vast majority of racial intermarriages occurred between Negro men and white women and that most of these white women were "second-class" individuals whose social standing was so low that they "had nothing to lose."[119] For a Negro to marry across the color line was almost certain to prompt an outpouring of criticism from opponents of amalgamation in the black community.

Those who espoused assimilation, including many of the fair-complexioned upper class, tended to be more tolerant of racial intermarriages. In responding positively to the question "Is Intermarriage Between the Races to Be Encouraged?" Theophilius J. Minton, a Philadelphia attorney and a member of the city's black elite, declared in 1886: "No benefit can come to the Negro by withholding himself apart from the white people. A distinctive Negro community, a distinctive Negro civilization, distinctive Negro organizations and social orders . . . are not only not desirable, but indeed are reprehensible for they create class distinctions, and foster the race prejudice of which we desire to free ourselves."[120] While few upper-class Negroes would have gone as far as Minton in endorsing mixed marriages, Blanche Bruce, Charles B. Purvis, George L. Ruffin, and many others of comparable status rushed to the defense of Douglass when he married a white woman.[121]

Some aristocrats of color practiced what they preached in regard to amalgamation by marrying across the color line. Among them were Charles B. Purvis, William S. Scarborough, Garnet Baltimore, Leondus Wilson, John S. Durham, Archibald Grimké, and Stephen Wall. Cora and Maud Clamorgan, members of an extremely fair-complexioned old mulatto family of St. Louis which persisted in its claim to a "vast estate" granted ancestors by the Spanish government, married white men of prominence in the city. But those who entered such marriages did so at considerable risk. Archibald Grimké's marriage to Sarah Stanley, which was denounced by her father, a minister in Indiana, as "revolting," ended in divorce. Archibald apparently reared their daughter, Angelina Weld Grimké; and through his influence she secured a teaching position in the Washington Negro schools. Those who denounced Durham as "a benedict to the race" for marrying a white woman and probably drove him to spend much of his married life outside the United States, also maintained that Scarborough could have been a more effective president of Wilberforce University had his wife been black rather than white. The Clamorgans' marriages across the color line led to a series of complicated legal actions, accusations of "passing," and "no little gossip."[122]

Negroes, especially the light-skinned elite, who married across the color line not only confronted the scorn of the ethnocentric advocates of race loyalty and solidarity but also often encountered a cold welcome from those in the black community from whom they might have expected a cordial reception. As Du Bois pointed out in 1897, "the average Negro" married one of his own race and frowned "darkly on his fellows unless they do likewise." But as Du Bois recognized, this view was not restricted to "the average Negro." "In those very circles of Negroes who have a large infusion of white blood, where freedom of marriage is most strenuously advocated," he noted, "white wives have always been treated with disdain bordering on insult, and white husbands never received on any terms of social recognition."[123] As one socially prominent black woman remarked about Douglass's second wife: "I don't consider her, socially, the equal of our Washington society." The position of Mary Church Terrell in regard to an anti-intermarriage measure before Congress in 1915 lends additional support to Du Bois's contentions. Along with four of her fair-complexioned aristocratic friends, she lobbied strenuously against passage of the measure, even though she "never advocated marriage between the races." Like others of her social class, she argued that marriage was a matter "that should be settled by the individual and not by the state."[124]

In the absence of precise data on racial intermarriage it is difficult to generalize, but it appears that the total number of such marriages between about 1877 and 1918 was small. According to conventional wisdom, a preponderance of such marriages involved Negro men and Caucasian women, but the official records of New York State indicate that the number of white males marrying black females was approximately the same as that of black males marrying white females. At any rate, a substantial percentage of these "mixed marriages" involved middle- or lower-middle-class people according to stratification criteria as applied in Negro and white communities respectively. Upper-class representation was minuscule among both black and white partners.[125]

The responses of fair-complexioned, upper-class Negroes to racial intermarriage, "passing," and other issues involving color revealed the extent to which they became enmeshed in a web of ambiguities and incongruities. As the staunchest advocates of "freedom of marriage," they rarely exercised the right themselves to breach the color line at the wedding altar and often treated the white spouses of those who did with disdain. This apparent inconsistency resulted partly from their being caught between pressures from within the black community, which placed a premium on race loyalty and solidarity, and those from the "dominant race," which was increasingly determined to place severe proscriptions on all Negroes of whatever color or condition. It also seems reasonable to assume that some aristocrats of color, while willing to advocate the *right* of intermarriage, were nonetheless loath to exercise that right because it promised to saddle them with yet another burden. Undoubtedly, their class consciousness also operated to prevent marriages across racial lines; as aristocrats of color, they were unwilling to compromise their status by choosing as a mate any white who did not occupy a "co-equal" status in the white community. They insisted on marriage partners who placed a premium on family heritage, education, culture, and gentility. It might be acceptable for a female member of the Wormley family to marry a French diplomat and for a beautiful wealthy "quadroon" widow from Macon, Georgia to become the wife of the Nicaraguan minister, especially since neither would have to live in the United States;[126] but it was not acceptable to cross the color line in marriage if the spouse was merely an ordinary, respectable white or "second-class white person," as "mulatto baiters" were wont to call them.

In the late nineteenth and early twentieth centuries, Negroes in the United States lived in a world dominated and tightly controlled by Caucasians whose culture equated white with good and black with evil. Small wonder that color "appeared mysteriously in everything" within the black community. Whether real or imaginary, it was a point of contention in politics, church affairs, education, club membership, and, most important of all, social status. "The sliding scale of color," Pauli Murray recalled of her early years, "bedeviled everyone, irrespective of where one stood on the color chart."[127] There was always someone lighter with greater advantages to envy and always someone darker to look down on. Of course, Americans in general, both whites and blacks, were color conscious. The rhetoric invoked by "mulatto baiters" in the black community clearly demonstrated that color consciousness was by no means confined to fair-complexioned upper-class Negroes.

To an extraordinary degree, the concern over the equation of color and class in the Negro community focused on those of the upper class, commonly called the "colored aristocracy." Populated by a preponderance of fair-complexioned people, this elite partook of the culture, as well as the blood, of both white and black America. In the view of whites, these mixed bloods, though intellectually superior to blacks, were inferior to Caucasians. Adherence to the "one drop rule" required whites to consign the "mixed blood" to the Negro race. Negroes, especially those of darker complexion and outside the upper class, agreed with the white notion that mulattoes were mischief makers, but each had a different idea of the mischief they created. For whites, "mixed bloods" were agitators for social equality and civil rights; for their black critics, their pride in their own fair skins and their imposition of a sliding scale of color on the class system among Negroes thwarted efforts at unity and solidarity in the black community. Some blacks even argued that "all our trouble as a rule is precipitated by the conduct of those of the upper class whose opportunities have been superior to the middlers."[128] The mulatto upper class played what their black critics described as "the race racket," posing as leaders of blacks in order to win recognition and support from whites and in the process monopolizing the choicest positions open to blacks.

The characterizations of both white and black critics of the fair-complexioned Negro elite contained elements of truth. They insisted on first-class citizenship and often appeared in the vanguard of movements to achieve greater civil rights for blacks. In that sense they were "disturbers" of a racial peace based upon discrimination, segregation, and injustice. They could scarcely have been unconscious of the "color factor," especially in view of the attributes that Caucasians associated with a white skin and the acrimonious debates among Negroes regarding color gradations. While in appearance they often resembled whites more than blacks, few admitted that complexion was a matter of primary consideration. Contrary to the accusations of their critics, aristocrats of color were likely to insist that character and culture, far more than pigmentation, were the criteria used to determine who should enter their social sphere. Perceiving themselves as "quality people," they were unwilling to admit to their ranks anyone, including those of light skin, who failed to measure up to their standards of culture, gentility, refinement, and character. From their perspective, their monopoly of leadership positions resulted from their "mixed" status; as a people linked in culture and blood to both races, they were best equipped to act as intermediaries. On the one hand, they attempted to arrest or soften white prejudice; on the other, they charted a course for blacks that would ultimately persuade whites to accord them first-class citizenship, if not en masse, then one by one on the basis of individual merit and achievement.

7

◆

The Genteel Performance

ARISTOCRATS OF COLOR VIEWED THEMSELVES as the exemplary practitioners of the genteel performance within the black community. More than any other blacks, in their view, they exercised the self-restraint, both in the parlor and on the street, that were the prime attributes of gentility. For them, the genteel performance no more allowed boisterous laughter and conversation on a street-car than it did shouting during a church service.

In 1912, at the eighteenth Atlanta University Conference, on the topic "Morals and Manners Among Negro Americans," participants clearly found a close correlation between manners and social class. As one put it, manners varied "with the social grade and opportunities for contact with cultured peo-ple." The results of a nationwide survey regarding manners and deportment among blacks indicated that the higher one's social status the better one's manners. A high social status implied more education and culture, which were closely linked to proper conduct. It was generally agreed that the lower strata were "vulgar and loud and sometimes annoying," especially in public places. A respondent to the survey from Ohio, who was critical of the "boisterousness" of the masses, suggested that "loud talking and laughing" in public was "a trait of character not yet overcome by culture." Sharp division existed over whether blacks in the North or South exhibited better public manners. Northern blacks, who often compared their behavior to that of recent migrants from the rural South, viewed themselves as infinitely superior. Black Southerners, on the contrary, were certain that "the colored people of the North have not the good manners of the colored people of the South."[1]

From the perspective of the old black upper class, manners at the turn of the century exhibited a serious deterioration when compared to those of the previ-ous generation. In 1903, a writer in the Washington *Colored American*, who claimed that the "old antebellum Negro was a Chesterfield in comparison to his 'up to date' grandson," suggested that the cause lay in the tendency of parents to "spare the rod too much in bringing up our children."[2] In 1911 Mrs. Hester Griffin of Baltimore, a member of the old and highly respected Butler family, who for many years conducted a private school for the children of the city's black elite, publicly expressed her nostalgia for the decorous behavior of her own social set in the late nineteenth century: "I wish that youth would cultivate a more refined attitude. I sometimes think of my girlhood days when mothers would insist that their children only associate with refined people. . . . There are some who think that a good suit of clothes . . . is all that one needs to enter refined company, but back of it should be a respect for all those conventions which make for respectable living."[3] The "Clara-to-Louise" column in the *Washington Bee*, which regularly bemoaned the passing of polite society among blacks in the nation's capital, frequently expressed a similar nostalgia—a longing for the restoration of "all those conventions" equated with social respectability and for the return of an era when people "were very careful with whom they associated."[4]

The behavior of the upper class adhered rigidly to the rules spelled out in scores of etiquette books that circulated in "the larger society" and that were the subject of frequent interpretive comment in the black press. At one time or another many black newspapers published columns, usually called the "Women's Department," that included advice on manners and fashions. Florence Williams's column in the *New York Age* provided detailed information about the proper etiquette at everything from dinner parties to debutante balls. In the early twentieth century the *Half Century Magazine* regularly featured a section entitled "Etiquette"; like the writings of Florence Williams, it closely resembled the rules and regulations found in many etiquette manuals in general circulation in the United States.[5]

An early book-length work on etiquette designed specifically for blacks was written by E. M. Woods, a principal of a school in Little Rock. In 1896 he delivered a lecture entitled "The Gospel of Civility" at Lincoln Institute, in Missouri. It was later printed in pamphlet form and received such a cordial reception that Woods expanded it into a book. *The Negro in Etiquette: A Novelty* appeared in 1899 and covered a broad range of information regarding the attributes of polite society. Although Woods obviously used Lord Chesterfield's letter to his son as a basic source, his work was not aimed primarily at those on the top rung of the black class structure but at upwardly mobile, ambitious but unsophisticated persons of the middle and lower classes. In his discourse on proper etiquette in church, he counselled against spitting on the floor, moving around during worship services, and allowing dogs to enter the sanctuary. He denounced the use of too much cologne, the cakewalk and ragtime, the chewing of gum, and the abuse of servants as incompatible with polite society, and he maintained that unrefined parents were incapable of rearing refined children. "Refinement," he wrote, "is the legitimate offspring of refinement."

Race and racial themes pervaded Woods's volume. It discouraged blacks from accepting whites' standards of beauty and denounced Negroes who, unwilling to exhibit any consideration for ladies and gentlemen of their own race, were quick to become obsequious in the presence of whites. Yet Woods also insisted that the "black man is . . . the white man's pupil," and Negroes as grateful scholars should respect and honor their instructors.[6]

While Woods ridiculed the "old darkey" for being servile to whites, his severest criticism was reserved for the "upper tens" of black society and those who claimed to be models for their less fortunate fellows. Described as people "trying to get into another race," those of the upper class pursued an impracticable and impossible goal. Those "self-styled upper-ten negroes" who insisted on residing in white neighborhoods defied the laws of good breeding and refinement because "people of refinement don't go where they are not wanted." Woods claimed that upper-class blacks were constantly striving to "do like white folks" and as a result had suffered irreparable harm. In the matter of marriage, "upper ten colored society" had learned well to "do like white folks" by marrying for "wealth, honor, prestige and convenience" rather than for love. The results were an increasing number of "family ruptures and wrecks upon the matrimonial sea."[7]

In 1916 E. Azalia Hackley published a collection of "talks given to girls in colored boarding schools." Entitled *The Colored Girl Beautiful*, it covered a wide range of topics related to manners, dress, personal appearance, the home, relationships with men, and motherhood. One of the book's themes was "culture and self-control." According to Hackley, "repose of manner and a soft voice" were "two of the greatest charms that a woman may possess." Young women were encouraged to "affect modesty and purity" even if they "did not feel them." Talkativeness, especially in a loud voice and in public, was "a sign of lost control," which in turn was indisputable evidence of ill breeding and bad taste. "We must remove the stigma of loudness and coarseness that now rests upon the race," Hackley declared. "The less a person knows the bigger noise she generally makes." In brief, the control that a woman exercised over her emotions as well as her appetite determined whether she was "a Somebody or a Nobody."[8]

In 1920, four years after the appearance of Hackley's volume, Edward S. Green published his *National Capital Code of Etiquette*, which reflected the prevailing rules and regulations of polite society among the "black 400" in Washington. The work by Green, a government employee who moved in the highest social circle of the city's black society, appeared in the form of a traditional etiquette book. It provided detailed rules on correct dress and table manners; proper conduct in public; the staging of dinners, dances, and weddings; the art of conversation, visiting cards, and mourning. The longest chapter was devoted to "correct letter writing," with samples of letters for virtually every social occasion.

Green defined good manners as "the first absolutely essential qualification for the perfect lady or gentleman." Proper manners, he argued, were the means for gaining the respect and esteem of one's fellowman. While good manners were necessary, Green recognized that they could be a superficial veneer to obscure "a malicious and contemptible nature." To be an authentic lady or gentleman, therefore, required that good manners rest on "a foundation of human kindness, honesty and character." Like Hackley and others, Green emphasized the need for self-control through careful practice, so that restraint and polite behavior came naturally. "The person who has learned to act naturally," he declared, "has accomplished a great deal towards his aim for good manners."[9]

Amid the hundreds of minute rules of etiquette detailed in Green's volume were certain pronouncements that indicated his perception of the genteel performance. Thus, an introduction involved far more than "an announcement of the party introduced"; it was also a "recommendation and endorsement" by the person making the introduction. Conversation, Green insisted, was "one of the most important qualifications" for admission to polite society. The good conversationalist must not only possess a command of the English language, an ample vocabulary, and general information on many subjects, but also be a good listener and never monopolize a conversation. To lose one's temper during a conversation, even in a discussion of controversial topics, was as much evidence of being "ill-bred" as loud talking, picking the teeth, and cleaning fingernails in public.[10]

Green emphasized that the critical test of the genteel performance was the degree to which it was practiced in the privacy of the home: "At no time or place is *true* gentility and perfect manners so in evidence as in the home." The practice of courtesy at home by all members of the family established a solid foundation "for future perfect ladies and gentlemen." Those who shed their veneer of polished manners at home were in Green's view "the Pharisees of Society," whose "final disastrous finish is a matter of absolute certainty."[11]

In manuals like Green's and Hackley's and in etiquette columns in the black weeklies and in *Half Century Magazine*, several themes appeared regularly and frequently. One was the importance of restraint in all matters from emotion and expression to dress. Another focused on the necessity for good manners both in public places and in the privacy of the home. A third centered around the notion that familiarity did indeed breed contempt. While this adage was most often applied to the proper attitude for young ladies to assume toward the opposite sex, it was, either directly or indirectly, also invoked in discussion relating to the choice of friends and associates. The implication was clear: genteel people should not risk contamination by fraternizing with those who were not. Most of those who lectured to blacks on matters of etiquette echoed Hackley's advice to young ladies to pay close attention to "cleanliness, manners, and self-sacrifice" in order to "advance and change the prevalent opinion of the Negro."[12]

The behavior spelled out in etiquette manuals not only offered external evidence of culture, refinement, and character that equaled the best found among the "dominant race," but also served to advance the claim of blacks to first-class citizenship by demonstrating their capacity for assimilation into the larger society. In their lectures to lower-class blacks, those of the upper class often addressed the subject of proper decorum and conduct and implied at least that theirs constituted a model worth emulating. "The respectable and cultured of the race," a black resident of Denver remarked in 1908, "must set the pace for others to follow." Theirs was the responsibility to teach lower-class blacks how to behave and how to achieve "high planes of living." In 1907 a Chicago attorney who was part of the city's colored aristocracy claimed that the primary "excuse for the existence of 'society' is that it sets a standard for good manners."[13]

Throughout the late nineteenth and early twentieth centuries, upper-class blacks contrasted their own adherence to the genteel performance with the crude behavior with which they credited the lower classes. They singled out the public behavior of the lower classes for special condemnation because it was more visible to whites and hence more harmful to the aspirations of blacks, especially the "respectable people of the race."[14] In 1897 John E. Bruce, who often castigated aristocrats of color for their color-consciousness and social pretensions, directed his venom at lower-class blacks whom he observed in public conveyances en route to the Centennial Exposition in Nashville, Tennessee. Such people, he wrote, were "bumptious, overbearing and greasy in public places . . . sometimes insulting and . . . always looking for trouble." Their behavior, so conspicuously lacking in "the decency and decorum which become all citizens," intensified white prejudice against the entire black race.[15] For those of the upper class who considered themselves above "the average respectable Negro," the burden appeared all the more intolerable.

Few were so bluntly critical of "the very common Negro" as R. Henri Herbert, a native of Louisiana who had emigrated to New Jersey, where he moved in the "best circles." A charter member of Trenton's Eclectic Club, which had "close relations" with the New York and Newport Ugly Fishing Club, Herbert was for a time editor of *The Sentinel*, a black weekly in the New Jersey capital. In his view the "very common Negro"—the one lacking any of the attributes of gentility and refinement—was "as pervasive and as ubiquitous and as universal as the chaff in the wheat before it goes to the thrasher." "He is," Herbert exclaimed in 1895, "the gall and wormwood of the respectable, ambitious, charactered American citizen of African descent, a veritable thorn in the flesh." But the "very common Negro" who also possessed wealth was "more obnoxious than any other." Assuming "a wonderful superiority," he obtruded "himself into good society" and succeeded through his "vulgar ostentation and loud-mouthed vanity in converting into Aryan aristocrats everybody with whom he is thrown in contact."[16]

For some blacks there was a close link between the crudities of the lower classes and the passage of discriminatory legislation. While the Virginia legislature was considering the enactment of a Jim Crow law in 1900, a black Virginian reminded the state's white leaders that there were "thousands of Negroes . . . as refined in their ways and as pure in their lives as are the blue blood aristocracy of the South." Upper-class blacks, he argued, found the "indecent, unclean and boisterous Negro as repugnant" as did the "most refined white man or woman." Since the aristocrats of color held "no communication" with the lower-class black, "save as he comes into contact with him in his daily work," it was a gross injustice to humiliate "the genteel Negro because of the shortcomings of the few."[17]

Calvin Chase of the *Washington Bee*, who in 1901 pursued a similar argument, forthrightly claimed that the "noisy and dirty negro" was largely responsible for Jim Crow ordinances and statutes.[18] Others viewed the "lack of good manners" among the black masses as merely "a specious excuse for 'Jim Crowing' the race."[19] As late as 1916 the *New York Age* was still editorializing about "street manners." "Good manners are not just for the parlor," it declared. "They apply equally well to the street." In fact, bad parlor manners were not so detrimental as bad street manners, because they did "not affect and annoy so many people." The editor of the *Age* especially objected to "loud and coarse laughter," congregating on sidewalks, and the uninhibited spitting on the street so much in evidence among blacks in New York. Unfortunately, in the editor's view, offensive public manners played directly into the hands of white racists, who, convinced that all blacks were alike, used the behavior of those of the lower class as an excuse to impose upon the entire race, including its most cultured and refined members, degrading and insulting Jim Crow measures.[20]

J. Wilson Pettus, a high school teacher who spoke from the perspective of an aristocrat of color, claimed that upper-class Negroes, no less than whites of comparable status, were "disgusted at the dirty, sweaty, unkempt [black] majority who, without respect for themselves or anyone else, often made the conveyance almost intolerable by their boisterous conduct." But, according to Pettus, it was the duty of the upper class to teach the masses "the lesson of respectability and refinement—teach it by example, teach it by precept, in the school room, from the pulpit, in the pew, on the rostrum, through the press." Otherwise, all clamor against the "Jim Crow car law will be futile and barren of results."[21] "Similarly, in 1908 a black resident of Denver, who claimed to speak for "the respectable and cultured of the race," interpreted the role of his social set to be that of leading others to achieve "higher planes of living" exemplified by proper conduct and refined behavior in public.[22]

Throughout the late nineteenth and early twentieth centuries, upper-class blacks attempted simultaneously to pursue different and often contradictory strategies in regard to the "ill-mannered masses." They appeared to assume the obligation of instructing the lower classes in the essentials of the genteel performance. They discoursed at length on the "reprehensible impropriety" of loud talking and laughing in public places; on the need to repress coughing, spitting, and scratching; and on the virtues of personal cleanliness. To be considered a gentleman, a man must obey all of "the rules of polite society," especially in the presence of women; he must eschew all "vulgar expressions," avoid intoxication, and deport himself "in a quiet gentleman-like way." To be considered a lady, a woman should exhibit dignity and a self-respect that would prevent any violation of the prevailing sexual code.

In fact, modesty and reserve were important for members of both sexes who aspired to genteel status. "The more modesty, the more dignity we display, the more we are respected," a black writer counseled in 1909.[23] Modesty embraced a wide range of attributes, including the degree to which one restrained from ostentation and social pretention. In a letter to a friend, Charles B. Purvis was highly critical of Mary Church Terrell for what he considered her aggressiveness and immodesty. In his view such characteristics were altogether unbecoming a lady of her social standing. Purvis found especially distasteful the advertisements announcing her lectures, in which she was described as a fluent speaker in several languages.[24]

Although aristocrats of color lectured the masses on public etiquette and appeared to believe that their elevation "to a higher plane" was in their own self-interest, they never consistently pursued this strategy. For some, the task was of such monumental proportions that they chose to disassociate from the vulgar masses and confine themselves to a small circle with similar "tastes, abilities and character." A writer in the Ohio Standard in 1900 suggested that the appropriate strategy for those in "good society" was to place distance between themselves and those blacks who preferred ill manners, "rowdyism, loafing and the like."[25] But as others pointed out, any effort on the part of the higher classes "to get away from the Negro masses" was bound to fail because the race could "be saved [only] through the salvation of the masses." In fact, the responsibility for elevating the masses lay with those blacks who had enjoyed the "opportunities of experience and education."[26]

Some aristocrats of color alternated between the uplift approach and the stratagem of placing distance between themselves and the ill-mannered masses. Or, on occasion, they attempted both approaches simultaneously. Often the result was resentment by the lower classes, who accused the "refined and educated classes" of being haughty, overbearing, or, even worse, traitors to the race. "Our aristocracy," declared John M. Henderson of New York, "is at present more hurtful than helpful, because it stands with frowning face and open sneers at the threshold and sends shivers down the spine of the working middle class." In his view, aristocrats of color not only ridiculed breaches in etiquette committed by those outside their own social circle, but also made them "feel that labor, except of a certain sort," was a "badge of shame."[27] Notwithstanding the fact that members of the black upper class were "working" aristocrats, Julius F.

Taylor, the maverick editor of the *Broad Ax*, a black weekly in Chicago that alternately attacked and pampered one socially elite group or another in the city, often shared Henderson's views. In 1909 Taylor claimed that the most eminent black citizens expressed great contempt for "those members of the race who occupy humbler positions." Such behavior, he charged, was evidence of the Negro's self-hate, of his "innate desire . . . to get away from himself."[28]

To the charges of snobbery regularly leveled at them, aristocrats of color countered with a rationale for their efforts to place distance between themselves and the crude masses. The latter constituted a large, contaminating force likely to overwhelm and drag down the select few who exhibited evidences of refinement, culture, and gentility. "An excess of democracy," a black upper-class Chicagoan claimed in 1907, "exists among Negroes." As early as 1878, a writer in the highly respected A.M.E. *Christian Recorder* warned that there "was too much commonness . . . in colored people's society" and that the concept of social equality was "taken to too great an extreme."[29] Convinced that too much familiarity did indeed breed contempt, he expressed admiration for those people who bore "an air of aristocratic superiority and consequence" and advised them: "Think so much of yourselves that others will be made to feel their unfitness to associate with you until their lives and actions shall become as chaste, dignified, noble, polished and pure as yours. Then, you will have a true aristocracy." It was, he concluded, the obligation of the black aristocrat to bar from his company all those who were "vulgar and dissolute," so that his parlor would be comparable to the "Philadelphia drawing room" where only refinement prevailed.[30]

A dozen years later, in 1890, the Detroit *Plaindealer*, a weekly owned by the Pelhams, a black family that was conspicuous in the city's "cultured colored 40," warned of the dangers of the "indiscriminate mixing of all classes in public entertainments, public resorts, halls, picnics, boat rides, etc." Implicit in the discourse was the idea that the observance of proper conduct was an outward manifestation of one's inner virtue. The genteel performance constituted evidence of excellence in character, and therefore one should not associate with those whose knowledge and practice of etiquette indicated that they belonged among "the vicious, ignorant and unreliable." The writer in the *Plaindealer* counseled the "better classes" to place great social distance between themselves and the "vicious classes"; otherwise their own skirts would become "daubed with the mud of contamination" that would preclude securing "the recognition they deserve and clamor for." Those of the upper class must "draw the line themselves" because "the rest of the American people will not do it for them."[31]

For the black upper class, the display of good manners was more than a useful stratifier; it was also intimately linked to whites' perception of the race question and hence to the ability of the upper class to realize its aspirations to be assimilated in American society. For black aristocrats to become exemplars of genteel behavior was not enough. Convinced that whites were inclined to judge the race by its worst, rather than its best, elements, they also assumed the task of instructing the black masses in the fine points of decorous behavior—a task that often proved frustrating because of their belief that familiarity might result in "contamination" and therefore adversely affect their own lofty status. To an extraordinary degree, upper-class blacks, like whites of comparable status, either consciously or unconsciously, subscribed to Francis Grund's dictum that to be genteel in America necessitated knowing nobody who was not genteel. A frequent criticism leveled at upper-class blacks was that they preferred social intercourse among themselves to efforts to elevate the character of the poor.[32]

Few aristocrats of color were able to resolve satisfactorily the conflict between their notions of the genteel performance and the need for uplift of the masses. Gentility required an aloofness from the "baser classes," while conventional wisdom held that the black upper class would achieve recognition and rights at the hands of the white majority only to the degree that they succeeded in improving the condition and behavior of the black masses. The ambivalence prompted by this conflict was abundantly evident in the responses of the aristocrats of color to the problem they saw posed by the masses. While they engaged in instruction by example as well as diverse uplift activities, their approach often resembled that of late nineteenth-century "friendly visitors" who worked among the urban poor. Like the friendly visitors, aristocrats of color often displayed paternalism and condescension toward the lower classes, whom they tended to blame for the ills of the race.

The prevailing pattern of family life among the "emerged classes" in black society, no less than their behavior, culture, background and achievement, wealth, and even complexion, distinguished them from the "submerged masses." Shaped in part by a degree of wealth and economic security that separated them from lower-class blacks, aristocrats of color possessed a family life and style of living that was close to that of middle- and upper-class whites. The nuclear family and the traditional patriarchal structure were dominant features of upper-class black households. They prized marital stability and considered divorce "a terrible something"[33] that blighted children and ruined their prospects for the future. Although some critics claimed that the more black aristocrats imitated upper-class whites, especially in marrying for wealth or prestige rather than for love, the more "family ruptures" there were,[34] divorces and separations were rare among the "upper tens" of black society.

Although reliable statistical data are lacking, it appears that upper-class families were small, probably averaging two or three children. Parents lavished great attention on the welfare of their children. They expended extraordinary effort in shielding them from exposure to racial prejudice and in providing them with the best possible education, both formal and informal. It was not unusual for upper-class children to be educated at select public high schools or private academies before entering either a prestigious black college or a well-known white university north of Mason and Dixon's line. Scarcely less important than formal schooling was the more informal social education that took place in the home and within a well-defined group of their social peers. Upper-class parents recognized that the "origin of refinement" lay in the home and that children acquired the attributes of "good breeding"[35] through exposure to good manners and proper values exhibited at home. Some of the elite adult clubs had junior auxiliaries in which the fine points of proper social intercourse were practiced under the watchful eye and direction of parents.

Children whose conduct failed to exhibit the "aristocratic instincts" of the family were sources of great disappointment and embarrassment. To run afoul of the law or to be charged with a serious crime, as did one of John Mercer Langston's sons and one of Senator Bruce's grandsons, was to bring disgrace upon the family. When Frank Langston was arrested in 1887 in Petersburg, Virginia, his father became so ill "from the strain caused by anxiety for the fate of his son" that he was in bed for several days.[36]

Fathers and husbands in upper-class families were the authority figures. While few were as tyrannical as P. B. S. Pinchback,[37] the vast majority were clearly dominant in the marriage partnerships. Male members of the black upper class were virtually all "working aristocrats," who provided the principal source of income for their family. Most were employed in white-collar and managerial occupations. Many of the older members of the aristocracy of color were likely to be found in service trades—such as catering, barbering, and tailoring—or in government positions and small businesses. While some were attorneys, physicians, and teachers, a greater number of their children were more likely to be found in these professions.

Mothers and wives of upper-class black families were mainly "parlor ladies" who usually did not work outside the home. If they did, they were teachers, lecturers, or writers. Some served as occasional columnists for newspapers. Even Mary Church Terrell, who lectured extensively under the auspices of the Slayton Lyceum Bureau, claimed that she did so not to make money but rather "to create sentiment in behalf of my race."[38] Even though many upper-class women had servants to assist with housekeeping, they spent much of their time and energy in managing their households and on child-rearing and home-related activities. They organized the parties, receptions, and other social events that took place in their homes. Outside the home they participated in ladies' guilds, church societies, and cultural organizations whose memberships were limited to women of their own social class. They figured prominently in the formation of the National Association of Colored Women. Like white women, they were viewed as the guardians of culture upon whom rested "the greatest privilege and responsibility."

No less than in public life, aristocrats of color practiced the genteel performance in their private social world; shorn of the "baser classes," it included only those of similar tastes and refinement. They "studiously kept their family and social affairs out of the sight of the rest of the world."[39] Only on rare occasions did whites get a glimpse of blacks' private social lives, as in the case of Mary Church's marriage to Robert Terrell in 1891. Old upper-class families seldom attended "public entertainments" and viewed certain dances popular at such affairs as unacceptable in polite social circles. The "cakewalk" was identified with only "the lowest strata of society," for the "over-dressing, over-acting and over-prancing" that characterized the dance were directly contrary to the principles of the genteel performance.[40] While aristocrats of color traveled extensively, they rarely joined in sight-seeing excursions sponsored by religious and social organizations; and when they attended public "picnics," they were almost invariably appalled by the language and behavior of those present. Their taste in music tended in the direction of Wagner, Mozart, or Coleridge-Taylor; they shunned "plantation melodies" and especially ragtime.[41] Writing to his wife in 1899, after having observed couples dancing to ragtime, John Hope declared it was as "sensuous, alluring and degrading as that voluptuous music to which the Arab women rendered the *danse du ventre* in the streets of Cairo."[42]

The black press regularly chronicled the doings of society people, and in the process often embarrassed the old upper-class families by its penchant for extravagant and sensational prose. Press accounts of a reception given by the John P. Greens for Mr. and Mrs. George A. Myers of Cleveland, when they visited Washington, were offensive to both the hosts and the honored guests because they contained so much "gush." The Washington *Bee*, much to her horror, referred to Mrs. Myers as "the Queen of Cleveland's society." Her objection was not that the description was false but that it was not proper for publication. In explaining the tendency of the editors of the *Bee* and the *Colored American* to engage in overstatement, Green observed: "These fellows mean well, but they don't seem to understand the proprieties."[43]

Nor was the black press always careful in distinguishing between "real society" and what one aristocrat of color called "a host of upstart nobodies" whose gift for "vulgar display" was equaled only by their skill at self-advertisement. Augustus Michael Hodges, a journalist who wrote under the name "B. Square Bluster," occasionally addressed the issue of "black society" in his columns and never made the mistake of confusing the identity of the authentic Afro-American aristocrats of color with "upstart nobodies" who clamored for social recognition. Hodges himself was the descendant of a black family from Tidewater Virginia who had been free since the late eighteenth century. In a short story published in 1894, he ridiculed the pretentiousness of the social climbers. The story chronicled the career of Lem Dozier, an illiterate black man from the backwoods of North Carolina who emigrated to New York and got a job as a stableboy. He was taught to read and write by his employer, ultimately became a coachman, joined a few clubs, and printed calling cards that read "Prof. L. Wilson Dozier." In time, Dozier managed to have the black press describe him as "the leader of society." While Hodges was well aware that a coachman with the proper credentials could be a member of the "black 400," he also knew that one so lacking in family background and possessing such a thin veneer of culture as Dozier would not qualify.[44]

Old upper-class families who had long been recognized as leaders of society were appalled by newspaper accounts that transformed "upstart nobodies" into social arbiters. Edward Wilson, a black attorney in Chicago, provided a fictitious example that closely resembled accounts of social happenings that actually appeared in the black press: "Of all the exclusive functions given by exclusive persons that at Mrs. Newcomer's was the most exclusive. All society was out. Mrs. Newcomer's handsome parlors were decorated with lovely flowers that must have cost a fortune. Such an array of fine dresses and jewelry was never seen in Chicago. As space will not allow us to describe the costumes of all the ladies we will not risk the invidiousness of describing any portion of them. Suffice to say they were marvelous creations. Professor Basso's orchestra discoursed delightful music to which the guests tripped the light fantastic. . . . [Mrs. Newcomer] has established her right to the undisputed leadership of society."[45]

According to Wilson, "Mrs. Newcomer" lacked any trait that qualified her as a member of polite society. She had neither family name, education, nor cultural refinement; nor was her income sufficient to afford her social ambitions. Such "journalistic outbursts" regarding social pretenders not only prompted aristocrats of color like Mrs. George Myers to avoid publicity but also confused and misled the black public about the character of genteel black society. The result was frequent and regular criticism that people in society lived beyond their means and squandered their limited resources on lavish entertainments. Such criticism was often misdirected at old upper-class families. In contrast to the frantic activities of those whose primary claim to social status lay in their ambitions and pretensions, the small, highly select circles of authentic aristocrats appeared "like cool, shady nooks far removed from the heat, noise, strife and hurry of a town." In such circles one found "triumph over vulgarity" and a gentility that was both natural and sincere.[46]

While the "social Wigginses" boasted loudly and often of "their social gaiety and plans," the society editor of the New York Freeman declared in 1885, "the older and more settled people have begun their quiet series of social gatherings . . . in the form of Whist and supper parties varied with an occasional dinner." The social world of "the older and more settled society people," as old upper-class familes were often described, shunned the publicity and journalistic fanfare that often accompanied the social doings of those outside the "innermost inner circles."[47]

Legal and extralegal discrimination barred blacks of all classes from fashionable places of social amusement frequented by whites. For aristocrats of color, who favored assimilation into the larger society, such discrimination posed serious problems because they found most black-owned establishments socially unacceptable. Such places encouraged "indiscriminate mixing of all classes," and to patronize them was to risk exposure to the contaminating influences of the "vulgar and dissolute." Aristocrats of color believed that the more refined and cultured a person of color the more sensitive he or she was both to the behavior of the "very common Negro" and to the sting of white prejudice. By centering their social world in the home, they avoided the "baser classes" and the "upstart nobodies" of their own race as well as the "rebuffs, insults and contumely" that they encountered from prejudiced whites. As a result, the homes of old upper-class black families were frequently the scenes of receptions, dinners, musicales, literary gatherings, card parties, and dances to which only those whose public and private lives conformed to the requirements of the genteel performance were invited.[48]

Because of the importance of the home in the social life of aristocrats of color, they expended what often appeared to others as a disproportionate amount of their resources on acquiring commodious houses in respectable residential districts. Securing adequate housing in such areas proved to be a formidable task for many upper-class blacks. The difficulties of Robert and Mary Church Terrell in Washington were not uncommon.[49]

Writing in 1919, Howard A. Phelps noted that "a few years ago Chicago's best [black] people spoke proudly of Dearborn Street as their residential section," but "today they turn up their noses at the mention of the street." The influx of migrants from the South into the vicinity of Dearborn Street as well as into other areas of Chicago's black belt on the south side was largely responsible for this change in attitude. The "decay" that landlords allowed in these districts, coupled with the "inroads of fast life," prompted upper-class blacks to seek more desirable housing elsewhere, especially in the predominantly white residential areas of Kenwood, Hyde Park, and Woodlawn, where they sometimes encountered stiff resistance from whites. Those who fled the black ghetto became targets of bitter criticism by Julius Taylor's weekly, The Broad Ax, which in 1909 quoted a Negro physician as complaining that "the niggers have become so thick on Wabash Avenue" that one could "scarcely enter or leave his home." Taylor also claimed that in their search for homes elsewhere in the city, prominent blacks first inquired: "How many 'niggers' live in this block? You know we don't want to live among too many 'niggers.' " In Taylor's view, such reactions offered abundant evidence of the capacity of "the Negro to hate himself." Nevertheless, according to Louise Bowen's study in 1913, upper-class blacks in Chicago, including those in the "black belt," lived in houses averaging eight rooms each, which compared favorably to residences occupied by white families.[50]

Whether located in predominantly white residential areas or in enclaves in or near black neighborhoods, the homes of the black upper class in Chicago and other cities were comfortable, well-kept, and often spacious. In greater New York City, sections of Brooklyn remained the choice residential areas of the black elite until the second decade of the twentieth century. In Detroit, most of the city's aristocrats of color lived "in large three-story, single family dwellings on such tree-lined streets as Canfield, Alfred, Frederick and Adelaide." Others resided in predominantly white neighborhoods.[51] In the first fifteen years of the twentieth century, the black upper class in Cleveland encountered relatively few restrictions on housing and owned homes throughout the city. "I have a beautiful new home in the finest residence district of the better class of Jews and whites," George A. Myers of Cleveland bragged to a friend. By 1915, when the majority of the city's blacks were concentrated in the vicinity of Central Avenue, old upper-class black families had to a large extent abandoned the area.[52] A dozen years earlier a black observer reported that in San Francisco and Oakland it was difficult to assess the state of housing for blacks since they did "not live in groups as in other places of large [black] populations." Scattered throughout both cities were beautiful homes owned by members of the black upper class.[53]

At the turn of the century, residences of upper-class blacks in St. Louis were concentrated in a northwestern neighborhood known as the Ville, a shortened version of Elleardsville. The area took its name from Charles Elleard, a horticulturist whose large home and greenhouses once occupied the site. Early in the twentieth century, Sumner School, a well-known and prestigious black high school, was moved from the central business district to the Ville. In Atlanta the black upper class resided in many locations in the city but was concentrated in certain sections on the city's east side and especially in the area around Atlanta University. In 1884 Wheat Street was known as "the fashionable avenue of the colored population." A typical upper-class home in black Atlanta, according to a survey in 1900, was a two-story house of seven or eight rooms, with tiled hearths in spacious parlors and a bathroom. Their owners were, for the most part, teachers, mail carriers, merchants, physicians, dentists, and attorneys.[54]

While the influx of blacks from the rural South into cities throughout the nation occurred at different rates throughout the period 1890–1919, few aristocrats of color in urban areas escaped entirely the impact of the so-called Great Migration. In some instances their flights from emerging ghettoes invited the scorn of other blacks. But whether upper-class families remained residents in "black belts" or moved elsewhere, their homes were generally far removed, culturally and often spatially, from those of the black masses. In 1902 a white reporter in Detroit, in describing the houses of the city's black upper class, referred to the "excellent libraries, beautiful pictures, and musical instruments" that served as "an outward expression of the culture of the masters and mistresses that preside over them." In the Chicago home of S. Laing and Fannie Barrier Williams "the choices of pictures and an ample library" gave "an air of refinement and culture." One upper-class black woman considered any "house without books" as "an unfurnished home." In New York, Philadelphia, Washington, and Atlanta the homes of old upper-class families were often filled "with oaken and black mahogany furniture so popular at the time" and displayed oil portraits of prominent ancestors and mementoes of important events in the family's history.[55]

Elite black families often employed one or more servants. Mary Church Terrell, Josephine Bruce, and other women of high social status fretted over the "servant problem" in much the same way as white women of comparable standing. In Charleston and elsewhere in the South such servants were likely to be black, but in the North and Midwest servants in black upper-class families were often Scandinavian or German immigrants. The Langstons employed Miss Janie M. Percivel, an Englishwoman, as the family housekeeper for a quarter of a century. According to a black society matron in New York in the 1880s, Swedish and Polish women were preferable as maids because they were more tractable than others. In Cleveland Mrs. Charles Chesnutt employed German and Bohemian girls but found it "hard to make them wear shoes or wash their hair."[56]

A common complaint by aristocrats of color was that they could not secure black servants, and if they did, the blacks refused to show proper deference toward their employers. In 1902 John P. Green wrote his wife that their friends the Chesnutts had at last hired a black maid. "Sent up here from Tuskegee, Alabama," Green reported. "I suppose Brer' Booker sent her."[57] Seven years later, when Ralph Tyler and his wife had difficulty securing a housekeeper, he wrote a friend: "You can't get domestic help here [Washington] for love or money—that is colored people can't for the reason that nigger women will not work for their own color." According to Archibald Grimké, the "colored servant class" unfortunately had "adopted the white race's contempt for colored people" and preferred to remain unemployed rather than work for a colored family.[58]

On one occasion a socially prominent black woman in Washington who succeeded in securing a Negro maid discovered that her employee had mistaken her "for a white woman" because of her fair complexion. Speaking in 1905 before the National Negro Business League, Robert H. Terrell claimed that "the most serious phase of this servant question is the fact that it is almost impossible to get colored men and colored women to work for members of their own race." Such a situation, he maintained, was all the more tragic because it indicated a lack of self-respect among blacks. Terrell cited the experiences of one well-to-do black family which had advertised for a washerwoman: When a Negro woman, thinking the family was white, responded to the advertisement and called at their residence, she quickly concluded, "Lady, I can't wash for you because I am in society myself."[59] Such experiences prompted upper-class blacks ouside the South to seek domestic servants among certain immigrant groups despite problems of personal appearance and hygiene such as those encountered by Susan Chesnutt.

With or without servants, the commodious, tastefully furnished homes of aristocrats of color were the scenes of numerous social affairs. Except for church and fraternal activities, the social life of the elite was, to a large extent, home-centered. A few exclusive social organizations, such as the Society of the Sons of New York and Washington's Mu-So-Lit Club, acquired clubhouses, but most such organizations met in the homes of members, except for special events, when private banquet halls or ballrooms were rented. Whether their homes were the scenes of club affairs, small intimate dinners, or debutante parties, black aristocrats conformed strictly to the prevailing rules of social etiquette and good taste in both manners and dress. In the case of certain kinds of social functions, such as a reception or a dinner dance, engraved invitations were sent and a local orchestra provided music. Fresh flowers, even in winter, were much in evidence. No less important was the food, which was often elegant and abundant. For larger social functions in the home, locally prominent caterers served a variety of delicacies. Dinners, whether large or small, were often multiple-course meals with a variety of vintage wines. Writing in 1909, Mary Helm, a white woman, observed that the "society circle of colored people" entertained in much the same way as whites of comparable social standing.[60]

Proper entertainment, as aristocrats of color clearly understood, involved more than food, drink, and decoration. Florence Williams, the society editor of the *New York Age*, pointed out in 1889 that an essential ingredient in successful entertaining was conversation, which required hosts to select as guests "persons who are in good fellowship and on equality with one another." If the gathering was of a literary cast, then no one should be invited whose "only attribute is his good nature." Williams also counseled the host to avoid any attempt "to outrival his guests": "Everyone should be made to feel the warm hospitality of impartial attention," a feat which hosts could accomplish by "moving gracefully from one guest to another, saying a few pleasant words . . . and endeavoring to make all feel that their presence is regarded as an honor."[61] Old upper-class black families stressed the importance of polite conversation and exerted every effort to place each guest attending one of the social functions at ease. An atmosphere of warm hospitality, coupled with a scrupulous regard for correct etiquette, was the standard for social gatherings in their homes.

Guests at such functions were expected not only to display manners characteristic of gentlefolk but to dress appropriately for the occasion. In some instances formal attire was required. When Josephine St. Pierre Ruffin held a reception in July 1890 to introduce W. E. B. Du Bois and Clement Morgan, two black students at Harvard, to Boston society, it was strictly a full-dress affair. On less formal occasions guests were expected to exhibit good taste in their attire.[62] As Julius Avendorph, the so-called black Ward McAllister of Chicago, declared in 1910, there were few social sins more unforgivable than inappropriate attire or "overdressing." He advised those invited to social affairs either to dress in keeping with the occasion or to refuse to attend.[63] A few years later Azalia Hackley, in her *Colored Girl Beautiful*, claimed that dress indicated "the character of the wearer" and urged black women to avoid gaudy clothes. A black woman in Charleston agreed that one's dress revealed much about one's habits, personality, and character and counseled her daughter: "Dress, you never know."[64]

Hackley associated "exaggerated styles" with actresses and "Boulevard" women. "The exclusive dressers in high society," she noted, "study to get simple lines; with them severity in line is elegance." She stressed the importance of stifling "the desire to be conspicuous unless it is to be conspicuous in quietness." Far more significant than the quantity of a wardrobe was its quality, which in her view included tailored, conservative outfits. Women should always possess at least one good black dress. Like Avendorph, Hackley was emphatic about dressing in keeping with the occasion. A recurring theme of the arbiters of black upper-class society was that flamboyant, inappropriate dress was characteristic of those outside the pale of gentility. Neither one's clothes nor one's laughter should be "loud."[65]

Newspaper accounts of social events of the upper class sometimes exhibited, in their detailed descriptions of the attire of guests, the very extravagance and lack of restraint that aristocrats of color found so objectionable. Journalists often provided exaggerated accounts of the gowns, furs, and jewels worn by socially prominent black women at parties and receptions. When Dr. and Mrs. Charles E. Bentley honored Mrs. Daniel Murray with a musicale in their home during her visit to Chicago, the black press described the event in prose that scarcely conformed to the sedateness of the affair. "Mrs. Murray," wrote one columnist, "looked very regal in her exquisite gown of white satin and rare lace, with jewels flashing in her beautiful white hair." If Anna Evans Murray read these accounts, she surely was appalled by them.[66]

In the larger urban areas the homes of aristocrats of color were the scenes of a succession of social events from September until the advent of Lent. No sooner had they returned from summer sojourns at country places and resorts than the whirl of social activity began. Writing of the old upper-class families in Detroit in 1902, one observer noted: "They entertain most hospitably and have many dinners and teas during the winter. To these functions whole families are invited. If the mother goes the daughter is also invited and when the father is asked the sons are not forgotten. In this way the young and the old mingle and the need for chaperons is done away with." The reporter might also have suggested that this exposure to polite society and its practice of the genteel performance were important parts of the social education of the younger generation.[67]

The social calendar of the black upper class became increasingly crowded during the weeks around Christmas, a favorite season of dances, balls, and cotillions sponsored by exclusive social clubs, as well as "at homes" and receptions in private residences. Few Christmas social events anywhere in early twentieth-century black America equaled the elegance of the assemblies in Baltimore and Philadelphia. Numerous relatives and acquaintances from out of town were present at such functions, and they were often the honorees of teas, luncheons, and receptions during the Christmas season.

A social ritual in which old upper-class black families, especially in New York, showed special pride was "New Year's calling." By the early nineteenth century, the practice of "visiting and feasting," introduced presumably by the Dutch in New Amsterdam, had become a tradition faithfully practiced by New Yorkers. Women functioned as hostesses at open houses, and men did the calling, moving from one open house to another, partaking of the lavish food and drinks. By the late nineteenth century, when New Year's calling had become customary in other sections of the country, it began to decline in New York in large part because "the distinction between privacy and sociability was ignored and troops of unwanted guests descended on the open houses, using them as eating and drinking stations." But far more serious, according to one authority, "was the manner in which society women found their houses invaded by people with whom they had very slight or sometimes no acquaintance." Even the humblest employee of a company "felt at entire liberty to call upon the wife of the president of the firm" on New Year's Day.[68]

Few New Yorkers were more faithful in upholding the Dutch tradition of visiting on Sylvester Day than old black residents, including some who still bore Dutch names. The decline of the practice among New York's aristocrats of color, which was evident by the later 1880s, occurred for precisely the same reason that it did among white aristocrats: it temporarily lifted barriers that they had established against the "uncouth." It provided opportunities for those outside the "upper tens" to exhibit a familiarity that violated the code of gentility. In 1887, the *New York Age*, which repeatedly expressed regret at the decline of the old Dutch custom, reported that fewer society people than ever made preparations for "this festive day." The following year the newspaper blamed the degeneration of New Year's calling on "a certain conservative set of people who decry the custom, because it brought within their doors many who otherwise could not enter without the formality of an introduction."[69]

The ritual of New Year's calling continued to be practiced in New York and elsewhere until the 1890s, but with less participation by upper-class blacks. In Baltimore by the mid-1880s the custom was "rapidly going out of fashion among all classes," and the "set-outs," or refreshments, in homes that still held an open house were not as lavish as formerly. While New Year's calling was not generally observed in Philadelphia in 1890, the home of Andrew F. Stevens continued to be the scene of a lavish open house presided over by his daughter Helen, assisted "by a bevy of young ladies of social prominence." The practice had virtually disappeared in Savannah by 1893, when one resident recalled nostalgically: "In years gone by society people were accustomed to receive calls on New Year's Day. On that day the double parlors were thrown open, the single ladies as well as those married received gentlemen of their own circles, short speeches were engaged in, a card left and the hospitalities of the house received."[70]

What survived of the custom of New Year's calling was a practice that allowed the old black upper class to maintain its social distance from "upstart nobodies" and indeed all those whom it considered unworthy of polite society. Instead of an open house to which all were free to come, aristocrats of color, like their white counterparts, held receptions to which guests were admitted by invitation only. In Washington in 1903 more than fifty black upper-class families held receptions from two o'clock in the afternoon until midnight. According to one observer, "more generally than for years the many elegant homes were thrown open for the formal reception of gentlemen callers, and the ladies never looked so charming or exercised better taste in the arrangement of their toilettes." For ten hours "a procession of gallants" made the rounds of the fifty receptions. The metamorphosis of the "open house" into a reception by invitation presumably ensured that the male guests would indeed be "gallants."[71]

Entertaining continued among the black upper class until Lent. On occasion the week preceding Lent was one of frenzied social activity. But between Ash Wednesday and Easter all such activities ceased, for aristocrats of color were great observers of Lent. In 1890 there were so many parties in Brooklyn during the week before Ash Wednesday that "even the hardened party-goer welcomed the coming of Lent." Twenty years later, the "old Knickerbocker set of New York and Brooklyn" annually staged what was known as the Pre-Lenten Recital and Assembly, which usually included representatives of the old black upper class from Boston, Philadelphia, and Washington. The affair marked the cessation of social events until the end of Lent.[72] A visitor to Louisville during the 1908 Lenten season noted that there was "quite a dullness in . . . society circles." Whist clubs had ceased to meet, dancing had been suspended, and social functions in general were at a standstill until Easter.[73] No sooner was Lent over than the "social gaiety" resumed.

The "social whirl" of aristocrats of color virtually ceased during the summer months as those who could afford it traveled or vacationed at spas or mountain and seaside resorts and occasionally in Europe. Among the older generation, Saratoga Springs, New York remained a favorite summer vacation place into the early twentieth century. Here the Pinchbacks of New Orleans and Washington, the Churches of Memphis, the Pelhams of Detroit, and the Ruffins and Lewises of Boston vacationed regularly. In 1898 the Churches spent two months at Saratoga, where they socialized with aristocrats of color from Charleston, Richmond, and Nashville, as well as from larger urban centers in the North and Midwest. In the same year John E. Bruce reported that, because hotel accommodations for blacks at what Pinchback called "the incomparable spa" were scarce, "cottages were doing a brisk rental business in the Quartier de Africaine." For some years most black upper-class vacationers at Saratoga stayed at the Thompson Cottage or the Jackson Cottage, two small black-owned inns that provided acceptable accommodations.[74]

Resorts along the Atlantic coast, such as Newport, Atlantic City, Cape May, and Sea Isle, in time vied with Saratoga as the vacation rendezvous of the black upper class. In 1891 Atlantic City enjoyed great popularity among the younger set of this group and attracted sizable contingents from Philadelphia, Washington, and Albany, as well as the Gibbs girls from Little Rock. Whether one chose Atlantic City, Cape May, or some other coastal resort depended, in large part, on the adequacy of accommodations open to blacks. Cape May, for example, declined in popularity because of the deteriorating conditions of black-owned inns and cottages.[75]

Not all upper-class families spent their summer vacations at spas and resorts in the Northeast. Some preferred to stay closer to home and vacation at less expensive places. For the aristocrats of color in Washington and Baltimore, Harper's Ferry and Silcott Springs nearby in Virginia were for some years attractive vacation places. Daniel Murray and his family owned a summer place at Harper's Ferry, while other black Washingtonians, including Josephine Bruce, often stayed for several weeks at Webb's Cottage in Silcott Springs. Still others, such as the Wormleys, escaped the summer heat in Washington by moving to farms they owned outside the city.[76]

After the turn of the century, upper-class blacks in Washington and Baltimore as well as in midwestern cities had access to summer resorts designed exclusively for their group. Arundel-on-the-Bay, later known as Highland Beach and developed by Frederick Douglass's son, had become an exclusive retreat for the "black 400" of Washington and Baltimore. The Terrells, Curtises, Wormleys, and others of Washington's colored aristocracy ultimately purchased cottages at Highland Beach, and along with their acquaintances from elsewhere formed what was called the "summer colony."[77]

Early in the twentieth century, upper-class black families in Chicago, Cleveland, Detroit, and other midwestern cities began to frequent two exclusive "Negro summer resorts" in Michigan. One was the West Michigan Resort near Benton Harbor, where the patronage was "dignified and conservative." Advertised as the "Atlantic City of the Race," in 1910 it included bathing facilities and nine buildings, in addition to privately owned cottages. It was for a time especially popular with Dr. and Mrs. Daniel Williams, the Dennisons, and others of Chicago's black elite. When Dan Williams's arch rival, Dr. George Cleveland Hall, and his socially ambitious wife invaded Benton Harbor with their entourage of what some considered "upstart nobodies," the Williamses abandoned the resort and retreated to Idlewild in the lake country north of Grand Rapids. Between 1912 and 1930 Idlewild was perhaps the most exclusive resort for blacks in the Midwest. In time the clientele of the Oakmere Hotel included aristocrats of color from St. Louis, Washington, and throughout the South. The resort included a large clubhouse with great stone fireplaces, where friends and neighbors gathered on rainy days. Dr. Williams built a cottage there, as did a number of his friends. W. E. B. Du Bois purchased lots at Idlewild but never built a house. Aside from offering swimming, boating, fishing, horseback riding, and hiking, Idlewild became something of a summer cultural mecca, attracting concert artists and lecturers of national prominence. Among the frequent guests at the resort were the Chesnutts of Cleveland and Lemuel Foster, the president of Fisk University in Nashville.[78]

Summering together provided opportunities for aristocrats of color from throughout the nation to make new acquaintances and renew old ones, all among persons of "co-equal" social status. Children and sometimes grandchildren of the old upper-class families who played together at the spas or on the seashores established relationships that bound them for life and perpetuated the genteel tradition bequeathed by their elders. Some of those who became acquainted during childhood at a resort wound up at the marriage altar. By vacationing together in selected resorts, upper-class families reinforced the relationships that linked the colored aristocracy into a nationwide network.

A few aristocrats of color had sufficient resources for European tours. The Bruces went to Europe on their wedding trip. Mary Church Terrell, who had taken the Grand Tour upon the completion of her formal education, returned to Berlin and Paris in 1888. "My traveling dress was made at Lord and Taylor's," she wrote a friend on the eve of her departure, "and is a very neat suit according to my mother's and my taste."[79] Others of "our group" who traveled to Europe in the late nineteenth and early twentieth centuries were various members of the Shadd, Purvis, Wormley, Wilder, and Cook families of Washington; the Churches of Memphis; the Thomases of New York; and Harriet Gibbs, the daughter of Judge Mifflin W. Gibbs of Little Rock.[80]

Throughout the year aristocrats of color regularly exchanged visits. The barriers that white hotels had established against black guests meant that those traveling to another town or city had to find accommodations at a black hotel or stay with friends. Members of the upper class rarely visited places where they did not have acquaintances and friends, and many chose to stay with them rather than in black hotels or boardinghouses. During meetings of professional, religious, or political organizations, the black upper class in the host city was likely to have housefuls of guests. Alice Williams, the wife of the famous Negro surgeon, reported in September 1903 that within the previous month she had had a succession of house guests, including three members of the Minton family from Philadelphia and Mr. and Mrs. Josiah T. Settle and their two sons from Memphis. When the Williamses traveled in the South, they usually stopped in Memphis with the Churches or in Nashville with the Napiers or Stewarts.[81]

House guests were often the recipients of social favors such as teas and receptions. Those who traveled to Washington to attend inaugural balls, Grand Army of the Republic Encampments, or some other gathering were frequently honored by such social events. When Helen Chesnutt of Cleveland, daughter of the writer, visited Memphis in 1910, the Robert R. Churches entertained at a reception in her honor that included the Settles, Hookses, Thompsons, and others of the city's black elite. The press described the affair as "the most brilliant" that Memphis's black society had held in many years. Two years later, when Bessie Trotter Craft of Boston, who belonged among the city's "upper ten" families and was related to one of Charleston's best-known old families, visited Chicago, she was the object of numerous social courtesies.[82] Josephine Bruce, Mary Church Terrell, and other upper-class women, who lectured extensively to large audiences in cities throughout the country, were often the guests of acquaintances of comparable status in those cities. While they appeared before audiences that included a cross section of social and economic classes in the black community, the guests at receptions and teas given in their honor were almost invariably limited to those of their own station.

Among the most notable social occasions in the homes of the black upper class were those that introduced eighteen-year-old daughters "to the world of society." Some chose to have the debutante party on the daughter's birthday; others staged the affair in her eighteenth year at a time when it would either open or close the social season. In any event, every detail of the coming out party conformed to the prevailing rules of etiquette, and as the rules changed, so did the form of the party. Those held in the home of the debutante's parents, as most were, usually included a reception at which the young lady was introduced to the guests as they arrived. Dancing continued until midnight, and the event concluded with an elaborate supper served by a caterer.

The debut in 1889 of Katherine Bowers Smith, the youngest daughter of Mr. and Mrs. William H. Smith of New York, was typical of the fashionable form of the "coming out" party. The Smiths occupied a conspicuous place in the upper echelon of New York's black society. William H. Smith was prominent in the affairs of St. Philip's Episcopal Church and the New York and Newport Ugly Fishing Club. The debut of his daughter was an elaborate social event that attracted upper-class families from Philadelphia, Boston, and other cities as well as New York. Flanked by her parents and two close friends—Katherine White of New York, the daughter of Dr. and Mrs. Philip A. White, and Blanche Warrick of Philadelphia, whose family belonged to the social elite of that city—the debutante was introduced to the guests upon their arrival. The reception was followed by several hours of dancing to the music of Professor Craig's Trio. Shortly after midnight a catered supper was served.[83]

Few if any events assumed greater significance in the social life of aristocrats of color than weddings. Not only were they occasions for receptions, parties, and teas which, like many weddings, occurred in the home, but also they were crucial for the maintenance of proper family connections. A debutante was likely to marry either one of the "young gallants" invited to her coming out party or someone of comparable status. While some within the upper class obviously chose spouses outside their social circle, an overwhelming majority married within their own class. Whether at home or at church, upper-class weddings indicated that the contracting parties placed a premium on proper etiquette and good taste.

Letters exchanged by John Hope and Lugenia Burns during their engagement reveal their adherence to the genteel performance and their attention to the details of their wedding. Theirs was a protracted engagement, as was customary among the upper class. Hope was a professor at Roger Williams University in Nashville, and his fiancée resided with her mother in Chicago. From 1896 until their wedding, in 1897, they corresponded regularly, sometimes daily, in letters that often ran more than a dozen pages. While they exhibited much affection and tenderness, both Hope and Burns were always careful to observe the proprieties. A few months before their wedding John Hope wrote his fiancée: "It is not necessary to tell just how much we enjoy correspondence, and yet, Genie, I feel proud and happy and manly when I reflect that no conversation or letter, if brought to light, would cause either of us any shame. Our communication has been, with all its freedom and informality, at all times that of lady with gentleman. We have not grown cheap. Indeed, I think that as our acquaintance has grown our letters would bear even *closer* inspection than some of the very early correspondence. If that be true, it is almost remarkable. For the tendency is for men and women to drop a notch in proprieties."[84]

Nor did they display any less concern for the proprieties in planning their wedding. The wording of the invitation was the source of considerable discussion, especially whether the reference to Hope should read "Mister" or "Professor." "I know 'Mr.' is modest," Hope wrote. "If you prefer 'Professor' and find it admissible, have it that way. But we don't want to be laughed at as being conceited. I may be conceited but I don't care to appear so." The Hope-Burns wedding took place in Chicago on December 29, 1897 at Grace Presbyterian Church, which counted among it congregants many of the city's most prominent black families.[85]

In few cities was the marriage ceremony more important in establishing familial links among diverse elements of the old upper class than in Washington. The marriage in 1881 of Bettie Cox to Dr. John R. Francis linked two families at the top of Washington's black social structure. The bride was the niece of Milton M. Holland, the son of Captain Byrd Holland, a well-to-do white Texan. Milton Holland had been awarded the Congressional Medal of Honor for bravery during the Civil War. After the war, he settled in Washington, where at various times he held government appointments, practiced law, and served as president of the Capital Savings Bank. He was a man of considerable means, with a large home on University Hill. The bride counted among her closest friends the daughters of the Wormley, Parke, and other old families of Washington. The groom, scion of one of the city's best-known old families, was later described as a person who "sort of feels he's one of the elect." The wedding took place at the Fifteenth Street Presbyterian Church and was followed by a supper at the Holland home on University Hill, where the "brilliant assemblage" included the Bruces, Syphaxes, Cooks, and others from Washington as well as guests of equal social station from other cities.[86]

Such marriages led to exceedingly complicated genealogies among the first families in Washington's black community. In 1902 a black resident of the city insisted that it would be impossible to "furnish a comprehensive diagram of the exact kinship existing among . . . such families as the Wormleys, Syphaxes, Douglasses, Washingtons, Cardozos and Cooks." In fact, anyone attempting such a genealogical chart was likely to wind up enjoying "the hospitality furnished free by St. Elizabeth's [Hospital]."[87]

Press reports of weddings in "high life" rarely failed to indicate the social status of the families of the matrimonial pair. When Alice Wormley and John R. Francis, Jr., married in 1906, a black newspaper in Washington described the bride as a member of "one of the best and most widely known families in the city" and the groom as "highly connected . . . , from one of the oldest and leading families in the city." The names of those present at the Wormley-Francis wedding were virtually the same as those that appeared regularly on the guest lists of the Monocan Club's social functions.[88]

In other cities, weddings brought together aristocratic families of color in relationships no less complicated than those in Washington. In Philadelphia most of the old catering families, such as the Bogles, McKees, Prossers, Mintons, and Warricks, in time became related through marriage, as did many of the "first families" in Charleston, New Orleans, Nashville, and New York. In Boston the marriage in 1888 of Florida Yates Ruffin, the daughter of Judge George L. and Josephine St. Pierrre Ruffin, to Ulysses A. Ridley united two of the city's most socially prominent families. A similar union of old upper-class families occurred almost twenty years later in the same city, when Maude Trotter married Dr. C. G. Steward, a dentist and the son of United States Army Chaplain T. G. Steward. The Steward family, originally from New Jersey, possessed a long and unusual history. Miss Trotter, who was a student at Wellesley, was also an associate editor of the family-owned Boston *Guardian;* Dr. Steward had a lucrative practice, was president of the Boston Literary and Historical Association, and was active in the city's black social life.[89]

In Charleston aristocrats of color, like those elsewhere, preferred endogamous marriages, and as a result many of the old families—such as the Holloways and Browns, the Dereefs and Westons, and the McKinlays and Barnetts—were intimately related by marriage. The sons and daughters of old upper-class families, who sought greater opportunities in places other than that of their birth, chose their spouses of comparable social status.[90]

But marriages also extended the influence of the black aristocracy to virtually every part of the country. Mary Le Count Durham, who was related to the Appos as well as to the Le Count and the Durham families of Philadelphia, married Robert C. Francis, a writer and musician in San Francisco. Their son, Robert C. Francis, editor of the *Western Outlook,* exhibited the qualities of "genius, enterprise, culture and refinement" bequeathed by his ancestors, especially those of his respected Philadelphia forebears. In St. Louis descendants of the Vashon, Curtis, and Langston families, among others from the East, occupied places at the top of the social structure well into the twentieth century. On occasion, however, the movement of aristocrats of color was from west to east. This was the case of Sadie Ford of Denver, who married into the prestigious Wormley family of Washington in 1892. The wife of Dr. Austin M. Curtis of Washington was Namahoko Sockoume, a native of San Francisco, who became a fixture in the "black 400" of the nation's capital and an intimate of Mary Church Terrell, Josephine Bruce, Anna Murray, and others of "co-equal" status. Despite the appearance of her maiden name, Mrs. Curtis was not Oriental but of African, German, and Indian ancestry.[91]

As in the case of debutante parties, weddings, and other "notable occasions," the life style and routine social life of aristocrats of color, whether in Charleston, New York, St. Louis, or San Francisco, conformed to the requirements of the genteel performance. The social ritual was important as a tangible manifestation of "good breeding," a term that appeared often in the musings of aristocrats of color. Blacks used it, as did other Americans of the era, to refer to certain "habitual attitudes and a knowledge of the proprieties and manners."[92] It consisted of an amalgam of qualities inculcated and perpetuated through the family and through certain types of formal as well as social education. For aristocrats of color, their practice of the genteel performance in both private and public served as a model for the black masses to emulate and as a significant factor in advancing the "progress of the race." By eschewing loud and vulgar expressions and deporting oneself "in a quiet and gentleman-like way," a black individual presumably would assist in eradicating the prejudice displayed by whites.

While their wealth often placed aristocrats of color far above the masses and buttressed their practice of the genteel performance, they often assumed an antimaterialistic view. Wealth was not a prime requisite for membership in the upper class. In fact, well-to-do or new rich blacks who lacked proper family credentials, "good breeding," and education and who failed to display attributes of gentility were rarely admitted to the social upper crust. Most aristocrats of color appeared to agree with Henri Herbert's view that the most boorish and obnoxious creature was the person who intruded upon polite society with "naught to recommend him" except money.[93]

On occasion those of the upper class expressed disdain for what they interpreted as the crass materialism so evident in American society. They were critical of the rising middle-class black adherents of Booker T. Washington's philosophy and of those from their own ranks who were obsessed with making money. In 1897, John Hope confided to his fiancée that in his view "the mercenary man or woman" was utterly contemptible.[94] Writing to a friend five years later, John P. Green, long a fixture in Cleveland's black upper class, expressed an even stronger objection to what he perceived as "the mad quest for gold": "No one on earth appreciates [more than I] the possession of adequate money for the procuring of all reasonable comforts and pleasures of this life, yet I am constrained to say that I have only disgust and sorrow for any man who puts money before love of wife and children, health, intellectual and moral attainments and the good opinion of his fellow citizens." In Green's view, the entire Western world was obsessed with materialistic values and judged individuals by their financial assets.[95]

Some of those with "aristocratic instincts," usually the well educated but impecunious, smarted under what they perceived as the injustice of a system that denied them economic rewards commensurate with their talents and training. They were envious of middle-class blacks who had money but lacked culture and refinement. In 1897 John Swain chided his friend John Hope on his bold venture of entering into marriage "even with no bank account": "I think you will, as a refined man, often feel the gall of seeing other men, without this refinement, possess much that would make you happy: books, ennobling entertainments, classic travel, to say nothing of the things the barbarous element in us desires: horses, a fine house, servants, dresses. . . ." Swain admitted that he was puzzled about the source of his "luxurious tastes," because none of his ancestors were rich and his parents were people of simple tastes. Despite being the son of such a family, which "never even kept a butler," his expensive tastes were something that came natural to him. "I feel it in my bones," he wrote. "I crave servants, rich surroundings, . . ." But such cravings, he admitted, were a curse, because he would never acquire these luxuries; he did not even have the wherewithal to purchase all the good books he desired.[96]

For some aristocrats of color, like Swain, the acquisition of wealth posed a dilemma. On the one hand they viewed "the mad quest for gold" with disdain since it resulted in a materialistic society that placed little value on education, decorous behavior, appreciation of culture, and concern for service, especially of the sort that promoted "the progress of the race." On the other hand, the "aristocratic instincts" of upper-class blacks imbued them with desires for the tastefully furnished homes, libraries, travel, and entertainment that only a substantial degree of economic security could provide. Members of some old upper-class families, of course, resolved the dilemma by joining in the quest for the gold that would support their practice of the genteel performance.[97] The sons and daughters of those in high-status service trades—such as catering, barbering, and tailoring—often entered the medical, teaching, or legal professions in order to strengthen their claims on membership in the aristocracy of color. But from Reconstruction to the First World War, the black person who possessed wealth but lacked family credentials, education, "good breeding," refinement, and the other attributes of gentility rarely gained admission to the highest stratum of black society.

Aristocrats of color in the late nineteenth and early twentieth centuries pursued the elusive quality of gentility for the same reasons as other Americans: they assumed that proper conduct was indicative of character. But for the black upper class the genteel performance was also intimately related to the issue of race. Fully aware that they were not upper-class Americans but upper-class Negro Americans whose African blood identified them with a people considered inferior by "the larger society," they almost invariably linked adherence to the conventions governing manners, etiquette, and decorum with racial concerns. In their view the practice of the genteel performance would advance "the progress of the race." Assuming that the crudities and vulgarities displayed by the black masses, especially in public places, were responsible for much of the legal and extralegal discrimination against the whole race, they sought to eliminate a significant source of white prejudice by behaving in ways that conformed to the canons of respectibility embraced by the larger society and by encouraging other blacks to follow their example.

In her talks on manners and beauty "to girls in colored boarding schools," Hackley referred frequently to the responsibility of "conquering prejudice" and relieving the race of some of its burdens. She counseled each young lady to become a "race missionary."[98] Other upper-class black women, including Fannie Barrier Williams, Mary Church Terrell, and Josephine Bruce, conveyed a similar message in their addresses to women's groups. Mary Church Terrell probabaly inspired young black women as much by her appearance, "regal bearing," and air of refinement as by her lectures. When she lectured to a capacity crowd in Charleston on "The Modern Woman," a young woman in the audience was mightily impressed; she later recalled: "Oh, my when I saw her walk onto that podium in her pink evening dress and long white gloves, with her beautifully done hair, she was that Modern Woman."[99]

Perhaps the most significant aspect of Josephine Bruce's job at Tuskegee during her tenure as Lady Principal was to be a model of the genteel lady for female students. Like Madame Hackley, she believed that instruction in proper conduct, no less than uplift activities of a purely economic nature, was a critically important part of "service to the race." To inculcate Negro youth with ideals that produced patterns of behavior marked by dignity, decorum, and virtue was to strike a blow against the prejudice that whites showed against blacks in general. As Madame Hackley and others who discoursed on manners and conduct emphasized, each black person's welfare was "closely bound with that of the masses." "The race as a whole must progress and prosper," Hackley declared, "or else no unit may prosper."[100]

In theory upper-class blacks justified the genteel performance in large part on the grounds that it contributed to advancement of all blacks. But for a variety of reasons practice sometimes diverged sharply from theory. The widely held view among aristocrats of color that gentility required putting social distance between themselves and those considered vulgar and crude tended to isolate and alienate the upper class from blacks outside their social stratum.

For some, the genteel performance became an end in itself. Others, overwhelmed by the magnitude of the task of reforming the conduct of the masses and convinced that they themselves were the products of a natural selection process, simply abandoned the struggle and withdrew into their own private social world of people with similar tastes, values, and genteel qualities. Notwithstanding frequent references to the mutuality of interests of all "units" within the race, many aristocrats of color believed, for a time at least, that blacks would be accepted or assimilated into American society on a purely individual basis as each demonstrated merit and worthiness, including the capacity for proper behavior, both public and private. Naturally, they assumed that they themselves would be accorded such recognition first.

While the upper class continued to serve as a model of proper conduct and decorum, its withdrawal and alienation often invited the scorn and ridicule of other blacks. Described as self-centered, snobbish, and hypocritical "exclusives," aristocrats of color were accused of "playing the race racket" only when personal gain or preferment was in the offing; otherwise they were unwilling to identify with Negroes.[101] On occasion black critics appeared to express as much animosity toward the "black 400" as toward white purveyors of Jim Crowism. As for the aristocrats of color, they remained convinced that in their efforts to achieve respectability they had arrayed against them all "the lower dregs of colored society."[102]

8

◆

Upper–Class Club Life

THE CLUB AFFILIATIONS AND ACTIVITIES of Senator Bruce and especially his wife were not unusual for Americans of their social class, regardless of race, in the late nineteenth century. Throughout the century, the United States had witnessed a proliferation of voluntary organizations dedicated to a wide variety of purposes. Foreign visitors from Alexis de Tocqueville to Lord Bryce commented on the American "zeal for joining."[1] The tendency observed by de Tocqueville and described as "the habit of forming associations" by Lord Bryce accelerated rather than diminished in the decades after the Civil War, creating what historian Arthur M. Schlesinger termed a "vast and intricate mosaic of organizations." Writing in the mid-1940s, he argued that because of Americans' penchant for "associationalism," every community, large and small, had "assumed a cellular structure with the subdivision of humanity intricately interlaced and overlapping."[2]

In 1944, the same year that Schlesinger published his study of voluntary associations, the Swedish scholar Gunnar Myrdal produced his monumental study of black Americans, which included a discussion of the significance of such organizations in the black community. Myrdal claimed that Negroes were more inclined than whites to belong to voluntary associations, and that upper- and middle-class blacks belonged "to more associations than do lower-class people." Hence, in Myrdal's view these blacks were "exaggerated Americans."[3] A qualified endorsement of this view appeared the next year, in *The Black Metropolis* by St. Clair Drake and Horace Cayton, two sociologists who argued that Negro voluntary associations were primarily middle-class, and to a lesser extent, upper-class organizations.[4]

Since the publication of these studies, the debate over the relationship between voluntary associations and social class among black Americans has generated substantial sociological literature, but relatively little attention is paid to the historical aspects of the issue.[5] Regardless of which social class in the black community was most responsible for the proliferation of clubs and societies, the number of such organizations multiplied rapidly in the late nineteenth and early twentieth centuries. In 1891, a black resident of Brooklyn publicly stated that "the growing tendency of Afro-Americans to organize themselves into numberless and ofttimes useless associations is reaching an alarming extent."[6] No less obvious to blacks at the turn of the century was the correlation between voluntary organizations and social class. Knowledgeable observers within the black community were not likely to confuse the lofty status of the Social Circle in Cleveland or the Mu-So-Lit Club in Washington with that of the Galilean Fishermen and numerous other lower- and lower middle-class organizations. The black press rarely had difficulty in placing clubs and societies on the proper rung of the social ladder and was quick to identify those at the top, referring to the members of such organizations as the "best people," "our most aristocratic set," and the "upper tens," or in critical, even derisive, terms which nonetheless signified their high status.

Among the social institutions that reinforced the class consciousness of the black aristocracy in the decades after Reconstruction were a variety of clubs, societies, and associations. Some were restricted to male members, others to females, and many others embraced members of both sexes.[7] There were organizations for "the younger set" as well as for more mature members of the community. Because those of the upper class tended to be integrationists or "assimilationists," they sometimes held membership in predominantly white organizations. For purposes of maintaining contact with other blacks, aristocrats of color often belonged to voluntary organizations that represented a broad spectrum of the Negro class structure. Since P. B. S. Pinchback, Robert Harlan, Blanche Bruce, John P. Green, and many others of the upper class were involved in politics, it was essential for them to be associated with political and even nonpolitical organizations that included middle- and even lower middle-class blacks to keep in touch with "plain people." But such involvement did not eliminate the social distance that aristocrats of color maintained toward those outside their circle. Plain people who made the mistake of interpreting such involvement to mean "social equality" quickly discovered their error.[8]

Within the upper stratum of black society, clubs and organizations of almost every variety existed in abundance. A black resident of Washington noted in 1889 that "colored society [in the District] has within its bounds clubs galore. Clubs for nearly every conceivable object . . . [existed]."[9] Organizations identified with the upper class tended to be restrictive in membership and to include only those whose behavior and life style conformed to the genteel performance. Black journalists clearly understood the differences between upper-class organizations and those dominated by people lower in the social hierarchy. Even the language used in describing their activities was different. The upper class, for example, sponsored balls, cotillions, and dances but never "hops."

While most upper-class organizations were local in character and were tied to a specific community, a few had more cosmopolitan memberships. Even those identified with a particular locale accommodated individuals of "co-equal" social status outside that locale, either by inviting them as special guests or by making them honorary members. Most upper-class clubs, especially those of a social nature, were often of brief duration, sometimes no more than two or three years. The older the organization the more prestigious it tended to be. In some instances the older clubs owned buildings with dining facilities and ballrooms or assembly halls. Those identified with the upper class eschewed names that indicated status. A clear indication that an organization was not upper class was the name Elite, Select Ten, or Bon-Ton, as many clubs were called.

Black upper-class club life in the late nineteenth and early twentieth centuries pursued a variety of objects. Connected with virtually every church, regardless of its social status, was an assortment of societies whose functions were often only peripherally related to religion. Although the lives of the aristocrats of color tended to be less church-centered than those of other blacks, both men and women members of the high-status Episcopal, Presbyterian, and Congregational churches were active in a variety of guilds, societies, and other organizations sponsored by their denominations. City-wide choral and musical groups, specializing in the music of such composers as Dvorak and Coleridge-Taylor, sometimes brought together rival social factions within the upper class and also attracted members from the middle class.[10]

The number of secret and fraternal societies in the black community multiplied rapidly in the late nineteenth and early twentieth centuries. In addition to the Odd Fellows, Elks, Colored Knights of Pythias, Knights of Tabor, Grand Order of Galilean Fishermen, and other relatively large and well-known national societies, there existed scores of smaller, more regionally oriented fraternal orders by the turn of the century. Many of these societies had beneficial or insurance programs. So greatly had these orders proliferated by 1916 that one black journalist claimed that Negroes "are lodge mad."[11]

The oldest and most respected secret fraternity was Prince Hall Freemasonry. It traced its origins to 1775, when Prince Hall, a West Indian, and fifteen other free people of color were initiated into a British Army lodge in Boston. By the end of the Civil War, Prince Hall Masonic Lodges existed in sixteen states—in the Northeast and the Midwest and in California. By 1880 lodges had been established in fourteen more states, principally in the South. Until the turn of the century, Prince Hall Freemasonry remained "a solid, highly prestigious and relative small fraternity" that emphasized secrecy, ritualism, and social intercourse. Composed primarily of men of "education, prosperity and personal culture," it had "a strong mulatto caste" and left "few of the classic petty bourgeois mores unattended." Elitist and selective, Prince Hall Freemasonry provided such individuals with a close-knit environment and a national network that supported the values and life style which they represented. It also provided them with ideological if not institutional ties with middle- and upper-class whites. The order's membership came to view the black lower class as a "negative reference group," a fact of significance because it defined "what the black bourgeoisie is by demonstrating what it is not." For some, freemasonry became a family tradition; for others it was a means of enhancing or perpetuating one's social standing; for still others membership was desirable for political or economic reasons.[12]

In time Prince Hall Freemasonry became more of a mass middle-class order, and it was never as uniformly elitist as the Society of the Sons of New York and other purely social, nonsecret organizations. In Detroit black freemasonry was primarily "an association of the middle and working classes"; members of the city's black social elite who did belong, especially those involved in politics, did so primarily "to maintain some social connections with the bulk of black middling classes."[13] In other cities, representatives of old, upper-class families played more conspicuous roles in Prince Hall lodges than in those in Detroit. For many years Robert Harlan of Cincinnati, James Lewis of New Orleans, John F. Cook, Jr., and Robert H. Terrell of Washington, all of whom were active in politics, occupied positions of leadership in their respective lodges. Cook, a member of the "most seclusive family" in Washington's aristocracy of color, was for a dozen years grand master of the Eureka Lodge, the oldest and most prestigious Prince Hall lodge in the District. In New York, Peter W. Ray and Edward V. C. Eato, members of the city's most prestigious and socially promi-nent black families, held various posts in the Masonic Order, including that of State Grand Master.[14] Both men were active in several other high-status organizations. Multiple memberships among black freemasons were by no means unusual.

Even though freemasonry was not as exclusive as some other social organiza-tions in the black community, it was nonetheless a class-defining institution. "It has worked," wrote historian William A. Muraskin, "to separate its members, both socially and psychologically, from the black masses."[15] It reinforced the conviction of those admitted into lodges that they occupied an exceptional position among blacks. Although their attitude toward those of the lower class sometimes smacked of condescension, they viewed themselves as role models whose responsibility it was to transmit their values to their less fortunate brethren.[16]

In towns and cities throughout the United States, including those in which the black population was small, culture clubs existed in abundance and often included both male and female members. Literary societies were the most common variety, and those identified with the middle class were likely to bear the names of such famous blacks as Frederick Douglass, John Mercer Langston, Blanche K. Bruce, or Paul Laurence Dunbar. In 1907 a black journalist calcu-lated that there were at least 800 literary societies in the country named for Dunbar.[17] On the other hand, upper-class literaries tended to choose names that would not identify them as black organizations, except in the cases of those named for Benjamin Banneker and Phillis Wheatley.

The memberships of some literary societies, such as the Bethel Literary and Historical Association in Washington, the Monumental Literary and Scientific Association in Baltimore, and the Interstate Literary Association in Kansas City, were sufficiently inclusive to embrace representatives of both the upper and middle classes. Almost invariably, however, members of the upper class held the most important offices and made the major decisions. These broader-based organizations were valuable to aristocrats of color because they provided contact with the middle class and reinforced their claims of being racial spokesmen. Despite the appearance of "literary" and "historical" and even "scientific" in the titles of some of the larger, better-known organizations, many such associations devoted much of their energies to "race topics" and "questions of the hour." For example, the Bethel Literary sometimes issued public appeals on such matters as lynching, Jim Crow practices, and other forms of discrimination.[18]

In New Orleans the Iroquois Literary and Social Club, which early in the twentieth century owned a building with "spacious parlors," appeared to be more social than literary but in fact was neither. Rather it was a Republican organization whose membership included politically active men of the city's social elite, such as James Lewis, Aristide Dejoie, J. R. Joubert, and Walter Cohen.[19] The Pen and Pencil Club in Washington, which was one of the best-known elite male organizations in black America, began at the turn of the century as a literary society but quickly became devoted to social pursuits. The same was true of the prestigious Mu-So-Lit Club, also of Washington, whose original cultural concerns received less and less attention. In time its clubhouse became a retreat for upper-class black men to find respite of a purely social variety from the strife of race and "questions of the hour."[20]

In smaller, more local organizations the social and literary aspects of club life were intimately intertwined, especially in women's groups. During the 1890s the Woman's Club in Baton Rouge, Louisiana met weekly "for the purpose of fostering sociability, doing literary work and planning receptions and socials," but clearly the literary work was for some years of secondary importance. The exclusive Social Circle of Cleveland was more successful for a time in maintaining a balance between the literary and social aspects of club life, but it ultimately became the Euchre Club, devoted to the card game by that name.[21]

Small upper-class literary societies met in the homes of members, usually in the evening. Some met weekly, others less frequently. A couple of members were responsible for the program, which might involve the study of a particular book or author. On occasion members were expected to read certain works in preparation for meetings and to contribute to the discussion of the topic under study. The literaries devoted much attention to the study of classics, especially the works of Shakespeare. Scarcely less important was the concern with biography, particularly the lives of literary figures, artists, musicians, and statesmen.

Among those whose biographies received attention were Phillis Wheatley, Toussaint L'Ouverture, and both black and white antislavery leaders. At some point in the meetings of the small societies members enjoyed "the delicacies of the occasion" served by the hosts.

The larger, more inclusive literary organizations, such as the Monumental in Baltimore and the Bethel in Washington, usually met in churches or in other public halls open to blacks. While their programs often included topics of a literary and historical nature, they were more likely to focus on themes that illuminated the "progress of the race" or to address public issues of special interest to blacks. Frequently their programs included well-known speakers, such as Frederick Douglass, Richard Greener, Mary Church Terrell, or Booker T. Washington. In St. Louis the organization comparable to the Monumental and Bethel was the Forum Club, which in 1901 had 186 members and owned a club building. Dominated by most of the city's professional and prominent businessmen, the organization met monthly to study and discuss "race problems."[22]

A variety of the intellectual and cultural organizations that attracted aristocrats of color focused attention on history. Local literary societies as well as church associations and even the American Negro Academy devoted considerable attention to the Afro-American past. In 1883, when George Washington Williams, a black historian, called for the organization of a national "Negro Historical Society," his recommendation met with favorable response in the press.[23] Although no such organization came into existence, the formation of several societies with similar objectives indicated that there was widespread interest in Afro-American history, especially among the educated old upper class.

In 1890, Florida Ruffin Ridley of Boston, whose interest in history derived in part from her research into her own family background, spearheaded a movement that led to the organization of the Society for the Collection of Negro Folk-Lore. Present at the organizational meeting that took place in her home in March 1890 was a select group of Boston's black upper class, including representatives of the Chappelle, Ruffin, and Sparrow families, as well as young William E. B. Du Bois, then a student at Harvard. Unfortunately information regarding the society beyond this initial meeting is lacking, but the materials in the Ruffin-Ridley papers suggest that at least Florida Ridley retained a keen interest in Negro history and folklore.[24]

On October 25, 1897 the American Negro Historical Society of Philadelphia was organized. While it came to include individuals who were not among the city's colored aristocracy, virtually all of the organizers and leaders were educated, socially prominent members of Philadelphia's upper-class families. The individual mainly responsible for the organization of the society was Robert Mara Adger, whose father had been an abolitionist and a well-known merchant in the city for over fifty years. Adger himself held a position in the Post Office and was one of six surviving members of the old and prestigious Banneker Institute. Also figuring prominently in the initial efforts to organize the society was Theophilius J. Minton, a well-to-do attorney who was the son-in-law of John McKee and the son of a famous caterer. Adger was the first president, and Minton was an early vice president. The society's treasurer was Henry L. Phillips, the Jamaica-born rector at the Church of the Crucifixion, a high-status Episcopal congregation in Philadelphia, of which Adger was a member. Two other founding members of the society were Matthew Anderson, minister of the Berean Presbyterian Church, and William Henry Dorsey, a native of Philadelphia whose father was one of the city's most illustrious caterers. Dorsey, who inherited substantial wealth from his father, held a succession of minor posts in the municipal government. A bibliophile and numismatist, he traveled widely collecting books and artifacts "concerning the Negro race in the world."[25]

The American Negro Historical Society met the fourth Tuesday of each month in the Parish House of the Church of the Crucifixion, which became its headquarters. Membership was open to all interested persons "regardless of sex." The society published occasional pamphlets, including Henry M. Minton's *Early History of Negroes in Business in Philadelphia* in 1913, and devoted much energy to the collection of historical materials relating to the Afro-American past. Within six years after its establishment, the society had acquired a "valuable collection . . . of rare books, newspapers, pamphlets, clippings and pictures" donated largely by friends and members and concerned mainly with the history of black Philadelphia. The widow of Jacob S. White, a famous educator in the city, donated a substantial body of his papers to the society. From its beginning until its demise early in the 1920s, the society subscribed to the idea that "no country can record its history truthfully until all of its scrolls are unrolled." According to one black writer, in establishing a historical society Philadelphia had "set the pace" for Afro-Americans in other cities to follow.[26]

Perhaps the most important individual in the American Negro Historical Society, other than its founder, was William Carl Bolivar, a native Philadelphian whose family had been prominent for several generations. He was related to the Le Counts through his mother, and he was an active member of St. Thomas Episcopal Church. Bolivar held a position in a well-known banking house for almost a half century. He acquired a huge library relating primarily to the history of Afro-Americans and functioned in Philadelphia in much the same way that Samuel Scottron did in New York, by chronicling the past of the city's blacks. From the founding of the *Philadelphia Tribune* in the 1880s until his death late in 1914, Bolivar, under the pen name "Pencil Pusher," contributed a weekly column on the Afro-American history of Philadelphia.[27]

The formation of societies in Boston and Philadelphia devoted to the Afro-American past, as well as the publication of histories of the Negro in

America by Williams in 1883 and by Edward Austin Johnson in 1891, coincided with an increase of interest in historical activities in the United States in general. The Negro Society for Historical Research, which was similar in some respects to the Philadelphia society, was launched about 1911 by the journalist John E. Bruce and the bibliophile Arthur Schomburg, a native of Puerto Rico. In the same year Reverend W. R. Lawton of the prestigious St. James Presbyterian Church started the New York Historical and Literary Society. Four years later, the Association for the Study of Negro Life and History[28] was founded by Carter G. Woodson, a Harvard-educated teacher in the Washington schools and a member of the most elite intellectual and social organizations in black America, the American Negro Academy and Boulé.

Among the numerous musical organizations in Washington's black community none were more prestigious than the Treble Clef Club and its offspring, the Samuel Coleridge-Taylor Choral Society. In 1897 a select group of women representing the city's best-known black families organized the Treble Clef Club for the purpose of studying classical music. Several members and especially Mrs. Andrew F. Hilyer manifested a keen interest in the musical works of Samuel Coleridge-Taylor, an Afro-British composer whose fame had spread across the Atlantic by the turn of the century. On a visit to London in 1901, Mrs. Hilyer met the composer, and shortly after her return, she and her husband invited a few friends to their home to discuss the possibility of forming a choral group to perform the works of Coleridge-Taylor. The aim of the Samuel Coleridge-Taylor Choral Society was "to develop a wider interest in the masterpieces of the great composers and especially to diffuse among the masses a higher musical culture and appreciation for the works that tend to refine and cultivate."[29]

Incorporated in 1903, the society ultimately included 200 members. Andrew Hilyer served as a treasurer and general manager, and John F. Cook was president; other directors and officers constituted a virtual roster of the District's black aristocracy, including Francis L. Cardozo, Arthur S. Gray, and John W. Cromwell. Among the women were Harriet Gibbs and Mrs. Robert Pelham, gifted musicians who were members of the Treble Clef Club. The choral society's first concert, on April 23, 1903, presented the premiere of Coleridge-Taylor's *Trilogy*. This performance prompted the *New York Times* to wonder "whether so effective a chorus had ever been heard before in Washington." For many whites in the audience it came as a revelation to learn that blacks could perform "high class music."[30]

At the urging of Hilyer and the Choral Society, Coleridge-Taylor came to the United States in 1904 and again in 1906. In 1904 he conducted performances of his compositions in which the chorus was accompanied by the United States Marine Band. Critics extolled his artistry as a conductor and composer and described the singers as unquestionably the best to appear at any time in Washington and vicinity. Coleridge-Taylor's second visit, which in-

cluded performances in New York as well as Washington, was no less triumphant than the first, and his *Hiawatha* became "one of the most popular works
with choral groups of both races."[31]

The Choral Society continued to stage concerts for almost another decade
after Coleridge-Taylor's second visit. Its officers strived to "cultivate a taste for
the best music" within the black community. "I shall always love the S.
Coleridge-Taylor Choral Society," a well-known black tenor wrote Hilyer,
"because it is doing more than any similar society in the world for the culture
and refinement of our race." Following the deaths of Arthur Gray and several
other key members, the society ceased to be active after 1916, and, after a brief
revival five years later, it disbanded permanently.[32]

Perhaps the most ambitious organization of a cultural and intellectual
nature undertaken by the nation's aristocrats of color was the American Negro
Academy. It specifically involved the group generally known as "the educational
set"—professors, theologians, literary figures, and other intellectuals. Spearheading the movement was the erudite Alexander Crummell, founder and
minister of the prestigious St. Luke's Protestant Episcopal Church in Washington, who envisioned the society as an agency to promote "the integrity and
perpetuity of the black race as such." Limited to forty members, the Academy
was open to "graduates or Professors in Colleges; Literary characters; authors,
artists and distinguished writers." Its membership came to include a substantial
segment of Washington's "colored society" as well as prominent blacks from
throughout the nation. Among the latter was William S. Scarborough, a
well-known classical scholar and president of Wilberforce University in Ohio,
who counseled the Academy against admitting "every Tom, Dick and Harry *et id
omni genus.*" At the urging of another member, William Edward Burghardt Du
Bois of Atlanta University, who saw the academy as "the epitome and expression of the intellect of the black-blooded people of America," the organization
modified its qualifications for membership to read "men of Science, Letters and
Art, or those distinguished in other walks of life." The objectives of the academy
included the promotion of Negro culture and unity through literary and scholarly works, aid to "youths of genius in the attainment of high culture," the
establishment of historical and literary archives relating to blacks, and assistance
to publications that vindicated "the race from vicious assaults."[33]

The function of "trained and scholarly men" such as those invited to join
the academy, according to Crummell, was to shape and direct "the opinions and
habits of the crude masses." He believed that it was the responsibility of the
black elite to save the masses from "being crushed on the one hand by white
racism and on the other, by black primitiveness."[34] Addressing the academy in
1903 on "The Educated Negro and His Mission," Scarborough pursued a similar
theme: He argued that the mission of the educated elite was "to help form classes
of society where culture and refinement, high thinking and high living in its
proper sense, draw the line—classes made up of what one denominates an

'aristocracy' of intelligence and character that protects the masses from the foes from without and from their own folly and unrighteousness."[35] Du Bois, who served as president of the academy from 1898 to 1903, espoused the same view in his advocacy of the Talented Tenth, which stressed the leadership role of the college-educated black elite. "The work of the educated Negro," he declared, "is the work of leadership."[36]

T. Thomas Fortune, the preeminent black American journalist at the turn of the century and the leading proponent of the term "Afro-American" as the proper designation for blacks in the United States, was highly critical of the academy for including "Negro" in its title. Convinced that the term implied those of unmixed African ancestry, Fortune argued that by emphasizing "Negro" identity, the society would exacerbate the tension already existing between mulattoes and blacks. A light-complexioned man of African, Irish, and Indian descent, Fortune maintained that the academy's attention to racial integrity would have a divisive effect in the black community. He used the occasion to elaborate on what he perceived as the historic role of mixed bloods in American society; in his view they constituted a favored group that had rendered invaluable service by reducing the impact of white prejudice on the black masses and by articulating the needs of all Afro-Americans to whites. Fortune also noted that many of those who clamored loudest about racial purity, including Crummell, Du Bois, and Scarborough, had not chosen dark-skinned women as their wives.[37]

Fortune struck a sensitive nerve, and his criticism of the academy, published originally in a white newspaper, created a minor tempest. The dark-skinned Crummell was outraged at what he considered Fortune's "contemptible, jesuitical and lying" journalistic foray; he insisted that his wife was "not a mulatto." John W. Cromwell responded to Fortune, pointing out that the academy contained members ranging in color from black to near white and that the favored position of light-skinned blacks was not a matter of concern for the organization. Early in his career Crummell had suffered at the hands of the mulatto ruling class in Liberia. In 1896 he confided to a friend just as color prejudice was cresting in the United States that there had arisen "a fanatical junto, more malignant than white men, pushing themselves forward as leaders and autocrats of the [Negro] race and at the same time repudiating the race." The sole basis for the claim to superiority put forward by this "junto" of mulattoes was, he maintained, their "bastardy." Whether Crummell's death a little more than a year after the founding of the academy was a factor in easing the tensions over the issue of color is unclear.[38]

Whatever the significance of the color factor may have been in the life of the academy, notions of elitism and missionary paternalism were pervasive. Despite all the rhetoric about the mission of the educated elite in the uplift of the masses, the organization's accomplishments in this respect were meager. The most recent authority on the history of the academy has suggested that from the beginning its purpose was to "promote the status and influence of its elite members as much as to promote the 'civilization' of the black masses."[39]

In the mixing of cultural and social objectives, evident in so many black clubs, the cultural objectives often became obscured in the struggle to acquire and retain social superiority. Both large and small black communities were experiencing the so-called social revolution. In 1906 a black resident of Steubenville, Ohio wrote: "Our society is on the verge of a social revolution. The basis of the trouble seems to be that several social and literary clubs [are] striving to be the social arbiter of our people here. The new industries have brought in many new Afro-American residents, with new tastes and ideas, and the old time social leaders are about to be consigned to the seas of oblivion. First of all, we have the Reading Club, containing the older people and a few newcomers who seem to assimilate to a certain extent. The club with the high sounding title Fleur de Lis, containing younger members, but nearly all members of the old families, striving to wrest all honors from its older competitor, and dictate the social standard. The Elite [Club] is getting its second wind and will make a hot finish. The most exclusive, The Whist Club, is small, but Oh! My! . . . it is almost an entire alien membership. Last but by no means least comes the Silver Leaf [Club] which controls or seeks to control the destinies of several other organizations. . . . Banqueting seems to be its strong card."[40] This account emphasized the disruptiveness experienced by small, stable black communities as the influx of Negroes, especially from the South, accelerated in the early twentieth century. The struggle among the clubs in Steubenville for status, occasioned in large part by the aspirations of newcomers and by the determination of "old citizens" to hold on to their hard-won place in the social hierarchy, was no less divisive in larger cities in the East and Midwest.[41]

The migration of blacks from the South into these cities prompted the socially prominent "old cits" to withdraw into organizations which expressly excluded newcomers. Those who were responsible for the formation of such organizations undoubtedly shared the views of Miss Eleanor Elliott, a fictional character in Dorothy West's The Living is Easy. As a descendant of an old black family of Boston, she recoiled at the influx of "so many unfortunates of our race" because their presence would "diminish in the estimation of our better whites" those of her class who were "hardly thought of as colored" before the arrival in Boston of so many poor, untutored blacks from the South.[42] The best approach to the "problem" in the view of many old upper-class families was to place greater distance between themselves and the newcomers, whom they tended to hold responsible for the intensification of racial antagonism, especially in the era of the First World War. Southern blacks who poured into urban areas of the North and Midwest were not the "well meaning, industrious, progressive Negroes," according to a prominent black Ohioan, but were "the lazy, shiftless, worthless" ones.[43]

About 1903, as the influx of black Southerners into Boston was increasing, members of the city's elite old families organized the Society of the Descendants of Early New England Negroes. Beginning with seventeen charter members, the group drew up a constitution limiting membership to citizens who had lived in New England prior to 1830 and their descendants. The society's rules were so restrictive that they excluded many socially prominent families, such as the Trotters and Ruffins. It does not appear that the society made any provision for extending associate or auxiliary status to those of high social standing who could not meet all requirements for membership, as many exclusive organizations elsewhere did.[44]

As early as 1905 there existed in Chicago's black community an Old Settlers Club. It met each month for the purpose of allowing the old families to "mingle together and chat over olden times" and especially to exchange stories about fugitive slaves and the Underground Railroad. Clearly they perceived the black migrants from the South as little more than "hordes of barbarians" who threatened to undermine the status that they had achieved through long and often bitter struggle.[45]

A similar community of interest and consciousness of cultural kinship among old upper-class black families inspired the formation of the Pioneer Club and the Native Sons and Daughters of California, both in Los Angeles.[46] Even in the tiny black community in Seattle, in 1907 the "old families" organized the Pioneer Social Club, which met monthly.[47] In 1912 the old residents of Washington, D.C. founded the Association of Oldest Inhabitants; it was made up of men who had lived in the District for at least thirty years and the sons of such individuals who were twenty years old or older. Although the association claimed to be "aggressively alive to every racial interest" and "a liberal con-tributor to organized uplift efforts," its primary emphasis was on the reinforce-ment of group pride through the "preservation of the valuable personal and racial history" as it related to their own forebears. Such history emphasized their patriotism, involvement in the Underground Railroad, and cordial relations with influential whites.[48] By 1914 one of the strongest social clubs in the Indianapolis black community was the Old Settlers Club, consisting of persons who had resided in the city for thirty years or more and their children. Among those most active in the club were the Hill, Furniss, and Christy families.[49] Such organizations became important in nourishing class consciousness and unity at a time when a flood of blacks out of the South appeared to jeopardize the fragile place that aristocrats of color had carved out for themselves in urban America.

An early example of an exclusive organization based on nativity or length of residence was the Society of the Sons of New York, founded in 1884. It was followed two years later by the Society of the Daughters of New York, a select group of New York-born ladies who "banded together for mutual love, protection and elevation."[50] In 1892 the Sons purchased and outfitted a commodious clubhouse on Fifty-third Street at a cost of $20,000. By the mid-1880s, when the Sons came into existence, the monopoly on the most prestigious and lucrative positions held by the old families of New York, some of whom bore Dutch names or were of West Indian origins, was being threatened by talented newcomers, most of whom were new migrants from the South. Membership in the Sons required not only that an individual be born and reared in New York but also that he be eminently respectable. Few of the native-born blacks of the city became members; only those who met the "respectability" requirement and belonged to families that had been prominent for several generations actually received invitations to join the society.[51] According to the *New York Daily Tribune*, "to belong to the Society of the Sons of New York is the ambition of every respectable colored man of the city."[52]

Nothing so clearly revealed the class orientation of the Society of the Sons of New York as the way in which it accommodated "newcomers" to the city of "co-equal" rank. While it excluded ordinary people, natives and non-natives, it was careful to include as "honorary members" socially prominent residents who did not meet the nativity requirement but whose family background and connections entitled them to special consideration. Among the honorary members were James W. Mars, a socially prominent resident of Brooklyn who was a descendant of an old and well-known Connecticut family; T. Thomas Fortune, editor of the *New York Age* and a member of a prominent black family from Florida; and T. McCants Stewart, an attorney from Charleston, South Carolina. Those who were most active in the founding and early development of the society bore names long identified with the civic and social life of New York— Ten Eyck, Ray, Reason, Van Horn, Williams, Scottron, Downing, and Peterson.[53]

The Society of the Sons of New York was most visible in April, when it sponsored an annual "reception"—actually a ball replete with orchestra, dancing, and catered food. Although the organization claimed to be "purely social and philanthropic," it clearly paid little attention to philanthropy and focused its energies on social affairs, especially the April reception, which rarely failed to receive detailed coverage in the press as the epitome of the social life of the "black 400." Arriving in handsome carriages, the members and their guests were invariably described as bearing all the earmarks of good breeding, refined tastes, and the latest fashion. A black reporter wrote of the Sons' second annual reception: "Beauty, gallantry, toilets, flowers, smiles, compliments and wine, all compounded making one grand carnival of mutual congratulation and mutual admiration, where voices low with fashion, not with feeling, softly freighted the air. . . ."[54] But if the society's annual reception was a gathering of the city's social elite, there were gradations even within the elite itself. Whether the reception was at The Cosmopolitan, Webster's Hall, or Tammany Hall, those in the boxes—and usually there were no more than two dozen boxes—represented the pinnacle of New York's black social structure.[55]

The founding of the Society of the Sons of New York stirred considerable resentment among newcomers, especially those who occupied important positions in the churches, schools, and business life of the black community. It inspired the formation of several organizations which explicitly excluded native New Yorkers. Among these were the Sons of Virginia, the Sons of North Carolina, and the Sons and Daughters of South Carolina, each made up primarily of professionals. The largest and most important, however, was the Sons of the South, which was organized in 1885, the year following the founding of the Sons of New York. Shortly afterward it changed its name to the Southern Beneficial League and for some years staged an annual reception which rivaled that of the New Yorkers in lavishness if not in exclusiveness and "refinement."[56]

By the second decade of the twentieth century, the younger generation of the "old families" represented in the Society of the Sons of New York had become the dominant force in the social life of the black elite. The "younger set" was found in the Bachelor-Benedict Club, which sponsored at least one "assembly" each year. Organizations with the same name came into existence in Cleveland, Philadelphia, and other cities and were also made up of the children of the old, socially prominent families and others considered worthy of admission to membership.[57]

Some black residents of New York interpreted the proliferation of clubs and societies, each discriminating against one group or another in the city's black community, as an unhealthy development. In their view it contributed to divisiveness at a time when discrimination against all blacks required as much unity in their ranks as possible. In response to such criticism the leading black newspaper of New York stoutly defended the growth of exclusive clubs, arguing that their principal advantage was that they brought together in organized fashion persons "who know each other most intimately and are therefore prepared to work most harmoniously for the success of the objects contemplated."[58]

Considerable duplication in membership existed between the Society of the Sons of New York and the much older New York African Society for Mutual Relief. Founded in 1808 by the leading black men of New York, the latter began as a beneficial organization to relieve the occasional financial problems that members might encounter. In time it accumulated "a sizable bank account" and valuable property. While membership still involved significant economic benefits, by the turn of the century the social prestige that it conferred was even more important. From the beginning membership was limited to fifty persons, but the actual number was usually smaller. Although the society did not sponsor social events, such as receptions and balls, and reports of its activities rarely received attention in the black press, black residents of New York clearly understood that the organization was the preserve of the city's old families and that it conferred a social status that no other organization in the city did. One observer in 1887 declared that "it stands today [as] one of the most respected, wealthy and conservative landmarks of old New York." The sons and grandsons of the society's earliest members, those named Ray, Downing, Vogelsang, Varrick, and Eato, and others prominent in education, religious affairs, and business, were active in its affairs well into the twentieth century. In fact, Edward V. C. Eato, employee of the Queen Insurance Company for many years and a descendant of Reverend Timothy Eato, a founder of the society, served as president for more than twenty-five years beginning in the mid-1880s. Eato was also closely identified with the Sons of New York and served as Grand Master of Prince Hall Masonry in New York at the turn of the century. In 1908 he presided at the centennial anniversary meeting of the African Society at elaborate ceremonies in Saint Philip's Episcopal Church.[59] At his funeral in January 1914, at "Mother Zion" A.M.E. Zion church, where he was a lifelong member, the handsome floral wreaths from the Ugly Club, Masons, Society of the Sons of New York, and the African Society symbolized the role he had played in all these organizations.[60]

Four years before his death, Eato's twenty-five year tenure as president of the African Society came to an end in a successful revolt by the younger members of the Society. Leading the movement that "routed the old guard" was Charles Lansing, an employee of the Brooklyn Gas, Water and Electricity Department for a quarter of a century. His family had been conspicuous in the affairs of New York's black community for several generations. Smarting under the ultraconservative leadership of Eato and a small group of "elders" in the society, Lansing and the "young Turks" won control by focusing on the need to raise the death benefit paid to heirs of members from $600 to $1,000—a change unalterably opposed by the Eato faction. However, Lansing and the new leadership undertook no other changes. The society remained an exclusive organization that viewed itself as the repository of the best traditions of New York's black community.[61]

In the late nineteenth and early twentieth centuries, members of the African Society took great pride in the age of the organization and in the accomplishments of those identified with it. Organizations in other northern cities with similar objectives and names had been formed about the time of the New York Society or even earlier, but they had failed to survive so long. The longevity of the New York society was indisputable proof of "the soundness of its internal affairs." Samuel R. Scottron, the chronicler of blacks in "old New York," reminded twentieth-century black residents of the city that the African Society had been established "nearly twenty years before the final emancipation of slaves in New York State" and had been the "first organization among the colored people of the city to appear in a public parade." He also noted the advanced educational status of those who founded the society and the "cordial and fraternal feeling" that existed between them and the white gentry. "Other societies have their brigadier generals, colonels, majors, captains, lieutenants and privates, comparatively speaking," he wrote in 1905, "but here we have a society with no rank less than colonel, and ever so many major generals. In that respect, it can't be matched in the United States, among colored men."[62] While Scottron's claims in behalf of the New York African Society may have been extravagant, membership in few other black organizations conferred more prestige or signified with more certainty one's place in the aristocracy of color.

Among those that did equal the New York society in these respects and that were of comparable age were several organizations in Charleston, South Carolina. For example, the Brown Fellowship Society, "the preeminent mulatto organization in antebellum Charleston," founded in 1790 by free Negroes, was still in existence in the twentieth century. Like the New York society, it was a mutual aid organization that provided sickness and death benefits for members and their families. Notwithstanding the scholarly debate over whether the Brown Fellowship was a color-conscious enclave of the wealthiest mulattoes, who sought to separate themselves from blacks, membership in the organization was an indisputable mark of high social status. So was membership in the Friendly Moralist Society, another exclusive mulatto group, founded in 1838. It was composed of younger members of the city's mulatto elite, and although they represented substantially less wealth than did members of the Brown Fellowship, the Friendly Moralist Society was a "good training ground for prospective members" of the older and more prestigious organization. As in the case of the New York African Society, both Charleston organizations limited their memberships to fifty; emphasized respectability, good manners, and decorum; and represented the wealthiest components of the Afro-American population of their city. Given the similarities between the New Yorkers and the Charlestonians, they probably would have been at ease in each other's company.[63]

While few organizations could claim a continuous existence as long as the New York African Society or Charleston's Brown Fellowship and Friendly Moralist societies, there were some which continued to confer high status and prestige for years after the purpose for which they had been established was no longer of primary importance. Among these were two organizations in New Orleans, the Société d' Economie, which had been created in 1837 by "those Creoles [of color] with tendencies toward exclusiveness"; and the Société des Jeunes Amis de Bienfaisance et d'Assistance Mutuelle, another colored Creole society founded thirty years later, which kept its records in French until 1918. No less prestigious was the Female Lundy Society of Albany, New York, founded on June 13, 1833, by "a few ladies of color" primarily for "the dispensation of charity" to fugitive slaves en route to Canada. Its name derived from the antislavery leader Benjamin Lundy, whose portrait still hung in the society's meeting hall sixty years later. By 1890, when the society celebrated its fifty-seventh anniversary, its primary function was obviously not assisting runaway slaves or the dispensation of charity. Rather it was essentially a social enclave of "ladies of color" of old prominent families.[64] Ironically, it was from the ranks of such people that the latter-day "fugitives"—the poor ignorant black migrants from the South—encountered opposition and hostility rather than assistance and hospitality.

Black organizations whose sole purpose was social or recreational probably outnumbered all other types of clubs and societies. They ranged in size from a dozen or two to several hundred individuals. Some, such as the Whist clubs, met often and regularly; others existed primarily for one or two social events each year. In virtually every black community, one social club was recognized as representing "the best society." In New York after the mid-1880s, the Society of the Sons of New York was such an organization. In Baltimore it was the Baltimore Assembly, created in 1909, which sponsored exclusive social events twice a year. In Philadelphia the Crescent Club reigned virtually unchallenged as the premier black social organization in the city from the late 1870s until the 1890s. Famous for its annual Christmas balls, it included all of the city's "first families" as well as invited guests from Washington and New York. By the second decade of the twentieth century the Bachelor-Benedict Club had replaced the Crescent as the city's most exclusive black social organization. Its membership included the younger members of the Abele, Warrick, Stevens, Dorsey, and other "old families." The Bachelor-Benedict Club became famous for its annual Christmas ball and reception.[65]

Of comparable social standing was Pittsburgh's Loendi Club, whose permanent clubhouse was a handsome three-story brick building with a tastefully decorated interior. Its membership consisted exclusively of professional men and those who held white-collar jobs, including its longtime president William Maurice Randolph, an attorney who married the sister of John S. Durham of Philadelphia.[66] For several decades after 1887, the Home Social Club of Albany, New York represented the pinnacle of the city's black social structure. Limited to a membership of twelve, which included representatives of the Douge, Yopp, Price, Van Vranken, and Van Horn families, it was the male equivalent of the city's Female Lundy Society. The Home Social Club was noted for its annual Christmas dinner-dance, which was attended by members, their families, and their out-of-town guests. As young men, Dr. Daniel Hale Williams and Hutchins Bishop of Maryland were frequent guests at the club's annual social event. Both had relatives and a large circle of friends among Albany's aristocrats of color.[67]

Class differentiation in Washington's black community was most evident among the organizations of a purely social nature. From 1880, a succession of such organizations came into existence, representing one clique or another of Washington's colored aristocracy. In the 1880s one of the most prestigious social clubs for black men was the Diamond Back Club, which met monthly and included Bruce, Pinchback, Terrell, Murray, the Cook brothers, and others of the city's elite. Each meeting included a gourmet meal, which had to include terrapin in some form. The Diamond Back Club maintained "close fraternal relations with the famous Ugly Club of New York and its Philadelphia annex, both of which represent[ed] the highest standards of social life in their respective cities."[68]

During the late 1880s and the 1890s, two of the most prestigious gentlemen's organizations in Washington were the Manhattan and Acanthus clubs. Organized in 1888, the Manhattan Club limited its membership to 300 and had its headquarters in a ten-room, three-story brick house. It was dominated by men of high social standing whose residence in the city was of relatively recent date. Among its best-known members were James C. Matthews of New York, John S. Durham of Philadelphia, and H. Price Williams, the brother of the famous surgeon Dr. Daniel Williams. A year after the organization of the Manhattan Club, a group of native Washingtonians and longtime residents, including Daniel Murray, Albert Brodie, Christian Fleetwood, and John C. Nalle, incorporated the Acanthus Club, which took its name from a plant that flourished on the east coast of Africa. It consisted of 115 members, and its clubhouse, located on L Street near the homes of several United States senators, had a library, double parlors, and a spacious dining room.[69]

In 1899 a group of colored aristocrats in Washington, led by Francis L. Cardozo, Jr., formed the Cosmos Club for "the enjoyment of themselves and their friends." Patterned after the white society of the same name, the Cosmos Club sponsored a series of four "assemblies" annually. Being on the invitation lists for these affairs was indisputable evidence of one's membership in Washington's "charmed circle." For reasons which are not clear the Cosmos Club changed its name to the Monocan Club shortly after the turn of the century and increased the number of its "assemblies" to six each year. Despite its new name, the organization remained the preserve of colored aristocrats.[70]

Throughout the late nineteenth and early twentieth centuries, Baltimore witnessed the rise and demise of a succession of purely social organizations. For some years after its founding in 1879, the Banneker Social Club was the best known and most exclusive gentlemen's club in black Baltimore. Presided over by the Deavers, Myerses, and Briscoes, it sponsored a Christmas ball that was conceded to be the "grandest social event" of the year.[71] By 1890 the Baltimore Annex of the New York and Newport Ugly Fishing Club had eclipsed the Banneker as the city's most elite black social organization. But the difference in the membership of the two was slight; representatives of the old families dominated the Annex as they had the larger, more inclusive Banneker. Scarcely less prestigious than either was the Baltimore Auxiliary of Washington's Inauguration Committee, a group that came into existence every four years to sponsor social events in connection with the inauguration of the President of the United States.[72]

Social rivalry among the aristocrats of color in Baltimore, as in other places, spawned a succession of factions, each claiming to be superior to the other. On occasion a faction of the social elite, represented by a short-lived organization, such as the Manhattan Club, would be responsible for several major social events that attracted representatives of old upper-class families from various cities. In 1905, for example, the Manhattan Club, headed by John C. Matthews, sponsored a debutante ball at which the daughters of Baltimore's aristocrats of color, including the Bradford girls, were presented to society. Guests from Washington, New York, Chicago, and Annapolis were present for what was described as "the finest affair of the season."[73]

In 1908, William H. Bishop, Jr., invariably identified as "belonging to one of the oldest families in Maryland," who was a clerk in the Internal Revenue Service for thirty-five years, succeeded in pulling together the various rival factions in Baltimore's black elite into a single organization, known as The Baltimore Assembly. Bishop served as its president and John C. Matthews as vice-president. The annual mid-winter balls and post-Lenten receptions held under the auspices of The Assembly offered abundant evidence of "gentility." Indeed, in 1910 one black journalist insisted that the social affairs of the "better class of Afro-Americans" who made up The Assembly surpassed even those sponsored by people "who claim to belong to the 'smart set' of the white race." In order to insure that The Assembly would remain genteel, its officers decreed in 1912 that the Bunnie Hug, Turkey Trot, and Gavotte, dances in vogue with the "smart set" in other cities, would not be allowed at the mid-winter ball in Baltimore; the invitations that year included a card listing those dances considered appropriate.[74]

In the late nineteenth and early twentieth centuries, social organizations of a status comparable to The Baltimore Assembly included the Young Men's West Side Social Club of Atlanta; the Eclectic Club of Trenton, New Jersey, which was organized in 1876; the Detroit Social Club, founded in 1890, which included the Pelhams, Watsons, Fergusons, Miraults, and Barriers; the Bachbens Club in Boston; and the Uno Club in Hartford, Connecticut.[75] In Chicago there was a succession of high-status social organizations. Among the oldest was the Prudence Crandell Club, organized in 1887, which included most of the "first families" of black Chicago. Members of the same families were found in the Fellowship Club and the Lotus Social Club. The latter, established in 1889 and described as "the pride of society's devotees," aspired "to achieve something that will reflect upon the entire race." Presumably this something was related to efforts of the club members, through their dress, manners, performance of the social ritual, and public deportment to set a standard for the race. In addition to its debutante ball, the Lotus Club in 1891 took the unusual step of sponsoring a "Calico Fancy Dress Ball" to demonstrate that something other than fine dress was necessary for membership in Chicago's "best society." Regardless of whether the club was sponsoring a cotillion or a calico ball, numerous guests of comparable social standing from outside Chicago were likely to be present. In 1890, for example, the Pelhams of Detroit and the Mordecais of St. Louis attended the club's post-Lenten dance.[76]

The most elite social organizations in the larger cities on occasion engaged in fund-raising efforts on behalf of a designated charity. In Philadelphia, Chicago, Washington, and other cities, charity balls were held to assist black hospitals, day-care centers, homes for the aged, and a variety of other worthy causes. In the press the "charity benefit balls" often received far more criticism than praise. The general complaint was that such elaborate social events produced more "society" than revenue for charities. Charity balls, so the argument ran, provided aristocrats of color opportunities to exhibit their snobbish behavior. Some critics even accused the social elite of using the few receipts from charity benefits for purposes other than buying "wood, coal and provisions for the worthy colored poor of their town."[77] An observer at a charity ball in Chicago's Second Regiment Armory in 1892 was comparatively generous in his assessment of the affair: "The absence of restraint and snobbishness was one of the most commendable features of the evening. While it is true that the leaders of society confined their attentions to the friends with whom they are accustomed to associate in Society, they did not carry their exclusiveness to the extent of rudeness."[78]

In 1912 the *Washington Bee* was not so generous: "There is, a so-called 'charity' group of individuals in this city who delight in giving 'society' balls under the guise of charity dances. That the cause for which these dances have been given is a worthy one, there is no doubt, but that the principles under which these affairs have been given were founded upon gross hypocrisy is becoming more and more apparent every day."[79] Such affairs, according to the *Bee*, were bound to be financial failures because their sponsors were bent upon restricting attendance to the "social elect," who had neither the means nor the inclination to underwrite worthy causes.

Despite the charges leveled at aristocrats of color by the *Bee* and other critics, their charity balls and other social events staged for philanthropic purposes did generate revenue, sometimes substantial amounts, for black hospitals in Chicago, St. Louis, and Philadelphia and for settlement houses, homes for the aged, and various other projects elsewhere. That the income produced by such social events was relatively small undoubtedly reflected the limited financial means of the aristocrats of color, and while they sometimes displayed an attitude of paternalism and even condescension toward those who benefited from their balls and receptions, they did not perceive of their efforts as expressing "principles of gross hypocrisy."

In larger black communities, the most prestigious clubs often sponsored debutante balls in connection with their major annual social events, usually those held during the Christmas season. The debutantes, as would be expected, were the daughters of the old upper-class families, and invitations to their "coming out" parties included only guests of similar family background and social status. From the end of Reconstruction to the outbreak of the First World War, debutantes in black communities from Providence, Rhode Island to New Orleans, Louisiana were annually introduced to the world of society.[80] Debutante balls sponsored by elite social organizations constituted an important element in the associational relationships of the nation's aristocrats of color and undoubtedly reinforced the tendency of upper-class blacks to marry within their own "circle."

Social organizations of the aristocrats of color came into and went out of existence with regularity. This phenomenon appeared to depend in large part on the intensity of the struggle between social cliques or factions within "the upper reaches of society," which usually had little relationship with the rivalry between "newcomers" and "old cits." These were struggles between peers. In Boston in the 1890s there was acute rivalry between "two distinct fashionable social sets" in the black community, the "West End Set" and the "South End Set," whose credentials as aristocrats of color were virtually identical.[81] Writing in 1906, Archibald Grimké, who resided for some years in Boston, found the same factionalism among the social elite in the District of Columbia, although it was not identified with particular sections of the city. He despaired of the aristocrats' lack of cohesiveness and of their penchant for expending energy on matters of little significance at the expense of business enterprise and racial uplift. As evidence of the disunity in the upper reaches of black society, Grimké pointed to the struggle among the social factions over entertainment in connection with the inauguration of President Theodore Roosevelt in 1905.[82]

The struggle was especially intense that year, but it was not the first occasion in which rival factions of the District's "black 400" competed with each other to provide the most lavish and prestigious entertainment during Inauguration Week. At least since the Civil War there had been two series of inaugural festivities in Washington, one white and the other black. In 1901 the competition among the various factions of Washington's colored aristocracy for sponsorship of the inaugural ball in the black community assumed an intensity that had not previously been apparent. In that year the principal competitors for social preference were the Cosmos Club, led by Francis L. Cardozo, Jr., who claimed that his organization represented "the best people," and the Inaugural Welcome Committee, headed by Daniel Murray, who was no less certain that his group represented the same people. Both organizations sponsored lavish balls and both claimed to attract the *crème de la crème* of black society from Washington and other places throughout the nation.[83] "Washington in its social circles is rent asunder," Murray wrote to a friend shortly before the inauguration, "and we are on top. We have the finest hall in town and it's the talk of the town."[84] John P. Green, who was allied with Murray, viewed the struggle in generational terms and interpreted the Cosmos Club's bid for precedence as an effort of the younger members of the aristocracy to usurp the rightful place of their elders. "The Old

Guard," Green advised, "must stick together and each man do his duty when the time comes to down them."[85]

The rivalry of the social cliques in the District's black upper class had in no way abated by the inauguration of 1905, when the Monocan Club, the successor to the Cosmos, vied with the Citizens Committee for social supremacy. That year John P. Green headed the Citizens Committee, while Murray and his brother-in-law Bruce Evans held other key positions in the organization. In 1905 the membership of the Monocans included representatives of the best families in the District—the Cooks, Francises, Cardozos, Pinchbacks, and Terrells among them. A third organization, the Native Washingtonians, also sponsored an inaugural ball in 1905. Although the *Washington Bee* announced that "the real ball will be given by the Native Washingtonians," this observation was more revealing of the editor's prejudice and his failure to gain admission to the other two organizations than it was a statement of fact. The Native Washingtonians represented substantially less social prestige than the other two groups because a majority of the most socially prominent, native Washingtonians were identified with the Monocans and the Citizens Committee. If the Murray-Green faction had demonstrated its social superiority in 1901, clearly the honor four years later belonged to the Monocans, whose ball at the Light Infantry Armory was, by all accounts, the most lavish affair of its kind ever staged by the black people of the District.[86]

In 1909 the rivalry was less intense between the Monocans and the Murray-Evans group, again called the Inaugural Welcome Committee, but a new element was introduced by the decision of the prestigious Mu-So-Lit Club to sponsor a ball. Because the Mu-So-Lit drew heavily from the constituencies formerly identified with the other two groups, its entry into the competition seems to have had a unifying effect.[87] By 1913, when Woodrow Wilson was inaugurated as President, a semblance of harmony prevailed among the "black 400." For most of them, the entrance of a Southern-born Democrat into the White House was scarcely an occasion for celebration.

Although few factional struggles generated so much sound and fury as those in Washington, rival social factions among the black upper class, each claiming preeminence, existed in most sizable black communities. The "social situation" in Indianapolis, as described by one observer in 1890, was by no means unusual: "Society in this city is composed of a number of luminaries, each esteeming itself brighter and more luminous than its neighbor. Each luminary attracts to itself, by its own center of gravity, three or four satellites. In other words society has separated itself into clans; each clan has a leader. Each leader and each clan is opposed to his neighbor. This opposition engenders strife and keeps the members of society from that freedom of association and having that tender regard for this fellow as he ought to have."[88] In some instances, factions did indeed revolve around individual social luminaries whose whims and jealousies were sources of perennial discord. In others, the factionalism resulted from the refusal of "old cits," who emphasized family background, fairness of complexion, and length of residence, to admit to their circle newcomers of comparable or greater education and wealth. Such refusals almost invariably produced rival social cliques. Only those newcomers whom the "old cits" determined to be compatible—that is, those who possessed the necessary qualities of good breeding, education, ancestry, and color in proper proportion—were likely to gain admission to the older, most elite social organizations. One who possessed wealth, or even wealth and a fair complexion, but who lacked education, the attributes of gentility, and especially what was considered the proper ancestry and family background would still be considered little more than a "mulatto nobody." Blacks who had, in fact, pulled themselves "out of the depths," a phrase roughly equivalent to "the self-made man," and achieved a degree of wealth and influence did not take kindly to what they perceived as the hauteur and condescension of the old families.

But aristocrats of color were not without their defenders. Among those who publicly applauded "the coming of the Negro aristocrat" and his efforts through clubs and other means to "escape the rabble, the ignorant and the uncouth" was Fannie Barrier Williams of Chicago. She and her husband, S. Laing Williams, an attorney, moved in "the best circles" in the city and belonged to the most elite organizations there in the late nineteenth and early twentieth centuries. Fannie Williams admitted that the black community possessed its share of "shadow aristocrats," those who assumed that "fine dresses, fine homes and even a fine education" were adequate substitutes for character, intelligence, manners, refinement, and authentic "aristocratic instincts." She expressed regret that "no social rim can be made wide enough to include all the people who deserve a place within its sacred borders" and that the evolution of "an aristocratic cult" within black communities resulted in "petty envies and spites and sore hearts" in those "on the outside." Nonetheless, she believed that the development of such a cult was "in the right direction" and that the Negro aristocrat was "very much needed" and had "good services to perform." The Negro aristocrat must work out his "ideals from within and not from without" his race, and having done so, he would henceforth function as a model and inspiration for the masses, who desperately needed instruction in manners and deportment. Williams and others of the old upper class believed that so long as the black masses engaged in boisterous behavior in public and failed to abide by the conventions of Victorian society, all people of color, from the highest to the lowest, would continue to be targets of discrimination and oppression.[89]

While most of the social clubs identified with the aristocracy of color in the late nineteenth century were local in character, the New York and Newport Ugly Fishing Club came nearer than any other in providing a comprehensive social organization for those in the upper reaches of black society, especially in the East. The club originated in the mid-1860s with a group of prominent Negro men who were fishing companions. By 1885, when it had become one of the most prestigious social organizations in black America, its members had largely abandoned their interest in fishing and confined their activities to one or two exclusive social events each year. In time, the Ugly Club, as it became known, had branches or annexes in Philadelphia, Baltimore, and Charleston. In addition, the Diamond Back Club of Washington, while never officially an "annex," maintained close relations with the Ugly Club, whose headquarters was always in New York. By the 1880s the organization was generally perceived as representative of the elite of eastern black society.[90] In 1881, in the process of describing the Ugly Club as "the great society club," a black newspaper correspondent denounced its members as "mere toadies of society" and as "whitewashed" blacks.[91]

By the mid-1880s the principal object of the club was "to bring together at its annual dinners the best minds of the race in the country." Despite its claims about the "best minds," it was an organization of the social elite that had two banquets each year, one in the winter and the other following Lent. These affairs included not only representatives from the Ugly Club Annexes but also carefully selected guests from many places. Always held in New York, these banquets invariably attracted a large contingent from the annex in nearby Philadelphia. Those who occupied positions of leadership in the Ugly Club in the two decades after its founding were the same individuals found in the New York African Society for Mutual Relief. For example, James W. Mars served serveral terms as Commodore of the Club, the title held by the chairman or president, and E. V. C. Eato was for many years secretary.[92]

The organization avoided publicity and remained largely invisible except for the press accounts of its annual dinners. To celebrate its twenty-first anniversary, the club took the unusual step of sponsoring a reception at which wives of members and guests were invited. This reception was as near as the club ever came to opening its doors to the public. In describing the event, a reporter for a black newspaper wrote: "Elegantly engraved invitations, embellished with uniquely tinted specimens of piscatorial life announced one of those rare occasions in the history of the New York and Newport Ugly Fishing Club when their doors were open to the world of society, without restriction as to age and sex. For although this organization has reduced hospitality to a science, it has usually been displayed in the form of dinners which necessarily restricted its enjoyment to a few. But the attainment of its majority was marked by a departure from its exclusiveness and after deciding to give a reception, the club maintained its reputation for lavish but discriminating hospitality by an entertainment unsurpassed for elegance in the social annals of the city."[93] Commodore Mars and Vice-Commodore Philip A. White and their wives served as hosts at the affair, which included "the youth and beauty, learning and wealth of New York and Brooklyn, Philadelphia, and other cities."[94]

Although the Ugly Club was a social club, its members did concern themselves informally on occasion with "race topics." In December 1888, the members discussed "the industrial and political phases of the race problem" while they enjoyed refreshments. According to one writer, Ugly Club members were "public spirited" men, "and many a movement for the general good" grew out of their meetings. The organization became less visible after about 1890, perhaps because of the increasing social prominence of the Society of the Sons of New York. Most of those in leadership positions in the Ugly Club were also conspicuous in the Society, which created honorary memberships for individuals who were not natives of New York. The relationship between the original Ugly Club and a social organization known as the Ugly Club, Jr., which existed in Philadelphia until the First World War, is unclear.[95]

The formation, in 1904, of Sigma Pi Phi, better known as Boulé, in a sense represented an amalgam of the Ugly Club and the American Negro Academy. The object of Boulé was to bring together college-educated Afro-Americans for social purposes. It was forthrightly elitist and consistently exercised great care in enforcing rigorous standards of admission. It was a conscious attempt to bring together Negroes who had "demonstrated outstanding ability to compete successfully with whites." Boulé's members adhered to a code of unimpeachable personal conduct and in fact constituted a model of the genteel society. The organization shunned publicity, and therefore accounts of its activities rarely appeared in the black press. But contemporaries knowledgeable about the Negro community and social structure were fully aware that Boulé represented, in the words of one member, "the flower of the race."[96]

The founders of Sigma Pi Phi were two physicians, a dentist, and a pharmacist—Edwin C. Howard, Algernon B. Jackson, Richard J. Warrick, and Henry M. Minton—all connected with Mercy Hospital in Philadelphia and all members of the city's colored aristocracy. Long active in the social life of the black upper class, they were identified with civic and racial uplift enterprises. Joining the original four shortly after their initial meeting on May 15, 1904, in Howard's office, were Eugene T. Hinson and Robert J. Abele, two other physicians who were also well connected in Philadelphia. Abele, a descendant of an old and well-known family, was related through marriage to the family of John F. Cook in Washington.[97]

The idea of a social fraternity of college-educated black men originated with Henry M. Minton. Through his wife, Edith Wormley, he was connected with one of Washington's most prestigious families. The third generation of his family to occupy a conspicuous place in Philadelphia's black community, Minton possessed all the attributes of a late nineteenth-century Victorian gentleman. Sophisticated and polished, he had what Americans, regardless of race, considered the best education of his day. He attended public schools in Washington and then spent two years in the preparatory department of Howard University before enrolling at Phillips Exeter, where he compiled a remarkable record. He graduated from the Philadelphia College of Pharmacy in 1895. He was a founder of Douglass Hospital, the first black hospital in Philadelphia. Minton enrolled in Jefferson Medical College in 1902 and graduated four years later, at which time he and his close friends Howard, Warrick, and Jackson were the prime movers in the establishment of Philadelphia's second black hospital, Mercy.[98]

According to the official historian of Sigma Pi Phi, the purpose of the organization was to provide "inspiration, relaxation, intellectual stimulation and brotherhood . . . [for] those who participate."[99] To participate the basic requirement was a college degree. In elaborating on the object of Boulé, Minton was careful to note the way it differed from other organizations. Its purpose, he declared, was "not to visit the sick and bury the dead but to bind men of like qualities, tastes and attainments into close sacred union."[100] The organization attracted those of the "talented tenth," a phrase associated with W. E. B. Du Bois, who became a member of Boulé and occupied an important office in it. As Minton and others repeatedly emphasized, the possession of wealth alone would not win one admission into Boulé. Indeed, those whose source of wealth was considered illicit or even questionable were explicitly excluded. The Boulé membership did include men of wealth, but only those who also met other requirements regarding education, respectability, and congeniality. From the beginning the organization adhered to the notion that "quality not numbers is our aim."[101]

In view of its selectivity, it is not surprising that Sigma Pi Phi expanded slowly. Its second chapter was established in 1907 in Chicago, where Minton settled briefly following graduation from medical school. The Chicago chapter contained mostly physicians and dentists, including Daniel H. Williams and Charles E. Bentley, but Williams's adversary, Dr. Cleveland Hall, could never muster enough votes to gain admission. The following year a chapter was established in Baltimore; it included Ralph V. Cook, Mason Albert Hawkins, Samuel Mossell, the McCard brothers, and Thomas S. Hawkins. In 1910 Sigma Pi Phi organized a chapter in Memphis, its first expansion into the South. Among those in the original Memphis chapter were attorney Josiah T. Settle, several prominent physicians, and James C. Napier of Nashville. The organization of a chapter in Washington in 1911 brought into the ranks of Boulé a sizable contingent of doctors, teachers, and attorneys who bore some of the most prestigious family names in black America—Bruce, Terrell, Tyson, Francis, Gray, Douglass, Curtis, Wilder, Wormley, and Cobb among others. By 1920, when Boulé had undergone sixteen years of selective expansion and established additional chapters in St. Louis, Kansas City, Detroit, and Atlanta, its total membership amounted to only 177. In all these chapters, only the most highly educated, cultured, and sophisticated men, representing the highest stratum of black society, gained admission. The extraordinary prestige of membership in Boulé reinforced the high social standing of individuals invited to join.[102]

One of the early issues that arose in the organization concerned whether it should adopt and promote some program or line of action for the "betterment of our people." William C. McCard of Baltimore, among others, maintained that it was incumbent upon members to "do more than pat each other on the back and eat good food." While Mercy Hospital was sometimes considered "a creature of Sigma Pi Phi" and local chapters often sponsored charitable and civic projects, the fraternity remained essentially a social organization of the educated elite. In addition to the diverse social activities of local chapters and those of the wives of members, who constituted something resembling auxiliaries, the numerous social functions of the national meetings of the fraternity, known as the Grand Boulé, were strictly limited to members and their families. According to the chronicler of the fraternity, "receptions, whist parties, luncheons and banquets and a round of festivities made these occasions the events of a lifetime for those in attendance."[103]

Writing in 1965, a distinguished black social psychologist observed that there was an element of "pretense and artificiality about Boulé."[104] He noted that in an effort "to build a tradition of inherited status, the sons and grandsons of members may be admitted who do not quite match the high standards required by their fathers and grandfathers." Clearly, however, the early members of Boulé already possessed a tradition of inherited status. They were the sons and grandsons of those who had been members of elite organizations such as the Ugly Club, the New York African Society, Philadelphia's Crescent Club, and various clubs in Washington. According to Kenneth Clark, Boulé represented "a kind of family, a community of mutual acceptance, of congeniality and compatibility," and although it sometimes appeared to be snobbish, superficial, and stuffy, it nonetheless provided "a sense of belonging" and a refuge for aristocrats of color to escape from "the conflict and tensions of race." In brief, Boulé provided an oasis that allowed members to enjoy friendship without being continually reminded of the everyday problems of being a Negro.[105]

Although Sigma Pi Phi did not provide a national program of action for "the betterment of the race," many of its members were conspicuous in a variety of movements which did have such programs. The ideologies of both Booker T. Washington and W. E. B. Du Bois had adherents within Boulé, but the nature of the organization and the background of its members meant that it was more closely identified with Du Bois. Because Du Bois's Niagara Movement drew heavily from the integrationist-oriented, college-educated upper class, it naturally attracted the support of a substantial number of Boulé members. In fact, the organization of a Baltimore chapter of Sigma Pi Phi had its origins in a conversation that occurred at a meeting of the Niagara Movement in 1906. On that occasion Charles Bentley of Chicago discussed the fraternity with Mason Hawkins of Baltimore, and when Hawkins returned home he initiated efforts to organize a group of "like-minded college degree men" in Baltimore that ultimately became Gamma Boule of the fraternity.[106]

For a few years Boulé maintained two classes of members: one for college graduates, the other for undergraduates. Like the educated professionals, black students in white universities suffered from social isolation. To overcome this isolation and develop association with men of "like attributes, education, skills and attainments," they followed the example of their elders who established Boulé and formed fraternities. This development prompted Boulé to discontinue its undergraduate memberships after only two men had been admitted to it.

The first black college fraternity, Alpha Phi Alpha, was founded at Cornell University in 1906; it was followed five years later by Kappa Alpha Psi at Indiana University. Once these fraternities had been established by black students at white institutions, others at black colleges followed in quick succession, including Omega Psi Phi and Phi Beta Sigma at Howard University in 1912 and 1914 respectively. In the meantime, the first black sorority, Alpha Kappa Alpha, came into existence on the Howard campus. Five years later another group of young women at Howard formed what became Delta Sigma Theta.[107]

Existing alongside male organizations were those made up exclusively of upper-class black women, often the wives or female relatives of men prominent in the Ugly Club, Boulé, and others. In some cases the women's organizations were adjuncts to the males'. The Masonic order, for example, had its female auxiliary, as did the Society of the Sons of New York. Black clubwomen constituted what Fannie Barrier Williams described as the real "gentle folks."[108] They cultivated tastes for fine literature, music, and art; displayed elegant manners and other attributes of gentility; and manifested a paternalistic interest in what they viewed as the "submerged masses." In sizable black communities, upper-class women, like their husbands and male relatives, formed clubs that were as diverse in function as they were numerous. And like upper-class white women, they not only devoted much attention to the social graces, fashionable dress, and canons of good etiquette but also functioned as guardians of the home and culture. They took seriously their responsibilities for the "progress of racial civilization."

The evolution of the club movement among upper-class black women was, in some respects, similar to that among middle- and upper-class white women. In the immediate post–Civil War era the prevailing concept of the lady held that women embodied "the desirable traits of loving maternity, intuition and sensitivity." A moral and domestic creature, she was assumed to possess finer sensitivities than men. The "ideal lady" in the upper reaches of society was "leisured and ornamental, absorbed in learning the niceties that would render her amusing and enable her to beautify the home."[109] Upper-class blacks, both men and women, subscribed to this definition of the ideal lady. But the efforts of upper-class black women to embody such a concept in their lives were complicated in ways that those of middle- and upper-class white women were not. Compared to white women of similar social status, they lacked the financial resources necessary for equal leisure. But more serious was the widespread perception among whites that black women were immoral and possessed an "inherent tendency to sexual transgression."[110] Because whites tended to view blacks as an undifferentiated mass, such perceptions appeared to apply to all black women, regardless of class. Upper-class black women attempted to combat assertions and implications that called into question their moral rectitude.

By the turn of the century, upper-class black women began to express themselves in regard to the double jeopardy that they experienced as a result of being both black and female. While they blamed whites for much of the "degradation" and "bad name" borne by black women, they did not exempt black men from responsibility for their double burden. Some complained that black women, unlike their white sisters, did not "bask in the sunlight of man's chivalry, admiration and even worship." "We have all too many colored men," Fannie Barrier Williams asserted, "who hold the degrading opinions of ignorant white men that all colored girls are alike." She was also convinced that black men no less than whites were more attracted "by womanly appearance than womanly merit." She, as well as numerous others, argued that only when Negro men began to exalt "the beauty and character" of black women and "throw about them the chivalry of love and protection" would these women ever "command the recognition and respect of all the world."[111] Such recognition and respect were essential because no race could ever "rise higher than its women." "The higher the type of woman with which a race is blessed," Thomas Nelson Baker, a black clergyman, wrote in 1906, "the higher can the race rise in the moral, religious and the intellectual scale."[112] The notion that women held the key to racial progress was a source of strength and inspiration for the upper-class women who provided the leadership in establishing a national organization of black women's clubs.

In the late nineteenth century, the club movement among both black and white women enabled them to move beyond the sphere of domesticity and to acquire greater autonomy without abandoning domestic values. The emergence of women's organizations devoted to the study of literature, art, music, and history to replace those that focused on the home and child-rearing was in some ways a natural progression because of the belief that the innate sensitivity of women lent itself to cultural concerns. Such clubs, while nurturing pride in the lady's supposedly "special morality and domesticity," nonetheless served as a way station on women's road from the domestic to the public sphere.[113] Club experiences for both black and white women enhanced self-confidence and taught important lessons about the value of collective effort. By the turn of the century the organizations of black and white women alike had moved from culture study to civic reform and had established national organizations to advance causes of a public nature.

In both the white and the black communities there existed a social hierarchy of clubs reflecting class and status. If members of the most prestigious clubs of white women "valued their aristocratic credentials,"[114] so did members of similar organizations of black women. For black women, no less than for white, class was a complex matter because it reflected in part their own position and in part that of the men in their lives. Nevertheless, cliques and elitism were as much a part of black women's clubs as of their white counterparts. In both, some members attempted to use clubs for class consolidation and upward mobility. On occasion black women outside the "charmed circle" of the upper class made clubwomen the target of scathing criticism for what was perceived as their hauteur and condescension toward the masses. Upper-class black clubwomen were not oblivious to such perceptions. Josephine Bruce was careful to explain the role of such women in terms of "stewardship."[115] Another black clubwoman, while combating charges of snobbishness, emphasized the importance of comradeship and singularity of purpose among black women. But she betrayed her own class feelings when she wrote: "Cordial relations in the club with women whom we recognize as superior, but whom the prejudices of social usages deny a place on our social visiting list, make for freedom and the fuller life. Tolerance is born where women differing in thought, in talent and in station, yet animated by one aim, meet on the level of comradeship."[116] Class differences obviously posed serious obstacles to finding that common ground in which black women were able to discover what one called "a larger and hitherto undreamed-of self."[117]

Despite the racist and nativistic attitudes often exhibited by white women's clubs, a few black women did gain admission to such organizations. The best known were Josephine Saint Pierre Ruffin of Boston, Fannie Barrier Williams of Chicago, and Mary Church Terrell of Washington. All three were well-educated and sophisticated women of the highest social standing in the black community—and only slightly darker in complexion than their white colleagues.[118] Ruffin and Williams, with only "a slight indication of color," were of "old Yankee stock," and like their club associates across the color line, had inherited from their forebears a tradition of civic involvement, especially in Abolition and moral reform movements. One well-known black woman observed in 1905 that there was "nothing new" about black women's clubs which were merely alterations in old organizations to meet "the demands of age."[119] Black women in the North did in fact have a tradition of voluntary associations, usually single-issue organizations devoted to Abolition, temperance, moral reform, education, or similar causes. The Female Lundy Society of Albany, for example, began as an organization of "ladies of color" solely for the purpose of aiding runaway slaves.

Notwithstanding the similarities that existed between these aristocrats of color and upper- and upper middle-class white clubwomen, the two remained separated by race. An incident involving Josephine Ruffin dramatized just how separate they were. In 1893 Mrs. Ruffin and her daughter Florida Ruffin Ridley organized the New Era Club in Boston, which became a member of the Massachusetts State Federation of Women's Clubs. When Mrs. Ruffin appeared at the national convention of the General Federation on Women's Clubs in Milwaukee in 1900 as the representative of three organizations—the New Era Club, the Massachusetts Federation, and the New England Women's Press Association—admission of the New Era Club was opposed because it was a black organization. Although the General Federation offered to seat Mrs. Ruffin as the representative of the other two organizations, she refused and left the convention. The "Ruffin Incident" attracted considerable publicity and underscored the rigidity of the color line in women's organizations. "It is the 'high-caste' negroes," declared Mrs. Rebecca Lowe, the president of the General Federation, who led the fight against seating Mrs. Ruffin, "who bring about all the ill-feeling. The ordinary colored woman understands her position thoroughly."[120]

Social clubs formed by upper-class black women in the late nineteenth century were highly restrictive in membership, and whether devoted primarily to "social chat and . . . the delicacies of the occasion"[121] or to other purposes, they brought together women with a "similarity of tastes, abilities and character." In St. Paul, Minnesota, for example, the Adelphia Club, a literary and philanthropic organization founded in 1899, was "a select group of women whose new members were drawn from the daughters of charter members."[122] The wife of a physician in Nashville, Tennessee who was a member of the city's black elite insisted that wealth counted for little in determining those admitted to her social club, even though it included only wives of physicians, teachers, prosperous businessmen, and postal clerks. The wife of a postal clerk, who was a member of the same club, corroborated this view. "My associates," she declared, "are very intelligent people; they aren't rich by any means. They are people with background and they stand for something in Nashville."[123] The criteria for admission to the most prestigious women's club in Nashville were similar to those applied by upper-class black women throughout the United States. Whether one "fit into our group" was determined in large part by one's family background, education, and attention to the evidences of gentility.

Among the most popular social organizations among upper-class black women were clubs for playing card games, such as Whist and Euchre. Whist, described as a forerunner of Bridge, appears to have been a favorite of more mature, married women. What may be termed the Whist club ritual included not only card playing but also fashionable attire, elegant refreshments, and the exchange of news or "chit-chat."[124] Mary Church Terrell, who for many years was a member of the Matron's Whist Club in Washington, explained her membership in terms of what it contributed to satisfying her "social needs." Spending "an afternoon or an evening with congenial friends," all of whom belonged to what she termed "our group," was refreshing and relaxing.[125] Other women of Mary Terrell's social class elsewhere obviously shared her love of card games. Whist clubs existed in abundance from Seattle, where the Silver Leaf Whist Club was the "leading social club" in the city's tiny black community, to

Baltimore, where the Foster Whist Club included members of the city's new and old black elite.[126]

Even more important in the lives of upper-class black women were the numberous self-culture clubs. Literary clubs, according to Josephine Turpin Washington of Virginia, were important not merely in the intellectual development of black women but also in the building of their self-confidence. "Even the society woman, usually adept at what is known as 'small talk,' " she observed, "needs an opportunity to cultivate conversation that rises above the gossip of the drawing room and the inanities that too often mark the social whirl."[127] Self-culture organizations, which usually took the form of literary or reading clubs, focused on self-development through the study of what were considered great books, art, literature, history, music, or philosophy. Typical of the upper-class cultural organization in a large black community was the Idle Hour Literary Society in St. Louis, which included the Langstons, Vashons, Mordecais, and other members of the city's aristocracy of color. Organized in 1886, it met once a month throughout the year except during the summer, a schedule that was common among such organizations. Its programs included musical performances as well as literary study, and the last meeting in the spring included either a dinner or a dance or both.[128]

In Washington the Booklovers, organized in 1894 and limited to a dozen women of the highest social standing, met fortnightly to "pursue courses of reading and study for higher culture." Interspersed among programs devoted to Shakespeare and Wagner and to reports on members' European travel, were some that dealt with "child-rearing practices," heredity, and similar family-related topics. Not until 1939 did the Booklovers expand their membership and then only by one member, from twelve to thirteen.[129]

Upper-class black clubwomen, though described as "parlor ladies," were rarely persons of unrestricted leisure. The "fuss and feathers of pink teas, musicales, receptions and full dress banquets,"[130] while obviously a part of their social ritual, by no means occupied all of their time and energy. Many of those at the pinnacle of the black social structure in the late nineteenth century were business or professional women. Josephine Bruce managed extensive real estate holdings in the District of Columbia as well as her Mississippi plantations. Mary Church Terrell earned substantial income on the professional lecture circuit. Susie Revels Cayton of Seattle and Meta Pelham of Detroit ran family newspapers. Teachers in public and private schools and colleges, who constituted one of the largest components of the black upper class, figured prominently in club life. Many upper-class black women not only worked but also assumed civic responsibilities. Mary Terrell and Bettie Cox Francis served as members of the Board of Education in the District of Columbia; others elsewhere took advantage of limited opportunities to serve on official or quasi-official boards and agencies dealing with charity, education, and similar public concerns.

The proliferation of black women's clubs, coupled with the example set by white women, prompted upper-class black women in Washington and Boston to initiate movements that ultimately led to the formation of a national federation of black women's clubs. The Colored Women's League, organized in Washington in 1892, was the creation of the District's female aristocrats of color. Headed by Helen Appo Cook, the wife of John F. Cook, Jr., the League counted among its most active members Charlotte Forten Grimké, Josephine Bruce, Mary Church Terrell, and other women who two years later formed the Booklovers.[131] "As a woman of culture, refinement and financial independence," wrote a black clubwoman, "Mrs. John F. Cook has been, and is, a noted example and inspiration to women of her own social standing in the serious work of social reform." That Helen Cook and other female aristocrats of color, so the argument ran, availed themselves of the opportunities offered by the club movement "to make use of their superior training" in behalf of the race served to combat the notion that "colored women of education and refinement" had no sympathetic interest in their own race.[132]

In 1893 the league issued an appeal for the formation of a "national organization of colored women." Three years later, Josephine Ruffin and the New Era Club of Boston called a national conference of black women "composed of delegates from all regularly organized colored women's clubs in the country," a meeting that ultimately led to the formation of the Federation of Afro-American Women. In 1896 the Federation and the Colored Women's League merged to form the National Association of Colored Women (NACW), with Mary Church Terrell as its first president. Its motto was "lifting as we climb."[133]

By the turn of the century, the club life of upper-class black women had undergone considerable alteration. The emphasis had shifted from domestic concerns and self-culture to an interest in civic reforms and racial uplift efforts. Black clubwomen had become convinced that they owed "something to those outside the home-nest" and beyond themselves. For upper-class black women like Josephine Bruce and Fannie Barrier Williams, the attention to public issues emphasized by the NACW brought a "new found pleasure in doing something worthwhile" and in demonstrating to those skeptical of the club movement that its labors were of "utilitarian" value to the entire race. The purpose of women's clubs, according to Mrs. Williams, was "to cultivate among the people a finer sensitiveness as to rights and wrongs, the proprieties and improprieties that enter into—may regulate—the social status of the race."[134]

The same attributes that made women peculiarly fitted for the home and the pursuit of culture came to be viewed as of special value in addressing "larger issues of the day." Charles Alexander, a black journalist, made this point in 1905: "Woman's quicker sensibilities, her keener views, and perceptions of justice, her delicacy of touch, her admirable qualities of head and heart combine to give her advantage in approaching the problems of domestic life as well as the larger questions of civic concern and importance."[135] Two years later, a well-known black clubwoman defined the woman's club as owing its "existence to woman's desire to unite with her sisters in doing something for somebody outside her own home." It was, she said, "women's organized effort for humanity."[136] In addition to aiding humanity, the club movement enabled black women to do something for themselves. "Thus to their proverbial clearness of insight-intuition, women are adding the reasoning faculty," Josephine Bruce remarked, "and calm judgment is supplanting the excess of emotion with which women are generally charged."[137]

In 1908 a black newspaper sounded "a warning to club women" based on the findings of a physician in Kentucky who claimed that club life was injurious to the digestion of women and card games were a drain on their "nervous vitality." Josephine Turpin Washington responded with a lengthy commentary that revealed the shift in emphasis that had occurred in the voluntary organizations of upper-class black women: "Afro-American club women may well stand aghast at the statement [by the physician]. The ordinary club woman devoting herself to cards! The extraordinary one, for sooth, if any at all. Such may be clubs of the idle rich, of the self-indulgent votaries of fashion; and doubtless there are, in some of the large cities, Afro-American women who ape the follies of this class, but the average club woman . . . is a creature of another type. The colored woman's club is an eleemosynary organization. There may be a social feature and some attention may be given to self-culture, but these are secondary aims."[138] The primary purposes of women's clubs, in her view, were "to relieve suffering, to reclaim the erring and to advance the cause of education."[139] The concern of upper-class black clubwomen for humanity varied, of course, from community to community but manifested itself in efforts in behalf of temperance, antilynching crusades, libraries, rescue agencies, night schools, orphanages, hospitals, kindergartens, and homes for the aged.[140]

Notwithstanding the solidarity represented by the National Association of Colored Women, class differences continued to be a source of internal friction and external criticism. "The club movement among colored women," Fannie Barrier Williams wrote in 1904, "means something deeper than a mere imitation of . . . white women, because it has grown out of the organized anxiety of women who have only recently become intelligent enough to recognize their own social condition and strong enough to initiate and apply the forces of reform. It is a movement that reaches down into the sub-social condition of an entire race and has become the responsibility and effort of a few competent in behalf of the many incompetent."[141] From the perspective of upper-class black women, it was imperative that they assist in lifting the submerged masses, else they ran the risk of being dragged backward into the lower-class ranks. NACW officials repeatedly urged members "to come into the closest possible touch with the masses of our women," because, as Mary Church Terrell noted, "colored women of education and culture know that they cannot escape altogether the consequences of the acts of their most depraved sisters." Therefore, both humanitarian concerns and self-preservation demanded that "they go down among the lowly." In an effort to practice what she preached, Mrs. Terrell taught English literature and German in a night school in Washington sponsored by the Colored Women's League.[142]

Despite impressive achievements in the area of social service and racial uplift, the club movement among black, as well as white, women possessed its share of unattractive elements, including pettiness, social climbing, "unworthy ambitions," cliquishness, and incompetence.[143] Some of these elements were much in evidence in the second convention of the National Association of Colored Women in Chicago in 1899. One observer correctly described the gathering as one "alternately between light and shadow." The "light" consisted of reports of uplift activities by clubs throughout the country and thoughtful papers devoted to issues ranging from the "convict lease system" to "the necessity of an equal moral standard for men and women." The "shadow" cast upon the convention resulted from a bitter struggle over the eligibility of Mary Church Terrell to serve another term as president. Factions supporting various other candidates, especially Josephine St. Pierre Ruffin, argued that Mrs. Terrell was constitutionally ineligible for reelection. The proceedings became so rowdy that a black journalist concluded that assembled clubwomen were as unruly as "the horrid men."[144] Shortly after her reelection, Mary Church Terrell confided to a friend that both Fannie Barrier Williams and Mrs. Ruffin had opposed her. Furthermore, she added: "Our virtuous friend had done all in her evil power to prejudice the minds of the Illinois delegates against me."[145] Presumably, the "virtuous friend" referred to Ida Walls Barnett, a famous newspaper woman, lecturer, and clubwoman she had known in Memphis. Contrary to newspaper reports that Mary Church Terrell was conspiring to have her friend Josephine Bruce elected president, Mrs. Barnett claimed that Mrs. Terrell actually "wanted to be elected for a third term."[146]

In its early years the organization experienced a succession of internal struggles occasioned by "petty ambitions and unseemly vanity" on the part of those who aspired to its principal offices. One well-known clubwoman referred to the national conventions as "the biennial stirring up of ambitions." References to "the big three," "hidden conspiracies," and "secret caucuses" abounded with the approach of every biennial convention.[147] In an inelegant description of the "big three" in the organization, a male relative of a prominent Ohio clubwoman wrote to a friend in 1901: "Mary Church Terrell, Mrs. Washington and Mrs. Bruce all piss in the same pot through the National Women's Federation."[148] Accusations, whether true or not, that Mary Terrell conspired to have her old friend Josephine Bruce, who had introduced her to Washington society twenty years earlier, elected as her successor in the NACW merely confirmed the suspicions of those inclined to believe that a cabal of prominent upper-class women dominated the organization. The perception of some was that these women, like their husbands, came down among ordinary black people only when they sought offices, honors, or political plums.

The rivalry among educated, upper-class women who founded the NACW enabled ambitious middle-class women to assume direction of the organization. Although Mrs. Terrell won reelection in 1899, Ida Barnett claimed that the techniques she used to remain in office "somehow seemed to kill her influence." Josephine St. Pierre Ruffin thereafter focused her attention on the New Era Club and the Massachusetts Federation of Women rather than the NACW. Although Josephine Bruce served the NACW in various capacities, including that of first vice president and member of the Executive Board, she too became less active following the controversy over her complexion at the organization's 1906 convention.

Fully aware of the tendency of whites to believe that all blacks were alike and that black women generally were immoral creatures, care was taken to publicize the presence of those in clubs and voluntary organizations who were as "accomplished and graceful in all the manners, capabilities and charms of personality" as the "best women of the more favored race." Whites "who have known the Negro only as a menial," Fannie Barrier Williams observed, "would be surprised to observe so many black women of culture, social standing and independence" among those attending national meetings of the NACW. Clearly, such women—those who represented "the best society and highest accomplishments"—dominated the organization. It was this group, according to a black observer of an early meeting of the NACW, that "gave a superb finish in manners, deportment and dignity to it."[149]

The welfare activities of black clubwomen, as one historian has observed, often reflected a patronizing, condescending attitude in dealing with the poor and disadvantaged. Few female aristocrats of color had had direct contact with what Mary Church Terrell called "the poor, benighted sisters of the Black Belt," but most viewed them as socially and culturally retarded people who desperately needed to be taught "the A B C of living." In the process of instructing these benighted "loved ones" in "the culture of the head and the heart" and in introducing the standards of genteel Victorian domesticity into the cabins of the rural South and slum dwellings of the urban North, upper-class black women, perhaps understandably, exhibited an attitude of superiority and paternalism that aroused resentment and interfered with their effectiveness.[150]

Critics in the black community suggested that clubwomen were less concerned with "lifting" the masses than they were in enhancing their own status at the expense of the masses. In 1900, Nannie H. Burroughs, a well-known educator, issued a ringing indictment of upper-class black clubwomen: "For the past four or five years Negro women have had a mania for club life. But did you ever stop to think that the clubs and federations among us are doing actually nothing for the benefit of the masses? Women who constitute them are of 'the kid glove order' who think themselves too good to work among the lowly and who do little to tone up our club life. They leave the platform and applause after a flowing paper talk on some burning race question and retire to their parlors where whist and euchre and merry music are indulged in until early morning. They live unconcerned and at ease while four million of their black sisters are out yonder in the cold, in the bonds of iniquity and the galls of bitterness. The fact is that the secular clubs existing under the good name of charity are only agencies to bring together certain classes at the exclusion of the poor, ignorant women who need to be led by the 'educated class.' These rings confine their feasts to the great and their favors to those in power, and are not proverbial for their hospitality to those whom society never considers, and charity serves with protest."[151]

In spite of such criticism, black clubwomen performed a "large amount of socially useful work." While some, perhaps most, objected to being forced into close association with persons whose behavior they found objectionable, it did not mean that they despised "other blacks." Rather the upper-class black women primarily responsible for launching the NACW and guiding it in its early years conceived of themselves as the "civic mothers of the race" whose job it was to establish a "special relationship between those who help and those who need help."[152] In fact, black clubwomen emphasized race pride and race progress at the same time that they embraced assimilationist or integrationist ideology. Notwithstanding their elitism, according to Gerda Lerner, black clubwomen were more successful than their white counterparts in bridging class barriers and in addressing issues of importance to the poor and ignorant women of their race. The National Association of Colored Women also spanned barriers posed by regional and religious differences and early brought within its ranks rural as well as urban women.[153]

The rapid expansion of the NACW meant that large numbers of middle-class black women's clubs became affiliated with the organization. As a result, upwardly mobile middle-class women increasingly replaced those of the old upper class in positions of leadership. At least some of the jealousies and suspicions within the association, which Fannie Barrier Williams described as "little sins peculiar to human nature generally and to femininity in particular,"[154] had their origins in class rivalry. By the end of the first decade of the twentieth century, the NACW was overwhelmingly middle class in leadership and in membership. But Mary Church Terrell, looking back from the perspective of 1940, concluded that her three terms as its first president were the critical years of the organization, because at that time so few black women outside the upper class had any experience with secular club work. In her view she and a handful of "loyal co-workers"—those that she referred to on other occasions as persons of "our group"—established a high standard for the organization from the outset and provided the expertise and structure that allowed others to lift as they climbed.[155]

9

◆

The Education of the Elite

FROM THE END OF RECONSTRUCTION until the First World War, education was of major importance in determining the contours of the black class structure. Those at the top, the aristocrats of color, tended to be well educated in comparison to the vast majority of blacks. In the generation following Emancipation, those with education demonstrated the validity of W. E. B. Du Bois's oft-repeated declaration that the work of the educated Negro was "largely the work of leadership."[1] In 1890 William V. Tunnell, a black Episcopal minister who became a professor at Howard University, noted that however significant family background, complexion, and church affiliation might be as stratifiers, they were both singly and collectively less important than the disciplined, cultivated mind produced by higher education.[2] Education was assumed to bestow the refinement and culture essential for entry into the highest stratum of black society.[3]

Although the person with "naught but wealth" rarely won admission to high society, those with naught but education, such as honor graduates from well-known colleges and universities, often did. In fact, those with such educational credentials were in large measure responsible for the expansion in the ranks of the aristocracy of color. As Lura Beam noted, among aristocrats of color in the early twentieth-century South, a man without a distinguished family background and of dark complexion had no chance of being accepted into the highest social circles unless he possessed an advanced degree from a prestigious northern university, in which case "adjustments would be made."[4] For example, the Bond family of Kentucky, though fair in complexion, lacked most of the attributes required for membership in the aristocracy of color except that of education. The Bonds possessed neither a distinguished old family background nor wealth, but the educational achievements begun late in the nineteenth century by Henry and James Bond, and continued by their descendants, gained for the family a place in the upper stratum of black society.[5]

The family and the home environment were keys to the perpetuation of the tradition of literacy and education bequeathed by antebellum forebears. Ambitious for their children, upper-class parents, like other Americans, were imbued with the idea that education was essential for a productive life. Not only did they preach the gospel of education and mount crusades for more and better black schools, but also they made great sacrifices to secure for their children the education they considered essential for success. Because they often possessed greater financial resources and had fewer children than other blacks, the educational opportunities open to their children came closer to those of middle- and upper-class whites. The values and especially the emphasis on "respectability" that were part of the home life of upper-class children were reinforced by the atmosphere and philosophy of the schools they attended.

Parents not only placed a high priority on both the informal and the formal education of their children, but also provided models by their attention to self-culture. Parents hosted club meetings in their homes in which the topics of discussion were great books, art, and classical music; some regularly read and wrote in foreign languages. In 1916 an upper-class black woman in New York wrote to a friend that she "read a little bit of French and a little bit of German and a little bit of Greek every day and [I] try to go to the Metropolitan Museum of Art once a week."[6]

Upper-class children grew up in homes in which books, magazines, music, and art were an important part of everyday life. When possible, the informal education of upper-class children included exposure to art galleries, museums, concerts, and the theatre. Upper-class homes often possessed sizable and well-selected libraries which included works by both white and black authors. Few such homes were without a piano, violin, or other musical instruments, and it was not uncommon for upper-class children to receive private instruction in music and ballroom dancing. On occasion children especially talented in music would perform at evening musicales held in their parents' home.[7]

Another important aspect of the informal education of upper-class black children was travel. For such children in the South, summer travel to the North was considered essential. They visited large cities and often joined other upper-class families from throughout the country in selected seashore or mountain resorts. Traveling abroad, especially in Europe, became increasingly popular amng the black upper class after the turn of the century. Writing in 1913, one observer noted that black upper-class families brought back from these European journeys "not only many new and happy impressions but also a considerable amount of information in the art of living that they do not have the opportunity to get at home." Families which could afford the expense of a "grand tour" sent their children to Europe following graduation from preparatory school or from college.[8]

Many aristocrats of color obviously favored a system of racially integrated education. Some refused to allow their children to attend segregated black schools primarily because they believed that such schools were qualitatively inferior. In Boston, Cleveland, and certain other cities in the North, racially mixed schools were the norm, but in Washington the occasional Negro who attended white public schools when it was still possible to do so ran the risk of being ostracized by both blacks and whites.[9] Aristocrats of color who could afford to do so sent their children to private academies and boarding schools in the North. Their primary concern appears to have been with the quality of education, for aristocrats of color in Washington had few qualms about sending their children to the racially segregated M Street High School, which was probably superior to white high schools in the city.

The question of "mixed versus separate" schools was the subject of periodic discussion. In the mid-1880s, Theophilius J. Minton, an attorney and a member of a socially prominent black family of Philadelphia, argued that "assimilation" was essential, otherwise the Negro would remain distinct and separate, "occupying a subordinate place but little above his present condition." According to Minton, the only viable choice open to blacks was to destroy "all lines of distinction by assimilating the manners, customs and racial characteristics of the Caucasian." Judge George L. Ruffin of Boston fully agreed that there must be a merger of blacks and whites. The acquisition of "education, wealth and refinement" by blacks, he believed, was necessary to dispel whites' repugnance for Negroes. Nothing, A. C. C. Astwood, a black diplomat from Louisiana insisted, was more injurious to the progress of blacks than forcing them to attend segregated schools. Not the least of the benefits of integrated education was the racial harmony that resulted from "contact and association."[10]

Francis L. Cardozo, a proud, free-born black of Charleston, who might have been expected to agree with Astwood about the desirability of integrated education, argued instead for segregated schools, at least for the time being: "I do not advise separate schools and churches as a desirable thing in itself but simply as a means to an end." In Cardozo's view, poverty and lack of education were the primary causes of prejudice against blacks. By "educating ourselves, by and through ourselves," he argued, "it will cultivate the independence and manliness that are so essential to eradicate the servility and obsequiousness which are the unfortunate results of our previous condition of servitude and which incur the contempt of whites." Nor did he believe that separation necessarily involved inferiority. His success at Avery Normal Institute in Charleston during Reconstruction tended to substantiate this view. Although Cardozo believed that separate schools for blacks were necessary for an indefinite period of time, he looked forward to the day when blacks would be able to enter racially integrated schools "on terms of perfect equality" with whites.[11]

The question of racially mixed schools briefly became the topic of public discussion in 1898 when it was alleged that membership in the revived National

Afro-American Council required one to endorse mixed schools and mixed marriages. John H. Smythe, formerly minister to Liberia and one of those in attendance at the initial meeting of the Council, prompted the public discussion by vehemently opposing "intermarriage of the races." The issue of intermarriage elicited more debate than that of integration of schools, but few black spokesmen thought either issue was of primary concern in view of the rapidly deteriorating status of blacks and the mounting racial violence in the South. "What is to be gained by agitating such questons, especially at this time," the Washington *Colored American* asked, "when the life, property and civil status of the race hang so threateningly in the balance?" Of far more concern to the National Afro-American Council were the issues of lynching, Jim Crow laws, and disfranchisement.[12]

In certain cities in the North where integrated public education had existed for years, movements to segregate the schools accelerated after the turn of the century as the influx of black migrants into northern and midwestern cities increased. After 1900 Chicago witnessed racial clashes in its integrated educational system, followed by attempts to tighten the color line in schools as well as in housing and public accommodations. Upper-class blacks such as Charles Bentley, James Madden, and Edward Wilson, identified as opponents of Booker T. Washington's philosophy, spearheaded a movement to thwart efforts to resegregate Chicago schools. In 1903 they organized the Equal Opportunity League for such a purpose. Although the city's schools remained legally integrated in 1920, the rapid increase in the black population and the confinement of blacks to specific neighborhoods and blocks meant that a separate school system was emerging without formal authorization by state or municipal officials.[13]

The educated black elite that played a leadership role during the generation following Emancipation came primarily from the ranks of free blacks living in the North and South and from favored slaves in the South. It was derived overwhelmingly from what Horace Mann Bond termed a "Negro upper class." In the South, according to Bond, the educated elite originated in clusters of counties, a geographical phenomenon explained by the fact that families were involved—families that began a tradition of literacy before the Civil War and maintained a tradition of educational achievement in the postwar years.[14]

While access to formal education by Northern blacks was limited in the antebellum era, it was substantially greater than that available to blacks, free as well as slave, in the South. But despite legal restrictions imposed by southern states on the education of all blacks, a few managed, sometimes clandestinely, to secure schooling, however episodic and short-lived it may have been. In some instances favored slaves such as Blanche Bruce shared tutors with their masters' children.[15] Free people of color in the South were more likely to acquire formal education than were slaves. In the more racially liberal climate of New Orleans, free children of color attended special and parochial schools open to both races, and some of the wealthier free families of color educated their children in France.[16] Charleston witnessed the establishment of a succession of schools for free blacks beginning in the late eighteenth century. Even after the enactment of a measure abolishing such schools in 1835, they continued to exist largely because the law was not enforced. Even so, the imposition of such legal restrictions was responsible in part for the migration northward, especially to Philadelphia, of some well-to-do free families of color. Among the best-known schools in Charleston were those operated by the Brown Fellowship Society and by Thomas Bonneau, both of which attracted students primarily "from the upper echelons of free black society." A host of individuals, including Francis L. Cardozo, who assumed prominent roles in education in Charleston and elsewhere after the Civil War received their early education in the city's antebellum schools for free blacks.[17]

Notable among the schools open to blacks in the Midwest during the antebellum period was the Gilmore School in Cincinnati. Founded in 1844 by the Reverend Hiram S. Gilmore, "a gentleman of means and training," the school was large and well equipped. Gilmore School prepared students for college, and a fair proportion of them went from there "to Oberlin and such colleges as drew no colorline on matriculation."[18] Its classical curriculum attracted blacks from throughout the nation, including a sizable group of mulatto children of southern planters. Among the latter were P. B. S. Pinchback, James Monroe Trotter, and John Mercer Langston, whose descendants were also well educated.[19]

A similar black school was established in 1856 at Tawawa Springs, Ohio, a favorite summer resort of wealthy white southerners. Sponsored by the Methodist Episcopal Church and "managed almost entirely by white persons," the institution became known as Wilberforce University. Its first students "were largely the natural children of Southern and Southwestern planters." The outbreak of the Civil War sharply curtailed Southern patronage, and the school passed into the hands of the African Methodist Episcopal Church in 1863. In the postwar era Wilberforce, with its classical curriculum, was counted among the select black colleges in the nation.[20]

Another Ohio institution that attracted a sizable contingent of black students from the South as well as the North was Oberlin College. From its establishment in 1833 until the Civil War, blacks constituted about four or five percent of the student body. Before the war a substantial portion of them were enrolled in the preparatory department. Despite the college's celebrated role in the Abolition movement, black students at Oberlin "were never treated the same as whites." Nevertheless, the atmosphere was probably freer of prejudice than at virtually any other predominantly white institution in the country.

Many blacks who later achieved prominence were enrolled at Oberlin, either as preparatory or collegiate students.[21]

Throughout the North and Midwest, blacks acquired education either in racially mixed institutions, such as Oberlin, or in schools established specifically for blacks. Beginning in the eighteenth century, various religious and philanthropic agencies, such as the Society for the Propagation of the Gospel, created separate schools for blacks. Other evidences of white benevolence appeared in the form of "charity schools" and Sabbath schools for blacks in towns and cities in the North. All the while northern blacks themselves played a significant role in the establishment of schools. Black leaders in New York, Boston, and other cities in the North marshalled whatever resources they could to maintain black schools, while pressing white authorities to assume public responsibility for black education. Boston opened its first public school for blacks in 1820; New York did not follow suit until more than twenty years later.[22]

From these early schools, whether segregated or racially mixed, came a cadre of black men and women who were community leaders in the antebellum era and who, with their descendants, were conspicuous in black America in the postwar era. Scores of black leaders studied under John Peterson and Charles L. Reason, two pioneer black teachers in New York, whose influence was comparable to that of Thomas Bonneau in Charleston. Peterson was principal of the African School Number One for a half century. A modest, courtly gentleman, "sure of his Christian faith," he also served as assistant minister of Saint Philip's Episcopal Church and was prominent in the affairs of the New York African Society for Mutual Relief. Former students agreed that he was a demanding and beloved schoolmaster who also exercised a strong personal influence upon them. "His pupils," declared Alexander Crummell, the erudite clergyman who had studied under Peterson, "took up unconsciously his tones, his manner, his movements, his style and his faults, so that oft times, they were copies of the Old Master." The list of Peterson's students also included Henry Highland Garnet, James McCune Smith, Ira Aldridge, and Charles L. and Patrick Reason, among others who became prominent.[23]

Charles L. Reason, who served as Peterson's assistant at the normal school, was a teacher in the black schools of New York for most of the time between 1832 and 1892. His parents had fled Haiti to escape the revolution there and in 1793 settled in New York, where Reason was born. Like Peterson, Reason was a product of the Manumission School and served for a time as teacher there. In 1849 he became Professor of Belle-Lettres and of the French Language and Adjunct Professor of Mathematics in New York Central College, a racially mixed institution supported by abolitionists. A scholar and writer who achieved considerable fame as a poet, Reason exerted a profound influence on his students, one of whom was Edward Valentine Clark Eato, a conspicuous figure in the civic and social life of black New York until his death in 1914. Both

Reason and Peterson were intolerant of mediocrity, emphasized intellectual discipline, and inspired their students with pride and dignity.[24]

The only time during his sixty-year career that Reason did not occupy some educational position in New York was the period 1852–1855, when he was principal of the Institute for Colored Youth in Philadelphia, an institution that enjoyed great prestige among blacks both before and after the Civil War. It was chartered in 1842, financed through a bequest of a wealthy Quaker, and at the time the only private school in Philadelphia offering Negroes courses on the secondary level. Ten years later, when a new building had been constructed in the heart of the city's black community, Charles L. Reason was chosen as principal. During his tenure the Institute abandoned the agricultural emphasis suggested by its benefactor's will and became a strong academic institution. In time the Institute's curriculum of classics, sciences, and higher mathematics came to equal "that of the average college." Under the leadership of Reason's successors, especially Ebenezer Bassett and Fanny Jackson Coppin, the Institute continued to attract a corps of outstanding faculty members, including Edward Bouchet, who had attended Yale, and Mary Jane Patterson, who was a graduate of Oberlin. During the fifty years from Reason's tenure until 1902, when Coppin resigned and the Institute was transformed into an "industrial" school that conformed to Booker T. Washington's philosophy, it enjoyed an academic reputation possessed by few other black educational institutions and attracted students from throughout the United States.[25]

Among Institute alumni who became conspicuous leaders were several Philadelphians: John S. Durham, the journalist, lawyer, and diplomat; Charles A. Dorsey, also a graduate of Oberlin and a distinguished educator in New York until his death in 1907; Jacob C. White, Jr., the son of a well-to-do barber, who as principal of the Robert Vaux School in Philadelphia from 1864 to 1896 was the highest ranking black official in the city's school system; and Joseph E. Lee, who settled in Jacksonville and became a power in Republican politics in Florida for several decades after Reconstruction. Another distinguished alumnus, born free in Virginia but reared in Philadelphia, was John W. Cromwell, educator, editor, lawyer, and a founder of the American Negro Academy, who spent most of his career in Washington. Others included Furman J. Shadd, who became a physician and served for years as secretary-treasurer of Howard University's Medical School; and Josephine Silone Yates, an educator and clubwoman in Missouri who achieved national prominence.[26] A majority of the Institute's graduates became teachers, and many occupied some of the choicest faculty positions in the best black schools in both the North and the South.

Although a few black southerners attended the Institute, most of its students came from Philadelphia and the surrounding area. By the time Fanny Coppin assumed charge of the institution in September 1865, a variety of religious and philanthropic agencies were establishing schools for blacks in the South, substantially increasing the demand for teachers such as those produced by the Institute for Colored Youth. Members of black families, both inside and outside the South, who had benefited from a tradition of literacy and educational achievement, naturally assumed positions of leadership among blacks in the postwar South. Among the black masses in the region, the degree of illiteracy was matched only by their thirst for learning. A sizable contingent of the educated black elite, including natives of the South who earlier had migrated north or otherwise managed to secure formal training, participated in efforts to educate southern freedmen during Reconstruction. Others seeking the main chance in the postwar South and sometimes known as "black carpet baggers" assumed positions of leadership in areas other than education.

Among agencies and groups that created schools for blacks in the postwar South few were as important as the American Missionary Association, which had close ties with the Congregational Church. A.M.A. schools, whether they provided elementary, secondary, normal, or collegiate training, often had racially mixed faculties and were closely identified with upper-class blacks. One such A.M.A. institution was Avery Normal Institute in Charleston, South Carolina. It was organized in 1865 and achieved a reputation for academic excellence largely as a result of the labor of Francis L. Cardozo. The son of a respected Jewish businessman and a free black woman, Cardozo was educated in the schools for free blacks in Charleston and later became an apprentice carpenter. At the age of twenty-one he left South Carolina for Scotland. He graduated with honors from the University of Glasgow and later studied at seminaries in London and Edinburgh. Returning to the United States in 1864, he became pastor of the prestigious Temple Street Congregational Church in New Haven, Connecticut.[27]

A year later, Cardozo joined the American Missionary Association's educational enterprise in the South. At his request he was sent to Charleston, where he replaced his brother, Thomas, as principal of the A.M.A. school. The school was renamed Avery Normal Institute in 1868 in honor of its principal benefactor. Under Francis Cardozo's leadership Avery became a "normal," or teacher-training, institution with a classical curriculum and a commitment to academic excellence. Of the 400 students who had graduated from Avery by 1900, two-thirds had at some point served as schoolteachers. From the beginning the Institute had a racially mixed faculty, and after Cardozo left the school in 1868 to become Treasurer of the state of South Carolina, it had a succession of white principals until 1913. Avery Institute was generally recognized as one of the strongest preparatory and teacher-training schools established by the A.M.A. in the postwar South.[28]

From the beginning the institution had close ties with Charleston's old free brown elite, even though Cardozo may not have shown any preference for those of this class. Many of its early black teachers came from old, well-known free families of color, with names such as Weston, Shrewsbury, Holloway, and others of comparable status. Although most of Avery's students came from poor or modest backgrounds, the institution always attracted upper-class black children, "particularly those of the old free born elite." The monthly tuition required of Avery students operated to give the institution an upper-class cast. According to a white reporter, the school's advanced classes consisted "mainly of those who were born free and who constitute the aristocracy of color." Upper-class family names—such as Holloway, Dereef, McKinlay, and Ransier—appeared regularly on the lists of students who competed in the school's public examination. In the view of Charleston's old upper-class families Avery was an excellent "reserche seminary." It was one of several institutions in the city that "crystallized the *esprit de corps* of the upper class."[29] The Avery Alumni Association, whose annual meetings in Charleston attracted alumni from throughout the nation who had achieved distinction in many fields, tended to perpetuate that *esprit de corps*.[30]

Although Avery Institute challenged much of the conventional wisdom of whites about black education, the school provided a classic example of the extent to which antebellum social patterns persisted in the postwar era. According to the historian of Avery, the patterns existing in prewar Charleston, which included an emphasis on color, free status, and wealth, "promoted tendencies toward intra-racial segregation within the school itself." Visitors to the school remarked about the presence of so many blue-eyed, fair-skinned children "in a colored school." A black resident of Charleston later recalled that the question of color "mixed up the children and some of the teachers at Avery." As late as 1938, the school's principal lamented that it was difficult "for an organization which was created to destroy caste to have to admit that Avery has not escaped the temptations of aristocracy."[31]

Although few of the A.M.A. preparatory and normal schools equaled Avery's reputation for elitism, others also succumbed, in varying degrees, to "the temptations of aristocracy." Beach Institute, an A.M.A. school in Savannah, Georgia, founded in 1867, was for many years the only high school for Negroes in the city. Taught by racially integrated faculty (with five white teachers and one black teacher as late as 1916), Beach attracted black upper-class children from the surrounding area and was accused on occasion of discriminating against children of darker complexion.[32] In Thomasville, Georgia, a famous winter resort in the late nineteenth century, Allen Normal Institute, founded by the A.M.A. in 1885 was a well-equipped boarding school for girls which admitted boys as day students. Because it was "patronized almost exclusively by the better class of Negroes," a white observer remarked, Allen was an example of the "segregation within the race" that existed in black education.[33] While teaching at A.M.A. schools in Wilmington and Memphis, Lura Beam, a northern-born white teacher, learned for the first time the meaning of the term "colored aristocracy" from her students, many of whom were from families that considered themselves part of the highest social stratum of black society.[34]

An institution which began as an A.M.A. school and later evolved into one of the best-known elite black preparatory schools in the nation was Palmer Memorial Institute, located near Greensboro, North Carolina. When the A.M.A. withdrew its support from the school in 1901, Charlotte Hawkins Brown, a black woman born in North Carolina but reared in Cambridge, Massachusetts, assumed control with the aid of white philanthropists in New England. She transformed it into a school that emphasized industrial education of the type practiced at Tuskegee Institute under Booker T. Washington, whom she greatly admired. About 1930 Palmer Memorial Institute underwent a major shift in emphasis as a result of financial constraints, the longtime interests of Charlotte Hawkins Brown, and the expressed desires of its philanthropic supporters. Rather than focusing on industrial education, the school concentrated on becoming a school for well-to-do blacks comparable to the most exclusive finishing schools for whites. The highly selective student body received training in culture, "correct habits," and manners, with the expectation that Palmer graduates would prove to be leaders whose appearance, behavior, and values would inspire other blacks to "seek ideals of truth, beauty and goodness."[35] In 1941 Charlotte Hawkins Brown published *The Correct Thing,* a book of etiquette that in many respects resembled earlier works by E. M. Woods, Azalia Hackley, and Edward Green. It was perhaps ironic that an institution which began as a school for poor rural blacks in the South should evolve into the most exclusive finishing school for blacks. Rather than being patronized by those who belonged to the "old families," Palmer appears to have attracted primarily the children of wealthy, upwardly mobile black parents who went there "to polish off the rough edges."[36]

In A.M.A. schools and others in the South founded by the American Baptist Home Mission Society, the Presbyterian Board of Missions for Freedmen, and similar groups, "Yankee teachers," heirs to the abolitionist legacy and products of New England culture, sought to reproduce academic institutions that they had known in the North. Their goal, according to historian James M. McPherson, "was a one-way acculturation of black people to 'white' values and institutions." They often attempted, in their effort to educate blacks for leadership, to mold what W. E. B. Du Bois called the "talented tenth" into their own image. Pious and often paternalistic, these white teachers sought to inculcate in their students white middle-class values of morality, civility, discipline, and industry. At the same time they imposed a rigid code of behavior, replete with numerous prohibitions against "whatever is immoral or opposed to true culture."[37]

At the A.M.A.–related Atlanta University, according to George A. Towns, a graduate of the institution, the white New England professors exercised a profound influence on the manners, speech, personal appearance, and attitudes of the black students. Through regular and intimate associations with the proper New Englanders, Atlanta University students became keenly conscious of "those little outward signs of good breeding." The Presbyterian-related

Scotia Seminary, an institution for black girls in North Carolina, prohibited all behavior considered "unladylike and disorderly." At Avery the "lessons of chastity" received especial attention, and of the more than 400 graduates of the school by 1903 not one, according to a teacher there, "was living a dissolute life."[38] Efforts to banish the immoral and to inculcate "true culture" were remarkably successful. Indeed, some began to question whether the missionary teachers had not been too successful. An A.M.A. official observed in 1909 that alumni of the schools sponsored by his organization exhibited "a gravity of manner, a sobriety of expression [and] a restraint of religious utterances" to such an extent that they had ceased being Negroes and had become merely Congregationalists, which was inarguably "a change for the worse."[39] Blacks who attended A.M.A. schools and some others sponsored by northern philanthropic groups were likely to encounter the same criticisms as those who joined the Congregationalist, Presbyterian, or Episcopal churches; both were often considered by other blacks as being too "high toned" and too aloof from the masses.

In the late nineteenth and early twentieth centuries, public educational facilities in the South lagged far behind those in most other sections of the country. As inferior as facilities there may have been for whites, they were far superior to those for blacks. In an era when the vast majority of blacks still lived in the South, the emergence of a more virulent form of racism in the region took its toll on the already limited educational opportunities for black children.[40] Upper-class blacks, for whom education was of such central importance, responded in various ways to the lack of adequate schools for their children. Although financially they were better off than most blacks, they often had to make extraordinary sacrifices to secure high-quality education for their children.

Those unwilling to send their children to the ill-equipped, short-term public elementary schools sometimes placed them in private or parochial schools scattered throughout the South. In addition to those operated by the A.M.A., scores of similar "tuition" schools sponsored by other philanthropic and religious agencies and individuals existed in the region. Some were boarding schools; others accepted only day students. Although these private institutions varied in quality and in curricula, they provided an alternative for black families who could afford them.[41] With the exception of the A.M.A. schools, most of the historical literature devoted to black education in the South has focused on public schools rather than on the diverse types of private institutions. Nevertheless, it appears that many upper-class black children received their earliest formal education in such schools. The children of black Episcopalians in some cities attended parochial schools conducted in connection with black churches. St. Mary's in Annapolis, All Saints in Nashville, St. Philip's in Richmond, Emmanuel in Memphis, and the Church of Our Merciful Savior in Louisville sponsored such schools.[42] Early in the 1880s, Hutchins C. Bishop, the rector of St. Mark's Episcopal Church in Charleston, led a movement which resulted in the establishment of the Charleston Military Academy, for Negro boys, which attracted students from the city's old upper-class families. The academy, supported largely by those associated with St. Mark's, appears to have survived for only a few years.[43] Of much longer duration were the other Episcopal-related schools, such as St. Augustine's in Gainesville, Florida and St. Mark's in Birmingham, which catered to the children of upper-class families. Other private schools sponsored by the northern branches of the Presbyterian, Baptist, and Methodist churches, as well as those operated by black denominations, provided opportunities for elementary education for blacks in the South, especially those of the "better class." Even Lutherans sponsored black schools, such as the Lutheran Grace School in North Carolina.[44]

Upper-class black southerners of substantial means sometimes chose to send their children to schools in the North. Mary Church Terrell's parents arranged for her to board with a white family in Yellow Springs, Ohio so that she could attend a school connected with Antioch College.[45] Another prominent Memphis family, the Josiah T. Settles, sent their sons to Oberlin as soon as they were ready to enter the preparatory department.[46] Apparently the practice of sending children north to be educated was fairly widespread among affluent upper-class black families in the South. In some instances, mothers accompanied young children and secured temporary homes near private or public schools of high quality that admitted blacks; in others, children were sent to live with relatives residing in the North until they had completed elementary school.

The secondary education of upper-class black children often followed a similar pattern. They either attended private boarding schools in the North or public high schools with reputable classical curricula, if such schools existed locally. Oberlin High School and the preparatory department of Oberlin College attracted a sizable contingent of upper-class black southerners. A few joined upper-class blacks from elsewhere at well-known white preparatory academies in New England.[47] Children of some upper-class black Catholic families attended St. Frances Academy in Baltimore, founded in 1829 by the Oblate Sisters of Providence, St. Francis de Sales Institute, established in 1899 in Rock Castle, Virginia, or other Catholic preparatory schools for "colored youth." Few of the Catholic schools were more sophisticated or elitist than St. Mary's Academy for Young Ladies of Color in New Orleans, a finishing school for the daughters of well-to-do colored Creoles.[48] Upper-class blacks in some areas of the South had access to high schools of superior quality, such as the Mifflin W. Gibbs High School in Little Rock, Sumner High School in St. Louis, and Stanton High School in Jacksonville.[49] Such schools almost invariably had a classical curriculum, employed a corps of well-educated teachers, and were the objects of great pride in the black community. A few public high schools acquired national reputations for academic excellence. Among these was the M Street School in Washington.

The number and quality of educational institutions in Washington made the city a national center of black education. The roster of the city's black school personnel included numerous names of prestigious old families inside and outside the District. Even more renowned was Howard University, located in Washington and sometimes known as the "national Negro university." By the turn of the century its cadre of black scholars was unequaled in achievement and academic excellence by any other black institution in the nation.[50]

The segregated school system of the District had a black superintendent and a white superintendent until the reorganization of 1901, at which time the administrative head of the black schools became an assistant superintendent subordinate to the white superintendent. Most of those selected for administrative and teaching positions in the black school system were aristocrats of color, especially the superintendent and later the assistant superintendent and members of the District Board of Education. George F. T. Cook was for many years superintendent of black schools, and various members of his family held administrative and faculty posts. Dr. John R. Francis and his wife, Bettie Cox Francis, Blanche K. Bruce, Charlotte Forten Grimké, Mary Church Terrell, John R. Brooks, William V. Tunnell, and others of the District's black elite at one time or another, were members of the Board of Education. As board members they were, almost without exception, effective advocates of more and better schools for blacks.[51]

Because Washington's black school system had a national reputation for excellence and provided respectable employment for well-educated blacks, the competition for jobs there was fierce and the struggles between rival factions were often bitter. "The fuss in the schools [in Washington] keeps a-going," Josephine Bruce confided to her son in 1897, "but as long as some are in while those out want their places, just so long will there be strife."[52] Few black administrators or board members escaped charges of preferential treatment in the selection of school personnel. A common complaint was that their relatives and friends among the "upper tens" were appointed to the choicest positions. In 1894 a black resident of Washington asked "why so many members of certain families are employed in lucrative positions in the public schools to the exclusion of . . . others who are not so high on the social scale." In responding to criticism about the appointment of his sister-in-law to a faculty position, Dr. Francis maintained that a teacher "who moves in the best society" was far preferable to one whose parents "live in an alley." Such statements lent credence to suspicions that the separate public school system was the preserve of upper-class "old families."[53]

The *Washington Bee* regularly alleged that favoritism and nepotism existed in the black school system. While it generally supported Superintendent Cook and Assistant Superintendent Roscoe C. Bruce, it periodically lashed out at both, as well as at the teachers in the public schools, claiming that they constituted a self-conscious elite that held itself aloof from Negroes outside its "charmed circle." Of those afflicted with "color prejudice," according to the *Bee*, the teachers were among the worst because they blatantly drew the color line against their darker brethren. In its view, only the colorphobia of "government clerks" surpassed that of the teachers.[54]

The intensity of the struggles surrounding the black public school system of Washington was indicative of its significance to the black community. Because the quality of few other black schools equaled that of the schools in the District, they attracted persons of extraordinary talent and educational background from throughout the nation to serve as administrators and faculty members. Although Washington's colored schools provided instruction that was sometimes superior to that offered by white schools, they were part of a segregated school system in which blacks received lower salaries and heavier teaching loads than whites.[55]

Rivaling Howard in prestige was the centerpiece of the separate colored school system, the high school. Established in 1870, for the next century it was known by various names—Preparatory High School for Colored Youth, Sumner High School, M Street High School, and Dunbar High School. Few institutions were so intimately linked to the lives of Washington's aristocrats of color. The founder of the school was William Syphax, an employee of the Department of the Interior and the first chairman of the Board of Trustees of the Colored Public Schools, who belonged to one of the District's oldest and most prestigious black families. For one hundred years following its founding, Syphaxes were identified with the institution either as students or members of its faculty and administrative staff, as were others of the District's colored aristocracy.[56]

Financed originally by private funds from philanthropists, the Preparatory High School began classes in the basement of the Fifteenth Street Presbyterian Church. A few years later, after it became tax supported, the name was changed to Sumner High School. The school occupied several different buildings until 1891, when it moved into a brick structure on M Street and was known as the M Street High School. In 1916 the school acquired a new and more spacious building on First Street and changed its name to Dunbar High School, in honor of the poet Paul Laurence Dunbar.[57]

From the beginning the institution bore a special relationship to Washington's colored aristocracy and functioned as a preparatory school for what Du Bois called the "Talented Tenth."[58] In his commencement address in 1908, William H. Lewis, a well-known Harvard-educated black attorney from Boston, reminded the graduates that there was "no real aristocracy except that of accomplishment and achievement."[59] Their successful completion of the requirements of a school with such rigid academic standards entitled them to a place in this aristocracy. In time the school became the best high school, white or black, in the nation's capital. The so-called Dunbar phenomenon was unique. "It reflected variables that came together at a particular time and place," Kenneth B.

Clark has noted, "and that are not likely to be duplicated. It could scarcely have existed in any other part of the country."[60]

From its beginning the Preparatory High School attracted an excellent faculty, committed to a classical curriculum and high academic standards. During its first half century, the school was under the direction of men and women who were graduates of some of the nation's most prestigious institutions, including Harvard, Amherst, Dartmouth, and Oberlin. The principal during the 1872–1873 term was Richard T. Greener, a Harvard graduate, who married Genevieve Ida Fleet, a schoolteacher and a member of an old and prominent family. Greener left Washington in 1873 to become professor of philosophy at the University of South Carolina, where he also obtained a law degree. Returning to Washington in 1877 after the collapse of the Republican government in South Carolina, he served as dean of the Howard University School of Law and later practiced law in the District until he entered the diplomatic service.[61]

The second Harvard graduate to head the colored high school was Robert H. Terrell, an alumnus of the institution and a strong advocate of a "purely English education." During his tenure, from 1899 to 1901, he devoted much of his energy toward "channelling bright Negro boys to Exeter in preparation for Harvard." In effect, the school served as "the academy of Washington's black well-to-do." A graduate of the class of 1905 recalled that elitism, based in part on "color distinctions," pervaded the institution. He claimed that while dark-skinned youths received a good education there, the light-complexioned children of the District's aristocrats of color never accepted them as social equals.[62]

Few individuals had a more profound influence on the colored high school and its development than Francis L. Cardozo, who served as principal from 1884 to 1896. Described as a courtly gentleman, "dignified in his bearing and polished in his manner," Cardozo was a proud descendant of a free family of color, who on one occasion informed a group of northern whites that there were in the South "colored people who have *always been free.*" During his tenure as principal, the institution acquired a larger and better-equipped facility on M Street and emerged as the premier black preparatory school in America.[63] Aristocrats of color throughout the nation often made great effort and substantial sacrifices for their children to attend Professor Cardozo's school. Some arranged to have them live with friends and acquaintances. Others undoubtedly pursued the course of Dr. Alonzo C. McClennan of Charleston, South Carolina, who rented a house for his wife and children in Washington. Cardozo's two sons attended the M Street School; both later secured graduate training. One became an educator in Washington, and the other a socially prominent, civic-minded physician in Baltimore, where he was an early leader in the National Association for the Advancement of Colored People.[64]

By any standard the record of achievement of the high school alumni was outstanding. Those graduates who did not pursue collegiate study often became teachers and principals of black schools throughout the nation. Of those who attended college, the majority probably went to Howard or some other black institution, but the usual route of the "brightest and best" was to go to a New England preparatory school and then on to a prestigious white institution. Of these, none achieved more recognition or enjoyed a higher status than the graduates of Ivy League institutions, such as Roscoe Conkling Bruce, Clement Morgan, and Hugh Francis, all of whom attended Harvard. But whether graduates of Washington's colored high school entered Ivy League or black universities, they were likely to excel and to enter the professions of medicine, law, and education. McClennan's son became a physician, as did sons of the Cooks, Wormleys, Curtises, and Cardozos. Francis and Morgan, among others, became prominent attorneys; and a large contingent of the high school's alumni achieved distinction as educators.[65]

Ironically perhaps, it was through Cardozo's influence that the colored high school in the District added a commercial department, followed by the introduction of business and technical courses. These innovations deeply troubled those who, like Robert H. Terrell, believed that the high school should adhere strictly to a college preparatory curriculum. Terrell was opposed to the position of the "intensely practical men who see no gain in studying the humanities, and who pretend to think that the improvement and refinements that come to us from living in an atmosphere of culture are not worth the time we spent in attaining them."[66]

Cardozo's vocational courses ultimately led to the founding of the Armstrong Manual Training School in 1902 and the Cardozo Vocational School a decade later. These institutions came closer to the so-called Tuskegee Idea of industrial education advocated by Booker T. Washington. The establishment of Armstrong received enthusiastic support from many of the colored aristocracy, including Mary Church Terrell, who at the time was a member of the school board. The creation of a separate vocational school meant that the M Street High School could then concentrate on providing a "purely English education." Even more than ever, the school became the preserve of upper-class blacks; an increasingly disproportionate share of its students came "from the homes of doctors, lawyers, teachers and government officials." No matter how bright the darker-skinned children of working-class families who attended M Street and later Dunbar might be, they "just knew they didn't belong."[67]

Washington's Negro high school, under its various names, has been described as "the only example in our history of a separate black school that was able, somehow, to be equal." It was, in Kenneth Clark's view, essentially "a 'white' school in a segregated system." Whatever the validity of these observations, it is clear that if its record of academic excellence and achievement inspired pride in the black community, its elitism and reputed color consciousness aroused widespread resentment that increased with time. Those who took pride in the school's "illustrious past" bemoaned the dramatic decline in its quality and standards in the wake of the Brown decision of 1954. When twenty years later the demolition of the Dunbar High School building appeared imminent, this group of distinguished graduates and descendants of the "old families" of the District launched a vigorous campaign to save their "symbol of black excellence." Their efforts ultimately failed, because of the formidable strength of the "anti-Dunbar forces" among blacks who rose to power during the civil rights revolution of the 1960s and who saw the old school building as a tangible reminder of "an elitism . . . that should never happen again." Wrecking crews demolished the structure in July 1977, a little more than a century after William Syphax had founded it. In referring to the black political forces responsible for the razing of the old Dunbar building, Syphax's granddaughter, a Radcliffe graduate who taught at the high school for thirty-five years, claimed that "these new people hate and resent us for what we did there." In a vein worthy of her ancestors in the 1880s she dismissed "these new people" as "a disgrace to home rule in Washington."[68]

One of the most important and persistent campaigns in which Baltimore's aristocrats of color participated was that devoted to securing educational facilities for the city's black children. By the late nineteenth century, the old families—the Forties, Masons, Bishops, and others—had a long tradition of involvement in educational concerns. In the antebellum era their ancestors had founded schools and been instrumental in providing the rudiments of education to Baltimore's blacks. "The Negroes of Baltimore," historian Carter Woodson wrote in 1915, "were almost as self-educating as those in the District of Columbia" before the Civil War.[69] From the end of the war until the turn of the century, education was the focus of much of the black protest in the city. As a result of long struggles in which Isaac Myers, William H. Bishop, Dr. H. J. Brown, and others of the city's black aristocracy often acted as leaders, by the turn of the century Baltimore had not only established a system of public schools including the Colored High School but also acquiesced in demands for black schools staffed by black teachers. The Howard Normal School in the city began as a private institution founded and operated by whites in 1867. For a time three well-known black Baltimoreans, John H. Butler, Harrison Webb, and John H. Locks, served on its board of trustees. Many of the city's upper-class blacks were associated with Howard Normal either as students or as teachers. In 1917 the school was sold and the proceeds were donated to the new state-supported Maryland Normal and Industrial School.[70]

As far as members of the old black upper class and their children were concerned, the private educational institutions in the city were as important as the public schools. The daughters of colored aristocrats could receive instruction in the "culture and refinement" they so highly prized at St. Frances Academy. Scarcely less important in educating the children of the upper class were the preparatory schools sponsored by the Episcopalians. One of these, St. Mary's Girls' Academy, attracted students from upper-class black families from Washington and other nearby cities, as well as from Baltimore. In 1879 black Episcopalians in Baltimore and Washington launched a campaign to establish a companion school for boys, which also became known as St. Mary's. The board of trustees of the new school, which in its original advertisement announced that the annual cost of board and tuition would be $100, included Blanche K. Bruce, Congressman Joseph Rainey, Richard T. Greener, and Alexander Crummell from Washington; and Dr. H. J. Brown, John H. Locks, James T. Bradford, and William H. Bishop of Baltimore. Despite plans for St. Mary's Boys' Academy to be a boarding school, it apparently remained a day school.[71]

Of particular importance in the educational history of black Baltimore was Centenary Biblical Institute, an institution chartered in 1867 by the Methodist Episcopal Church to train black ministers. For the first five years of its existence, it had no building and operated out of the Sharp Street Methodist Church. By 1890, when its name was changed to Morgan College, Centenary had dramatically expanded its original curriculum and had acquired two "branch schools," in Princess Anne, Maryland and Lynchburg, Virginia. In addition to the black Marylanders educated at Centenary and Morgan who achieved distinction elsewhere, the college attracted students who eventually worked in Baltimore and became prominent members of the new black elite emerging in the city during the decade before the First World War.[72]

Among these were Mason Albert Hawkins of Virginia, who acquired degrees from Harvard and Columbia before returning to teach foreign languages in Baltimore's Colored High School in 1901. Nine years later he became principal of the school. Active in a variety of social and civic enterprises, he counted among his close personal friends W. E. B. Du Bois, who visited him frequently. As Hawkins's guest at the mid-winter ball of the Baltimore Assembly in 1911, Du Bois had an opportunity to become acquainted with "the younger set" as well as with members of the old families, people inclined to prefer his approach to race issues to that of Booker T. Washington. Another Centenary graduate who became a conspicuous member of Baltimore's black upper class was the attorney William Ashbie Hawkins, also a native of Virginia. He received his legal training at Howard and returned to Baltimore to open a law office in 1892, eight years after blacks were allowed to practice before the courts of Maryland. A prominent layman in the Methodist Episcopal church, he had a long career as a civil rights attorney and battled, often successfully, a variety of discriminatory laws and practices in Maryland. He won wide recognition for his legal fight against Baltimore's residential segregation ordinances. By the second decade of the twentieth century, Hawkins occupied a secure place in Baltimore's black upper class, as evidenced by his membership in the American Negro Academy, the Baltimore Assembly, and Boulé, probably the most exclusive social organization of black men in America.[73]

In the black community, educational achievement both promoted the upward mobility of those outside the aristocracy of color and enhanced the position of those inside it. Because attendance at or graduation from college by blacks, not to mention the acquisition of advanced degrees, was so rare, those who did have college diplomas enjoyed special distinction and were expected to assume leadership roles. Between 1826 and 1900 fewer than 2,500 black men and women graduated from college. Between 1900 and 1909 there were an additional 1,613 college graduates. One of the most exclusive organizations in Washington from the mid-1890s on was the Graduate Club. Organized by Kelly Miller of Howard University and composed of thirty-two college graduates, the club included those who made up a social elite sometimes referred to as Washington's "educational set." The members devoted their attention primarily to the study of sociological questions, including "the Negro Problem."[74]

In the late nineteenth and early twentieth centuries, the sons and daughters of caterers, barbers, tailors, teachers, government employees, and others of high-status occupations, who were also likely to possess a level of education and refinement that distinguished them from other blacks, strengthened their claims to places at the top of the black class structure by becoming educators, physicians, and attorneys. Teachers and educational administrators usually occupied a lofty status in the black community. A majority of the female "society leaders" of black Boston identified in a newspaper account in 1888 were teachers, all of whom were graduates of Boston or suburban high schools.[75] Physicians and their families also belonged to the "upper tens" of black society, in large part because a medical degree represented advanced formal education. While a majority of the black physicians received their education at Howard, Meharry in Nashville, Leonard in Raleigh, and the few other black medical schools in the United States, some were graduates of the most prestigious, predominantly white medical colleges. Black physicians and dentists sometimes enhanced their social standing by marrying into "old families," as did the Cabiness brothers of Virginia. James, a graduate of New York Dental College, married a member of the Holloway family of Charleston; and his brother George, a physician and graduate of Howard's medical school, married Ruth Tancil, from an old and socially prominent family of Alexandria, Virginia.[76] Attorneys might occupy a comparable standing, especially if they were graduates of reputable law schools.

Despite the existence of numerous black institutions that called themselves colleges and universities, many in fact scarcely qualified as solid secondary schools. Among those that did offer high-quality collegiate education were several institutions established by or somehow linked with the American Missionary Association and the Congregational church, such as Atlanta University, Howard University in Washington, and Fisk University in Nashville. These institutions, as well as Wilberforce in Ohio and Presbyterian-related Lincoln University in Pennsylvania, had racially mixed faculties and attracted the children of "the best-to-do colored families."[77] In discussing the several black institutions of higher education in Atlanta, John Hope observed in 1904 that the curricula of Spelman, Clark, Atlanta Baptist (Morehouse), Morris Brown, and Atlanta University sought to provide students with "broad learning and liberal culture" rather than manual training or what at the time was called industrial education.[78] On a smaller scale, Claflin College in South Carolina, founded by the Northern Methodist Church, strived to accomplish the same objective. Dominated in its early years by teachers and trustees "who had been free, fairly well educated and relatively economically secure during a part of the slave regime," Claflin became known as "an institution for the Negro aristocrat."[79] Wilberforce University, according to Reverdy Ransom, was "a community with an atmosphere of culture and refinement hardly equalled elsewhere among Negroes of the United States."[80] Alumni of Atlanta University, Fisk, Howard, and other prestigious black institutions probably would have made the same claim for their alma mater. Howard University viewed itself as the institution in which "choice youth of the race" could "assimilate the principles of culture and hand them down to the masses below."[81]

Beginning in the 1880s, an industrial education vogue developed throughout the United States. Among blacks the intense debate over liberal arts education versus industrial education came to focus on two individuals who represented divergent ideologies and strategies: Booker T. Washington, founder and principal of Tuskegee Institute, who was the foremost advocate of industrial education; and W. E. B. Du Bois, who was educated at Fisk and Harvard, taught at Atlanta University, and advocated higher (liberal) education for the so-called talented tenth of the race. The rivalry between the higher education and the industrial education enthusiasts on occasion became so bitter it poisoned faculty relations in some institutions. A graduate of Cornell University who was on the faculty at Tuskegee confided to a friend in 1909 that she was ridiculed because of her education. "It was a crime for you to say 'college,' " she reported, "or if you happened to mention 'degree' you are termed an egotistic pedant."[82]

In 1908 Kelly Miller, a highly respected scholar and Howard University professor, characterized the controversy over industrial versus liberal arts education as the work of "one eyed enthusiasts," unable or unwilling to understand that both types of education were beneficial to blacks. To insist that a single curriculum was suitable for all blacks, was, in his view, "both mischievous and silly."[83] In a sense, aristocrats of color exhibited the "binocular vision" on the debate that rival enthusiasts lacked: while most upper-class blacks probably favored industrial education for the masses, they insisted on higher education for their own children.

Among those who condemned all attempts to confine blacks to industrial education was James Weldon Johnson, a graduate of Stanton High School in Jacksonville and Atlanta University. Since Emancipation, he wrote in 1902, blacks had classified themselves "into almost as many grades, as regards ability and capacity as . . . found among whites." Whether a black person should receive higher education or industrial training depended "entirely upon the individual."[84] Andrew F. Hilyer, a graduate of the University of Minnesota and a conspicuous figure in Washington's "black 400," agreed that it would be a "grievous wrong" to restrict blacks, regardless of ability, to a program of industrial education. Hilyer believed that higher education had practically the same effect on blacks as on whites, with the salient difference that higher education "raises the colored youth from a lower social scale, as a rule, and places him on a social plane, relatively, among his own people, higher than it does in the case of the white youth."[85]

Some children of upper-class black families enrolled at prestigious white institutions in the North. Those who graduated from Harvard acquired a degree of prestige perhaps unequaled by graduates of any other institution. Among those who held Harvard degrees were Richard T. Greener, Robert Terrell, and Roscoe C. Bruce of Washington; Mason A. Hawkins of Baltimore; Edwin Clarence Howard of Boston and Philadelphia; and William Monroe Trotter of Boston.[86] In 1912 Trotter's sister Bessie married a Harvard graduate, Henry K. Craft, a member of an old and socially prominent family of Charleston, South Carolina.[87] One student of the M Street High School whom Robert Terrell directed to Exeter in preparation for Harvard was Haley Douglass, a grandson of Frederick Douglass.[88] By 1914 the "colored alumni of Harvard in the Middle Atlantic States" had organized an informal association that periodically held "Harvard Smokers." Clearly, such groups, which were well represented in Boulé and other exclusive gentlemen's organizations, constituted an elite within an elite.[89] Ranking only slightly below the "Harvard men" were the graduates of other Ivy League schools. The brothers Jefferson and George Ish of Little Rock, whose parents were graduates of Talladega College, an A.M.A. institution in Alabama, were both Yale graduates. For more than a half century they occupied places of leadership in the professional and social life of Little Rock's black community. Ebenezer Bassett, the principal of Philadelphia's Institute for Colored Youth, and his two sons attended Yale.[90]

The sons and daughters of aristocrats of color attended a variety of other prestigious white institutions. Willis M. Menard, the grandson of John Willis Menard, the first of the black Reconstruction politicians to be elected to Congress, graduated from Williams College. In the 1890s Maud Cuney, the daughter of the well-known politician of Galveston, Texas, Norris Wright Cuney, and Florida Desverney, whose father was a prosperous cotton dealer in Savannah, were classmates at the New England Conservatory of Music in Boston.[91] Fannie Barrier of Brockport, New York also attended the Conservatory and taught in the public schools of Washington before her marriage to S. Laing Williams, a graduate of the University of Michigan.[92] Two other prominent blacks who graduated from Michigan were the physicians Samuel Le Count Cook and John Richard Francis of Washington, members of two of the most-respected families in the District.[93] Francis, the son of a well-known caterer, had four sons, all of whom became professional men: the eldest, a physician, was a graduate of Howard's medical school; the second was a dentist who graduated from the University of Pennsylvania; the third, a Harvard law school graduate, practiced law in San Juan, Puerto Rico; and the youngest was a graduate of Dartmouth who taught in the District schools.[94]

Oberlin College was probably the alma mater of more aristocrats of color than any other white institution, and in some instances it was the college of several generations of the same black family. A son, a grandson, and a great-grandson of John Mercer and Caroline Wall Langston were, like their forebears, graduates of Oberlin.[95] Several members of the Alexander family of Helena, Arkansas, including John H. Alexander, the second black graduate of West Point, attended Oberlin.[96] When the daughters of Mary Church Terrell reached college age, she enrolled them at her alma mater, Oberlin, because she believed it would be "wrong to bring them up having contact with nobody but their own racial group."[97] While numerous considerations figured in the decision of black parents to send their children to Oberlin and other white institutions, their "assimilationist" approach to the racial question undoubtedly played some role in such decisions.

A considerable correlation existed between upper-class status and educational achievement in the black community in the forty years following Reconstruction, as it did in previous generations. It was no mere coincidence that the two most prestigious black organizations in the United States early in the twentieth century, the American Negro Academy and Sigma Pi Phi (Boulé), required scholarly and educational credentials for admission to membership. To a considerable degree, the descendants of literate antebellum blacks reinforced their claims to positions at the top of the class structure by perpetuating traditions of educational achievement. The children and grandchildren of those who before the Civil War had acquired some education— whether in college, at preparatory schools, or even on lower levels—constituted a disproportionately large segment of those in post–Reconstruction America who held college diplomas and advanced degrees. The records of "old families" other than the Francises and Langstons demonstrated a continuity in educational achievement. Among them were the Curtis-Childs families of Alabama; the Dibbles of South Carolina; the Daniel family of Virginia, which traced its origins back to John Mercer Langston's sister, Maria; and numerous others whose academic genealogies have been charted by Horace Mann Bond.[98]

No less noteworthy in this respect was the Gibbs family, originally from Philadelphia, which produced several generations of teachers, physicians, and other individuals dedicated to higher education for blacks. Mifflin W. and Jonathan C. Gibbs, the sons of a Philadelphia Methodist minister, grew up in the "best circles" of the city's antebellum black society. Mifflin Gibbs apparently was self-educated, but read law, became a judge, and played a prominent role in late nineteenth-century Arkansas politics. Two of his daughters graduated from Oberlin in the 1880s: Ida was for a time a teacher; and Harriet, who married a Harvard graduate, established a conservatory of music in Washington. None of Judge Gibbs's children left offspring, but those of his equally prominent brother did. Jonathan Gibbs was educated at Dartmouth and Princeton. As a Presbyterian minister he occupied several prestigious pulpits in the North before moving South during Reconstruction. He finally settled in Florida, where he served as both secretary of state and superintendent of education. In the latter position he was credited with establishing public schools in Florida. His son, Thomas Van Rensselaer Gibbs, spent a year at West Point and later married Alice Menard, the daughter of J. Willis Menard. Thomas served in the Florida legislature and was largely responsible for the establishment of Florida A. & M. College for blacks, where for a time his cousin Ida Gibbs was a member of the faculty. A grandson and a great-grandson of Jonathan Gibbs became physicians, and many of his other descendants taught in schools from Florida to New Jersey.[99]

One of the most frequent themes pursued by upper-class educated blacks was the obligation to render "service to the race," which, as William S. Scarborough declared in 1903, "is peculiarly the mission of the educated Negro."[100] In the same year Roscoe C. Bruce discoursed on a similar theme in his commencement address to the M Street High School in Washington. He spoke in terms of the spirit of *noblesse oblige* that ought to inspire educated blacks to assist in the uplift of the less fortunate masses. While service by the educated elite took many forms, one of the most significant was that of setting an example for the less privileged to follow. It was the responsibility of educated black men and women "to steady the nerves of a staggering people and make the word Negro more than a reproach."[101] Scarborough pointed out that while blacks, like other races, had an abundance of idlers and pretenders, Negroes could not afford to tolerate such people in view of the prevailing racial climate. Therefore, he argued, one of the most important functions of the black educated elite was "to form classes of society where culture and refinement, high thinking and high living, in its proper sense, draw the line."[102]

Few other organizations in the black community exhibited a stronger commitment to the idea of "service to the race" than women's clubs. The founders and early leaders of the National Association of Colored Women were well-educated individuals who placed kindergartens, schools, and libraries among the highest priorities of the organization. Implicit in the efforts of the NACW and its affiliates was the recognition that the educational advancement of blacks was essential to the elimination of prejudice and to the overall "progress of the race." In Atlanta and other cities, black women's organizations lobbied vigorously in behalf of improved educational facilities for blacks. In Arkansas the state federation of women's clubs organized and supported "School Improvement Associations" throughout the state. The Michigan federation, as well as those in other states, emphasized the need for providing the black masses with industrial education—"education that shall fit the Negro to do the work that he can get to do." While the most socially prominent leaders in the club movement among black women, such as Mary Church Terrell, Josephine St. Pierre Ruffin, and Josephine Bruce, advocated industrial training for the masses, they did not believe that Booker T. Washington's educational philosophy was applicable to their families or to others of the "higher classes."[103]

Despite the value blacks in general placed on education and the deference they displayed toward those with academic training, the educated elite did not escape criticism at the hands of those whose formal schooling was often slight. Some characterized the educated elite as "learned, verbose and voluble" and inclined to criticize "men who hustle and succeed" in business.[104] Others condemned educated blacks as self-centered and "dominated by a narrow, individualistic conception of things" that made it impossible for them "to get collectively" with others in efforts to benefit the race.[105] In 1903 a resident of Topeka, Kansas echoed a common complaint of older blacks when he condemned the younger, better-educated generation for lacking the "quiet manners" that education was supposed to bestow: "When such conduct is observed among the 'smart set,' what can be expected from the socially, mentally and morally submerged?"[106] A writer in the *Cleveland Journal* in 1908 roundly condemned "society girls" of the city for spurning all suitors who were not educated. According to him, a young man without a college diploma, regardless of his other attributes, had no chance of winning the hand of any of Cleveland's upper-class girls.[107]

Perhaps the most frequent criticism of the black educated elite related to its aloofness from the masses. Benjamin Davis, the volatile editor of the *Atlanta Independent,* condemned the administrators and faculty of the black colleges in Atlanta, including John Hope and W. H. Crogman, for their failure either to come "in touch with the community life" or to be identified with movements in "the interest of the masses." "You can't do us any good," he declared in 1907, "[by] standing off trying to lift us up with a forty-foot pole."[108] Two years later Davis suggested that if the black colleges of Atlanta wished to "serve the people," their administrators should visit Tuskegee and learn what Booker T. Washington's school was contributing to the uplift of the masses.[109]

Critics of educated, upper-class blacks sometimes accused them of being "lamp black whites" or of aping the ways of middle- and upper-class whites. While there was obviously some truth to the accusation, it is difficult to see how it could have been otherwise. Reared in homes that placed a premium on middle-class values and a Victorian code of behavior, they then often attended schools and colleges in which white New England faculties stressed the same kind of virtues and pieties. The pattern of education found at Oberlin, Fisk, Atlanta University, and Howard also prevailed in numerous other schools, black and white, throughout the nation; the objectives, ideologies, and even faculties were strikingly similar. The curricula devoted virtually no attention to the cultural heritage of Africa, but emphasized Anglo-Saxon or American culture. The educational experience of the black upper class, then, conspired to mold it into a replica of middle- and upper-class white America. Its values, style of living, and patterns of behavior, collectively known as "respectability" and highly prized in the black community, bore a remarkable resemblance to those of "respectable" white Americans. Elite blacks were educated to take a paternalistic view toward blacks less fortunate than themselves, in much the same way as the well-educated, white New England teachers and professors had often manifested toward them. Although upper-class blacks generally looked upon Africa as a benighted land, as did other Americans, this did not mean that they sought to deny either their racial identity or their black heritage. In fact, it was precisely individuals such as Henry Minton, Florida Ruffin Ridley, W. E. B. Du Bois, and Carter Woodson who organized black historical societies, recorded black history, and promoted black culture.

Despite complaints about their aping of whites, the educated black elite enjoyed extraordinary prestige in the larger black community. Whether in the M Street High School in Washington or a small school in a southern village, teachers were at or near the top of the class structure, as were physicians, dentists, certain clergymen, and others with academic credentials. The largest component of the "black 400" in Washington, other than government employees, consisted of teachers in the separate colored school system and members of the Howard University faculty. If one were both educated and a member of an "old family," it was virtually assured that he or she would be included among the "upper tens" of black society. On the other hand, if one were educated and exhibited "true gentility" but lacked a distinguished family heritage, admittance to the "upper tens" was highly likely.

10

♦

Churches of the Aristocracy

THE CHURCH HAS PLAYED A VITAL ROLE in Negro life in the United States. Early in the twentieth century W. E. B. Du Bois referred to it as "the social center of Negro life" and Booker T. Washington as the institution most representative of the black masses and the one that had "the strongest hold upon them."[1] In a later treatment of the role of the church in the black community, E. Franklin Frazier, a sociologist, interpreted it as a multifunctional institution that served as an agency of social control, education, and economic cooperation; it also provided blacks with both an arena of political life and a refuge from a hostile environment.[2] Notwithstanding the influence of the African past and the slave experience on the development of the black church, most students of Afro-American history agree that as the black population became more differentiated socially, economically, and culturally, "Negro religion likewise has become more varied."[3]

Overwhelmingly Protestant, a majority of Negro Americans affiliated with various types of Methodist and Baptist churches. In the late eighteenth and early nineteenth centuries, separate black Baptist churches were established in Georgia, South Carolina, and Virginia, but in part because of the Baptist tradition of religious freedom and diversity, it was not until seventy-five years later that the National Baptist convention came into existence. In 1816 Richard Allen and others created the African Methodist Episcopal Church at a meeting convened in Philadelphia. Five years later another step in the independence movement occurred with the formation of the African Methodist Episcopal Zion Church in New York. Other denominations, such as Colored Methodist and Colored Cumberland Presbyterian churches, came into existence after the Civil War. In addition, blacks continued to hold memberships in the Protestant Episcopal, Presbyterian, Methodist Episcopal, Congregational, and other predominantly white congregations. Regardless of denominational affiliations, black clergymen throughout the nineteenth and early twentieth centuries enjoyed great prestige and often occupied positions of leadership in the community. While some black clergymen were uneducated and known as "jackleg preachers," their ranks also included individuals, especially in the Episcopal, Presbyterian, and Congregational churches, who were erudite theologians.[4]

Blacks identified by sociologists of religion as belonging to the lower classes, in both rural and urban areas, practiced a religion that was less formal, more otherworldly, and more inclined to congregational participation in worship services than that of most whites or of middle- and upper-class blacks. By the late nineteenth century, the religious services and beliefs of upper- and upper middle-class blacks in urban areas appear to have been similar to those of white Protestants of comparable education, social status, and economic standing.[5]

Writing in 1908, Monroe Work, a black scholar and observer of black society, reported a change in the status of the Negro minister: "The tendency is for the Negro minister to assume a position in the community similar to that of the white minister; that is, to become the spiritual leader of the people and leave the guidance of social and economic matters to other persons." The primary cause for this change, according to Work, was the emergence of a better-educated laity and the prominence in black congregations of doctors, lawyers, teachers, and other professionals who were competent to assume direction of nonreligious activities. But black ministers still occupied more conspicuous roles in the general life of the black community than did white clergymen[6] in the white community. Francis J. Grimké and Alexander Crummell of Washington, Hutchins C. Bishop of New York, and Henry H. Proctor of Atlanta, who presided over upper-class black congregations, as well as an assortment of well-known A.M.E. bishops and other black religious leaders, were well-educated, sophisticated ministers whose influence extended far beyond the religious sphere.

The relationship between social class and church affiliation among blacks in the late nineteenth and early twentieth centuries does not lend itself to easy generalization. In this era blacks generally perceived Episcopal, Presbyterian, Congregational, and to a lesser degree Methodist Episcopal and Catholic churches as those made up of "high-toned" people who, undemonstrative during worship services, adhered to "book religion." "There was a time and it is within the memory of this generation," a black observer noted in 1888, "when a colored man [who] was other than a Methodist or Baptist was the target of derision and contempt." That blacks had become affiliated with the Episcopal, Presbyterian, Catholic, and even Unitarian churches "without unpleasant comment," he concluded, was primarily the result of education and intellectual sophistication. It constituted abundant evidence of "the Negro's growing intelligence."[7] For some blacks, especially those identified as upper class and "old family," it was not a matter of becoming affiliated with these denominations but of perpetuating a family tradition that had existed, in some instances, for several generations.

But the individual church, regardless of denomination, was sometimes more important than the denominational label in determining social status. African Methodist Episcopal, African Methodist Episcopal Zion, and Baptist churches often included representatives of the upper class, especially families descended from founding members. The style of worship, education of the minister, and collective social standing of members combined to confer upper-class status on some congregations within these black denominations. In Washington, the Nineteenth Street Baptist Church, founded in 1839, counted among its lay leaders some of the most prominent black families in the district, including those by the name of Syphax, Parke, and Pierre. Walter H. Brooks, originally a Presbyterian educated at Lincoln University, served as minister of the church for more than a third of a century. By the turn of the century, Nineteenth Street Baptist Church was considered a "high-tone" church[8] that bore little resemblance to lower-class Baptist congregations scattered throughout the rural South or poor districts of cities.

Editors and others in black communities expressed admiration for what they perceived as the "progress from rude to civilized worship."[9] They were highly critical of the emotionalism evident in a vast majority of black churches. In 1865 free-born Thomas Cardozo chose to avoid the freedmen's churches in his native Charleston because of their barbaric behavior.[10] Twenty years later a black resident of Washington, in a devastating critique of the pulpit antics of black ministers, observed: "Making a noise in the pulpit is not preaching."[11] Other characterized shouting and noise making during worship services, as well as the tendency to "beat and lacerate themselves to appease the supposed wrath of God," as painful reminders of slavery. Such behavior in churches, others argued, ought to be put aside since it was inconsistent with the growing intelligence and sophistication of blacks. Along with "gyrations," blacks ought to abandon "their hankering for plantation melodies" and sing decorous sacred music. For many upper-class blacks the "moaning and shouting" preacher was a major obstacle to the progress of civilization among blacks: he symbolized ignorance and thwarted enlightenment among his followers.[12]

In 1898 William Taylor Burrell Williams, a graduate of Harvard who returned to his native Virginia after an absence of seven years, was appalled at both the form and the substance of a church service that he attended. For several hours he listened to two ministers, one "an old man and the other a mere boy." "The former," he confided to a friend, "was simply reciting the identical words, to say nothing of the thought, that he used to charm his audience into physical ecstasy when I was a child. The second was a mere understudy of the older minister." No less disturbing to him was the behavior of the communicants, who, constantly "swaying to and fro" virtually drowned out the voices of the speakers with their shouting and moaning: "In the face of the

enlightenment of this day, there they were happy and bigoted in their ignorance."[13]

Upper-class blacks were repelled not only by the flamboyant antics of black
preachers but by those of whites as well. In 1915, when Mary Church Terrell
attended a service conducted by Billy Sunday, she expressed almost as much
disgust with his behavior as with his racism. In addition to being "the worst Jim
Crow" she ever encountered, she wrote in her diary, he also "hops up and down
a ladder, chants . . . pulls his collar off and does everything else."[14]

Upper-class blacks, as well as others who openly criticized the "barbarism"
displayed by black congregations, elicited sharp responses from adherents of
traditional forms of black religion. The language used to describe those who had
abandoned "emotional" religion for the more sedate liturgical forms revealed
both respect and resentment. The sentiment expressed by a black resident of
Washington, writing in the *Star of Zion* in 1889, was typical. "I have heard much
talk lately of 'bon-tons'; 'upper crust' and 'high tone' members in the church." In
the writer's view such elements were "worthless," if not downright malevolent,
forces in the black church, because of their condescension toward less fortunate
blacks. This "crowd," he observed, had emerged in virtually all denominations
and was busily engaged in its destructive work.[15] Such critics sometimes displayed their hostility toward upper-class blacks who objected to demonstrative
religion by actions as well as words. A Harvard-educated Episcopalian who was
eager to lecture to the masses in his hometown and who expected an invitation
to do so from one of the all-black denominations was shocked when he received
none. "I was not an 'Ironside Baptist' and therefore was disqualified."[16]

The denomination that perhaps included more aristocrats of color than any
other was the Protestant Episcopal church, which was also generally considered
a high-status church by whites. In the antebellum South substantial numbers of
blacks, slave and free, were communicants in the Episcopal church, especially in
Virginia, the Carolinas, and Georgia. For example, in 1860, of the 6,126
communicants in South Carolina, 2,960 were black. "Prior to emancipation,"
one historian of black Episcopalians has observed, "southern black Episcopalians
were under the paternalistic control of southern bishops, while their more
independent brethren suffered from the benign neglect of northern bishops."[17]
White Episcopalians exhibited a racism that prompted them to treat their black
brethren as step-children separated from the main body of the flock. Although
the Episcopal church did not split over slavery, as other major Protestant
denominations did, its Negro membership both before and after the war remained "a delicate subject." In 1903 W. E. B. Du Bois, who was baptized in the
Episcopal church, claimed that it had "probably done less for black people than
any other aggregation of Christians."[18]

Regardless of the accuracy of Du Bois's observation, the Episcopal church
witnessed what has been described as a "wholesale exodus" of blacks from its
ranks right after the Civil War. Most of those who withdrew apparently shifted

their allegiance to the black denominations, principally Methodist and Baptist. One authority claims that the Episcopal church suffered the greatest losses among blacks in rural areas and hypothesizes that it was chiefly former field slaves who abandoned the church, leaving free blacks and privileged slaves as the two primary components of black Episcopal congregations after the war. "The hypothesis," he concludes, "would be consistent with the fact that black parishes were located in urban centers and with evidence that they were composed largely of the more privileged blacks. It would also help to explain the limited appeal that the Episcopal Church has continued to have among blacks."[19]

The popular perception, among blacks as well as whites, was that communicants of the Episcopal church did indeed constitute a "privileged" group. The ranks of the black Episcopalians included a disproportionately large number of the most respected "old families," professional people, and others whose education and affluence often set them apart from other blacks. The small number of black Episcopalians, amounting to only 15,000 by 1903, also contributed to an image of exclusiveness.[20] Based on observations in Mobile in 1867, a black writer noted that communicants in a local black Episcopal congregation had adopted "the high and aristocratic ideas of white people" and spoke of themselves as "the better class, the well-to-do class, Episcopal element."[21] In their view the Episcopal church contained the "select few," while the "common multitude" filled other denominations. Forty years later, George Freeman Bragg, Jr., one of the best-known black Episcopal clergymen in the United States, admitted that the church still contained "a small contingent of dandiacal colored people" who used the church "to get as far as possible from the ordinary Negro."[22]

Arnold Hamilton Maloney, another black Episcopal clergyman, agreed that his parishioners too often considered the church as "a play house," consisting of social cliques: "Only those in the community who could qualify according to terms laid down by the clique were wanted for membership."[23] The idea that Episcopalians were more of a social class than a religious denomination found expression in a joke repeatedly told by Booker T. Washington and which prompted prolonged applause from audiences. An elderly black woman in Mississippi, according to Washington, wandered into an Episcopal church and took a seat in a rear pew. When she began to moan and clap her hands, a church official inquired whether she was ill. "No sir, I'se happy; I'se got religion. Yes, sir, I'se got religion!" To this enthusiasm the official responded: "Why, don't you know that this isn't the place to get religion?"[24]

Although the degree to which congregations exhibited social exclusiveness varied from parish to parish, the idea of Episcopalians being "the select few" was sufficiently widespread to prompt upwardly mobile blacks to transfer their allegiance from Baptist and Methodist denominations to the Episcopal church. Some, especially those tied economically or politically to the black ghetto, tried to have it both ways: they attended high-prestige churches such as the Episcopal church but retained membership in Baptist and Methodist churches.[25]

Throughout the late nineteenth and early twentieth centuries, black Episcopalians constituted a tiny minority in a white church. Most were members of separate all-black congregations. A few congregations were self-supporting, but the majority were dependent on white parishes. As they struggled to become self-supporting parishes rather than dependent missions, they also sought to gain recognition as full-fledged members of the faith with a voice in church affairs comparable to that of other communicants. Their efforts came to focus in a thirty-year struggle over the issue of black bishops—a struggle that posed for them a cruel dilemma. The choice was between black parishes organized into a separate Negro diocese or suffragan bishops without the right of succession. Among those who opposed a racially separate episcopate was All Saints Episcopal Church of St. Louis. Inasmuch as the rector of All Saints, the Baltimore-born C. M. S. Mason, and its vestry, which included "the leading colored citizens," shared the assimilationist perspective, they considered a separate racial district within the church as a form of Jim Crowism. In the final analysis, the suffragan bishop plan prevailed, and the first such bishop was elected in 1917. While the suffragan bishop plan could be viewed as a victory, black Episcopalians were still second-class communicants.[26]

Whatever their status in the Episcopal church, black communicants perceived themselves as being of the social "upper crust" and were also seen by other blacks as occupying a lofty status. Those who worshipped at St. Philip's in New York, St. Thomas's in Philadelphia, St. Luke's in Washington, All Saints in St. Louis, and St. Mark's in Charleston were the same people who occupied the top rung of black society and who enjoyed a special relationship with the white community. By the turn of the century, perhaps the best-known and reputedly the wealthiest black Episcopal parish in the United States was St. Philip's in New York, founded in 1818. "Fully entitled to rank as one of the historic churches of New York," a speaker observed on its fiftieth anniversary, St. Philip's prospered not only because of the nurture provided by the "ancient Trinity Church" but also because it attracted blacks "of a different stamp" from those who founded Baptist, Methodist, or even Presbyterian churches in the city. Those who established St. Philip's, in his view, possessed "a superior respect for ecclesiastical order and authority."[27] Their number also included some of the city's best-known and most prosperous people of color. Peter Williams, Jr., the chief founder and first pastor of the church, was the son of a well-known tobacconist. Wardens and vestrymen of the church throughout the century were likely to possess old family names like Ten Eyck, Ray, Guignon, Mars, White, Bowser, and Smith. In fact, there was a close correlation between leadership in St. Philip's and membership in the Newport and New York Ugly Fishing Club and The Society of the Sons of New York. In the sanctuary on Center Street there was an especially beautiful chancel, a gift of Joseph Ten

Eyck. When the church moved to Twenty-fifth Street in 1889, Dr. Peter Ray and Mrs. Cornelia Guignon equipped it with a "pure white marble" altar in memory of their parents; and Dr. Philip A. White outfitted a small chapel as a memorial to his niece. Throughout its first hundred years, in its various locations, first near Peck's Slip; then on Center, Mulberry, and Twenty-fifth streets, in succession; and finally in Harlem, in 1910, the church attracted "the most outstanding members of the race to its membership." It remained New York's "most fashionable" black church and the only one in Manhattan to retain until the late nineteenth century a "pew system" by which members bid for choice seats in the sanctuary.[28]

For more than a generation, beginning in 1886, the central figure in the evolution of St. Philip's was Hutchins C. Bishop, a member of an old and respected Episcopal family in Maryland. For many years his ancestors were prominent in St. James Church in Baltimore; and his father and older brothers and sisters were among the upper-class blacks who established the second congregration of black Episcopalians in the city, the Chapel of St. Mary the Virgin, in 1867. Sponsored by and closely linked to the elite white Mount Calvary Church, the Chapel of St. Mary the Virgin in time eclipsed the older St. James church and became the church of Baltimore's aristocrats of color. Hutchins Bishop's father, William H., for years combined the office of warden with that of treasurer, "often at his own cost, but always to the advantage of the church." In addition to the Bishops, other old families prominent in the life of St. Mary's included the Masons, Prices, Butlers, and Webbs. Black Episcopalians in Baltimore, like those elsewhere at the time, were relatively well-to-do people who had acquired property "as barbers, caterers, sextons, undertakers and the like." According to a white observer, they were "among the most intelligent, modest, courteous and upright men among their people."[29]

From the families identified with St. Mary's came two nationally prominent Episcopal clergymen: Cassius M. C. Mason, who married a sister of Hutchins Bishop, served for many years as rector of All Saints Church in St. Louis; and Hutchins Bishop, himself, who, after serving parishes in Albany, New York and Charleston, South Carolina, spent almost a half century at Saint Philip's in New York. Bishop's "mentor, life-long friend, and spiritual guide" was Calbraith B. Perry, a white Episcopal clergyman who served as rector of St. Mary's and supervised the schools sponsored by the chapel. Educated in these schools, Bishop was the first black student admitted to the General Theological Seminary in New York, an achievement that owed much to Perry's influence. Following graduation in 1881 and ordination in Albany two years later, Bishop became rector of St. Mark's Church in Charleston. In 1885, at St. Philip's, Bishop married Estelle Gilliam of New York, whose family was among the most socially prominent in the city's black community. Soon after Bishop became rector of St. Philip's.[30]

In 1889 the church acquired a larger building on West Twenty-fifth Street. In 1906 Bishop started purchasing property in Harlem with a view toward locating his church nearer the new center of the city's black population. A tall, slender man of very fair complexion, he acquired the property in his own name because white residents of Harlem refused to sell to blacks. Assuming from his appearance that he was white, the Harlem landlords candidly told him that they "would never sell to blacks." In 1910 Bishop transferred the titles to the property he had acquired in Harlem to the congregation. A new St. Philip's, which included a beautiful large sanctuary, a parish house, and facilities for diverse activities, opened a year later.[31]

Described as "an administrative genius" as well as a "shepherd of his flock and beloved leader of his community," Hutchins Bishop was largely responsible for the increase in the church's membership, property value, and outreach into the community. When he became rector in 1886, the church had 350 communicants; by 1913 it had almost 1,200. Its property was valued at a million dollars; and its programs, designed to benefit the less fortunate, underwent continual expansion.[32]

Because of Bishop's talents as an administrator, the church appears to have been spared factional squabbles that sometimes caused deep divisions in congregations. Members of well-to-do old families monopolized the most important offices in the church, and on at least one occasion, in 1912, the competition between two highly respected families triggered a brief flare-up. The contest was between William H. Smith, Jr., Bishop's son-in-law, and J. Eugene Mars for election to the vestry. When Smith lost, his father, who was senior warden, resigned his post. While the press billed the affair as "trouble in the church," its impact appears to have been minimal, and at the next election neither Smith nor Mars won a place on the vestry.[33]

Although Saint Philip's remained the wealthiest and most fashionable black church in New York, not all aristocrats of color worshipped there. Those of the Episcopal persuasion were scattered among several other congregations in greater New York. The one that ranked second in prestige to St. Philip's was St. Augustine's in Brooklyn, which by 1909 had almost 400 members. Among its most prominent families were the Lansings. For many years Charles E. Lansing, who married the daughter of Dr. Philip White, served as senior warden. Under the guidance of the rector, William Victor Tunnell, an 1887 graduate of General Theological Seminary, St. Augustine's moved from the status of a mission to a parish. Tunnell later accepted a professorship at Howard University and became a conspicuous figure in Washington's upper-class social life. "Rev. Tunnell and wife," John P. Green confided to a friend in 1900, "are of our social elite."[34]

The Episcopal church outside New York which ranked close to Saint Philip's in prestige was St. Thomas in Philadelphia. Founded in 1794, St.

Thomas was "the first and oldest colored Episcopal church in this country." In 1787 Absalom Jones and Richard Allen were among the Philadelphia blacks expelled from St. George's Methodist Episcopal Church. Allen and Jones formed the Free African Society, which became an "undenominational" church. When the society membership voted to join the Episcopal church, Allen dissented and formed the African Methodist Episcopal church. When the Episcopal church accepted the conditions laid down by Jones and other members of the African Society, St. Thomas African Episcopal Church was established. Jones was ordained deacon in 1795 and priest in 1804. Other considerations aside, one observer noted, an important reason why St. Thomas never achieved the degree of national prestige enjoyed by New York's St. Philip's was that its founders were Methodists rather than Episcopalians and only "in maturer life, in a body, conformed to the [Episcopal] church."[35]

Regardless of the religious background of its founders, St. Thomas was the church of a disproportionately large number of upper-class black Philadelphians. They had great pride in the "ancient age" of their institution and in the fact that Benjamin Rush had taken great interest in its welfare. "In the century or more of its existence," W. E. B. Du Bois wrote in 1899, "St. Thomas has always represented a high grade of intelligence, and today it still represents the most cultured and wealthiest of the Negro population and the Philadelphia born residents." Among those who figured prominently in the life of St. Thomas were members of the Forten, Stevens, Bogle, Bustill, Warrick, Howard, and Jackson families. Always small in size, the congregation still consisted of fewer than 400 persons at the end of its first century.[36]

Almost from the beginning St. Thomas Church sponsored a society known as the Sons of St. Thomas. It appears to have begun as a beneficial society comparable to the St. James Male Beneficial Society connected with St. James Episcopal Church in Baltimore. Nevertheless, over the years, the membership of the Sons of St. Thomas included numerous representatives of Philadelphia's most prominent black families. One member of the society, writing in 1912, compared the Sons to the Brown Fellowship Society of Charleston and the New York African Society of Mutual Relief. He suggested that all three were high-prestige organizations perpetuated "mainly by the sons and grandsons" of their founders.[37]

While the social service of St. Thomas does not appear to have been as diverse as that of St. Philip's in New York or even of its sister parish in Philadelphia, the Church of the Crucifixion, it nonetheless engaged in a variety of good works and had "many public spirited Negroes on its rolls." Despite its service to the black community, many blacks viewed St. Thomas, as they did other black Episcopal congregations, as aristocratic and snobbish. While Du Bois seemed unsure whether "there is some justice to this charge," he was certain St. Thomas was "by no means a popular *church among* the masses."[38]

Though established more than a half century later than St. Philip's in New York and St. Thomas's in Philadelphia, St. Luke Episcopal Church in Washington had become one of the most prestigious churches in America by 1900. The erudite Alexander Crummell founded the church shortly after his return from Liberia in 1873 and remained its rector until his death twenty-five years later. Located on Fifteenth Street, close to two other prestigious churches, the Fifteenth Street Presbyterian and St. Augustine Roman Catholic, St. Luke's was an imposing stone structure with a large stained-glass window behind the chancel. A majority of its communicants, according to a black resident of Washington in 1891, had "more than a generation of culture behind them."[39] A few years later, an observer noted "the fashionable colored churches of the city [Washington] have refined congregations dressed in perfect taste, well trained choirs, pipe organs, diamonds and rich lace worn, especially if the ladies are quadroons and mulattoes. At St. Luke's (P.E.), St. Augustine (Catholic), and the Fifteenth Street Presbyterian, a visitor will see the colored aristocracy at church."[40] Nor was it unusual on Sundays for St. Luke's to have present a dozen or more whites who resided in the neighborhood and attended as a matter of convenience. Episcopalian aristocrats of color who moved to Washington from elsewhere tended to gravitate to St. Luke's rather than to St. Mary's or some other missions established by white churches.[41]

In nearby Baltimore, St. James First African Church, organized in 1827, was especially proud of being the "first truly missionary effort by a black priest below the Mason-Dixon!" For many years, few other congregations in Baltimore, a city of numerous black churches, included so many aristocrats of color as St. James. Among the most active black Episcopalians in the city were the most socially prominent families: the Bishops, Browns, De Courseys, Deavers, and Masons. Sons of the Bishop, Mason, and Deaver families, among others at St. James, became prominent Episcopal clergymen in New York, St. Louis, and Atlantic City respectively. St. James remained the church home of many if not a majority of Baltimore's aristocrats of color until the early 1870s, when a contingent of younger communicants, led by William H. Bishop, Jr., and Cassius M. Mason, organized the Chapel of St. Mary the Virgin. St. Mary's flourished and became numerically larger and more influential than the older church. St. James "was much weakened" by the transfer of the rising generation of Bishops, Masons, and other old families to the newer church.[42]

Few if any other black Episcopal congregations acquired a reputation for exclusiveness equal to that of St. Mark's in Charleston. Founded in 1865 by fair-complexioned people of color who had been free before the Civil War, St. Mark's was for years the center of a controversy prompted by its effort to obtain representation in the Diocesan convention of South Carolina. Composed of what one observer called "the flower of the city," St. Mark's counted among its founders and communicants the Dereefs, Kinlochs, McKinlays, Bennetts,

Holloways, and others of Charleston's social elite likely also to be found in the Brown Fellowship Society and Friendly Moralist Society.[43] An ex-slave who wandered into St. Mark's a few years after the Civil War articulated a widely held view of this congregation: "When I was trampin' round Charleston, dere was a church dere called St. Mark, dat all the de society folks of my color went to. No black nigger welcome dere, they told me. Thinkin' as how I was bright enough to git in, I up and goes dere one Sunday. Oh, how they did carry on, bow and scrape and ape de white folks. . . . I was uncomfortable all de time though, 'cause they was too 'hifalootin' in de ways, in de singin', and all sorts of carryin' on."[44]

In addition to its "hifalootin" ways, St. Mark's acquired a reputation for color consciousness that was probably unequaled in black America. Stories circulated to the effect that no one darker than an octoroon was allowed to join the church. Another story about St. Mark's that persisted well into the twentieth century was that it was founded by white slave owners for their mulatto children, some of whom "were inclined toward their fathers."[45] In fact, St. Mark's was established for the elite of Charleston's antebellum free people of color who found themselves without a place to worship at the end of the war.[46] In terms of their culture, wealth, color, and antebellum social status, a gulf existed between them and the newly freed slaves that caused the latter to view St. Mark's as a bastion of snobbery.

Throughout the United States in the generation after Reconstruction, the notion persisted that black communicants in Episcopal churches were upper class and "old family." In 1907, Richard W. Thompson, a black journalist and an astute observer of black society, noted that black Episcopal churches were generally "made up of Negroes of education, social standing and means."[47] When in the same year St. Thomas Episcopal Church in Chicago decided to abandon its building on Dearborn Street in the "black belt" for an imposing structure on Wabash Avenue, "one of the choicest streets of the city," Fannie Barrier Williams observed: "St. Thomas has been looked upon as the church home of the Afro-American aristocracy in this city. It is not an easy thing to be a real aristocrat on a street in the 'black belt.' "[48]

As in Chicago, a substantial portion of the Afro-American aristocracy of other cities worshiped in Episcopal churches. In Savannah, Georgia, St. Stephen's Church had a reputation for social snobbery and color consciousness that resembled that of St. Mark's in Charleston. In Memphis the Settles, Churches, and other elite families were members of Emmanuel Episcopal Church. The Church family boasted of having been Episcopalians for several generations and took pride in the fact that an ancestor had "been the first colored person to be confirmed in the Episcopal Church in Arkansas."[49] In Detroit the membership of St. Matthew's, established in 1846, read like "the blue book of colored society" and included the Fergusons, Lamberts, Pelhams, and other elite families. As black migration from the South into Detroit increased in tempo around the turn of the century, St. Matthew's attempted to preserve its elite status by erecting barriers to memberships by instituting such devices as pew rentals.[50] All Saints' Church in St. Louis and St. Philip's in Omaha were the "church homes" of an overwhelming majority of the aristocrats of color in those cities. In Cleveland, St. Andrew's, a congregation of relatively recent origin, was restricted largely to old families, who displayed little interest in accepting working-class blacks into its membership. While Holy Trinity in Nashville and St. Philip's in Indianapolis attracted some aristocrats of color, most of the social elite in those cities were members of other denominations. St. Luke's in New Haven, founded in the 1840s, attracted many of the city's blacks "who aspired to education, to New England standards of conduct [and] to upper class practices," but even more such people gravitated to the local Congregational church.[51]

In the northern cities, aristocrats of color, such as the Chesnutts in Cleveland, were members of white Episcopal congregations. In Boston, blacks "attended white churches for a long time before they had any of their own." By 1914, after the establishment of numerous black churches in the city, most of those who continued to worship in predominantly white congregations were members of Boston's Afro-American aristocracy. They were found in Episcopal churches more than in any other. As in Philadelphia, New York, and elsewhere, some of the black upper class in Boston who were descendants of West Indian and Canadian blacks steeped in the Anglican tradition, naturally joined Episcopal congregations. Others joined the Episcopal churches for the same nonreligious reasons as whites—"because they think it savors of distinction." By the turn of the century, blacks had become numerous enough in certain Episcopal churches, Trinity in Boston and St. James's and St. Peter's in Cambridge, that whites began to complain of their presence and to initiate efforts that resulted in the creation of separate all-black congregations. In 1909, under headlines that read "Boston Churches Drawing Colorline," the *New York Age* explained that so long as the number of black Episcopal communicants was small, white churches extended them a welcome; but when it became noticeably larger, they attempted to consign blacks to Jim Crow congregations.[52] In 1914 sociologist John Daniels reported a "distinct decrease in Negro attendance at white churches," Episcopal as well as others. A significant segment of Boston's black elite remained loyal to the Episcopal church, despite the inhospitable attitude of whites, and worshipped in the separate, all-black Episcopal congregations established in Cambridge (St. Bartholomew's) and Boston (St. Cyprian's). "All the nice colored families send their children to the Episcopal Church in Cambridge," a character in Dorothy West's novel, *The Living Is Easy*, explained: "You don't have to be a shouting Baptist to be a child of God."[53]

In terms of social status, membership in Presbyterian congregations ranked second only to that in the Episcopal church. In fact, Presbyterians occupied the most elite status in some black communities. Historically, its clergymen had included some of the best-known black intellectuals in America: Samuel Cornish, Henry Highland Garnet, J. W. C. Pennington, and John Chavis, among others. Always small in number, black Presbyterians affiliated with the northern and southern branches of the church amounted to only 25,000 in 1906. Black Presbyterians, like black Episcopalians, made up few self-supporting congregations. Within both the Presbyterian and Episcopal churches, blacks formed organizations—the Afro-American Presbyterian Council and the Conference of Church Workers Among Colored People respectively—to secure equitable treatment at the hands of predominantly white denominations that were inclined to relegate their black brethren to subordinate if not separate spheres. Progress toward this objective was slow and incomplete by the First World War.[54]

It may well be, as Gayraud S. Wilmore has argued, that black Presbyterians were as much a part of the "Black church" in America as the African Methodists and the Baptists. Focusing on Philadelphia, which may be viewed as a birthplace of African Methodism, Wilmore observed: "Most Black Presbyterian congregations may be somewhat more formal and may lack some of the ardor of a Baptist or Methodist church, but Black Presbyterianism, as a whole, is a constituent part of what we call the Black Church. . . ."[55] Even though black Presbyterians as well as black Episcopalians may be considered participants in what was called the "Black Church," many blacks considered them "outside the pale." Both acquired a reputation for social exclusiveness that persisted into the mid-twentieth century. To claim that this was largely a myth is to discount perceptions shared by many blacks, including at least some within the Presbyterian fold.[56]

A widespread view of black Presbyterians was that they lacked warmth, were snobbish, belonged to a denomination legally owned and operated by whites, and embraced an intellectual form of worship that had no room for ardor and emotion. In 1916 a black critic claimed that Presbyterianism was weak among blacks, and few of its black churches were strong and forceful because the black people who joined them were "seeking personal advancement" and engaged in social climbing rather than serving the spiritual needs of the race.[57] The idea that the Presbyterian church was made up of upper-class blacks who desired to place distance between themselves and those who belonged to the "mass" denominations found support in both the actions and the words of the congregations and black Presbyterian spokesmen. Siloam Presbyterian Church in Brooklyn, which counted among its members a substantial contingent of the city's aristocrats of color, continued its pew system even though many outside the church viewed it as merely a device "to maintain its exclusiveness"; visitors to the church regularly complained of being treated coldly by "pew renters." Despite arguments that pew rents constituted a substantial element in the church's budget, Reverend William H. Dickerson led the movement which finally abolished the pew system in 1889.[58]

In the same year J. R. Riley, pastor of the Ninth Avenue Presbyterian Church in Indianapolis, addressed a civic club on the topic, "The Colored Man as a Presbyterian," which betrayed a certain condescension toward blacks outside the "high-status" churches. Riley, a well-known black Presbyterian who later served briefly as a minister of the prestigious Fifteenth Street Church in Washington, argued that most blacks naturally went to Baptist and Methodist churches because "the emotional element in the colored man's nature was also better satisfied with these forms of religion than with the more purely intellectual Presbyterianism." In addition, he declared, blacks shied away from what they considered "the white folks' church," especially "the aristocratic bearing of Presbyterians." In explaining the ingredients that went into making blacks devout Presbyterians, he concluded: "Education, hard work, prayer and money are essential elements in developing the colored man as a Presbyterian." Such statements, reprinted widely in the black press, reinforced the idea that black Presbyterians were "high muck-a-muck church people."[59]

Almost invariably Presbyterians were ranked along with Episcopalians and Congregationalists as constituting "upper-crust" congregations in the black community. In 1903, at the Eighth Conference for the Study of the Negro Problems, sponsored by Atlanta University and directed by W. E. B. Du Bois, an investigator reporting on the condition of churches in Atlanta provided a typical example of the status of Presbyterian, Episcopal, and Congregationalist congregations. According to him the clergy of these churches were "excellent characters," with a degree of education and sophistication rarely found among other black ministers. He described the membership of the Presbyterian, Episcopal, and Congregationalist churches in Atlanta as made up of people of lofty character who occupied positions of leadership in the community: "They are quiet and intelligent, and there is no emotionalism in churches. . . . Most of the members of these churches are at least high school graduates, a large percent is composed of business and professional men and women." Included in the proceedings of the same conference was a communication from A. J. McKelway, the editor of a southern Presbyterian journal, who commented on black Presbyterians in Charlotte, North Carolina, which was located "in a Presbyterian section." McKelway claimed that the old white families in the area were "largely Presbyterian, and the best Negro stock is the same." In his view the presence in the city of Biddle University, a black institution sponsored by Presbyterians, exercised "a helpful influence."[60]

Black Presbyterian congregations elsewhere were, in general, similar to those in Atlanta and Charlotte. They were small in size, relatively well educated, and prosperous; their religious services were sedate, and like other black upper-class denominations, they were opposed to using church sanctuaries for concerts, entertainments, and other nonreligious purposes, as was often the case in some Baptist and Methodist churches.

At the turn of the century, black Presbyterian congregations in large northern cities, even though some had been in existence for seventy-five years or more, remained small in size and relatively few in number. In Philadelphia the combined membership of the city's three black Presbyterian churches, First African, Central, and Berean, all of which were high-prestige institutions, was about 650 compared to 5,500 in the seventeen black Baptist churches and the 3,200 in the fourteen A.M.E. churches in the city.[61] Comparable in status to the Presbyterian congregations in Philadelphia were Grace Church in Chicago; St. James, Shiloh, and Siloam in New York; Ninth Street in Indianapolis; and Madison Street in Baltimore. All of them counted among their members a large number of the most prominent black families in these cities.[62]

Although these congregations were upper class, few black Presbyterians in the country enjoyed a wider reputation of being "an upper-set" church than those in the Fifteenth Street Presbyterian Church in Washington.[63] Founded by John Francis Cook, an educator and former member of the A.M.E. Church, the church was linked to one of the District's most prominent families. In 1841 a group of free blacks who attended a white Presbyterian church decided "to withdraw from circumstances over which we have no control." Under Cook's leadership the group petitioned for a church of its own. The Presbytery granted their request, and Cook became pastor of the new First Colored Presbyterian Church, a post that he held until his death, in 1855. Under his direction the congregation grew and prospered. A few years before his death a new church building was constructed on Fifteenth Street, and the name was changed to the Fifteenth Street Presbyterian Church.[64]

A succession of outstanding clergymen filled the Fifteenth Street pulpit during the forty-five years after Cook's death, including J. Sella Martin, Henry Highland Garnet, and J. R. Riley. In 1889 Francis J. Grimké accepted the call to the Fifteenth Street Church, where he remained for most of the next forty years. Grimké had been educated at Princeton and was married to Charlotte Forten of Philadelphia. He transformed the Fifteenth Street Church into one of the most prestigious black churches in the Presbyterian denomination.[65] The congregation that gathered in the sanctuary each Sunday to hear Grimké's polished and provocative sermons included many of Washington's most prominent old families. By 1901 it had increased to 350 members. An activist in the cause of black rights and a Puritan in matters of personal morality, Grimké did not hesitate to lecture his congregation on the question of social classes. He warned his parishioners of the dangers in the attitude of "the so-called upper classes" in assuming that they were "entitled to greater consideration than those in the so-called lower classes," for both, he insisted, will "stand on precisely the same footing in the matter of Judgment."[66]

Despite Grimké's discourses on the equality of divine judgment, those outside his church (and some inside) often viewed the communicants at Fifteenth Street as among the "upper circles," whose "wealth, position [and] influence" entitled them to greater consideration than others.[67] Indeed, Grimké's church included a disproportionately large number of blacks who were highly educated, occupied the most lucrative posts open to their race in the federal and District governments, and held membership in Washington's most exclusive social organizations. Some observers claimed that the first step taken by a socially ambitious new resident in Washington was to seek membership in Grimké's church.[68]

A black journalist writing in 1881 described the Fifteenth Street congregation as exhibiting "our possibilities and excellences" rather than "the average conditions of our people."[69] More than twenty years later, Mrs. John A. Logan observed that while membership in the church was small in comparison to that of other black congregations, "the quality, however, is unmistakable."[70] In 1896 Julian Ralph, despite his obvious racism and condescension, corroborated Mrs. Logan's observation. He was surprised to discover at the Fifteenth Street Church "women with lorgnettes," men "with pointed beards and button-hole bouquets," an altar banked with fresh flowers and a melodious choir; young men, "dressed like the best dressed young men on Fifth Avenue," drove up "in fine carriages for mothers and sisters." "The Presbyterian Church," he wrote, "is known as the religious rendezvous of the educated set and is necessarily small. The Rev. F. J. Grimké, a Negro and a Princeton graduate, is the pastor. His flock is composed of school teachers, doctors, lawyers, dentists and those colored folk from all over America who come to Washington when they have money to get the worth of it. You see nothing to laugh at, no darky peculiarities in that edifice. The people dress, look and behave precisely like nice white people, only some are black, and others shaded off from white."[71] Mrs. Logan later noted that "some of these women, just a shade off the white, are among the handsomest in the city." In 1907 an old black resident of Washington commented on the complexion of Fifteenth Street's congregation: "There are probably not a dozen black persons who attend that church. Not that they are unwelcome, but it just happens that way."[72] Nine years later, in 1916, Grimké's old friend Richard T. Greener wrote him: "I dare venture to believe there is scarcely another church of our race in the United States which may boast a brighter array of talent, a more refined cultural auditory, or that has more competent, faithful, God-fearing, Gospel-serving, public spirited pastors, men of brain, heart and true piety than the Fifteenth Street Presbyterian Church in Washington, D.C."[73]

Like Presbyterians and Episcopalians, blacks who belonged to the Congregationalist church were often considered by those of the black denominations as "outside the pale," that is, outside the "Black Church" and dependent on whites. Before the Civil War, Congregationalism was centered in New England and the Old Northwest, where relatively few blacks resided, and only a small number of black residents in these regions identified with the predominantly white Congregationalist churches. An early example of a separate black Congregationalist church was Temple Street Church in New Haven, Connecticut. Founded in 1820 and later renamed Dixwell Avenue Church, it was sponsored and for some years supported by whites of the Center Congregational Church. In New Haven, as in other cities in New England, "congregationalism had prestige, and Temple Street was the foremost Negro church." Most of the city's leading black families belonged to Temple Street, including an impressive proportion of the barbers, waiters at Yale, and artisans. Among a succession of well-educated clergymen who filled the Temple Street pulpit, perhaps the most notable were Amos Beman, who exemplified the church's close association with militant abolitionism, and Francis L. Cardozo, who later became prominent in South Carolina during Reconstruction. Temple Street's congregation, which exhibited "good Connecticut mores and folkways," remained the city's most exclusive and aristocratic black church for a hundred years after its establishment.[74]

The chief instrument for introducing black southerners to Congregationalism in the post–Civil War era was the American Missionary Association. It was founded in 1846 as a nonsectarian antislavery missionary organization, but it ultimately became an arm of the Congregational church. In its effort to organize Congregational churches among blacks in the South, the A.M.A. sought to avoid offending black denominations. The first Congregationalist churches came into existence near or in conjunction with A.M.A. schools for freedmen, enterprises that dominated the efforts of the organization. By 1871 the A.M.A. had established forty-five black Congregationalist churches in the South, with a total of 2,577 members; by 1885 the number of churches had increased to 118, with a membership of 7,512. The growth slowed substantially by the 1890s, and few black Congregationalist churches in the South survived without an A.M.A. school nearby, because a large percentage of their membership was drawn from A.M.A. teachers, students, and former students.[75]

Despite their circumspection in establishing churches, Congregationalists encountered hostility from A.M.E. and black Baptist churches. Nor did their religion have mass appeal for black southerners, who tended to reject "its soberness, its simplicity and its leaning toward intellectualism" as well as its paternalism and its tendency to appoint white ministers for urban churches. Black Congregationalists who attended Christ Church in Wilmington, North Carolina, organized in 1870, frequently encountered the charge that they had abandoned "heartfelt religion" for "book religion," an accusation commonly made by members of A.M.E. and Baptist denominations. Members of the First Congregational Church in Mobile, which was organized in 1876 by two blacks who had formerly worshipped at a white Presbyterian church, encountered similar criticism for their "higher sense and taste of worship."[76]

As one historian has suggested, the failure of Congregationalism to win more adherents among blacks in the postwar South was largely because it was "too unfamiliar, its services too alien, too white and the attraction of the black churches was too great."[77] Coupled with perceptions of Congregationalism as an exotic and intellectual religion was the notion that it was prone to exclusiveness and snobbery. In 1902 John W. Whittaker, a prominent black Congregationalist minister in the South, admitted that the congregations of his denomination were, in intelligence, "far removed from the masses," who described them as too "high-tone," too well-educated, and too well-dressed.[78] The strong Congregationalist churches in Savannah, Atlanta, Nashville, and other cities that possessed well-known A.M.A. schools also attracted blacks of education, property, and high social status. A member of Nashville's prestigious Howard Congregational Church told an interviewer: "As you know, most of the Negroes who aren't intelligent are emotional; they like to shout, and thus the minister must preach fiery sermons. Well, the Congregational Church [in Nashville] has an intelligent pastor, his sermons aren't the shouting kind. Therefore the emotional class doesn't attend that church, rather the dignified people go there—the Napiers etc."[79] She might have added that the church membership also drew heavily from Fisk University. Others observed that they "felt themselves better than the commonality of their brethren," an impression that scarcely endeared them to members of the black denominations.[80]

This elitist tendency was perhaps inherent in Congregationalism. A historian of Congregationalism among blacks in the South argues that from the beginning it "was destined . . . to become a movement for the social and intellectual elite." While the A.M.A. stood firm against caste on the grounds that it excluded people from common rights, it was not opposed to class. In fact, it held the view that class distinctions were necessary insofar as class rested on companionship, indeed "sympathetic or selective companionship" that had "its own qualifications." To accomplish its own mission among black southerners, the A.M.A. and the Congregational churches, often organized in conjunction with their schools, selected their "companions" with great care. Convinced that the future of black Americans rested with leadership drawn from their privileged minority, Congregationalists sought out potential leaders, brought them into their churches and schools, and attempted to lay claim on them as vehicles for advancing the New England Congregational Way among blacks in the South. The first blacks brought into the Congregational fold were free people of color, often more Anglo-Saxon than African in appearance. For them, Congregationalism provided a means to reinforce their privileged position through institutions that allowed for upward mobility on the basis of merit.[81]

Black Congregationalists in the South and elsewhere often competed with Episcopalians and Presbyterians for possessing the "high tone" church in a particular community. When the "high-toned colored folks" in Washington withdrew from Union Bethel A.M.E. Church early in 1880 to form Plymouth Congregational Church, a local black newspaper described their action as the "throwing off the yoke of Methodism," whose "heathenish" behavior such as

"bawling and knocking down benches" repulsed blacks of education and sophistication. Such behavior, he noted, was unbecoming to Congregationalists, who
were "reputed to be the broadest thinkers." Plymouth "abounded in evidences of
culture."[82]

Late in 1896 a small group of colored aristocrats who gathered at the home
of Robert and Mary Church Terrell launched another Congregational church in
Washington. The group included Blanche K. Bruce, John M. Langston, Alice
Strange Davis, and several other Oberlin alumni. The new church became
University Park Temple and was located near Howard University. Its first
minister was Sterling N. Brown, a graduate of Fisk and Oberlin who had served
as pastor of Plymouth before joining the theology faculty at Howard. In 1901,
University Park Temple united with Lincoln Memorial Congregational Church
to form Lincoln Congregational Temple, and Brown continued to occupy the
pulpit. In the year of the merger a prominent black Congregationalist minister
observed that churches of his denomination had made little effort to reach the
masses. Although such an attitude undoubtedly had existed in the past, the new
Lincoln Temple exerted itself in that direction by sponsoring a variety of
programs and facilities for the less privileged.[83]

In Louisville the Plymouth Congregational Church, founded in 1877,
rivaled the Episcopal congregation at the Church of Our Merciful Savior as the
elite church of the city's black community. Many of those who attended these
churches did so because they believed that it conferred status upon them. Some
who attended Plymouth and Our Merciful Savior never officially joined, but
maintained membership in Baptist and A.M.E. churches.[84] A resident of Little
Rock, writing in 1898, described the First Congregational Church in that city as
"well situated and tastefully furnished" and its members as among "the best
people," including the Ish family: "The tone and character of the services are
highly spiritual and intellectual and bespeak the culture and refinement of its
pastor and members."[85] In Nashville one of the most prestigious congregations
in the city was that at Howard Congregational Church, organized in 1876. Its
ministers included such erudite men as D. W. Culp, J. E. Moreland, and James
Bond. Among its members were numerous representatives of Nashville's "best
society"—black families whose high status rested on a "basis of good breeding,
culture, refinement and wealth."[86] In Nashville, as in Louisville, Washington,
and elsewhere, the size of black Congregationalist churches remained small,
rarely with a membership over 150.

One of the largest and best-known black churches in America was the First
Congregational Church in Atlanta, established in 1867 and tied closely to
Storrs School, one of the stronger A.M.A. secondary schools in the South, and
to Atlanta University. During the tenure of Henry H. Proctor, a Fisk and Yale
Divinity School graduate, as minister between 1894 and 1919, the church
became one of the first black institutional churches in the South to provide a
free library, a home for girls, a prison mission, and a kindergarten on a

nonsectarian basis. Although the First Congregational Church was the most socially conscious church in Atlanta's black community, it encountered hostility and resentment among certain blacks. Proctor's deliberative sermons and sedate worship services set his church apart from the more "emotional" churches, as did the fact that its congregation, from the beginning, included whites, primarily faculty members from Atlanta University.[87] It was the church of Atlanta's aristocrats of color to such an extent that one scholar claimed that its membership list read like "a black Atlantan Social Register." Among the families on that list were the Whites, Ruckers, Townses, and others of high social standing.[88]

If members of the church were socially conscious, they were also class conscious. Distinguished from other black congregations in Atlanta by their education and wealth, as well as by the erudition of their minister and the sedateness of their services, members of the First Congregational Church displayed an attitude of condescension toward the black masses, including those who benefited from the social programs that the church sponsored. In 1897, in the course of discussing the need for churches to "come into personal touch with the masses," Proctor asserted that such contact would not intrude "upon our social reserve":

"We must come into close personal touch with the masses. To this some will put in objections: will not these people presume upon our social reserve? Will not the upper class be dragged down by contact with the lower? These questions are not unnatural. They demand a reasonable answer. To the first objection I would say there is not the least danger in the plainest people mistaking our kindly interest as an invitation to our private social functions. The plain people have wonderfully keen instincts. To the other I would say that it is not contact with the lower element that injures the higher; it is the kind of contact. The distinction is vital. 'He is armed without who is innocent within.' Virtue is its possessor's shield. The immaculate swan comes unspotted from the vilest sewer. . . . You can not elevate society by lifting from the top; you must put the jackscrews under the mudsills of society. Put the unfailing dynamics of friendly visitation under the homes of the poor and the whole people will rise."[89] In making the distinction between social uplift and social intercourse, Proctor revealed the same sense of superiority and paternalism that characterized nineteenth-century white "friendly visitors," whose primary objectives included character reformation among the lower classes that would lead them to embrace upper- and middle-class values such as sobriety, economy, and industry.

Proctor's wife, who was active in a variety of civic movements in Atlanta, shared his views of class. In a discussion of Negro women, she began by refuting the peculiar white man's idea that all Negroes were alike. Rather, she insisted any discerning observer well knew that "the Negro in his home, at his work and worship, on the street and in places of amusement" differed greatly. Mrs. Proctor divided blacks into three classes: the lower class, often immoral and vicious, filled prisons and tolerated abandoned mothers and fatherless children; the middle class, though poor and ignorant, was moral and strived after better things; and the upper class, necessarily much smaller, possessed property, education, and character. Even though the daily press rarely mentioned the third class, blacks who belonged to it constituted "a prophecy of the possibilities of the race."[90]

Despite the services rendered by the various agencies of the First Congregational Church, both the minister and the congregation were targets of criticism, especially from upwardly mobile middle-class blacks. Few were more persistent or vitriolic than Benjamin J. Davis, the editor and publisher of the *Atlanta Independent*. A colorful personality who was often the center of controversy, Davis was prominent in the Grand United Order of Odd Fellows. Despite its emphasis on fraternal affairs, the *Independent* also specialized in denouncing the First Congregational Church. In addition to criticizing its minister, snobbish members, and religious services alien to the typical Negro revivalistic tradition, the newspaper described its plans for an institutional church as an absurd effort "to mix a church, bathroom, cook kitchen and card room," and suggested that such plans should be deferred until blacks had acquired an ability to pursue "Christian living and conduct." Davis reserved his most acid remarks for Proctor, whom he characterized as a black leader in Atlanta chosen by the city's white elite and as a black man who regularly drew "the color line." The Proctors, Ruckers, and other upper-class members of the congregation, according to Davis, belonged to "that class of Negroes in our community who are known as mulattoes and . . . draw the color line by having exclusive mulattoes in their society and for their associates." The First Congregational Church, he maintained, had "an unwritten law that mulattoes *were preferred*" as members.[91]

Although the Episcopal, Presbyterian, and Congregational churches possessed the largest representation of old upper-class black families, members of this class were found in a variety of other Protestant denominations, including those that were predominantly white and those that were all black. By the turn of the century, the Methodist Episcopal church (Northern Methodist) had a black membership of over 245,000. After the Civil War the Northern Methodist church was one of the most successful white denominations in recruiting black members and in establishing black schools and colleges through its Freedmen's Aid Society. Within the denomination black congregations were segregated into separate annual conferences, and the *Southwestern Christian Advocate* served as the mouthpiece for its black communicants. In a manner similar to black Episcopalians, blacks in the Northern Methodist church waged a prolonged fight to secure black bishops, an effort that finally succeeded in 1920.[92]

While struggling to win equitable treatment at the hands of white Methodists, blacks in the Methodist Episcopal church had to defend themselves against critics in the black Methodist denominations—the A.M.E. and the A.M.E. Zion churches. These critics accused them of racial treason for identifying with a white denomination and characterized them as belonging to the "cringing class of Negroes" who allowed themselves to be "bossed" by whites in order to share in "a rich missionary treasury, a wealthy extension society, and a rapidly increasing super-annuate's fund." To such charges blacks in the Northern Methodist church responded by insisting that in theory at least theirs was not a self-proclaimed "caste church," as was the case of the A.M.E. and A.M.E. Zion denominations. "We do not go out of the [Northern Methodist] church," declared a black minister, "because we are men and propose to stand up side by side with the best white membership in the church and show them and the world that in the great work being done . . . for the evangelization of the world . . . we can bear our share of the burden." In his view the "best way for the Negro to advance intellectually, morally, and religiously" was through contact with other races rather than through self-imposed segregation. Such an argument coincided with the view of upper-class blacks whose objective was "assimilation into the larger society."[93]

Whether blacks of the upper class chose to identify with Methodist Episcopal churches depended on a variety of circumstances, such as the quality of the clergy, the identity of old families in founding the church, and the presence of a college or school supported by the denomination. In Atlanta the two black congregations of the Methodist Episcopal church indicated their diversity: one was made up primarily of uneducated people who responded positively to "loud and emotional" worship services; the other consisted of "the best class of working people with a large number of educated people and graduates of the schools who preferred a greater, more intellectual form of worship." The latter was identified with Clark College and Gammon Theological Seminary, both located in Atlanta and supported by the Methodist Episcopal church.[94] In Baltimore the Sharp Street Methodist Episcopal church, which had close ties with Morgan College, attracted a substantial portion of the city's aristocrats of color, as did the Center Street Church in Louisville and Simpson Chapel in Indianapolis. In New York, St. Mark's Methodist Episcopal Church, founded in 1872 and distinguished by the quality of its ministers, including Ernest Lyon and William H. Brooks, had in its large congregation members of the city's black upper class. But few Methodist Episcopal congregations included so many aristocrats of color as Centenary Church in Charleston, South Carolina. Established in 1866, Centenary rivaled St. Mark Episcopal Church as the religious home of Charleston's black elite.[95]

Upper-class families in various cities were also found in the black Methodist and Baptist denominations. This was especially true of families whose ancestors had been instrumental in the founding of the A.M.E. and the A.M.E. Zion churches. In New York, Philadelphia, Baltimore, Charleston, and other cities, congregations of these denominations, sometimes known as Mother Bethel or

Big Bethel, included a sizable contingent of upper-class families. For example, the Bradfords in Baltimore were identified with the A.M.E. church for several generations, as were the Myerses of Baltimore and Cleveland. The Varick and Eato families in New York were active in the A.M.E. Zion church from its founding.[96]

Nor were representatives of the black upper class entirely absent from Baptist congregations, such as the First African Baptist in Louisville, Morris Street Church in Charleston, and Nineteenth Street Church in Washington. As in the case of the First African Church in Louisville, these Baptist churches usually had long histories and retained at least some old upper-class families whose ancestors had been antebellum free people of color. But black Methodist and Baptist congregations that attracted aristocrats of color were exceptional; they had levels of education, culture, and wealth among the clergy and the memberships that were considerably above that of the rank and file congregation in these denominations and a form of worship barely distinguishable from that in the higher-status churches. Edward M. Brawley of the Morris Street Baptist Church in Charleston, for example, was the scion of a free family of color and was educated at Philadelphia's Institute for Colored Youth, Howard University, and Bucknell. Early in the twentieth century a British visitor to Philadelphia's premier A.M.E. church likened its Sunday service to that of the Anglican church.[97]

The overwhelming majority of church-going black Americans of all classes was Protestant, but a small percentage of the total black population belonged to the Roman Catholic church. Precise figures are difficult to obtain, but Catholic sources indicated that in 1890 there were approximately 160,000 Negro Catholics in the United States. Black Catholics, like members of the A.M.E. and the A.M.E. Zion churches, cut across class lines. Some congregations tended to be predominantly upper and middle class in composition, while others, perhaps a majority, were clearly lower and lower-middle class. Those of the black upper class who had been identified with Catholicism longest were usually found in New Orleans and other places among the Gulf coast which shared the French and Spanish cultural influence, as well as in Baltimore and cities along the seaboard that became the home of West Indian Negro refugees in the 1790s. Not until the late nineteenth and early twentieth centuries did the Catholic church undertake a concerted effort to bring black Americans into its ranks, an effort that coincided with the emergence of a more virulent form of anti-Negro prejudice in the United States.[98]

Writing in the 1920s, a chronicler of the Catholic church's missionary effort among black Americans outlined a series of difficulties that confronted "the missioner to the Negro." One of these was the existence of a class structure: "To the casual observer, the colored people of the United States form but one homogeneous group. The actual condition is quite different." At the top of the black social structure were, in his view, two groups closely allied: the so-called cultural group consisted of those of refinement and economic independence who resented being included with the black masses, whom they considered inferior; the other, termed the "blood" group, were mulattoes who strenuously objected to "anything that smacked of segregation," such as churches for the exclusive use of Negroes. Each group possessed its own peculiar social difficulties and problems. The problem of the Catholic missioner whose church recognized "no distinction as to color or caste" was to "steer his bark through the maelstroms of social feuds which are brought over into the church." His was the complicated task of fusing into a single harmonious flock, under a single shepherd, different classes whose "social animosities have their sources outside the church."[99]

Another difficulty encountered by the Catholic church was the intensification of racial tensions that coincided with its expanded missionary efforts among blacks. Even in areas in which blacks and whites had worshipped together for years, the emergence of a more virulent form of racism led to the creation of segregated congregations. In New Orleans, where racially integrated religious services had been the accepted practice, especially in the St. Louis Cathedral, for years even before the Civil War, the church hierarchy inaugurated a plan for racially separate churches in the 1890s. Descendants of the old free families of color, who "accepted the privileges granted to them during the antebellum period in their church parishes as a matter of right," strenuously opposed the plan, in part because they objected to any effort that classified them with ex-slaves and their progeny. But their opposition was of no avail, and the first separate all-black Catholic church in New Orleans, St. Katherine's, was dedicated in 1895.[100]

Black Catholics elsewhere in the nation encountered similar experiences, and like blacks identified with the predominantly white Protestant denominations, waged a persistent struggle to prevent Jim Crowism in the church. When late in the 1890s black Catholics in Boston were encouraged "to withdraw their membership from the great Cathedrals" of the city, a black editor suggested that the request was prompted because "both races cannot get the Virgin Mary's attention at the same time, nor should dip their hands into the holy water during the same service."[101] From her observations in travels throughout the nation, Mary Church Terrell concluded in 1918 that the Catholic church, "once so broad and generous in its treatment of Colored people, has been led astray and allowed itself to become tainted with a cruel, unreasonable, unChristlike race prejudice." Even in Baltimore, a city with a sizable black Catholic population, Negro communicants found themselves relegated to backless benches in the rear of the city's cathedral.[102]

According to one historian, it was natural that "out of Baltimore, as the center of Catholic life in Maryland, there would spring the first fruits of the fullness of Catholicism among the Negroes of the state." Baltimore was the home of the Oblate Sisters of Providence, the first sisterhood for black Catholic nuns in the United States. The sisterhood originated with French-speaking mulatto refugees from San Domingo in the late eighteenth century. Organized in 1829, the order had grown substantially by the Civil War and was known for the academy it operated in Baltimore for the daughters of "well-to-do Negro Catholics." By 1890, when it was sixty years old, St. Frances Academy had a college preparatory curriculum that enrolled many boarding scholars from various states. Generally recognized as an exclusive preparatory school for the daughters of the nation's black elite, the institution counted among its graduates many individuals who occupied prominent positions throughout the United States.[103]

In 1863, shortly after Emancipation, a church was established in Baltimore under the patronage of St. Francis Xavier which claimed to be the "first Catholic church in the United States for the use of an all-colored congregation." From this congregation came Charles Uncles, a member of a moderately well-to-do black Baltimore family. He was ordained in 1891 and served as priest of the St. Francis Xavier parish for more than a third of a century. By the early twentieth century Baltimore had two additional black Catholic congregations, St. Peter Claver and St. Barnabas. Although the black Catholic congregations were never large, even when compared to the relatively high status Protestant churches, their membership included some who clearly belonged to Baltimore's colored aristocracy.[104] In terms of social status, however, black Catholics in the city appear generally to have occupied a place below that of the Episcopal, Presbyterian, and Methodist Episcopal congregations but substantially above that of most Baptist, A.M.E., and A.M.E. Zion churches.

Few black Catholic congregations in the United States equaled that of St. Augustine's Church in Washington in terms of social prestige. Located on Fifteenth Street, it enjoyed a status comparable to that of two nearby congregations, St. Luke's Episcopal and Fifteenth Street Presbyterian. St. Augustine's began as a parish sponsored by St. Matthew's in 1863. It prospered and grew in membership; the handsome church on Fifteenth Street, constructed in 1874, was "the largest, most costly church for Negro Catholics in the country." The congregation included "some of the best and most intelligent members of the race here [Washington]: doctors, dentists, educators and businessmen." Among its most conspicuous members were William Henry Smith, who served for many years as assistant librarian of the House of Representatives, and William S. Lofton, a prominent dentist and a graduate of Howard. Archibald Grimké claimed that St. Augustine's was "perhaps the only church in the city where the races worship side by side on terms of Christian equality."[105]

St. Augustine's hosted the first Colored Catholic Congress, in January 1889. It brought together a large body of the leading black Catholic laity throughout the nation. In this and succeeding congresses Lofton, Smith, Charles H. Butler, and other communicants of St. Augustine's, who were also members of Washington's "black 400," played conspicuous roles. At the Congress in Cincinnati in 1890 Lofton emerged as a lay leader of national promi-nence. He, along with Butler, Frederick McGhee of St. Paul, Minnesota, and others, pressed the church hierarchy to establish schools for black youth and to oppose American racism. They spearheaded a movement to create a national organization to coordinate the activities of numerous Negro Catholic societies. This organization, established in 1893 and called St. Peter Claver's Catholic Union, along with the Catholic Congress, provided Negro Catholics a sense of identity at a time of increasing antiblack prejudice.[106]

The Catholic missionary efforts among blacks in the late nineteenth and early twentieth centuries resulted in a proliferation of black churches. Most were mission churches, and relatively few became self-supporting. The Church of St. Benedict the Moor, established in New York in 1883, was perhaps typical. Rather than being the religious home of the city's black elite, it was considered remarkable principally for its parishioners' "great love for their church, for their constant zeal in preaching their faith and for their generous loyalty in supporting every project their priest undertakes for the spiritual or material advancement of their mission." Other black mission churches were organized specifically to labor among the poor. Such was the mission of St. Monica's in Baltimore, a "slum church in the waterfront section of the city," where a few dozen poor black families worshipped alongside "some Italian immigrants, Chinese converts and even Indians."[107]

Virtually all major churches and denominations, both those that were all black and those that were predominantly white, included the names of aristo-crats of color on their membership rolls. Upper-class blacks avoided con-gregations that engaged in "emotional" religion and "heathenish" behavior and identified with those emphasizing liturgy and ritual. Although a dis-proportionately large percentage of the old black upper class was found in the Episcopal church, sizable numbers were also Presbyterians and Con-gregrationalists. Even though blacks in these denominations, regardless of class, might be treated as second-class communicants by the church hierarchies, their membership expressed their assimilationist attitudes and signified their opposi-tion to overtly "caste" churches such as the A.M.E. and black Baptist de-nominations. It also provided opportunities for identity and association with the white elite, which conferred status as well as power. "The traditional Negro upper class," historian Joseph R. Washington, Jr., has observed, "distinguished itself from the folk culture through its religious affiliation—becoming Episcopa-lians, Presbyterians, Congregationalists and Roman Catholics instead of Baptists and Methodists." Another distinguishing characteristic of the black upper class was that its life was less church-centered than that of other Afro-Americans. Like the family of W. E. B. Du Bois, many aristocrats of color were "placidly religious." Or as Azalia Hackley remarked in 1916, "the best representative people go to church if only for example's sake."[108]

In Chicago, Boston, Cleveland, and other northern cities, some members of the black upper class, who rejected "caste" implications of all-black congregations within predominantly white denominations as well as those evident in black Methodist and Baptist churches, were members of white congregations. Blacks who chose to express their opposition to "caste" religion in such a way risked compromising their position as "leaders of the race." Senator and Mrs. Bruce encountered considerable criticism from blacks when they chose to attend a white Episcopal church in Indianapolis, and Dr. Charles E. Bentley of Chicago became the target of bitter denunciation for his failure to "go among Negroes." "If Dr. Bentley wants to be a leader among Negroes," a black editor wrote, "let him join Bethel A.M.E. Church and take his membership out of the white church where he is a member."[109]

For black churches in northern and midwestern cities, the influx of black southerners in the two decades after 1900 posed a series of problems. The pressure to assimilate and adjust to thousands of migrants fell heaviest on the black Methodist and Baptist churches, which witnessed dramatic increases in membership. In some cities the number of churches affiliated with these denominations increased by 150 percent between 1916 and 1926. Increases in the black membership of congregations of predominantly white denominations, such as the Episcopal and Presbyterian, were comparatively slight. While some upper-class congregations in these denominations attempted to provide services to ease the transition of migrants from a rural to an urban environment, others clearly exhibited apathy, if not antipathy, for the new arrivals. Few apparently went so far as St. Matthew's Episcopal Church in Detroit, which instituted pew rentals, but others were scarcely less subtle in indicating that they were no more inclined to embrace the new arrivals from the South than they had been to allow the urban lower class to intrude upon their "social reserve." Aristocrats of color identified with high-status churches were likely to be among the most active members of organizations like the Old Settlers of Chicago and the Association of the Oldest Inhabitants of Washington, whose purpose was to establish a line of demarcation between "old cits" and recent migrants. Some blacks from the rural South who emigrated to the urban North undoubtedly had experiences similar to that of the man who wandered into St. Mark's Episcopal Church in Charleston shortly after the Civil War and discovered that it was too "highfalootin" for him; others, for a variety of reasons, felt no less uncomfortable in the older, well-established black Methodist and Baptist churches. From their ranks came the congregations of store-front churches, an urban phenomenon that proliferated after the First World War.[110]

Church affiliation, like club membership, reflected the prevailing social structure of the black community, and association with certain denominations provided an index of social preferment. For those of the old upper class, church preferences often served as a means to cultivate group consciousness and exclusivity and to preserve their privileged heritage. Whether one belonged to an

Episcopal, Presbyterian, or some other church frequently owed more to the prestige of the local congregation than to the denomination's overall reputation for being "high tone." Few disputed the primacy of St. Philip's Episcopal Church as the home of New York's aristocrats of color, but in Charleston such families were about evenly divided between St. Mark's Episcopal and Centenary Methodist Episcopal Church. In Washington membership in any one of the churches on Fifteenth Street—St. Luke's Episcopal, St. Augustine's Roman Catholic, or Fifteenth Street Presbyterian—signified high social standing. In Louisville the most prestigious congregation was probably that of the First Baptist Church, while in New Orleans the elite of the city's black society was likely to be Roman Catholic. Regardless of church or denominational labels, aristocrats of color were likely to identify with congregations whose emphasis on education, culture, and gentility was evident in the practice of religion.

11

◆

Aristocrats of Color and Jim Crow

THE TWO DECADES FOLLOWING 1890 witnessed a hardening of racial lines and the proliferation of legal and extralegal Jim Crow contrivances. Although legalized segregation and racial violence, especially lynching, flourished in the South, blacks in other regions also felt the heavy hand of *de facto* segregation and racial discrimination. The "one drop rule," by which a person with any Negro blood, however minuscule, was considered black and therefore subject to all the restrictions imposed on the "proscribed race," prevailed throughout the United States. Regardless of the class to which blacks belonged, their access to hotels, restaurants, Pullman cars, and other public accommodations was restricted either by law or by custom. In the South blacks were denied suffrage through a variety of disfranchisement stratagems. Baltimore, St. Louis, and other cities enacted residential segregation ordinances which accelerated the growth of black ghettoes. Churches, especially the high-prestige denominations that attracted upper-class blacks, either implemented or attempted to implement segregated arrangements for their black parishioners. National professional organizations, such as those of physicians and attorneys, virtually closed their doors to blacks, forcing them to create parallel organizations of their own. With few exceptions public schools for blacks were unequal to and separate from those of whites. Few blacks enjoyed equality with whites in the administration of justice.

Because many of the aristocrats of color were committed to racial progress through assimilation, they were, of all blacks, perhaps most acutely sensitive to racial discrimination. But their responses to Jim Crowism were by no means identical. At one extreme were those who shunned involvement in racial affairs altogether and withdrew into the safe oasis of their own making in an effort to isolate themselves from the conflict and tensions of race. "Racial prejudices," declared one aristocrat of color in 1907, "are so flagrant and ofttimes shown in so vulgar and offensive a manner that the self-respecting citizen rather prefers to ignore them than humiliate himself by their notice."[1] Purely social organizations, such as chapters of Boulé or Washington's Mu-So-Lit Club, which brought together upper-class blacks of similar tastes, provided peaceful havens for such people. At the other extreme were those of the upper class, also found in Boulé and the Mu-So-Lit Club, who became activists in the cause of racial justice. Perhaps a majority of the aristocrats of color occupied a position somewhere between these two extremes: they remained committed to an integrated society and, while not militant, lent support to those who boldly challenged racial prejudice. Like Roscoe Bruce, they were inclined to believe that culture, rather than race, was or should be the "basis of sound nationality." As educated, cultured Americans, they considered the ignorance and crude behavior of the black masses an unwarranted burden that they, of the upper class, were forced to bear. Some aristocrats of color were convinced, at least for a time, that if it were not for the behavior of the masses, the "better class of whites" would extend to the black elite the full privileges of citizenship. In 1901, a black editor who alternately functioned as a critic and as a defender of the black aristocracy observed that no one expected all Negroes to be recognized simultaneously as first-class citizens, but rather that those of education and property individually would "be placed upon a footing with his more fortunate brother[s] in white."[2]

By the end of the first decade of the twentieth century, it became evident that such expectations were unrealistic in view of the hardening of racial lines throughout the country. Even those who possessed wealth, along with ancestry, education, and other attributes of upper-class status, found it increasingly difficult to avoid the strictures of the color line. Roscoe Bruce's encounter with it at Harvard may have come later than comparable experiences of others of his social status, but it was by no means exceptional. In 1914 Mary Church Terrell complained bitterly to President H. C. King of her alma mater, Oberlin, where her daughters were then enrolled, that the institution had become far more discriminatory toward blacks since her days as a student there. She especially resented limitations on the number of black students, the special arrangements for them in housing, and the college administration's concern about offending white students.[3]

Six years later, when Mary Church Terrell was in Dover, Delaware, in her capacity as Director of Work Among Colored Women in the Republican party, she had an encounter with a railroad ticket agent that resulted in her arrest for disorderly conduct. Although the charge was ultimately dismissed, it proved to Mary Terrell, a woman of education and refinement who belonged to Washington's "best society," just "how easily a serious charge based upon a trivial incident may be trumped up against a colored woman or man." She clearly understood that no matter how genteel, educated, and well-dressed she was, she was still a Negro and as such subject to the same treatment at the hands of certain whites as a black field hand in the South. The one significant difference was that Mary Church Terrell had an important and influential white friend in Delaware's Republican Senator Coleman DuPont, who interceded in her behalf.[4]

Similar incidents in 1908 and 1909 in Washington had resulted in the arrests of Judson Lyons of Augusta, Georgia, formerly Register of the Treasury, and Robert Pelham of Detroit, both of whom figured prominently in the District's aristocracy of color. Like Mrs. Terrell later, Lyons and Pelham had influential white friends on Capitol Hill who intervened in their behalf.[5] Such incidents demonstrated to some members of the black upper class the extent to which many whites viewed them as indistinguishable from the lower-class blacks they sought to keep at arm's length. For some aristocrats of color such experiences with racial prejudice undoubtedly confirmed the validity of what others had long maintained, namely, that efforts to place distance between themselves and the masses were futile and that no group or class of blacks could achieve equality with whites unless blacks of all classes did so.

In 1896 the Supreme Court decision in the case of *Plessy* v. *Ferguson* laid down the "separate but equal" doctrine, which was a blow to black Americans who still clung to notions of black equality and assimilation into American society and culture. The death of Frederick Douglass a year earlier removed from the scene the most fearless and eloquent advocate of first-class citizenship for Afro-Americans. His place as the principal spokesman for blacks fell to Booker T. Washington,[6] who was born a slave in West Virginia and never knew the identity of his white father. He was educated at Hampton Institute and founded Tuskegee Institute in Alabama, an institution that he transformed into the showpiece of black education in America. Chosen by whites to represent blacks at the Cotton States Exposition in Atlanta in 1895, Washington outlined in a brief address what became known as the Atlanta Compromise, which acquiesced in segregation and emphasized economic initiative and self-help rather than civil rights. As the foremost champion of so-called industrial education for blacks, he maintained that the most appropriate schooling for his race was vocational rather than literary or higher education. A complex, enigmatic man whose formula for racial progress eschewed protest for peace, he publicly embraced the tactics of conciliation, compromise, and accommodation while secretly subsidizing efforts to undermine the legal structure of Jim Crowism. By the turn of the century Washington had emerged as an influential power broker for blacks. In 1905, one of his most loyal journalistic lieutenants boldly proclaimed: "Dr. Booker T. Washington has reached the point where he is not called upon to explain."[7]

Endorsed and supported by influential whites who subscribed to his formula of race relations, Washington wielded enormous power over the distribution of white philanthropy among blacks, especially among black educational institutions. To ensure his leadership in the black community, he maintained an elaborate publicity apparatus, employed spies and detectives, and created a nationwide network of lieutenants, known as the Tuskegee Machine, which assisted in quelling incipient rebellion among blacks. Anyone who seriously challenged either his program or his personal prestige was likely to feel the full weight of the Tuskegee Machine. The National Negro Business League, which Washington created in 1900 and headed until his death, proved useful in cementing his relations with the new black entrepreneurial class in northern cities. He also either dominated or exerted influence over other national black organizations, including the Afro-American Council and fraternal orders.[8] Reaching the zenith of his power in the last dozen or so years before his death, in 1915, Washington clearly had preempted the role of mediator and broker previously performed by those drawn largely from the aristocracy of color.

Washington assiduously cultivated what were called "representative men of the race," many of whom belonged to the upper class. Nor were his efforts unsuccessful, for he brought within his circle numerous black aristocrats who were willing to acquiesce in Washington's leadership in return for his assistance in securing jobs and political preferment. At one time or another a sizable group of those whose families had long been identified as the "upper tens" in black America were on the Tuskegee payroll. Such an arrangement benefited both the institution and the individual. In view of the lack of employment opportunities open to well-educated blacks, those of the upper class who had attended prestigious universities and colleges often welcomed jobs at Tuskegee. As Washington was undoubtedly aware, moreover, their presence on campus not only lent prestige to his institution but also provided the student body, drawn largely from less-privileged backgrounds, with examples of sophistication and gentility.

Perhaps the most conspicuous aristocrats of color identified with Washington and Tuskegee were Josephine Bruce and her son, Roscoe. Among others attracted to Tuskegee were Lloyd Wheeler of Chicago and his son, Hiram. The elder Wheeler, as the son-in-law of the well-to-do and socially prominent John Jones, moved in the "best circles" of Chicago society. The son of Francis L. Cardozo, the grandson and namesake of John Mercer Langston, two children of Charles Chesnutt of Cleveland, and a son of Dr. Austin M. Curtis of Washington, who was also a physician, joined the Tuskegee staff either as faculty members or as administrators. Henry Kempton Craft, a Harvard-educated engineer and scion of two old Charleston families, the Crafts and the Kinlochs, taught at Tuskegee from 1908 to 1911.[9]

The tenure of aristocrats of color at Tuskegee was usually short, rarely more than two or three years. The specific reasons for their brief stays varied from person to person, but the atmosphere at Tuskegee, located in the black belt of the Deep South, resembled that of a company town; and the emphasis was on industrial training rather than higher education, making it an uncongenial place for sophisticated, well-educated, upper-class blacks, especially for those who had been reared in large cities.[10] Even so, a succession of prominent black men and women who belonged to the most exclusive circles of black society in Chicago, Washington, New York, and other cities visited Tuskegee at Washington's invitation and were his guests at "The Oaks," his large, well-appointed residence on the campus. Few failed to be impressed by his work among the "submerged masses" in the rural South.

In addition to providing younger members of the nation's black elite with jobs at Tuskegee, Booker T. Washington courted aristocrats of color in other ways, especially by using his considerable influence in securing political appointments for them. Although Washington counseled blacks to eschew politics for economics, he was in fact a "black Warrick," a confidant of Presidents Theodore Roosevelt and William Howard Taft.[11] As a minority political boss, he distributed patronage, constructed alliances, and rooted out malcontents. Blacks who held political appointments or who desired to receive them, including those of the upper class, understood the risks involved in being designated anti-Bookerites.

The District of Columbia, especially during the Roosevelt administration, became a Bookerite stronghold. In the capital city the awarding of a presidential appointment to a black, as Louis Harlan has noted, "gave its holder an elite status that even followed him out of office and clung as an aura to his descendants."[12] To a large extent Booker T. Washington controlled such appointments for more than a decade after 1901. Because of his assistance, past and future, a sizable group of the District's black elite rallied to the Tuskegee banner. Robert H. Terrell owed his municipal judgeship to Washington's influence, as did John C. Dancy his appointment as recorder of deeds. P. B. S. Pinchback's declining fortunes, political and otherwise, prompted him to curry the favor of Washington, whose influence also enabled Richard T. Greener to win a diplomatic post. Perhaps Washington's most-trusted ally in the District was Whitefield McKinlay, scion of a well-known free black family of Charleston who had been educated at Avery Institute. McKinlay operated a prosperous real estate and loan business in the capital city. Francis and Archibald Grimké were for a time friendly toward the Tuskegeean, but ultimately they cast their lot with his opponents.[13]

Although Washington's influence was weaker in Baltimore and Philadelphia than in the District, he nonetheless could rely on the support of certain aristocrats of color in both cities. In Philadelphia, John S. Durham was an outright Bookerite. Less reliable was Henry Minton.[14] Boston was even less of a Bookerite stronghold and was viewed as the center of anti-Washington sentiment. Although the Tuskegeean possessed friends in Boston, such as his former student Samuel E. Courtney, a socially prominent physician, the city's "old families" were wedded to the abolitionist tradition. The Trotters, Forbeses, and Butlers, as well as the very old New England black families, such as those who made up the Society of the Descendants of Early New England Negroes, found little about Washington and his philosophy to recommend them. Few critics were more vitriolic or persistent in opposing the Tuskegee Idea than William Monroe Trotter, especially through the columns of his *Boston Guardian.*[15]

Unlike Boston, New York was in some respects a pro-Washington city, especially in Harlem, where men such as the realtor Philip Payton, Charles W. Anderson, and the restaurateur John B. Nail were trusted lieutenants. Nail was the father-in-law of James Weldon Johnson, whose appointment to a diplomatic post owed much to Washington's recommendation. Ultimately Johnson joined the opposition and became an official of the National Association for the Advancement of Colored People. Washington, however, had little support in Brooklyn, where most of New York's aristocrats of color lived. An exception was Samuel R. Scottron, a well-known businessman and the great-grandfather of Lena Horne, who was related to several of the city's "old families."[16]

In Chicago, Cleveland, and other cities, the Tuskegee Machine gained its greatest support from the new economic elite rather than from the old leadership. The new elite, which was less educated and less articulate than the old, consisted largely of self-made men, tied almost exclusively to the black ghetto, who espoused Washington's philosophy of self-help. In Chicago two of his most reliable allies among the city's black upper crust were S. Laing Williams, an attorney, and his wife, Fannie Barrier Williams, a clubwoman who frequently interpreted and praised the city's black "gentle folks." While Daniel Williams, the eminent physician, remained on friendly terms with Washington, it was Dr. George Cleveland Hall, his arch rival, both professionally and socially, who was most closely identified with Washington and served as his personal physician.[17] Among the social elite in Cleveland who supported Washington, though not always enthusiastically, was George A. Myers. Charles Chesnutt, while friendly to Washington, scarcely subscribed to his philosophy. John P. Green, a close friend of both Myers and Chesnutt, probably expressed a view common among black aristocrats when he praised Washington for his uplift activities in behalf of disadvantaged blacks in the rural South but questioned the validity of his racial philosophy and the wisdom of his political strategy.[18]

Washington also counted among his supporters a sizable contingent of upper-class blacks in the South. James C. Napier of Nashville was a loyal adherent of the Tuskegee philosophy and figured prominently in the National Negro Business League. He owed his appointment as Register of the Treasury in 1911 in part to Washington's influence with President Taft. In Charleston, William Demos Crum, a politically active and socially prominent physician, was a staunch ally of Washington.[19] Robert R. Church, the wealthy Memphis banker and businessman and father of Mary Church Terrell, was a close personal friend of Booker Washington, but they subscribed to different philosophies and policies.[20] As elsewhere in the nation, Washington's allies in southern cities included influential editors and publishers, such as Benjamin Davis of the *Atlanta Independent.* The target of many of Davis's bitterest editorials, Henry

Hugh Proctor, minister of Atlanta's prestigious First Congregational Church, was, like Robert Church, a personal friend of the Tuskegeean but was scarcely a consistent proponent of the Tuskegee philosophy.[21]

The relationship of aristocrats of color to Booker T. Washington was as complex as it was diverse. Although some aristocrats of color undoubtedly gravitated to Washington out of a genuine commitment to his philosophy, the loyalty of many, if not most, rested on their personal indebtedness to him for jobs, political appointments, and other favors. As was the case with many Bookerites, regardless of class, their support of the Tuskegeean resulted more from mutual interest than from ideology. Cultural differences obviously separated many aristocrats of color from the man whose ideological position on the race issue was often at variance with their own. It would have been easy enough for those who placed a premium on ancestry and education to dismiss Washington as merely a "mulatto nobody." It was possible, however, for aristocrats of color who joined Washington's circle often out of self-interest to convince themselves that he was one of "our group" by emphasizing his attributes other than family background and education. Like Washington, they were usually conservatives, except in regard to civil rights. Certainly they could identify with his paternalistic attitude toward the black masses and with his attention to proper decorum. They could appreciate the life style of the "royal family" at Tuskegee, where Washington presided in the manner of the "master of Tuskegee plantation" and lived in an imposing residence. Like the aristocrats of color, he seemed to think of industrial education as proper for the children of the less fortunate while his own attended New England preparatory schools, Fisk, and Wellesley and studied music in Paris.[22]

Despite the exertions of the Tuskegee Machine to silence all who challenged Washington, and despite the steady flow of publicity that exaggerated the success of his economic and educational programs, white aggression against the rights of blacks contributed to keeping alive discontent with his leadership. Among the discontented was a disproportionately large number of aristocrats of color, who still insisted on equality, full civil rights, and assimilation into American society and culture. Although such people were found in virtually all cities and regions, perhaps the most vocal and visible group was the so-called Boston radicals. This well-educated, upper-class group included Archibald Grimké, Clement Morgan, and Butler Wilson, all of whom were attorneys; and George Forbes and William Monroe Trotter, who launched the *Boston Guardian* in 1901 "to protest forever against being proscribed or shut off in any caste from equal rights with other citizens."[23] In the same year Trotter and the Boston radicals founded the Boston Literary and Historical Association, which became a forum for militant race opinion. Both the *Guardian* and the association early assumed an anti-Tuskegee position.[24]

Unlike Washington, who was born in slavery, grew up in poverty, and struggled through Hampton Institute, Trotter and his sisters, Maude and Bessie, grew up in genteel affluence in Boston's "polite Negro society" in the predominantly white suburb of Hyde Park. His father, who had attended the famous Gilmore School in Cincinnati, settled in Boston, secured a job in the Post Office, and remained there except for two years in Washington as Recorder of Deeds during Grover Cleveland's first term. Trotter's mother was, according to oral tradition, a descendant of Thomas Jefferson; her sister was married to William H. Dupree, who was a fixture in Boston's upper-class black society and, like his friend Trotter, a militant on racial matters. A Phi Beta Kappa graduate of Harvard and heir to a small fortune from his father, William Monroe Trotter gained a position with a white real estate firm. He settled in a predominantly white neighborhood with his bride, Geraldine Pindall, a talented, vivacious "blonde, blue-eyed" woman whose family had led in the struggle to integrate Boston schools in the antebellum era. Later, his sister Maude married a physician, Dr. Charles G. Steward, the son of an army chaplain and the descendant of an extraordinary biracial family from Gouldtown, New Jersey; and his younger sister, Bessie, married Henry K. Craft, an engineer and former faculty member at Tuskegee.[25]

Proud of Boston as "freedom's birth place," Trotter espoused what his biographer described as "an elitist militancy" that was characteristic of Boston's black upper class. Alarmed by the deteriorating status of blacks in the South and the accommodationist, optimistic approach of Booker T. Washington, Trotter and his upper-class friends challenged the Tuskegeean first through the National Afro-American Council, an organization created in 1898 as the successor to the defunct Afro-American League. When the Tuskegee Machine assumed control of the Council, Trotter established the *Guardian*, which regularly attacked "the person, prestige and racial policies of Booker T. Washington." Over the years he created a succession of anti-Bookerite organizations. In 1903, two years after the launching of the *Guardian*, Washington made a speech in Boston under the auspices of the city's chapter of the National Negro Business League. Trotter, his sister Maude, and several friends attended the meeting, where they jeered, laughed, and asked Washington embarrassing questions. Arrested and jailed for the disturbance that Bookerites termed the "Boston riot," Trotter became the target of Washington's vindictiveness. The Tuskegeean sought to intimidate and silence Trotter and the *Guardian*, and failing that, he subsidized a rival newspaper in Boston. Trotter and the *Guardian* survived as unrestrained critics of Washington, whom Trotter characterized as the "great surrenderer," but he did so at great personal sacrifice. To keep his newspaper alive he and his family moved from a position of relative affluence to one of genteel poverty. Nor was Trotter ever able to coordinate the potential anti-Bookerites into an effective opposition, in large part because of his temperament and personality. Stubborn, arrogant and inflexible, self-righteous and priggish, he was suspicious of "everyone's motives except his own."[26] A pro-Washington newspaper in New York observed in 1911 that the "constant and often senseless agitation of the 'color question' " by a small group of elitist blacks in Boston was responsible for the steady deterioration in the condition of black Bostonians. The most obvious result of this agitation, the New York editor declared, was that blacks no longer had representatives in the Massachusetts legislature or on the Boston city council.[27]

Although Trotter was incapable of galvanizing the opposition to Washington, he had nonetheless raised the flag of dissent and boldly challenged the Tuskegee formula of race relations. The "Boston riot" and Washington's response to it accelerated the polarization of black sentiment that was already under way. Increasingly, Washington classified blacks as either friends or enemies. Not only did Trotter go to jail and fall into eclipse as a result of his part in the "riot," but the names of those who had indicated sympathy for him found their way onto a blacklist compiled by Washington and his associates. Among those on this list were such representatives of the black aristocracy as Judson W. Lyons of Augusta, Francis Grimké and Lafayette M. Hershaw of Washington, and W. E. B. Du Bois and his colleague George A. Towns of Atlanta. Grimké, as minister of Washington's upper-class Fifteenth Street Presbyterian Church, was perhaps the least vulnerable to Tuskegee pressure. Hershaw was an employee of the Interior Department and might have been subject to such pressure except for the fact that his position was covered by civil service. Washington brought pressure on Du Bois and Towns, both of whom were on the staff of Atlanta University, through the institution's white benefactors. Lyons ultimately lost his post as Register of the Treasury, at least in part through Washington's influence. Bookerites in Boston also sought without success to remove from office two individuals who had supported Trotter: Napoleon Marshall, a Harvard-educated employee of the city tax office and the husband of Harriet Gibbs; and George Forbes, Trotter's early cohort on the *Guardian*, who was employed in a Boston public library.[28]

Other aristocrats of color, though not involved in the struggle between Trotter and Washington, engaged in civil rights activities that were scarcely consistent with Tuskegee accommodationism. Even before Washington emerged as the spokesman for black Americans, Robert J. Harlan, a member of Cincinnati's upper-class black society, sued a theatre in 1891 for refusing his children seats.[29] A group of upper-class blacks and Creoles of color in Louisiana had instituted the suit by Homière Plessy that resulted in the "separate but equal" decision in 1896.[30] Aristocrats of color were among the most outspoken critics of and lobbyists against the separate coach laws enacted in the South in the 1890s and opening years of the twentieth century. Among those who led the opposition against such a statute in Maryland were members of the socially prominent Bishop family of Annapolis and Baltimore. When San Antonio, Texas passed a Jim Crow streetcar ordinance in 1904, the "better class of colored people" in the city led a boycott "in order to retain the respect they have for the wives and daughters." In fact, a view widely held among upper-class blacks was that Jim Crow measures were aimed not at the lower classes but at the "better class of colored people," who no more desired to be herded together in dirty, crowded "separate coaches" with uncouth, noisy, and unkempt lower-class blacks than did whites.[31]

It was, perhaps, more than coincidence that at the height of his dispute with Washington, Trotter was feted in December 1903 at a banquet in the District of Columbia which was attended by such aristocrats of color as John F. Cook, John W. Cromwell, Owen M. Waller, W. S. Lofton, and John P. Green. Although some of these men were on friendly terms with Washington, their presence at a dinner for Trotter indicated where their ideological sympathies lay.[32] Even those of the upper class who were on intimate terms with Washington, such as Dr. Austin M. Curtis, head of the Freedman's Hospital, and his wife, on occasion acted in ways that were more reminiscent of Trotter than of Washington. In 1907, while Mrs. Curtis was having lunch at the restaurant in Kahn's Department Store, she saw a waitress refuse to serve a Negro nursemaid who was attending a white child. After protesting to the store's owner, she vowed "never set foot" in the store again. Her action received considerable notice in the *Bee* and other Washington papers.[33]

In view of the risks involved, few upper-class blacks unsympathetic to the Tuskegee formula were willing to say publicly what they might reveal privately. John Hope, a native of Augusta, Georgia and Judson Lyons's brother-in-law, confided his opinion of Booker T. Washington in a letter to his fiancée, Lugenia Burns, in 1897. Hope was a young instructor at Roger Williams University in Nashville at the time. The reason for his references to Washington was that his financée had been invited to take part in a reception for the Tuskegeean in Chicago. "We can recognize greatness," Hope wrote, "even when we do not agree with it." Although he characterized Washington as "the greatest Negro . . . since Douglass," he was nonetheless convinced that the Tuskegeean was "certainly not doing our cause *all* good and *no* harm."[34] In another letter to Lugenia Burns, Hope wrote more forthrightly: "We in the South have suffered so much from Booker Washingtonism and I have not the heart to be even a small part of any festivities, the purpose of which is to make greater a man whose increasing greatness means increasing humiliation. Any colored man who talks to Southern white people as he does about the Negro cannot receive my commendation."[35] After Hope moved to Atlanta Baptist College in 1898 (he became president there eight years later), his lack of sympathy for the Tuskegee philosophy became more overt. Because he was considered an enemy by Washington, Hope found the doors to white philanthropic agencies closed to him until about 1909. At that time a mutual friend patched up his differences with Washington, and with the Tuskegeean's help Hope secured a gift for his college from Andrew Carnegie.[36]

The polarization of black sentiment regarding Booker T. Washington and his formula of race relations increasingly cast William Edward Burghardt Du Bois in the role of the Tuskegeean's most formidable adversary. In a sense Trotter's mantle fell to Du Bois, who shared certain of the Bostonian's personality traits but was nonetheless capable of galvanizing the anti-Bookerite opposition. In terms of family background, cultural orientation, and concern for civil rights, many aristocrats of color found Du Bois a natural ally and a congenial spokesman. Born in Great Barrington, Massachusetts, of African, Dutch, and French ancestry, he belonged to a family that was "among the oldest inhabitants" of a town in which the "bulk of the well-to-do people belonged to the Episcopal and Congregational churches." Du Bois grew up in the Congregational Sunday school of his mother and occasionally attended the Episcopal church of his grandmother. Because he enrolled in the college preparatory curriculum in the local high school, he was by his own account, "thrown with the upper rather than the lower classes and [was] protected in many ways." Although his family owned little property, and wealth "had no particular lure" for him, Du Bois consciously identified with the rich and wellborn. "I cordially despised the poor Irish and South Germans who slaved in the mills," he later recalled, "and annexed the rich and well-to-do as my natural companions."[37]

Those who knew Du Bois after he reached maturity suggested that he adopted the air and manner of those natural companions. They spoke of his aristocratic bearing, inaccessibility, and dapper attire, with the ever-present gloves and walking stick; "even his laughter was reserved." Some interpreted his behavior as that of "a man who thought so much of himself that he couldn't stoop" to be familiar with ordinary folks. Booker T. Washington considered him downright arrogant and haughty.[38] "Whatever can be said in praise of Dr. W. E. B. Du Bois," one black journalist wrote, "even his staunchest supporters have to admit that he . . . disdains to mix with 'the common clay.' "[39] A leading Bookerite in Atlanta who was acquainted with Du Bois maintained that "the only way he can help his race is for him to pull off his gloves and specks and get down off his bicycle long enough to speak to a colored gentleman when he meets him in the streets."[40] Fully aware that he was often perceived as a snob, Du Bois explained that he was too thoroughly a New Englander and possessed too much "Dutch taciturnity" to be as voluble and emotional as many of the blacks he encountered in the South.[41]

After completing high school, Du Bois wanted to attend Harvard, but because of a lack of money, he went instead to Fisk University in Nashville, Tennessee. Here, for the first time he was among people of his own race who exhibited an extraordinary range of colors. In Nashville's black community he moved in "the best circles," dominated by old families such as the Napiers and other members of Howard Congregational Church. Upon graduation from Fisk, he fulfilled his ambition to attend Harvard; he entered as a junior in 1888 and remained for the Ph.D. degree, granted seven years later. Following post-graduate study at the University of Berlin, he held appointments at Wilberforce and at the University of Pennsylvania as a special investigator of social conditions among Philadelphia Negroes. In 1897 he returned to the South, to Atlanta University, where he remained for more than a dozen years, teaching and carrying on significant sociological investigations. Among his special friends in Atlanta were John Hope, George A. Towns, and H. H. Proctor, the Yale-educated minister of the First Congregational Church.[42]

At various times Du Bois's ideas included elements from diverse streams of black thought regarding ways to combat prejudice and discrimination. At the heart of his thought lay a paradox that he described as the "two-ness" inherent in Afro-Americans. The Afro-American was both a Negro and an American, with "two souls, two thoughts, [and] two unreconciled strivings" as well as "two warring ideals in one dark body." On the one hand, Du Bois insisted that blacks be full participants in American society and that all caste distinctions based on race and color be abolished. On the other, he advocated a sense of black pride, racial unity, and identification with the darker races in other parts of the world. Throughout his long career, Du Bois confronted the paradox of attempting to create black Americans as a separate cultural group at the same time that he sought to integrate them into the larger white society. Convinced that the black ethos would enrich American life, he advocated a form of cultural pluralism by which peoples of different backgrounds "live together on a basis of equality, tolerance, justice and harmony." Despite the paradox in his thought, according to his biographer, Du Bois "learned to compartmentalize and move freely between his two contradictory goals."[43]

Early in his career Du Bois viewed Booker T. Washington's industrial education program and gradualist philosophy with favor. But shortly after the turn of the century a shift in his thinking became evident as he increasingly placed emphasis on the civil rights of blacks. He became convinced that major social change—the solution to the race problem in America—could only be achieved through agitation and protest. In an era that witnessed mounting evidence of anti-black prejudice in the form of Jim Crow laws, disfranchisement, peonage, and racial violence, Du Bois concluded that the accommodation, subterfuge, and "half truths" that he believed characterized Booker T. Washington's leadership were not only inadequate but harmful—a position his friend John Hope had arrived at earlier. Under the circumstances only a bold assault on the bastions of prejudice and discrimination and a forthright emphasis on the civil rights of blacks would suffice. Central to Du Bois's formula was the elitist concept of the "talented tenth," which maintained that college-educated blacks such as himself, rather than those trained at "industrial schools," should provide leadership for the elevation of the black masses. His idea of the "talented tenth" was one with which many well-educated aristocrats of color could identify. In fact, it bore considerable resemblance to the role they had played until the emergence of Booker T. Washington.[44]

Despite evidence of increasing alienation between Washington and Du Bois, the relationship between the two men remained overtly cordial until

1903–1904; Du Bois taught summer school at Tuskegee in 1903 but spent the remainder of the summer with Trotter in Boston. His book *The Souls of Black Folk* had appeared that spring, and the chapter entitled "Of Mr. Booker T. Washington and Others" severed Du Bois's relationship with the Tuskegeean and cast him in the role of the anti-Bookerite leader. Having publicly indicted Washington for condoning white racism and for placing on blacks the primary responsibility for their deprivation, Du Bois ultimately accepted the responsibility for organizing an anti-Washington black rights movement. In popular terminology the Du Bois forces became known as the "radicals" or "militants" and those of Washington as the "conservatives." But it was scarcely a battle in which the forces were evenly matched, for Washington was a skilled politician with considerable resources at his command, including the Tuskegee Machine and a preponderance of the black press.[45]

Always a popular speaker, Du Bois was in even greater demand on the lecture circuit following the publication of *The Souls of Black Folk*, which some considered "the political bible" of the black educated elite. In December 1903 he lectured at the All Souls Unitarian Church in Chicago, which had a racially mixed congregation including some of the most outstanding members of the city's black social elite. Following the lecture, he was entertained at the home of Dr. Charles E. Bentley at a reception attended by most of Chicago's socially prominent blacks. The following March Du Bois lectured on "The Negro Problem" at the Mount Zion Congregational Church in Cleveland, where he was introduced by Charles W. Chesnutt. According to one observer, his audience was "composed of Cleveland's most enlightened Afro-Americans." In fact, wherever Du Bois appeared on the lecture circuit he attracted a sizable segment of the black elite, often described as those Afro-Americans with "advanced ideas."[46]

His visits throughout the country enabled Du Bois to gauge the extent of the anti-Tuskegee sentiment. Fully aware of Washington's power and of the risk of being accused of leading a movement of status-hungry elitists, he nonetheless decided to organize a militant anti-Washington campaign. His first step in initiating what became known as the Niagara Movement was to call together twenty-nine carefully screened delegates, mostly college-educated black professionals. These individuals represented, as Du Bois had hoped, the most "thoughtful" and "dignified" blacks, in fact, "the very best class" of Afro-Americans. Many of those in attendance were at or near the top of the social structure of the cities in which they resided: Morgan and Trotter from Boston, John Hope from Atlanta, Bentley from Chicago, and Hershaw and Owen M. Waller from Washington.[47] Waller, an Oxford-educated clergyman who succeeded Crummell as rector of St. Luke's Episcopal Church, was in some respects even more militant than Du Bois in his opposition to Washington. Denouncing the Tuskegeean's "unsound doctrine" in a speech in 1904, Waller declared that he preferred "the vision of Toussaint L'Ouverture defying Napoleon to Mr.

Washington, bowing hat in hand, to an unwashed cracker."[48] Another Episcopal clergyman involved in the Niagara Movement was George F. Bragg of Baltimore, who, unlike Waller, attempted to maintain cordial relations with Washington by claiming that the difference between him and Du Bois was one of methods, not ultimate objectives. Also representing Maryland was Du Bois's old friend Mason A. Hawkins, a graduate of Harvard who at the time taught foreign languages in the Colored High School in Baltimore.[49]

For several years after its initial session in 1905, the Niagara Movement held annual meetings at which it issued declarations of protest that stood in sharp contrast to Washington's philosophy. In 1905, for example, the delegates denounced his tactics of gradualism, contradicted his assertions that blacks were primarily responsible for their problems, and pointed out the inequities of the "separate-but-equal" doctrine. "Persistent manly agitation," the Niagaraites maintained, "is the way to liberty."[50]

Two events in 1906—the Atlanta race riot, and President Roosevelt's preemptory dismissal of a battalion of black troops as a result of the so-called Brownsville affray—dramatized the flaws in Washington's accommodationist policy. Both seemed to corroborate the contention of Niagaraites that under the Tuskegeean's leadership Roosevelt's promises of keeping open "the door of opportunity" for blacks were empty rhetoric. Despite the blow dealt to Washington by these two events, the Niagara Movement failed to become either popular or effective. It lacked significant white support, had scant financial resources, and encountered formidable opposition from the Tuskegee Machine. But as the historian of the Niagara Movement has noted, another significant factor figured in the ineffectiveness of the Movement: the Niagaraites were a privileged group psychologically isolated from the black masses. They were, as Du Bois described them, "a splendid set of people" fully conscious of their lofty status within black society.[51] Perhaps their most notable contribution was in laying the foundation for the National Association for the Advancement of Colored People.

The NAACP was a biracial organization, founded in 1909 in response to the declining status of black Americans in general and to a race riot in Springfield, Illinois the previous year. Bringing together some of the Niagaraites with white descendants of old abolitionists, the NAACP was sometimes referred to as "the new Abolition" movement. Among blacks who figured prominently in the founding of the organization and signed the original "call" were Du Bois, Mary Church Terrell, Owen Meredith Waller, and Archibald Grimké. Still others, including Hutchins C. Bishop of New York, Butler Wilson of Boston, F. N. Cardozo of Baltimore, and George W. Cook of Washington, became members of the NAACP board of directors by 1915. Du Bois became the director of publicity and research and published the first issue of The Crisis, the NAACP organ, in November 1910.[52]

During the next decade, the organization waged campaigns against segregation and discrimination on many fronts. Among its most notable efforts were a campaign to improve black education, a crusade against lynching, efforts to ban the showing of the film *Birth of a Nation,* an attempt to win equal treatment for black soldiers in the First World War, and a successful legal battle against urban residential segregation ordinances. The Baltimore branch of the NAACP early entered the struggle against residential segregation under the leadership of two well-known and socially prominent individuals, F. N. Cardozo, a physician and son of the Washington and Charleston educator who headed the Baltimore branch of the NAACP, and W. Ashbie Hawkins, an attorney and a member of Boulé, who handled the legal challenge to the ordinance.[53]

In an effort to expand the NAACP outside New York, the organization moved quickly to establish branches in Boston, Chicago, and Philadelphia. A driving force in the Boston branch was Butler R. Wilson, the son of a black physician in Georgia, a graduate of Atlanta University, and the holder of a law degree from Boston University. Owing to his elitist background, Wilson possessed the manner of "a member of the black aristocracy . . . all of his life." He settled in Boston, married Mary L. Evans, the sister of Mrs. Daniel Murray of Washington, practiced law for a time with Archibald Grimké and George L. Ruffin, and early manifested an interest in civil rights cases. His legal clientele was biracial, including more whites than blacks. Wilson and his wife moved in Boston's most elite black society. A principal ally of Trotter in the Boston opposition to Washington, Wilson had been active in the Niagara Movement. An early member of the NAACP, he and other members of the Boston branch, including Clement Morgan and influential whites, scored a significant victory in 1913 against the racially discriminatory policies of the city's Y.M.C.A. swimming pool. Wilson's old ally, the irascible Trotter, remained on the periphery of NAACP activities and ultimately broke with both Wilson and the organization. Trotter came to view Wilson as a politician who remained aloof from the black masses and "worked for genteel causes in the company of upper-class whites." Such a view, of course, closely resembled that which many Bookerites took of all blacks who identified with the NAACP.[54]

In Chicago, according to historian Allan Spear, those who constituted the city's aristocracy of color were "by and large, antagonistic to the ideology of self-help and racial solidarity of Booker T. Washington." From the ranks of the old elite in the city, the NAACP initially drew its most active members, such as the black dentist Charles E. Bentley, a personal friend of Du Bois and a participant in his Niagara Movement. Bentley's friend Dr. Daniel Williams, the eminent surgeon, was not temperamentally inclined to be involved with protest movements; for a time he had been friendly toward Washington but ultimately became sympathetic to the efforts of the Niagara Movement and the NAACP. In fact, the latter organization received its largest bequest from his sizable estate. Like those of comparable status elsewhere, some of Chicago's black social elite eschewed protest activities and organizations altogether. Among the most notable of these were Julius Avendorph, long considered the "Ward McAllister" of the city's upper crust, and Charles J. Smiley, a socially prominent, wealthy caterer.[55]

In Philadelphia, Cleveland, and other cities in the North where the NAACP initially established its most active branches, it generally followed the same pattern in attracting its local leadership from the old elite. The Philadelphia branch counted among its most active members Dr. Nathan F. Mozell and George H. White, formerly a congressman from North Carolina.[56] In Cleveland the involvement of the old elite was less clear-cut than elsewhere. Charles Chesnutt supported the NAACP but was reluctant to become too deeply involved in anti-Washington movements. Others who were viewed as part of the city's "blue vein" upper crust, such as John P. Green and George A. Myers, both of whom were fully aware of the deterioration in race relations, remained aloof from NAACP activities. Both were dependent on whites for their political influence, and Myers alternated between the contradictory beliefs that discrimination was caused by white racism and that blacks were responsible for their own plight. The most conspicuous early NAACP supporter in Cleveland was Harry Smith, editor of the *Gazette,* who was a member of the old leadership group but was never part of Cleveland's social elite. Smith sometimes criticized the NAACP for not being militant enough.[57]

The NAACP branch in Washington was organized in 1912 and attracted the support of "the most able of the upper class Negro community." It provided legal aid to the victims of discrimination, battled all forms of segregation, and acted as an effective lobbying group and as a watchdog regarding federal legislation. But more was involved in the District's upper-class association with the NAACP than abstractions about civil rights and race progress. Opportunities for government employment, on which many of them depended for a livelihood, were rapidly slipping away, especially under the administration of Woodrow Wilson. The elimination of blacks from government offices and the introduction of segregation in the federal bureaucracy, where it had not previously existed, undoubtedly prompted some aristocrats of color to become involved in the NAACP. For those dependent on government jobs, as the historian of the NAACP has suggested, "it was a case of bread and butter—of personal involvement." From the beginning, several members of Washington's aristocracy of color were active in NAACP affairs at both national and local levels. Under the leadership of Archibald Grimké, the Washington branch became the largest and one of the most active in the nation. Unlike the New York and Boston branches, it included few whites but a large segment of the city's "black 400," such as Andrew F. Hilyer, Neval Thomas, and Mary Church Terrell. The District membership also proved to be one of the most liberal in financial contributions to the national coffers.[58]

By 1914 the Tuskegeean's grip on the black community in Washington was clearly slipping. Visiting the city in October, T. Thomas Fortune reported that it was "a hot bed of association for the advancement of colored people sentiment and opposition to Dr. Washington."[59] Earlier in the year, Ralph Tyler, a Bookerite in Washington, informed the Tuskegeean that Roscoe Bruce had proved to be a "despicable ingrate" by becoming the "high priest" of the local NAACP branch, "hurtling from his past friends who saved him to hoped for new friends." Tyler claimed that Bruce was not only subsidizing Calvin Chase's *Bee*, which accounted for its sudden anti-Tuskegee position, but also writing a column for the paper under a pen name and saying uncomplimentary things about Washington. In June 1914 Tyler reported that "all 'our friends' joined and contributed financially to the N.A.A.C.P." Even Judge Terrell had promised a twenty-five dollar contribution. Although Whitefield McKinlay, one of the most reliable Bookerites in the District, had joined the NAACP, Tyler excused his action on the grounds that he was ignorant of "its real purpose, and largely influenced by his relatives, the Grimké brothers."[60]

As was the case with other local branches of the NAACP, the one in Washington on occasion suffered from factionalism and from involvement in local disputes that were irrelevant to organizational objectives. In the controversy over the Moens affair, for example, the District branch was a target of attack by some of those intent on using the case to depose Roscoe Bruce as assistant superintendent of schools. Convinced that the local branch was the preserve of those who belonged to the same high social status as the Bruces, they claimed that the NAACP in the District provided a strong base of support for the assistant superintendent. Such an allegation rested on evidence that was circumstantial at best.[61]

Despite the polarization of the black community between Bookerites and anti-Bookerites, some aristocrats of color more or less divided their allegiance between the philosophies of Washington and Du Bois. It was not unusual for individuals to be active in both the National Negro Business League and the NAACP. Not all aristocrats of color, any more than other blacks, possessed coherent philosophies of racial advancement; they did not view the strategies of Washington and Du Bois as incompatible. In the highly polarized atmosphere of the era such individuals were likely to be characterized as "straddlers." One of these was Kelly Miller, the well-known scholar at Howard University. In some respects George Dereef, a Wisconsin attorney, was more typical. The descendant of a slave-holding free family of color from Charleston, South Carolina whose members had belonged to the Brown Fellowship Society, Dereef had settled in Milwaukee in 1913 and figured prominently in the local branches of the NAACP and the National Negro Business League. As with others of similar background, Dereef's activities graphically demonstrated "ways in which the ideology of self-help and racial solidarity overlapped with an emphasis on racial protest and integration."[62]

Although the extent to which the NAACP won support from old upper-class black families varied from place to place, the evidence suggests that local NAACP leadership was primarily "drawn from the upper strata of the Negro community," especially from the ranks of professional people.[63] Substantial correlation existed between those who assumed leadership roles in the NAACP and those who held membership in the American Negro Academy, Boulé, and the most exclusive local social clubs. The role of aristocrats of color in the affairs of the NAACP was sufficiently conspicuous to allow some critics, especially those identified with Washington and the Tuskegee Machine, to characterize it as a self-serving, elitist organization. The Bookerite *Atlanta Independent* continually heaped ridicule on Du Bois and the NAACP, which it characterized as Du Bois's "exclusive bunch." Hubert H. Harrison, a Virgin Islander prominent in Harlem in the 1920s, was credited with slurring the NAACP as the "National Association for the Advancement of *Certain* People"; but the idea was present much earlier in criticisms made by other blacks.[64]

Calvin Chase's *Washington Bee* was for a time a bitter critic of the NAACP and its District branch. "Any attempt," the *Bee* warned the local branch in 1914, "to establish a Negro aristocracy to the disadvantage and embarrassment of the common people will be promptly exposed and condemned." Later the newspaper cited the NAACP as proof of its oft-repeated charge that there was "as much color prejudice among certain classes of colored people" as there was "among certain classes of whites." Chase's reference to the NAACP as "a caste organization" resembled nothing so much as his earlier tirades against the Lotus Club and the Monday Night Literary Club, both of which had been accused of color-conscious snobbery. For Chase and his *Bee* the organization was mere "social bombast," and those associated with it were engaged "in more discriminating stunts than the 98 Southerners who voted for the recent Jim Crow bill in Congress." In Chase's view the NAACP was merely another elitist social club that contributed about "as much as the Mu-So-Lit Club" to the welfare of the black masses.[65]

In response to an address in which the District NAACP spokesman, Archibald Grimké, assailed the "color prejudice" rampant in the country, the *Bee* asked whether whites possessed any more "color prejudice" than Grimké, who had chosen a white woman as his wife. Furthermore, it charged that when Grimké lived in Boston, he "never associated with people of his own race because he thought he was too good to associate with them."[66]

In an editorial in 1917, Chase expressed his disdain for the NAACP without ever mentioning the organization by name. He maintained that there was developing alongside the "caste based on complexion," another "caste based on book learning and professional career." The tendency, he argued, was for college-trained "highbrows" to "withdraw themselves from the masses." Teachers, preachers, doctors, and lawyers formed associations ostensibly for the purpose of advancing the welfare of the masses, but in reality their ends were purely selfish. Since the black "highbrows" liked to travel, they wanted to abolish Jim Crow rail cars, hotels, and restaurants. Since they were likely to be "either an office holder or an office seeker," they demanded an end to discrimination in

government employment. According to the *Bee*, Negroes who flocked to organizations like the NAACP, whether because of "color prejudice" or "caste of
book learning," did so primarily because of a desire to remove barriers to their
own personal advancement and comfort. Only when personally affected was the
upper-"caste" black likely to lodge protests and lead crusades. In short, according
to the *Bee*, upper-class blacks took little interest in goals designed to benefit the
masses directly, such as proper housing and health facilities.[67]

Although Chase and the *Bee* scarcely provided objective critiques of the
NAACP, the notion that the organization was roughly comparable to an
exclusive social club was not confined to those hostile to it. At least some
aristocrats of color viewed admission to the NAACP as by "invitation only," in
much the same way that one gained entry to the Booklovers or Mu-So-Lit clubs.
In January 1915, as Mary Church Terrell and her friend Namahoko Sockoume
Curtis, the wife of the well-known physician, walked home from Capitol Hill,
where they had been lobbying against a bill to prohibit interracial marriage,
Mrs. Curtis "complained that she had never been invited to join the NAACP."
When an invitation was properly issued, she joined and became an active
member.[68]

On some occasions local branches of the NAACP appeared to function
more as social clubs than as militant civil rights groups. In 1915, when Josephine
Bruce and several members of the Cook family traveled to San Francisco to
attend the World Purity Federation, the Northern California Branch of the
NAACP hosted a round of receptions and sight-seeing tours for them. *The Crisis*
may have unwittingly contributed to the image of the NAACP as merely
another elite social organization by publishing double-page pictures of Baltimore's Mid Winter Assembly, New York's Bachelor Benedict Assembly, and the
annual dinner of Pittsburgh's Leondi Club to depict "social life in colored
America." But on some occasions what critics termed the "social bombast" of
the organization were actually fund-raising affairs. In Boston Mrs. Butler Wilson
held a series of musicales and receptions, or what were termed "parlor parties,"
to which the black elite was invited along with prominent whites for the purpose
of raising money for the NAACP.[69]

Until his death, in 1915, Booker T. Washington remained hostile to the
NAACP. Viewing the organization as a threat to his own power and prestige, he
sought by any means to thwart its growth and influence. Although his own
power was on the wane, especially with the Democrats in control of the White
House, the Tuskegeean was still a force to be reckoned with in the black
community. Even those upper-class blacks who by tradition and instinct might
have been expected to cast their lot with the NAACP were hesitant to incur the
wrath of Washington and his followers. Their reputation for ruthlessness toward
those whom they considered "enemies" was often sufficient to force acquies-
cence on the part of some who might otherwise have rallied to the cause of Du
Bois and the NAACP. Mary Church Terrell was obviously correct in asserting

that it "required a bit of courage" for blacks to join the NAACP in its initial years or, more specifically, so long as Washington was alive. "There is no doubt," she recalled, "that when the Association was formed there were many colored people who believed in the principles for which it stood, who hesitated or refused to join it because they feared membership in it would cause them to lose their jobs or hurt their influence in the communities in which they lived."[70]

Such reluctance was especially evident in the South, where a majority of blacks still lived and where racial discrimination appeared in its most extreme form. Although John Hope of Atlanta was a member of the NAACP's first General Committee in 1910, a branch of the organization was not established in Atlanta until 1917, two years after Washington's death. In 1919 Robert R. Church, Jr., a wealthy Memphis businessman and Mary Church Terrell's half-brother, was the "first distinctly southern member" of the NAACP to be elected to the organization's board of directors.[71]

An organization that came into existence at about the same time as the NAACP and that provided an alternative for some blacks interested in the uplift of the masses was the National Urban League (NUL). An interracial community service organization established in 1910, the NUL employed the tools and methods of social work, economics, law, and various other disciplines to assist black migrants from the South in finding jobs and housing and in adjusting to an urban environment in northern cities. Although there were obvious points of convergence between the NAACP and the NUL in both ideology and personnel, the Urban League was the type of organization more likely to win support from Booker T. Washington and his allies. In fact, Washington encouraged his lieutenants in northern cities to join the League, and in 1914 he accepted an invitation to become a member of its national board. While both organizations attracted upper-class blacks, those who became involved with the NUL tended to be more representative of the newer socioeconomic elite, which was closely tied to the black ghetto and was sympathetic with the Tuskegee philosophy and strategy. Robert S. Abbott, publisher of the *Defender,* and Dr. George Cleveland Hall, Washington's personal physician, who was unable to gain admission to Chicago's charmed circle of the old elite, were the most active figures in the city's NUL. Despite the fact that individuals such as John Hope, among others, who were closely identified with the NAACP also supported the NUL, the black leadership of the NAACP tended to be more representative of socially prominent "old families" who viewed themselves as heirs to the Abolitionist tradition and who opposed Washington's accommodationist approach.[72]

The death of Washington in 1915 not only elevated Du Bois to the position of the nation's best-known black spokesman but also meant that the NAACP moved to a more "centrist" position. For a time the black community was no longer polarized into "conservatives" and "radicals." Even before Washington's death, a shift in sentiment among prominent blacks was evident in the successful efforts of the NAACP to organize local branches and increase its membership. But the removal of Booker T. Washington from the scene undoubtedly accounted for the proliferation of branches in cities throughout the South. From a national membership of 9,000 in 1916, shortly after Washington's death, the NAACP climbed to almost 80,000 by the fall of 1919.[73]

Although the removal of Washington from the scene undoubtedly contributed to the expansion of the NAACP, especially in the South, other factors also figured significantly in its growth. The triumphant march of Jim Crow was responsible, in large part, for a change in sentiment, especially among the upper class, that promoted a degree of unity in the black community. As early as 1901, Owen M. Waller, who had served as chaplain to the National Afro-American Council and who later participated in the founding of both the Niagara Movement and the NAACP, claimed that blacks were "being so persecuted and crowded together" as a result of racial prejudice that all lines of division in the black community were gradually being obliterated.[74] Because Jim Crow laws made no distinction between "the educated gentleman or lady" and "the noisiest tough of the slums," upper-class blacks came to see the futility of hoping for acceptance as first-class citizens. It became increasingly evident that no matter how educated and refined they were or how much distance they placed between themselves and the "submerged masses," they were subjected to the same proscriptions and humiliation as the supposedly ignorant and vulgar members of their race. Impressive personal achievement, lofty social status, and a fair complexion did not exempt any Negro from the strictures of Jim Crow.[75] One observer noted that all blacks had to assume the role of being "their brothers' keeper" inasmuch as every black was held responsible by whites for the negative behavior of every other black person.[76] That the membership of the NAACP expanded so dramatically between 1916 and 1920 suggested the degree to which it had become a broad-based organization in which the black elite had made common cause with the masses.

Despite the death of Washington and the growth of the NAACP, neither the organization nor its most conspicuous black spokesman, Du Bois, escaped criticism from blacks. In an article in *Crisis* in 1918, Du Bois called upon black Americans to forget their "special grievances" and close ranks with their white fellow citizens in the fight for democracy. Even the Washington branch of the NAACP condemned the editorial as an unfortunate deviation from the traditional position of the organization. But A. Philip Randolph, a black socialist and editor of *The Messenger*, was considerably less generous in his rejection of the editorial. He characterized Du Bois as a "hand picked, me-too-boss, hat-in-hand, sycophant, lick spittling" Negro.[77]

During and immediately after the war, Du Bois's involvement in the Pan-African movement prompted a clash with Marcus Garvey, a native of Jamaica and popular leader of the Universal Negro Improvement Association. The flamboyant Garvey appealed to the black masses with bellicose rhetoric about conquering Africa and with overtly hostile references to the NAACP as an elitist organization. He characterized Du Bois as a "white man Negro" who associated only with whites and "upper ten Negroes" while ignoring the black masses. Du Bois, he thundered, worshipped a "bastard aristocracy" and was all talk and no action. Garvey asked, "Where did he get this aristocracy from?" and then proceeded to explain that Du Bois "just got it into his head that he should be an aristocrat and ever since that time has been keeping his very beard as an aristocrat." Thunderous applause and laughter greeted Garvey's reference to Du Bois as a Negro leader who tried to "be everything else but a Negro."[78]

Du Bois, however, was by no means the only target of the bitter attacks of the Garveyites. They railed against the "black 400," whom they associated with organizations such as the NAACP. Garvey sometimes referred to upper-class blacks as "aristocrats" or as "upper tens" but usually preferred "dicties" or "dickties," a term that had become popular by 1920.[79] In Garvey's opinion virtually every black community in urban America had its share of "dickties" whose self-serving antics had thwarted the progress of Afro-Americans. Boasting that he had the support of the black masses and was engaged in activities to promote their welfare, Garvey claimed in 1920 that he had routed the "four hundred" in Boston and several other cities and that the days of the self-appointed "upper tens" were numbered. "This isn't the age of the dicties," he concluded.[80]

Of course, the notion that organizations such as the NAACP were mere instruments of a snobbish, self-serving elite did not originate with Garvey. Rather he made an existing perception the basis for his demagogic appeals to the black masses. The enthusiasm with which the masses responded to his references to the "four hundred" and the "dicties" suggested the extent to which class considerations figured in the workings of protest organizations.

Throughout the late nineteenth and early twentieth centuries, aristocrats of color provided much of the inspiration and leadership for organized efforts in behalf of black civil rights. Viewing themselves as heirs to the Abolitionist tradition and wedded to the idea of assimilation into American society and culture, they represented the best-educated, most articulate segment of the black population. They were usually what Daniel Murray referred to as "composite" people, both racially and culturally. Fair in complexion, they were members of families that had been free for several generations. Fully acquainted with both black and white culture, they assumed the role of brokers, speaking to blacks and for blacks to whites while exhibiting an elitism toward other blacks that was compounded of both condescension and sympathy for those who did not share their privileged background. Their uplift and civil rights activities generally exhibited an interplay of race consciousness and class consciousness. When class interests were seen to conflict with race consciousness, those outside the upper class viewed the NAACP as more relevant to the desires of the elite than to the needs of the masses.

By the time Garvey began unleashing his tirades against the "dicties" and what he saw as their posturing on behalf of the masses, the NAACP had evolved into an organization substantially different from what earlier critics termed Du Bois's "exclusive bunch." By the 1920s, when its membership and program had undergone extraordinary expansion, descriptions of it as an organization dedicated to the advancement of "certain people" became increasingly inappropriate and irrelevant. Individuals of the upper class continued to occupy a disproportionately large number of leadership positions, and the class biases of certain members on occasion still posed problems, but the objectives and methods of the NAACP had become generally accepted throughout black America.

PART IV

◆

Changes and Continuities

PROLOGUE

DURING HIS FOURTEEN YEARS AS HEAD of the colored schools in Washington, Roscoe Bruce, his wife, and his mother belonged to the District's black social elite. They moved among the "best families" and were members of the most prestigious clubs (Bruce was an early member of Sigma Pi Phi, or Boulé). In 1913 he succeeded Dr. John Francis, an old family friend, as head of the board of trustees of the Colored Social Settlement, a social uplift agency sponsored by upper-class blacks for the benefit of the "unfortunates."[1] The troubles Bruce encountered as assistant superintendent were linked in part to his social standing in the District. The series of controversies in which he was involved almost invariably included charges, especially from upwardly mobile middle-class blacks, that he showed favoritism toward those of his own class in the appointment of teachers and other school personnel.

Controversy marked Roscoe Bruce's tenure as assistant superintendent of Washington's colored schools almost from the beginning. In 1909 a group of parents petitioned the Board of Education to remove him from office. Two years later, the three black members of the board spoke out strongly against his reappointment, but the white majority voted for Bruce. In 1912 he again alienated a sizable segment of Washington's aristocracy of color by dismissing W. Bruce Evans as principal of Armstrong Manual Training School for "insufficient academic and pedagogic equipment." Evans, who was Daniel Murray's brother-in-law and had powerful connections in the District, sued Bruce and the school board to be reinstated.[2]

The almost annual fights on Bruce's reappointment usually involved charges of favoritism, illegal promotions and demotions, and dictatorial methods. Some of the opposition, especially among upper-class blacks, resulted from his cordial relationship with Booker T. Washington and the perception that Bruce desired to emphasize industrial education in his curriculum. By 1915 the *Washington Bee* characterized him as "the most despised man in the city." Despite the growing opposition among blacks, however, he remained in good standing with the white majority of the Board of Education.[3]

The last six years of his tenure, from 1915 to 1921, were especially tumultuous. In April 1915, Bruce, his secretary, and three teachers—Miss Jessie Wormley, Mrs. Marion Wormley Lewis, and Mrs. Wormley Anderson—were en route to Baltimore in his Cadillac when they were involved in an accident. Bruce suffered a serious concussion and was incapacitated for several months. The accident prompted much "unfavorable gossip" and intimations of "excessive hilarity among a party of joy riders." Rumors spread to the effect that the District of Columbia chapter of the NAACP had split over whether to support Bruce "in his troubles." As earlier, a Parents' League was organized to protest Bruce's reappointment, but to no avail. In 1919 the "joy riding" incident resurfaced when Bruce was the target of a much more serious charge.[4]

Upon the recommendation of the Dutch embassy, the white superintendent of District schools granted Herman Moens permission to photograph some black schoolchildren in order to secure comparative anthropological data. Bruce directed Charlotte Hunter, a black teacher, to assist with the photographing. The Parents' League, claiming a membership of thousands, insisted that Moens had taken advantage of innocent children to obtain obscene photographs. Moens was arrested in July 1919 and charged with possessing indecent photographs. The Moens affair was the source of numerous rumors about Bruce's "moral delinquencies." The *Washington Bee,* claiming that Moens had been lionized by the social elite, cited the affair as an example of the decadence of the "upper tens." Despite pressure from the Parents' League, a majority of the Board of Education, including Coralie Cook, a black member and a close friend of Bruce's mother, labeled the charges against Bruce as unsubstantiated and false.[5] Nevertheless, his effectiveness was at an end. Some members of the old elite families who had long been intimate with Bruce's family were among his most persistent critics. In 1921, after years of strife, Bruce finally resigned under pressure.

Bruce accepted an offer to organize and serve as principal of a Negro high school in Kendall, West Virginia, a small town located in the heart of coalmining country. The county superintendent of public schools there, R. C. Cook, was also a Harvard graduate and had learned of Bruce through professors at Cambridge who had known both men as students. Cook considered Bruce "one of the strongest Negro educators in the entire country" and was delighted to secure his services in organizing what was known as the Brown's Creek District High School. Although the position was scarcely a choice one, Bruce accepted it for lack of any other employment.[6]

When Bruce moved to Kendall, he left his mother, wife, and three children at Kelso Farm, the family's summer home outside the District of Columbia in Maryland. He hesitated to relocate his family in a "place so far away from everybody and everything." Notwithstanding that the residents of Kendall, black and white, treated Bruce with consideration and even deference, he found the people and the environment strange and uncongenial. His first difficulty was in finding a place to live that was consistent with his "personal and official *dignity.*" For Bruce, few blacks in the small West Virginia town could be classified as "enlightened people," and even fewer bore resemblance to his friends in Washington.[7] After a few months in Kendall, Bruce wrote his mother: "But Mama, dear, I do not want you and Caree [his wife] and dear little Woogs [his son, Burrill] to be mixed up in this Negro society of the coal mines. It would be exceedingly humiliating to me. Of course, they'd act as nicely as they know how; but, O, the devilishness of their lives. I'm a man and it hurts my sensibilities daily and hourly. How could you folks stand it? T'would be almost impossible. The only way you can get a friend to talk with who'd understand your language would be to take the train and go a thousand miles. That's a fact."[8] While Bruce expressed relief at being far away from what he called the "nigger mess" over the Washington schools, he nonetheless experienced a growing sense of loneliness and frustration in Kendall. He not only missed his family but also longed to regain a position that gave him the power and influence that he had enjoyed in "the Athens of colored America."[9] His bitterness toward his "so-called friends" in Washington, whom he felt had manipulated and betrayed him, became more intense with time. Compounding his problems was the deterioration of his financial condition, which forced him to rely increasingly on his mother's resources.[10]

Clearly, Bruce never intended to remain for long in the small West Virginia community. In fact, he was scarcely settled into his new position when he wrote a friend that he intended to become a lawyer and open his practice by July 1924. He ordered law books and began a systematic program of reading that would help him in law school; his plans were to enter the law school at the University of Chicago, where he had been accepted for admission for the fall term of 1923.[11] Despite his plans to enter law school, Bruce sought in vain to win a more attractive position in education early in 1922, presumably by the opening of the fall term. His most likely prospect was a faculty position at Lincoln University in Jefferson City, Missouri, a town far preferable to Kendall, where the soot was "external, internal and eternal." Even with the influence exerted in his behalf by Congressman L. C. Dyer, Bruce failed to get the Lincoln University post, so he was condemned to another term in the West Virginia coal-mining town.[12] Some time before the opening of the 1922 school year, his mother, wife, and children joined him there. But even before their arrival an event occurred that Bruce considered nothing less than a family catastrophe.

On August 29, 1922 Bruce's daughter Clara Josephine secretly married Barrington Guy, a singer and actor. Both of them were only eighteen years old. They eloped to Rockville, Maryland, where they were married by a justice of the peace after falsifying their ages and names. Roscoe Bruce was outraged at his daughter for bringing such disgrace to the family's good name. Convinced that the elopement of a teenage couple was illegal as well as inconsistent with behavior expected of those of his social class, he attempted without success to have the marriage annulled. His objection was not so much to the husband, who was a member of an old Washington family, but to what he regarded as the immaturity of his daughter and Guy. He wrote Guy's father that the Bruce family considered "a university education" an essential prerequisite to marriage.[13]

Barrington Guy, who was later described as a "brilliant baritone, talented legitimate actor and ballet dancer," was a strikingly handsome man with a fair complexion. He was the son of Nathaniel Guy, an instructor in drama and "one of the greatest Negro Shakespearean actors" of his day, and Louise Antoinette Guy, a shrewd businesswoman of Italian descent. The younger Guy did well in vaudeville until theatre owners discovered he was a Negro. "I never tried to pass," he remarked in 1939: "Folks thought I was white and I didn't enlighten them." But two years later, Guy changed his stage name to Barrington Shamar and claimed that his father "came from India." Despite Roscoe Bruce's anger at their elopement, Clara and Barrington Guy apparently had a long and happy life. Their marriage produced two sons, Barrington, Jr. (born 1928), and Bruce (born 1934).[14]

The Bruces had scarcely recovered from the trauma of Clara's secret marriage, when Josephine Bruce died in Kendall, West Virginia, in February 1923. Her death left an enormous void in the life of her son, for whom she had been a source of strength and inspiration. Bruce made no important decisions without first consulting her, and he rarely failed to follow her advice. Although Josephine Bruce had given generously of her own financial resources so that her son's family could live in a style she considered appropriate, she still left a sizable estate, which enabled her grandchildren to attend college.[15]

Bruce decided not to return to the Brown's Creek District High School in the fall of 1923 even though he had been unable to get another, more prestigious position. Instead of pursuing a career in law himself, his wife, Clara, entered law school, while he returned to Kelso Farm and started a poultry operation. His wife and children settled in Cambridge, Massachusetts, where Clara entered Boston University School of Law and their youngest child, Burrill, enrolled in the public schools of the city. Clara Bruce won the Robinson Prize for academic excellence and served as editor-in-chief of the *Boston University Law Review* in her senior year. She passed the Massachusetts bar examination in 1926 and claimed "to be the second Negro woman to do so."[16]

In the mid-1920s the Bruces suffered serious financial reverses. The cause of these reverses is unclear, but by the time Clara Bruce graduated from law school, the family was in straitened circumstances. Bruce moved to New York in 1925 and became head of the Phillis Wheatley Publishing Company, whose main business apparently was the compilation and publication of *Who's Who in Colored America*. His editorial board included an impressive list of well-known Afro-Americans, such as W. E. B. Du Bois and Mary McCleod Bethune. "The career of no person will be treated in this book," Bruce declared, "unless the fact of his Negro descent is clearly demonstrated." He also made a point of announcing that the name of Marcus Garvey would not be included because "no one had recommended it."[17]

Bruce did not oversee the completion of the volume but instead became resident manager of the Paul Laurence Dunbar Apartments in 1927. Financed by John D. Rockefeller, Jr., and designed to aid in solving the housing crisis in Harlem, the Dunbar complex consisted of six apartment houses located on more than five acres and surrounded by parks, gardens, and playgrounds. A philanthropic project intended to "help the Negro help himself," the Dunbar Apartments were rented on a cooperative basis with the aim of eventually having tenants own their apartments. As "one of the best known Negroes in the United States" and the Harvard-educated son of a United States senator, Bruce as manager lent substantial prestige to the project. For Bruce the job provided an annual income of $12,000; Clara served as his assistant. Bruce took great pride in this model of the "new philanthropy" and let it be known that "the sporting fraternity, the daughters of joy and the criminal element" would not be tolerated in his Dunbar complex. He personally screened and interviewed each prospective resident. Throughout his tenure in the Dunbar project Bruce served on the board of directors of the Dunbar National Bank, a Rockefeller-backed bank located in the complex. During his ten years as resident manager of the Dunbar, Bruce achieved considerable distinction as an expert in urban housing and served as consultant on projects built elsewhere.[18]

Despite its auspicious beginning, Harlem's "adventure in community building" for blacks proved to be a disappointment. The project accumulated a large deficit and suffered increasing competition from New Deal housing projects constructed in New York in the 1930s. Finally, late in 1936 John D. Rockefeller foreclosed on the Dunbar Apartments. In January 1937, following a reorganization of the project, Bruce was removed as manager. When his hopes of heading a New Deal housing project in New York failed to materialize, he organized his own real estate company, Bruce Realty and Associates, which in time managed various New York apartment houses "occupied by colored tenants."[19]

Throughout his career in New York, Bruce and his wife engaged in a variety of civic and uplift activities. As manager of the Dunbar Apartments, he edited the *Dunbar News*, a biweekly journal on economic cooperation. He belonged to several local and national organizations concerned with housing. In addition to his activities in the NAACP, he was a loyal supporter of the Association for the Study of Negro Life and History. In Harlem he was an organizer of the Citizens Committee on More and Better Jobs. Largely as a result of his persistent efforts, "many newspapers and magazines treated the word Negro as a proper noun or adjective, printing it with a capital letter." Clara Bruce, all the while, was active in the New York League of Women Voters, the Welfare Council of New York City, and the Municipal Affairs Commission. She occasionally published poetry in magazines such as *Crisis* and *The Saturday Evening Post*.[20]

Both Roscoe and Clara Bruce showed a deep interest in the education of their children. Their two sons attended Harvard, their father's alma mater. The elder, Roscoe, Jr., prepared for college at Phillips Exeter Academy. Despite the public controversy in 1923 between his father and President A. Lawrence Lowell about reserving a room in a dormitory, he entered Harvard College in 1926 and remained for two years. He graduated from the City College of New York, where he was elected to Phi Beta Kappa. After studying medicine for a time at the Sorbonne in Paris, he returned to the United States, married Bessie Humbles, a member of an old and well-known Lynchburg, Virginia family, and served his apprenticeship in housing management under his father at Dunbar Apartments. In 1935 he became manager of the Richard B. Harrison Apartments, a low-cost housing project in Newark, New Jersey, financed by the Prudential Life Insurance Company.[21]

Early in April 1937, less than three months after his father had been removed as manager of the Dunbar, Roscoe, Jr., became involved in an affair that humiliated his proud parents. As early as the previous November, a bookkeeper had discovered shortages in the account of the Harrison Apartments. Bruce failed to report them to the Prudential Insurance Company, apparently for fear of being accused of theft. On April 3, 1937, according to press accounts, he was robbed of apartment rental receipts. An investigation by the Newark police resulted in Bruce's being charged with masterminding a "fake hold-up" to camouflage a shortage in receipts of almost $2,000.[22] The Bruces used their considerable influence to secure a mild sentence from the presiding judge, Daniel Brennan. According to newspaper reports, virtually everyone expected Bruce to avoid imprisonment and be placed on probation.[23] But the sentence proved to be a distinct surprise: "You are suffering from the self-delusion that you are not guilty," Judge Brennan said to Bruce; "Because of your background and training, I am giving you eighteen months [in the penitentiary]."[24]

The trial made front-page news in the black press under such headlines as "18 Months in Penitentiary for Harvard Man" and "Harvard to Hoosegow." Described as the "scion of an illustrious family" and as the Harvard-educated grandson of a United States senator, Bruce was reported at one point of being on the verge of suicide and at another of being estranged from his wife.[25] Despite the family's original intention to pursue the "seemingly hopeless battle to free young Bruce," no appeal of the case was instituted and he began serving his prison sentence. Assigned to the "rockpile," he developed large calluses on his hands and lost over fifteen pounds within a few weeks; the *New York Amsterdam News* reported that Bruce's "Harvardian accent" had disappeared and that his spirit was broken.[26]

After his release from prison, Bruce returned to France, presumably to continue his medical studies, but he did not secure a degree. Divorced from his first wife, he married Jacqueline Marie Therese Moison and returned to New

York, where he entered the mercantile business. He died in 1966, survived by his wife and two daughters.[27] Not even the *Amsterdam News,* which had lavished so much attention on his trial and imprisonment, printed a notice of his death.

The second Bruce son, Burrill Kelso, graduated from Harvard Law School in 1936 and practiced law in New York until his death, in 1978. The Bruce's daughter, Clara Josephine, graduated from Dunbar High School in Washington in 1921, spent a year at Howard University, and enrolled at Radcliffe College, her mother's alma mater, in 1923. She attended Radcliffe under her maiden name, and college officials never knew that she was at the time married to Barrington Guy. Because of the family's financial condition she did not return to Radcliffe for her senior year in 1926–1927.[28] Sometime after the 1940s, Clara Bruce Guy and her husband seem to have disappeared from the black community.

Despite a decline in Roscoe and Clara Bruce's financial status, they managed to send their children to colleges and universities of the highest quality. The family name was sufficient to admit them to the "best circles" of black society. That they were the son, daughter-in-law, and grandchildren of a United States senator bestowed upon them a substantial measure of prestige in the black community. As a character in Gertrude Sanborn's 1923 novel remarked of his own family, the second and third generation of Bruces were "aristocrats under the veil— . . . worthy men and women caught by a mad fate in a prison built of prejudice!"[29]

Even though they were well educated and eminently respectable, Roscoe and Clara Bruce encountered the strictures placed on all people of the race with which they were identified. Roscoe Bruce came of age just as blacks in America confronted a rising tide of racial violence and Jim Crow laws. Such an atmosphere thwarted the hopes of and commitment to racial progress through assimilation into American white culture that had characterized his parents and others of their generation and class. Although Roscoe Bruce shared the commitment of his parents, his choices were severely limited, despite his background and Harvard degree. As an educator he was restricted to black institutions, first at Tuskegee Institute and then as head of Washington's separate school system. In New York he managed a black apartment complex built by a white philanthropist and became a real estate broker whose clientele was all black. Although Bruce never completely abandoned his dream of an integrated society and culture and certainly never lost the style and tastes of an aristocrat of color, his encounters with white prejudice forced a closer identity with blacks. While he believed that culture rather than race was the "basis of sound nationality," he was by 1923 unwilling to deny "his blood or tradition."[30]

12

◆

Into the 1920s

D<small>URING THE HALF CENTURY FOLLOWING</small> the end of the Civil War, a combination of developments, including rapid industrialization and urbanization, an enormous influx of European immigrants, and vast technological changes, dramatically altered American life and profoundly affected traditional class arrangements in white society. The crop of newly minted millionaires produced by the industrial revolution posed serious challenges to the old elite, whose claims to primacy rested on ancestry, culture, and continuity as much as on wealth. In many instances fashionable society came to mean something other than polite society. In New York, the relatively modest, unpublicized social life of the old families who dominated the Academy of Music and demonstrated a sense of *noblesse oblige* gave way to the conspicuous consumption and lavish, much-publicized social affairs of the new rich. "Plutocracy," according to one authority, "triumphed over aristocracy in New York's high society, thus opening it to the newly risen, denying it the refinement of ancient status [and] making it uncertain of traditions and prerogatives. . . ."[1]

Although the impact of the changes in American society between 1880 and 1920 on blacks and whites was by no means identical, it nonetheless had a significant effect on Afro-Americans. The era witnessed the emergence of a more virulent expression of racism, which became institutionalized in the South in a maze of laws and ordinances designed to keep the Negro "in his place," while the rest of the country achieved similar ends through less formal, extralegal practices. At the same time the "great migration" of blacks out of the South, especially after the turn of the century, meant that the black population of cities in the North, Midwest, and even far West increased dramatically. Blacks who had lived in these cities, often for generations, and had carved out privileged places for themselves resented the influx of southern migrants, whom they blamed for the spread of anti-Negro prejudice among whites. Convinced that the uncouth, loud, and unkempt "riff-raff" from the black belt of the South flowing into Philadelphia, Boston, Chicago, and other cities was responsible for the erection of racial barriers which had not existed previously, the old residents withdrew into exclusive organizations in an effort to place distance between themselves and the new arrivals "who happened to have some ancestors of the same race."[2] While many of the newcomers did exhibit unacceptable conduct and customs, some possessed the family background, education, and attributes of gentility that gained them admission into the best society. The "old families" might accommodate such people but only after careful screening to ensure that they were of "co-equal" status.

In addition to the massive shift in the black population accelerated by the First World War, there were other developments that significantly affected class relationships in the black community. The discrimination encountered by black soldiers during the war and the outbreak of race riots in East St. Louis, Washington, Chicago, and elsewhere in 1917 and 1919, coupled with the emergence of a revived Ku Klux Klan, encouraged blacks of all classes to close ranks. It became increasingly apparent that the assimilation of any group of Afro-Americans into the larger society was an unrealistic expectation and drove home, for a time at least, the truth of the oft-repeated warning that any attempt by the black elite to "draw off from the masses" was folly. Voicing a theme that appeared frequently in the black press, the Indianapolis *Freeman* in 1900 had observed that while Negroes were not all alike, every black person, regardless of education, complexion, and wealth, would "stand charged to some degree with every crime committed by Negroes everywhere."[3] The closing of ranks by blacks of all classes, while significant, proved to be less than permanent. In Washington, for example, the old upper class families, or "cave dwellers," weary of making common cause with those below them on the social scale, had by the middle of the 1920s "washed their hands of every group but their own."[4]

By the 1920s a new economic elite had emerged in urban black communities and posed a serious threat to the place traditionally occupied by the old upper class in the black social structure. While the wealth of this new elite was relatively small compared with the great fortunes amassed by whites in industry, railroads, and banking in the late nineteenth and early twentieth centuries, they did not escape the spirit of acquisitiveness that characterized the age. Booker T. Washington's message was, in a sense, a black version of the gospel of wealth because of the priority it placed on the accumulation of property. For those who subscribed to the Tuskegee ideology, wealth became an increasingly significant criterion for determining one's place on the social scale. This is not to suggest that the old elite, those who made up what was known as the colored aristocracy, disparaged the possession of wealth. Indeed, their style of living, the educational opportunities provided their children, and the leisure enjoyed by such families suggested a degree of wealth unknown to the vast majority of blacks. Their objection was not to wealth *per se*, but rather to attempts to equate money with high social standing without regard for ancestry, culture, and continuity. The new black economic elite, unlike the old upper class, whose occupations brought it into frequent contact with upper-class whites, was tied almost exclusively to the black ghetto and less concerned about assimilation into the larger society. Increasingly, the new elite challenged the primacy of the old in ways that resembled the competition in white society between the "old Knickerbocker set" of New York and the "old Philadelphians" on the one hand and the new rich on the other. Black businessmen and professionals, who possessed money or prestige or both, pressed for admission to the highest social stratum which was traditionally dominated by the "old families." While the aristocracy of color had never been a closed circle admissible only by birthright, blacks with "naught but wealth" still found entry into its ranks difficult. Adjustments were made to include those of the new rich who, though lacking proper family credentials, had talent and education and who practiced the genteel performance. Those excluded for one reason or another from the charmed circle came in time to constitute a parallel elite whose penchant for conspicuous consumption and publicized social affairs was not unlike that of its counterparts in white society.

Among these was Sarah Breedlove Walker, better known as Madame C. J. Walker, a poor black woman from Louisiana who married at fourteen and was widowed five years later. Beginning with a process for "dekinking" hair, she eventually expanded her enterprise to include the manufacture of various beauty products for blacks. In time she amassed a large fortune, acquired several elaborate homes, including a cream-colored mansion built in 1917 at Irvington-on-the-Hudson, and entertained lavishly. Among her frequent guests were Booker T. Washington, Marcus Garvey, and other well-known blacks. After acquiring wealth, she employed a tutor to teach her "to speak well." She also learned to draw "social lines as closely as any white society leader ever essayed to do." Although Madame Walker lacked both education and distinguished ancestry, the sheer size of her fortune enabled her, in the words of an observer, to become "one of the first 'outsiders' to break into black society." Her daughter, A'Lelia, owned a townhouse in New York known as the Dark Tower, which was a gathering place for the literati of the Harlem Renaissance. A'Lelia spent money recklessly and wore extravagant gowns and exotic turbans. More than 1,500 guests crowded into St. Philip's Episcopal Church for the so-called million-dollar wedding of A'Lelia's daughter. Such ostentatious displays, according to one observer, "caused the securely familied folk to frown."[5]

For all their wealth, lavish entertainment, and attention from the press, Madame Walker and her family were scarcely a part of what the old upper class called "real society." In writing about black New York in 1925, George S. Schuyler claimed that "society here is not based on money, but on culture, refinement and sophistication." Langston Hughes might prefer Seventh Avenue in Washington or Lenox Avenue in Harlem, where people were less class-conscious and manifested little interest in family background, but many of those whose ancestry resembled his still found uncongenial the people represented by references to these neighborhoods. Schuyler heard upper-class black women in New York boast that "they never go on Lenox Avenue," which they viewed as the "habitat of the rough proletariat."[6]

By the 1920s the new black elite had come of age, eclipsing, at least in the public view, the "old families," who still thought of themselves as "aristocrats." The "upstart nobodies" were, according to a member of an old upper-class family in Chicago, "people struggling to get where we were born."[7] Commenting in 1957 on the death of the genteel tradition among blacks, in his controversial *Black Bourgeoisie*, the sociologist E. Franklin Frazier conceded that the "ascendency of the 'gentleman' was not completely undermined until the mass migrations of Negroes to cities and the resulting occupational differentiation of the Negro population." Frazier was imprecise about time and suggested that the tradition of the gentleman ceased having influence in the black community "during a decade or so following the first World War."[8]

By the 1920s the black aristocracy was scarcely the same that had existed twenty years earlier. The rising tide of racism and the fading of hopes for an integrated society, as well as the decline in the economic base of the old upper class, eroded the prestige and influence of a group that had nurtured ties with whites and advocated assimilation into the larger society. The ranks of the old guard, who had displayed pride in family tradition and been most insistent on drawing the line against what they considered the vulgar and uncouth, had been depleted by death. The decade beginning around 1912 witnessed the passing from the scene of a host of those who for a generation had been conspicuous members of the aristocracy of color. This generational changeover did not go unnoticed within the ranks of the "upper tens." Writing to his friend George A. Myers in 1914, upon receiving word of James Lewis's death, Robert H. Terrell remarked: "All of that old crowd just beyond you and me are falling away. It is sad to contemplate, yet they ran their race and fought a good struggle."[9] Some died childless; the family names of others who had only daughters disappeared. In the case of Pinchback, his sons, who failed to live up to his high expectations, had no male offspring; and his twice-married daughter, Nina, had one child, Jean Toomer, who achieved literary fame. But descendants of "old families" such as the Cooks, Mintons, Francises, and Syphaxes perpetuated both the family name and the lofty status identified with it.

Some of the genteel families, as Frazier claimed, chose not to compete with the new economic elite and instead preserved their traditions in splendid isolation from the black community. Others, especially members of the younger generation of the "old families," came to terms with the new economic elite without completely abandoning the legacies bequeathed by their forebears. Among them were the children of those who had been engaged in what had formerly been viewed as high-status occupations for blacks, such as catering, barbering, and tailoring. By becoming physicians, educators, attorneys, and other professionals, these children perpetuated and often enhanced the prestige of their family names. They were less sanguine than their ancestors about the possibility of assimilation into white society and employed less restrictive criteria for determining those of "co-equal" status. They nonetheless continued the tradition of service and leadership in behalf of racial progress. Their role as cultural brokers between the black and white worlds underwent transition, shifting from an emphasis on assimilation to an emphasis on black culture and a closer identity with the black masses.

As early as 1910, observers of the black social scene in Washington had noted the emergence of an "educational set," which existed alongside those of the upper stratum known as the "government official set." The latter had traditionally been the social arbiters of the city's black community. But as one commentator noted, "the government official set, quickly recognizing the intellectuality and culture of the educational set, not only welcomed them but accorded them such a division of the social spoils as to leave little cause for complaint." By the second decade of the twentieth century, the two had in many instances become "bound together by blood relation," because in Washington, as in other cities, "the impetuosity of the young lovers disregards social barriers." Although both "sets," civil servants and those identified with Howard University and the separate colored school system, were relatively affluent, wealth alone did not insure admission to either. One might be "poor in worldly goods" and still belong to the upper stratum of society if one possessed "some special qualities," such as proper family credentials, education, and an appreciation for the "genteel performance."[10]

Older members of the aristocracy of color on occasion expressed regret and even bitterness at what they perceived as efforts by vulgar interlopers and adventurers to usurp the place they had traditionally held at the pinnacle of black social life. In 1914, when a British journalist, Anita Westlake, included in her investigation of Washington's social scene a "side glance at colored society," she quickly became aware of the disdain that the "dowagers" of black society exhibited toward changes taking place in what was considered the "best society." Among those whom Westlake interviewed was the eighty-year-old widow of John Mercer Langston, who still lived at Hillside Cottage, near Howard University, and whose annual reception still signaled the opening of the social season among aristocrats of color in the nation's capital. The Langston home remained a retreat for "the best in Washington society who love the dear old lady and who love to swap reminiscences of the days when it required a real introduction buttressed by a pedigree to break through the stiff upper crust of colored society in Washington." "But alas those days are gone," Westlake was informed, "and Washington's colored society in the second decade of the twentieth century bore little resemblance to that existing a quarter of a century earlier."

When Westlake inquired about the causes of the deterioration, one elderly matron replied, "schools and automobiles." It became clear in the course of her explanation that what she meant was that college degrees and money had become the principal prerequisites for admission into the "best society." In her view, the disregard of family pedigree and good breeding represented a catastrophic lowering of standards, so that "society" had become "a conglomeration into which enters good, bad or indifferent upon an equality—a bizarre alignment of the fit and unfit." Fashionable society by 1914, in the opinion of Caroline Langston's generation, had become something quite different from polite society.[11]

The eclipse of the old upper class was neither as sudden nor as complete as some observers suggested. The rate and degree of change that occurred in its influence and composition differed from place to place. In the older cities of the East, its eclipse appeared to occur more slowly than in the newer cities of the Midwest and West, where those known as "the black 400" had always been fewer in number, less well entrenched, and more inclined to attach greater importance to wealth than to ancestry and good breeding. Washington continued to hold its place as the capital of the "colored aristocracy" until well after the First World War, but even there the old upper class underwent modification. The older generation of the aristocracy of color in the nation's capital, as elsewhere, equated change with an erosion of standards and cherished virtues.[12]

The increasing number of black physicians, lawyers, and other professionals as well as certain well-to-do entrepreneurs whose education and income conferred high status served to expand the ranks of the upper class. The upper-class came to consist of two strata or components: the "old families," at least in their own view, occupied the top rung, and the "newcomers" the one just below it.[13] Although aristocrats of color generally engaged in endogamous marriages, they occasionally married members of the new educational or economic elites, provided the latter exhibited evidences of good breeding and "respectability" as well as high standing in their profession or occupation. For the professional without a distinguished family background, marriage into one of the prestigious old families often provided the missing ingredient for admission into the aristocracy of color.

According to the historian of Washington's black community, the phenomenon of "passing" in that city substantially increased after the First World War, and light-complexioned people of the upper class were frequently involved in it. "Passing" apparently became so common in the 1920s that one theatre in Washington employed "a black doorman to spot and bounce intruders whose racial origins were undetectable by whites." If passing for white permanently as opposed to part-time, or convenience, passing to avoid the strictures of Jim Crow was as widespread as some claimed, it obviously did disrupt the solidarity and deplete the ranks "of the top level of Washington's colored world."[14] While passing undoubtedly had an impact on the composition of the traditional aristocracy, it is virtually impossible to determine the extent of it because of the secretive nature of the whole phenomenon.

Notwithstanding the fragile foundations upon which it rested and the dilution that it experienced, the aristocracy of color that matured in the decades following Reconstruction proved to be remarkably resilient. That it continued to be the subject of so much discussion and criticism suggests that while its influence may have diminished, it had by no means disappeared. Much of the criticism of the old upper class in the 1920s and afterward bore a striking resemblance to that expressed throughout the previous forty years. Critics continued to accuse black aristocrats of being snobbish, aloof, and disdainful of those beneath them on the social scale; they poked fun at their emphasis on ancestry and expressed outrage at their alleged color consciousness.

Among the severest critics of the black aristocracy was the poet Langston Hughes, great-nephew of John Mercer Langston, who first achieved fame during the Harlem Renaissance. He lived for a time with the "more intellectual and high class branch" of his family in Washington's Le Droit Park, where he observed the city's "Negro society" at close range. Writing in 1927 in *Opportunity*, the Urban League's publication, Hughes condemned Washington's "black 400" in a vein worthy of John E. Bruce or Calvin Chase earlier. Even as a child in Kansas, Hughes had heard of Washington's "colored society," which was reputed to be "the finest in the country, the richest, the most cultured, the most worthy." Once among the "best people" of the nation's capital, he found that they did indeed exhibit grand manners, speak "frightfully correct English," and boast of distinguished ancestry, but he found their culture superficial, their conversation intellectually sterile, and their concern for the tangible evidences of wealth, such as automobiles and fur coats, obsessive. Their adherence to ideals that were "most Nordic and un-Negro," indicated to him that they were "moving away from the masses . . . rather than holding an identity with them." Hughes was repelled by their insistence on drawing "rigid class and color lines within the race against Negroes who worked with their hands or who were dark in complexion and had no degrees from college." To escape the pretensions of this "unbearable and snobbish" group, he fled to Washington's Seventh Street, which was frequented by "ordinary Negroes . . . with practically no family tree at all" and who drew no color line between those of lighter and darker hues. For Hughes, the folk culture of the black masses was infinitely preferable and richer than the superficial culture of the city's aristocrats of color. Conceding that he may have been prejudiced or that his values, rather than those of the black aristocracy, were awry, he nonetheless was happy to get to Harlem, "where people are not quite so ostentatiously proud of themselves, and where one's family background is not of such great concern."[15]

Such a critique of "black society" was by no means limited in the 1920s to that found in Washington. In 1927–1928 A. H. Maloney, a black Episcopal minister in Indianapolis, contributed a series of articles to a black weekly on the history of blacks in that city. He devoted a lengthy piece to the "absurdities of an aristocracy." Convinced that social distinctions in general within a democracy were "out of place," Maloney argued that they were especially absurd among blacks who were less than three-quarters of a century away from slavery. Nevertheless, he admitted, there did exist in Indianapolis a group which claimed membership in an aristocracy. The characteristics that he noted among the elite of the city were, in many respects, similar to those that Langston Hughes found in Washington: snobbery, pretentiousness, preoccupation with light skin color and fine clothes, "lust for luxury," and intellectual superficiality. In Maloney's view, the gatherings of Indianapolis's elite were "barbaric carica-tures" because "the butler, the chauffeur, the professor [and] the doctor finds himself promiscuously thrown together with the fellow fresh from the coal yard, the hod, the pig-joint counter and the cabaret." Unlike Hughes's critique, however, Maloney's made no reference to ancestry and education and accused the elite of immorality and "refined debauchery."[16]

Late in the 1920s a black South Carolinian, Asa H. Gordon, claimed that while a "growing group consciousness" was evident among blacks throughout his state, even in Charleston, there were still "many Negroes . . . who believe in the principles of aristocracy." Their dissatisfaction with the existing "arrangement" in the South was not rooted in a belief in democracy or equality but in their conviction that the prevailing caste system failed "to recognize all the aristo-crats, especially themselves, who are due special considerations suitable to their proper 'station in life' and their extraordinary inherited talents." Such "aristo-cratic" blacks were for the most part descendants of antebellum free people of color who, in Kelly Miller's phrase, had "lived in self satisfied complacency in a little world below the whites and above the slaves." According to Gordon, these people still believed firmly "in the value of 'blue blood' " and in the privileges that it presumably conferred. A black native of Charleston returning to the city in 1985 after an absence of twenty-two years observed many changes there but "noted sadly that the class system, even among Blacks, is still intact."[17]

Writing in Scribner's in 1930, Eugene Gordon of the Boston Post attempted to identify the chief attributes of "negro society" in general. He agreed with Hughes that family background continued to be an important stratifier, but since relatively few blacks were able to "boast of family traditions," they often had to invoke "the white man's secondary measurement of social eminence, occupation." Gordon agreed with Maloney that any gathering of the black social elite was likely to present the spectacle of "the barber seated by the bank president." The reason, he argued, that in such gatherings one was likely to find the sheep "rubbing noses with the goats" was that the goat was probably "the big ram's father or brother or some other close relative." Nevertheless, Gordon claimed that Negro society was "becoming more discriminating of those who compose it."[18]

As was often the case with impressionistic observations, such as those by Maloney, Gordon, and Hughes, it was not always clear whether the writers were describing the old-family aristocracy or the new economic elite. All three emphasized the importance of wealth in social stratification in black society and made virtually no reference to the significance of manners, decorum, and the "genteel performance." It would hardly have been surprising in the 1920s, "the dollar decade," for the younger generation of the old upper class to become enamored of money. One's family background might still be important, but as Langston Hughes observed, it scarcely kept "a fellow who's penniless from getting hungry."[19] Even if those who possessed proper ancestry, education, and manners increasingly attached importance to wealth, individuals and families "with naught but wealth" were still not automatically accepted into the upper stratum of black society. But those poor in worldly goods—the "goats" as Gordon called them—continued to be counted among the social elite if they possessed other attributes, especially that of family background.

Despite the criticism and ridicule aimed at the "well-ancestored people" of the old upper class, family name continued to perform a crucial function in determining those at the pinnacle of the class structure. Even descendents of old upper-class families whose educational and income levels were below contemporary standards could rely upon their family name and reputation to accord them a substantial measure of social status. Over the years, the Brown Fellowship Society, Boulé, and other elite organizations had some success in building a tradition of inherited status. Writing about black New Haven in 1940, Robert Warner claimed that the lack of economic continuity from one generation to the next had seriously eroded the position once held by the old families, but he admitted that the "shreds and fragments of aristocracy" still existed, especially in " 'old family' ancestry, in being a 'Yankee' or an 'Old New Havener.' "[20]

In 1929 P. L. Prattis, a close observer of "black society" in Chicago, wrote an essay on the city's black "400," a misleading label, as he suggested, because the ranks of the elite contained considerably fewer than 400 persons. While this special group included individuals and families who had long been a part of Chicago's aristocracy of color, the overwhelming majority were "new blood." In addition to the thousands of poor, untutored blacks who flowed into Chicago during the Great Migration, there were also lawyers, physicians, dentists, affluent entrepreneurs, and others of high social standing. By the late 1920s this "new blood," especially those of "co-equal" rank from elsewhere, had become part of the highest social stratum of the city's black community.

Despite changes in the composition of Chicago's black upper class in the decade after the First World War, Prattis indicated that at least some traditional criteria for admission into it were still operative: He listed first "birth" or ancestry, "the standing of one's family," and the "duration of its residence in the community and its record." Other traditional criteria still used in Chicago in the 1920s were education and culture, especially when one had achieved distinction in his or her "devotion to the cultural arts" or had "made a notable record for scholarship"; and "the cultivation of the social graces." To enter the ranks of the upper tens a person also had to possess "character," which prevented one from "making a common exhibition of one's weakness"; and "achievement," signified by one's status in a profession or success in business. While no one of these factors or even a combination of them was a guarantee of admission to the "peak of Olympus," Prattis pointed out, the failure to possess one or more of them was certain to result in exclusion from the social pinnacle.[21]

Even Langston Hughes, who in the 1920s and later wrote critically of the "best people" in Washington, recognized the significance of family connections. In his autobiography he recalled that he intended his first novel to be about the typical black family in the Midwest, like his own. But he soon discovered that his was not a typical black family: "My grandmother never took in washing or worked in service or went to church much. She lived in Oberlin and spoke perfect English, without a trace of dialect. She looked like an Indian. My mother was a newspaper woman and a stenographer then. My father lived in Mexico City. My granduncle had been a congressman and there were heroic memories of John Brown's raid and the underground railroad in the family storehouse." Hughes was descended from the Clays of Kentucky and "the Indian tribe to which Pocahontas belonged," and his grandfathers were Sheridan Leary, who died in John Brown's raid on Harper's Ferry, and Charles Langston, who achieved political prominence in post–Civil War Kansas. The midwestern branch of the Langston family participated little in "society" because they could not afford it. Nevertheless, their family background and achievement were not without significance. "We were poor—," Hughes admitted, "but different."[22] Hughes's kin and connections within the upper class undoubtedly shared his perception, as did others outside the so-called charmed circle.

Starting with the First World War, the "old families," with their devotion to ancestry, culture, and refinement, were periodically the subjects of obituaries. In its early years Ebony magazine, established in 1945, devoted a good deal of attention to the origins of and changes in the black upper class. The consensus seemed to be that "the old family aristocracy" still prevailed in a few cities, such as Boston, Charleston, and Philadelphia, but that its ranks were thinning and its power as social arbiter waning. Taking its place was a "new crowd" that "zoomed to the top after the depression and during the prosperous war years." By 1949, if the Ebony commentators were correct, "a hefty bank account" and high professional standing were rapidly replacing "the family tree as the measuring rod of society." By the early 1950s the process was presumably complete.[23] During the civil rights revolution of the following decade, topics like the "black aristocracy" and "black blue bloods" declined in popularity. References to them often took the form of critical or even satirical comments reminiscent of those that had periodically appeared during the previous half century.

Washington was still considered a stronghold of the "color-conscious" black upper crust. "The Negroes in Washington," declared a black resident of the city, "had to do their own integrating after 1954."[24] Writing about the District's aristocracy of color in *Look* magazine a decade later, Sidney Hyman did not directly address the color issue but described in some detail the "pride that descendants of the old families" manifested in their distinguished (and often miscegenated) family trees and in their educational achievements. Few could be considered wealthy but most were "in comfortable circumstances." Some lived in ancestral Victorian homes in neighborhoods that had begun to decline, but most resided in what was known as the "Gold Coast" near Rock Creek Park. They socialized together in a few, highly selective organizations that resembled the Monocan and Mu-So-Lit clubs of their ancestors. References to the descendants of the "old families" being "restrained in manner" indicated the degree to which they perpetuated the emphasis on the "genteel performance." Hyman claimed that the traditional role of the black elite in serving as "a bridge between the white community and the submerged Negroes" was in the process of undergoing significant change in the wake of desegregation. While their activities helped blacks as individuals, their children took a more militant position by demanding the elimination of "barriers that stand in the way of Negroes as a group." Whether or not the descendants of Washington's "old families" provided adequate leadership in meeting the needs of the "submerged Negro" was all the more important, in Hyman's view, because theirs still served "as a model for many other urban communities."[25]

One of the most perceptive analyses of the state of the old upper class during the 1960s appeared in a treatment of the "Black Establishment" by Lerone Bennett, a historian and astute observer of black America. "For many years," he noted, "the elite of family, education, property and, yes, color, was, in part, an interlocked directorate of several large families tied together by marriage and a larger group who stood candidacy for power—and marriage." Linked by formal and informal ties, the members of the black establishment were the lineal descendants of favored slaves, free people of color, and the "black Puritan class," which placed a premium on respectability, responsibility, and what were called the middle-class values of thrift, sobriety, and steadiness. Though basically conservative themselves, the members of the old upper class "tilled the ground and prepared the way" for the civil rights revolution of the 1960s. Their common educational, cultural, and familial background, coupled with an access to institutionalized power, produced leaders with a "rather aristocratic and not altogether realistic concept of noblesse oblige." They were, in Bennett's view, leaders who "felt they were responsible for the masses and discharged that responsibility at a safe distance." Despite a long history of "in group mating and a certain snobbishness based on status and color," Bennett noted, the black establishment had never been entirely closed to talent, especially if it were backed by "money and/or organization and if possible respectability." While Bennett detected evidence that the establishment was "losing some of its caste and color flavor," it had by no means ceased to exert influence. He reminded his readers, lest the upheaval of the Negro Revolution mislead them in assessing the resiliency of the old upper class, that it had successfully weathered a number of previous onslaughts, including Marcus Garvey in the 1920s, "black Lenins" in the 1930s, and A. Philip Randolph in the 1940s.[26]

In the bicentennial year of 1976, Geraldyn Hodges Major, who was in her eighty-second year, produced a large and lavishly illustrated volume chronicling "Black Society" in the United States for two centuries. Having been society editor for several black publications, Major decided to write her history in order "to set the record straight." She had been part of that "society" for eight decades, and her ancestors had also "lived it." From the vantage point of the mid-1970s, she claimed that black "society" had undergone "a virtual revolution" in which the "miscegenated family tree" had been "supplanted by stocks, bonds, bank accounts, real estate and/or high professional standing as a standard for acceptance." In her opinion the "blue-veined" elite, which for generations had constituted the upper crust of black social structure, had been replaced by those of high financial and professional standing who proclaimed their black identity proudly. Descendants of the old ruling families no longer displayed interest in perpetuating the carefully structured arrangement of their forebears and even went "far afield in mate selection." She was not willing to admit that the "old family" elite no longer exercised any influence. "The doors to the clubhouse," she concluded, "while not wide open, are at least ajar."[27] At one time or another, in the first three-quarters of a century after 1900, commentators on the black aristocracy had made similar observations: the door was always at least ajar, never completely closed or open.

For at least a half century, the aristocracy of color that emerged in the post–Civil War era continued to exercise influence in black America. Tracing its origins to free people of color, favored slaves, and other privileged groups in the antebellum era, the postwar aristocracy viewed itself as the product of "the process of natural selection," whose culture, achievement, and sophistication not only entitled its members to positions of leadership but also made them models for other blacks. For more than a generation, they dominated and often monopolized the choicest positions open to blacks in education, politics, government, and business. Aristocrats of color sometimes considered themselves neither black nor white but as "an ambiguous something-between."[28] Reluctant even in the face of hardening racial lines and the triumphant march of Jim Crow to abandon hopes for first-class citizenship and assimilation into American society, they were often in the vanguard of efforts to thwart movements that they believed would perpetuate a segregated society.

Members of the aristocracy of color, especially those of the old elite in the East, had great pride in family background, education, and what was called "respectability," a term that included good breeding, manners, and proper conduct. Enamored of royalty and nobility, as were white Americans of the era, they drew up family trees in which names of African princes, Madagascan noblemen, Caucasian statesmen, and Indian chieftains occupied prominent places. If upper-class blacks, whose physical appearance often made their white inheritance obvious, recognized and expressed pride in white ancestors, they were scarcely less unstinting in their praise of their black forebears, especially those who had been well-to-do free people of color or who had figured prominently in religious and civic affairs, the Underground Railroad, the Abolition movement, and the nation's wars. That they were pioneers in the establishment of organizations dedicated to the study and preservation of the Afro-American past suggested a deep concern for their heritage.

Of no less importance was the striking emphasis that aristocrats of color placed on education. Formal schooling in the liberal arts and in medicine, law, and other professions by the sons and daughters of caterers, barbers, civil servants, and others in occupations that possessed elite status in the black community strengthened their claims to high social standing. Upper-class children often prepared for college at private academies, especially in New England or at well-known public schools, such as Dunbar in Washington, then attended Howard, Fisk, Atlanta, and other elite black institutions or white universities in the North. An indication of the significance of education as a stratifier among blacks was the great social prestige enjoyed by educators at all levels. Although one might lack a distinguished family background, one could compensate for the deficiency by possessing ample educational qualifications and other attributes of upper-class status.

Aristocrats of color often linked education with their quest for respectability and their practice of the genteel performance. Attendance at Howard, Atlanta, Fisk, and certain other elite black institutions not only contributed significantly in shaping and solidifying the upper class but also facilitated the acquisition of a genteel style. Like other Americans, they assumed that proper conduct, manners, and other evidence of good breeding were indicative of one's character. But unlike whites, they believed that the genteel performance would in fact promote racial progress. Convinced that the crudities and vulgarities of the black masses, especially in public places, constituted a major source of prejudice and discrimination against all blacks, they themselves behaved in ways that conformed to the prevailing canons of respectability embraced by the dominant race and encouraged other blacks to follow their example. Yet while aristocrats of color sought to reform the conduct of the masses, they also held that gentility required one to place social distance between oneself and those considered vulgar and crude. Such a conviction translated into actions that isolated the upper class from other blacks and prompted scorn from them.

Neither immune to the strictures of white prejudice imposed on all blacks nor insensitive to the plight of the submerged masses, aristocrats of color figured prominently in a variety of civic, social uplift, and civil rights causes. Although they were sometimes overwhelmed by the magnitude of the problems facing black Americans, they exhibited a sense of mission and took seriously their responsibility for the less fortunate of the race, even if they discharged that responsibility "at a safe distance." They used their access to the white power structure not only to advance their own careers but also to shield the black community from the more blatant forms of white prejudice. To be fair, some of those most critical of the upper class had unrealistic expectations of what it was able to achieve in removing discriminatory barriers and providing greater opportunities for blacks. Nor was the record of the aristocrats as barren of good works as some critics suggested. Because virtually all were "working" aristocrats whose wealth was modest by white standards, they were not able to engage in the kind of philanthropy that was expected of them. Nevertheless, their efforts in establishing schools, hospitals, homes for the aged, settlement houses, protest organizations, and other institutions designed to aid disadvantaged blacks bore a substantial harvest.

The perception of those outside the small black upper class was that it was extraordinarily color conscious, snobbish, and self-serving. Such perceptions, while not without foundation, often suffered from exaggeration and distortion. While the question of color was likely to crop up in almost any black community from time to time, the "blue-vein foolishness" was linked especially with those in Washington, Cleveland, Charleston, and a few other cities. The situation in New Orleans appears to have been considered special or even unique. The color consciousness of the upper class was a persistent theme of certain black editors who contributed significantly to the notion that a fair complexion was the primary or even sole prerequisite for admission to the upper reaches of black society. Most aristocrats of color were in fact light-skinned, but it did not follow that all mulattoes belonged to the upper class. Color alone, without proper family credentials, education, or evidences of good breeding and respectability, did not constitute a passport to the upper stratum of black society. Even if the fair-complexioned elite was as color conscious as its black critics claimed, such a condition would scarcely have been extraordinary. American society was a color-conscious society in which whites equated the color of their skin with superiority and that of Negroes with inferiority. That skin bleaches and hair straighteners found ready markets among blacks outside the upper class suggests the degree to which whites imposed their standards on blacks of all classes.[29]

Blacks who claimed that those of the upper tens were snobbish usually referred to the distance that they placed between themselves and those they considered outside polite society. They confined their social lives to their own group and usually married within the bounds of their class. Intermarriage, in fact, constituted a major strategy for maintaining group cohesion. Theirs was a tightly closed society that outsiders found difficult but not impossible to penetrate, provided they possessed a combination of at least several attributes considered essential by the aristocracy of color. Viewing the race problem from afar, upper-class blacks often assumed a paternalistic, even patronizing, attitude toward the less fortunate of their race.

Critics interpreted such attitudes and actions to mean that upper-class blacks were forever attempting to get away from the race. Some took the argument a step further by asserting that they identified with whites rather than with blacks. The truth is that while members of the black aristocracy were probably as well acquainted with white culture as with black, they identified with each other rather than with either whites or other blacks. It was within the small group at the top of the social structure that there existed a mutuality of values, interests, and views more than between this group and whites or other blacks.

A persistent theme of certain critics was that aristocrats of color constituted a self-serving elite that exploited those whom they viewed with disdain in order to monopolize the few opportunities open to blacks. Implicit in much of the criticism was that the elite formed a mutual-aid society that perpetuated their privileged place within the race. Undoubtedly upper-class blacks like other Americans, white and black, were motivated by self-interest, and they did in fact occupy a large if not disproportionate share of the most prestigious positions within the black community. From their ranks came a sizable contingent of educators, physicians, attorneys, clergymen, and government employees, whose education, income, style of living, and "respectability" separated them from those below them in the social structure. However limited their power may have been, it was far more substantial than that of other blacks. From the perspective of those of the upper class, such an arrangement was entirely appropriate since they represented what W. E. B. Du Bois labeled the Talented Tenth. Despite charges of playing the "race racket" to garner rewards for themselves, aristocrats of color were not unmindful of their responsibility toward the masses. Langston Hughes, who could hardly be classified as an admirer of the black aristocracy, was probably correct when he observed, in 1951, "My guess is that more upper class Negroes are socially and racially conscious of their obligations to the masses than a proportionate number of upper class whites are."[30]

Reflecting upon the social circle he had known as a youth in Washington, Jean Toomer described it as "a natural but transient aristocracy thrown up by the . . . creative conditions of the postwar period." Composed of racially mixed people who possessed "personal refinement, a certain inward culture and beauty [and] a warmth of feeling" that he rarely encountered elsewhere, the Washington "colored aristocracy" was "comfortably fixed financially" and had "a satisfying social life." Above all, according to Toomer, they "were conscious that they were and had something in themselves."[31] Although Washington was perceived as the "mecca of the colored aristocracy," upper-class blacks in Chicago, Philadelphia, and other places were convinced that they were similar. Often related by blood or marriage, aristocrats of color maintained a nationwide network of social and familial relationships, shared similar values and ideals, embraced the same code of conduct, and functioned as "the carriers of white culture into the black world" that contributed significantly to the making of an authentic Afro-American culture.

The aristocracy of color spawned by what Toomer called the creative conditions in the immediate post–Civil War era existed in a society that proclaimed adherence to the ideals of democracy and equality while practicing a racism that contradicted these ideals. As a result, aristocrats of color never possessed the power, prestige, or affluence usually associated with upper classes. No less limited was their ability to ensure the perpetuation of high status to their descendants.

Yet, some families included in the aristocracy of color proved to be remarkably successful in maintaining places at the top of the social structure over several generations. To be sure, Toomer's own family, the Pinchbacks, suffered declining fortunes and, like others, failed to produce sons who perpetuated the family name. But others, like the Wormleys, from the eighteenth century to the present, were conspicuous in the social, civic, and economic life of the black community. Marrying within the confines of their own social class, the Wormleys became linked by marriage to the Mintons of Philadelphia, the Francises of Washington, and the Cheathams of North Carolina. Scarcely less impressive in terms of pedigree and continuity of achievement were two other old families of the District, the Cooks and the Syphaxes. The Cooks, descended from John F. Cook, who was born in 1790, furnished a host of educators and entrepreneurs from the Atlantic to the Pacific and through marriage became linked to the Appos and Abeles of Philadelphia and the Masons of Baltimore. The Syphaxes were no less successful in maintaining transgenerational records of prominence and achievement. Similarly the Revelses, Learys, Evanses, and Murrays, who married into the equally prestigious Perry and Imboden families, produced a succession of leaders in diverse fields. Old families originating among Charleston's well-to-do and often slave-owning free people of color, though often dispersed throughout the United States, continued from one generation to another to perpetuate the high status occupied by their forebears. Such records, by American standards, could scarcely be considered "transient." Although members of these old black upper-class families often refused to lean on the "crutch of illustrious ancestors" and desired to be considered on their merits as individuals, theirs was, in the view of one knowledgeable observer, "a most honorific crutch."[32]

Born within the antebellum period, the aristocracy of color came to distinct self-consciousness during the Reconstruction era and flourished during the forty years that followed, only to have its social supremacy and class cohesion seriously challenged, especially in the years after the First World War. Culturally identified with the white world, the aristocracy shared the biases of middle- and upper-class whites toward family background, education, respectable occupation, and genteel behavior. It flourished at a time when the white world shared a firm consensus on such matters and when the mass of the black population was just entering the first generations of freedom and geographic mobility. Its most serious challenges came, predictably perhaps, in the decades after the turn of the century as the Great Migration got under way and black ghettoes came into existence, as alternative modes of social advancement became possible within the black community, and as the ruling white elite found its consensus eroding on the very values that the aristocracy of color so eagerly emulated. It was scarcely surprising, in view of white society's racism, that the toleration accorded the small group of black aristocrats rapidly diminished as the larger black population became more geographically and economically mobile. One may, indeed, speak of the *pathos* of the aristocrats of color, who operated from a position of weakness and on an erroneous assumption: possessing small numbers and slight wealth and power, they convinced themselves that they could win for the black masses an acceptance and toleration by whites that they incorrectly believed they themselves were coming to enjoy. Beguiled by their self-perceptions and by their self-congratulations, aristocrats of color succumbed to the same trend toward "tribal exclusivity" that attracted so many other Americans in the late nineteenth and early twentieth centuries. Such a trend could and often did have the effect of keeping new talent out of the "talented tenth." "Under the weight of time and human frailty," Emma Jones Lapsansky has observed regarding the evolution of the black elite, "self-appreciation acquired a patina of snobbery; ambition shaded in self-importance; intellectual curiosity could drift into intellectual display."[33] But notwithstanding charges of aloofness from the masses, irresponsibility, and a preoccupation with the frivolous leveled at aristocrats of color, they never in fact abandoned one legacy inherited from their ancestors, namely, the "mission of service" to less fortunate blacks, a legacy that they in turn bequeathed to their descendants. The persistent commitment to racial uplift evidenced by the "old families," generation after generation, has been of significant and enduring value to the larger black community.

Notes

Part I: Origins

Prologue

1. *New York Times*, May 9, 10, 1878; *Washington Post*, June 24, 1878.

2. *Washington Post*, June 24, 1878; Cleveland *Plain Dealer*, June 24, 1878; the Willson family apparently dropped one *l* in its name sometime in the late nineteenth century and thereafter spelled it *Wilson*.

3. Russell Davis, *Black Americans in Cleveland, from George Peake to Carl B. Stokes, 1796–1969* (Washington, D.C.: Associated Publishers, 1972), p. 99. For a sketch of Dr. Joseph Wilson, see obituaries in *Washington Bee*, September 7, 1895, and *Indianapolis News*, August 21, 1895; Helen M. Chesnutt, *Charles Waddell Chesnutt: Pioneer of The Color Line* (Chapel Hill: University of North Carolina Press, 1952), pp. 61–62; *Cleveland Gazette*, October 30, 1886. It is probable that this Joseph Wilson was the author of the small book on the "higher classes of colored society" in Philadelphia, published in 1841; see below, p. 10 and *Philadelphia Tribune*, February 7, 1917.

4. William J. Simmons, *Men of Mark: Eminent, Progressive and Rising* (Chicago: Johnson Publishing Co., 1970), pp. 448–455; William C. Harris, "Blanche K. Bruce of Mississippi: Conservative Assimilationist," *Southern Black Leaders of the Reconstruction Era*, edited by Howard N. Rabinowitz (Urbana: University of Illinois Press, 1982), pp. 3–4; Melvin I. Urofsky, "Blanche K. Bruce: United States Senator, 1875–1881," *Journal of Mississippi History*, XXIX (May, 1967), 118–120; G. David Houston, "A Negro Senator," *Journal of Negro History*, VII (July, 1922), 243–256; Samuel L. Shapiro, "Blanche Kelso Bruce," in Rayford W. Logan and Michael Winston (eds.), *Dictionary of American Negro Biography* (New York: W. W. Norton, 1982), pp. 74–76.

5. Emma V. Brown to Emily Howland, March 31, 1875, in Dorothy Sterling, *We Are Your Sisters: Black Women in the Nineteenth Century* (New York: Norton, 1984), p. 293.

6. *Colored American* (Washington, D.C.), March 26, 1898.

7. James B. Murphy, *L. Q. C. Lamar: Pragmatic Patriot* (Baton Rouge: Louisiana State University Press, 1973), pp. 186–187.

8. David S. Barry, *Forty Years in Washington* (Boston: Little, Brown, 1924), pp. 60–61; see also Samuel D. Smith, *The Negro in Congress, 1870–1901* (Chapel Hill: University of North Carolina Press, 1940), p. 27.

9. *Boston Herald*, quoted in *Washington Bee*, September 12, 1891.

10. *Washington Post*, June 25, 1878; unidentified newspaper clipping, Blanche K. Bruce Papers, Library of Congress; Bruce Grit, "Character of B. K. Bruce," Washington *Colored American*, March 26, 1898.

11. *Washington Post*, June 25, 27, 1878; *New York Tribune*, June 26, 27, 1878; *New York Times*, June 25, 1878; *The Leader* (Cleveland), June 25, 1878.

12. *Washington Post*, June 24, 1878.

13. Smith, *The Negro in Congress*, pp. 33–34; *New York Times*, December 7, 1878.

14. Undated clipping, *Boston Journal*, Bruce Papers; John Mercer Langston, *From the Virginia Plantation to the National Capitol* (Hartford: American Publishing Co., 1894), p. 521.

1. Background and Antecedents

1. *Harper's Weekly*, XVII (September 20, 1873), 840.

2. *Hartford Courant*, quoted in *New York Globe*, November 3, 1883; for a discussion of "social distinctions among Negroes," see *New York Times*, August 1, 7, 1906; P. M. Thompson, Letter to the Editor, August 2, 1906, ibid., August 6, 1906.

3. Quoted in *World* (Indianapolis), October 22, 1887.

4. On Lewis see sketches in Cleveland *Gazette*, February, 2, 1884; Washington *Colored American*, March 29, 1902; *Freeman* (Indianapolis), July 25, 1914.

5. *New York Times*, July 12, 1914.

6. *Philadelphia Record*, quoted in Indianapolis *Freeman*, March 5, 1894; see also a copyrighted story entitled "Colored Aristocracy" by A. C. B., in *The Augusta Chronicle* (Augusta, Georgia), September 18, 1893.

7. George L. Knox, in *Indianapolis Freeman*, March 26, 1898.

8. Constance M. Green, *The Secret City: Race Relations in the Nation's Capital* (Princeton: Princeton University Press, 1967), p. 141.

9. See Charles S. Johnson et al., *Deep South: A Social Anthropological Study of Caste and Class* (Chicago: University of Chicago Press, 1941), pp. 237–251. The pioneer work on black class structure in the late nineteenth and early twentieth centuries is August Meier, "Negro Class Structure and Ideology in the Age of Booker T. Washington," *Phylon*, XXIII (Fall, 1962), 258–266.

10. Jay R. Williams, "Social Stratification and the Negro American: An Exploration of Some Problems in Social Class Measurement," Ph.D. diss., Duke University, 1968, p. 12.

11. Sutton Griggs, *Overshadowed* (Nashville: Orion Publishing Co., 1901), p. 71.

12. Williams, "Social Stratification and the Negro American," pp. 2, 132, 139; see also Daniel C. Thompson, *Sociology of the Black Experience* (Westport, Conn.: Greenwood Press, 1974), pp. 221–223; Andrew Billingsley, *Black Families in White America* (Englewood Cliffs, N.J.: Prentice Hall, 1968), pp. 8–9, 124–130.

13. Sarah Grimké to Theodore Weld, December 17, 1837, in Gilbert Barnes and Dwight L. Dumond, *Letters of Theodore Weld, Angelina Grimké Weld and Sarah Grimké, 1822–1844*, 2 vols. (New York: D. Appleton-Century, 1934), Vol. I, p. 498; see also Jane H. Pease and William H. Pease, *They Who Would Be Free: Blacks' Search for Freedom, 1830–1861* (New York: Atheneum, 1974), pp. 291–294.

14. [Joseph Willson], *Sketches of the Higher Classes of Colored Society in Philadelphia* (Philadelphia: Merriheu and Thompson, 1841), pp. 23–39, 66. For a sophisticated analysis of the antebellum black upper class in Philadelphia, see Emma Jones Lapsansky, "Friends, Wives and Strivings: Networks and Community Values Among Nineteenth-Century Afroamerican Elites," *The Pennsylvania Magazine of History and Biography*, CVIII (January, 1984), 3–24.

15. Willson, *Sketches*, pp. 37–49.

16. Fannie Barrier Williams, "A Northern Negro's Autobiography," *Independent*, LVII (July 14, 1904), 91–96.

17. James Weldon Johnson, *Along This Way: The Autobiography of James Weldon Johnson* (New York: Viking Press, 1933), pp. 137–138.

18. Wendell P. Dabney, *Cincinnati's Colored Citizens* (Cincinnati: Dabney Publishing Co., 1926), pp. 44–45, 150–152.

19. See Ira Berlin, *Slaves Without Masters: The Free Negro in the Antebellum South* (New York: Pantheon Books, 1974); Marina Wikramanayake, *A World in Shadow: The Free Black in Antebellum South Carolina* (Columbia: University of South Carolina Press, 1973); Laura Foner, "The Free People of Color in Louisiana and St. Dominigue," *Journal of Social History*, III (Summer, 1970), 406–430; Linda V. Ellsworth, "Pensacola's Creoles: Remnants of a Culture," pp. 1–66 (unpublished paper in possession of the author); Marilyn Mannhard, "Free People of Color in Mobile County, Alabama," M.A. thesis, University of South Alabama, 1982.

20. "Charles Waddell Chesnutt," Notes, Daniel Murray Papers, State Historical Society of Wisconsin, Madison (microfilm); see also "Power of Blood Inheritance," ibid.

21. See Ira Berlin, "The Structure of the Free Negro Caste in the Antebellum United States," *Journal of Social History*, IX (Spring, 1976), 297–318.

22. Virginia R. Dominguez, *White By Definition: Social Classification in Creole Louisiana* (New Brunswick: Rutgers University Press, 1986), p. 136; see also Arthe Agnes Anthony, "The Negro Creole Community in New Orleans, 1880–1920: An Oral History," Ph.D. diss., University of California, Irvine, 1978, pp. 16–18, 44–47; Donald E. Everett, "Free Persons of Color in New Orleans, 1803–1865," Ph.D. diss., Tulane University, 1952.

23. H. C. Bruce, *The New Man: Twenty-Nine Years A Slave, Twenty-Nine Years A Free Man* (York, Pa.: Anstadt and Son, 1895), p. 79; Sara Iredell to Christian Fleetwood, February 21, 1868, Christian A. Fleetwood Papers, Library of Congress.

24. Robert L. Harris, "Charleston's Free Afro-American Elite: The Brown Fellowship Society and the Humane Brotherhood," *South Carolina Historical Magazine*, LXXII (January, 1981), 289–310; Horace Fitchett, "The Traditions of the Free Negro in Charleston, South Carolina," *Journal of Negro History*, XXV (April, 1940), 144–152; Larry Koger, *Black Slaveowners: Free Black Slave Masters in South Carolina, 1790–1860* (Jefferson, N.C.: McFarland & Co., 1985), pp. 98–99.

25. Theodore D. Jervey, *The Slave Trade: Slavery and Color* (Columbia, S.C.: The State Co., 1925), pp. 221–225; G. S. Dickerson, "A Glimpse of Charleston History," *Southern Workman*, XXXVI (January, 1907), 15–23; Koger, *Black Slaveowners*, pp. 167–168. In the notes for his encyclopedia Daniel Murray claims that the Brown Fellowship Society inspired the formation of similar groups in cities throughout the South and even in the border states and the North. He claimed that their "purpose was to enroll all free mixed blood people in the various centers of the South to create a middle class of free mixed blood people, a third color line as found in Jamaica, Trinidad and Barbados." See "Brown Fellowship Society," Notes, Murray Papers.

26. J. H. Holloway to Whitefield McKinlay, June 20, 1902, Whitefield McKinlay Papers, Carter Woodson Collection, Library of Congress; Jervey, *Slave Trade*, p. 225.

27. Lawrence O. Christensen, ed., "Cyprian Clamorgan, The Colored Aristocracy of St. Louis (1858)," *Bulletin of the Missouri Historical Society*, XXXI (October, 1974), 9–31.

28. Ibid., pp. 16–17; *The Western Appeal* (Chicago), November 30, 1890, June 20, July 4, 1891.

29. William R. Hogan and Edwin A. Davis, eds., *William Johnson's Natchez: The Ante-Bellum Diary of A Free Negro* (Baton Rouge: Louisiana State University Press, 1951), pp. 11, 48, 187, 215, 257, 372, 482–483, 764–765.

30. Paul D. Escott, *Slavery Remembered: A Record of Twentieth-Century Slave Narratives* (Chapel Hill: University of North Carolina Press, 1979), pp. 59–63; Eugene D. Genovese, *Roll, Jordan Roll: The World the Slaves Made* (New York: Pantheon, 1974), pp. 113–123.

31. Bruce, *New Man*, pp. 38–39, 171–172.

32. Samuel Mordecai, *Richmond in By-Gone Days* (Richmond: Deitz Press, 1860, 1946), pp. 353–360.

33. Daniel R. Hundley, *Social Relations in Our Southern States*, edited by William J. Cooper (Baton Rouge: Louisiana State University Press, 1979), pp. 351–352; *New York Globe*, November 3, 1883.

34. Leon Litwack, *Been in the Storm So Long: The Aftermath of Slavery* (New York: Knopf, 1979), p. 156.

35. Indianapolis *Freeman*, July 7, 1906.

36. Carter Woodson, "What Makes a Family Distinguished," *Negro History Bulletin*, XIII (October, 1949), 2.

37. Roi Ottley, *'New World A-Coming': Inside Black America* (Boston: Houghton Mifflin, 1943), p. 177; see also E. Franklin Frazier, *The Negro Family in the United States* (Chicago: University of Chicago Press, 1939), p. 408.

38. See James Haskins, *Pinckney Benton Stewart Pinchback* (New York: Macmillan, 1973); on Harlan, see Washington, *Colored American*, March 28, 1903; on Cheatham, Willard B. Gatewood, Jr., "Henry Plummer Cheatham," in *Dictionary of North Carolina Biography*, edited by William S. Powell (Chapel Hill: University of North Carolina Press, 1979), pp. 359–360; on Cuney, Maud Cuney Hare, *Norris Wright Cuney: A Tribune of the Black People* (New York: Crisis Publishing Co., 1913).

39. Mary Church Terrell, *A Colored Woman in a White World* (Washington: Ransdell, Inc., 1940), pp. 1–12; Annette E. Church and Roberta Church, *The Robert R. Churches of Memphis* (Ann Arbor: Edwards Brothers, 1974), p. 6; Emily L. Byers to R. R. Church, December 24, 1891, Emily L. Byers to R. R. Church, December 31, 1891, P. B. B. Hynson to R. R. Church, February 17, 1901, Robert Reed Church Family Papers, Mississippi Valley Collection, Memphis State University, Memphis, Tennessee; the quotation from Lewis is in James Lewis to R. R. Church, January 31, 1901, Church Papers.

40. Langston, *From the Virginia Plantation to the National Capitol*, pp. 14–15, 21–22, 142; W. E. B. DuBois, *Dusk of Dawn: An Essay Toward an Autobiography of a Race Concept* (New York: Harcourt, Brace, 1940), p. 10; B. F. Wheeler, *The Varick Family* (n.p., n.p., 1907), pp. 9, 16–17, 26, 36–38.

41. Langston, *From the Virginia Plantation to the National Capitol*, pp. 14–15, 21–22, 142.

42. "Mrs. Warren Logan," *Twentieth Century Negro Literature*, edited by D. W. Culp (Naperville, Ill.: J. L. Nichols, 1902), p. 198; Caroline Bond Day, *A Study of Negro-White Families* (Cambridge: Harvard University Press, 1932), pp. 33–34; Adele Logan Alexander, "How I Discovered My Grandmother," *MS. Magazine*, November, 1983, pp. 29–30, 32, 36. Adele Logan Alexander, "Ambiguous Lives: Free Women of Color in Rural Georgia, 1787–1879," M. A. thesis, Howard University, 1987, is an extraordinarily perceptive account of the Hunt family.

43. "J. T. Settle," in James T. Haley, *Afro-American Encyclopedia* (Nashville: Haley and Florida, 1896), pp. 43–49.

44. Langston, *From the Virginia Plantation to the National Capitol*, pp. 14–15, 21–22, 142; Pinchback quoted in the Washington *Colored American*, April 10, 1898.

45. Langston, *From the Virginia Plantation to the National Capitol*, pp. 12–13, 30, 61; see also *The Big Sea: An Autobiography* (New York: Knopf, 1940) by Langston's great-nephew Langston Hughes, especially pp. 12–13, 303–304.

46. See Edwin A. Davis and William R. Hogan, *The Barber of Natchez* (Baton Rouge: Louisiana State University Press, 1973), pp. 56–57, 241–242; Clamorgan, "Colored Aristocracy of St. Louis," pp. 24, 26, 28.

47. Clamorgan, "Colored Aristocracy of St. Louis," p. 12; see also Lapsansky, "Friends, Wives and Strivings," 22–24.

48. See especially John S. Durham, "Three Types of Growth," *A.M.E. Church Review*, XIV (1897), 121–130; Washington *People's Advocate*, May 15, 1880.

49. *Colored Citizen* (Fort Scott, Kansas), June 14, 1878; see also Washington *People's Advocate*, May 15, 1880; W. E. B. Du Bois, *The Black North in 1901: A Social Study* (New York: Arno Press, 1969), p. 46.

50. *Washington Bee*, August 17, 1901.

51. *Savannah Tribune*, December 21, 1889.

52. J. C. Price, "Does the Negro Seek Social Equality?" *The Forum*, X (January, 1891), 563; See also Indianapolis *Freeman*, December 10, 1904, January 14, 1905.

53. Du Bois, quoted in *New York Age*, June 13, 1891; *New Orleans Crusader*, July 19, 1890.

54. For an analysis of the black aristocracy predicated on the natural selection theory, see especially Washington *People's Advocate*, May 15, 1880.

55. Indianapolis *Freeman*, September 19, 1896.

56. Ibid., October 17, 24, 1896.

57. Ibid., November 7, 1896.

58. John M. Henderson, "The Forces Upon Which the Race Depends for Success," *Colored American Magazine*, XIV (January, 1908), 70–71.

59. *New York Age*, May 12, 1888; *Indianapolis World*, November 23, 1889; September 26, 1891; *Washington Bee*, January 18, 1890.

60. See "Class Distinction Among Negroes," *Southern Workman*, XXVIII (October, 1899), 371; Washington *Colored American*, August 11, 1894; Topeka *Weekly Call*, June 18, 1893.

61. Quoted in Indianapolis *Freeman*, March 4, 1893.

62. J. Simon Flipper, "Is the Young Negro an Improvement over his Father?" in Culp, *Twentieth Century Negro Literature*, p. 257.

63. "Colored Aristocracy," in *Historic Times* (Lawrence, Kansas), August 29, 1891.

64. See Indianapolis *Freeman*, June 15, 1895; Ralph Tyler, "Real Society," *Colored American Magazine*, XIII (November, 1907), 391–392. For a satirical song on the "Colored Aristocracy" from the black musical *Dahomey*, see Dorothy Sterling, ed., *We Are Your Sisters* (New York: W. W. Norton and Co., 1984), p. 429.

65. Langston, *From the Virginia Plantation to the National Capitol*, pp. 234–235.

66. Peter Kolchin, *First Freedom: Responses of Alabama's Blacks to Emancipation and Reconstruction* (Westport, Conn.: Greenwood Press, 1972), pp. 128–145; Litwack, *Been in the Storm So Long*, pp. 513–514, 536; Thomas Holt, *Black Over White: Negro Political Leadership in South Carolina During Reconstruction* (Urbana: University of Illinois Press, 1977), pp. 17, 20–21, 37–38, 63–65; see also William C. Hine, "Black Politicians in Reconstruction Charleston, South Carolina: A Collective Study," *Journal of Southern History*, XLIX (November, 1983), 555–571.

67. Joel Williamson, *New People: Miscegenation and Mulattoes in the United States* (New York: The Free Press, 1980), p. 130.

68. Andrew F. Hilyer, "An Analysis of American Color Prejudice and How to Overcome It," Andrew F. Hilyer Papers, Moorland-Spingarn Research Center, Howard University, Washington, D.C.

69. "Antipathy of the Upper and Lower Classes," *Christian Recorder*, X (October 26, 1872), 1; Francis J. Grimké, "Some Things that Lie Across the Pathway of Our Progress," *Southern Workman*, XXVII (September, 1897), 185–190.

70. Williamson, *New People*, pp. 75–82; James Weldon Johnson, *The Autobiography of an Ex-Colored Man* (New York: Alfred A. Knopf, 1979), p. 82.

Part II: People and Places

Prologue

1. *New York Graphic*, November 20, 1878; undated clippings, *Baltimore American* and *Boston Journal*, Blanche K. Bruce Papers, Library of Congress; hereafter cited as Bruce Papers (L.C.).

2. *People's Advocate* (Washington), February 15, 1879; undated clipping, *Baltimore American*, Bruce Papers (L.C.); see also Cleveland *Leader*, February 21, 1879.

3. Constance M. Green, *The Secret City: A History of Race Relations in the Nation's Capital* (Princeton: Princeton University Press, 1967), p. 119.

4. Undated clippings, Bruce Papers (L.C.); *New York Graphic*, February 20, 1879.

5. Mary Church Terrell, *A Colored Woman in a White World* (Washington: Ransdell, Inc., 1940), p. 50.

6. *New York Graphic*, February 20, 1879; *The Gazette* (Huntsville, Alabama), July 13, 1889.

7. *People's Advocate*, August 2, 1879; see also *Weekly Louisianian* (New Orleans), August 9, 1879.

8. Josephine Bruce to R. C. Bruce, October 18, 1897, Roscoe C. Bruce Papers, Moorland-Spingarn Collection, Howard University, Washington; Terrell, *Colored Woman in a White World*, p. 50.

9. Undated clipping, *Washington Republican*, Bruce Papers (L.C.); see also William C. Harris, "Blanche K. Bruce: Conservative Assimilationist," in *Southern Black Leaders of the Reconstruction Era*, edited by Howard N. Rabinowitz (Urbana: University of Illinois Press, 1982), pp. 12–13.

10. Harris, "Blanche K. Bruce," pp. 15–31; Melvin Urofsky, "Blanche K. Bruce: United States Senator," *Journal of Mississippi History*, XXIX (May, 1867), 118–141.

11. The black press, especially the *Washington Bee*, Washington *Colored American*, and Indianapolis *Freeman*, covered his frequent lecture tours.

12. Indianapolis *World*, December 6, 1890; Indianapolis *Freeman*, November 21, 1902; Samuel L. Shapiro, "Blanche Kelso Bruce," *Dictionary of American Negro Biography*, edited by Rayford W. Logan and Michael B. Winston (New York: W. W. Norton, 1982), pp. 74–76; Terrell, *Colored Woman in a White World*, p. 49; Frank G. Carpenter, *Carp's Washington* (New York: McGraw-Hill, 1960), pp. 245–246; Annette E. Church and Roberta Church, *The Robert R. Churches of Memphis* (Ann Arbor: Edwards Brothers, 1974), p. 37; B. K. Bruce to John P. Green, July 25, 1897, John P. Green Papers, Western Reserve Historical Society, Cleveland.

13. Green, *Secret City*, pp. 119, 123; undated clipping, Bruce Papers (L.C.). For an analysis of changes in race relations in Washington, see Thomas Reed Johnson, "The City on the Hill: Race Relations in Washington, D.C., 1865–1885," Ph.D. diss., University of Maryland, 1975.

14. Green, *Secret City*, p. 140; *Cleveland Gazette*, November 29, 1884; Mrs. E. N. Chapin, *American Court Gossip, or Life at the National Capital* (Marshalltown, Iowa: Chapin and Hartwell Brothers, 1887), p. 39; Mrs. John A. Logan, in San Francisco *Pacific Coast Appeal*, December 21, 1901.

15. Darwin T. Turner, ed., *The Wayward and the Seeking: A Collection of Writings by Jean Toomer* (Washington: Howard University Press, 1980), p. 84.

16. Terrell, *Colored Woman in a White World*, p. 50.

17. Indianapolis *Freeman*, February 27, 1892; see also Cleveland *Gazette*, October 30, 1886. For Josephine Bruce's reaction to Tuskegee, see her letter to Roscoe Bruce, April 6, 1902, R. C. Bruce Papers.

18. Booker T. Washington to Josephine Beall Wilson Bruce, September 6, 1899, in Louis Harlan et al., *The Booker T. Washington Papers* (Urbana: University of Illinois, 1976), V, 196–197; see also Booker T. Washington to Hollis B. Frissell, October 23, 1896, ibid., IV, 226–227.

19. Indianapolis *Freeman*, September 23, 1899; *Seattle Republican*, April 6, 1900.

2. Washington: Capital of the Colored Aristocracy

1. Haynes Johnson, *Dusk At the Mountain—The Negro, The Nation and The Capital—A Report on Problems and Progress* (Garden City: Doubleday, 1963), p. 172.

2. *North Star* (Rochester), July 6, 1849; see also John Francis Cook Diary 1850–1851, Cook Family Papers, Moorland-Spingarn Research Center, Howard University, Washington; Francis J. Grimké, "Anniversary Address," *The Works of Francis J. Grimké*, edited by Carter G. Woodson (Washington: Associated Publishers, n.d.), I, 531–540; *History of the Schools for the Colored Population in the District of Columbia* in *Special Report of the Commission on Education*, Executive Document 315, 41st Congress, 2d Session (Washington: Government Printing Office, 1871), pp. 200–202.

3. Genealogical Records, Cook Family Papers; see also "Rev. John Francis Cook," and "The Appo Family," in Daniel Murray Papers (microfilm), State Historical Society, Madison, Wisconsin; E. S. Lewis, "The Cook Family," *Negro History Bulletin*, V (January, 1942), 83; Chapin, *American Court Gossip*, p. 38.

4. *Norfolk Virginian*, June 14, 1869.

5. *Washington Bee*, May 26, 1900.

6. *Mobile Adviser*, quoted in *New York Age*, July 27, 1881; *Washington Bee*, October 4, 1884; for a sketch of George F. T. Cook, see ibid., November 30, 1895.

7. Carter G. Woodson, "The Wormley Family," *Negro History Bulletin*, XI (January, 1948), 75–84; Francis J. Grimké to G. Smith Wormley, August 23, 1934, Carter G. Woodson Collection, Library of Congress; James H. Whyte, *The Uncivil War: Washington During the Reconstruction, 1865–1878* (New York: Twayne Publishers, 1958), pp. 29, 36, 166, 248–249, 251–253, 258–259; Chapin, *American Court Gossip*, p. 41.

8. On the Syphax family, see Letitia Brown and Elsie Lewis, *Washington in the New Era, 1870–1970* (Washington, D.C.: Educational Department, National Portrait Gallery, 1972), p. 12; Gerri Major, *Black Society* (Chicago: Johnson Publishing Company, 1976), pp. 40–41, 398–399; E. Delorius Preston, "William Syphax, A Pioneer in Negro Education in the District of Columbia," *Journal of Negro History*, XX (October, 1955), 448–476.

9. Whyte, *The Uncivil War*, pp. 29, 106, 144, 161, 166, 251, 258, 283.

10. Andrew Hilyer, "The Progress of Color People in Washington," Andrew Hilyer Papers, Moorland-Spingarn Research Center, Howard University, Washington.

11. *Washington Bee*, August 18, 1883.

12. See family deeds and diary in the Whitefield McKinlay Papers, Carter Woodson Collection, Library of Congress; various Cardozo family documents and "Folk's Ways," a book-length manuscript by Francis L. Cardozo, Jr., in Francis L. Cardozo Family Papers, Library of Congress; "Charles B. Purvis," in William J. Simmons, *Men of Mark: Eminent, Progressive and Rising* (Chicago: Johnson Publishing Co., 1970), pp. 477–479; Angelina Grimké, "A Biographical Sketch of Archibald H. Grimké," *Opportunity*, III (February, 1925), 44–47; "Frank J. Grimké," in Simmons, *Men of Mark*, pp. 416–419.

13. E. Menard, "John Willis Menard: First Negro Elected to the U.S. Congress," *Negro History Bulletin*, XXVIII (December, 1964), 53–54; *Washington Bee*, October 14, 1893, December 26, 1903; *Cleveland Gazette*, October 12, 1889.

14. Robert L. Harris, Jr., "Daniel Murray and the Encyclopedia of the Colored Race," *Phylon*, XXXVII (Fall, 1976), 270–272; "Estate of Daniel Murray," Murray Papers; Edwin A. Lee, "Daniel Murray," *Colored American Magazine*, V (October, 1902), 432–440.

15. On Pinchback's career, see Haskins, *Pinckney Benton Stewart Pinchback*; Turner, *The Wayward and the Seeking*, pp. 22–27; Nellie McKay, *Jean Toomer, Artist: A Study of His Literary Life and Work, 1894–1936* (Chapel Hill: University of North Carolina Press, 1984), pp. 13–14.

16. John W. Blassingame, *Black New Orleans* (Chicago: University of Chicago Press, 1973).

17. *New York Age*, November 3, 1883.

18. *Washington Bee*, December 20, 1890; Indianapolis *Freeman*, January 13, 1894; Turner, *The Wayward and the Seeking*, pp. 29, 57.

19. Indianapolis *Freeman*, January 13, 1894.

20. Turner, *The Wayward and the Seeking*, pp. 25–26, 29–30, 86; see also S. P. Fullinwider, "Jean Toomer: Lost Generation or Negro Renaissance?" *Phylon*, XXVII (Winter, 1966), 396–397; Cynthia E. Kerman and Richard Eldridge, *The Lives of Jean Toomer: A Hunger for Wholeness* (Baton Rouge: Louisiana State University Press, 1987), pp. 15–47.

21. On Harrison Terrell, see *New York Age*, September 28, 1889, July 12, 1906; on Robert H. Terrell, see Terrell, *Colored Woman in a White World; Class of 1884, Harvard College: Fortieth Anniversary Report of the Secretary* (Cambridge: Harvard University Press, 1924), p. 102.

22. Indianapolis *Freeman*, June 15, 1895.

23. Indianapolis *Recorder*, January 29, 1910.

24. Indianapolis *Freeman*, June 15, 1895.

25. Diary, February 6, 1909, p. 37, Mary Church Terrell Papers, Library of Congress.

26. Diary, September 14, 1905, p. 257, ibid.

27. The District's black press faithfully chronicled the migration out of Washington each summer; see, for example, *Washington Bee*, June 7, 1884, August 20, 1892, August 17, 1895, June 19, 1915; Washington *Colored American*, July 18, 1903; and also Terrell, *Colored Woman in a White World*, pp. 240–42; Turner, *The Wayward and the Seeking*, pp. 26, 87.

28. Terrell, *Colored Woman in a White World*, pp. 239–240; Green, *Secret City*, p. 209; Mary Church Terrell to Thomas Church, August 10, 1917, M. C. Terrell Papers; Paul Laurence Dunbar, "Negro Society in Washington," *Saturday Evening Post*, CLXXIV (December 14, 1901), 9, 18.

29. Green, *Secret City*, pp. 127, 162; *The Elite List: A Compilation of Selected Names of Residents of Washington City, D.C. 1888* (Washington: Elite Publishing Co., 1888), pp. 59, 103, 109, 134, 149, 171; Rayford Logan, *Howard University: The First Hundred Years, 1867–1967* (New York: New York University Press, 1969), pp. 110–111; Chapin, *American Court Gossip*, pp. 38–40.

30. *Washington Bee*, August 17, 1901; see also *Broad-Ax* (Chicago), May 8, 1909.

31. Terrell, *Colored Woman in a White World*, pp. 397–398.

32. Steven Mintz, "An Historical Ethnography of Black Washington, D.C.," unpublished paper in possession of the author, p. 28.

33. Terrell, "Society Among the Colored People of Washington," *Voice of the Negro*, I (March, 1904), pp. 151–152; *Washington Bee*, August 1, 1885, August 1, 1903, June 27, 1914, November 14, 1914.

34. Green, *Secret City*, pp. 145–147; *Washington Bee*, June 20, 1885, August 2, 1902, December 17, 1904, December 28, 1912, April 27, June 22, 1918.

35. *Washington Bee*, December 17, 1904, February 11, 1905, January 16, 1909, January 21, 1911; Mary Church Terrell, "The Social Functions During Inauguration Week," *Voice of the Negro*, II (April, 1905), 238–241.

36. Terrell, "Society Among the Colored People of Washington," p. 155.

37. Ibid., p. 186; Washington *Colored American*, October 18, 1902.

38. Terrell, Diary, November 30, 1905, p. 334, M. C. Terrell Papers; Washington *Colored American*, April 5, 1905; Lasalle D. Lafall, Jr., "Austin Maurice Curtis," in Logan and Winston, *Dictionary of American Negro Biography*, pp. 152–154.

39. Ralph Tyler, "Affairs at Washington," *Colored American Magazine*, XVI (April, 1909), 230.

40. See Indianapolis *Freeman*, June 1, 1895, April 17, 1897, January 13, 1906.

41. *Washington Bee*, February 24, 1906.

42. Green, *Secret City*, p. 145.

43. Ibid., pp. 145–148; Washington *Colored American*, January 31, 1903; *Washington Bee*, May 24, 1902, May 28, 1904, December 31, 1910.

44. *Washington Bee*, February 1, 1890.

45. James Borchert, *Alley Life in Washington: Family, Community, Religion, and Folklife in the City, 1850–1970* (Urbana: University of Illinois Press, 1980), pp. 208–209; see also *Washington Bee*, May 31, 1890, April 29, May 13, 1893, April 21, 1900; Washington *Colored American*, April 1, 1899.

46. *Washington Bee*, May 31, 1890, April 29, 1893.

47. Indianapolis *Freeman*, May 13, 1893.

48. See *State Capital* (Springfield, Ill.), November 7, 1891; *American Citizen* (Kansas City), April 5, 1901.

49. Mrs. John A. Logan, *Thirty Years in Washington, or Scenes in Our National Capital* (Hartford: A. D. Worthington and Co., 1901), p. 521.

50. *Daily Inter-Ocean* (Chicago), January 17, 1886; Eric Anderson, *Race and Politics in North Carolina, 1872–1901: The Black Second* (Baton Rouge: Louisiana State University Press, 1981), pp. 130–131.

51. See New Orleans *Weekly Louisianian*, November 1, 1879; *Washington Bee*, September 27, 1884.

52. Quoted in *The Boston Guardian*, December 20, 1902.

53. *Chicago Blade*, quoted in *Washington Bee*, October 17, 1891; see also *New York Globe*, January 5, 1884; *New York Times*, February 15, 1891.

54. Henry Loomis Nelson, "The Washington Negro," *Harper's Weekly*, XXXVI (July 9, 1892), 654; see also Katherine G. Busbey, *Home Life in America* (New York: Macmillan, 1910), pp. 217–218.

55. Washington *People's Advocate*, May 15, 1880.

56. *New York Globe*, January 5, 1884.

57. *Washington Bee*, December 29, 1883, January 12, 19, 1884.

58. See below, p. 162.

59. "Washington Colored Society," John E. Bruce Papers, Schomburg Center for Research in Black Culture, New York Public Library; see also "John Edward Bruce," Logan and Winston, *Dictionary of American Negro Biography*, pp. 76–77.

60. *Washington Bee*, January 18, 1890; Washington *People's Advocate*, February 12, 1881; Cleveland *Gazette*, April 15, 1891.

61. Washington *People's Advocate*, January 8, 1881, March 11, 1882, January 12, 1884.

62. See Willard B. Gatewood, Jr., "Edward Elder Cooper: Black Journalist," *Journalism Quarterly*, LV (Summer, 1978), 269–275, 324.

63. Washington *Colored American*, August 11, 1894, September 3, 1898.

64. Hal Chase, "William C. Chase and *The Washington Bee*," *Negro History Bulletin*, XXXVI (December, 1973), 172–174.

65. *Washington Bee*, December 29, 1883.

66. Ibid., April 18, 1885, January 2, September 18, 1886.

67. Ibid., January 19, February 2, 16, March 15, 1884, January 2, 1886, September 28, October 5, 1918.

68. Ibid., November 17, 1883, September 25, 1886, February 2, 1889, May 28, 1904, June 27, September 19, November 14, 1914, April 15, 1915.

69. Ibid., March 15, 1884.

70. Ibid., November 17, 1883, January 19, 1884, August 1, 1885, June 21, 1890.

71. Washington *People's Advocate*, January 12, 1884.

72. *Washington Bee*, August 1, 1885, September 18, 1886, June 21, December 20, 1890, February 24, 1906, August 5, 1911.

73. Ibid., August 8, 15, 1891.

74. Ibid., October 27, December 1, 1894, July 4, 1896, October 16, 1897, November 7, 1908.

75. Paul Laurence Dunbar, "Negro Life in Washington," *Harper's Weekly*, XLIV (January 13, 1900), 32. This article is much more critical of Washington's aristocrats of color than Dunbar's "Negro Society in Washington," *Saturday Evening Post*, CLXXIV (December 14, 1901), 9, 18.

76. Washington *People's Advocate*, July 14, 1883; Kansas City *American Citizen*, September 6, 1895; *Pittsburgh Courier*, March 23, 1912.

77. Mary Church Terrell, "Society Among The Colored People of Washington," pp. 150–156.

78. Ibid.

79. Ibid.

80. Richard W. Thompson, "Phases of Washington Life," in Indianapolis *Freeman*, June 8, 15, 1895.

81. Archibald Grimké, in *New York Age*, March 8, 1906.

82. Green, *Secret City*, pp. 154–168, 171–179; *Washington Bee*, January 10, 1903.

83. *Washington Bee*, November 10, 24, 1894; Edward Ingle, *The Negro in the District of Columbia* (Baltimore: The Johns Hopkins Press, 1893), pp. 43–47; W. Montague Cobb, *The First Negro Medical Society: A History of the Medico-Chirurgical Society of the District of Columbia, 1884–1939* (Washington: Associated Publishers, 1939), pp. 1, 7–39, 42–43, 127.

84. "What It Means To Be Colored in the Capital of the United States," *Independent*, XII (January 17, 1907), 181–186.

85. Washington *People's Advocate*, June 4, 1881; Indianapolis *Freeman*, June 15, 1895; Terrell, *Colored Woman in a White World*, pp. 113–119; Ronald M. Johnson, "From Romantic Suburb to Racial Enclave: Le Droit Park, Washington, D.C., 1880–1920," *Phylon*, XLV (December, 1984), 264–270.

86. Indianapolis *Freeman*, September 18, 1897; *Pittsburgh Courier*, August 2, 1912; Chapin, *American Court Gossip*, p. 38; G. F. Richings, *Evidences of Progress Among Colored People* (Philadelphia: George S. Ferguson Co., 1900), pp. 429–435; Washington *Colored American*, February 25, 1899.

87. McKay, *Jean Toomer: Artist*, p. 20.

88. On the Pelham case, see *New York Age*, May 6, 1909.

89. Terrell, Diary, December 6, 1909, p. 340; M. C. Gibbs to Robert H. Terrell, July 12, 1916, M. C. Terrell Papers.

90. *Washington Bee*, December 26, 1914; *New York Age*, December 26, 1914.

3. Aristocrats of Color in the South

1. Washington *People's Advocate*, June 10, 1876.

2. Robert Lewis Waring, *As We See It* (Washington, D.C.: Press of C. F. Sudworth, 1910), p. 5.

3. Washington *Colored American*, March 15, 1902.

4. Ray Stannard Baker, *Following the Color Line* (New York: Doubleday, Page and Co., 1908).

5. A South Carolinian, "South Carolina Society," *Atlantic Monthly*, XXXIX (June, 1877), 677.

6. Quoted in the Cleveland *Gazette*, January 10, 1885.

7. Samuel J. Barrows, "What the Southern Negro is Doing for Himself," *Atlantic Monthly*, LXVII (June, 1891), 810; A South Carolinian, "South Carolina Society," p. 677; Bessie Blanden, "Our Colored Society," unidentified newspaper clipping, dated April 5, 1890, in the Robert Reed Church Family Papers, Mississippi Valley Collection, Memphis State University, Memphis, Tennessee; McMinnville Correspondent in Indianapolis *Freeman*, May 20, 1893.

8. Lura Beam, *He Called Them By Lightning: A Teacher's Odyssey of the Negro South, 1908–1919* (Indianapolis: Bobbs-Merrill, 1967), pp. 40, 88.

9. Ibid., pp. 88–90.

10. Indianapolis *Freeman*, February 3, 1894; W. E. Burghardt Du Bois, "The Negroes of Farmville, Virginia: A Social Study," *Bulletin of the Department of Labor*, No. 14 (Washington, D.C.: Government Printing Office, 1898), pp. 1–38; H. Paul Douglass, *Christian Reconstruction in the South* (Boston: Pilgrim Press, 1909), pp. 85–96.

11. Quoted in William Archer, *Through Afro-America* (Westport, Conn.: Negro Universities Press, 1970), p. 95.

12. Indianapolis *Freeman*, February 11, 1893.

13. Electa C. Wiley, *Black Elitism: Hope, Arkansas 1900–1935* (n.p., n.p., 1981), pp. 2–11.

14. Indianapolis *Freeman*, August 26, 1899.

15. Leroy Graham, *Baltimore: The Nineteenth Century Black Capital* (Lanham, Md: University Press of America, 1982), p. 295; Paul Laurence Dunbar, "Negro Society in Washington," *Saturday Evening Post*, CLXXIV (December 14, 1901), 11; Baltimore *Afro-American Ledger*, February 15, 1913, July 3, 1915.

16. On free blacks in antebellum Baltimore, see Leonard P. Curry, *The Free Black in Urban America, 1800–1850* (Chicago: University of Chicago Press, 1981), pp. 123, 145–146, 220–221; Jeffrey R. Brackett, *The Negro in Maryland: A Study of the Institution of*

Slavery (Baltimore: Johns Hopkins University Press, 1889), chap. V; "The Condition of the Colored Population of Baltimore," *Baltimore Literary and Religious Magazine,* IV (April, 1838), 168–176; James M. Wright, *The Free Negro in Maryland, 1634–1860* (New York: Columbia University Press, 1921).

17. Jeffrey R. Brackett, *Notes on the Progress of the Colored People of Maryland Since the War* (Baltimore: Johns Hopkins University Press, 1890), pp. 26, 57–58; see also "Colored Society in Maryland," *Indianapolis World,* October 22, 1887.

18. Graham, *Baltimore,* pp. 198–199, 263–267; Baltimore *Afro-American Ledger,* May 17, 1902; *New York Globe,* November 8, 1884; Philip S. Foner, "Isaac Myers (1835–91)," *Dictionary of American Negro Biography,* pp. 468–469; George F. Bragg, Jr., *Men of Maryland* (Baltimore: Church Advocate Press, 1925), pp. 70, 94–98.

19. Graham, *Baltimore,* pp. 201–203, 268; *New York Freeman,* February 19, 1887; Baltimore *Afro-American Ledger,* October 25, 1902; see also Allison Blakely, "Richard T. Greener and the 'Talented Tenth's' Dilemma," *Journal of Negro History,* LIX (October, 1974), 305–321.

20. Edwin A. Lee, "Daniel Murray," *Colored American Magazine,* V (October, 1902), 432–440; see also Graham, *Baltimore,* pp. 269–271; Robert L. Harris, Jr., "Daniel Murray and the Encyclopedia of the Colored People," *Phylon,* XXXVII (Fall, 1976), 260–282.

21. Washington *People's Advocate,* August 9, 1879, July 3, 1880; Baltimore *Afro-American Ledger,* June 13, 1903; Graham, *Baltimore,* p. 269; *Cleveland Gazette,* July 23, 30, 1887; Bragg, *Men of Maryland,* p. 136.

22. Sallie Ives, "Formation of the Black Community in Annapolis, 1870–1885," *Geographical Perspectives on Maryland's Past.* Occasional Papers in Geography, No. 4, edited by Robert Mitchell and Edward K. Miller (College Park: University of Maryland, 1979); Harold W. Hurst, "The Northernmost Southern Town: A Sketch of Pre-Civil War Annapolis," *Maryland Historical Magazine,* LXXVI (September, 1981), 240–249; George F. Bragg, *History of the Afro-American Group of the Episcopal Church* (Baltimore: Church Advocate Press, 1922), p. 136; Washington *People's Advocate,* July 3, 1880; Baltimore *Afro-American Ledger,* June 13, 1896.

23. Washington *People's Advocate,* May 1, June 12, 1880; Graham, *Baltimore,* pp. 136–137; *New York Age,* February 25, 1885.

24. *New York Freeman,* November 28, 1885, May 14, 1887; *New York Age,* April 7, 1888; Indianapolis *Freeman,* November 28, 1891, April 9, 1892; Graham, *Baltimore,* p. 267.

25. *New York Globe,* April 11, 1883.

26. Baltimore *Afro-American Ledger,* February 24, 1906.

27. On Bethel A.M.E. Church, see Graham, *Baltimore,* pp. 72–74, 147–149, 152–153, 198.

28. See Bragg, *Afro-American Group of the Episcopal Church,* pp. 90–96, 98; Washington *People's Advocate,* March 18, 1880; *New York Age,* February 8, 1890.

29. Washington *People's Advocate,* August 30, 1879.

30. *New York Freeman,* June 26, 1886; for other descriptions of upper-class weddings, see ibid., January 15, 1887; Baltimore *Afro-American Ledger,* February 28, 1903.

31. Bragg, *Afro-American Group of the Episcopal Church,* p. 97; for a brief history of the Saint James Beneficial Society, see Baltimore *Afro-American Ledger,* April 12, 1913.

32. *New York Freeman,* December 18, 1886. The Baltimore *Afro-American Ledger* published extensive news about the Empty Stocking and Fresh Air Circles; see the issues of January 7, 1906 and April 19, 1913 especially.

33. Brackett, *Colored People of Maryland Since the War,* pp. 28–30; Graham, *Baltimore,* pp. 201–202; see also "Wealthy Colored Baltimoreans," in *Cleveland Gazette,*

February 28, 1885, October 23, 1886; "Colored Men in Business," *A.M.E. Church Review*, VI (July, 1889), 106–109.

34. Washington *People's Advocate*, August 9, 1879, July 24, 1880.

35. Ibid., September 4, 1880; Washington *Colored American*, July 18, 1903; Baltimore *Commonwealth*, July 24, 31, 1915.

36. Baltimore *Afro-American Ledger*, July 14, 1906.

37. See Ronald M. Johnson, "From Romantic Suburb to Racial Enclave: Le Droit Park, Washington, D.C., 1880–1920," *Phylon*, XLV (December, 1984), 264–270; Hollis Lynch, *The Black Urban Condition: A Documentary History, 1866–1971* (New York: Crowell, 1973), pp. 39–40.

38. Baltimore *Afro-American Ledger*, September 17, October 8, November 26, 1910, January 14, 1911; William George Paul, "The Shadow of Equality: The Negro in Baltimore, 1864–1911," Ph.D. diss., University of Wisconsin, 1972, pp. 391–399.

39. Paul, "The Shadow of Equality," pp. 190–193, 236.

40. *New York Age*, July 18, 1891; see also January 8, 1888.

41. Baltimore *Afro-American Ledger*, February 22, 1902. On the attempts at disfranchisement, see James B. Crooks, *Politics and Progress: The Rise of Urban Progressivism in Baltimore, 1895 to 1911* (Baton Rouge: Louisiana State University Press, 1968), pp. 54–70. On blacks on the Baltimore City Council, see Suzanne E. Green, "Black Republicans on the Baltimore City Council, 1890–1931," *Maryland Historical Magazine*, LXXIV (September, 1979), 203–222.

42. Baltimore *Afro-American Ledger*, May 5, 1906.

43. Paul, "Shadow of Equality," pp. 346, 397.

44. Baltimore *Afro-American Ledger*, September 6, 1906; see also March 24, August 26, 1906.

45. August Meier, *Negro Thought in America, 1880–1915: Racial Ideologies in the Age of Booker T. Washington* (Ann Arbor: University of Michigan Press, 1963), p. 111, 180, 223; Baltimore *Afro-American Ledger*, April 6, 1912, November 22, 1913, July 18, 1914.

46. Baltimore *Afro-American Ledger*, January 2, 1915.

47. Ibid., November 18, 1911.

48. Ibid., March 23, 1912, April 26, 1913, November 28, 1914.

49. Ibid., May 20, 1911.

50. Asa H. Gordon, *Sketches of Negro Life and History in South Carolina* (Columbia: University of South Carolina Press, 1971), p. 69. On Charleston's antebellum free black elite, see Marina Wikramanayake, *A World in Shadow: The Free Black in Antebellum South Carolina* (Columbia: University of South Carolina Press, 1973), pp. 15–17, 71–81, 88–89, 109–111. On the postbellum elite, see Bernard Edward Powers, Jr., "Black Charleston: A Social History, 1822–1885," Ph.D. diss., Northwestern University, 1982, pp. 146–177.

51. Kelly Miller, "The 'Colored' United States: South Carolina," *The Messenger*, VII (December, 1925), 377. For two works by Michael P. Johnson and James R. Roark which offer rich insight into the outlook and values of Charleston's antebellum mulatto aristocracy, see *No Chariot Let Down: Charleston's Free People of Color on the Eve of the Civil War* (Chapel Hill: University of North Carolina Press, 1984); and *Black Masters: A Free Family of Color in the Old South* (New York: W. W. Norton and Co., 1984).

52. "Impressions of Charleston," *Christian Recorder*, V (September 8, 1866), 142; *New York Globe*, September 1, 1883; Gordon, *Sketches*, pp. 77, 139, 141; Amelia Merriam, "Avery Normal Institute, Charleston, S.C.," *American Missionary*, XLV (May, 1891), 181–183; *New York Age*, July 6, 1889; see also Larry Koger, *Black Slaveowners:*

Free Black Slave Masters in South Carolina 1790–1860 (Jefferson, N.C.: McFarland and Co., 1985).

53. Joe W. Trotter, Jr., *Black Milwaukee: The Making of an Industrial Proletariat, 1915–1945* (Urbana: University of Illinois Press, 1985), pp. 103–105, 125–126.

54. *Charleston News and Courier*, quoted in *New York Age*, May 30, 1907; E. Franklin Frazier, *The Free Negro Family* (New York: Arno Press, 1969), pp. 27–33; "Whitefield McKinlay," *Journal of Negro History*, XXVII (January, 1942), 129–130; *The Works of Francis J. Grimké*, edited by Carter G. Woodson, 4 vols. (Washington: Associated Publishers, n.d.), I, 541; IV, 283; Lulu Singleton to Whitefield McKinlay, May 18, 1908, Whitefield McKinlay Papers in the Carter G. Woodson Collection, Library of Congress.

55. On the infusion of "new groups" into Charleston's elite, see Powers, "Black Charleston: A Social History, 1822–1885," pp. 175–177. On Crum, see Willard B. Gatewood, Jr., *Theodore Roosevelt and the Art of Controversy* (Baton Rouge: Louisiana State University, 1970), pp. 100–101, 117.

56. "A Pace Maker," an eleven-page sketch of McClennan by his daughter in McClennan Family Papers, Amistad Research Center, Tulane University, New Orleans; Alonzo McClennan to Ida Ridley, August 11, 1880, ibid.; *New York Globe*, February 17, 1883; *New York Age*, February 18, 1888; Washington *Colored American*, March 14, 1903; Charleston *News and Courier*, July 20, 1902, October 16, 1912.

57. *New York Age*, May 24, 1890.

58. Powers, "Black Charleston: A Social History, 1822–1885," p. 176.

59. Bruce, quoted in Washington *Colored American*, January 31, 1903.

60. Grimké in *New York Age*, July 5, 1906; *South Carolina Messenger*, quoted in *Washington Bee*, December 2, 1905.

61. John W. Blassingame, *Black New Orleans, 1860–1880* (Chicago: University of Chicago Press, 1973), VI.

62. Loren Schweninger, ed., *From Tennessee Slave to St. Louis Entrepreneur: The Autobiography of James Thomas* (Columbia: University of Missouri Press, 1984), p. 113. See also Laura Foner, "Free People of Color in Louisiana and St. Dominque," *Journal of Social History*, III (Summer, 1970), 406–430; Charles B. Rousseve, *The Negro in Louisiana* (New Orleans: Xavier University Press, 1937); H. E. Sterkx, *The Free Negro in Ante-Bellum Louisiana* (Rutherford, N.J.: Fairleigh Dickinson University Press, 1972); Gary Mills, *The Forgotten People: Cane River's Creoles of Color* (Baton Rouge: Louisiana State University Press, 1977); Linda V. Ellsworth, "Pensacola's Creoles: Remnants of a Culture," unpublished paper in the author's possession; Marilyn Manhard, "The Free People of Color in Antebellum Mobile County, Alabama," M.A. thesis, University of South Alabama, 1982.

63. Sterkx, *The Free Negroes in Ante-Bellum Louisiana*, p. 160; Donald E. Everett, "Free Persons of Color in New Orleans, 1803–1865," doctoral diss., Tulane University, 1952.

64. Blassingame, *Black New Orleans*, pp. xvi, 10–15, 21–22, 127–128, 139; David C. Rankin "The Origins of Black Leadership in New Orleans During Reconstruction," *Journal of Southern History*, XL (August, 1974), 417–436. On colored Creoles, see Virginia R. Dominguez, *White By Definition: Social Classification in Creole Louisiana* (New Brunswick: Rutgers University Press, 1986), especially pp. 250–261.

65. Rodolphe Lucien Desdunes, *Our People and Our History* (Baton Rouge: Louisiana State University Press, 1973), pp. xxvii, 109.

66. Rankin, "Origins of Black Leadership in New Orleans During Reconstruction," pp. 435–436; Desdunes, *Our People and Our History*, pp. 29–30; V. P. Thomas, "Colored New Orleans," *Crisis*, II (February, 1916), pp. 188–192.

67. *Weekly Louisianian* (New Orleans), August 2, 1879.

68. *New York Globe*, October 6, 1883; see also Dale A. Somers, "Black and White Relations in New Orleans, 1865–1900," *Journal of Southern History*, XL (February, 1974), 19–42.

69. Rankin, "Origins of Black Leadership in New Orleans During Reconstruction," p. 421.

70. Arthe Agnes Anthony, "The Negro Creole Community in New Orleans, 1880–1920: An Oral History," Ph.D. diss., University of California, Irvine, 1978, pp. 47, 51.

71. Ibid., pp. 26, 135–150.

72. Ibid., pp. 94–99. For the educational activities of the colored Creole-dominated Justice, Protective, Social and Educational Club, which campaigned for a school in the third ward, see New Orleans *Weekly Pelican*, May 7, June 4, 1887.

73. Anthony, "The Negro Creole Community in New Orleans," pp. 94–95.

74. *The Crusader* (New Orleans), July 19, 1890.

75. Desdunes, *Our People and Our History*, pp. xv, 141–148; see also Otto H. Olsen, *The Thin Disguise: Turning Point in Negro History* (New York: Humanities Press, 1967), chap. 3.

76. Hollis R. Lynch, *The Black Urban Condition: A Documentary History, 1866–1971* (New York: Thomas Y. Crowell Co., 1973), pp. 58–59.

77. Desdunes, *Our People and Our History*, p. 18.

78. Anthony, "Negro Creole Community," p. 47.

79. On T. T. Allain, see *New York Globe*, August 4, 1884; *New York Freeman*, May 29, 1886; New Orleans *Southern Republican*, May 7, 28, 1887; *New York Freeman*, July 17, 1886, March 30, 1889; Washington *Colored American*, June 25, 1898, February 17, 1900; Alice Ruth Moore to Paul Laurence Dunbar, July 6, 1895, Paul Laurence Dunbar Papers, Ohio Historical Society, Columbus (microfilm); William J. Simmons, *Men of Mark: Eminent, Progressive and Rising* (Chicago: George M. Rewell and Co., 1887), pp. 125–141.

80. Indianapolis *Freeman*, May 22, 1897.

81. Ibid., March 29, 1902.

82. Ibid., June 16, 1909. The upper class in the New Orleans black community in the era after 1920 is treated in Allison Davis and John Dollard, *Children of Bondage* (Washington, D.C.: American Council on Education, 1940), especially chaps. VI and VIII; and in John H. Rohrer and Munro S. Edmonson, *The Eighth Generation: Cultures and Personalities of New Orleans* (New York: Harper and Brothers, 1960).

83. Alice Ruth Moore to Paul L. Dunbar, July 6, 1895, Dunbar Papers.

84. Dominguez, *White By Definition*, pp. 30, 164, 214, 258.

85. Rohrer and Edmonson, *The Eighth Generation*, pp. 215–233.

86. Dominguez, *White By Definition*, pp. 163–166.

87. Cleveland *Gazette*, January 10, 1885; Indianapolis *Freeman*, November 27, 1897, July 8, 1905; Mary Church Terrell, *A Colored Woman in A White World* (Washington: Ransdel, Inc., 1940), pp. 3–9; Annette Church and Roberta Church, *The Robert R. Churches of Memphis* (Ann Arbor: Edwards, 1974), p. 32–36; Preston R. Merry, "Josiah T. Settle," *Negro History Bulletin*, V (February, 1942), 113–114; G. P. Hamilton, *The Bright Side of Memphis: A Compendium of Information Concerning the Colored People of Memphis, Tennessee* (Memphis: n.p., 1908), pp. 30, 72–75, 101, 212; *Solvent Savings Bank and Trust Company, Eighth Semi-Annual Statement* (c. 1910); John M. Langston to R. R. Church, December 31, 1892, B. K. Bruce to R. R. Church, December, 1897, P. B. S. Pinchback to R. R. Church, February 20, 1885, March 16, 1886, July 13, 1898, January 23, 1903, Church Family Papers.

88. Indianapolis *Freeman*, June 20, 1896; on Nashville's black community, see ibid., January 1, 1898, October 24, 1908; Topeka *Plaindealer*, October 3, 1893; Washington *Colored American*, August 1, 1903; Howard Rabinowitz, *Race Relations in the Urban South, 1865–1890* (Urbana: University of Illinois Press, 1980), pp. 239–242, 246–251; Faye Robbins, "A World-Within-A-World: Black Nashville, 1880–1915," Ph.D. diss., University of Arkansas, 1980.

89. *The Globe* (Nashville), September 27, 1907.

90. "Structure of Nashville's Negro Society," Folder #5, E. Franklin Frazier Papers, Moorland-Spingarn Research Center, Howard University, Washington, D.C.; see also Charles Foster Smith, "The Negro in Nashville," *Century*, XLII (May, 1891), 154–156.

91. George C. Wright, "Blacks in Louisville, Kentucky, 1890–1930," Ph.D. diss., Duke University, 1977, pp. 65, 96–97.

92. James Weldon Johnson, *Along This Way: The Autobiography of James Weldon Johnson* (New York: Viking Press, 1933), pp. 58, 133–134; Washington *People's Advocate*, July 19, 1879; Indianapolis *Freeman*, November 17, 1894.

93. Ridgely Torrence, *The Story of John Hope* (New York: Macmillan, 1948), pp. 54–58; see also Richard R. Wright, Jr., *87 Years Behind the Black Curtain: An Autobiography* (Philadelphia: Rare Book Co., 1965), pp. 60–66.

94. J. Morgan Kousser, "Separate But *Not* Equal: The Supreme Court's First Decision on Discrimination in Schools," *Social Science Working Paper*, No. 204 (California Institute of Technology, 1978), pp. 15–21; Torrence, *John Hope*, p. 59.

95. On Savannah's black community, see Whittington B. Johnson, "Free Blacks in Antebellum Savannah: An Economic Profile," *Georgia Historical Quarterly*, LXIV (Winter, 1980), 418–431; John W. Blassingame, "Before the Ghetto: The Making of the Black Community in Savannah, Georgia, 1865–1880," *Journal of Social History*, VI (Summer, 1973), 463–488; Robert Perdue, *The Negro in Savannah, 1865–1900* (New York: Exposition Press, 1973); Wright, *87 Years Behind the Black Curtain*, pp. 66–67; *Savannah Tribune*, January 13, February 4, December 30, 1893; Roi Ottley, *The Lonely Warrior: The Life and Times of Robert S. Abbott* (Chicago: Henry Regnery, 1955), p. 35.

96. August Meier and David Lewis, "History of the Negro Upper Class in Atlanta, Georgia, 1890–1958," *Journal of Negro Education*, XXVIII (Spring, 1959), 130; Clarence Bacote, "Some Aspects of Negro Life in Georgia, 1880–1908," *Journal of Negro History*, XLIII (July, 1958), 190; Edward R. Carter, *The Black Side: A Partial History of the Business, Religious, and Educational Side of the Negro in Atlanta* (Atlanta: n.p., 1894), pp. 207–208; Robert J. Alexander, "Negro Business in Atlanta," *Southern Economic Journal*, XVII (April, 1951), 452–454; John Dittmer, *Black Georgia in the Progressive Era* (Urbana: University of Illinois Press, 1965), pp. 59–61.

97. Torrence, *John Hope*, p. 57; Indianapolis *Freeman*, June 28, 1890; Caroline Bond Day, *A Study of Some Negro-White Families in the United States* (Cambridge: Harvard University Press, 1932), p. 37.

98. Walter White, *A Man Called White: The Autobiography of Walter White* (New York: Viking Press, 1948), pp. 3–21.

99. Clarence Bacote, *The Story of Atlanta University: A Century of Service 1865–1965* (Atlanta: Atlanta University, 1965); Dittmer, *Black Georgia*, pp. 61–64; Johnson, *Along This Way*, pp. 75–76; *Atlanta Independent*, May 7, 1904, November 5, 1905, September 28, November 2, 1907, January 30, 1909; *Washington Bee*, October 13, 1894; Indianapolis *Freeman*, February 20, 1897.

100. Paul D. Lack, "An Urban Slave Community: Little Rock, 1831–1862," *Arkansas Historical Quarterly*, XLI (Autumn, 1982), 264–269.

101. D. B. Gaines, *Racial Possibilities As Indicated by the Negroes of Arkansas* (Little

Rock: Philander Smith College, 1898), pp. 62–83; Lack, "An Urban Slave Community," 268–269; *Biographical and Historical Memoirs of Central Arkansas* (Chicago: Goodspeed Publishing Co., 1889), pp. 795–808; Tom W. Dillard, "Isaac Gillam: Black Pulaski Countian," *Pulaski County Historical Review*, XXIV (March, 1876), 6–11; Adolphine Fletcher Terry, *Charlotte Stephens: Little Rock's First Black Teacher* (Little Rock: Academic Press, 1973).

102. C. Calvin Smith, "John E. Bush of Arkansas, 1890–1910," *Ozark Historical Review*, II (Spring, 1973), 48–59; John E. Bush, "Afro-American People of Little Rock," *Colored American Magazine*, VIII (January, 1905), 39–42; Joe Neal, "Fraternal Cemetery: Reflections on a Southern Negro Graveyard," *Pulaski County Historical Review*, XXV (March, 1977), 5; Dillard, "Isaac Gillam," 6–11.

103. Carter Woodson, "The Gibbs Family—The Hunts, The Marshalls, The Muses, The Laws and The Millers," *Negro History Bulletin*, XI (October, 1947), 3–12, 22; Tom W. Dillard, "The Black Moses of the West: A Biography of Mifflin Wistar Gibbs, 1823–1915," M.A. thesis, University of Arkansas, 1974.

104. *Biographical and Historical Memoirs of Central Arkansas*, pp. 803–804, 807–808; Barbara Garvey Jackson, "Florence Price, Composer," *The Black Perspectives in Music*, Spring, 1977, pp. 31–35; Fred W. Dietrich, *The History of Dentistry in Arkansas* (Little Rock: Arkansas Dental Association, n.d.), pp. 45–46; J. H. Smith, *Maudelle: A Novel* (Philadelphia: Mayhew Publishing Co., 1906).

105. J. G. Ish, "An Object of Life," *Christian Recorder*, XVIII (February 5, 1880), 1; Gaines, *Racial Possibilities*, pp. 67–68, 74–75; *New York Age*, November 21, 1907; *Who's Who in the Colored Race 1915*, edited by Frank L. Mather (Chicago: n.p., 1915), p. 149; *Who's Who in Colored America, 1938–40* (Brooklyn: Thomas Yenser, 1940), p. 275; Marla Manor, "The Ish House and the Doctor," *Arkansas Democrat Sunday Magazine*, June 9, 1968, pp. 1–3.

106. William Grant Still, "My Arkansas Boyhood," *Arkansas Historical Quarterly*, XXVI (Autumn, 1967), 285–292; Judith Anne Still, "Carrie Still Sheppardson: The Hallows of Her Footsteps," ibid., XLII (Spring, 1983), 37–46. On churches in Little Rock, see the analysis by E. M. Saddler in Indianapolis *Freeman*, September 21, 1901; Jackson, "Florence Price," 33.

4. The "Upper Tens" in the Northeast

1. Arthur Shadwell, *Industrial Efficiency*, 2 vols. (London: Longmans, Green, 1906), I, 311. For a perceptive account of blacks in nineteenth-century Philadelphia, see Theodore Hershberg and Henry Williams, "Mulattoes and Blacks: Intra-Group Color Differences and Social Stratification in Nineteenth Century Philadelphia," in *Philadelphia: Work, Space, Family, and Group in the Nineteenth Century*, edited by Theodore Hershberg (New York: Oxford University Press, 1981), pp. 392–434.

2. Ray A. Billington, ed., *The Journal of Charlotte Forten* (New York: Collier Books, 1961), pp. 13–20; Richard R. Wright, Jr., *The Negro in Pennsylvania: A Study in Economic History* (New York: Arno Press, 1969), pp. 26–54; *Philadelphia Tribune*, March 9, 1912; on "old families," see also Julie Winch, "The Leaders of Philadelphia's Black Community, 1789–1848," Ph.D. diss., Bryn Mawr College, 1982.

3. *Philadelphia Tribune*, May 11, 1912, March 1, 9, 1913; Henry M. Minton, *Early History of Negroes in Business in Philadelphia* (n.p., 1913), pp. 11–14; Carter Woodson, "The Bustill Family," *Negro History Bulletin*, XI (April, 1948), 147–148; W. E. B. Du Bois, *The Philadelphia Negro: A Social Study* (Philadelphia: University of Pennsylvania Press, 1899), pp. 18–19, 23, 34–35; Pauline Hopkins, "Famous Women of the Negro Race," *Colored American Magazine*, IV (August, 1912), 173.

4. "Catering," "Robert Bogle," Notes, Daniel Murray Papers, State Historical Society of Wisconsin, Madison (microfilm); Minton, *Early History of Negroes in Business in Philadelphia*, pp. 11–14; *Philadelphia Tribune*, May 11, 1912.

5. "Thomas Joshua Dorsey," Notes, Murray Papers; *New York Freeman*, August 8, 1885; Minton, *Early History of Negroes in Business in Philadelphia*, pp. 11–15.

6. *New York Globe*, December 15, 1883; Velma J. Hoover, "Meta Vaux Warrick Fuller: Her Life and Art," *Negro History Bulletin*, XL (March–April, 1977), 678–681; Harrison Wayman, "Meta Vaux Warrick," *Colored American Magazine*, VI (March, 1903), 325–331; Florence Bentley, "Meta Warrick, A Promising Sculptor," *Voice of the Negro*, IV (March, 1904), 116–118.

7. Minton, *Early History of Negroes in Business in Philadelphia*, pp. 11–15; *New York Globe*, June 2, 1883; *Cleveland Gazette*, February 21, 1891; Washington *Colored American*, April 19, 1902; H. Harrison Wayman, "The Quaker City," *Colored American Magazine*, VI (December, 1903), 888; Indianapolis *Freeman*, August 16, 1890. Andrew F. Stevens, the *doyen* of Philadelphia caterers in the late nineteenth century, was an active Episcopalian and the founder of the Citizens Republican Club in 1884, a political as well as a social uplift organization that was still in existence forty years later. Stevens died in 1898, but his descendants continued to be prominent in Philadelphia's black society; see Du Bois, *Philadelphia Negro*, p. 119; *Philadelphia Tribune*, December 14, 1912; "Andrew Stevens of Philadelphia," Murray Papers.

8. Anna Bustill Smith, "The Bustill Family," *Journal of Negro History*, X (October, 1925), 638–644; *New York Freeman*, April 4, 1885; *Philadelphia Tribune*, June 27, July 4, 1914. On the Mossell family, see Arthur O. White, "The Black Movement Against Jim Crow Education in Lockport, New York, 1835–1876," *New York History*, L (July, 1969), 276, 279.

9. *Indianapolis Freeman*, May 24, 1890; "John Stephens Durham," *Negro History Bulletin*, V (December, 1941), 67; Oliver G. Waters, "The Smoky City: Glimpses of Social Life," *Colored American Magazine*, IV (November, 1901), 14–15.

10. *New York Globe*, March 15, 1884; *New York Age*, January 4, 1890.

11. Du Bois, *The Philadelphia Negro*, pp. 317–320, 359.

12. H. W. Scott in *Washington Bee*, May 19, 1888.

13. *New York Age*, December 14, 1905; Du Bois, *The Philadelphia Negro*, p. 19; Wright, *The Negro in Pennsylvania*, pp. 42–43; *The Christian Recorder*, organ of the A.M.E. Church published in Philadelphia, regularly featured "local news" in the 1870s and 1880s. On the Scientific and Art Association of Philadelphia, see ibid., XVIII (October 28, 1880), 5; ibid., XIX (February 24, 1881), 3; see also "Think Well of Yourself," ibid., XVI (April 11, 1878), 1; *Philadelphia Tribune*, January 2, 1915.

14. "Nella," in *Indianapolis World*, July 6, 1889; Harrison, "The Quaker City," *Colored American Magazine*, VI (November, 1903), 769; *New York Age*, April 7, 1888.

15. Jessie Fauset, *The Chinaberry Tree: A Novel of American Life* (Philadelphia: J. B. Lippincott, 1931), pp. 23, 131, 188, 256, 286.

16. *Philadelphia Tribune*, February 10, 1917.

17. R. R. Wright, "The Negroes of Philadelphia," *A.M.E. Church Review*, XXIV (October, 1907), 142.

18. See below, pp. 234–237.

19. Rhoda G. Freeman, "The Free Negro in New York City in the Era Before the Civil War," Ph.D. diss., Columbia University, 1966, pp. 424–425; "Charles A. Dorsey," Notes, Murray Papers.

20. *New York Freeman*, March 7, 1885, June 5, 1887; *New York Age*, August 15, 1888, January 10, 1891; August 3, 1905; S. R. Scottron, "The New York Negro a Century Ago," *Colored American Magazine*, XII (June, 1907), 437–442; Samuel R.

Scottron, "New York African Society for Mutual Relief, Ninety-seventh Anniversary," *Colored American Magazine*, IX (December, 1905), 685–690; Helen Boardman, "First Families of Manhattan," *Phylon*, V (Spring Quarter, 1944), 138–141; Mary White Ovington, *Half A Man: The Status of the Negro in New York* (New York: Longmans, Green and Co., 1911), p. 176; W. E. B. Du Bois, *The Black North in 1901: A Social Study* (New York: Arno Press, 1969), p. 18; Carleton Mabee, *Black Education in New York State From Colonial to Modern Times* (Syracuse: Syracuse University Press, 1979), pp. 111–113; *Washington Bee*, April 14, 1900.

21. *New York Age*, January 12, 1889.

22. *New York Globe*, June 2, 1883.

23. *New York Freeman*, April 17, 1887; *New York Age*, January 31, 1885, March 23, 1889; David P. Thelan and Leslie H. Fishel, Jr., "Reconstruction in the North: The *World* Looks at New York's Negroes, March 16, 1867," *New York History*, XLIX (October, 1968), 432–438; Roi Ottley and William Weatherby, *The Negro in New York* (New York: New York Public Library, 1967), pp. 133–135; Gilbert Osofsky, *Harlem: The Making of a Ghetto: Negro New York, 1890–1930* (New York: Harper and Row, 1966), pp. 5–6. On Scottron, see Gail L. Buckley, *The Hornes: An American Family* (New York: Alfred A. Knopf, 1986), pp. 63–66.

24. "James W. Mars," "Charles Henry Lansing," Notes, Murray Papers.

25. *New York Times*, July 14, 1895; Ottley and Weatherby, *The Negro in New York*, p. 133; Du Bois, *The Black North in 1901*, p. 18.

26. *New York Globe*, June 21, 1884; *New York Age*, May 9, 1891; "Mrs. E. V. C. Eato," in Monroe A. Majors, *Noted Negro Women: Their Triumphs and Activities* (Chicago: Donohue and Henneberry, 1893), pp. 272–273.

27. Nail, quoted in Jervis Anderson, *This Was Harlem: A Cultural Portrait, 1900–1950* (New York: Farrar, Straus, Giroux, 1981), p. 28.

28. Quoted in Indianapolis *World*, July 9, 1887.

29. Anderson, *This Was Harlem*, pp. 28–29; Du Bois, *The Black North in 1901*, p. 18.

30. See extant copies of the *New York Globe*, *New York Freeman*, and *New York Age*, 1880–1918.

31. *New York Freeman*, March 13, 1886, June 4, 1887; *New York Age*, November 9, 1889, June 7, 1890.

32. *New York Freeman*, January 17, 31, 1885.

33. Seth M. Scheiner, *Negro Mecca: A History of the Negro in New York City, 1865–1920* (New York: New York University Press, 1965), pp. 20–21; James Weldon Johnson, *Black Manhattan* (New York: Alfred A. Knopf, 1930), p. 59.

34. Quoted in Scheiner, *Negro Mecca*, p. 20; see also Lionel M. Yard, "Blacks in Brooklyn," *Negro History Bulletin*, XXXVII (August–September, 1974), 289–293; Harold X. Connolly, "Blacks in Brooklyn From 1900 to 1960," Ph.D. diss., New York University, 1972, pp. 52, 115.

35. "Our Social Observer," in *New York Freeman*, November 29, 1884.

36. Johnson, *Along This Way*, pp. 202–203.

37. *New York Age*, March 23, 1889, August 15, 1891; New Orleans *Weekly Louisianian*, November 1, 1879.

38. On the black upper class in Albany, see *New York Globe*, October 20, 1883; *New York Freeman*, December 6, 1884, June 6, 1885, February 5, 1887; *New York Age*, June 25, 1890, January 16, 1892; Helen Buckler, *Daniel Hale Williams: Negro Surgeon* (New York: Pitman Publishing Co., 1954), pp. 56–58; *Cleveland Gazette*, October 23, 1886; Ira D. Reid, "American Cities—Albany, New York," *Opportunity*, VII (June, 1929), 179.

39. "Bruce Grit," in Washington *Colored American*, May 6, 1889.

40. *New York Age*, January 5, 1889, February 8, 1890.

41. *New York Age*, February 25, 1909, January 27, 1910, February 22, 1912, February 6, 1913, February 26, 1914.

42. Ibid., June 1, 1911, April 25, May 2, 1912, January 29, 1914.

43. On "The Frogs," see ibid., June 30, 1910, June 19, 1913.

44. John Daniels, *In Freedom's Birthplace: A Study of Boston Negroes* (Boston: Houghton Mifflin Co., 1914), pp. 163, 168, 181; see also George W. Harris, "Boston Colored People," *Colored American Magazine*, XIV (January, 1908), 28–31; Adelaide Cromwell Hill Gulliver, "The Negro Upper Class in Boston—Its Development and Present Social Structure," Ph.D. diss., Radcliffe College, 1952, pp. 52–54. On Brazillia Lew, see "Negroes Who Fought at Bunker Hill," *Ebony*, XIX (February, 1964), 44–53, 75. On Boston's antebellum black community, see James Oliver Horton and Lois E. Horton, *Black Bostonians: Family Life and Community in the Antebellum North* (New York: Holmes and Meier Publishers, 1979).

45. "James H. Wolff," *Colored American Magazine*, VI (March, 1903), 358–359; Topeka *Plaindealer*, April 8, 1904.

46. Daniels, *In Freedom's Birthplace*, pp. 121–126.

47. Ibid., p. 183.

48. *Boston Journal*, August 18, 1883; "May It Please Your Honor," *The Alumni Journal* [Hampton Institute], III (January, 1884), 1; *Boston Symphony Orchestra Fifty-Ninth Season 1939–40*; Ruffin Family Bible, in Heslip-Ruffin Papers, Amistad Research Center, Tulane University, New Orleans.

49. Washington *People's Advocate*, August 27, 1881; *New York Freeman*, October 30, 1886; *New York Age*, May 12, 1888; Indianapolis *Freeman*, November 23, 1912; Harris, "Boston Colored People," pp. 29–30.

50. Walter J. Stevens, *Chip on My Shoulder: Autobiography* (Boston: Meador Publishing Co., 1946), pp. 80–90; Gulliver, "The Negro Upper Class in Boston," pp. 99–100; Stephen R. Fox, *The Guardian of Boston: William Monroe Trotter* (New York: Atheneum, 1971), pp. 9–10, 15–22.

51. Daniels, *In Freedom's Birthplace*, p. 182

52. Harris, "Boston Colored People," p. 28.

53. "Boston's Smart Set," *Colored American Magazine*, II (January, 1901), 204–209.

54. Dorothy West, *The Living Is Easy* (New York: Arno Press, 1969), pp. 169–170, 172.

55. *Boston Sunday Globe* (clipping), July 22, 1894, entitled "In Colored Society," Ruffin Family Papers, Moorland Spingarn Research Center, Howard University, Washington, D.C.

56. Stevens, *Chip on My Shoulder*, pp. 16–17.

57. Ibid., p. 85; Gulliver, "Negro Upper Class in Boston," pp. 101–102; *New York Freeman*, October 30, 1886.

58. See Florida Ruffin Ridley, "Out of New England," unpublished manuscript, Ruffin Family Papers, Moorland-Springarn Research Center, Howard University, Washington, D.C.; Florida Ruffin Ridley, "Other Bostonians," unpublished manuscript, Heslip-Ruffin Papers; *Christian Recorder*, XIV (December 2, 1886), 2, for an obituary of George Lewis Ruffin.

59. Robert A. Warner, *New Haven Negroes: A Social History* (New Haven: Yale University Press, 1940), pp. 92–94, 169–171, 173–176, 182, 185.

60. George S. Schuyler, *Black and Conservative: The Autobiography of George S. Schuyler* (New Rochelle: Arlington House, 1966), pp. 3–5, 9, 11–12, 24.

61. Ibid., p. 3; J. E. Bruce to J. W. Cromwell, December 1, 1902, Alain Locke Papers, Moorland-Spingarn Research Center, Howard University, Washington, D.C.

62. Schuyler, *Black and Conservative*, pp. 6, 13, 47–48.

63. Washington *People's Advocate*, October 20, 1883; *New York Freeman*, April 6, 1886; Washington *Colored American*, August 1, 1903.

5. Elites in the Midwest and West

1. *American Citizen* (Kansas City), January 15, 1897.

2. *Historic Times* (Lawrence, Kansas), November 7, 1891.

3. Wendell P. Dabney, *Cincinnati's Colored Citizens* (Cincinnati: Dabney Publishing Co., 1926), pp. 150–153; Richard Pih, "Negro Self-Improvement Efforts in Antebellum Cincinnati," *Ohio History,* LXXVIII (Summer, 1969), 179–187; Henry L. Taylor, "On Slavery's Fringe: City Building and Black Community Development in Cincinnati: 1800–1850," *Ohio History*, LXLV (Winter-Spring, 1986), 5–33; David A. Gerber, *Black Ohio and the Color Line, 1860–1915* (Urbana: University of Illinois Press, 1976), pp. 21–22, 130–131, 328–329; Frank Quillin, *The Color Line in Ohio* (New York: Negro Universities Press, 1969), pp. 125–133; *Cleveland Gazette*, December 1, 1883, January 9, 1884, May 7, 1887; Carter G. Woodson, "The Negroes of Cincinnati Prior to the Civil War," *Journal of Negro History*, I (January, 1916), 1–22. On the relationships between education and status in Cincinnati's black community, see David L. Calkins, "Black Education and the 19th Century City: An Institutional Analysis of Cincinnati's Colored Schools," *Cincinnati Historical Society Bulletin*, XXXIII (Fall, 1975), 161–171.

4. Gerber, *Black Ohio*, pp. 117–118, 216, 221, 241–242; *Cleveland Gazette*, May 1, 1886, May 10, 1890, October 2, 1897; *Weekly Anglo-African* (New York), September 10, 1859; Paul McStallworth, "Robert James Harlan," *Dictionary of American Negro Biography*, pp. 287–288.

5. Simmons, *Men of Mark*, pp. 421–422; McStallworth, "Robert James Harlan," 288.

6. *The Appeal* (St. Paul), November 14, 1891; *Cleveland Gazette*, June 25, 1887; "Robert Gordon: A Successful Businessman," *Negro History Bulletin*, I (November, 1937), 1, 3.

7. See Judy Day and M. James Kedro, "Free Blacks in St. Louis: Antebellum Conditions, Emancipation, and the Postwar Era," *Bulletin of the Missouri Historical Society*, XXX (January, 1974), 117–135; Lawrence O. Christensen, ed., "Cyprian Clamorgan, The Colored Aristocracy of St. Louis," *Missouri Historical Review*, XXXI (October, 1974), 3–31; Lawrence O. Christensen, "Race Relations in St. Louis, 1865–1916," *Missouri Historical Review*, LXXVIII (January, 1984), 123–136; Lillian Brandt, "The Negroes of St. Louis," *Journal of the American Statistical Association*, VIII (March, 1903), 203–269. Among the most prominent members of the black elite of St. Louis both before and after the Civil War was James Thomas, the son of John Catron, Chief Justice of the Tennessee Supreme Court, and a slave mother who purchased his freedom in 1834. Thomas settled in St. Louis, where he prospered and married Antoinette Rutgers, whose mother was the richest free Negro in Missouri. On Thomas, see Loren Schweninger, ed., *From Tennessee Slave to St. Louis Entrepreneur: The Autobiography of James Thomas* (Columbia: University of Missouri Press, 1984).

8. Joan R. Sherman, "George Boyer Vashon," *Dictionary of American Negro Biography*, p. 617; *St. Paul Appeal*, December 5, 1891; *Crisis*, XXVIII (September, 1923), 216.

9. *New York Age*, June 9, 1888; *St. Louis Palladium*, May 16, July 4, October 3, 1903, February 13, October 29, December 3, 17, 1904; *Indianapolis Freeman*, December 27, 1890; Brandt, "The Negroes of St. Louis," p. 257.

10. Horace Mann Bond, *Black American Scholars: A Study of their Beginnings* (De-

troit: Bolamp Publishing, 1972), pp. 34–49; Lawrence O. Christensen, "Black St. Louis: A Study in Race Relations," Ph.D. diss., University of Missouri, 1972, p. 237; John Mercer Langston, *From the Virginia Plantation to the National Capitol* (Hartford: American Publishing Co., 1894), p. 75.

11. Quoted in *St. Louis Palladium*, April 8, 1905.

12. Ibid.

13. Allan H. Spear, *Black Chicago: The Making of A Negro Ghetto, 1890–1920* (Chicago: University of Chicago Press, 1967), pp. 5–8, 54; St. Clair Drake and Horace R. Cayton, *Black Metropolis: A Study of Negro Life in A Northern City* (New York: Harcourt, Brace and Co., 1945), pp. 531–538, 563.

14. Washington *People's Advocate*, June 21, 1879; Spear, *Black Chicago*, pp. 55, 77, 101, 111; Helen Buckler, *Daniel Hale Williams: Negro Surgeon* (New York: Pitman Publishing Co., 1954), pp. 25–27; New Orleans *Weekly Louisianian*, May 31, 1879; Charles A. Gliozzo, "John Jones: A Study of A Black Chicagoan," *Illinois Historical Journal*, LXXX (Autumn, 1987), 177–188.

15. Buckler, *Daniel Hale Williams*, pp. 26–27, 50–52; St. Paul *Western Appeal*, February 11, 1888; Springfield *Illinois Record*, December 25, 1897; Washington *Colored American*, October 11, 1903; Spear, *Black Chicago*, pp. 56–57, 66, 86.

16. Washington *Colored American*, April 2, 1898; Buckler, *Daniel Hale Williams*, pp. 147–148, 228–229.

17. Spear, *Black Chicago*, chap. 3; Edward E. Wilson, "Negro Society in Chicago," *Voice of the Negro*, IV (July, 1907), 306–309; *Broad Ax* (Chicago), December 25, 1909; Springfield *Illinois Record*, January 7, February 18, 1899; Indianapolis *Freeman*, April 2, 1907; "Dr. Bentley at the Dentists' Congress," *Voice of the Negro*, I (October, 1904), 443–444; Fannie Barrier Williams, "A Northern Negro's Autobiography," *Independent*, LVII (July 14, 1904), 91–96; Mary D. Crowe, "Fannie Barrier Williams," *Negro History Bulletin*, V (May, 1942), 190–191.

18. Quoted in *New York Age*, September 14, 1905.

19. Spear, *Black Chicago*, pp. 56, 167–168; Drake and Cayton, *Black Metropolis*, pp. 543–563. On Mollison, see Washington *Colored American*, July 11, 1903; Indianapolis *Freeman*, June 14, 1924; see also E. Franklin Frazier, *The Negro Family in Chicago* (Chicago: University of Chicago Press, 1932), pp. 82–83, 238.

20. Buckler, *Daniel Hale Williams*, pp. 77, 175–177, 189, 236–237, 250–252, 260–265; see also P. L. Prattis, "Chicago's '400,' " in Frederic H. Robb, *The Negro in Chicago, 1779 to 1929* (Chicago: Atlas Printing Co., 1929), pp. 84, 96–97, for changes in the upper class by 1929.

21. Indianapolis *World*, September 24, 1887; *Cleveland Gazette*, September 17, 1887; see also Springfield *Illinois Record*, December 25, 1897.

22. St. Paul *Western Appeal*, February 11, 1888.

23. Wilson, "Negro Society in Chicago," 306–309; for Wilson's later comments on the same topic, see Chicago *Broad Ax*, December 25, 1909.

24. *New York Age*, September 14, 1905; see also Fannie Barrier Williams, ibid., July 25, 1907.

25. *Chicago Whip*, quoted in *The Appeal* (Minneapolis), May 19, 1923.

26. David M. Katzman, *Before the Ghetto: Black Detroit in the Nineteenth Century* (Urbana: University of Illinois Press, 1973), pp. 3–9, 13–14, chap. V; W. B. Hartgrove, "The Story of Maria Louise Moore and Fannie M. Richards," *Journal of Negro History*, I (January, 1916), 23–33; Fred H. Williams, "Richard De Baptiste," *Negro History Bulletin*, XXII (May, 1959), 178; June B. Woodson, "The Negro in Detroit Before 1900," ibid., XXII (January, 1959), 90–91.

27. Katzman, *Before the Ghetto*, pp. 186–189; Indianapolis *Freeman*, April 17, 1897; Aris A. Mallas, Jr., Rea McCain, and Margaret Hedelen, *Forty Years in Politics: The Story of Ben Pelham* (Detroit: Wayne State University Press, 1957), pp. 2–3, 49–50, 84–87.

28. *Detroit News-Tribune*, April 27, 1902.

29. *Plaindealer* (Detroit), June 26, 1891.

30. Katzman, *Before The Ghetto*, p. 83.

31. Mallas, McCain, and Hedelen, *Forty Years in Politics*, p. 45.

32. Katzman, *Before The Ghetto*, p. 83; Washington *Colored American*, August 22, 1903; Indianapolis *Freeman*, January 13, 1906.

33. Detroit *Plaindealer*, August 15, 1890.

34. For a perceptive, sophisticated study of Cleveland's black community, see Kenneth L. Kusmer, *A Ghetto Takes Shape: Black Cleveland, 1870–1930* (Urbana: University of Illinois Press, 1976).

35. Quoted in Russell H. Davis, *Black Americans in Cleveland* (Washington: Associated Publishers, 1972), p. 46.

36. Ibid., pp. 31, 57; *Cleveland Gazette*, May 28, 1904; Kusmer, *A Ghetto Takes Shape*, pp. 9–10.

37. Indianapolis *Freeman*, August 26, 1899.

38. Kusmer, *A Ghetto Takes Shape*, pp. 27–28.

39. See above, p. 4.

40. See Helen M. Chesnutt, *Charles Waddell Chesnutt: Pioneer of the Color Line* (Chapel Hill: University of North Carolina Press, 1952).

41. Charles W. Chesnutt, *The House Behind the Cedars* (Boston: Houghton Mifflin Co., 1901), pp. 209–210.

42. John P. Green, *Fact Stranger Than Fiction: Seventy-Five Years of a Busy Life* (Cleveland: Riehl Printing Co., 1920), pp. 3–8; John P. Green to George A. Myers, September 16, 1899, George A. Myers Papers, Ohio Historical Society, Columbus; Lewis Chesnutt to John P. Green, February 17, 1898, John P. Green Papers, Western Reserve Historical Society, Cleveland.

43. Carrie Clifford, "Cleveland and Its Colored People," *Colored American Magazine*, IX (July, 1905), 365–380; Gerber, *Black Ohio*, pp. 82–83, 308, 340, 345–370; John P. Green to George A. Myers to John P. Green, December 11, 1902, Green Papers.

44. Newark *Daily Advocate*, quoted in Cleveland *Gazette*, October 9, 1886. On "blue veinism," see Cleveland *Gazette*, October 27, 1888, January 18, February 1, 1896; Nashum D. Brascher, "Cleveland—A Representative American City," *Voice of the Negro*, II (August, 1905), 534; *Cleveland Journal*, July 11, 1908.

45. Richard P. Wright, Jr., "The Negroes of Xenia, Ohio," *Bulletin of the Bureau of Labor*, No. 47 (July, 1903), p. 1042; see also on Steubenville, Ohio, Cleveland *Gazette*, March 24, 1906, and on other Ohio towns, Quillen, *Color Line in Ohio*, pp. 141–153, and Le Roy T. Williams, "Black Toledo: Afro-Americans in Toledo, Ohio, 1890–1930," Ph.D. diss., University of Toledo, 1977.

46. David V. Taylor, "Pilgrim's Progress: Black St. Paul and The Making of An Urban Ghetto, 1870–1930," Ph.D. diss., University of Minnesota, 1977, pp. 73–78, 90, 116–118.

47. George L. Knox, *Slave and Freeman: The Autobiography of George L. Knox*, edited by Willard B. Gatewood, Jr. (Lexington: University Press of Kentucky, 1979), pp. 20–23; A. H. Maloney, "The Negro of Indianapolis," in *Indianapolis Recorder*, January 14, 1928; Indianapolis *World*, April 16, 1887, November 1, 1889, February 1, April 20, August 23, 1890; Indianapolis *Freeman*, June 11, 1892, July 16, 1896, June 28, 1897, December 26, 1914.

48. For a perceptive study of blacks in San Francisco, see Douglas Henry Daniels, *Pioneer Urbanites: A Social and Cultural History of Black San Francisco* (Philadelphia: Temple University Press, 1980).

49. Ibid., pp. 22–24; Delilah L. Beasley, *The Negro Trailblazers of California* (New York: Negro Universities Press, 1969), chaps. X, XII; Philip M. Montesano, *Some Aspects of the Free Negro Question in San Francisco, 1849–1870* (San Francisco: R and E Research Associates, 1973), pp. 11–32; Roger W. Lotchin, *San Francisco, 1846–1956; From Hamlet to City* (New York: Oxford University Press, 1974), pp. 129–132; *Pacific Coast Appeal* (San Francisco), February 13, 1904, April 23, 1906.

50. *Daily Morning Call* (San Francisco), November 1, 1892; *The Elevator* (San Francisco), October 25, 1867, March 6, 1868, November 8, 1873.

51. Francis M. Lortie, *San Francisco's Black Community, 1870–1890: Dilemmas in the Struggle for Equality* (San Francisco: R and E Research Associates, 1973), pp. 28–29; see also *New York Globe*, July 7, September 29, 1883.

52. San Francisco *Elevator*, September 5, 1874.

53. Daniels, *Pioneer Urbanites*, pp. 135–137.

54. *Western Outlook* (Oakland), January 2, July 24, August 7, 1915; May 15, 1926.

55. See Laurence B. de Graaf, "The City of Black Angels: Emergence of the Los Angeles Ghetto, 1890–1930," *Pacific Historical Review*, XXXIX (August, 1970), 323–352; J. Max Bond, *The Negro in Los Angeles* (San Francisco: R and E Research Associates, 1972), p. 33.

56. Bond, *The Negro in Los Angeles*, pp. 13–15, 34.

57. Ibid., pp. 12–13; Beasley, *Negro Trailblazers*, p. 109; James W. Johnson, "Robert C. Owens: A Pacific Coast Successful Negro," *Colored American Magazine*, IX (July, 1905), 391–393; Max B. Thrasher, "An Account of Washington's California Four, January 31, 1905," in *Booker T. Washington Papers*, VII, 18–25; see Sue Bailey Thurman, *Pioneers of Negro Origin in California* (San Francisco: Acme Publishing Co., 1971), pp. 44–47.

58. Bond, *The Negro in Los Angeles*, pp. 13–14; W. Sherman Savage, *Blacks in the West* (Westport, Ct.: Greenwood Press, 1976), p. 127.

59. *The California Eagle*, October 13, 1914, March 25, 1916.

60. George F. Bragg, *History of the Afro-American Group of the Episcopal Church* (Baltimore: Church Advocate Press, 1922), p. 241.

61. Bond, *The Negro in Los Angeles*, p. 69.

62. See Phyllis Scott, "Titus Alexander," *California Eagle*, November 13, 1947; *Opportunity*, XI (May, 1933), 129; Thurman, *Pioneers of Negro Origin in California*, "Foreword," no pagination.

63. Calvin F. Schmid, *Social Trends in Seattle* (Seattle: University of Washington Press, 1944), pp. 139–140; W. Sherman Savage, "Negro Pioneers in the State of Washington," *Negro History Bulletin*, XXI (January, 1958), 93–95; Quintard Taylor, "The Emergence of Black Communities in the Pacific Northwest, 1865–1910," *Journal of Negro History*, LXIV (Fall, 1979), 343.

64. *Seattle Republican*, April 5, December 13, 1901, January 3, February 21, 28, December 5, 1902, August 17, 1906, February 8, 1907.

65. Horace Cayton, *Long Old Road* (New York: Trident Press, 1965), pp. 1–9; *Seattle Republican*, October 12, 1900; "Horace Roscoe Cayton," *Current Biography, 1946* (Chicago: H. W. Wilson Co., 1947), 103–104.

66. Cayton, *Long Old Road*, pp. 17–21.

67. Ibid.

68. *Seattle Republican*, March 29, 1901.

69. Ibid., January 25, 1907.

70. Lyle W. Dorsett, *The Queen City: A History of Denver* (Boulder, Colorado: Pruett Publishing Co., 1977), pp. 52–53.

71. "Henry Oscar Wagoner: 'The Douglass of Colorado,' " *Colored American Magazine*, V (July, 1902), 188–192; Simmons, *Men of Mark*, pp. 469–472.

72. Washington *People's Advocate*, March 26, August 6, 13, 1881; *Colorado Statesman* (Denver), April 24, 1909; Forbes Parkhill, *Mister Barney Ford: A Portrait in Bistre* (Denver: Sage Books, 1963), p. 100.

73. Information on Barney Ford and his family is based on Parkhill, *Mister Barney Ford.*

74. *Colorado Statesman*, February 13, 1903, October 28, 1905, January 20, March 31, July 21, 1906, January 4, 1908, October 22, 1910; "Denver, The City Beautiful—Denver, The City of Lights," *Colored American Magazine*, XII (May, 1907), 336–338.

75. "Denver, The City Beautiful," p. 338; Denver *Colorado Statesman*, April 14, 1906, October 22, 1910; Bragg, *Afro-American Group of the Episcopal Church*, p. 240.

76. M. Marguerite Davenport, *Azalia: The Life of Madame E. Azalia Hackley* (Boston: Chapman and Grimes, 1947), pp. 20–23, 31, 38, 42–44, 66, 74, 75, 90; "Booker T. Washington's Stay in Denver, January 28, 1900," in *Booker T. Washington Papers*, V, 423–427; Katzman, *Before The Ghetto*, pp. 150, 153, 163.

Part III: Color, Culture, and Behavior

Prologue

1. Edward E. Wilson, in Chicago *Broad Ax*, December 25, 1909.

2. See Arna Bontemps, *Free At Last: The Life of Frederick Douglass* (New York: Dodd, Mead, 1971), pp. 275–276.

3. Washington *People's Advocate*, August 2, 1879; *Cleveland Gazette*, October 10, 1886; Indianapolis *News*, March 22, 1888.

4. Indianapolis *Freeman*, July 28, 1906.

5. *New York Age*, August 16, 1906; Chicago *Broad-Ax*, June 30, July 28, 1906; see also undated newspaper clippings on the NACW convention in 1906 in the Mary Church Terrell Papers, Library of Congress, Washington, D.C.

6. Karen Halttunen, *Confidence Men and Painted Women: A Study of Middle Class Culture in America, 1830–1870* (New Haven: Yale University Press, 1982), p. 93.

7. David S. Barry, *Forty Years in Washington* (Boston: Little, Brown, 1924), pp. 59–61; Samuel D. Smith, *The Negro in Congress, 1870–1901* (Chapel Hill: University of North Carolina Press, 1940), pp. 27–38; undated newspaper clippings, Blanche K. Bruce Papers, Library of Congress; *Cleveland Gazette*, May 4, 1889.

8. Mary Church Terrell to Robert Terrell, June 25, 1902, Mary Church Terrell Papers, Library of Congress.

9. Clara Burrill to R. C. Bruce, August 7, 1901, R. C. Bruce Papers, Moorland-Spingarn Research Center, Howard University, Washington, D.C.

10. R. C. Bruce to Clara Burrill, November ?, 1902, R. C. Bruce Papers; Ralph Tyler, "Real Society," *Colored American Magazine*, XIII (November, 1907), 391.

11. Barry, *Forty Years in Washington*, p. 60; Washington *Colored American*, March 26, 1898; Cleveland *Plaindealer*, June 24, 1878.

12. Clara Burrill to R. C. Bruce, June 2, 1903, R. C. Bruce Papers.

13. Fannie Barrier Williams, "Club Movement Among Negro Women," in J. W. Gibson and W. H. Crogman, *Progress of a Race* (Miami: Mnemosyne Publishing Co.,

1969), p. 207; Josephine Bruce, "The Afterglow of the Women's Convention," *Voice of the Negro*, I (November, 1904), 541–543.

14. "Bruce Grit," in Washington *Colored American*, March 26, 1898; William C. Harris, "Blanche K. Bruce: Conservative Assimilationist," *Southern Black Leaders of the Reconstruction Era*, edited by Howard N. Rabinowitz (Urbana: University of Illinois Press, 1982), pp. 27–28.

15. Cleveland *Plain Dealer*, June 24, 1878.

16. *Washington Bee*, January 31, February 21, 1885.

17. "Roscoe Conkling Bruce," Notes, Daniel Murray Papers, State Historical Society of Wisconsin, Madison; Washington *Colored American*, May 6, 1899, June 13, 1903.

18. Louis R. Harlan, *Booker T. Washington: Wizard of Tuskegee, 1901–1915* (New York: Oxford University Press, 1983), pp. 144, 149–150.

19. "Roscoe Bruce," Notes, Murray Papers.

20. Washington *Colored American*, March 26, 1898.

21. Josephine Bruce to Roscoe Bruce, January 22, 1897, R. C. Bruce Papers.

22. Indianapolis *News*, March 22, 1888; Indianapolis *Freeman*, March 26, 1898.

23. Roscoe Bruce to Clara Burrill, January ?, 1902, R. C. Bruce Papers.

24. Harris, "Blanche K. Bruce," pp. 25–28, 32–33; "Bruce Grit," in the Washington *Colored American*, March 26, 1898.

25. Harris, "Blanche K. Bruce," p. 28.

26. Booker T. Washington to the Faculty of Harvard University, April 23, 1898, *Papers of Booker T. Washington*, edited by Louis R. Harlan et al., IV, 411; Jere A. Brown to George Myers, November 16, 1901, George A. Myers Papers, Ohio Historical Society, Columbus.

27. See *Results of an Investigation Authorized by the Board of Education Into the Educational and Administrative Efficiency of Roscoe Conkling Bruce, Assistant Superintendent of Schools of the District of Columbia* (n.p., n.p., 1919), especially pp. 5, 8, 9–11.

28. R. C. Bruce to Josephine Bruce, December 22, 1903, R. C. Bruce Papers; R. C. Bruce to Archibald Grimké, January 4, 1914, Archibald Grimké Papers, Moorland-Spingarn Research Center, Howard University, Washington, D.C.

29. Josephine Bruce to R. C. Bruce, April 6, 1902, R. C. Bruce Papers.

30. R. C. Bruce to Josephine Bruce, ?, 1922, R. C. Bruce Papers.

31. For the Lowell-Bruce correspondence, see *New York Times*, January 12, 1923; Marcia Graham Synnott, *The Half-Opened Door: Discrimination and Admission at Harvard, Yale and Princeton, 1900–1970* (Westport, CT: Greenwood Press, 1979), pp. 49–50, 52.

32. *New York Times*, January 13, 24, 26, 27, February 1, 1923; see Folder 96 entitled "Harvard Exclusion Policy" in R. C. Bruce Papers.

6. The Color Factor

1. E. Franklin Frazier, *The Negro Family in the United States* (Chicago: University of Chicago Press, 1939), chap. XIX, especially pp. 405–406.

2. John G. Mencke, *Mulattoes and Race Mixture: American Attitudes and Images, 1865–1918* (n.p.: UMI Research Press, 1979), x; Thomas Holt, *Black Over White: Negro Political Leadership in South Carolina During Reconstruction* (Urbana: University of Illinois Press, 1977), p. 61; David G. Neilson, *Black Ethos: Northern Urban Negro Life and Thought, 1890–1930* (Westport: Greenwood Press, 1977), pp. 162–181.

3. See Joel Williamson, *New People: Miscegenation and Mulattoes in the United States* (New York: Free Press, 1980); Edward Reuter, *Race Mixture: Studies in Intermarriage and Miscegenation* (New York: McGraw-Hill, 1931); Mencke, *Mulattoes and Race Mixture*,

especially p. 132; Patricia Morton, "From Invisible Man to 'New People': The Recent Discovery of American Mulattoes," *Phylon*, XLVI (June, 1985), 106–122.

4. Alfred Holt Stone, *Studies in the American Race Problem* (New York: Doubleday, Page, 1908), pp. 398–439.

5. H. Paul Douglass, *Christian Reconstruction in the South* (Boston: Pilgrim Press, 1909), p. 85.

6. Mary Helm, *The Upward Path: The Evolution of a Race* (New York: Eaton and Mains, 1909), pp. 158–161.

7. For a similar opinion by a prominent black, see Josiah T. Settle, in *Colored American* (Washington), August 29, 1903.

8. Helm, *The Upward Path*, p. 161.

9. Williamson, *New People*, p. 108.

10. Lura Beam, *He Called Them By Lightning: A Teacher's Odyssey in the Negro South, 1908–1919* (Indianapolis: Bobbs-Merrill, 1967), pp. 88–90.

11. *Washington Bee*, August 23, 1891; *Cleveland Gazette*, December 6, 1890; Indianapolis *Freeman*, October 23, 1897; Charleston, West Virginia *Advocate*, quoted in Denver *Colorado Statesman*, March 5, 1910; see also letter to the editor entitled "Aristocracy of Color," in *The Sun* (New York), July 24, 1913.

12. John M. Henderson, "The Forces Upon Which the Race Depends for Success," *Colored American Magazine*, XIV (January, 1908), 71.

13. *Washington Bee*, May 13, 20, 1893; *Cleveland Gazette*, April 25, 1891.

14. Sutton E. Griggs, *Overshadowed* (Nashville: Orion Publishing Co., 1901), p. 63.

15. "Class Distinctions Among Negroes," *Southern Workman*, XXVIII (October, 1899), 371; Nannie H. Burroughs, "Not Color But Character," *Voice of the Negro*, I (July, 1904), 277–279.

16. Samuel Barrett, "A Plea for Unity," *Colored American Magazine*, VII (January, 1904), 49.

17. Kansas City *American Citizen*, March 22, 1895; Emma Lou Thornbrough, *T. Thomas Fortune: Militant Journalist* (Chicago: University of Chicago Press, 1972), p. 132.

18. Griggs, *Overshadowed*, p. 71; in 1905 the Post Office Department launched a campaign against companies that advertised products that promised to turn black skins white and to remove the "kink" from hair; see *New York Times*, June 19, 1905.

19. Leon Litwack, *Been in the Storm So Long: The Aftermath of Slavery* (New York: Alfred Knopf, 1979), p. 467.

20. Burroughs, "Not Color But Character," 277–279.

21. Pine Bluff *Echo*, quoted in Topeka *Times-Observer*, October 10, 1891.

22. *Cleveland Gazette*, January 4, 1902.

23. Barrett, "A Plea for Unity," 49.

24. Majors, in Indianapolis *Freeman*, December 31, 1910.

25. Chicago *Broad Ax*, December 25, 1909.

26. Indianapolis *Freeman*, May 25, 1889; James S. Stemons, "Negroes of Pure and Negroes of Mixed Blood," in Chicago *Broad Ax*, March 23, 1907; Washington *Colored American*, December 13, 1902.

27. "Mulattoes, Negroes and the Jamestown Exhibit," *Colored American Magazine*, XIII (August, 1907), 87–88.

28. Walter White, "The Paradox of Color," in *The New Negro: An Interpretation*, edited by Alain Locke (New York: Albert and Charles Boni, 1925), p. 367.

29. Baltimore *Afro-American Ledger*, March 7, 1903.

30. "Colored People of Charleston," *African Repository*, XXIII (June, 1847), 190.

31. Marina Wikramanayake, *A World in Shadow: The Free Black in Antebellum*

South Carolina (Columbia: University of South Carolina Press, 1973), p. 51; Bernard E. Powers, Jr., "Black Charleston: A Social History, 1822–1885," Ph.D. diss., Northwestern University, 1982, p. 177.

32. Beam, *He Called Them By Lightning*, p. 170.

33. *The Works of Francis J. Grimké*, edited by Carter G. Woodson, 4 vols. (Washington: Associated Publishers, 1942), I, 541; see also Amelia Merriman, "Avery Normal Institute," *American Missionary*, XLV (May, 1891), 181–183; *New York Age*, October 3, 1885.

34. John E. Bruce, in Washington *Colored American*, January 31, 1900; Mamie Garvin Fields, *Lemon Swamp and Other Places: A Carolina Memoir* (New York: Free Press, 1983), p. 24; Kelly Miller, "The 'Colored' United States: South Carolina," *The Messenger*, VII (December, 1925), 377.

35. *Works of Francis J. Grimké*, I, p. 541; "Frances L. Cardozo," Notes, Daniel Murray Papers (microfilm), State Historical Society of Wisconsin, Madison; see also book manuscript "Folks Ways," by F. Elsee [Francis L. Cardozo, Jr.], in Francis L. Cardozo Family Papers, Library of Congress.

36. Howard N. Rabinowitz, *Race Relations in the Urban South, 1865–1890* (New York: Oxford University Press, 1978), p. 249; "Structure of Nashville's Negro Society," E. Franklin Frazier Papers, Moorland-Spingarn Research Center, Howard University, Washington, D.C.; see also Faye W. Robbins, "A World-Within-A-World: Black Nashville, 1880–1915," Ph.D. diss., University of Arkansas, 1980, pp. 245–248; Louis C. Perry, "Studies in the Religious Life of the City of Nashville, Tenn.," *Vanderbilt University Quarterly*, IV (Summer, 1904), 90–91.

37. Indianapolis *Freeman*, May 20, 1893.

38. Baltimore *Afro-American Ledger*, March 7, 1903.

39. See Robert Perdue, *The Negro in Savannah, 1865–1900* (New York: Exposition Press, 1973), pp. 91–92; Roi Ottley, *The Lonely Warrior: Life and Times of Robert S. Abbott* (Chicago: Henry Regnery and Co., 1955), pp. 34–36.

40. *Atlanta Independent*, January 9, 1909, May 30, 1914, October 23, 1915.

41. See Chicago *Broad Ax*, September 20, 1902, September 17, 1904, October 27, 1907, October 16, 1909.

42. Indianapolis *Freeman*, June 27, July 18, August 15, 1896.

43. Kansas City *American Citizen*, August 2, 1894.

44. *St. Louis Palladium*, October 28, 1905.

45. Wichita *Torchlight*, April 24, June 19, 1909.

46. *Cleveland Gazette*, February 21, 1885, March 13, 1886, May 7, 1887; Indianapolis *World*, July 26, 1890.

47. Cleveland *Gazette*, October 9, 1886, January 18, December 6, 1890; N. D. Brascher, "Cleveland—A Representative American City," *Voice of the Negro*, II (August, 1905), 532–536.

48. David A. Gerber, *Black Ohio and the Color Line, 1860–1915* (Urbana: University of Illinois Press, 1976), p. 135; Kenneth L. Kusmer, *A Ghetto Takes Shape: Black Cleveland, 1870–1930* (Urbana: University of Illinois Press, 1976), pp. 130–133.

49. *Cleveland Gazette*, January 18, February 1, 1890.

50. Brascher, "Cleveland—Representative American City," 534; see also *Cleveland Journal*, July 11, 1908; R. W. Thompson, in Indianapolis *Freeman*, October 23, 1897.

51. See Bruce's columns in *Cleveland Gazette*, December 11, 1886; Washington *Colored American*, May 6, 1899, August 11, 1900; J. E. Bruce, "Color Prejudice Among Negroes," in *The Selected Writings of John Edward Bruce*, edited by Peter Gilbert (New York: Arno Press, 1971), pp. 106–108; J. E. Bruce to J. W. Cromwell, December 1,

1902, December 29, 1904, June 5, 1902, August 5, 1912, Alain Locke Papers, Moorland-Spingarn Research Center, Howard University, Washington, D.C.

52. John E. Bruce, "Colored Society in Washington," typescript, Schomburg Center for Research in Black Culture, New York Public Library; large portions of this manuscript are quoted in Frazier, *Negro Family in the United States*, pp. 397–400.

53. *Cleveland Gazette*, March 20, 1886; *Washington Bee*, January 18, 1890; Kansas City *American Citizen*, April 5, 1901.

54. Based on a reading of *Bee* editorials from 1882 to 1922.

55. Washington *Colored American*, August 18, 1900; Alexander Walters, *My Life and Work* (New York: Fleming H. Revell, 1917), pp. 123–124; Denver *Colorado Statesman*, January 9, 1909.

56. *Washington Bee*, December 20, 1890; see also June 7, 1890, April 23, 1891, June 3, December 23, 1893, May 6, 1897, August 5, 1911.

57. Ibid., September 18, 1886, April 23, 1891, June 3, 1893, February 24, 1906.

58. Ibid., February 2, 1884, October 27, 1894, November 7, 1908, September 18, 1918.

59. Ibid., November 1, 1884.

60. Ibid., September 4, 1897.

61. Ibid., February 12, 1916.

62. Ibid.

63. Ibid., October 27, 1894; see also "The Negroes and the Near Negroes," *Colored American Magazine*, XIII (July, 1907), 9–10.

64. "Charles B. Purvis," in William J. Simmons, *Men of Mark, Eminent, Progressive and Rising* (Chicago: Johnson Publishing Co., 1970), p. 478.

65. Washington *People's Advocate*, July 21, 1883; Washington *National Leader*, February 23, 1889.

66. *Cleveland Gazette*, July 25, 1891.

67. Ibid., February 7, 1885, May 9, 1914.

68. John Roy Lynch, *Reminiscences of an Active Life: The Autobiography of John Roy Lynch*, edited by John Hope Franklin (Chicago: University of Chicago Press, 1970), pp. ix–xxviii, 9–22.

69. Kolchin, *First Freedom: Responses of Alabama's Blacks to Emancipation and Reconstruction* (Westport, Ct.: Greenwood, 1972), p. 141; Lynch, *Autobiography*, pp. 301–304; New Orleans *Weekly Louisianian*, November 1, 1879; *Washington Bee*, September 27, December 20, 1884.

70. *Washington Bee*, September 27, December 20, 1884; Lynch, *Autobiography*, p. 304.

71. *Washington Bee*, December 20, 17, 1884; *New York Freeman*, December 13, 1884.

72. *Washington Bee*, January 10, March 28, 1885.

73. *Wall v. Oyster, Reports of Cases Adjudged in the Court of Appeals of the District of Columbia, 1910–1911*, vol. 36, 50–58.

74. Ibid., See also Baltimore *Afro-American Ledger*, December 24, 1910; Indianapolis *Freeman*, January 7, 1911; *New York Age*, December 8, 1910; Mary Church Terrell, *A Colored Woman in a White World* (Washington: Ransdell, 1940), pp. 131–132.

75. *Washington Bee*, June 4, 1910.

76. Ibid., June 3, 1893, January 4, 1894, May 6, 1897, January 14, August 5, 1911, January 30, 1915, September 28, 1918.

77. Ibid., November 14, 1914.

78. Ibid., March 22, 29, 1913.

79. Ibid., September 19, 1914, April 29, 1916.

80. Ibid., January 18, 1890; Cleveland *Gazette*, April 25, 1891.

81. Indianapolis *Freeman*, October 26, 1907.

82. Transcript of an interview with Julia Moore Griffin by Margot Dashiell, August, 1979; Denver *Colorado Statesman*, August 27, 1907.

83. Thornbrough, *T. Thomas Fortune*, pp. 131–135; Bruce, *Selected Writings*, pp. 50–52, 106–108.

84. Chicago *Broad Ax*, September 20, 1902.

85. John P. Green to Mrs. John P. Green, July 16, 1902, John P. Green Papers, Western Reserve Historical Society, Cleveland.

86. P. B. S. Pinchback to Whitefield McKinlay, August 18, 1912, Whitefield McKinlay Papers in Carter G. Woodson Collection, Library of Congress.

87. Kansas City *American Citizen*, April 25, 1902.

88. E. Azalia Hackley, *The Colored Girl Beautiful* (Kansas City: Burton Publishing Co., 1916), pp. 33–38.

89. On one occasion, Robert Terrell wrote a friend: "Paul Dunbar, our neighbor, has just married that pretty 'yaller' girl—Miss Alice Ruth Moore." See R. H. Terrell to R. R. Church, April 18, 1898, Robert Reed Church Papers, Mississippi Valley Collection, Memphis State University, Memphis, Tennessee.

90. Washington *Colored American*, April 18, 1898; *Pittsburgh Courier*, June 14, 1912.

91. Darwin T. Turner, ed., *The Wayward and the Seeking: A Collection of Writings by Jean Toomer* (Washington: Howard University Press, 1980), pp. 22–24; S. P. Fullinwider, "Jean Toomer: Lost Generation or Negro Renaissance?" *Phylon*, XXVII (Winter, 1966), 397; Cynthia E. Kerman and Richard Eldridge, *The Lives of Jean Toomer: A Hunger for Wholeness* (Baton Rouge: Louisiana State University Press, 1987), pp. 18–19, 85; John C. Griffin, Jr., "Jean Toomer: American Writer," Ph.D. diss., University of South Carolina, 1976, pp. 1–29.

92. John P. Green, *Fact Stranger Than Fiction: Seventy Five Years of a Busy Life* (Cleveland: Riehl Printing Co., 1920), chap. I. On Harlan, see *Cleveland Gazette*, May 1, 1886, May 10, 1890, October 2, 1897; Paul Stallworth, "Robert James Harlan," *Dictionary of American Negro Biography*, 287–288. The story of the Syphax family is found in Gerri Major, *Black Society* (Chicago: Johnson Publishing Co., 1976), pp. 40–41, 398–399; and E. Delorus Preston, Jr., "William Syphax, A Pioneer in Negro Education in the District of Columbia," *Journal of Negro History*, XX (October, 1935), 448–454; see also Carter Woodson, "The Beginnings of the Miscegenation of Whites and Blacks," *Journal of Negro History*, III (October, 1918), 335–353; Pauli Murray, *Proud Shoes: The Story of an American Family* (New York: Harper, 1956), p. 33. On some occasions mulatto descendants of well-to-do white families were successful in their legal actions to share in estates; among them were Alice Strange Davis, a music director in Washington schools, and Bettie Thomas Lewis of Richmond; see St. Paul *Western Appeal*, July, 1892 and *New York Age*, May 3, 1890.

93. Quotation on genealogy from Ella Sheppard Moore, *Negro Womanhood: Its Past* (Boston: American Missionary Association, n.d.), p. 1. On the Downing family, see *New York Freeman*, March 7, 1885; Washington *Colored American*, August 1, 1903; *New York Times*, November 18, 1904; "George T. Downing," Notes, Murray Papers.

94. Michael Flusche, "On the Color Line: Charles Waddell Chesnutt," *North Carolina Historical Review*, LIII (January, 1976), 18.

95. Traveling in Florida, Mary Terrell who was probably temporarily "passing," had a conversation with a white woman who had no idea she "was colored" and asked her: "Are you related to Governor Terrell of Georgia? Your eyes are just like his." Terrell, Diary, April 8, 1909, Terrell Papers.

96. Fanny Garrison Villard to Mr. Ely, December 8, 1910 (copy), Mary Church Terrell Papers.

97. Terrell, *Colored Woman in a White World,* p. 427; Andrew F. Hilyer, "An Analysis of American Color Prejudice and How to Overcome It," March 22, 1892, Andrew F. Hilyer Papers, Moorland-Spingarn Research Center, Howard University, Washington, D.C.

98. J. Douglas Wetmore to W. E. B. Du Bois, October 20, 1903, *Correspondence of W. E. B. Du Bois, Selections, 1877–1934,* edited by Herbert Aptheker (Amherst: University of Massachusetts Press, 1973), p. 60.

99. James Weldon Johnson, *The Autobiography of an Ex-Colored Man* (New York: Alfred A. Knopf, 1979), pp. 157–167.

100. John Hope to Lugenia Hope, August 2, 1899, John Hope Papers (microfilm), Atlanta University, Atlanta, Georgia.

101. Quoted in Reverdy C. Ransom, *The Pilgrimage of Harriet Ransom's Son* (Nashville: Sunday School Union, n.d.), p. 83.

102. *Cleveland Journal,* July 1, 1905; *New York Age,* July 20, 1905; Helen M. Chesnutt, *Charles Waddell Chesnutt: Pioneer of the Color Line* (Chapel Hill: University of North Carolina Press, 1952), pp. 209–211.

103. *Odd Fellows Journal,* quoted in Washington *Colored American,* July 14, 1900.

104. See Edwin A. Lee, "Daniel Murray," *Colored American Magazine,* V (October, 1902), 432–440.

105. See Daniel Murray, "The Power of Blood Inheritance," manuscript, 41 pp., Murray Papers.

106. See "Notes and Sketches for Encyclopedia," Murray Papers.

107. Daniel Murray, "Color Problem in the United States," *Colored American Magazine,* VII (December, 1904), 719–724.

108. "Passing" is the subject of a substantial body of both popular and scholarly literature; see especially William M. Kephart, "The 'Passing' Question," *Phylon,* X (Fourth Quarter, 1948), 336–340; Joseph R. Washington, Jr., *Marriage in Black and White* (Boston: Beacon Press, 1970), chap. 4; Johnson, "Crossing the Color Line," *Outlook and Independent,* CLVIII (August 20, 1931), 526–527, 542–543; "The Adventures of a Near White," *Independent,* LXXV (August 14, 1913), 373–374; "I Pass for White," *Abbott's Monthly,* IV (February, 1932), 14–15, 52–53, 54–55, 56. On "passing" among New Orleans Creoles of color, see Arthe A. Anthony, "The Creole Community in New Orleans, 1880–1920: An Oral History," Ph.D. diss., University of California, Irvine, pp. 84–87; and on the "passing" of the McCarys of Natchez, see *Cayton's Weekly* (Seattle), August 2, 1919.

109. Johnson, "Crossing the Color Line," 527.

110. Fannie Barrier Williams, "Perils of the White Negro," *Colored American Magazine,* XIII (December, 1907), 421–423. Among those of the old upper class who "passed" was Theophilius John Minton Syphax; he was related to three well-known families (Mintons, Syphaxes, and McKees) and for many years "passed" as a Wall Street lawyer under the name T. John McKee; see Dan Burley, "The Strange Will of Colonel McKee," *Negro Digest,* X (November, 1951), 17–22.

111. Kephart, "The 'Passing' Question," 336; Washington, *Marriage in Black and White,* p. 314; see also Denver *Colorado Statesman,* August 3, 1907.

112. Terrell, *Colored Woman in a White World,* pp. 295–307; Chicago *Broad Ax,* September 20, 1902, September 17, 1904; October 27, 1907.

113. Fannie Barrier Williams, "A Northern Negro's Autobiography," *Independent,* LVII (July 14, 1904), 91–96.

114. W. E. B. Du Bois, *The Philadelphia Negro: A Social Study* (Philadelphia: University of Pennsylvania, 1899), pp. 364–365.

115. Ransom, *Pilgrimage of Harriet Ransom's Son*, pp. 91–93; *Cleveland Gazette*, April 9, 1892; Detroit *Plaindealer*, April 8, 1892; *Indianapolis World*, April 16, 1892; "The Case Against Mixed Marriage," *Ebony*, V (November, 1950), 54–55.

116. *Cleveland Gazette*, April 9, 1892.

117. Ransom, *Pilgrimage of Harriet Ransom's Son*, p. 92.

118. *Atlanta Independent*, August 22, 1908; see also May 7, 1904, October 24, 1908, October 23, 1915.

119. *Cleveland Gazette*, April 9, 1892.

120. Theophilius J. Minton, "Is Intermarriage Between the Races to Be Encouraged?" *A.M.E. Church Review*, III (October, 1886), 286.

121. August Meier, *Negro Thought in America, 1880–1915: Racial Ideologies in the Age of Booker T. Washington* (Ann Arbor: University of Michigan Press, 1963), pp. 54–55; see also Benjamin Quarles, *Frederick Douglass* (New York: Atheneum, 1968), pp. 298–300.

122. Angelina Weld Grimké, "Archibald H. Grimké," unpublished manuscript, Archibald H. Grimké Papers, Moorland-Spingarn Research Center, Howard University, Washington, D.C.; M. C. Stanley to Sarah Stanley Grimké, February 21, 1897, ibid.; *Indianapolis World*, July 11, 1891. On Durham's white wife, see Roscoe C. Bruce to Josephine Bruce, ?, 1902, R. C. Bruce Papers; "Notable Mixed Marriages" and "Cora Clamorgan Collins," Notes, Murray Papers; *Cleveland Gazette*, October 7, 1911; Indianapolis *Freeman*, July 10, 17, 1897; *St. Louis Post-Dispatch*, June 9, 10, 16, 1911.

123. Du Bois, *Philadelphia Negro*, p. 359.

124. Terrell, *Colored Woman in a White World*, pp. 165–166, 409.

125. In 1895 there were 729 mixed marriages in New York State, with 369 Negro men having married white women and 360 white men having married Negro women; while in 1900 there were 1,846 mixed marriages, with 926 Negro men married to white women and 920 white men married to Negro women; see Chicago *Broad Ax*, June 29, 1901.

126. "Notable Mixed Marriages," Notes, Murray Papers; *Cleveland Gazette*, January 14, 1905.

127. Murray, *Proud Shoes*, pp. 90–91.

128. *Atlanta Independent*, November 2, 1907.

7. The Genteel Performance

1. W. E. B. Du Bois, ed., *Morals and Manners Among Negro Americans* (Atlanta: Atlanta University Press, 1914), pp. 17–24.

2. Washington *Colored American*, March 14, 1903.

3. Baltimore *Afro-American Ledger*, September 3, 1911.

4. See especially *Washington Bee*, February 2, March 15, 1884.

5. *New York Age*, 1889–1890; *Half Century Magazine*, 1916–1919.

6. E. M. Woods, *The Negro in Etiquette: A Novelty* (St. Louis: Baxton and Skinner, 1899), especially pp. 9–11, 21–24, 34–36, 37–46, 73–75, 137–139.

7. Ibid., pp. 59, 98–102, 147.

8. E. Azalia Hackley, *The Colored Girl Beautiful* (Kansas City: Burton Publishing Co., 1916), pp. 17–24.

9. Edward S. Green, *National Capital Code of Etiquette* (Washington: Austin Jenkins Co., 1920), pp. 6–7.

10. Ibid., pp. 43, 50–54.

11. Ibid., pp. 123–131.

12. Hackley, *Colored Girl Beautiful*, p. 31. No group of Negroes adhered more closely to such themes than the New Orleans Creoles of color; see Arthe A. Anthony, "The Negro Creole Community in New Orleans, 1880–1920: An Oral History," Ph.D. diss., University of California, Irvine, 1978, pp. 57, 94–96, 125.

13. Denver *Colorado Statesman*, July 18, 1908; Edward E. Wilson, "Negro Society in Chicago," *Voice of the Negro*, VI (July, 1907), 307.

14. *Indianapolis World*, May 20, 1891.

15. Raleigh *Gazette*, August 7, 1897.

16. Indianapolis *Freeman*, February 23, 1895.

17. Birmingham *Wide Awake*, January 24, 1900.

18. *Washington Bee*, August 10, 1901.

19. Du Bois, *Morals and Manners*, p. 18.

20. *New York Age*, December 3, 1908, June 3, 1916; see also *Richmond Planet*, August 11, 1900.

21. *Washington Bee*, August 24, 1901.

22. Denver *Colorado Statesman*, July 18, 1908.

23. Ibid., September 15, 1909; see also Hackley, *Colored Girl Beautiful*, pp. 109–113.

24. Charles B. Purvis to Francis J. Grimké, July 11, 1918, *Works of Francis H. Grimké*, IV, 219.

25. Xenia *Ohio Standard*, January 27, 1900; see also *Washington Bee*, May 19, 1888; Baltimore *Afro-American Ledger*, September 3, 1911. On the colored Creoles' efforts at disassociating themselves from other Negroes, see Anthony, "The Negro Creole Community in New Orleans, 1880–1920: An Oral History," especially pp. 94–95, 122–124.

26. Parsons, Kansas *Weekly Blade*, March 3, 1900.

27. Indianapolis *Freeman*, November 7, 1896.

28. Chicago *Broad Ax*, October 16, 1909.

29. Wilson, "Negro Society in Chicago," p. 309; "Think Well of Yourself," *Christian Recorder*, XVI (April 11, 1878), 1; see also Indianapolis *World*, November 1, 1889.

30. "Think Well of Yourself," 1.

31. Detroit *Plaindealer*, August 8, 1890; see also Indianapolis *Freeman*, June 11, 1892.

32. See especially Washington *People's Advocate*, January 12, 1884; Elsie J. McDougald, "The Task of Negro Womanhood," in *The New Negro*, edited by Alain Locke (New York: Boni, 1925), pp. 370–371.

33. Hackley, *The Colored Girl Beautiful*, p. 170.

34. Woods, *The Negro in Etiquette*, p. 101.

35. Ibid., p. 87.

36. *Cleveland Gazette*, August 20, 1887.

37. See Darwin T. Turner, ed., *The Wayward and the Seeking: A Collection of Writings by Jean Toomer* (Washington: Howard University Press, 1980), pp. 21–37.

38. Mary Church Terrell, *A Colored Woman in a White World* (Washington: Ransdell, Inc., 1940), p. 185.

39. Roi Ottley and William Weatherby, *The Negro in New York: An Informal Social History* (Dobbs Ferry, N.Y.: Oceana Publications, 1967), p. 134.

40. Indianapolis *Freeman*, September 9, 1899; Joel Williamson, *New People: Miscegenation and Mulattoes in the United States* (New York: Free Press, 1980), p. 155; see also James Weldon Johnson, *The Autobiography of an Ex-Colored Man* (New York: Alfred A. Knopf, 1979), pp. 85–87.

41. Indianapolis *Freeman*, June 28, 1897, July 8, 1899; *New York Freeman*, September 5, 1885; *New York Age*, December 30, 1909; Denver *Colorado Statesman*, January 14, 1905, February 17, 1906; *Boston Guardian*, April 4, 1903.

42. John Hope to Lugenia Hope, July ?, 1899, John and Lugenia Burns Hope Papers, Atlanta University.

43. John P. Green to Mrs. John P. Green, August 26, 1902, John P. Green Papers, Western Reserve Historical Society, Cleveland.

44. Augustus Michael Hodges, "Professor L. Wilson Dozier: The Leader of the '400,' " in Indianapolis *Freeman*, February 24, 1894; see also Willard B. Gatewood, Jr., ed., *Free Man of Color: The Autobiography of Willis Augustus Hodges* (Knoxville: University of Tennessee Press, 1982).

45. Wilson, "Negro Society in Chicago," p. 307.

46. Ibid.; see also *New York Age*, March 8, 1906; *Cleveland Journal*, November 21, 1903.

47. *New York Freeman*, November 14, 1885.

48. See W. S. Scarborough, "What the Omen?" in *Twentieth Century Negro Literature*, edited by D. W. Culp (Naperville, Ill.: J. L. Nichols Co., 1902), p. 416; *New York Freeman*, April 18, 1885; Washington *Colored American*, October 18, 1902; *New York Age*, December 14, 1905; *Washington Bee*, September 23, 1905, January 11, 1913.

49. See above, pp. 65–66.

50. Howard A. Phelps, "Negro Life in Chicago," *Half Century Magazine*, VI (May, 1919), 12–14; Chicago *Broad Ax*, August 28, October 16, 1909; Louise D. Bowen, *The Colored People of Chicago* (Chicago: n.p., 1913), pp. 12–13; Allan H. Spear, *Black Chicago: The Making of a Ghetto* (Chicago: University of Chicago Press, 1967), pp. 11–19, 142, 150, 210–213.

51. David Katzman, *Before the Ghetto: Black Detroit in the Nineteenth Century* (Urbana: University of Illinois Press, 1973), pp. 77–78.

52. George A. Myers to Daniel Murray, July 9, 1920, Daniel Murray Papers, State Historical Society of Wisconsin, Madison; Kenneth Kusmer, *A Ghetto Takes Shape: Black Cleveland, 1870–1930* (Urbana: University of Illinois Press, 1976), pp. 46–47, 101.

53. San Francisco *Pacific Coast Appeal*, January 17, 1903; Douglas Henry Daniels, *Pioneer Urbanites: A Social and Cultural History of Black San Francisco* (Philadelphia: Temple University Press, 1980), pp. 99–101.

54. Sandra Schoenberg and Charles Bailey, "The Symbolic Meaning of an Elite Black Community: The Ville of St. Louis," *Bulletin of the Missouri Historical Society*, XXXIII (January, 1977), 94–99; William A. Crossland, *Industrial Conditions Among Negroes in St. Louis* (St. Louis: Mendle Printing Co., 1914), pp. 10–11; W. E. B. Du Bois, ed., *The Negro American Family* (Atlanta University Press, 1908), pp. 65–67; see also Jerry J. Thornberry, "The Development of Black Atlanta, 1865–1885," Ph.D. diss., University of Maryland, 1977, pp. 161, 164; Michael L. Porter, "Black Atlanta: An Interdisciplinary Study of Blacks on the East Side of Atlanta, 1890–1930," Ph.D. diss., Emory University, 1974; Barbara Richardson, "A History of Blacks in Jacksonville, Florida, 1860–1895: A Socio-Economic and Political Study," D.A. thesis, Carnegie-Mellon University, 1975, p. 121.

55. See "Detroit's Most Exclusive Social Clique, The Cultural Colored '40,' " in *Detroit News-Tribune*, April 27, 1902; Mrs. N. F. Mossell, *The Work of the Afro-American Women* (Freeport, N.Y.: Books for Libraries, 1971), p. 112; Hackley, *Colored Girl Beautiful*, pp. 146–147.

56. Ottley and Weatherby, *Negro in New York*, p. 134; "The Home," in San Francisco *Pacific Coast Appeal*, February 2, 1903; John M. Langston, *From the Virginia Plantation to the National Capitol* (New York: Arno Press, 1969), p. 533; H. Paul

Douglass, *Christian Reconstruction in the South* (Boston: Pilgrim Press, 1909), p. 88; W. E. B. Du Bois, "The Negroes of Farmville, Virginia: A Social Study," *Bulletin of the Department of Labor*, No. 14 (Washington: Government Printing Office, 1898), p. 21; Helen M. Chesnutt, *Charles Waddell Chesnutt: Pioneer of the Color Line* (Chapel Hill: University of North Carolina Press, 1952), p. 49.

57. John P. Green to Mrs. John P. Green, October 27, 1902, Green Papers.

58. Ralph Tyler to George Myers, September 12, 1911, George A. Myers Papers, Ohio Historical Society (microfilm), Columbus; Grimké in *New York Age*, March 15, 1906.

59. R. H. Terrell, "The Negro in Domestic Service," *Colored American Magazine*, IX (November, 1905), 631–633; see also John W. Paynter, in Denver *Colorado Statesman*, August 10, 1907.

60. Mary Helm, *The Upward Path: The Evolution of a Race* (New York: Eaton and Mains, 1909), p. 158; see also Robert E. Park, "Negro Home Life and Standards of Living," *The Negro's Progress in Fifty Years* (Philadelphia: American Academy of Political and Social Sciences, 1913), pp. 160–161.

61. *New York Age*, February 16, 1889. On the importance of the art of conversation, see Walter J. Stevens, *Chip on My Shoulder: Autobiography* (Boston: Meador Publishing Co., 1946), pp. 86–87.

62. *New York Age*, July 5, 1890.

63. *Chicago Defender*, December 3, 1910.

64. Hackley, *Colored Girl Beautiful*, pp. 71–75; Mamie Garvin Fields with Karen Fields, *Lemon Swamp and Other Places* (New York: Free Press, 1983), p. 167.

65. Hackley, *Colored Girl Beautiful*, pp. 71–75.

66. *Chicago Defender*, October 7, 1911.

67. *Detroit News-Tribune*, April 27, 1902.

68. William S. Walsh, *Curiosities of Popular Customs* (Philadelphia: J. B. Lippincott, 1897), pp. 738–740; Jane M. Hatch, ed., *The American Book of Days* (New York: H. W. Wilson Co., 1978), pp. 6–7.

69. *New York Age*, January 8, 1887, January 7, 1888; see also January 5, 1889.

70. Washington *People's Advocate*, January 8, 1881; *New York Freeman*, January 9, 1886; *Cleveland Gazette*, January 7, 1888; *New York Age*, January 14, 1888, January 11, 1890, January 9, 1892; *Savannah Tribune*, December 30, 1893. For information on the practice of New Year's calling in Montgomery, Alabama, see *The Huntsville Gazette*, January 6, 1894.

71. Washington *Colored American*, January 10, 1903.

72. *Detroit News-Tribune*, April 27, 1902; *New York Age*, March 7, 1885, February 25, 1909, January 27, 1910, February 22, 1912.

73. Indianapolis *Freeman*, March 28, 1908.

74. *New York Freeman*, August 21, 1886; *New York Age*, August 4, 1888, July 5, August 23, 1890, September 5, 1907; Washington *Colored American*, August 13, 1898, September 5, 1903; P. B. S. Pinchback to Whitefield McKinlay, August 10, McKinlay Papers.

75. Washington *People's Advocate*, July 31, September 4, 1880; *New York Age*, August 29, 1891; "Vacation Days," *Crisis*, IV (August, 1912), 186–188.

76. Daniel Murray to George A. Myers, June 23, 1907, Myers Papers; *Washington Bee*, August 17, 1895.

77. Washington *Colored American*, August 11, 1894, August 18, 1900, July 13, August 17, 1901; *Washington Bee*, September 3, 1910, July 18, 1914, September 15, 1917, June 15, 1918.

78. Indianapolis *Freeman*, July 30, August 20, 1910; Helen Buckler, *Daniel Hale*

Williams: Negro Surgeon (New York: Pitman Publishing Co., 1954), pp. 269–271; Benjamin C. Wilson, "Idlewild: A Black Eden in Michigan," Michigan History, LXV (Sept.–Oct., 1981), 33–37.

79. Mary Church Terrell to Frances Settle, July 19, 1888, Terrell Papers.

80. William E. Matthews, "A Summer Vacation in Europe," Christian Recorder, VI (January, 1890), 292–306; Washington Bee, December 11, 1886, October 27, 1888, May 28, 1910, October 19, 1912; see also William H. Hunt Papers, Moorland-Spingarn Research Center, Howard University. John P. Green provides accounts of his European travel in his autobiography, Fact Stranger than Fiction: Seventy-five Years of a Busy Life (Cleveland: Riehl Printing Co., 1920).

81. Alice Williams to John P. Green, September 14, 1903, Green Papers; see also Alice Williams to John P. Green, June 14, 1904, ibid.

82. New York Age, June 16, 1910; Indianapolis Freeman, November 23, 1912.

83. New York Age, November 9, December 7, 1889.

84. John Hope to Lugenia Burns, January 25, 1898, Hope Papers.

85. John Hope to Lugenia Burns, December 22, 1897, Hope Papers; Jacqueline Rouse, "Lugenia D. Burns Hope: A Black Female Reformer in the South, 1871–1947," Ph.D. diss., Emory University, 1983.

86. Washington People's Advocate, December 31, 1881; St. Paul Appeal, December 20, 1890; Cleveland Gazette, April 2, 1887; "William H. Holland," Dictionary of American Negro Biography, pp. 318–319; Washington Bee, September 9, 1911.

87. Washington Colored American, March 15, 1902.

88. Washington Bee, November 24, 1906.

89. New York Age, October 20, 1888; Washington Bee, March 2, 1907; Adelaide Cromwell Hill Gulliver, "The Negro Upper Class in Boston—Its Development and Present Social Structure," Ph.D. diss., Radcliffe College, 1952, p. 127.

90. Bernard E. Powers, Jr., "Black Charleston: A Social History, 1822–1885," Ph.D. diss., Northwestern University, 1982, p. 164; Lula Singleton to Whitefield McKinlay, May 18, 1908, McKinlay Papers.

91. San Francisco Pacific Coast Appeal, April 5, 1902; Forbes Parkhill, Mister Barney Ford: A Portrait in Bistre (Denver: Sage Books, 1963), pp. 194–195; "Namahyoko Sockoume Curtis," Notes, Murray Papers.

92. Robert A. Warner, New Haven Negroes: A Social History (New Haven: Yale University Press, 1940), p. 184.

93. See Lawrence, Kansas Historic Times, August 29, 1891; Indianapolis Recorder, September 17, 1910; W. E. B. Du Bois, The Black North in 1901: A Social Study (New York: Arno Press, 1969), pp. 18, 27–29, 34–35.

94. John Hope to Lugenia Burns, April 22, 1897, Hope Papers.

95. John P. Green to George A. Myers, June 30, 1902, Myers Papers; see also Robert H. Terrell to E. H. Hall, January 6, 1890, Robert H. Terrell Papers, Library of Congress.

96. John Swain to John Hope, December 22, 1897, Hope Papers.

97. See William E. Matthews, "Money as a Factor in Human Progress," Christian Recorder, XXIII (August 20, 1885), 1.

98. Hackley, Colored Girl Beautiful, p. 30.

99. Fields, Lemon Swamp, p. 23.

100. Hackley, Colored Girl Beautiful, p. 163.

101. William Morris to Benjamin Harrison, November 6, 1891, Benjamin Harrison Papers (microfilm), Library of Congress; Kansas City American Citizen, January 8, 1897; Springfield Illinois Record, December 25, 1897; Cleveland Journal, February 2, 1907,

December 4, 1909; Baltimore *Afro-American Ledger*, May 20, 1911; Karl F. Phillips, "The 'Gap,' Let's Close It," *Conservator*, III (Jan.–Feb., 1921), 12, 53.

102. See G. N. Gresham, "Social Betterment," *Southern Workman*, XXIX (October, 1900), 577–580.

8. Upper-Class Club Life

1. Alexis de Tocqueville, *Democracy in America* (New York: Alfred A. Knopf, 1959), 2 vols., II, 114.

2. Arthur M. Schlesinger, "Biography of a Nation of Joiners," *American Historical Review*, L (October, 1944), 13, 16, 21.

3. Gunnar Myrdal, *An American Dilemma: The Negro Problem and American Democracy* (New York: Harper, 1944), p. 952.

4. See St. Clair Drake and Horace R. Cayton, *Black Metropolis: A Study of Negro Life in a Northern City* (New York: Harcourt, Brace, 1945), pp. 669–715.

5. See especially Nicholas Babchuk and Ralph V. Thompson, "The Voluntary Associations of Negroes," *American Sociological Review*, XXVII (October, 1962), 647–652; Anthony M. Orum, "A Reappraisal of the Social and Political Participation of Negroes," *American Journal of Sociology*, LXXII (July, 1966), 32–46.

6. W. E. H. Chase to the Editor, *New York Age*, January 17, 1891.

7. *New York Freeman*, April 18, 1885; Saint Louis *Palladium*, October 8, December 17, 24, 1904.

8. H. H. Proctor, "The Need of Friendly Visitation," in *Social and Physical Condition of Negroes in Cities*, edited by W. E. B. Du Bois (Atlanta: Atlanta University Press, 1897), pp. 44–45.

9. *Washington Bee*, February 9, 1889.

10. *Cleveland Gazette*, March 20, 1886; "The Dvorak Musical Society," *Colored American Magazine*, III (October, 1901), 454–455; on the Coleridge-Taylor society, see below pp. 217–218.

11. Edward Nelson Palmer, "Negro Secret Societies," *Social Forces*, XXII (December, 1944), 207–212; Seth Scheiner, *Negro Mecca: A History of the Negro in New York City, 1865–1920* (New York: New York University Press, 1965), p. 94. *The Colored American Magazine* (1900–1909) and *Alexander's Magazine* (1905–1909) regularly featured "Masonic Departments," as did newspapers such as the Indianapolis *Freeman* and *New York Age*.

12. See Loretta J. Williams, *Black Freemasonry and Middle-class Realities* (Columbia: University of Missouri Press, 1980); William H. Grimshaw, *Official History of Freemasonry Among Colored People in North America* (New York: Broadway Publishing Co., 1902). The best single work on the subject is William A. Muraskin, *Middle Class Blacks in A White Society: Prince Hall Freemasonry in America* (Berkeley: University of California Press, 1975), see especially pp. 32–41, 292.

13. David Katzman, *Before the Ghetto: Black Detroit in the Nineteenth Century* (Urbana: University of Illinois Press, 1973), p. 148.

14. Grimshaw, *Official History*, pp. 124–130, 141–164, 234.

15. Muraskin, *Middle-Class Blacks*, p. 26.

16. Ibid., p. 297.

17. Indianapolis *Freeman*, March 16, 1907.

18. John W. Cromwell, *History of the Bethel Literary and Historical Association* (Washington: Press of R. L. Pendleton, 1896); Bethel Literary and Historical Association Papers, Moorland-Spingarn Research Center, Howard University; *New York Free-*

man, November 28, 1885, May 14, 1887; Indianapolis *Freeman*, April 9, 1892; Kansas City *American Citizen*, January 21, 1896.

19. Indianapolis *Freeman*, January 7, 1905.

20. "The Pen and Pencil Club," Sketches, Daniel Murray Papers, State Historical Society of Wisconsin, Madison; *Washington Bee*, February 21, 1903, February 3, March 23, 1912, March 1, 1919; Washington *Colored American*, February 21, March 7, 21, 1903; Minutes of the Executive Committee, October 9, 1919, May 4, 1920, Mu-So-Lit Club Papers, Moorland-Spingarn Research Center, Howard University, Washington, D. C.

21. Indianapolis *Freeman*, January 26, 1895; Helen M. Chesnutt, *Charles Waddell Chesnutt: Pioneer of the Color Line* (Chapel Hill: University of North Carolina Press, 1952), pp. 61–62, 185.

22. Generalizations about club characteristics were drawn from diverse newspaper accounts and some club records from the mid-1880s to 1920; see Cromwell, *History of the Bethel Literary and Historical Association*; Minute Book and Roster of Members, 1898–1900, Bethel Literary and Historical Association Papers; *New York Freeman*, November 28, 1886, May 14, 1887; *New York Age*, April 7, 1888; Indianapolis *Freeman*, November 28, 1891, April 9, 1892; Lillian Brandt, "The Negroes of St. Louis," *Journal of the American Statistical Association*, VIII (March, 1903), 258.

23. John Hope Franklin, *George Washington Williams: A Biography* (Chicago: University of Chicago Press, 1985), p. 125; *New York Globe*, June 30, 1883.

24. *New York Age*, March 8, 1890; see also Florida Ruffin Ridley materials in the Heslip-Ruffin Papers, Amistad Research Center, Tulane University, New Orleans.

25. "The American Negro Historical Society of Philadelphia and Its Officers," *Colored American Magazine*, VI (February, 1903), 287–294; Indianapolis *Freeman*, December 4, 1897; James G. Spady, "The Afro-American Historical Society: The Nucleus of Black Bibliophiles, 1897–1923," *Negro History Bulletin*, XXXVII (June-July, 1974), 254–257; *Philadelphia Tribune*, June 1, 1912, February 17, 1913.

26. "The American Negro Historical Society of Philadelphia and Its Officers," 287–294; *Philadelphia Tribune*, Feburary 17, April 5, 1913.

27. *Philadelphia Tribune*, November 14, 21, 1914.

28. See Charles H. Wesley, "Racial Historical Societies and the American Heritage," *Journal of Negro History*, XXXVII (January, 1952), 27–33; *New York Age*, July 4, 1912; *Cleveland Gazette*, August 7, 1915.

29. Ellsworth Janiter, "Samuel Coleridge-Taylor in Washington," *Phylon*, XXVIII (Summer, 1967), 188–189; "Constitution of the S. Coleridge-Taylor Choral Society of the District of Columbia," Hilyer Papers; Maud Cuney-Hare, *Negro Musicians and Their Music* (Washington: Associated Publishers, 1936), pp. 244–246.

30. William Tortolano, *Samuel Coleridge-Taylor: Anglo-Black Composer, 1875–1912* (Metuchen, N.J.: Scarecrow Press, 1977), pp. 33, 72–73; *Washington Bee*, November 17, 1900; Andrew F. Hilyer to "Dear sir," November 7, 1903, Andrew F. Hilyer to Alice Clark, November 30, 1905, Hilyer Papers; Janiter, "Samuel Coleridge-Taylor," pp. 190–191.

31. Janiter, "Samuel Coleridge-Taylor," pp. 192–193; Cuney-Hare, *Negro Musicians*, pp. 246–247; Washington *Colored American*, January 10, April 10, 1903.

32. Terrell, *Colored Woman in a White World*, p. 400; J. Arthur Freeman to Andrew F. Hilyer, December 4, 1904, Hilyer Papers; Cuney-Hare, *Negro Musicians*, pp. 246–247; Mary Church Terrell, "Samuel Coleridge-Taylor," *Voice of the Negro*, V (January, 1905), 665–669.

33. Alfred N. Moss, *The American Negro Academy: Voice of the Talented Tenth* (Baton Rouge: Louisiana State University Press, 1981), pp. 23–57; Indianapolis *Freeman*, October 31, 1897.

34. Moss, *American Negro Academy*, p. 40.

35. W. S. Scarborough, "The Educated Negro and His Mission," *American Negro Academy Occasional Papers* No. 8 (Washington: American Negro Academy, 1903), p. 7.

36. W. E. B. Du Bois and A. G. Dill, eds., *The College-Bred Negro American* (Atlanta: Atlanta University Press, 1910), 73.

37. Moss, *American Negro Academy*, p. 55; Emma Lou Thornbrough, *T. Thomas Fortune: Militant Journalist* (Chicago: University of Chicago Press, 1972), pp. 131–132.

38. Moss, *American Negro Academy*, pp. 22, 54–57.

39. Ibid., p. 294.

40. *Cleveland Gazette*, March 24, 1906.

41. See Florette Henri, *Black Migration: Movement North, 1900–1920* (Garden City: Doubleday, 1975), pp. 187–191.

42. Dorothy West, *The Living Is Easy* (New York: Arno Press, 1969), p. 172.

43. Ralph Tyler to George A. Myers, August 13, 1908, George A. Myers Papers, Ohio Historical Society, Columbus.

44. Adelaide Cromwell Hill Gulliver, "The Negro Upper Class in Boston—Its Development and Present Social Structure," Ph.D. diss., Radcliffe College, 1952, pp. 219–222.

45. Chicago *Broad Ax*, May 20, August 19, 1905; Indianapolis *Freeman*, August 21, 1909; Allan H. Spear, *Black Chicago: the Making of a Ghetto, 1890–1920* (Chicago: University of Chicago Press, 1967), p. 108.

46. Los Angeles, *California Eagle*, June 20, October 3, 1914, March 25, 1916.

47. *Seattle Republican*, February 8, 1907.

48. *Washington Bee*, December 28, 1912, September 5, 1914, April 27, June 22, 1918, August 2, 1919.

49. Indianapolis *Freeman*, December 26, 1914, April 17, 1915.

50. *New York Freeman*, November 13, 1886, April 5, 1890.

51. Jervis Anderson, *This Was Harlem: A Cultural Portrait, 1900–1950* (New York: Farrar Straus Giroux, 1981), pp. 26–27; *New York Freeman*, April 2, 23, 1887; April 21, 1888; December 21, 1889, February 13, 1892.

52. *New York Daily Tribune*, March 20, 1892.

53. Ibid.; *New York Freeman*, April 2, 9, 23, August 20, 1887; *New York Age*, April 19, 1890.

54. *New York Age*, April 21, 1888.

55. *New York Freeman*, April 23, 1887; *New York Age*, April 21, 1888, May 4, 1889, April 19, 1890, April 11, 1891. The Benevolent Sons of New York, organized in 1903, claimed to be the successor to the Sons of New York, whose rules for membership it adopted; see Indianapolis *Freeman*, August 12, 1905.

56. *New York Freeman*, October 3, 1885; *New York Age*, January 19, 1889, April 6, 1905; Washington *Colored American*, August 4, 1900; Chicago *Broad Ax*, January 13, 1912, January 4, 1913.

57. *New York Age*, April 10, 1913, January 2, 1914, February 22, 1917; *Cleveland Journal*, May 20, 1905, January 6, 1906.

58. *New York Freeman*, December 11, 1886.

59. Daniel Perlman, "Organizations of the Free Negro in New York City, 1800–1860," *Journal of Negro History* (July, 1971), 182–184; *New York Freeman*, February 5, 1887; *New York Age*, September 15, 1888, January 4, 1900, June 18, 1908, January 23, 1914; Samuel R. Scottron, "New York African Society for Mutual Relief—Ninety-Seventh Anniversary," *Colored American Magazine*, IX (December, 1905), 685–690.

60. Scottron, "New York African Society for Mutual Relief," pp. 687–688.

61. *New York Age*, October 20, 1910.

62. Scottron, "New York African Society for Mutual Relief," pp. 687–688.

63. Robert L. Harris, "Charleston's Free Afro-American Elite: The Brown Fellowship Society and the Humane Brotherhood," *South Carolina Historical Magazine*, LXXXII (January, 1981), 289–310; Marina Wikramanayake, *A World in Shadow: The Free Black in Antebellum South Carolina* (Columbia: University of South Carolina Press, 1973), pp. 81–85; Horace Fitchett, "The Traditions of the Free Negro in Charleston, South Carolina," *Journal of Negro History*, XXV (April, 1940), 144–152; Michael P. Johnson and James L. Roark, "A Middle Ground; Free Mulattoes and the Friendly Moralist Society of Antebellum Charleston," *Southern Studies*, XXI (Fall, 1982), 246–265.

64. Rodolphe L. Desdunes, *Our People and Our History* (Baton Rouge: Louisiana State University Press, 1973), pp. 29–30; Arthe A. Anthony, "The Creole Community in New Orleans, 1880–1920," Ph.D. diss., University of California, Irvine, 1978, p. 113; New Orleans *Weekly Pelican*, March 2, 1889; *New York Freeman*, February 5, 1887; *New York Age*, January 28, 1888, June 28, 1890.

65. Washington *People's Advocate*, January 10, 1880; *New York Freeman*, January 12, 1885, January 9, 1886; *New York Age*, April 7, 1888, January 4, 1890; *Philadelphia Tribune*, January 2, 1915.

66. On the Loendi Club, see Oliver Waters, "The Smoky City," *Colored American Magazine*, IV (November, 1901), 11–17.

67. *New York Age*, January 7, 1888, January 16, 1892; *New York Times*, January 17, 1907; Helen Buckler, *Daniel Hale Williams: Negro Surgeon* (New York: Pitman Publishing Co., 1954), p. 56.

68. *The National Leader* (Washington), December 8, 1888.

69. *New York Age*, December 20, 1890; A.C.B., "Colored Aristocracy," in *Augusta Chronicle* (Augusta, Georgia), September 18, 1893; *Washington Bee*, May 10, 1890.

70. Washington *Colored American*, November 11, 1899, May 9, 1900, March 9, 1901; *Washington Bee*, January 12, 19, 1901; Andrew F. Hilyer, *Twentieth Century Union League Directory* (Washington, D.C.: n.p., 1903), p. 148.

71. Washington *People's Advocate*, June 7, August 30, 1879, January 3, 1880.

72. *New York Age*, February 22, 1890; for the composition of the Baltimore Auxiliary in 1905, see *Afro-American Ledger*, February 18, 1905.

73. Baltimore *Afro-American Ledger*, March 11, 18, 1905.

74. Indianapolis *Recorder*, January 8, 1910; Baltimore *Afro-American Ledger*, December 28, 1912.

75. *The Sentinel* (Trenton, N.J.), March 5, 1881; *New York Age*, February 7, 1907; Washington *Colored American*, January 20, 1900; *Boston Guardian*, January 3, February 28, 1903; Detroit *Plaindealer*, May 8, 1891; Indianapolis *Freeman*, March 26, 1898.

76. Spear, *Black Chicago*, p. 108; Chicago *Broad Ax*, July 5, 1902, April 4, 1908; Detroit *Plaindealer*, April 11, 1890; Indianapolis *Freeman*, January 10, 1891; *New York Age*, February 27, 1908.

77. Indianapolis *Freeman*, January 6, 1894; Kansas City *American Citizen*, May 9, 1902; Chicago *Broad Ax*, April 29, May 13, 1905, January 25, 1908, December 25, 1909, January 11, 1911.

78. Chicago *Appeal*, March 5, 1892.

79. *Washington Bee*, June 12, 1912. For a different view of charity balls, see Baltimore *Afro-American*, March 31, 1906.

80. New Orleans *Weekly Pelican*, August 6, 1887; *New York Freeman*, February 1, 1890; see also *New York Age*, December 7, 1889, June 7, 1890; Baltimore *Afro-American Ledger*, March 11, 18, 1905.

81. *Boston Sunday Globe*, July 22, 1894.

82. Archibald Grimké, "The Four Hundred of Washington," in *New York Age*, March 8, 1906.

83. *Washington Bee*, January 12, 1901; Daniel Murray to George A. Myers, March 16, 1901, Myers Papers; Washington *Colored American*, March 9, 1901.

84. Daniel Murray to George A. Myers, February 23, 1902, Myers Papers.

85. J. P. Green to George A. Myers, February 12, 1901, Myers Papers.

86. *Washington Bee*, December 10, 17, 1904, February 11, 1905; Mary Church Terrell, "The Social Functions During Inauguration Week," *Voice of the Negro*, II (April, 1905), 237–242.

87. *Washington Bee*, January 16, 23, 1909.

88. Indianapolis *World*, August 23, 1890.

89. Fannie Barrier Williams in *New York Age*, September 24, 1905, July 25, 1907.

90. *New York Globe*, June 21, December 20, 1884; *New York Freeman*, May 15, 1885, May 15, 1886, January 29, 1887.

91. Trenton *Sentinel*, June 11, 1881.

92. *New York Freeman*, May 15, 1885, January 29, 1887; *Washington Bee*, January 10, 1885.

93. *New York Freeman*, May 15, 1886.

94. Ibid.

95. *New York Age*, January 5, 1889; "Andrew Stevens of Philadelphia," Sketches, Murray Papers; *Philadelphia Tribune*, May 25, 1912, January 16, 1915.

96. Kenneth Clark, *Dark Ghetto: Dilemma of Social Power* (New York: Harper and Row, 1965), p. 190; see also Charles H. Wesley, *History of Sigma Pi Phi* (Washington: Association for the Study of Negro Life and History, n.d.), p. 99.

97. Wesley, *Sigma Pi Phi*, pp. 15–36.

98. Ibid., pp. 21–25; *New York Globe*, June 2, 1883; *Cleveland Gazette*, August 29, 1891.

99. Wesley, *Sigma Pi Phi*, pp. 15–36.

100. Quoted in Gerri Major, *Black Society* (Chicago: Johnson Publishing Co., 1976), p. 323.

101. Wesley, *Sigma Pi Phi*, pp. 26, 45, 49, 117; Clark, *Dark Ghetto*, p. 191.

102. Wesley, *Sigma Pi Phi*, pp. 43–79; Buckler, *Daniel Hale Williams*, p. 254.

103. Wesley, *Sigma Pi Phi*, pp. 40, 99–100, 117.

104. Clark, *Dark Ghetto*, p. 191.

105. Ibid., p. 192.

106. Wesley, *Sigma Pi Phi*, 49–52.

107. Wesley, *Sigma Pi Phi*, pp. 26–27; *Washington Bee*, May 25, 1912; January 18, 1913; "Living Fraternity Founders," *Ebony*, XII (October, 1958), 58–63; Herman Dreer, *The History of Omega Psi Fraternity: A Brotherhood of College Men* (n.p., n.p., 1940); Marjorie H. Parker, *Alpha Kappa Alpha: Sixty Years of Service* (n.p., n.p., 1966).

108. *New York Age*, September 14, 1905.

109. Karen J. Blair, *The Clubwoman As Feminist: True Womanhood Redefined, 1868–1914* (New York: Holmes and Meier Publishers, 1980), p. 1.

110. Thomas Nelson Baker, "The Negro Woman," *Alexander's Magazine*, III (December 15, 1906), 77.

111. Fannie Barrier Williams, "The Colored Girl," *Voice of the Negro*, II (June, 1905), 400–403.

112. Baker, "The Negro Woman," p. 75.

113. See Blair, *The Clubwoman As Feminist*, chap. 4.

114. Ibid., p. 63.

115. See Josephine Bruce, "The Afterglow of the Women's Convention," *Voice of the Negro*, I (November, 1904), 541–542.

116. Josephine T. Washington, "What the Club Does For the Club-Woman," *Colored American Magazine*, XII (February, 1907), 124.

117. Ibid.

118. Fanny Garrison Villard to Mr. Ely, December 8, 1910, Mary Church Terrell Papers, Library of Congress.

119. Quoted in Robert G. Sherer, "The Origins of the National Association of Colored Women," p. 3 (paper delivered at the 1978 Missouri Valley History Conference, Omaha, Nebraska. Copy in the possession of the author).

120. See Adelaide Cromwell Hill, "Josephine St. Pierre Ruffin," in *Notable American Women*, edited by Edward T. James, 3 vols. (Cambridge: Harvard University Press, 1971), III, 206–208; Williams, "Club Movement Among Negro Women," *Progress of a Race*, pp. 218–228; Mrs. Rebecca Lowe quoted in Rayford W. Logan, *The Betrayal of the Negro from Rutherford B. Hayes to Woodrow Wilson* (New York: Collier Books, 1965), p. 241.

121. Nashville *Globe*, June 7, 1910.

122. David V. Taylor, "Pilgrim's Progress: Black St. Paul and the Making of an Urban Ghetto, 1870–1930," Ph.D. diss., University of Minnesota, 1977, p. 202.

123. Quoted in "Structure of Nashville Society Among the Negro Group," E. Franklin Frazier Papers, Moorland-Spingarn Research Center, Howard University, Washington, D.C.

124. For a description of a Whist party, see *Boston Guardian*, April 4, 1903.

125. Terrell, *Colored Woman in a White World*, pp. 400–401; *Washington Bee*, December 25, 1909.

126. *Seattle Republican*, April 5, 1901.

127. Washington, "What the Club Does for the Club-Woman," p. 122.

128. Indianapolis *Freeman*, August 6, 1896; *Seattle Republican*, December 13, 1901; *New York Age*, June 9, 1888.

129. Information on the Booklovers, including the "Creed," is found among the papers of Ida Gibbs Hunt, who was a member, in the William H. Hunt Papers, Moorland-Spingarn Research Center, Howard University, Washington, D.C.

130. Fannie Barrier Williams, "Work Attempted and Missed in Organized Club Work," *Colored American Magazine*, XIV (May, 1908), 285.

131. Fannie Barrier Williams, "Club Movement Among Negro Women," in Nichols and Crogman, *Progress of a Race*, p. 207; Indianapolis *Freeman*, August 1, 1896; Washington *Colored American*, January 31, 1903.

132. Williams, "Club Movement Among Negro Women," p. 207.

133. Ibid., pp. 207–210; Terrell, *Colored Woman in a White World*, pp. 148–153; see also Elizabeth L. Davis, *Lifting As They Climb*, (n.p., n.p., 1933).

134. Washington, "What the Club Does for the Club-Woman," p. 124; Bruce, "Afterglow of the Women's Convention," p. 542; Fannie Barrier Williams, "Club Movement Among the Colored Women," *Voice of the Negro*, I (March, 1904), 101.

135. Charles Alexander, "The Ohio Federation at Dayton," *Alexander's Magazine*, I (August 15, 1905), 7.

136. Washington, "What the Club Does for the Club-Woman," p. 123.

137. Bruce, "Afterglow of the Convention," p. 542.

138. Quoted in Addie W. Hunton, "The National Association of Colored Women: Its Real Significance," *Colored American Magazine*, XIV (July, 1908), 418–419.

139. Ibid.

140. See *Efforts for Social Betterment Among Negro Americans*, edited by W. E. Burghardt Du Bois (Atlanta: Atlanta University Press, 1909), pp. 47–63; "Club Work as a Factor in the Advance of Colored Women," *Colored American Magazine*, XI

(August, 1906), 83–90; Mary T. Blauvelt, "The Race Problem as Discussed by Negro Women," *American Journal of Sociology*, VI (March, 1901), 662–672.

141. Williams, "Club Movement Among the Colored Women," p. 101.

142. Mary Church Terrell, "What Role Is the Educated Negro Woman to Play in the Uplifting of Her Race?" in *Twentieth Century Negro Literature*, edited by D. W. Culp (Naperville, IL: J. L. Nichols & Co., 1902), p. 175; Terrell, *Colored Woman in a White World*, p. 148.

143. Williams, "Club Movement Among Colored Women," in Nichols and Crogman, *Progress of a Race*, p. 229; Blair, *Clubwoman as Feminist*, p. 71; see Fannie Barrier Williams, "Some Perils of Women's Clubs," in *New York Age*, December 25, 1905.

144. Chicago *Broad Ax*, August 26, 1899; see also Washington *Colored American*, August 19, 26, 1899; *Press Comments: Second Convention of the National Association of Colored Women, Held at Quinn Chapel, Chicago, Illinois, August 14–16, 1899* (n.p., n.d.).

145. Mary Church Terrell to Frances Settle, September 5, 1899, Mary Church Terrell Papers, Library of Congress; see also a nine-page handwritten, undated document entitled "Refutation of False Charges," ibid.

146. Ida Wells Barnett, *Crusade for Justice: The Autobiography of Ida Wells Barnett*, edited by Alfreda M. Duster (Chicago: University of Chicago Press, 1970), pp. 258–60.

147. Williams, "Club Movement Among the Colored Women," 98–100.

148. Jere A. Brown to George Myers, November 16, 1901, Myers Papers.

149. Williams, "Club Movement Among Negro Women," in Nichols and Crogman, *Progress of a Race*, p. 215–216.

150. Mary Church Terrell, "Club Work Among Women," in *New York Age*, January 4, 1900; Wilson J. Moses, *The Golden Age of Black Nationalism, 1850–1925* (Hamden, Conn.: Archon Press, 1978), p. 104.

151. *National Baptist Union*, quoted in Topeka *Plaindealer*, February 7, 1902.

152. Moses, *Golden Age of Nationalism*, p. 125; Williams, "Club Movement Among the Colored Women," p. 100.

153. Gerda Lerner, "Early Community Work of Black Club Women," *Journal of Negro History*, LIX (April, 1974), 167; see also extensive collection of reports, minutes, and other documents concerning the NACW in Papers of Mary Church Terrell.

154. Williams, "Club Movement Among Negro Women," in Nichols and Crogman, *Progress of a Race*, p. 229.

155. Terrell, *Colored Woman in a White World*, pp. 155–156.

9. The Education of the Elite

1. W. E. B. Du Bois, *The College-Bred Negro American* (Atlanta: Atlanta University Press, 1910), p. 73; see also Rutledge M. Dennis, 'Du Bois and the Role of the Educated Elite," *Journal of Negro Education*, XLVI (Fall, 1977), 388–402.

2. W. V. Tunnell, "The Necessity of Higher Education," *A.M.E. Church Review*, VI (1890), 173–180.

3. *Indianapolis World*, August 2, 1890.

4. Lura Beam, *He Called Them By Lightning: A Teacher's Odyssey in the Negro South, 1908–1919* (Indianapolis: Bobbs-Merrill, 1967), p. 90.

5. See Roger M. Williams, *The Bonds: An Americam Family* (New York: Atheneum, 1971).

6. "Kitt" to Mary Church Terrell, October 25, 1916, Mary Church Terrell Papers, Library of Congress, Washington.

7. Beam, *He Called Them By Lightning*, p. 40; Mary Church Terrell, *A Colored Woman in a White World* (Washington: Ransdell, Inc., 1940), pp. 246–248; Daniel

Murray to George A. Myers, January 21, 1901, George A. Myers Papers, Ohio Historical Society, Columbus.

8. Robert E. Park, "Negro Home Life and Standards of Living," *Annals of the American Academy of Political and Social Sciences* (Philadelphia: n.p., 1913), pp. 160–161; *Washington Bee*, October 19, 1912; Mary B. Talbert to Mary Church Terrell, November 25, 1910, Terrell Papers.

9. *Cleveland Gazette*, July 25, 1891; "*Wall* v. *Oyster*," in *Reports of Cases Adjudged in the Court of Appeals of the District of Columbia, 1910–1911*, XXXVI, 50–58.

10. Theophilius J. Minton, "Is Intermarriage Between the Races to Be Encouraged?" *A.M.E. Church Review*, III (1886), 283–286; H. C. C. Astwood, "Shall Our Schools Be Mixed or Separated?" ibid., 369–76.

11. Francis L. Cardozo, "Shall Our Schools be Mixed?" *A.M.E. Church Review*, III (1886), 160–64.

12. Washington *Colored American*, October 8, 15, November 12, 26, 1898.

13. Michael W. Homel, *Down From Equality: Black Chicagoans and the Public Schools, 1920–41* (Urbana: University of Illinois Press, 1984), pp. 1–22; Allan H. Spear, *Black Chicago: The Making of a Ghetto, 1890–1920* (Chicago: University of Chicago Press, 1967), pp. 85, 201.

14. Horace Mann Bond, *Black American Scholars: A Study of Their Beginnings* (Detroit: Balamp Publishing, 1972), pp. 20, 32.

15. See Carter G. Woodson, *The Education of the Negro Prior to 1861* (New York: G. P. Putnam's Sons, 1915); William C. Harris, "Blanche K. Bruce of Mississippi," in *Southern Black Leaders of the Reconstruction Era*, edited by Howard Rabinowitz (Urbana: University of Illinois Press, 1982), p. 3.

16. Woodson, *The Education of the Negro*, pp. 128–129; Ira Berlin, *Slaves Without Masters: The Free Negro in the Antebellum South* (New York: Pantheon Books, 1974), pp. 304–306; H. E. Sterkx, *The Free Negro in Antebellum Louisiana* (Rutherford, N.J.: Fairleigh Dickinson University Press, 1972), pp. 269–274.

17. Marina Wikramanayake, *A World in Shadow: The Black in Antebellum South Carolina* (Columbia: University of South Carolina Press, 1973), pp. 86–87; C. W. Birnie, "The Education of the Negro in Charleston, South Carolina Before the Civil War," *Journal of Negro History*, XII (January, 1927), 13–21.

18. Frederick A. McGinnis, *The Education of Negroes in Ohio* (Wilberforce, Ohio: Curless Printing Co., 1962), pp. 39–40; Carter Woodson, "The Negroes of Cincinnati Prior to the Civil War," *Journal of Negro History*, I (January, 1916), 19–20; Wendell P. Dabney, *Cincinnati's Colored Citizens* (Cincinnati: Dabney Publishing Co., 1926), pp. 103–105.

19. Darwin T. Turner, ed., *The Wayward and the Seeking: A Collection of Writings by Jean Toomer* (Washington: Howard University Press, 1980), p. 26; Stephen R. Fox, *The Guardian of Boston: William Monroe Trotter* (New York: Atheneum, 1971), pp. 3–17; Bond, *Black American Scholars*, p. 51.

20. Emma C. Bowles, ed., "Concerning the Origin of Wilberforce," *Journal of Negro History*, VIII (July, 1923), 335–337; S. T. Mitchell, "Grand Old Wilberforce," in *The Freeman* (Indianapolis), February 24, 1894; G. F. Richings, *Evidences of Progress Among Colored People* (Philadelphia: George S. Ferguson, 1900), pp. 117–129.

21. W. E. Bigglestone, "Oberlin College and the Negro Student, 1865–1940," *Journal of Negro History*, LVI (July, 1971), 198–219; John Mercer Langston, *From the Virginia Plantation to the National Capitol* (Hartford: American Publishing Co., 1894), pp. 140–143. For a list of the 120 "colored graduates" of Oberlin College as of 1911, see George M. Jones to Mary Church Terrell, April 13, 1911, Terrell Papers.

22. Carleton Mabee, *Black Education in New York State from Colonial to Modern Times* (Syracuse: Syracuse University Press, 1979), chaps. 1–5; Woodson, *Education of the Negro,* p. 96.

23. Mabee, *Black Education in New York State,* pp. 105–107; *New York Freeman,* July 18, 1895.

23. Mabee, *Black Education in New York State,* pp. 105–107; *New York Freeman,* July 18, 1895.

24. Mabee, *Black Education in New York State,* pp. 105–107; "Edward Valentine Clark Eato," Notes, Murray Papers.

25. Linda M. Perkins, "Quaker Beneficence and Black Control: The Institute for Colored Youth, 1852–1903," in *New Perspectives on Black Educational History,* edited by Vincent P. Franklin and James D. Anderson (Boston: G. K. Holland Co., 1978), pp. 19–40; Milton James, "Institute for Colored Youth," *Negro History Bulletin,* XXI (January, 1958), 83–85; *Philadelphia Tribune,* March 27, 1912.

26. "Charles Alexander Dorsey," Notes, Murray Papers; *New York Freeman,* June 25, 1887; Washington *People's Advocate,* July 7, 1883; Harry C. Silcox, "Philadelphia Negro Educator: Jacob C. White, Jr.," *Pennsylvania Magazine of History and Biography,* XCVII (January, 1973), 75–98; Washington *Colored American,* June 24, 1899, September 28, 1901: for other distinguished alumni of the Institute for Colored Youth, see Baltimore *Afro-American,* August 10, 1895.

27. See Joe M. Richardson, "Francis L. Cardozo: Black Educator During Reconstruction," *Journal of Negro Education,* XLVII (Winter, 1979), 73–83; "Francis L. Cardozo," Notes, Murray Papers; various items in F. L. Cardozo Family Papers, Library of Congress, Washington, D.C.

28. Edmund L. Drago and Eugene C. Hunt, *A History of Avery Normal Institute from 1865 to 1954* (Charleston: College of Charleston, n.d.), no pagination [pp. 1, 2]. See also the superb work by Edmund L. Drago, *Initiative, Paternalism, and Race Relations: Charleston's Avery Normal Institute* (Athens: University of Georgia Press, 1989).

29. Bernard E. Powers, Jr., "Black Charleston: A Social History, 1822–1885," Ph.D. diss., Northwestern University, 1982, pp. 260–263.

30. *New York Freeman,* July 18, 1885; *New York Age,* July 6, 1889, June 21, 1906.

31. Drago and Hunt, *Avery Normal Institute,* p. 2; Amelia Merriam, "Avery Normal Institute, Charleston, S.C.," *American Missionary,* XLV (May, 1891), 181–183; Mamie G. Fields, *Lemon Swamp and Other Places: A Carolina Memoir* (New York: Free Press, 1983), p. 24; Mary Deas, quoted in W. E. B. Du Bois, *The Negro Church* (Atlanta: Atlanta University Press, 1903), p. 181.

32. Thomas Jesse Jones, *Negro Education: A Study of the Private and Higher Schools for Colored People in the United States,* 2 vols., Bureau of Education Bulletin No. 39, 1916 (Washington: Government Printing Office, 1917), I, 197–198; Robert E. Perdue, *The Negro in Savannah, 1865–1900* (New York: Exposition Press, 1973), pp. 76–80, 91; *Savannah Tribune,* December 21, 1889.

33. Jones, *Negro Education,* pp. 243–244; H. Paul Douglass, *Christian Reconstruction in the South* (Boston: Pilgrim Press, 1909), pp. 95–96.

34. Beam, *He Called Them By Lightning,* p. 40.

35. Sandra N. Smith and Earle H. West, "Charlotte Hawkins Brown," *Journal of Negro Education,* LI (Summer, 1982), 191–206; see also Constance Marteona, *The Lengthening Shadow of a Woman* (New York: Exposition Press, 1977).

36. Stephen Birmingham, *Certain People: America's Black Elite* (Boston: Little Brown, 1977), pp. 4–12.

37. James M. McPherson, *The Abolitionist Legacy: From Reconstruction to the*

NAACP (Princeton: Princeton University Press, 1975), chap. 11, especially pp. 188–197; see also Cynthia Flemming, "The Effect of Education on Black Tennesseeans After the Civil War," *Phylon*, XLIV (September, 1983), 209–216.

38. George A. Towns, "The Sources of the Tradition of Atlanta University," *Phylon*, III (Second Quarter, 1942), 121; Clarence Bacote, *The Story of Atlanta University: A Century of Service, 1865–1965* (Atlanta: Atlanta University, 1969), p. 328; Richings, *Evidences of Progress*, p. 155; Du Bois, *The Negro Church*, p. 181; Richard R. Wright, Jr., *87 Years Behind the Black Curtain: An Autobiography* (Philadelphia: Rare Book Co., 1965), p. 29.

39. Douglass, *Christian Reconstruction in the South*, p. 379; McPherson, *The Abolitionist Legacy*, p. 196.

40. See Henry A. Bullock, *A History of Negro Education in the South From 1619 to the Present* (Cambridge: Harvard University Press, 1967), chap. 3; Louis R. Harlan, *Separate and Unequal: Public School Campaigns and Racism in the Southern Seaboard States, 1901–1915* (Chapel Hill: University of North Carolina Press, 1958).

41. For private schools still existing in 1916, see Thomas, *Negro Education*, II.

42. *New York Globe*, July 19, 1884; *Indianapolis World*, March 2, 1889; *Nashville Globe*, September 27, 1907.

43. *New York Globe*, October 20, 1883, November 8, 1884.

44. Sadie E. Beach DeVigne, "St. Mark's School, Birmingham, Alabama," *Colored American Magazine*, XIII (December, 1907), 417–420; Harry A. Kersey, "St. Augustine School: Seventy-five Years of Negro Parochial Education in Gainesville, Florida," *Florida Historical Quarterly*, LI (July, 1972), 58–63; James B. Dudley, "Education for Negroes in Guilford County, North Carolina," *Alexander's Magazine*, VI (October 15, 1908), 255–257.

45. Terrell, *Colored Woman in a White World*, p. 18–24.

46. *The Globe* (Nashville), September 27, 1907; Frances Settle to Mary Church Terrell, December 29, 1908, Terrell Papers.

47. Upper-class blacks attended New England preparatory academies such as Lawrence, Kimball, and Williston, in addition to Phillips Exeter.

48. Washington *People's Advocate*, August 16, 1879; *New York Age*, September 13, 1890; Michael F. Rouse, *A Study of the Development of Negro Education Under Catholic Auspices in Maryland and the District of Columbia* (Baltimore: Johns Hopkins Press, 1935), pp. 37–43, 78–79. On other Catholic schools, see *Alexander's Magazine*, IV (June 15, 1907), 97–107. In the antebellum era St. Frances Academy in Baltimore attracted a sizable contingent of students from southern states, who in most instances were "Daughters of wealthy planters, the Negro blood in their veins barring them from the schools for whites" (Rouse, *Negro Education Under Catholic Auspices*, p. 42). On St. Mary's in New Orleans, see Arthe A. Anthony, "The Negro Creole Community in New Orleans, 1880–1920," Ph.D. diss., University of California, Irvine, 1978, p. 97; *The Crusader* (New Orleans), July 19, 1890.

49. Willard B. Gatewood, Jr., "William Grant Still's Little Rock," in *William Grant Still Studies at the University of Arkansas: A Congress Report, 1984* (Fayetteville: n.p., 1985), pp. 10–12; James Weldon Johnson, *Along This Way: The Autobiography of James Weldon Johnson* (New York: Viking Press, 1933), pp. 33–36; Jones, *Negro Education*, I, 128, 165; Henry S. Williams, "The Development of the Negro Public School System in Missouri," *Journal of Negro History*, V (April, 1920), 162.

50. George F. T. Cook, "Historical Sketch of the Colored Schools, Past and Present," in *First Report of the Board of Trustees of the Public Schools of the District of Columbia, 1874–1875* (Washington: McGill and Witherow, 1876), pp. 89–94; Green, *The Secret City*, pp. 7–8, 23–24, 67–70, 85–90, 136–139, 210–211; Kelly Miller,

"Howard: The National Negro University," in *The New Negro: An Interpretation*, edited by Alain Locke (New York: Albert and Charles Boni, 1928), pp. 312–322; see also Rayford Logan, *Howard University: The First Hundred Years, 1867–1967* (New York: New York University Press, 1969).

51. Green, *Secret City; Washington Bee*, September 29, 1900.

52. Josephine Bruce to R. C. Bruce, November 23, 1897, Roscoe C. Bruce Papers, Moorland-Spingarn Research Center, Howard University, Washington, D.C.

53. *Washington Bee*, October 27, 1894, April 23, 1891.

54. Ibid., April 23, 1891, May 20, 1893, May 6, 1897.

55. Green, *Secret City*, pp. 136–137.

56. E. Delorius Preston, "William Syphax, A Pioneer in Negro Education in the District of Columbia," *Journal of Negro History*, XX (October, 1955), 448–476; Mary Church Terrell, "History of the High School for Negroes in Washington," ibid., II (April, 1917), 252–266; Henry S. Robinson, "The M Street High School, 1891–1916," *Records of the Columbia Historical Society of Washington D.C.*, LI (1984), 119–143.

57. *Washington Bee*, December 25, 1915, January 1, 8, 22, 1916.

58. Jervis Anderson, "A Very Special Monument: The Dunbar High School on First Street," *The New Yorker*, March 20, 1978, pp. 101–102; see also Mary Gibson Hundley, *The Dunbar Story, 1870–1955* (New York: Vantage Press, 1965).

59. W. H. Lewis, "Commencement Address to Graduates of M Street High School," *Colored American Magazine*, XIV (July, 1908), 425–426.

60. Quoted in Anderson, "A Very Special Monument," p. 108.

61. On Greener, see Allison Blakeley, "Richard T. Greener and the Dilemma of the 'Talented Tenth,' " *Journal of Negro History*, LIX (October, 1974), 305–321; Richard Bardolph, *The Negro Vanguard* (New York: Holt, Rinehart and Winston, 1959), p. 88.

62. On Terrell, see Washington *Colored American*, October 20, 1900; see also Anderson, "A Very Special Monument," pp. 96–97.

63. Leon Litwack, *Been in the Storm So Long: The Aftermath of Slavery* (New York: Knopf, 1979), pp. 495–496; Green, *Secret City*, pp. 137–138; *Washington Bee*, July 4, 1896.

64. A. C. McClennan to Whitefield McKinlay, September 15, 1902, McKinlay Papers; "Contents of Poll of the Press on the Cardozo Case Arranged by R. C. Doggett," Terrell Papers.

65. Hundley, *The Dunbar Story*, pp. 75–88; Anderson, "A Very Special Monument," pp. 108–117; Terrell, "History of the High School for Negroes in Washington," pp. 62–65.

66. Robert H. Terrell to E. H. Hall, January 6, 1890, R. H. Terrell Papers.

67. G. Smith Wormley, "Educators of the First Half Century of Public Schools of the District of Columbia," *Journal of Negro History*, XVII (April, 1932), 137–138; Terrell, "History of the High School for Negroes in Washington," pp. 257–258; Anderson, "A Very Special Monument," p. 96; *Washington Bee*, January 27, 1912.

68. Anderson, "A Very Special Monument," pp. 110–121.

69. Washington *People's Advocate*, August 16, September 20, 1879; *New York Age*, February 8, 1890.

70. G. F. Richings, *Evidences of Progress Among Colored People* (Philadelphia: Geo. S. Ferguson, 1900), p. 112; "An Old and Worthy Institution," *Colored American Magazine*, XIV (January, 1908), 72–73. "Morgan State University," in *Encyclopedia of Black America*, edited by W. A. Low and Virgil A. Clift (New York: McGraw Hill Book Company, 1981), pp. 567–568.

71. J. L. Nichols and William H. Crogman, *Progress of a Race* (Naperville, Ill.: J. L. Nichols and Co., 1920), pp. 384–385; Alfred Moss, *American Negro Academy: Voice of*

the Talented Tenth (Baton Rouge: Louisiana State University Press, 1981), pp. 120, 214, 258–259; Charles F. Kellogg, *NAACP: A History of the National Association for the Advancement of Colored People, 1909–1920* (Baltimore: Johns Hopkins University Press, 1967), pp. 184, 186, 196, 204.

72. Woodson, *The Education of the Negro Prior to 1861*, p. 138.

73. Bettye C. Thomas, "Public Education and Black Protest in Baltimore, 1865–1900," *Maryland Historical Magazine*, LXXI (Fall, 1976), 381–391; William George Paul, "The Shadow of Equality: The Negro in Baltimore, 1864–1911," Ph.D. diss., University of Wisconsin, 1972, chaps. 7 and 9; Baltimore *American Citizen*, April 19, 1879; Baltimore *Afro-American*, February 22, 1896; Martha S. Putney, "The Baltimore Normal School for the Education of Colored Teachers: Its Founders and Its Founding," *Maryland Historical Magazine*, LXXII (Summer, 1977), 238–252.

74. W. E. B. Du Bois, *The College-Bred Negro* (Atlanta: Atlanta University Press, 1900), p. 37; W. E. B. Du Bois, *The College-Bred Negro American* (Atlanta: Atlanta University Press, 1910), p. 45; W. E. B. Du Bois, *Social and Physical Condition of Negroes in Cities* (Atlanta: Atlanta University Press, 1897), p. 70; Washington *Colored American*, January 21, 1899.

75. *New York Age*, May 12, 1888; see also R. R. Wright, "The Negroes of Philadelphia," *A.M.E. Church Review*, XXIV (October, 1907), 141–142.

76. *New York Age*, May 8, 1913; "George W. Cabiness," Notes, Murray Papers.

77. See Clarence A. Bacote, *The Story of Atlanta University: A Century of Service, 1865–1965* (Atlanta: Atlanta University, 1965); Logan, *Howard University*; Joe M. Richardson, *A History of Fisk University, 1865–1946* (Tuscaloosa: University of Alabama Press, 1980).

78. John Hope, quoted in Hollis R. Lynch, ed., *The Black Urban Condition: A Documentary History, 1866–1971* (New York: Thomas Y. Crowell, 1973), p. 61.

79. E. Horace Fitchett, "The Influence of Claflin College on Negro Family Life," *Journal of Negro History*, XXIX (October, 1944), 429–460; E. Horace Fitchett, "The Role of Claflin College in Negro Life in South Carolina," *Journal of Negro Education*, XII (Winter, 1943), 42–68.

80. Reverdy C. Ransom, *The Pilgrimage of Harriet Ransom's Son* (Nashville: Sunday School Union, n.d.), p. 29.

81. Kelly Miller, "Howard University," in *From Servitude to Service* (Boston: American Unitarian Association, 1905), p. 15; Zora Neale Hurston, *Dust Tracks on a Road: An Autobiography* (Urbana: University of Illinois Press, 1984), p. 156.

82. Hallie E. Queen to Mary C. Terrell, January 2, 1909, Terrell Papers.

83. Miller, "Howard University," p. 28.

84. James Weldon Johnson, "Should the Negro Be Given an Education Different from that Given to the Whites?" in *Twentieth Century Negro Literature*, edited by D. W. Culp (Naperville, Illinois: J. L. Nichols, 1902), p. 78.

85. Andrew F. Hilyer, "The Higher Education for Negro Youth," *Popular Science Monthly*, LVII (August, 1900), 437–438.

86. See Charles H. Wesley, *History of Sigma Pi Phi* (Washington: Association for the Study of Negro Life and History, 1954), pp. 32–33.

87. Joseph J. Boris, ed., *Who's Who in Colored America, 1928–29* (New York: Who's Who in Colored America, 1929), p. 90.

88. Washington *Colored American*, October 20, 1900.

89. See *Washington Bee*, May 30, 1914.

90. "Outstanding Yale Graduates," *Ebony*, V (July, 1950), 18; Chicago *Broad Ax*, May 7, 1908.

91. *New York Age*, November 15, 1890; *Washington Bee*, January 2, 1908.

92. Mary D. Crowe, "Fannie Barrier Williams," *Negro History Bulletin*, V (May, 1942), 190–191. On S. Laing Williams, see Indianapolis *Freeman*, August 2, 1904.

93. *Washington Bee*, February 1, 1890; May 31, 1913.

94. *New York Age*, May 29, 1913.

95. Bond, *Black American Scholars*, p. 51.

96. Willard B. Gatewood, Jr., "John Hanks Alexander of Arkansas: Second Black Graduate of West Point," *Arkansas Historical Quarterly*, XLI (Summer, 1982), 103–128; see also Phyllis Scott, "Titus Alexander," *The California Eagle* (Los Angeles), November 13, 1947.

97. Terrell, *Colored Woman in a White World*, pp. 243–244.

98. Bond, *Black American Scholars*, pp. 34–58, 170–179.

99. Carter G. Woodson, "The Gibbs Family—The Hunts, The Marshalls, The Muses, The Laws and the Millers," *Negro History Bulletin*, XI (October, 1947), 3–12, 22; Thomas V. Gibbs, "John Willis Menard: The First Colored Congressman Elect," *A.M.E. Church Review*, LII (1886), 426–432.

100. W. S. Scarborough, *The Educated Negro and His Mission*, American Negro Academy Occasional Papers, No. 8 (Washington: American Negro Academy, 1903), p. 5.

101. R. C. Bruce, "Service By the Educated Negro," *Colored American Magazine*, VI (December, 1903), 850–857.

102. Scarborough, *The Educated Negro*, p. 7.

103. See Cynthia Neverdon-Morton, "The Black Woman's Struggle for Equality in the South, 1895–1925," in *The Afro-American Woman: Struggles and Images*, edited by Sharon Harley and Rosalyn Terborg-Penn (Port Washington, N.Y.: Kennikat Press, 1978), pp. 43–57; W. E. B. Du Bois, *Efforts for Social Betterment Among Negro Americans* (Atlanta: Atlanta University Press, 1909), pp. 52–53; Gerda Lerner, "Early Community Work of Black Club Women," *Journal of Negro History*, LXI (April, 1974), 158–167.

104. *New York Age*, June 29, 1905.

105. *Washington Bee*, July 17, 1920.

106. Quoted in *Indianapolis Recorder*, July 18, 1903; for a similar view, see *Washington Bee*, May 22, 1886.

107. *Cleveland Journal*, January 18, 1908.

108. *Atlanta Independent*, October 5, 1907; see also *Dallas Express*, in *Cleveland Journal*, December 4, 1909.

109. *Atlanta Independent*, September 25, 1909; see also November 11, 1905, September 28, 1907.

10. Churches of the Aristocracy

1. Quoted in Milton C. Sternett, *Afro-American Religious History: A Documentary Witness* (Durham, N.C.: Duke University Press, 1985), p. 3.

2. See E. Franklin Frazier, *The Negro Church in America* (New York: Schocken Books, 1974).

3. Norval Glenn, "Negro Religion and Negro Status in the United States," in *Religion, Culture and Society*, edited by Louis Schneider (New York: John Wiley, 1964), pp. 623, 639.

4. Ibid.; Carter G. Woodson, *The History of the Negro Church* (Washington: Associated Publishers, 1972); see also Joseph R. Washington, Jr., *Black Religion: The Negro and Christianity in the United States* (Boston: Beacon Press, 1964), chaps. 2 and 3; Harry V. Richardson, *Dark Salvation: The Story of Methodism As It Developed Among Blacks in America* (Garden City: Doubleday, 1976), chaps. 6 and 7; Francis J. Grimké, "The Defects of Our Ministry and Its Remedy," *A.M.E. Church Review*, III (February, 1887), 154–157.

5. Glenn, "Negro Religion and Negro Status in the United States," pp. 637–38.

6. Monroe N. Work, "The Negro Church in the Negro Community," *Southern Workman*, XXXVII (August, 1908), 428–433.

7. Quoted in Indianapolis *Freeman*, August 18, 1888. On social class and church membership, see Vattel Elbert Daniel, "Negro Classes and Life in the Church," *Journal of Negro Education*, XIII (Winter, 1944), 19–29.

8. Detroit *Plaindealer*, April 10, 1901; "Walter H. Brooks," in *Twentieth Century Negro Literature*, edited by D. W. Culp (Naperville, Illinois: J. L. Nichols, 1902), p. 315.

9. Washington *People's Advocate*, May 26, 1883.

10. Quoted in Leon F. Litwack, *Been in the Storm So Long: The Aftermath of Slavery* (New York: Alfred A. Knopf, 1979), p. 458.

11. *Washington Bee*, July 26, 1884.

12. Washington *People's Advocate*, May 26, 1883; Francis L. Broderick, *W. E. B. Du Bois: Negro Leader in a Time of Crisis* (Palo Alto: Stanford University Press, 1959), p. 33; Indianapolis *Freeman*, June 9, 1894, August 12, 1904; *Seattle Republican*, October 19, 1900; Kansas City *American Citizen*, May 31, 1901; *Christian Index*, quoted in *Indianapolis Recorder*, September 5, 1903; Chicago *Broad Ax*, March 26, 1910.

13. W. T. B. Williams to John Hope, September 17, 1898, John and Lugenia Burns Hope Papers, Atlanta University Library (microfilm).

14. Mary Church Terrell, Diary, January 18, 1915, Mary Church Terrell Papers, Library of Congress.

15. *Star of Zion*, XIII (November 28, 1889), 2.

16. W. T. B. Williams to John Hope, September 18, 1898, Hope Papers.

17. Robert A. Bennett, "Black Episcopalians: A History from the Colonial Period to the Present," *Historical Magazine of the Protestant Episcopal Church*, XLIII (September, 1974), 237.

18. W. E. B. Du Bois, *The Negro Church* (Atlanta: Atlanta University Press, 1903), p. 139; John Hope Franklin, "Negro Episcopalians in Antebellum North Carolina," *Historical Magazine of the Protestant Episcopal Church*, XIII (September, 1944), 234.

19. J. Carleton Hayden, "After the War: The Mission and Growth of the Episcopal Church Among Blacks in the South, 1865–1877," *Historical Magazine of the Protestant Episcopal Church*, XLII (December, 1973), 403, 426–428.

20. Department of Commerce, Bureau of the Census, *Special Report: Religious Bodies, 1906*, Part I (Washington: Government Printing Office, 1910), p. 538.

21. "The Episcopal Church," *The Christian Recorder*, VII (April 6, 1867), 54.

22. George F. Bragg, Jr., in *New York Age*, June 13, 1907.

23. Arnold Hamilton Maloney, *Amber Gold: An Adventure in Autobiography* (Boston: Meador Publishing Co., 1946), pp. 120, 134–135.

24. Louis R. Harlan et al., *The Papers of Booker T. Washington* (Urbana: University of Illinois Press, 1976), V, 67n.

25. See George C. Wright, *Life Behind A Veil: Blacks in Louisville, Kentucky, 1865–1930* (Baton Rouge: Louisiana State University, 1985), p. 134.

26. See Bennett, "Black Episcopalians," 238–242; David Reimers, "Negro Bishops and Diocesan Segregation in the Protestant Episcopal Church, 1870–1954," *Historical Magazine of the Protestant Episcopal Church*, XXXI (September, 1962), 231–240; "Afro-American Episcopalians," *Western Outlook* (San Francisco), February 27, 1915; *New York Age*, August 17, 1905, December 7, 1916, May 17, 1917; George F. Bragg, Jr., *History of the Afro-American Group of the Episcopal Church* (Baltimore: Church Advocate Press, 1922); "Color Question in the Protestant Episcopal Church," *A.M.E. Church Review*, XXI (January, 1905), 268–269.

27. Benjamin F. De Costa, *Three Score and Ten: The Story of St. Philip's Church* (New York: The Parish, 1889), pp. 11–17.

28. Ibid.; Shelton H. Bishop, "A History of St. Philip's Church, New York City," *Historical Magazine of the Protestant Episcopal Church*, XV (December, 1946), 298–317; *New York Age*, April 11, 1885, February 23, 1889, April 17, 1886, April 16, 1887, December 9, 1909, December 24, 1889, March 30, 1911, January 16, 1913; *Indianapolis Recorder*, February 10, 1910.

29. For the story of the Chapel of St. Mary the Virgin and the role of the Bishop family in its origins and growth, see Calbraith B. Perry, *Twelve Years Among the Colored People: A Record of the Work of Mount Calvary Chapel of St. Mary the Virgin, Baltimore* (Baltimore: James Pott and Co., 1894), especially pp. 75–77, 121–123.

30. Bragg, *Afro-American Group of the Episcopal Church*, pp. 88, 172–174; Bishop, "History of St. Philip's Church," pp. 307–308; Perry, *Twelve Years Among the Colored People*, pp. 101–108.

31. Gilbert Osofsky, *Harlem: The Making of A Ghetto, Negro New York, 1890–1930* (New York: Harper and Row, 1966), pp. 115–116; *New York Age*, March 30, 1911.

32. *New York Age*, January 16, 1913.

33. Ibid., April 18, May 2, 1912, March 12, 1913.

34. Ibid., April 22, May 6, 1909, May 15, 1909; "Charles Henry Lansing, Jr.," Sketches, Daniel Murray Papers, State Historical Society of Wisconsin, Madison (microfilm); on Tunnell, see Bragg, *Afro-American Group of the Episcopal Church*, pp. 178–181; John P. Green to George A. Myers, June 21, 1900, George A. Myers Papers, Ohio Historical Society, Columbus.

35. Ann C. Lammers, "The Rev. Absalom Jones and the Episcopal Church: Christian Theology and Black Consciousness in New Alliance," *Historical Magazine of the Protestant Episcopal Church*, LI (June, 1982), 159–184; Bragg, *Afro-American Group of the Episcopal Church*, p. 81.

36. W. E. B. Du Bois, *The Philadelphia Negro* (Philadelphia: University of Pennsylvania Press, 1899), p. 198; "St. Thomas Episcopal Church, Philadelphia," Notes, Murray Papers; *Richmond Planet*, February 9, 1901. The column in the *Philadelphia Tribune* by "Pencil Pusher" (William C. Bolivar) regularly chronicled the history of St. Thomas, where Bolivar was a communicant; see *Philadelphia Tribune*, November 23, 1912, March 29, 1913, October 31, 1914, February 7, 1917. On Benjamin Rush, see also L. H. Butterfield, *Letters of Benjamin Rush*, 2 vols. (Princeton: Princeton University Press for the American Philosophical Society, 1951), I, 599–601.

37. *Philadelphia Tribune*, May 25, 1912; see also May 18, 1912, May 10, 1913.

38. Du Bois, *The Philadelphia Negro*, p. 199n.; on the Church of the Crucifixion in Philadelphia, see *Philadelphia Tribune*, March 16, 1912.

39. Allen J. Johnston, "Surviving Freedom: The Black Community of Washington, D.C., 1860–1880," Ph.D. diss., Duke University, 1980, pp. 97–98; *Washington People's Advocate*, January 8, 1881, see also November 29, 1879; *New York Times*, February 15, 1891.

40. Mrs. E. N. Chapin, *American Court Gossip, or Life at the National Capitol* (Marshalltown, Iowa: Chapin and Hartwell, 1887), p. 38.

41. Julian Ralph, *Dixie, or Southern Scenes and Sketches* (New York: Harper and Brothers, 1896), p. 368.

42. Bragg, *Afro-American Group of the Episcopal Church*, pp. 90–96, 98, 172–176; *Washington People's Advocate*, March 18, 1880; *New York Age*, February 8, 1890; Baltimore *Afro-American Ledger*, May 17, October 18, 1902.

43. Register, 1864–1965, St. Mark's Protestant Episcopal Church, Charleston, South Carolina Historical Society (microfiche); *Christian Recorder*, V (September 8, 1866), 142; *New York Globe*, September 1, 1883; George F. Bragg, Jr., "The Episcopal Church and the Negro Race," *Historical Magazine of the Protestant Episcopal Church*, IV (March, 1935), 50; "Some Historical Facts About St. Mark's Episcopal Church, Charles-

ton, S.C., 100th Anniversary" (mimeographed), St. Mark's Church, Charleston; A. Toomer Porter, *Led On! Step by Step: Scenes from Clerical, Military, Educational and Plantation Life in the South, 1828–1898* (New York: G. P. Putnam's Sons, 1898), pp. 307–311, 330–339.

44. Quoted in Litwack, *Been in the Storm So Long*, p. 467.

45. A. N. Fields, "Colorline Within the Race," *Abbott's Monthly*, VII (July, 1933), 2–3; Mamie Garvin Fields with Karen Fields, *Lemon Swamp and Other Places: A Carolina Memoir* (New York: Free Press, 1983), p. 24.

46. "Some Historical Facts About St. Mark's Episcopal Church."

47. Indianapolis *Freeman*, January 26, 1907.

48. Quoted in *New York Age*, March 21, 1907.

49. Robert E. Perdue, *The Negro in Savannah, 1865–1900* (New York: Exposition Press, 1973), pp. 91–92; Annette E. Church and Roberta Church, *The Robert R. Churches of Memphis* (Ann Arbor, Michigan: Edwards Brothers, 1974), pp. 4, 28–29; P. B. B. Hynson to R. R. Church, February 17, 1901, E. Thomas Demby to R. R. Church, May 1, 1911, Robert Reed Church Family Papers, Mississippi Valley Collection, Memphis State University, Memphis, Tennessee.

50. David M. Katzman, *Before the Ghetto: Black Detroit in the Nineteenth Century* (Urbana: University of Illinois Press, 1973), pp. 136–139.

51. Indianapolis *Freeman*, July 14, 1906; *New York Age*, May 30, 1907; Indianapolis *World*, March 2, 1889; *Cleveland Journal*, December 2, 1905, November 16, 1907; Nashville *Globe*, September 27, 1907; *The Enterprise* (Omaha), April 4, 1896; Kenneth L. Kusmer, *A Ghetto Takes Shape: Black Cleveland, 1870–1930* (Urbana: University of Illinois Press, 1976), p. 94; George C. Wright, "Blacks in Louisville, Kentucky, 1890–1930," Ph.D. diss., Duke University, 1977, pp. 84–85; Robert A. Warner, *New Haven Negroes: A Social History* (New Haven: Yale University Press, 1940), pp. 84–88.

52. *New York Age*, April 1, 1909. Two years earlier a white Episcopal congregation in New York voiced complaints about the presence of blacks; see "Negroes in White Churches," *Colored American Magazine*, XII (April, 1907), 247.

53. John Daniels, *In Freedom's Birthplace: A Study of the Boston Negroes* (Boston: Houghton Mifflin, 1914), pp. 225–234, 244–247; "St. Cyprian P. E. Church, Boston," Notes, Murray Papers; Dorothy West, *The Living Is Easy* (New York: Arno Press, 1969), p. 309.

54. For a study of black Presbyterians, see Andrew E. Murray, *Presbyterians and the Negro: A History* (Philadelphia: Presbyterian Historical Society, 1966); the entire issue of *The Journal of Presbyterian History*, LI (Winter, 1973).

55. Gayraud S. Wilmore, *Black and Presbyterian: The Heritage and the Hope* (Philadelphia: Geneva Press, 1983), p. 75. For arguments that blacks should become Presbyterians, see Matthew Anderson, *Presbyterianism: Its Relation to the Negro Illustrated by the Berean Presbyterian Church, Philadelphia* (Philadelphia: John McGill White and Co., 1897).

56. Wilmore, *Black and Presbyterian*, p. 74.

57. Ibid., p. 74; *New York Age*, September 30, 1916.

58. *New York Age*, November 23, 1889.

59. Quoted in Indianapolis *Freeman*, February 16, 1889.

60. Du Bois, *The Negro Church*, pp. 73, 174.

61. Du Bois, *The Philadelphia Negro*, pp. 199–201; *Philadelphia Tribune*, January 13, 1913, October 20, 1917; Richard R. Wright, Jr., *The Negro in Pennsylvania: An Economic Study* (Philadelphia: A.M.E. Book Concern, 1912), pp. 117–118; on Berean Church, see Anderson, *Presbyterianism: Its Relation to the Negro*.

62. *New York Globe*, July 28, 1883; *New York Freeman*, June 5, 1889; *Indianapolis*

World, May 23, 1891; *New York Age*, November 23, 1889, July 30, 1905; *Illinois Record* (Springfield), July 2, 1898; Jervis Anderson, *This Was Harlem: A Cultural Portrait, 1900–1950* (New York: Farrar, Straus, Giroux, 1981), pp. 5–6; Allan H. Spear, *Black Chicago, 1890–1920* (Chicago: University of Chicago Press, 1967), p. 94; see also "Colored Presbyterians," *A.M.E. Church Review*, XV (October, 1898), 671–673; *Richmond Planet*, May 27, 1905.

63. Records of Session and Church, 1841–1868, Fifteenth Street Presbyterian Church, Moorland-Spingarn Research Center, Howard University, Washington, D.C.

64. Ibid., November 3, 1841; *The National Era* (Washington), November 9, 1854, March 29, 1855; *Daily National Intelligencer* (Washington), March 23, 1855.

65. On Grimké, see Louis B. Weeks, "Racism, World War I, and the Christian Life: Francis J. Grimké in the Nation's Capital," *Journal of Presbyterian History*, LI (Winter, 1973), 471–488.

66. Carter G. Woodson, ed., *The Works of Francis J. Grimké*, 4 vols. (Washington: Associated Publishers: n.d.), I, 477–478.

67. Ibid.

68. *Washington Bee*, November 17, 1883.

69. Washington *People's Advocate*, January 8, 1881.

70. Mrs. John A. Logan, *Thirty Years in Washington Or Life and Scenes in Our National Capital* (Hartford, Conn.: A.D. Worthington and Co., 1901), p. 522.

71. Ralph, *Dixie or Southern Scenes and Sketches*, pp. 368–369.

72. Paynter, in *Colorado Statesman*, August 27, 1907.

73. Richard T. Greener to Francis J. Grimké, November 16, 1916, in *Works of Francis J. Grimké*, IV, 181.

74. Warner, *New Haven Negroes*, pp. 88–94; Alice M. Bacon, "A Negro District in New Haven," *Southern Workman*, XXXVI (July, 1907), 82.

75. Joe M. Richardson, "The Failure of the American Missionary Association to Expand Congregationalism Among Southern Blacks," *Southern Studies*, XVIII (Spring, 1979), 58–66; see also Augustus F. Beard, *A Crusade of Brotherhood: A History of the American Missionary Association* (Boston: Pilgrim Press, 1909), chaps. V–XI.

76. Richardson, "Failure of the American Missionary Association," pp. 66, 73; "Christ Church, Wilmington," *American Missionary*, XLVI (June, 1892), 195–196; "First Congregational Church of Mobile," ibid., pp. 182–183.

77. Richardson, "Failure of the American Missionary Association," p. 77.

78. John W. Whittaker, "Are Other than Baptist and Methodist Churches Adapted to the Present Negro?" in Culp, *Twentieth Century Negro Literature*, pp. 359–361; see also Lura Beam, *He Called Them By Lightning: A Teacher's Odyssey in the Negro South, 1908–1919* (Indianapolis: Bobbs-Merrill, 1967), p. 49.

79. "Structure of Nashville Society Among the Negro Group," E. Franklin Frazier Papers, Moorland-Spingarn Research Center, Howard University.

80. Whittaker, "Are Other than Baptist and Methodist Churches Adapted to the Present Negro?" pp. 361–362.

81. A. Knighton Stanley, *The Children Is Crying: Congregationalism Among Black People* (Boston: Pilgrim Press, 1979), pp. 74–77; Beard, *A Crusade of Brotherhood*, pp. 229–231.

82. Washington *People's Advocate*, July 7, 1883, September 22, 1883. Washington *Colored American*, October 1, 1898.

83. *Washington Bee*, December 5, 1896; Mary Church Terrell, *A Colored Woman in A White World* (Washington: Ransdell, Inc., 1940), p. 114; *University Park Temple* (pamphlet), in John P. Green Papers, Western Reserve Historical Society, Cleveland, Ohio.

84. Wright, "Blacks in Louisville, Kentucky, 1890–1930," pp. 84–85; Benjamin D. Berry, Jr., "The Plymouth Congregational Church of Louisville, Kentucky," *Phylon*, XLII (September, 1981), 224–232; see also *Cleveland Journal*, August 1, November 14, 1903; "Organization of the First Congregational Christian Church of Lexington, Kentucky," *American Missionary*, XLV (May, 1891), 199.

85. D. B. Gaines, *Racial Possibilities As Indicated By the Negroes of Little Rock* (Little Rock: Philander Smith College, 1898), p. 125.

86. "Structure of Nashville's Negro Society," Frazier Papers; *Nashville Globe*, April 12, October 4, 1907; Roger M. Williams, *The Bonds: An American Family* (New York: Atheneum, 1971), pp. 34–49.

87. Henry Hugh Proctor, *Between Black and White: Autobiographical Sketches* (Freeport, N.Y.: Books for Libraries Press, 1971), pp. 28–36, 93–110; H. Paul Douglass, *Christian Reconstruction in the South* (Boston: Pilgrim Press, 1909), pp. 156, 164; Jerry John Thornberry, "The Development of Black Atlanta, 1865–1885," Ph.D. diss., University of Maryland, 1977, pp. 151–156, 178. Unfortunately the Henry H. and Adeline L. Davis Proctor Papers at the Amistad Research Center, Tulane University, New Orleans, Louisiana, include primarily materials from after 1919.

88. Michael L. Porter, "Black Atlanta: An Interdisciplinary Study of Blacks on the East Side of Atlanta," Ph.D. diss., Emory University, 1974, p. 72.

89. Quoted in *Social and Physical Condition of Negroes in Cities*, edited by W. E. B. Du Bois (Atlanta: Atlanta University Press, 1897), pp. 44–45.

90. Mrs. H. H. Proctor, *Negro Womanhood* (New York: American Missionary Association, n.d.), pp. 3–4.

91. John Dittmer, *Black Georgia in the Progressive Era, 1900–1920* (Urbana: University of Illinois Press, 1977), p. 62; *Atlanta Independent*, May 23, June 6, 1908, January 23, 1909, January 30, October 2, 9, 23, 1915, July 1, 1916.

92. David Reimers, *White Protestantism and the Negro* (New York: Oxford University Press, 1965), pp. 21–25, 71–75; J. C. Hartzell, "Methodism and the Negro in the United States," *Journal of Negro History*, VIII (July, 1923), 301–315.

93. Edward L. Gilliam, quoted in Indianapolis *Freeman*, November 2, 1901; ibid., February 23, 1895; Willard B. Gatewood, Jr., ed., *Slave and Free Man* (Lexington: University Press of Kentucky, 1982), pp. 21–22; *New York Freeman*, April 9, May 21, 1887; *Christian Recorder*, XXIII (November 26, 1885), 2; L. M. Hagood, *The Colored Man in the Methodist Episcopal Church* (Cincinnati: Cranston and Stowe, 1890).

94. Du Bois, *The Negro Church*, pp. 76, 78.

95. *New York Globe*, September 1, 1883; Washington *People's Advocate*, June 5, 1880; Baltimore *Afro-American*, May 17, 1902; "St. Mark's Methodist Episcopal Church," *Colored American Magazine*, X (May, 1906), 381–385; Wright, "Blacks in Louisville," p. 77; Powers, "Black Charleston," pp. 193, 219–220.

96. Leroy Graham, *Baltimore: The Nineteenth Century Black Capital* (Lanham, Md.: University Press of America, 1982), pp. 202–203; "E. V. C. Eato," Sketches, Murray Papers.

97. Wright, "Blacks in Louisville," p. 77; Powers, "Black Charleston," pp. 184–185; Wright, *The Negro in Philadelphia*, p. 121.

98. On black Catholics, see John T. Gillard, *The Catholic Church and the American Negro* (Baltimore: St. Joseph's Society Press, 1929); *New Catholic Encyclopedia*, 17 vols. (New York: McGraw Hill, 1967), X, 310–314; Robert Reinders, "The Churches and the Negro in New Orleans, 1850–1860," *Phylon*, XXII (Fall, 1961), 241–248. Much of *Alexander's Magazine*, IV (June 15, 1907) is devoted to the work of the Catholic church among blacks.

99. Gillard, *The Catholic Church and the American Negro*, pp. 252–253.

100. John W. Blassingame, *Black New Orleans, 1860–1880* (Chicago: University of Chicago Press, 1973), pp. 199–201; Dolores Egger Labbe, *Jim Crow Comes to Church: The Establishment of Segregated Catholic Parishes in South Louisiana* (New York: Arno Press, 1978), especially chaps. III–V; Arthe A. Anthony, "The Negro Creole Community in New Orleans, 1880–1920: An Oral History," Ph.D. diss., University of California, Irvine, 1978, pp. 53–54.

101. Quoted in Salt Lake City *Broad Ax*, February 25, 1899.

102. Mary Church Terrell to Anna Coveney, March 10, 1918, Terrell Papers; Albert S. Foley, *God's Men of Color: The Colored Catholic Priests in the United States* (New York: Farrar, Straus and Co., 1955), p. 42; *New York Age*, September 13, 1890; Gillard, *Catholic Church and the American Negro*, pp. 16, 139–140; Grace E. Sherwood, *The Oblates' Hundred and One Years* (New York: Macmillan, 1931), pp. 29–35, 130–133, 152; *Cleveland Gazette*, July 16, 1904.

103. Foley, *God's Men of Color*, pp. 43–51; Baltimore *Afro-American Ledger*, December 2, 1895, October 26, 1912, September 27, 1913; Michael F. Rouse, *A Study of the Development of Negro Education Under Catholic Auspices in Maryland and the District of Columbia* (Baltimore: The Johns Hopkins Press, 1935), pp. 37–43.

104. Gillard, *Catholic Church and the American Negro*, pp. 29–30; Foley, *God's Men of Color*, pp. 42–51.

105. David Spalding, "The Negro Catholic Congresses, 1889–1894," *Catholic Historical Review*, LV (October, 1969), 340; Archibald Grimké, "Colored Catholics in Washington, D.C.," *Alexander's Magazine*, IV (June 15, 1907), 108–110; Ralph, *Dixie or Southern Scenes and Sketches*, p. 369.

106. Spalding, "The Negro Catholic Congresses," pp. 337–357; see also *Three Catholic Afro-American Congresses* (New York: Arno Press, 1978) for the proceedings of the congresses held in 1889, 1890, and 1892.

107. *New York Age*, February 20, 1913; Foley, *God's Men of Color*, p. 60.

108. Washington, *Black Religion*, p. 222; W. E. B. Du Bois, *Dusk of Dawn* (New York: Harcourt, Brace, 1940), p. 17; E. Azalia Hackley, *The Colored Girl Beautiful* (Kansas City: Burton Publishing, 1916), p. 89.

109. Springfield *Illinois Record*, October 15, 1898.

110. Benjamin E. Mays and Joseph W. Nicholson, *The Negro's Church* (New York: Institute of Social and Religious Research, 1933), see especially pp. 94–102.

11. Aristocrats of Color and Jim Crow

1. Denver *Colorado Statesman*, August 6, 1907.

2. *Washington Bee*, August 17, 1901.

3. Mary Church Terrell to Henry C. King, January 26, 1914, Mary Church Terrell Papers, Library of Congress, Washington, D.C.; see also Florence Fitch to Mary Church Terrell, November 4, 1913, Oswald Garrison Villard to Mary Church Terrell, January 13, 1914, Henry C. King to Mary Church Terrell, February 4, 1914, Terrell Papers.

4. Mary Church Terrell, *A Colored Woman in a White World* (Washington: Ransdell, 1940), pp. 311–315; *Washington Bee*, October 30, 1920.

5. *Washington Bee*, May 30, 1908; *New York Age*, May 6, 1909.

6. The interpretation of Booker T. Washington relies heavily on Louis R. Harlan's two-volume biography, *Booker T. Washington: The Making of a Black Leader, 1856–1901* and *Booker T. Washington: The Wizard of Tuskegee, 1901–1915* (New York: Oxford University Press, 1972, 1983). See also Willard B. Gatewood, Jr., "Booker T. Washington," in *Encyclopedia of Black America*, edited by W. A. Low and Virgil A. Clift (New York: McGraw-Hill, 1981), pp. 839–845.

7. Quoted in Chicago *Broad-Ax*, September 23, 1905.

8. Gatewood, "Booker T. Washington," pp. 843–844. The Afro-American Council, organized in 1898 as the successor to the moribund Afro-American League, was dominated by Washington's forces almost from the beginning; see Emma L. Thornbrough, "The National Afro-American League, 1887–1908," *Journal of Southern History*, XXVII (November, 1961), 494–512.

9. Indianapolis *Freeman*, June 15, 1901, December 6, 1902; Washington *Colored American*, October 3, 1903; *New York Age*, July 12, 1906, September 9, 1909, December 7, 1918; *Washington Bee*, October 30, 1915. Laura Terrell Jones, who served on the Tuskegee staff for several decades, carried on regular correspondence with her sister-in-law Mary Church Terrell; see her letters in Terrell Papers.

10. Hallie Queen was desperate to leave Tuskegee, claiming that "another year will make me a mental and physical wreck." See Hallie Queen to Mary Church Terrell, April 16, 1909, Terrell Papers.

11. Gatewood, "Booker T. Washington," p. 843.

12. Harlan, *The Wizard of Tuskegee*, p. 94.

13. Ibid., pp. 94–95. For extensive correspondence between Washington and Whitefield McKinlay, see the Whitefield McKinlay Papers in Carter Woodson Collection, Library of Congress. For references to "the anti-Washington social set" in the District of Columbia, see *Washington Bee*, March 3, 1906.

14. Harlan, *Wizard of Tuskegee*, p. 95; *New York Age*, August 28, 1913.

15. Stephen R. Fox, *The Guardian of Boston: William Monroe Trotter* (New York: Atheneum, 1971), pp. 41–46.

16. Harlan, *The Wizard of Tuskegee*, pp. 96–97; Gail L. Buckley, *The Hornes: An American Family* (New York: Alfred A. Knopf, 1986), p. 63.

17. Allan H. Spear, *Black Chicago: The Making of a Negro Ghetto, 1890–1920* (Chicago: University of Chicago Press, 1967), pp. 66–75.

18. Kenneth L. Kusmer, *A Ghetto Takes Shape: Black Cleveland, 1870–1930* (Urbana: University of Illinois Press, 1976), pp. 140–144; John P. Green to George A. Myers, February 4, 1904, George A. Myers Papers, Ohio Historical Society, Columbus.

19. On Napier, see Harlan, *The Wizard of Tuskegee*, pp. 345, 349; on Crum, see Willard B. Gatewood, Jr., *Theodore Roosevelt and the Art of Controversy: Episodes of the White House Years* (Baton Rouge: Louisiana State University Press, 1970), pp. 96, 98, 100, 109, 110.

20. Annette E. Church and Roberta Church, *The Robert R. Churches of Memphis* (Ann Arbor: Edwards Brothers, 1974), p. 43.

21. See above, pp. 19–20.

22. Harlan, *The Wizard of Tuskegee*, Chapter 5.

23. Fox, *William Monroe Trotter*, p. 30.

24. Ibid., p. 28.

25. Ibid., pp. 8–25; Charles W. Puttkammer and Ruth Worthy, "William Monroe Trotter, 1872–1934," *Phylon*, XLIII (October, 1958), 298–316.

26. Fox, *William Monroe Trotter*, pp. 49–57; Harlan, *The Wizard of Tuskegee*, pp. 32–62; Thornbrough, "National Afro-American League," pp. 503–506.

27. *New York Age*, February 16, 1911.

28. Harlan, *The Wizard of Tuskegee*, p. 53.

29. St. Paul *Western Appeal*, January 31, 1891.

30. See above pp. 86, 302.

31. Baltimore *Afro-American Ledger*, February 22, 1902, May 5, 1906; *Topeka Plaindealer*, April 15, 1904.

32. *Washington Bee*, December 19, 1903.

33. Ibid., April 6, 1907.

34. John Hope to Lugenia Burns, June 10, 1897, John and Lugenia Burns Hope Papers, Atlanta University (microfilm).

35. John Hope to Lugenia Burns, June 20, 1897, Hope Papers.

36. August Meier, *Negro Thought in America, 1880–1915: Racial Ideologies in the Age of Booker T. Washington* (Ann Arbor: University of Michigan Press, 1963), p. 114.

37. W. E. B. Du Bois, *Dusk at Dawn: An Essay Toward An Autobiography of A Race Concept* (New York: Harcourt, Brace, 1940), pp. 8–21; W. E. B. Du Bois, *Darkwater: Voices from Within the Veil* (New York: Harcourt, Brace and Howe, 1920), p. 10; see also Francis L. Broderick, *W. E. B. Du Bois: Negro Leader in a Time of Crisis* (Palo Alto: Stanford University Press, 1959), pp. 1–4.

38. Dorothy C. Yancey, "William Edward Burghardt Du Bois, The Atlanta Years: The Human Side—A Study Based on Oral Sources," *Journal of Negro History*, LXIII (January, 1978), 59–67; Elliott Rudwick, "W. E. B. Du Bois: Propagandist of the Afro-American Protest," in *Black Leaders of the Twentieth Century*, edited by John Hope Franklin and August Meier (Urbana: University of Illinois Press, 1982), p. 66.

39. *Washington Bee*, July 27, 1918.

40. *Atlanta Independent*, December 2, 1905.

41. Du Bois, *Dusk at Dawn*, p. 19.

42. Elliott Rudwick, *W. E. B. Du Bois: Propagandist of Negro Protest* (New York: Atheneum, 1972), chaps. 1 and 2; Broderick, *W. E. B. Du Bois*, p. 54.

43. Rudwick, "W. E. B. Du Bois," pp. 63–65.

44. Ibid., pp. 66–67; Rudwick, *W. E. B. Du Bois*, pp. 54–68; Broderick, *W. E. B. Du Bois*, p. 74; W. E. B. Du Bois, "The Talented Tenth," in Booker T. Washington et al., *The Negro Problem* (New York: AMS Press, 1970), pp. 31–75.

45. Rudwick, *W. E. B. Du Bois*, pp. 68–76; see also W. E. B. Du Bois, *The Souls of Black Folk* (Milwood, N.Y.: Kraus-Thomason, 1973).

46. Chicago *Broad Ax*, December 19, 1903; *Cleveland Journal*, March 19, 1904; Denver *Colorado Statesman*, May 27, 1911.

47. Elliott M. Rudwick, "The Niagara Movement," *Journal of Negro History*, XLIII (July, 1957), 177–182; see also W. E. B. Du Bois to Archibald Grimké and Kelly Miller, March 21, 1905, W. E. B. Du Bois to Messrs. Grimké and Miller, August 13, 1905, Archibald Grimké Papers, Moorland-Spingarn Research Center, Howard University, Washington, D.C.

48. Chicago *Broad Ax*, May 7, 1904; Indianapolis *Freeman*, October 28, 1905.

49. Baltimore *Afro-American Ledger*, March 24, August 24, September 6, 1906, January 6, 1912. During the social hour of a fund-raising party of the Niagara Movement, when a participant remarked that "there were no dark skinned persons present," she was told to avoid that "touchy subject"; see "Washington, D.C. Letter," Denver *Colorado Statesman*, August 24, 1907.

50. Rudwick, "W. E. B. Du Bois," p. 69; see also J. Max Barber, "The Niagara Movement at Harper's Ferry," *Voice of the Negro*, III (October, 1906), 402–411.

51. Rudwick, "The Niagara Movement," p. 199; Broderick, *W. E. B. Du Bois*, p. 78.

52. For the history of the founding and early years of the NAACP, I have relied principally on the interpretations of Charles Flint Kellogg, *NAACP: A History of the National Association for the Advancement of Colored People, 1909–1920* (Baltimore: Johns Hopkins Press, 1967). See also the voluminous NAACP Papers in the Library of Congress; Meier, *Negro Thought in America*; and Minutes, Board of Directors, NAACP, January 21, 1913, November 4, 1914, NAACP Papers.

53. Baltimore *Afro-American Ledger*, November 22, 1913, July 18, 1914; W.

Ashbie Hawkins, "A Year of Segregation in Baltimore," *Crisis*, III (November, 1911), 27–30. On the NAACP response to *Birth of a Nation*, see Thomas R. Cripps, "The Reaction of the Negro to the Motion Picture Birth of a Nation," *The Historian*, XXV (May, 1963), 344–362.

54. Kellogg, *NAACP*, pp. 120–121; Fox, *William Monroe Trotter*, p. 137; Minutes of the Meeting of Members and Friends of the NAACP, Boston, May 10, 1911, NAACP Papers; Clarence C. Contee, "Butler R. Wilson and the Boston N.A.A.C.P. Branch," *Crisis*, LXXXI (December, 1974), 346–348.

55. Spear, *Black Chicago*, pp. 56–66; Helen Buckler, *Daniel Hale Williams: Negro Surgeon* (New York: Pitman Publishing Co., 1954), pp. 272–273.

56. *Philadelphia Tribune*, January 25, 1913.

57. Kusmer, *A Ghetto Takes Shape*, p. 243; David A. Gerber, *Black Ohio and the Color Line, 1860–1915* (Urbana: University of Illinois Press, 1976), pp. 463–467.

58. Kellogg, *NAACP*, pp. 126–127; *Washington Bee*, July 25, 1914, June 22, 1918; *Crisis*, X (September, 1915), 243; Minutes, Board of Directors, January 3, 1916, NAACP Papers. Much of the history of the Washington, D.C. branch of the NAACP is found in the voluminous Grimké Papers.

59. T. Thomas Fortune to Emmett J. Scott, October 14, 1914, in Harlan, ed., *Washington Papers*, XIII, 145–146.

60. Ralph Tyler to Emmett J. Scott, January 6, 1914, ibid., XII, 404–405; Ralph Tyler to Emmett J. Scott, March 1, 1914, ibid., 462–464; Ralph Tyler to B. T. Washington, June 3, 1914, ibid., XIII, 43.

61. *Washington Bee*, May 3, 17, 24, June 14, July 5, 1919.

62. Meier, *Negro Thought in America*, pp. 217–218; Joe W. Trotter, Jr., *Black Milwaukee: The Making of an Industrial Proletariat, 1915–45* (Urbana: University of Illinois Press, 1985), pp. 103–104.

63. Wilson Record, "Negro Leadership in the National Association for the Advancement of Colored People: 1910–1940," *Phylon*, XVII (4th Quarter, 1956), 383.

64. *Atlanta Independent*, March 7, 1914; Claude McKay, *A Long Way From Home* (New York: Lee Furman, Inc., 1937), pp. 113–114. For a refutation of the view that the NAACP was a conservative, middle-class organization that ignored the masses, see Bernard Eisenberg, "Only for the Bourgeois? James Weldon Johnson and the NAACP, 1916–1930," *Phylon*, XLIII (Summer, 1982), 110–124.

65. *Washington Bee*, May 23, 1914, February 27, 1915.

66. Ibid., June 26, 1915.

67. Ibid., August 4, 1917; despite his prolonged opposition to the NAACP, Chase had become a member of the organization by 1918.

68. Mary Church Terrell, Diary, January 18 [?], 1915, p. 18, Terrell Papers.

69. San Francisco *Western Outlook*, July 24, August 7, 1915; *Crisis*, III (February, 1912), 154–155; VII (March, 1914), 234; VIII (August, 1914), 182; Minutes, Board of Directors, NAACP, July 12, 1915, NAACP Papers; Contee, "Butler R. Wilson," p. 347; see also F. D. Wilkinson to Neval Thomas, March 3, 1915, Grimké Papers.

70. Terrell, *Colored Woman in a White World*, pp. 194–195; see also Minutes, Board of Directors, NAACP, January 3, 1916, NAACP Papers.

71. Kellogg, *NAACP*, p. 136; Minutes, Board of Directors, NAACP, November 11, 1918, NAACP Papers. In May 1917, James Weldon Johnson, in speaking of the growth of the NAACP in the South, declared that there was "a new spirit awakening in the region"; see *Crisis*, XIV (May, 1917), 18.

72. Nancy J. Weiss, *The National Urban League 1910–1940* (New York: Oxford University Press, 1974), pp. 58–60; see also Jesse T. Moore, Jr., *A Search for Equality: The National Urban League, 1910–1961* (University Park: Pennsylvania State University

Press, 1981); Arvarh E. Strickland, *History of the Chicago Urban League* (Urbana: University of Illinois Press, 1966).

73. Rudwick, "W. E. B. Du Bois," p. 76; Minutes, Board of Directors, NAACP, September 8, 1919, NAACP Papers.

74. Quoted in Chicago *Broad Ax*, July 9, 1901.

75. For an expression of this view, see Francis Grimké, "Some Things that Lie Across the Pathway of Our Progress," in *Works of Francis Grimké*, 4 vols. (Washington: Associated Publishers, n.d.), I, 552.

76. Editorial in Indianapolis *Freeman*, March 24, 1900.

77. Rudwick, "W. E. B. Du Bois," p. 76.

78. Rudwick, *W. E. B. Du Bois*, p. 219; Robert A. Hill, ed., *The Marcus Garvey and Universal Negro Improvement Association Papers*, 4 vols. (Berkeley: University of California Press, 1983), III, 125, 583.

79. From a Garvey speech in 1920; see Hill, *The Marcus Garvey and UNIA Papers*, II, 251.

80. Ibid., p. 459.

Part IV: Changes and Continuities

Prologue

1. *Washington Bee*, December 6, 1913; Charles H. Wesley, *History of Sigma Pi Phi* (Washington: Association for the Study of Negro Life and History, 1954), pp. 77, 89.

2. "Roscoe C. Bruce," Notes, Murray Papers; *New York Age*, September 21, October 12, 1911; *Washington Bee*, October 30, December 18, 1915.

3. *New York Age*, March 12, December 24, 1914, January 7, 1915; *Washington Bee*, July 31, 1915; see also Roscoe C. Bruce, "A Plea for Negro Trade Schools in Cities," *Southern Workman*, XXXIII (December, 1904), 650–654; G. Smith Wormley, "Educators of the First Half Century of the Public Schools of the District of Columbia," *Journal of Negro History*, XVII (April, 1932), 138–139.

4. "Roscoe C. Bruce," Notes, Murray Papers; *New York Age*, April 29, 1915; *Washington Bee*, July 31, December 4, 1915.

5. Constance M. Green, *The Secret City: A History of Race Relations in the Nation's Capital* (Princeton: Princeton University Press, 1967), p. 179; "Roscoe C. Bruce," Notes, Murray Papers; *Washington Bee*, April 26, March 29, May 3, 1919.

6. Mary Wilson to Josephine Bruce, September 10, 1921, R. C. Bruce to Coralie Cook, November 29, 1921, R. C. Cook to John W. Davis, March 21, 1922, Roscoe C. Bruce Papers, Moorland-Spingarn Research Center, Howard University, Washington, D.C.

7. R. C. Bruce to Josephine Bruce, September 8, 1921, R. C. Bruce to Josephine Bruce, September 24, 1921, Bruce Papers.

8. R. C. Bruce to Josephine Bruce, ?, 1922, Bruce Papers.

9. R. C. Bruce to Josephine Bruce, March 16, 1922, Bruce Papers; R. C. Bruce to Archibald Grimké, December 7, 1922, Archibald Grimké Papers, Moorland-Spingarn Research Center, Howard University, Washington, D.C.

10. R. C. Bruce to Josephine Bruce, ?, 1921; R. C. Bruce to Josephine Bruce, March 16, 1922, R. C. Bruce to Josephine Bruce, ?, 1922, Bruce Papers.

11. R. C. Bruce to Coralie Cook, November 29, 1921, Bruce Papers; R. C. Bruce to Archibald Grimké, December 7, 1922, Grimké Papers.

12. Arthur M. Hyde to L. C. Dyer, February 9, 1922, R. C. Bruce to Josephine Bruce, March ?, 1922, Bruce Papers.

13. Marriage certificate, John W. Guy and Margery G. Bruce, August 29, 1922, Montgomery County, Maryland, (copy), R. C. Bruce to Nathaniel Guy, September 22, 1922, Nathaniel Guy to R. C. Bruce, October 24, 1922, Nathaniel Guy to R. C. Bruce, November 6, 1922, R. C. Bruce to Nathaniel Guy, November 9, 1922, Bruce Papers.

14. Interview with Barrington Guy, *New York Amsterdam News*, April 12, 1939; interview with Barrington Shamar in an unidentified newspaper clipping dated 1941, in Bruce Papers; see also Errol Hill, *Shakespeare in Sable: A History of Black Shakespearean Actors* (Amherst: University of Massachusetts Press, 1984), p. 86; Allen Woll, *Dictionary of the Black Theatre: Broadway, Off Broadway, and Selected Harlem Theatre* (Westport, CT: Greenwood Press, 1983), pp. 4, 21, 32, 43, 67, 102.

15. *Cleveland Gazette*, May 26, 1923.

16. Arthur J. Gray, "Biography of Roscoe Conkling Bruce" (WPA Research Paper, March 30, 1939), Schomburg Center for Research in Black Culture, New York Public Library; "Roscoe Conkling Bruce," in *The Harvard Class of 1902*, p. 90; "Mrs. Clara Burrill Bruce," *Who's Who in Colored America 1928–1929*, edited by Joseph Boris (New York: Who's Who in Colored America Corp., 1929), p. 56; Radcliffe Alumnae information for the 1934 directory (Clara Washington Burrill Bruce), Radcliffe College Archives, Cambridge, Massachusetts.

17. *New York Times*, May 10, 1926; see also Langston Hughes to Arna Bontemps, April 11, 1937, in *Arna Bontemps-Langston Hughes Letters, 1925–1967*, edited by Charles H. Nichols (New York: Dodd, Mead and Co., 1980), p. 27.

18. Gray, "Roscoe C. Bruce," p. 2; R. C. Bruce, "The Dunbar Apartment House: An Adventure in Community Building," *The Southern Workman*, LX (October, 1931), 417–428; Alfred Alexander, "Housing of Harlem," *Crisis*, XXXV (October, 1928), 333–336, 351–353; "An Experiment in Negro Housing," *Monthly Labor Review*, XXIX (September, 1929), 107–108; "Experiments in Negro Housing in New York and Cincinnati," ibid., XXXIV (January, 1932), 124–130; "Dunbar National Bank," *Crisis*, XXXV (November, 1928), 370, 387.

19. Undated newspaper clipping, Daniel Murray Papers, State Historical Society of Wisconsin, Madison (microfilm); "Roscoe C. Bruce," *Harvard Class of 1902*, p. 90.

20. Ibid., pp. 90–91; Radcliffe Alumnae information for the 1934 directory (Clara Washington Burrill Bruce).

21. *Harvard Alumni Directory* (Cambridge: Harvard University Press, 1948), p. 577; *Harvard Class of 1930*, p. 84; *Opportunity*, XIII (June, 1935), 188.

22. *New York Amsterdam News*, April 10, 17, 24, 1937; *Newark Evening News*, October 22, 1937.

23. *Newark Evening News*, November 18, 1937; *New York Amsterdam News*, October 23, November 6, 13, 1937.

24. Quoted in *New York Amsterdam News*, November 20, 1937.

25. *Washington Afro-American*, November 27, 1937; *New York Amsterdam News*, November 13, 1937.

26. *New York Amsterdam News*, December 11, 1937; *Cleveland Call and Post*, December 23, 1937.

27. *Harvard Class of 1930*, p. 84.

28. *Harvard Alumni Directory*, p. 576; Kathleen A. Markee (Harvard University Archives) to the author, November 10, 1987; L. B. R. Briggs to R. C. Bruce, June 1, 1922, L. B. R. Briggs to R. C. Bruce, June 7, 1922, L. B. R. Briggs Collection, Radcliffe College Archives, Cambridge, Massachusetts; Jane Knowles (Radcliffe College Archives) to the author, January 11, 1988.

29. Gertrude Sanborn, *Veiled Aristocrats* (Washington: Associated Publishers, 1923), p. 40.

30. See above, p. 147.

12. Into the 1920s

1. Frederic C. Jahr, "Style and Status: High Society in Late Nineteenth Century New York," in *The Rich, The Well-Born and the Powerful: Elites and Upper Classes in History,* edited by Frederic C. Jahr (Urbana: University of Illinois Press, 1973), p. 283.

2. Florette Henri, *Black Migration: Movement North, 1900–1920* (Garden City: Doubleday, 1975), p. 189.

3. Indianapolis *Freeman,* March 24, 1900.

4. Constance M. Green, *The Secret City: A History of Race Relations in the Nation's Capital* (Princeton: Princeton University Press, 1967), p. 207.

5. Roi Ottley and William J. Weatherby, eds., *The Negro in New York: An Informal History* (New York: New York Public Library, 1967), pp. 237–238; Gerri Major, *Black Society* (Chicago: Johnson Publishing Co., 1976), p. 292; Roi Ottley, *'New World A-Coming': Inside Black America* (Boston: Houghton-Mifflin, 1943), p. 173; "Queen of Gotham's Colored 400," *Literary Digest,* LV (October 13, 1917), 75–76, 78–79.

6. George S. Schuyler, "These Colored United States: New York, Utopia Deferred," *The Messenger,* VII (October-November, 1925), 348.

7. Quoted in E. Franklin Frazier, *The Negro Family in the United States* (Chicago: University of Chicago Press, 1939), p. 393.

8. E. Franklin Frazier, *Black Bourgeoisie: The Rise of a New Middle Class* (New York: Free Press, 1957), p. 114.

9. Robert H. Terrell to George A. Myers, July 17, 1914, George A. Myers Papers, Ohio Historical Society, Columbus.

10. Indianapolis *Recorder,* January 29, 1910.

11. Anita Hodges Westlake, quoted in *Washington Bee,* December 26, 1914; see also *New York Age,* December 26, 1914; Whitefield McKinlay to T. McCants Stewart, October 5, 1922, Whitefield McKinlay Papers in Carter G. Woodson Collection, Library of Congress.

12. See Gertrude Sanborn's novel, *Veiled Aristocrats* (Washington, D.C.: Associated Publishers, 1923).

13. For the emergence of new or rival elites in two cities, see Allan Spear, *Black Chicago: The Making of a Ghetto* (Chicago: University of Chicago Press, 1967), chap. 4; Kenneth L. Kusmer, *A Ghetto Takes Shape: Black Cleveland, 1870–1930* (Urbana: University of Illinois Press, 1976), pp. 103–106.

14. Green, *The Secret City,* pp. 207–208.

15. Langston Hughes, "Our Wonderful Society: Washington," *Opportunity* (August, 1927), 226–227; see Hughes's poem, "High to Low," in his *Montage of A Dream Deferred* (New York: Henry Holt, 1951), pp. 43–44.

16. A. H. Maloney, "Absurdities of An Aristocracy," in *Indianapolis Recorder,* January 14, 1928.

17. Asa H. Gordon, *Sketches of Negro Life and History in South Carolina* (Columbia: University of South Carolina Press, 1971), p. 69; *The Charleston Chronicle,* July 13, 1985.

18. Eugene Gordon, "Negro Society," in *The Black Man and the American Dream: Negro Aspirations in America, 1900–1930,* edited by June Sochen (Chicago: Quadrangle Books, 1971), pp. 124–133.

19. Hughes, "Our Wonderful Society," 227.

20. Robert A. Warner, *New Haven Negroes: A Social History* (New York: Arno Press, 1969), pp. 185–186.

21. P. L. Prattis, "Chicago's 400," *The Negro in Chicago, 1779 to 1929*, edited by Frederic H. Robb (Chicago: Atlas Printing Co., 1929), pp. 84–87; see also *Chicago Whip*, quoted in *The Appeal* (Minneapolis), May 19, 1923; St. Clair Drake and Horace Cayton, *Black Metropolis: A Study of Negro Life in a Northern City* (New York: Harcourt, Brace, 1945), pp. 531–563; St. Clair Drake and Horace Cayton, "Chicago Today: Metropolis Revisited," *Negro Digest*, XII (April, 1963), 20–25. For evidence of the survival of traditional criteria, especially ancestry and "culture," for determining upper-class status, see the thirty-four case studies entitled "Documents on Higher Class Families in Chicago," in E. Franklin Frazier Papers, Moorland-Spingarn Research Center, Howard University, Washington, D.C.

22. Langston Hughes, *The Big Sea: An Autobiography* (New York: Knopf, 1940), pp. 12–13, 303–304.

23. "Society Rulers in 20 Cities," *Ebony*, IV (May, 1949), 62–63; see also "How Society Had Its Birth," ibid., II (May, 1947), 13; "Society," ibid., II (May, 1947), 9; Langston Hughes and John C. Alston, "Atlanta: Society and Slums," ibid., III (January, 1948), 19, 22; "Is Negro Society Phony?" ibid., VIII (September, 1953), 56; "Negroes Who Hate Negroes," ibid., VIII (December, 1952), 112; "Negro Bluebloods," ibid., X (September, 1955), 55; Franklin Fosdick, "The Truth About Negro Society," *Negro Digest*, VIII (July, 1950), 3–6.

24. Haynes Johnson, "Caste and Class in Washington, D.C.," *Negro Digest*, XI (December, 1961), 40–44.

25. Sidney Hyman, "Washington's Negro Elite," *Look*, April 6, 1965, pp. 60–63; see also Bill Davidson, "Our Negro Aristocracy," *Saturday Evening Post*, CCXXXV (January 13, 1962), 14–16.

26. Lerone Bennett, "The Black Establishment," *Negro Digest*, XIII (July, 1964), 81–96.

27. Major, *Black Society*, p. 3.

28. John Daniels, *In Freedom's Birthplace* (New York: Arno Press, 1969), p. 183.

29. See Indianapolis *Freeman*, October 23, 1897; "Color Lines Among the Colored People," *Literary Digest*, LXII (March 18, 1922), 42; A. N. Fields, "Color Line Within the Race," *Abbott's Monthly*, VII (July, 1933), 2–3, 41–42; "Are Mulattoes Ruling the Race?" *Ebony*, IX (October, 1954), 62. For a later critique, see Nathan Hare, *The Black Anglo-Saxons* (New York: Collier Books, 1965, 1970).

30. Langston Hughes, "Do Big Negroes Keep Little Negroes Down?" *Negro Digest*, X (November, 1951), 82.

31. Darwin T. Turner, ed., *The Wayward and the Seeking: A Collection of Writings by Jean Toomer* (Washington: Howard University Press, 1980), p. 85.

32. Hyman, "Washington's Negro Elite," p. 60.

33. Emma Jones Lapsansky, "Friends, Wives and Strivings: Networks and Community Values Among Nineteenth-Century Philadelphia Afroamerican Elites," *The Pennsylvania Magazine of History and Biography*, CVIII (January, 1984), 24.

Bibliography

Manuscript Collections

Bethel Literary and Historical Association Papers: Moorland-Spingarn Research Center, Howard University, Washington, D.C.

L. B. R. Briggs Collection: Radcliffe College Archives, Cambridge, Massachusetts.

Blanche K. Bruce Papers: Manuscript Division, Library of Congress, Washington, D.C.

John Edward Bruce Papers: Schomburg Center for Research in Black Culture, New York Public Library, New York.

Roscoe Conkling Bruce Papers: Moorland-Spingarn Research Center, Howard University, Washington, D.C.

Francis L. Cardozo Family Papers: Manuscript Division, Library of Congress, Washington, D.C.

Robert Reed Church Family Papers: Mississippi Valley Collection, Memphis State University, Memphis, Tennessee.

Cook Family Papers: Moorland-Spingarn Research Center, Howard University, Washington, D.C.

Paul Laurence Dunbar Papers (microfilm): Ohio Historical Society, Columbus, Ohio.

Records of the Fifteenth Street Presbyterian Church, Washington, D.C.: Moorland-Spingarn Research Center, Howard University, Washington, D.C.

Christian A. Fleetwood Papers: Manuscript Division, Library of Congress, Washington, D.C.

E. Franklin Frazier Papers: Moorland-Spingarn Research Center, Howard University, Washington, D.C.

Gray, Arthur J., "Biography of Roscoe C. Bruce," WPA Research Paper, March 30, 1939: Schomburg Center for Research in Black Culture, New York Public Library, New York.

John P. Green Papers (microfilm): Western Reserve Historical Society, Cleveland, Ohio.

Archibald Grimké Papers: Moorland-Spingarn Research Center, Howard University, Washington, D.C.

Benjamin Harrison Papers (microfilm): Manuscript Division, Library of Congress, Washington, D.C.

Heslip-Ruffin Papers: Amistad Research Center, Tulane University, New Orleans, Louisiana.

Andrew F. Hilyer Papers: Moorland-Spingarn Research Center, Howard University, Washington, D.C.

John and Lugenia Burns Hope Papers (microfilm): Atlanta University, Atlanta, Georgia.

William H. Hunt Papers: Moorland-Spingarn Research Center, Howard University, Washington, D.C.

Alain Locke Papers: Moorland-Spingarn Research Center, Howard University, Washington, D.C.

McClennan Family Papers: Amistad Research Center, Tulane University, New Orleans, Louisiana.

Whitefield McKinlay Papers in the Carter G. Woodson Collection: Manuscript Division, Library of Congress, Washington, D.C.

Daniel Murray Papers (microfilm): State Historical Society of Wisconsin, Madison, Wisconsin.

Mu-So-Lit Club Papers: Moorland-Spingarn Research Center, Howard University, Washington, D.C.

George A. Myers Papers: Ohio Historical Society, Columbus, Ohio.

National Association for the Advancement of Colored People Papers (microfilm): Manuscript Division, Library of Congress, Washington, D.C.

Radcliffe Alumnae Information for the 1934 Directory: Radcliffe College Archives, Cambridge, Massachusetts.

Ruffin Family Papers: Moorland-Spingarn Research Center, Howard University, Washington, D.C.

Mary Church Terrell Papers (microfilm): Manuscript Division, Library of Congress, Washington, D.C.

Robert H. Terrell Papers: Manuscript Division, Library of Congress, Washington, D.C.

Official Reports, Documents, and Directories

Class of 1884, Harvard College, Fortieth Anniversary: Report of the Secretary. Cambridge: Harvard University Press, 1924.

Department of Commerce, Bureau of the Census, Special Report: Religious Bodies, 1906. Washington: Government Printing Office, 1910.

The First Report of the Board of Trustees of the Public Schools of the District of Columbia, 1874–75. Washington: McGill and Witherow, 1876.

Harvard Alumni Directory. Cambridge: Harvard University Press, 1948.

Jones, Thomas Jesse, Negro Education: A Study of the Private and Higher Schools for Colored People in the United States. 2 vols. Bureau of Education Bulletin No. 39, 1916. Washington: Government Printing Office, 1917.

Reports of Cases Adjudged in the Court of Appeals of the District of Columbia, 1910–1911. Vol. 36.

Results of an Investigation By the Board of Education Into the Educational and Administrative Efficiency of Roscoe Conkling Bruce, Assistant Superintendent of Schools of the District of Columbia. n.p.,: n.p., 1919.

Special Report of the Commission on Education [in the District of Columbia]. Executive Document 315, 41st Cong., 2d sess. Washington: Government Printing Office, 1871.

Memoirs, Autobiographies, and Published Correspondence and Writings

Aptheker, Herbert, ed., Correspondence of W. E. B. Du Bois: Selections, 1877–1934. Boston: University of Massachusetts Press, 1973.

Barnes, Gilbert, and Dwight L. Dumond, eds., Letters of Theodore Weld, Angelina Grimké Weld and Sarah Grimké. 2 vols. New York: D. Appleton-Century Company, 1934.

Barry, Davis S., *Forty Years in Washington*. Boston: Little, Brown, 1924.

Beam, Lura, *He Called Them By Lightning: A Teacher's Odyssey in the Negro South, 1908–1919*. Indianapolis: Bobbs-Merrill, 1967.

Billington, Ray A., ed., *The Journal of Charlotte Forten*. New York: Collier Books, 1961.

Bruce, H. C., *The New Man: Twenty-nine Years a Slave, Twenty-nine Years a Free Man*. York, Pa.: Anstadt and Son, 1895.

Butterfield, L. H., ed., *Letters of Benjamin Rush*. 2 vols. Princeton: Princeton University Press, 1951.

Carpenter, Frank G., *Carp's Washington*. New York: McGraw-Hill, 1960.

Cayton, Horace R., *Long Old Road*. New York: Trident Press, 1965.

Chapin, Mrs. E. N., *American Court Gossip, or Life at the National Capital*. Marshalltown, Iowa: Chapin and Hartwell Brothers, 1887.

Christensen, Lawrence O., ed., "Cyprian Clamorgan, The Colored Aristocracy of St. Louis (1858)," *Bulletin of the Missouri Historical Society*, XXXI (October, 1974), 9–31.

Du Bois, William E. B., *Darkwater: Voices From Within the Veil*. New York: Harcourt, Brace and Howe, 1920.

———, *Dusk of Dawn: An Essay Toward an Autobiography of a Race Concept*. New York: Harcourt, Brace, 1940.

Duster, Alfreda, M., ed., *Crusade for Justice: The Autobiography of Ida Wells Barnett*. Chicago: University of Chicago Press, 1970.

Fields, Mamie Garvin, *Lemon Swamp and Other Places: A Carolina Memoir*. New York: Free Press, 1983.

Franklin, John Hope, ed., *Reminiscences of an Active Life: The Autobiography of John Roy Lynch*. Chicago: University of Chicago Press, 1970.

Gatewood, Willard B., ed., *Free Man of Color: The Autobiography of Willis Augustus Hodges*. Knoxville: University of Tennessee Press, 1982.

———, ed., *Slave and Freeman: the Autobiography of George L. Knox*. Lexington: University Press of Kentucky, 1979.

Gilbert, Peter, ed., *Selected Writings of John Edward Bruce*. New York: Arno Press, 1971.

Green, John P., *Fact Stranger Than Fiction: Seventy-five Years of a Busy Life*. Cleveland: Riehl Printing Co., 1920.

Harlan, Louis, et al., eds., *The Booker T. Washington Papers*. 13 vols. Urbana: University of Illinois Press, 1972–1984.

Hill, Robert A., ed., *The Marcus Garvey and Universal Negro Improvement Association Papers*. 4 vols. Berkeley: University of California Press, 1983.

Hogan, William R., and Edwin A. Miles, eds., *William Johnson's Natchez: The Antebellum Diary of a Free Negro*. Baton Rouge: Louisiana State University Press, 1951.

Hughes, Langston, *The Big Sea: An Autobiography*. New York: A. Knopf, 1940.

Hurston, Zora Neale, *Dust Tracks on a Road: An Autobiography*. Urbana: University of Illinois Press, 1984.

Johnson, James Weldon, *Along This Way: The Autobiography of James Weldon Johnson*. New York: Viking Press, 1933.

———, *The Autobiography of an Ex-Colored Man*. New York: Knopf, 1979.

Johnson, Michael P., and James R. Roark, eds., *No Chariot Let Down: Charleston's Free People of Color on the Eve of the Civil War*. Chapel Hill: University of North Carolina Press, 1984.

Langston, John Mercer, *From the Virginia Plantation to the National Capitol*. Hartford: American Publishing Co., 1894.

BIBLIOGRAPHY

Logan, Mrs. John A., *Thirty Years in Washington, or Scenes in Our National Capital*. Hartford: A. D. Worthington and Co., 1901.

McKay, Claude, *A Long Way From Home*. New York: Lee Furman, 1937.

Maloney, Arnold Hamilton, *Amber Gold: An Adventure in Autobiography*. Boston: Meador Publishing Co., 1946.

Mordecai, Samuel, *Richmond in By-Gone Days*. Richmond, Va.: Deitz Press, 1860, 1946.

Murray, Pauli, *Proud Shoes: The Story of An American Family*. New York: Harper, 1956.

Nichols, Charles H., ed., *Arna Bontemps–Langston Hughes Letters, 1925–1967*. New York: Dodd, Mead, 1980.

Perry, Calbraith B., *Twelve Years Among the Colored People: A Record of Work of Mount Calvary Chapel of St. Mary the Virgin*. Baltimore: James Pott and Co., 1894.

Porter, A. Toomer, *Led On! Step by Step: Scenes from Clerical, Educational and Plantation Life in the South, 1828–1898*. New York: G. P. Putnam's Sons, 1898.

Proctor, Henry Hugh, *Between Black and White: Autobiographical Sketches*. Freeport, New York: Books for Libraries, 1971.

Ralph, Julian, *Dixie, or Southern Scenes and Sketches*. New York: Harper and Brothers, 1896.

Ransom, Reverdy C., *The Pilgrimage of Harriet Ransom's Son*. Nashville: Sunday School Union, n.d.

Schuyler, George S., *Black and Conservative: The Autobiography of George S. Schuyler*. New Rochelle: Arlington House, 1966.

Schweninger, Loren, ed., *From Tennessee Slave to St. Louis Entrepreneur: The Autobiography of James Thomas*. Columbia: University of Missouri Press, 1984.

Sterling, Dorothy, ed., *We Are Your Sisters: Black Women in the Nineteenth Century*. New York: W. W. Norton and Co., 1984.

Stevens, Walter J., *Chip on My Shoulder: Autobiography*. Boston: Meador Publishing Co., 1946.

Still, William Grant, "My Arkansas Boyhood," *Arkansas Historical Quarterly*, XXVI (Autumn, 1967), 285–292.

Terrell, Mary Church, *A Colored Woman in a White World*. Washington: Ransdell, 1940.

Turner, Darwin T., ed., *The Wayward and the Seeking: A Collection of Writings of Jean Toomer*. Washington: Howard University Press, 1980.

Walters, Alexander, *My Life and Work*. New York: Fleming R. Revell, 1917.

Waring, Robert Lewis, *As We See It*. Washington: Press of C. F. Sudworth, 1910.

White, Walter, *A Man Called White: The Autobiography of Walter White*. New York: Viking Press, 1948.

Williams, Fannie Barrier, "A Northern Negro's Autobiography," *The Independent*, LVII (July 14, 1904), 91–96.

Woodson, Carter G., ed., *The Works of Francis J. Grimké*. 4 vols. Washington: Associated Publishers, n.d.

Wright, Richard R., *87 Years Behind the Black Curtain: An Autobiography*. Philadelphia: Rare Book Co., 1965.

Newspapers

Afro-American, Baltimore
Afro-American, Washington
Afro-American Ledger, Baltimore
American Citizen, Kansas City, Missouri
Amsterdam News, New York
Atlanta Independent

BIBLIOGRAPHY

The Augusta Chronicle, Augusta, Georgia
Boston Guardian
Boston Journal
Broad Ax, Salt Lake City and Chicago
The California Eagle, Los Angeles
Call and Post, Cleveland
Cayton's Weekly, Seattle
The Charleston Chronicle, Charleston, South Carolina
Chicago Defender
Cleveland Gazette
Cleveland Journal
Colorado Statesman, Denver
The Colored American, Washington, D.C.
The Colored Citizen, Fort Scott, Kansas
The Commonwealth, Baltimore
The Crusader, New Orleans
Daily Inter-Ocean, Chicago
Daily Morning Call, San Francisco
Daily National Intelligencer, Washington, D.C.
Detroit News-Tribune
The Elevator, San Francisco
The Enterprise, Omaha, Nebraska
The Freeman, Indianapolis, Indiana
The Globe, Nashville, Tennessee
Historic Times, Lawrence, Kansas
The Huntsville Gazette, Huntsville, Alabama
Illinois Record, Springfield, Illinois
Indianapolis Recorder
The Leader, Cleveland, Ohio
The National Era, Washington, D.C.
National Leader, Washington, D.C.
New York Age
New York Daily Tribune
New York Freeman
New York Globe
New York Times
Newark Evening News, Newark, New Jersey
The News, Indianapolis
The News and Courier, Charleston, S.C.
Norfolk Virginian
North Star, Rochester, New York
Ohio Standard, Xenia, Ohio
Pacific Coast Appeal, San Francisco
People's Advocate, Washington, D.C.
Philadelphia Tribune
Pittsburgh Courier
The Plain Dealer, Cleveland, Ohio
The Plaindealer, Detroit
The Plaindealer, Topeka, Kansas
Richmond Planet, Richmond, Virginia
St. Louis Palladium

St. Louis Post-Dispatch
Savannah Tribune, Savannah, Georgia
Seattle Republican
The Sentinel, Trenton, New Jersey
Southern Republican, New Orleans
State Capital, Springfield, Illinois
The Sun, New York
Times-Observer, Topeka
Torchlight, Wichita, Kansas
Washington Bee
Washington Post
Weekly Anglo-African, New York
Weekly Blade, Parsons, Kansas
The Weekly Call, Topeka, Kansas
Weekly Louisianian, New Orleans
Weekly Pelican, New Orleans
Western Appeal, Chicago
Western Outlook, Oakland, California
Wide Awake, Birmingham
The World, Indianapolis

Novels and Poetry

Chesnutt, Charles W., *The House Behind the Cedars*. Boston: Houghton, Mifflin, 1901.
Fauset, Jessie, *The Chinaberry Tree: A Novel of American Life*. Philadelphia: J. B. Lippincott, 1931.
Griggs, Sutton, *Overshadowed*. Nashville: Orion Publishing Company, 1901.
Hughes, Langston, *Montage of a Dream*. New York: Henry Holt, 1951.
Sanborn, Gertrude, *Veiled Aristocrats*. Washington: Associated Publishers, 1923.
Smith, J. H., *Maudelle: A Novel*. Philadelphia: Mayhew Publishing Co., 1906.
West, Dorothy, *The Living Is Easy*. New York: Arno Press, 1969.

Dissertations, Theses, and Unpublished Papers

Alexander, Adele Logan, "Ambiguous Lives: Free Women of Color in Rural Georgia, 1787–1879," M.A. thesis, Howard University, 1987.
Anthony, Arthe Agnes, "The Negro Creole Community in New Orleans, 1880–1920: An Oral History," Ph.D. diss., University of California, Irvine, 1978.
Christensen, Lawrence O., "Black St. Louis: A Study in Race Relations," Ph.D. diss., University of Missouri, 1972.
Connolly, Harold X., "Blacks in Brooklyn from 1900 to 1960," Ph.D. diss., New York University, 1972.
Dillard, Tom W., "The Black Moses of the West: A Biography of Mifflin Wistar Gibbs, 1823–1915," M.A. thesis, University of Arkansas, 1974.
Ellsworth, Linda V., "Pensacola's Creoles: Remnants of a Culture," unpublished paper in possession of the author.
Everett, Donald E., "Free Persons of Color in New Orleans, 1803–1865," Ph.D. diss., Tulane University, 1952.
Freeman, Rhoda G., "The Free Negro in New York City in the Era Before the Civil War," Ph.D. diss., Columbia University, 1966.

BIBLIOGRAPHY

Griffin, John C., "Jean Toomer: American Writer," Ph.D. diss., University of South Carolina, 1976.

Gulliver, Adelaide Cromwell Hill, "The Negro Upper Class in Boston—Its Development and Present Social Structure," Ph.D. diss., Radcliffe College, 1952.

Johnson, Thomas Reed, "The City On the Hill: Race Relations in Washington, D.C., 1865–1885," Ph.D. diss., University of Maryland, 1975.

Mannhard, Marilyn, "Free People of Color in Mobile County, Alabama," M.S. thesis, University of South Alabama, 1982.

Mintz, Steven, "An Historical Ethnography of Black Washington, D.C., unpublished paper in possession of the author.

Paul, William George, "The Shadow of Equality: The Negro in Baltimore, 1864–1911," Ph.D. diss., University of Wisconsin, 1972.

Porter, Michael L., "Black Atlanta: An Interdisciplinary Study of Blacks on the East Side of Atlanta, 1890–1930," Ph.D. diss., Emory University, 1974.

Powers, Bernard E., "Black Charleston: A Social History, 1822–1885," Ph.D. diss., Northwestern University, 1982.

Richardson, Barbara, "A History of Blacks in Jacksonville, Florida, 1860–1895: A Socio-Economic and Political Study," D.A. thesis, Carnegie-Mellon University, 1975.

Robbins, Faye W., "A World-Within-A-World: Black Nashville, 1880–1915," Ph.D. diss., University of Arkansas, 1980.

Rouse, Jacquelene, "Lugenia D. Burns Hope: A Black Female Reformer in the South, 1871–1947," Ph.D. diss., Emory University, 1983.

Scherer, Robert G., "The Origins of the National Association of Colored Women," unpublished paper in possession of the author.

"Some Historical Facts About St. Mark's Episcopal Church, Charleston, S.C., 100th Anniversary," St. Mark's Protestant Episcopal Church, Charleston, South Carolina (mimeographed).

Taylor, David V., "Pilgrim's Progress: Black St. Paul and the Making of an Urban Ghetto, 1870–1930," Ph.D. diss., University of Minnesota, 1977.

Thornberry, Jerry J., "The Development of Black Atlanta, 1865–1885," Ph.D. diss., University of Maryland, 1977.

Transcript of an Oral Interview with Julia Moore Griffin by Margot Dashiell, August, 1979.

Williams, Jay R., "Social Stratification and the Negro American: An Exploration of Some Problems in Social Class Measurement," Ph.D. diss., Duke University, 1968.

Williams, Leroy T., "Black Toledo: Afro-Americans in Toledo, Ohio, 1890–1930," Ph.D. diss., University of Toledo, 1977.

Winch, Julie, "The Leaders of Philadelphia's Black Community, 1789–1848," Ph.D. diss., Bryn Mawr College, 1982.

Wright, George C., "Blacks in Louisville, Kentucky, 1890–1930," Ph.D. diss., Duke University, 1977.

Articles

"The Adventures of a Near White," Independent, LXXV (August 14, 1913), 373–374.

Alexander, Adele Logan, "How I Discovered My Grandmother," MS. Magazine, November, 1983, pp. 29–30, 32, 36.

Alexander, Alfred, "Housing in Harlem," Crisis, XXXV (October, 1928), 333–336, 351–353.

BIBLIOGRAPHY

Alexander, Charles, "The Ohio Federation at Dayton," *Alexander's Magazine*, I (August 15, 1901), 7.

Alexander, Robert J., "Negro Business in Atlanta," *Southern Economic Journal*, XVII (April, 1951), 452–454.

"The American Negro Historical Society of Philadelphia and Its Officers," *Colored American Magazine*, VI (February, 1903), 287–294.

Anderson, Jervis, "A Very Special Monument: The Dunbar High School on First Street," *The New Yorker*, LIV (March 20, 1978), 93–94, 100–102, 104–108, 110–121.

"Antipathy of the Upper and Lower Classes," *Christian Recorder*, X (October 26, 1872), 1.

"Are Mulattoes Ruling the Race?" *Ebony*, IX (October, 1954), 62.

Babchuk, Nicholas, and Ralph V. Thompson, "The Voluntary Associations of Negroes," *American Sociological Review*, XXVII (October, 1962), 647–652.

Bacote, Clarence, "Some Aspects of Negro Life in Georgia, 1880–1908," *Journal of Negro History*, XLIII (July, 1958), 186–213.

Baker, Thomas Nelson, "The Negro Woman," *Alexander's Magazine*, III (December 15, 1906), 71–85.

Barber, J. Max, "The Niagara Movement at Harper's Ferry," *Voice of the Negro*, III (October, 1906), 402–411.

Barrett, Samuel, "A Plea for Unity," *Colored American Magazine*, VII (January, 1904), 49.

Barrows, Samuel J., "What the Southern Negro Is Doing for Himself," *Atlantic Monthly*, LXVII (June, 1891), 805–815.

Bennett, Lerone, "The Black Establishment," *Negro Digest*, XIII (July, 1964), 81–96.

Bennett, Robert A., "Black Episcopalians: A History from the Colonial Period to the Present," *Historical Magazine of the Protestant Episcopal Church*, XLIII (September, 1974), 231–245.

Bentley, Florence, "Meta Warrick: A Promising Sculptor," *Voice of the Negro*, IV (March, 1904), 116–118.

Berlin, Ira, "The Structure of the Free Negro Caste in the Antebellum United States," *Journal of Social History*, IX (Spring, 1976), 297–318.

Berry, Benjamin D., "The Plymouth Congregational Church of Louisville, Kentucky," *Phylon*, XLII (September, 1981), 224–232.

Bigglestone, W. E., "Oberlin College and the Negro Student, 1865–1940," *Journal of Negro History*, LVI (July, 1971), 198–219.

Birnie, W. C., "The Education of the Negro in Charleston, South Carolina Before the Civil War," *Journal of Negro History*, XII (January, 1927), 13–21.

Bishop, Shelton H., "A History of St. Philip's Church, New York City," *Historical Magazine of the Protestant Episcopal Church*, XV (December, 1946) 298–317.

Blakely, Allison, "Richard T. Greener and the 'Talented Tenth's' Dilemma," *Journal of Negro History*, LIX (October, 1974), 305–321.

Blassingame, John W., "Before the Ghetto: The Making of the Black Community in Savannah, Georgia, 1865–1880," *Journal of Social History*, VI (Summer, 1973), 463–488.

Blauvelt, Mary T., "The Race Problems as Discussed by Negro Women," *American Journal of Sociology*, VI (March, 1901), 662–672.

Boardman, Helen, "First Families of Manhattan," *Phylon*, V (Spring, 1944), 138–141.

"Boston's Smart Set," *Colored American Magazine*, II (January, 1901), 204–209.

Bowles, Emma C., ed., "Concerning the Origin of Wilberforce," *Journal of Negro History*, VIII (July, 1923), 335–337.

Bragg, George F., "The Episcopal Church and the Negro Race," *Historical Magazine of the Protestant Episcopal Church*, IV (March, 1935), 47–52.

Brandt, Lillian, "The Negroes of St. Louis," *Journal of the American Statistical Association*, VIII (March, 1903), 203–269.

Brascher, N. D., "Cleveland—A Representative American City," *Voice of the Negro*, II (August, 1905), 534.

Bruce, Josephine, "The Afterglow of the Women's Convention," *Voice of the Negro*, I (November, 1904), 541–543.

Bruce, Roscoe Conkling, "The Dunbar Apartment House: An Adventure in Community Building," *Southern Workman*, LX (October, 1931), 417–428.

———, "A Plea for Negro Trade Schools in Cities," *Southern Workman*, XXXIII (December, 1904), 650–654.

———, "Service by the Educated Negro," *Colored American Magazine*, VI (December, 1903), 850–857.

Burley, Dan, "The Strange Will of Colonel McKee," *Negro Digest*, X (November, 1951), 17–22.

Burroughs, Nannie H., "Not Color But Character," *Voice of the Negro*, I (July, 1904), 277–279.

Bush, John E., "Afro-American People of Little Rock," *Colored American Magazine*, VIII (January, 1905), 39–42.

Calkins, David L., "Black Education and the 19th Century City: An Institutional Analysis of Cincinnati's Colored Schools," *Cincinnati Historical Society Bulletin*, XXXIII (Fall, 1971), 161–171.

"The Case Against Mixed Marriage," *Ebony*, V (November, 1950), 54–55.

Chase, Hal, "William C. Chase and *The Washington Bee*," *Negro History Bulletin*, XXXVI (December, 1973), 172–174.

"Christ Church, Wilmington," *American Missionary*, XLVI (June, 1892), 195–196.

Christensen, Lawrence O., "Race Relations in St. Louis, 1865–1916," *Missouri Historical Review*, LXXVIII (January, 1984), 123–136.

"Class Distinctions Among American Negroes," *Southern Workman*, XXVIII (October, 1899), 371.

Clifford, Carrie, "Cleveland and Its Colored People," *Colored American Magazine*, IX (July, 1905), 365–380.

"Color Lines Among the Colored People," *Literary Digest*, LXXII (March 18, 1922), 42.

"Color Question in the Protestant Episcopal Church," *A. M. E. Church Review*, XXI (1905), 268–269.

"Colored Men in Business," *A. M. E. Church Review*, VI (July, 1889), 106–109.

"Colored People of Charleston," *African Repository*, XXIII (June, 1847), 190.

"Colored Presbyterians," *A. M. E. Church Review*, XV (1898), 671–673.

"The Condition of the Colored Population of Baltimore," *Baltimore Literary and Religious Magazine*, IV (April, 1838), 168–176.

Contee, Clarence C., "Butler R. Wilson and the Boston N.A.A.C.P. Branch," *Crisis*, LXXXI (December, 1974), 346–348.

Cripps, Thomas R., "The Reaction of the Negro to the Motion Picture Birth of A Nation," *The Historian*, XXV (May, 1963), 344–362.

Crowe, Mary D., "Fannie Barrier Williams," *Negro History Bulletin*, V (May, 1942), 190–191.

Daniel, Vattel E., "Negro Classes and Life in the Church," *Journal of Negro Education*, XIII (Winter, 1944), 19–29.

Davidson, Bill, "Our Negro Aristocracy," *Saturday Evening Post*, CCXXXV (January 13, 1962), 14–16.

Day, Judy, and M. James Kedro, "Free Blacks in St. Louis: Antebellum Conditions, Emancipation and the Postwar Era," *Bulletin of the Missouri Historical Society*, XXX (January, 1974), 117–135.

Dennis, Rutledge M., "Du Bois and the Role of the Educated Elite," *Journal of Negro Education*, XLVI (Fall, 1977), 388–402.

"Denver, The City Beautiful—Denver, The City of Lights," *Colored American Magazine*, XII (May, 1907), 336–338.

DeVigne, Sadie E. Beach, "St. Mark's School, Birmingham, Alabama," *Colored American Magazine*, XIII (December, 1907), 417–420.

Dickerson, G. S., "A Glimpse of Charleston History," *Southern Workman*, XXXVI (January, 1907), 15–23.

Dillard, Tom W., "Isaac Gillam: Black Pulaski Countian," *Pulaski County Historical Review*, XXIV (March, 1976), 6–11.

Drake, St. Clair, and Horace R. Cayton, "Chicago Today: Metropolis Revisited," *Negro Digest*, XII (April, 1963), 20–25.

Du Bois, W. E. Burghardt, "The Negroes of Farmville, Virginia: A Social Study," *Bulletin of the Department of Labor*, No. 14. Washington: Government Printing Office, 1898.

Dudley, James B., "Education for Negroes in Guilford County, North Carolina," *Alexander's Magazine*, VI (October 15, 1908), 255–257.

Dunbar, Paul Laurence, "Negro Life in Washington," *Harper's Weekly*, XLIV (January 13, 1900), 32.

———, "Negro Society in Washington," *Saturday Evening Post*, CLXXIV (December 14, 1901), 9, 18.

"Dunbar National Bank," *Crisis*, XXXV (November, 1928), 370, 387.

Durham, John S., "Three Types of Growth," *A. M. E. Church Review*, XIV (1897), 121–130.

"The Dvorak Musical Society," *Colored American Magazine*, III (October, 1901), 454–455.

Eisenberg, Bernard, "Only for the Bourgeois? James Weldon Johnson and the NAACP, 1916–1930," *Phylon*, XLIII (Summer, 1982), 110–124.

"Etiquette—Debutante Dances," *Half Century Magazine*, II (May, 1917), 11.

"An Experiment in Negro Housing," *Monthly Labor Review*, XIX (September, 1929), 107–108.

"Experiments in Negro Housing in New York and Cincinnati," *Monthly Labor Review*, XXXIV (January, 1932), 124–130.

Fields, A. N., "Colorline Within the Race," *Abbott's Monthly*, VII (July, 1933), 2–3.

"First Congregational Church of Mobile," *American Missionary*, XLVI (June, 1892), 182–183.

Fitchett, E. Horace, "The Influence of Claflin College on Negro Family Life," *Journal of Negro History*, XXIX (October, 1944), 429–460.

———, "The Role of Claflin College in Negro Life in South Carolina," *Journal of Negro Education*, XII (Winter, 1943), 42–68.

———, "The Traditions of the Free Negro in Charleston, South Carolina," *Journal of Negro History*, XXV (April, 1940), 144–152.

Flemming, Cynthia, "The Effect of Education on Black Tennesseans After the Civil War," *Phylon*, XLIV (September, 1983), 209–216.

Flusche, Michael, "On the Color Line: Charles Waddell Chesnutt," *North Carolina Historical Review*, LIII (January, 1976), 1–24.

Foner, Laura, "The Free People of Color in Louisiana and St. Dominique," *Journal of Social History*, III (Summer, 1970), 406–430.

Fosdick, Franklin, "The Truth About Negro Society," *Negro Digest*, VIII (July, 1950), 3–6.

Franklin, John Hope, "Negro Episcopalians in Antebellum North Carolina," *Historical Magazine of the Protestant Episcopal Church*, XIII (September, 1944), 216–234.

Fullinwider, S. P., "Jean Toomer: Lost Generation or Negro Renaissance?" *Phylon*, XXVII (Winter, 1966), 396–403.

Gatewood, Willard B., "Edward Elder Cooper: Black Journalist," *Journalism Quarterly*, LV (Summer, 1978), 269–275, 324.

———, "John Hanks Alexander of Arkansas: Second Black Graduate of West Point," *Arkansas Historical Quarterly*, XLI (Summer, 1982), 103–128.

Gersman, Elinor M., "The Development of Public Education for Blacks in Nineteenth Century St. Louis, Missouri," *Journal of Negro Education*, XLI (Winter, 1972), 35–47.

Gibbs, Thomas V., "John Willis Menard: The First Colored Congressman Elect," *A. M. E. Church Review*, LII (1886), 426–432.

Gliozzo, Charles A., "John Jones: A Study of a Black Chicagoan," *Illinois Historical Journal*, LXXX (Autumn, 1987), 177–188.

de Graaf, Lawrence D., "The City of Black Angels: Emergence of the Los Angeles Ghetto, 1890–1930," *Pacific Historical Review*, XXXI (August, 1970), 323–352.

Green, Suzanne E., "Black Republicans on the Baltimore City Council,, 1890–1931," *Maryland Historical Magazine*, LXXIV (September, 1979), 203–222.

Gresham, G. N., "Social Betterment," *Southern Workman*, XXIX (October, 1900), 577–580.

Grimké, Angelina, "A Biographical Sketch of Archibald H. Grimké," *Opportunity*, III (February, 1925), 44–47.

Grimké, Archibald, "Colored Catholics in Washington, D. C.," *Alexander's Magazine*, IV (June 15, 1910), 108–110.

Grimké, Francis J., "The Defects of Our Ministry and Its Remedy," *A. M. E. Church Review*, III (1887), 154–157.

———, "Some Things That Lie Across the Pathway of Our Progress," *Southern Workman*, XXVII (September, 1897), 185–190.

Harris, George C., "Boston Colored People," *Colored American Magazine*, XIV (January, 1908), 28–30.

Harris, Robert L., "Charleston's Free Afro-American Elite: The Brown Fellowship Society and the Humane Brotherhood," *South Carolina Historical Magazine*, LXXII (January, 1981), 289–310.

———, "Daniel Murray and the Encyclopedia of the Colored Race," *Phylon*, XXXVII (Fall, 1976), 270–282.

Hartgrove, W. B., "The Story of Maria Louise Moore and Fannie B. Richards," *Journal of Negro History*, I (January, 1916), 22–33.

Hartzell, J. C., "Methodism and the Negro in the United States," *Journal of Negro History*, VIII (July, 1923), 301–315.

Hawkins, A. Ashbie, "A Year of Segregation in Baltimore," *Crisis*, III (November, 1911), 27–30.

Henderson, John M., "The Forces Upon Which the Race Depends for Success," *Colored American Magazine*, XIV (January, 1908), 70–71.

"Henry Oscar Wagoner: 'The Douglass of the West,'" *Colored Amerian Magazine*, V (July, 1905), 188–192.

Hilyer, Andrew F., "The Higher Education of Negro Youth," *Popular Science Monthly*, LVII (August, 1900), 437–438.

Hine, William C., "Black Politicians in Reconstruction Charleston, South Carolina: A

Collective Study," *Journal of Southern History*, XLIX (November, 1983), 555–571.

Hoover, Velma J., "Meta Vaux Warrick Fuller: Her Life and Art," *Negro History Bulletin*, XL (March–April, 1977), 678–681.

Hopkins, Pauline, "Famous Women of the Negro Race," *Colored American Magazine*, IV (August, 1912), 173.

Houston, G. David, "A Negro Senator," *Journal of Negro History*, VII (July, 1922), 243–256.

"How Society Had Its Birth," *Ebony*, II (May, 1947), 13.

Hughes, Langston, "Do Big Negroes Keep Little Negroes Down?" *Negro Digest*, X (November, 1951), 79–82.

————, "Our Wonderful Society: Washington," *Opportunity* (August, 1927), 226–227.

————, and John C. Alston, "Atlanta: Society and Slums," *Ebony*, III (January, 1948), 19, 22.

Hunton, Addie W., "The National Association of Colored Women: Its Real Significance," *Colored Amerian Magazine*, XIV (July, 1908), 418–419.

Hurst, Harold W., "The Northernmost Southern town: A Sketch of Pre-Civil War Annapolis," *Maryland Historical Magazine*, LXXVI (September, 1981), 240–249.

Hyman, Sidney, "Washington's Negro Elite," *Look*, April 6, 1965, pp. 60–63.

"I Pass for White," *Abbott's Monthly*, IV (February, 1932), 14–15, 52–53, 54–55, 56.

"Impressions of Charleston," *Christian Recorder*, V (September 8, 1866), 142.

"Is Negro Society Phoney?" *Ebony*, VIII (September, 1953), 56.

Ish, J. G., "An Object in Life," *Christian Recorder*, XVIII (February 5, 1880), 1.

Jackson, Barbara G., "Florence Price, Composer," *Black Perspectives on Music*, Spring, 1977, pp. 31–35.

James, Milton, "Institute for Colored Youth," *Negro History Bulletin*, XXI (January, 1958), 83–85.

"James H. Wolff," *Colored American Magazine*, VI (March, 1903), 358–359.

Janiter, Ellsworth, "Samuel Coleridge-Taylor in Washington," *Phylon*, XXVIII (Summer, 1967), 187–194.

"John Stephens Durham," *Negro History Bulletin*, V (December, 1941), 67.

Johnson, Caleb, "Crossing the Color Line," *Outlook and Independent*, CLVIII (August 20, 1931), 526–527, 542–543.

Johnson, Haynes, "Caste and Class in Washington, D. C.," *Negro Digest*, XI (December, 1961), 40–44.

Johnson, James W., "Robert C. Owens: A Pacific Coast Successful Negro," *Colored American Magazine*, IX (July, 1905), 391–393.

Johnson, Michael P., and James L. Roark, "A Middle Ground: Free Mulattoes and the Friendly Moralist Society of Antebellum Charleston," *Southern Studies*, XXI (Fall, 1982), 246–265.

Johnson, Ronald M., "From Romantic Suburb to Racial Enclave: Le Droit Park, Washington, D.C., 1880–1920," *Phylon*, XLV (December, 1984), 264–270.

Johnson, Whittington B., "Free Blacks in Antebellum Savannah: An Economic Profile," *Georgia Historical Quarterly*, LXIV (Winter, 1980), 418–431.

Kephart, William M., "The Passing Question," *Phylon*, X (Fourth Quarter, 1948), 336–340.

Kersey, Harry A., "St. Augustine School: Seventy-five Years of Negro Parochial Education in Gainesville, Florida," *Florida Historical Quarterly*, LI (July, 1972), 58–63.

Lack, Paul D., "An Urban Slave Community: Little Rock, 1831–1862," *Arkansas Historical Quarterly*, XLI (Autumn, 1982), 258–287.

Lammers, Ann C., "The Rev. Absalom Jones and the Episcopal Church: Christian

Theology and Black Consciousness in New Alliance," *Historical Magazine of the Protestant Episcopal Church*, LI (June, 1982), 159–184.

Lapsansky, Emma Jones, "Friends, Wives and Strivings: Networks and Community Values Among Nineteenth-Century Philadelphia Afroamerican Elites," *The Pennsylvania Magazine of History and Biography*, CVIII (January, 1984), 3–24.

Lee, Edwin A., "Daniel Murray," *Colored American Magazine*, V (October, 1902), 432–440.

Lerner, Gerda, "Early Community Work of Black Club Women," *Journal of Negro History*, LIX (April, 1974), 158–167.

Lewis, E. S., "The Cook Family," *Negro History Bulletin*, V (January, 1942), 83.

Lewis, W. H., "Commencement Address to Graduates of M Street High School," *Colored American Magazine*, XIV (July, 1908), 425–426.

"Living Fraternity Founders," *Ebony*, XII (October, 1958), 58–63.

Manor, Marla, "The Ish House and the Doctor," *Arkansas Democrat Sunday Magazine*, June 9, 1968, pp. 1–3.

Matthews, William E., "Money As a Factor in Human Progress," *Christian Recorder*, XXIII (August 20, 1885), 1.

———, "A Summer Vacation in Europe," *Christian Recorder*, VI (January, 1890), 292–306.

"May It Please Your Honor," *The Alumni Journal* [Hampton Institute], III (January, 1884), 1.

Meier, August, "Negro Class Structure and Ideology in the Age of Booker T. Washington," *Phylon*, XXIII (Fall, 1962), 258–266.

———, and David Lewis, "History of the Negro Upper Class in Atlanta, Georgia, 1890–1958," *Journal of Negro Education*, XXVIII (Spring, 1958), 128–139.

Menard, E., "John Willis Menard: First Negro Elected to the U.S. Congress," *Negro History Bulletin*, XXVIII (December, 1964), 53–54.

Merriam, Amelia, "Avery Normal Institute, Charleston, S.C.," *American Missionary*, XLV (May, 1891), 181–183.

Merry, Preston R., "Josiah T. Settle," *Negro History Bulletin*, V (February, 1942), 113–114.

Miller, Kelly, "The 'Colored' United States: South Carolina," *The Messenger*, VII (December, 1925), 377.

Minton, Theophilius J., "Is Intermarriage Between the Races to Be Encouraged?" *A. M. E. Church Review*, III (October, 1886), 284–287.

Moore, Larry, "Across the Great Divide: The Memphis Black Elite," *Memphis*, VII (November, 1982), 37, 47, 49–50.

Morton, Patricia, "From Invisible Man to 'New People': The Recent Discovery of American Mulattoes," *Phylon*, XLVI (June, 1985), 106–122.

"Mulattoes, Negroes and the Jamestown Exhibit," *Colored American Magazine*, XIII (August, 1907), 87–88.

Murray, Daniel, "Color Problem in the United States," *Colored American Magazine*, VII (December, 1904), 719–724.

Neal, Joe, "Fraternal Cemetary: Reflections on a Southern Negro Graveyard," *Pulaski County Historical Review*, XXV (March, 1977), 4–8.

"Negro Bluebloods," *Ebony*, X (September, 1955), 55.

"The Negroes and Near Negroes," *Colored American Magazine*, XIII (July, 1907), 9–10.

"Negroes in White Churches," *Colored American Magazine*, XII (April, 1907), 247.

"Negroes Who Fought At Bunker Hill," *Ebony*, XIX (February, 1964), 44–53, 75.

"Negroes Who Hate Negroes," *Ebony*, VIII (December, 1952), 112.

Nelson, Henry Loomis, "The Washington Negro," *Harper's Weekly*, XXXVI (July 9, 1892), 654.

"An Old and Worthy Institution," *Colored American Magazine*, XIV (January, 1908), 72–73.

Orum, Anthony M., "A Reappraisal of the Social and Political Participation of Negroes," *American Journal of Sociology*, LXXII (July, 1966), 32–46.

"Outstanding Yale Graduates," *Ebony*, V (July, 1950), 18.

Palmer, Edward Nelson, "Negro Secret Societies," *Social Forces*, XII (December, 1944), 207–212.

Park, Robert E., "Negro Home Life and Standards of Living," *Annals of the American Academy of Political and Social Sciences*. Philadelphia: n.p., 1913.

Perlman, Daniel, "Organizations of the Free Negro in New York City, 1800–1860," *Journal of Negro History*, XVI (July, 1971), 181–197.

Perry, Louis E., "Studies in the Religious Life of the City of Nashville, Tenn.," *Vanderbilt University Quarterly*, IV (Summer, 1904), 90–91.

Phelps, Howard A., "Negro Life in Chicago," *Half Century Magazine*, VI (May, 1919), 12–14.

Phillips, Karl F., "The 'Gap,' Let's Close It," *Conservator*, III (January–February, 1921), 12, 53.

Pih, Richard, "Negro Self-Improvement Efforts in Antebellum Cincinnati," *Ohio History*, LXXVIII (Summer, 1969), 179–187.

Preston, E. Delorius, "William Syphax, A Pioneer in Negro Education in the District of Columbia," *Journal of Negro History*, XX (October, 1955), 448–476.

Price, J. C., "Does the Negro Seek Social Equality?" *The Forum*, X (January, 1891), 558–564.

Putney, Martha S., "The Baltimore Normal School for the Education of Colored Teachers: Its Founders and Its Founding," *Maryland Historical Magazine*, LXXII (Summer, 1977), 238–252.

Puttkammer, Charles W., and Ruth Worthy, "William Monroe Trotter, 1872–1934," *Phylon*, XLIII (October, 1958), 298–316.

"Queen of Gotham's Colored 400," *Literary Digest*, LV (October, 13, 1917), 75–76, 78–79.

Rankin, David C., "The Origins of Black Leadership in New Orleans During Reconstruction," *Journal of Southern History*, XL (August, 1974), 417–436.

Record, Wilson, "Negro Leadership in the National Association for the Advancement of Colored People: 1910–1940," *Phylon*, XVII (4th Quarter, 1956), 375–389.

Reid, Ira D., "American Cities—Albany, New York," *Opportunity*, VII (June, 1929), 179.

Reimers, David, "Negro Bishops and Diocesan Segregation in the Protestant Episcopal Church, 1870–1954," *Historical Magazine of the Protestant Episcopal Church*, XXXI (September, 1962), 231–240.

Reinders, Robert, "The Churches and the Negro in New Orleans, 1850–1860," *Phylon*, XXII (Fall, 1961), 241–248.

Richardson, Joe M., "The Failure of the American Missionary Association to Expand Congregationalism Among Southern Blacks," *Southern Studies*, XVIII (Spring, 1979), 58–66.

———, "Francis L. Cardozo: Black Educator During Reconstruction," *Journal of Negro Education*, XLVII (Winter, 1979), 73–83.

"Robert Gordon: A Successful Businessman," *Negro History Bulletin*, I (November, 1937), 1, 3.

Robinson, Henry S., "The M Street High School, 1891–1916," *Records of the Columbia Historical Society of Washington, D.C.*, LI (1984), 119–143.

Rothrock, Thomas, "Joseph Carter Corbin and Negro Education in the University of Arkansas," *Arkansas Historical Quarterly*, XXX (Winter, 1971), 277–314.

Rudwick, Elliott, "The Niagara Movement," *Journal of Negro History*, XLIII (July, 1957), 177–182.

"St. Mark's Methodist Episcopal Church," *Colored American Magazine*, X (May, 1906), 381–385.

Savage, W. Sherman, "Negro Pioneers in the State of Washington," *Negro History Bulletin*, XX (January, 1958), 93–95.

Scarborough, W. S., "The Educated Negro and His Mission," *American Negro Academy Occasional Papers*, No. 8. Washington: American Negro Academy, 1903.

Schlesinger, Arthur M., "Biography of a Nation of Joiners," *American Historial Review*, L (October, 1944), 1–25.

Schoenberg, Sandra, and Charles Bailey, "The Symbolic Meaning of an Elite Black Community: The Ville of St. Louis," *Bulletin of the Missouri Historical Society*, XXXIII (January, 1977), 94–102.

Schuyler, George S., "These Colored United States: New York, Utopia Deferred," *The Messenger*, VII (October–November, 1925), 348.

Scottron, Samuel R., "New York African Society for Mutual Relief, Ninety-Seventh Anniversary," *Colored American Magazine*, IX (December, 1905), 685–690.

———, "The New York Negro a Century Ago," *Colored American Magazine*, XII (June, 1907), 437–442.

Silcox, Harry C., "Philadelphia Negro Educator: Jacob C. White, Jr.," *Pennsylvania Magazine of Biography and History*, XCVII (January, 1973), 75–98.

Smith, Anna Bustill, "The Bustill Family," *Journal of Negro History*, X (October, 1925), 638–644.

Smith, C. Calvin, "John E. Bush of Arkansas, 1890–1910," *Ozark Historical Review*, II (Spring, 1973), 48–59.

Smith, Charles F., "The Negro in Nashville," *Century*, XLII (May, 1891), 154–156.

Smith, Sandra N., and Earle H. West, "Charlotte Hawkins Brown," *Journal of Negro Education*, LI (Summer, 1982), 191–206.

"Society," *Ebony*, II (May, 1947), 9.

"Society Rulers in 20 Cities," *Ebony*, IV (May, 1949), 62–63.

Somers, Dale A., "Black and White Relations in New Orleans, 1865–1900," *Journal of Southern History*, XL (February, 1974), 19–42.

A South Carolinian, "South Carolina Society," *Atlantic Monthly*, XXXIX (June, 1877), 670–684.

Spady, James G., "The Afro-American Historical Society: The Nucleus of Black Bibliophiles, 1897–1923," *Negro History Bulletin*, XXXVIII (June–July, 1974), 254–257.

Spalding, David, "The Negro Catholic Congresses, 1889–1894," *Catholic Historical Review*, LV (October, 1969), 337–357.

Still, Judith A., "Carrie Still Sheppardson: The Hallows of Her Footsteps," *Arkansas Historical Quarterly*, XLII (Spring, 1983), 37–46.

Taylor, Henry L., "On Slavery's Fringe: City Building and Black Community Development in Ohio: 1800–1850," *Ohio History*, LXLV (Winter–Spring, 1986), 5–33.

Taylor, Quintard, "The Emergence of Black Communities in the Pacific Northwest, 1865–1910," *Journal of Negro History*, LXIV (Fall, 1979), 342–354.

Terrell, Mary Church, "History of the High School for Negroes in Washington," *Journal of Negro History*, II (April, 1917), 252–266.

————, "Samuel Coleridge-Taylor," *Voice of the Negro*, II (January, 1905), 665–669.

————, "Social Functions During Inauguration Week," *Voice of the Negro*, II (April, 1905), 238–241.

————, "Society Among the Colored People of Washington," *Voice of the Negro*, I (March, 1904), 150–156.

Terrell, Robert H., "The Negro in Domestic Service," *Colored American Magazine*, IX (November, 1905), 631–633.

Thelan, David, and Leslie H. Fishel, "Reconstruction in the North: The *World* Looks at New York's Negroes, March 16, 1867," *New York History*, XLIX (October, 1968), 432–438.

"Think Well of Yourself," *Christian Recorder*, XVI (April 11, 1878), 1.

Thomas, Bettye C., "Public Education and Black Protest in Baltimore, 1865–1900," *Maryland Historical Magazine*, LXXI (Fall, 1976), 381–391.

Thomas, V. P., "Colored New Orleans," *Crisis*, II (February, 1916), 188–192.

Thornbrough, Emma L., "The National Afro-American League, 1887–1908," *Journal of Southern History*, XXVII (November, 1961), 494–512.

Towns, George A., "The Sources of Tradition of Atlanta University," *Phylon*, III (Second Quarter, 1942), 117–134.

Tunnell, W. V., "The Necessity of Higher Education," *A. M. E. Church Review*, VI (1890), 173–180.

Tyler, Ralph, "Affairs at Washington," *Colored American Magazine*, XVI (April, 1909), 230.

————, "Real Society," *Colored American Magazine*, XIII (November, 1907), 391–392.

Urofsky, Melvin I., "Blanche K. Bruce: United States Senator, 1875–1881," *Journal of Negro History*, XXIX (May, 1967), 118–141.

"Vacation Days," *Crisis*, IV (August, 1912), 186–188.

Washington, Josephine T., "What the Club Does for the Club-Woman," *Colored American Magazine*, XII (February, 1907), 121–124.

Waters, Oliver G., "The Smoky City: Glimpses of Social Life," *Colored American Magazine*, IV (November, 1901), 14–17.

Wayman, Harrison, "Meta Vaux Warrick," *Colored American Magazine*, VI (March, 1903), 325–331.

————, "The Quaker City," *Colored American Magazine*, VI (December, 1903), 765–769.

Weeks, Louis B., "Racism, World War I and the Christian Life: Francis J. Grimké in the Nation's Capital," *Journal of Presbyterian History*, LI (Winter, 1973), 471–488.

Wesley, Charles H., "Racial Historical Societies and American Heritage," *Journal of Negro History*, XXXVII (January, 1952), 25–33.

"What It Means to be Colored in the Capital of the United States," *The Independent*, XII (January 17, 1907), 181–186.

White, Arthur O., "The Black Movement Against Jim Crow Education in Lockport, New York, 1835–1876," *New York History*, L (July, 1969), 265–282.

"Whitefield McKinlay," *Journal of Negro History*, XXVII (January, 1942), 129–130.

Williams, Fannie Barrier, "Club Movement Among the Colored Women," *Voice of the Negro* I (March, 1904), 99–107.

————, "The Colored Girl," *Voice of the Negro*, II (June, 1905), 400–403.

————, "Perils of the White Negro," *Colored American Magazine*, XIII (December, 1907), 421–423.

————, "Work Attempted and Missed in Organized Club Work," *Colored American Magazine*, XIV (May, 1908), 283–285.

BIBLIOGRAPHY

Williams, Fred H., "Richard De Baptiste," *Negro History Bulletin*, XXII (May, 1959), 178.
Williams, Henry S., "The Development of the Negro Public School System in Missouri," *Journal of Negro History*, V (April, 1920), 137–165.
Wilson, Benjamin C., "Idlewild: A Black Eden in Michigan," *Michigan History*, LXV (September–October, 1981), 33–37.
Wilson, Edward E., "Negro Society in Chicago," *Voice of the Negro*, IV (July, 1907), 306–309.
Woodson, Carter G., "The Beginnings of Miscegenation of Whites and Blacks," *Journal of Negro History*, II (October, 1918), 335–353.
———, "The Bustill Family," *Negro History Bulletin*, XI (April, 1948), 147–148.
———, "The Gibbs Family—The Hunts, the Marshalls, the Muses, the Laws, and the Millers," *Negro History Bulletin*, XI (October, 1947), 3–12, 22.
———, "The Negroes in Cincinnati Prior to the Civil War," *Journal of Negro History*, I (January, 1916), 1–22.
———, "What Makes A Family Distinguished," *Negro History Bulletin*, XIII (October, 1949), 2.
———, "The Wormley Family," *Negro History Bulletin*, XI (January, 1948), 75–84.
Woodson, June B., "The Negro in Detroit Before 1900," *Negro History Bulletin*, XXII (January, 1959), 90–91.
Work, Monroe N., "The Negro Church in the Negro Community," *Southern Workman*, XXXVIII (August, 1908), 428–433.
Wormley, G. Smith, "Educators of the First Half Century of Public Schools of the District of Columbia," *Journal of Negro History*, XVII (April, 1932), 124–140.
Wright, Richard R., "The Negroes of Philadelphia," *A. M. E. Church Review*, XXIV (October, 1907), 141–144.
———, "The Negroes of Xenia, Ohio," *Bulletin of the Bureau of Labor*, No. 47 (July, 1903).
Yancey, Dorothy C., "William Edward Burghardt Du Bois, The Atlanta Years: The Human Side—A Study Based on Oral Sources," *Journal of Negro History*, LXIII (January, 1978), 59–67.
Yard, Lionel M., "Blacks in Brooklyn," *Negro History Bulletin*, XXXVII (August–September, 1974), 289–293.

Other Sources

Anderson, Eric, *Race and Politics in North Carolina, 1872–1901: The Black Second.* Baton Rouge: Louisiana State University Press, 1981.
Anderson, Jervis, *This Was Harlem: A Cultural Portrait, 1900–1950.* New York: Farrar, Straus, Giroux, 1981.
Anderson, Matthew, *Presbyterianism: Its Relation to the Negro as Illustrated by the Berean Presbyterian Church, Philadelphia.* Philadelphia: John McGill White and Co., 1897.
Archer, William, *Through Afro-America.* Westport: Negro Universities Press, 1970.
Bacote, Clarence, *The Story of Atlanta University: A Century of Service, 1865–1965.* Atlanta: Atlanta University, 1965.
Baker, Ray S., *Following the Color Line.* New York: Doubleday, Page, 1908.
Bardolph, Richard, *The Negro Vanguard.* New York: Rinehart and Winston, 1959.
Beard, Augustus F., *A Crusade of Brotherhood: A History of the American Missionary Association.* Boston: Pilgrim Press, 1909.

Beasley, Delilah, *The Negro Trailblazers of California*. New York: Negro Universities Press, 1969.

Berlin, Ira, *Slaves Without Masters: The Free Negro in the Antebellum South*. New York: Pantheon Books, 1974.

Billingsley, Andrew, *Black Families in White America*. Englewood Cliffs: Prentice-Hall, 1968.

Biographical and Historical Memoirs of Central Arkansas. Chicago: Goodspeed Publishing Co., 1889.

Birmingham, Stephen, *Certain People: America's Black Elite*. Boston: Little, Brown, 1977.

Blair, Karen J., *The Clubwoman As Feminist: True Womanhood Redefined, 1868–1914*. New York: Holmes and Meier, 1980.

Blassingame, John W., *Black New Orleans, 1860–1880*. Chicago: University of Chicago Press, 1973.

Bond, Horace Mann, *Black American Scholars: A Study of Their Beginnings*. Detroit: Balamp Publishing Co., 1972.

Bond, J. Max, *The Negro in Los Angeles*. San Francisco: R and E Associates, 1973.

Bontemps, Arna, *Free at Last: The Life of Frederick Douglass*. New York: Dodd, Mead, 1971.

Borchert, James, *Alley Life in Washington: Family, Community, Religion and Folklife in the City, 1850–1890*. Urbana: University of Illinois Press, 1980.

Boris, Joseph J., ed., *Who's Who in Colored America, 1928–29*. New York: Who's Who in Colored America, 1929.

Bowen, Louise D., *The Colored People of Chicago*. Chicago: n.p., 1913.

Brackett, Jeffrey R., *The Negro in Maryland: A Study of the Institution of Slavery*. Baltimore: Johns Hopkins University Press, 1889.

————, *Notes on the Progress of the Colored People of Maryland Since the War*. Baltimore: Johns Hopkins University Press, 1890.

Bragg, George F., *History of the Afro-American Group in the Episcopal Church*. Baltimore: Church Advocate Press, 1922.

————, *Men of Maryland*. Baltimore: Church Advocate Press, 1925.

Broderick, Francis L., *W. E. B. Du Bois: Negro Leader in a Time of Crisis*. Palo Alto: Stanford University Press, 1959.

Brown, Letitia, and Elsie Lewis, *Washington in the New Era, 1870–1970*. Washington, D.C.: Educational Department, National Portrait Gallery, 1972.

Buckler, Helen, *Daniel Hale Williams: Negro Surgeon*. New York: Pitman Publishing Co., 1954.

Buckley, Gail Lumet, *The Hornes: An American Family*. New York: Knopf, 1986.

Bullock, Henry A., *A History of Negro Education in the South from 1619 to the Present*. Cambridge: Harvard University Press, 1967.

Busbey, Katherine G., *Home Life in America*. New York: Macmillan, 1910.

Carter, Edward R., *The Black Side: A Partial History of the Business, Religious and Educational Side of the Negro in Atlanta*. Atlanta: n.p., 1894.

Chesnutt, Helen M., *Charles Waddell Chesnutt: Pioneer of the Colorline*. Chapel Hill: University of North Carolina Press, 1952.

Church, Annette, and Roberta Church, *The Robert R. Churches of Memphis*. Ann Arbor: Edwards Brothers, 1974.

Clark, Kenneth, *Dark Ghetto: Dilemma of Social Power*. New York: Harper and Row, 1965.

Cobb, W. Montague, *The First Negro Medical Society: A History of the Medico-Chirurgical Society of the District of Columbia, 1884–1939*. Washington, D.C.: Associated Publishers, 1939.

BIBLIOGRAPHY

Cromwell, John W., *History of the Bethel Literary and Historical Association*. Washington, D.C.: Press of R. L. Pendleton, 1896.

Crooks, James B., *Politics and Progress: The Rise of Urban Progressivism in Baltimore, 1895 to 1911*. Baton Rouge: Louisiana State University Press, 1968.

Crossland, William A., *Industrial Conditions Among Negroes in St. Louis*. St. Louis: Mendle Printing Co., 1914.

Culp, W. D., ed., *Twentieth Century Negro Literature*. Naperville, Illinois: J. L. Nichols, 1902.

Curry, Leonard P., *The Free Black in Urban America, 1800–1850*. Chicago: University of Chicago Press, 1981.

Dabney, Wendell P., *Cincinnati's Colored Citizens*. Cincinnati: Wendell Publishing Co., 1926.

Daniels, Douglas, *Pioneer Urbanites: A Social and Cultural History of Black San Francisco*. Philadelphia: Temple University Press, 1980.

Daniels, John, *In Freedom's Birthplace: A Study of Boston Negroes*. Boston: Houghton, Mifflin, 1914.

Davenport, M. Marguerite, *Azalia: Madame E. Azalia Hackley*. Boston: Chapman and Grimes, 1947.

Davis, Allison, and John Dollard, *Children of Bondage*. Washington: American Council on Education, 1940.

Davis, Edwin A., and William R. Hogan, *Barber of Natchez*. Baton Rouge: Louisiana State University Press, 1973.

Davis, Elizabeth, *Lifting As They Climb*. n.p.: n.p., 1933.

Davis, Russell, *Black Americans in Cleveland, from George Peake to Carl B. Stokes, 1796–1969*. Washington, D.C.: Associated Publishers, 1972.

Day, Caroline Bond, *A Study of Negro-White Families in the United States*. Cambridge: Harvard University Press, 1932.

De Costa, Benjamin F., *Three Score and Ten: The Story of St. Philip's Church*. New York: The Parish, 1889.

Desdunes, Rodolphe L., *Our People and Our History*. Baton Rouge: Louisiana State University Press, 1973.

Detels, Claire, ed., *William Grant Still Studies at the University of Arkansas: A 1984 Congress Report*. Fayetteville: n.p., 1985.

Dietrich, Fred W., *The History of Dentistry in Arkansas*. Little Rock: Arkansas Dental Association, n.d.

Dittmer, John, *Black Georgia in the Progressive Era*. Urbana: University of Illinois Press, 1965.

Dominguez, Virginia R., *White by Definition: Social Classification in Creole Louisiana*. New Brunswick: Rutgers University Press, 1986.

Dorsett, Lyle W., *The Queen City: A History of Denver*. Boulder: Pruett Publishing Co., 1977.

Douglass, H. Paul, *Christian Reconstruction in the South*. Boston: Pilgrim Press, 1909.

Drago, Edmund L., *Initiative, Paternalism, and Race Relations: Charleston's Avery Normal Institute*. Athens: University of Georgia Press, 1989.

————, and Eugene C. Hunt, *A History of Avery Normal Institute From 1865 to 1954*. Charleston: College of Charleston, n.d.

Drake, St. Clair, and Horace R. Cayton, *Black Metropolis: A Study of Negro Life in a Northern City*. New York: Harcourt, Brace, 1945.

Dreer, Herman, *The History of Omega Psi Fraternity: A Brotherhood of College Men*. n.p.: n.p., 1940.

Du Bois, W. E. B., *The Black North in 1901: A Social Study*. New York: Arno Press, 1969.

———, *The Philadelphia Negro: A Social Study*. Philadelphia: University of Pennsylvania Press, 1899.

———, *The Souls of Black Folk*. Milwood, New York: Kraus-Thomason, 1973.

———, ed., *Efforts for Social Betterment Among Negro Americans*. Atlanta: Atlanta University Press, 1909.

———, ed., *Morals and Manners Among Negro Americans*. Atlanta: Atlanta University Press, 1914.

———, ed., *The Negro American Family*. Atlanta: Atlanta University Press, 1908.

———, ed., *The Negro Church*. Atlanta: Atlanta University Press, 1903.

———, ed., *Social and Physical Condition of Negroes in Cities*. Atlanta: Atlanta University Press, 1897.

———, and A. G. Dill, eds., *The College-Bred Negro American*. Atlanta: Atlanta University Press, 1910.

The Elite List: A Compilation of Selected Names of Residents of Washington City, D.C. [1888–1907]. Washington, D.C.: Elite Publishing Co., 1888–1908.

Escott, Paul D., *Slavery Remembered: A Record of Twentieth-Century Slave Narratives*. Chapel Hill: University of North Carolina Press, 1979.

Foley, Albert S., *God's Men of Color: The Colored Catholic Priests in the United States*. New York: Farrar, Straus, 1955.

Fox, Stephen R., *The Guardian of Boston: William Monroe Trotter*. New York: Atheneum, 1971.

Franklin, John Hope, *George Washington Williams: A Biography*. Chicago: University of Chicago Press, 1985.

———, and August Meier, eds., *Black Leaders of the Twentieth Century*. Urbana: University of Illinois Press, 1982.

Franklin, Vincent P., *The Education of Black Philadelphia: The Social and Educational History of a Minority Community, 1900–1950*. Philadelphia: University of Pennsylvania Press, 1979.

———, and James D. Anderson, eds., *New Perspectives on Black Educational History*. Boston: G. K. Holland Co., 1978.

Frazier, E. Franklin, *Black Bourgeoisie: The Rise of a New Middle Class*. New York: Free Press, 1957.

———, *The Free Negro Family*. New York: Arno Press, 1969.

———, *The Negro Church in America*. New York: Schocken Books, 1974.

———, *The Negro Family in Chicago*. Chicago: University of Chicago Press, 1932.

———, *The Negro Family in the United States*. Chicago: University of Chicago Press, 1939.

From Servitude to Service. Boston; American Unitarian Association, 1905.

Gaines, D. B., *Racial Possibilities As Indicated By the Negroes of Arkansas*. Little Rock: Philander Smith College, 1898.

Gatewood, Willard B., *Theodore Roosevelt and the Art of Controversy*. Baton Rouge: Louisiana State University Press, 1970.

Genovese, Eugene D., *Roll, Jordan Roll: The World the Slaves Made*. New York: Pantheon, 1974.

Gerber, David A., *Black Ohio and the Color Line, 1860–1915*. Urbana: University of Illinois Press, 1976.

Gibson, J. W., and W. H. Crogman, *Progress of a Race*. Miami: Mnemosyne Publishing Co., 1969.

Gillard, John T., *The Catholic Church and the American Negro*. Baltimore: St. Joseph Society Press, 1929.

Gordon, Asa H., *Sketches of Negro Life and History in South Carolina*. Columbia: University of South Carolina Press, 1971.

Graham, Leroy, *Baltimore: The Nineteenth Century Black Capital*. Lanham, Md.: University Press of America, 1982.

Green, Constance M., *The Secret City: A History of Race Relations in the Nation's Capital*. Princeton: Princeton University Press, 1967.

Green, Edward S., *National Capital Code of Etiquette*. Washington: Austin Jenkins Co., 1920.

Grimshaw, William H., *Official History of Freemasonry Among Colored People in North America*. New York: Broadway Publishing Co., 1902.

Hackley, E. Azalia, *The Colored Girl Beautiful*. Kansas City: Burton Publishing Co., 1916.

Hagood, L. M., *The Colored Man in the Methodist Episcopal Church*. Cincinnati: Cranston and Stowe, 1890.

Haley, James T., *Afro-American Encyclopedia*. Nashville: Haley and Florida, 1896.

Halttunen, Karen, *Confidence Men and Painted Women: A Study of Middle-Class Culture in America, 1830–1870*. New Haven: Yale University Press, 1983.

Hamilton, G. P., *The Bright Side of Memphis: A Compendium of Information Concerning the Colored People of Memphis*. Memphis: n.p., 1908.

Hare, Maud Cuney, *Negro Musicians and Their Music*. Washington: Associated Publishers, 1936.

———, *Norris Wright Cuney: A Tribune of the Black People*. New York: Crisis Publishing Co., 1913.

Hare, Nathan, *The Black Anglo-Saxons*. New York: Collier Books, 1965, 1970.

Harlan, Louis R., *Booker T. Washington: The Making of a Black Leader, 1856–1901*. New York: Oxford University Press, 1972.

———, *Booker T. Washington: Wizard of Tuskegee, 1901–1915*. New York: Oxford University Press, 1983.

———, *Separate and Unequal: Public School Campaigns and Racism in the Southern Seaboard States, 1901–1915*. Chapel Hill: University of North Carolina Press, 1958.

Harley, Sharon, and Rosalyn Terborg-Penn, eds., *The Afro-American Woman: Struggles and Images*. Port Washington, New York: Kennikat Press, 1978.

Haskins, James, *Pinckney Benton Stewart Pinchback*. New York: Macmillan, 1973.

Hatch, Jane M., ed., *The American Book of Days*. New York: H. W. Wilson Co., 1978.

Helm, Mary, *The Upward Path: The Evolution of a Race*. New York: Eaton and Mains, 1909.

Henri, Florette, *Black Migration: Movement North, 1900–1920*. Garden City: Doubleday, 1975.

Hershberg, Theodore, ed., *Philadelphia: Work, Space, Family and Group Experience in Nineteenth Century Philadelphia*. New York: Oxford University Press, 1981.

Hill, Errol, *Shakespeare in Sable: A History of Black Shakespearean Actors*. Amherst: University of Massachusetts Press, 1984.

Hilyer, Andrew, *Twentieth Century Union League Directory*. Washington, n.p., 1903.

Holt, Thomas, *Black Over White: Negro Political Leadership in South Carolina During Reconstruction*. Urbana: University of Illinois Press, 1977.

Homel, Michael W., *Down From Equality: Black Chicagoans and the Public Schools, 1920–1941*. Urbana: University of Illinois Press, 1984.

Horton, James O., and Lois E. Horton, *Black Bostonians: Family Life and Community in the Antebellum North*. New York: Holmes and Meier Publishers, 1979.

Hundley, Daniel R., *Social Relations in Our Southern States*. Baton Rouge: Louisiana State University Press, 1979.

Hundley, Mary Gibson, *The Dunbar Story, 1870–1955*. New York: Vantage Press, 1965.

Ingle, Edward, *The Negro in the District of Columbia*. Baltimore: The Johns Hopkins Press, 1893.

BIBLIOGRAPHY

Jahr, Frederic C., ed., *The Rich, The Well-Born and the Powerful: Elites and Upper Classes in History*. Urbana: University of Illinois Press, 1973.

James, Edward T., *Notable American Women*. 3 vols. Cambridge: Harvard University Press, 1971.

Jervey, Theodore D., *The Slave Trade: Slavery and Color*. Columbia, S.C.: The State Co., 1925.

Johnson, Charles S., et al., *Deep South: A Social Anthropological Study of Caste and Class*. Chicago: University of Chicago Press, 1941.

Johnson, Haynes, *Dusk at the Mountain—The Negro, The Nation and the Capital—A Report on Problems and Progress*. Garden City: Doubleday, 1963.

Johnson, James Weldon, *Black Manhattan*. New York: Knopf, 1930.

Johnson, Michael P., and James R. Roark, *Black Masters: A Free Family of Color in the Old South*. New York: W. W. Norton and Co., 1984.

Katzman, David M., *Before the Ghetto: Black Detroit in the Nineteenth Century*. Urbana: University of Illinois Press, 1973.

Kellogg, Charles F., *NAACP: A History of the National Association for the Advancement of Colored People, 1909–1920*. Baltimore: Johns Hopkins Press, 1967.

Kerman, Cynthia E., and Richard Eldridge, *The Lives of Jean Toomer: A Hunger for Wholeness*. Baton Rouge: Louisiana State University, 1987.

Koger, Larry, *Black Slaveowners: Free Black Slave Masters in South Carolina, 1790–1860*. Jefferson, N.C.: McFarland and Co., 1985.

Kolchin, Peter, *First Freedom: Responses of Alabama's Blacks to Emancipation and Reconstruction*. Westport: Greenwood Press, 1972.

Kousser, J. Morgan, "Separate But Not Equal: The Supreme Court's First Decision on Discrimination in Schools," *Social Science Working Paper*, No. 204. Pasadena: California Institute of Technology, 1978.

Kusmer, Kenneth L., *A Ghetto Takes Shape: Black Cleveland, 1870–1930*. Urbana: University of Illinois Press, 1976.

Labbe, Delores E., *Jim Crow Comes to the Church: The Establishment of Segregated Catholic Parishes in South Louisiana*. New York: Arno Press, 1978.

Litwack, Leon, *Been in the Storm So Long: The Aftermath of Slavery*. New York: Knopf, 1979.

Locke, Alain, ed., *The New Negro: An Interpretation*. New York: Albert and Charles Boni, 1925.

Logan, Rayford W., *The Betrayal of the Negro from Rutherford B. Hayes to Woodrow Wilson*. New York: Collier Books, 1965.

———, *Howard University: The First Hundred Years, 1867–1967*. New York: New York University Press, 1969.

———, and Michael Winston, eds., *Dictionary of American Negro Biography*. New York: W. W. Norton and Co., 1983.

Lortie, Francis M., *San Francisco's Black Community, 1870–1890: Dilemmas in the Struggle for Equality*. San Francisco: R and E Associates, 1973.

Lotchin, Roger W., *San Francisco, 1846–1956: From Hamlet to City*. New York: Oxford University Press, 1974.

Low, W. A., and Virgil A. Clift, eds., *Encyclopedia of Black America*. New York: McGraw-Hill, 1981.

Lynch, Hollis, ed., *The Black Urban Condition: A Documentary History, 1866–1971*. New York: Crowell, 1973.

Mabee, Carleton, *Black Education in New York State from Colonial to Modern Times*. Syracuse: Syracuse University Press, 1979.

McGinnis, Frederick A., *The Education of Negroes in Ohio*. Wilberforce, Ohio: Curless Printing Co., 1962.

McKay, Nellie, *Jean Toomer, Artist: A Study of His Literary Life and Work, 1894–1936*. Chapel Hill: University of North Carolina Press, 1984.

McPherson, James M., *The Abolitionist Legacy: From Reconstruction to the NAACP*. Princeton: Princeton University Press, 1975.

Major, Gerri, *Black Society*. Chicago: Johnson Publishing Co., 1976.

Majors, Monroe A., *Noted Negro Women: Their Triumphs and Activities*. Chicago: Donohue and Henneberry, 1893.

Mallas, Aris A., et al., *Forty Years in Politics: The Story of Ben Pelham*. Detroit: Wayne State University Press, 1957.

Marteona, Constance, *The Lengthening Shadow of a Woman*. New York: Exposition Press, 1977.

Mather, Frank L., ed., *Who's Who in Colored America, 1915*. Chicago: n.p., 1915.

Mays, Benjamin E., and Joseph W. Nicholson, *The Negro's Church*. New York: Institute of Social and Religious Research, 1933.

Meier, August, *Negro Thought in America, 1880–1915: Racial Ideologies in the Age of Booker T. Washington*. Ann Arbor: University of Michigan Press, 1963.

Mencke, John G., *Mulattoes and Race Mixture: American Attitudes and Images, 1865–1918*. [Ann Arbor]: UMI Research Press, 1979.

Mills, Gary, *The Forgotten People: Cane River's Creoles of Color*. Baton Rouge: Louisiana State University Press, 1977.

Minton, Henry M., *Early History of Negroes in Business in Philadelphia*. n.p.: n.p., 1913.

Mitchell, Robert, and Edward K. Miller, eds., *Geographical Perspectives on Maryland's Past*. Occasional Papers in Geography, No. 4. College Park: University of Maryland, 1979.

Montesano, Philip M., *Some Aspects of the Free Negro Question in San Francisco, 1849–1870*. San Francisco: R and E Associates, 1973.

Moore, Jesse T., *A Search for Equality: The National Urban League, 1910–1961*. University Park: Pennsylvania State University Press, 1981.

Moses, Wilson J., *The Golden Age of Black Nationalism, 1850–1925*. Hamden, Ct.: Archon Press, 1978.

Moss, Alfred N., *The American Negro Academy: Voice of the Talented Tenth*. Baton Rouge: Louisiana State University Press, 1981.

Mossell, Mrs. N. F., *The Work of Afro-American Women*. Freeport, NY: Books for Libraries, 1971.

Muraskin, William A., *Middle Class Blacks in a White Society: Prince Hall Freemasonry in America*. Berkeley: University of California Press, 1975.

Murray, Andrew E., *Presbyterians and the Negro: A History*. Philadelphia: Presbyterian Historical Society, 1966.

Myrdal, Gunnar, *An American Dilemma: The Negro Problem and American Democracy*. New York: Harper, 1944.

Negro Progress in Fifty Years. Philadelphia: American Academy of Political and Social Sciences, 1913.

Negro Womanhood: Its Past. Boston: American Missionary Association, n.d.

Neilson, David G., *Black Ethos: Northern Negro Urban Life and Thought, 1890–1930*. Westport: Greenwood Press, 1977.

Olsen, Otto H., *Thin Disguise: Turning Point in Negro History*. New York: Humanities Press, 1967.

Osofsky, Gilbert, *Harlem: The Making of a Ghetto: Negro New York, 1890–1930*. New York: Harper and Row, 1966.

Ottley, Roi, *The Lonely Warrior: The Life and Times of Robert S. Abbott*. Chicago: Henry Regnery, 1955.

———, *'New World A-Coming': Inside Black America*. Boston: Houghton, Mifflin, 1943.

————, and William Weatherby, *The Negro in New York.* New York: New York Public Library, 1967.

Ovington, Mary White, *Half A Man: The Status of the Negro in New York.* New York: Longmans, Green, 1911.

Parker, Majorie H., *Alpha Kappa Alpha: Sixty Years of Service.* n.p.: n.p., 1966.

Parkhill, Forbes, *Mister Barney Ford: A Portrait in Bistre.* Denver: Sage Books, 1963.

Pease, Jane H., and William H. Pease, *They Who Would Be Free: Blacks' Search for Freedom, 1830–1861.* New York: Atheneum, 1974.

Perdue, Robert, *The Negro in Savannah, 1865–1900.* New York: Exposition Press, 1973.

Powell, William S., ed., *Dictionary of North Carolina Biography.* Chapel Hill: University of North Carolina Press, 1979.

Proctor, Mrs. H. H., *Negro Womanhood.* New York: American Missionary Association, n.d.

Quarles, Benjamin, *Frederick Douglass.* New York: Atheneum, 1968.

Quillin, Frank, *The Color Line in Ohio.* New York: Negro Universities Press, 1969.

Rabinowitz, Howard, *Race Relations in the Urban South, 1865–1890.* Urbana: University of Illinois Press, 1980.

————, ed., *Southern Black Leaders of the Reconstruction Era.* Urbana: University of Illinois Press, 1982.

Reimers, David, *White Protestantism and the Negro.* New York: Oxford University Press, 1965.

Reuter, Edward, *Race Mixture: Studies in Intermarriage and Miscegenation.* New York: McGraw-Hill, 1931.

Richardson, Harry V., *Dark Salvation: The Story of Methodism As It Developed Among Blacks in America.* Garden City: Doubleday, 1976.

Richardson, Joe M., *A History of Fisk University, 1865–1965.* Tuscaloosa: University of Alabama Press, 1980.

Richings, G. F., *Evidences of Progress Among Colored People.* Philadelphia: George S. Ferguson Co., 1900.

Robb, Frederic H., *The Negro in Chicago, 1779 to 1929.* Chicago: Atlas Printing Co., 1929.

Rohrer, John H., and Munro S. Edmonson, *The Eighth Generation: Cultures and Personalities of New Orleans.* New York: Harper and Brothers, 1960.

Rouse, Michael P., *A Study of the Development of Negro Education Under Catholic Auspices in Maryland and the District of Columbia.* Baltimore: Johns Hopkins Press, 1935.

Rousseve, Charles B., *The Negro in Louisiana.* New Orleans: Xavier University Press, 1937.

Rudwick, Elliott, *W. E. B. Du Bois: Propagandist of Negro Protest.* New York: Atheneum, 1972.

Savage, W. Sherman, *Blacks in the West.* Westport: Greenwood Press, 1976.

Scheiner, Seth M., *Negro Mecca: A History of the Negro in New York City, 1865–1920.* New York: New York University Press, 1965.

Schmid, Calvin F., *Social Trends in Seattle.* Seattle: University of Washington Press, 1944.

Schneider, Louis, ed., *Religion, Culture and Society.* New York: John Wiley, 1964.

Shadwell, Arthur, *Industrial Efficiency.* 2 vols. London: Longmans, Green, 1906.

Sherwood, Grace, *The Oblates' Hundred and One Years.* New York: Macmillan, 1931.

Simmons, William J., *Men of Mark: Eminent, Progressive and Rising.* Chicago: Johnson Publishing Company, 1970.

Smith, Samuel D., *The Negro in Congress, 1870–1901.* Chapel Hill: University of North Carolina Press, 1940.

Sochen, June, ed., *The Black Man and the American Dream: Negro Aspirations in America, 1900–1930*. Chicago: Quadrangle Books, 1971.

Spear, Allan H., *Black Chicago: The Making of a Negro Ghetto, 1890–1920*. Chicago: University of Chicago Press, 1967.

Stanley, A. Knighton, *The Children is Crying: Congregationalism Among Black People*. Boston: Pilgrim Press, 1979.

Sternett, Milton C., *Afro-American Religious History: A Documentary Witness*. Durham: Duke University Press, 1985.

Sterkx, H. E., *The Free Negro in Antebellum Louisiana*. Rutherford, N.J.: Fairleigh Dickinson University, 1972.

Stone, Alfred Holt, *Studies in the American Race Problem*. New York: Doubleday, Page, 1908.

Strickland, Arvarh E., *History of the Chicago Urban League*. Urbana: University of Illinois Press, 1966.

Synnott, Marcia G., *The Half-Opened Door: Discrimination and Admission at Harvard, Yale and Princeton, 1900–1970*. Westport: Greenwood Press, 1979.

Terry, Adolphine F., *Charlotte Stephens: Little Rock's First Black Teacher*. Little Rock: Academic Press, 1973.

Thompson, David C., *Sociology of the Black Experience*. Westport: Greenwood Press, 1974.

Thornbrough, Emma Lou, *T. Thomas Fortune: Militant Journalist*. Chicago: University of Chicago Press, 1972.

Thurman, Sue Bailey, *Pioneers of Negro Origin in California*. San Francisco: Acme Publishing Co., 1971.

de Tocqueville, Alexis, *Democracy in America*. 2 vols. New York: Knopf, 1959.

Torrence, Ridgely, *The Story of John Hope*. New York: Macmillan, 1948.

Tortolano, William, *Samuel Coleridge-Taylor: Anglo-Black Composer, 1875–1912*. Metuchen, N.J.: Scarecrow Press, 1977.

Trotter, Joe W., *Black Milwaukee: The Making of An Industrial Proletariat, 1915–1945*. Urbana: University of Illinois Press, 1985.

Walsh, William S., *Curiosities of Popular Customs*. Philadelphia: J. B. Lippincott, 1897.

Warner, Robert A., *New Haven Negroes: A Social History*. New Haven: Yale University Press, 1940.

Washington, Booker T., et al., *The Negro Problem*. New York: AMS Press, 1970.

Washington, Joseph R., *Black Religion: The Negro and Christianity in the United States*. Boston: Beacon Press, 1964.

————, *Marriage in Black and White*. Boston: Beacon Press, 1970.

Weiss, Nancy J., *The National Urban League, 1910–1940*. New York: Oxford University Press, 1974.

Wesley, Charles H., *History of Sigma Pi Phi*. Washington, D.C.: Association for the Study of Negro Life and History, n.d.

Wheeler, B. F., *The Varick Family*. n.p.: n.p., 1907.

Who's Who in Colored America, 1938–40. Brooklyn: Thomas Yenser, 1940.

Whyte, James H., *The Uncivil War: Washington During the Reconstruction, 1865–1878*. New York: Twayne, 1958.

Wikramanayake, Marina, *A World in Shadow: The Free Black in Antebellum South Carolina*. Columbia: University of South Carolina Press, 1973.

Wiley, Electa C., *Black Elitism: Hope, Arkansas, 1900–1935*. n.p.: n.p., 1981.

Williams, Loretta J., *Black Freemasonry and Middle Class Realities*. Columbia: University of Missouri Press, 1980.

Williams, Roger M., *The Bonds: An American Family*. New York: Atheneum, 1971.

BIBLIOGRAPHY

Williamson, Joel, *New People: Miscegenation and Mulattoes in the United States.* New York: The Free Press, 1980.

Willson, Joseph, *Sketches of the Higher Classes of Colored Society in Philadelphia.* Philadelphia: Merrihew and Thompson, 1841.

Wilmore, Gayraud S., *Black and Presbyterian: The Heritage and the Hope.* Philadelphia: Geneva Press, 1983.

Woll, Allen, *Dictionary of the Black Theatre: Broadway, Off-Broadway and Selected Harlem Theatre.* Westport: Greenwood Press, 1983.

Woods, E. M., *The Negro in Etiquette: A Novelty.* St. Louis: Baxton and Skinner, 1899.

Woodson, Carter G., *The Education of the Negro Prior to 1861.* New York: G. P. Putnam's Sons, 1915.

————, *The History of the Negro Church.* Washington, D.C.: Associated Publishers, 1972.

Wright, George C., *Life Behind A Veil: Blacks in Louisville, Kentucky, 1865–1930.* Baton Rouge: Louisiana State University, 1985.

Wright, James M., *The Free Negro in Maryland, 1634–1860.* New York: Columbia University Press, 1921.

Wright, Richard R., *The Negro in Pennsylvania: A Study in Economic History.* New York: Arno Press, 1969.

Index

INDEX

INDEX

◆

WILLARD B. GATEWOOD is Alumni Distinguished Professor of History at the University of Arkansas, Fayetteville, and author of nine other books, including *Black Americans and the White Man's Burden, 1898–1903;* "*Smoked Yankees*" *and the Struggle for Empire: Letters from Negro Soldiers, 1898–1902; Slave and Freeman: The Autobiography of George L. Knox;* and *Free Man of Color: Autobiography of Willis Augustus Hodges.*